argin

The Narrow Margin, the book on which the
screenplay of the film 'The Battle of Britain' was
based, is the most authoritative work ever written
about those sixteen historic weeks in the summer of
1940 when the future of Britain was at stake.

Since its first publication in 1961, a great deal of
additional material has come to light and this new
edition has not only been extensively revised but also
contains more than two hundred photographs (from
both British and German sources), many of which
have never been published before, and which in
themselves make a fascinating pictorial study.

For all its indisputable authority, *The Narrow
Margin* is first and foremost a magnificently readable
book about The Battle of Britain, one which is
never likely to be superseded.

PEN & SWORD MILITARY CLASSICS

We hope you enjoy your Pen and Sword Military Classic. The series is designed to give readers quality military history at affordable prices. Below is a list of the titles that are planned for 2003. Pen and Sword Classics are available from all good bookshops. If you would like to keep in touch with further developments in the series, including information on the Classics Club, then please contact Pen and Sword at the address below.

2003 List

Series No.		
	JANUARY	
1	The Bowmen of England	*Donald Featherstone*
2	The Life & Death of the Afrika Korps	*Ronald Lewin*
3	The Old Front Line	*John Masefield*
4	Wellington & Napoleon	*Robin Neillands*
	FEBRUARY	
5	Beggars in Red	*John Strawson*
6	The Luftwaffe: A History	*John Killen*
7	Siege: Malta 1940–1943	*Ernle Bradford*
	MARCH	
8	Hitler as Military Commander	*John Strawson*
9	Nelson's Battles	*Oliver Warner*
10	The Western Front 1914–1918	*John Terraine*
	APRIL	
11	The Killing Ground	*Tim Travers*
12	Vimy	*Pierre Berton*
	MAY	
13	Dictionary of the First World War	*Pope & Wheal*
14	1918: The Last Act	*Barrie Pitt*
	JUNE	
15	Hitler's Last Offensive	*Peter Elstob*
16	Naval Battles of World War Two	*Geoffrey Bennett*
	JULY	
17	Omdurman	*Philip Ziegler*
18	Strike Hard, Strike Sure	*Ralph Barker*
	AUGUST	
19	The Black Angels	*Rupert Butler*
20	The Black Ship	*Dudley Pope*
	SEPTEMBER	
21	The Argentine Fight for the Falklands	*Martin Middlebrook*
22	The Narrow Margin	*Wood & Dempster*
	OCTOBER	
23	Warfare in the Age of Bonaparte	*Michael Glover*
24	With the German Guns	*Herbert Sulzbach*
	NOVEMBER	
25	Dictionary of the Second World War	*Pope & Wheal*
26	Not Ordinary Men	*John Colvin*

PEN AND SWORD BOOKS LTD

47 Church Street • Barnsley • South Yorkshire • S70 2AS

Tel: 01226 734555 • 734222

E-mail: enquiries@pen-and-sword.co.uk • **Website:** www.pen-and-sword.co.uk

THE NARROW MARGIN

The Battle of Britain
and the rise of air power
1930-1940

Derek Wood
with Derek Dempster

Foreword by Air Chief Marshal the
Lord Dowding GCB GCVO CMG

PEN & SWORD MILITARY CLASSICS

First published in 1961 by Hutchinson & Company
Published in 2003, in this format, by
PEN & SWORD MILITARY CLASSICS
an imprint of
Pen & Sword Books Limited,
47, Church Street,
Barnsley,
S. Yorkshire,
S70 2AS

© Derek Wood and Derek Dempster, 1961, 2003

ISBN 0 85052 915 8

A CIP record for this book is
available from the British Library

Printed in England by
CPI UK

All the great struggles of history have been won by
superior will-power wresting victory in the teeth
of odds or upon the narrowest of margins

WINSTON S. CHURCHILL

Contents

Foreword

Air Chief Marshal the Lord Dowding G C B G C V O C M G

This is undoubtedly the best account that I have read of the factual history of the Battle of Britain, and it is a pleasure for me to be able to say that I agree so much with the opinions that are expressed and the verdicts that have been reached.

It was not until quite recently, after re-reading this excellent book, that I discovered that both the authors were too young to have been able to participate in the battle. They were, in fact, still at school during the time when it was fought. I must say that it is greatly to their credit that they have written about what happened with such understanding, basing it on the most meticulous research. That is particularly commendable when one realises that there was no way in which they could have been exposed to a first-hand contact with the problems and tensions faced by those who were actually involved in the battle. The authors have hit off most accurately the attitude that was mine, as the Commander-in-Chief of Fighter Command, at the time – to say nothing of the others who participated in the battle – and they have given a splendid accounting of the work of the pilots who were so deeply involved.

This is a perceptive and moving book as well as being an excellent history of the events that led up to and the course that was followed by the battle in the summer of 1940.

Authors' introduction to original edition

In 1940 one of the most significant battles of history was fought in the skies over Britain. Its outcome had a profound effect on the future of the civilised world.

The Battle of Britain saved the country from invasion. If the R.A.F. had been defeated all the efforts of the Army and Navy could hardly have averted defeat in the face of complete German air superiority. With all Europe subjugated, Germany and Japan would later have met on the borders of India.

The undivided weight of the German war effort would then have fallen on Russia with the United States completely isolated.

It is unlikely that there will ever be a parallel to the Battle of Britain where armies and navies, immobilised on either side of the Channel, watched a few thousand combatants meet in the air above.

The battle was not, however, won in the period from July to October 1940 alone. The outcome was the culmination of the preparation, good judgment and error made in the preceding seven years.

On the face of it the Luftwaffe should have won the battle. It possessed superiority in numbers and bases stretching round two-thirds of Britain, but lacked any effective plan of campaign, intelligence facilities and above all operational scientific knowledge.

The battle marked the advent of controlled scientific warfare, which is the basis of defence strategy today. Science and enlightenment were employed in the British and not the German camp.

We have endeavoured to show, step by step, how the military machines of both sides were built up and how they finally came to grips in the summer of 1940. The battle has been laid out for the first time in the form of a complete operational day-to-day diary.

Most previous accounts of the battle have been divided into four phases, but close analysis of official records reveals a clear cut separation for the R.A.F. into five phases between July 11th and October 30th. The diary has accordingly been divided in this form.

German historians still persist in regarding the '*Luftkrieg gegen England*' (air war against England) as one continuous battle from the summer of 1940 up to May 1941. Their own records refute this assertion. The beginning of all-out night blitz in November 1940 and the fading out of day bombing marked the end of a complete chapter in the air war. Invasion was no longer possible and direct assault on the R.A.F. and southern England gave way to a war against industry, the shipping lifelines and morale.

We have therefore ended the narrative in October,

by which time Hitler had cancelled operation Seelöwe and already turned his eyes to the east.

The appendices have been made as comprehensive as possible to avoid the use of lengthy footnotes and cross-references. Original official British and German designations and nomenclature have been used except in one case where the prefix Me is given for the Messerschmitt Company. The abbreviation Me was not officially used until 1944 and Messerschmitt fighters were known by the letters Bf (Bayerische Fleugzeugwerke).

So many official German sources adopted the prefix Me in 1940 that it became a generic term in the Luftwaffe and the R.A.F. We have therefore used it to avoid confusion.

Throughout, the losses quoted for both sides are the official figures and not estimates. Suggestions have been made from time to time that the Luftwaffe casualty figures put out by the Air Ministry after the war were based on original records which were falsified for German propaganda purposes. Close examination of these records has shown that they are completely accurate. Losses were laid down in great detail in the Luftwaffe Quartermaster General's returns for the period, and these were used as a basis for the replacement of aircraft and crews for pensions and administrative purposes. It is impossible to imagine any commander deliberately understating his casualties and thus losing the fresh aircraft and personnel he so vitally needed.

A military history which casts a net as wide as *The Narrow Margin* cannot be written without the help and goodwill of those who witnessed the events described. In the two years it took to write the book the paths of inquiry have led us to many people in Britain and the Continent of Europe to whom we should like to record our gratitude.

Particularly we are indebted to John Chappell, who advised on both layout and text from the early stages and who undertook the arduous task of reading the manuscript and the proofs.

We should also like to record our debt to the Air Ministry, in particular to Mr. L. A. Jackets and Mr. W. H. Martin of the Air Historical Branch. Much of the manuscript could not have been compiled or checked without their unfailing efforts. We are grateful, too, for the access permitted to official documents, some of which are quoted in this book. These are Crown Copyright.

Our thanks also go to General a. D. Paul Deichmann,

Oberstlt d. O. Greffrath, and Herr F. W. Fischer of the German Air Historical Branch (Studiengruppe Luftwaffe bei der Führungsakademie der Bunderswehr), who supplied valuable material.

John Blake spent many hours ensuring the high accuracy of the maps and drawings. Our thanks go to him, and also to Flight Lieutenant J. H. Holloway, who compiled the full list of aircrew in the Battle of Britain which is appended at the end of this book.

In addition we are grateful to the Right Honourable The Earl of Swinton; Air Chief Marshal The Lord Dowding; Air Chief Marshal Sir Keith Park: Air Marshal W. P. G. Pretty; Air Commodore F. R. Banks; the late Air Marshal Sir Raymund Hart; Professor R. V. Jones; Sir Sydney Camm; Group Captain E. Fennessy; Group Captain R. Scott-Farnie; Professor P. M. S. Blackett; Dr. E. C. Williams; Mr. M. N. Golovine; Group Captain J. A. Kent; Group Captain A. C. Deere; Group Captain J. H. Hill; Group Captain T. P. Gleave; Wing Commander Havercraft; Wing Commander R. M. Milne; Wing Commander J. Seldon; Wing Commander J. Cherry; Squadron Leader R. M. Dye; Observer Commander F. W. Mitchell; Observer Commander G. A. D. Bourne; Observer Lieutenant R. D. T. Onions; Mr. E. C. Baker (G.P.O. Archivist); Major C. H. Vallence; Dr. and Mrs. H. Rieck; Field Marshal Erhard Milch; General W. Martini; General W. Gosewisch; Kapitän Zür See H. Giessler; General A. Galland; General J. Steinhoff and Dr. Gaertner.

We gratefully acknowledge the assistance of the late Dr. E. E. Heiman, founder and proprietor of *Interavia*, and of the staff of the magazine, who were most helpful in providing material for this book.

There are many others who gave freely of their time, memories, documents and photographs; to them also we express our thanks.

The authors thank Cassell & Co., the publishers of Sir Winston Churchill's *History of the Second World War*, for permission to quote from Volume Three of that work.

Introduction to revised, illustrated edition

It is unusual for an author to find himself writing a fresh introduction to a book which first appeared eight years before.

In this case, it is necessary because this is not just another edition, but a complete revision with a great deal of new material, plus more than two hundred illustrations. The only omission is the synopsis chapter which has made way for more pressing items.

When I approached the problem of illustrations my one fear was that there would be insufficient genuine pictures to do justice to the project. In fact the opposite has been the case and the only difficulty has been one of selection. On the British side long hidden photographs have come to light in private collections, while in Germany the Bundesarchiv collection of thousands of top-grade official illustrations of the 1940 period proved a revelation.

So many have assisted with this new volume that it is difficult to enumerate them all. First, however, I must place on record my gratitude to my colleague Derek Dempster for his continued aid.

I am deeply indebted to Lord Dowding for writing the Foreword and for the terms he has used. Robert Wright, whose book on Lord Dowding is shortly to appear, has also given most valuable assistance and guidance.

Wing Commander K. J. Powell gave unstinted help with both the first edition and this new version. An old friend and colleague, Mr. Roger Gillyns, provided many leads and introductions.

Mr. Christopher Elliott loaned a number of most useful maps and publications from his collection and also provided valuable information. Mr. Dennis Knight made available a great deal of new factual material and rare photographs from the very comprehensive Knight-Foote Collection.

I am very grateful to Mrs. Gillian Howell and Mr. Henry Howell for their help and permission to use documents, log books and photographs of the late Squadron Leader F. J. Howell.

Lt. Colonel Aviateur BEM M. Terlinden possesses an encyclopaedic knowledge of the Belgian Air Force and gave freely from his files. The Belgian Ministry of Defence kindly gave access to their excellent records.

The Imperial War Museum, as always, proved to be a mine of useful photographs and Mr. Hine was most helpful.

Mr. William Green gave freely of his time and his excellent archives, while Mr. W. O. J. Pyemont of Image In Industry Ltd. performed the impossible in turning out prints and copy negatives at a moment's notice.

Thanks are also due to Lt. General Baron Donnet, Air Commodore P. M. Brothers, Professor Dr. Gley, Herr H. Walther, Group Captain J. Kent, Colonel P. Hordern, Mr. J. M. Bruce, Mr. John W. R. Taylor, Captain J. H. Mann, Mr. T. Angelle Weisse, Group Captain T. F. U. Lang, Herr Horst Burgsmuller, Wing Commander Asher Lee, Wing Commander R. P. Beamont, Mr. G. Squire and Mrs. J. Wiltsher.

Finally I would like to thank my wife who has not only done a great deal of work from the beginning, but has provided constant encouragement and put up with the midnight oil being burned on many occasions.

DEREK WOOD

Cuckfield, March, 1969

Prologue

In the spring of 1939 the giant airship *Graf Zeppelin* was presumed to be in honourable retirement in its shed at Frankfurt-am-Main after nearly eleven years of flying.

Instead, it was being prepared for the first military electronics reconnaissance in history, twenty-one years before the American U-2 hit the headlines with its crash in Russia.

General Wolfgang Martini, head of the Luftwaffe signals organisation, had for many months been interested to discover whether Britain possessed a workable radar for detecting aircraft. German firms were busy developing such equipment, and his suspicions had been heightened by the appearance of unusual 350-foot-high aerial masts round the south and east coasts of England.

When the first masts had gone up at Orfordness in Suffolk the German Air Force maps labelled them as belonging to a radio-transmitting station. Then Bawdsey showed similar towers and these were followed by others at Dunkirk and Dover in Kent and Canewdon in Essex. By early 1939 masts were up, or in process of erection, from the Isle of Wight to the Orkneys.

Martini urgently required to know the state of British radar, its wavelength and the number of sites operational. The tall masts with their crossed lattice aerials appeared, however, to be unsuited to the wavelengths which German scientists had deemed best for their own secret Freya and Würzburg radars. Accordingly, at a meeting with Göring, Milch and other air force commanders, Martini proposed that twelve airships be made available for high-frequency 'research'.

At first the assembly was hostile to the idea, but began to show a more helpful attitude as Martini explained his purpose. He could not, he pointed out, use an aeroplane, as it was too small, lacked endurance and could not remain motionless in the air. With an airship he would have all the space necessary, many hours of flying time and the ability to stop and take readings where necessary.

Göring and Milch felt that any production of airships would use up large quantities of materials urgently needed for aircraft. Finally, however, it was agreed that Martini should use the two existing Zeppelins, L.Z.127 and L.Z.130, and if the experiments were successful four more should be ordered.

Work was immediately started on converting one of them into an airborne radio interrogation station. A number of new high-frequency receivers were installed and an aerial array rigged underneath the gondola.

Towards the end of May 1939 preparations were completed. Under cover of night the 776-foot-long airship slipped her moorings at Frankfurt and headed out over the North Sea. Her course stood westwards in the direction of the Bawdsey Research Station in Suffolk where the tall radio-transmitting masts were situated.

General Martini himself was on board for this trial run, which was mainly concerned with testing the receivers. Off Bawdsey, *Graf Zeppelin* turned north and flew parallel to the British east coast. The operators and technicians in the gondola anxiously waited for some response from the radio receivers, but each set emitted a loud crackling noise and nothing else.

At Canewdon and at Bawdsey the staff were amazed to find the largest 'blip' they had ever seen, travelling very slowly across the cathode-ray-tubes.

Fighter Command filter and operations rooms immediately began tracking on the map tables. It became evident that the strange visitor, because of its size and speed, could only be an airship. From its course along the coast it was correctly deduced that some sort of radar interrogation was in progress.

One by one the east coast Chain Home radars picked up *Graf Zeppelin* as it progressed northwards. Over the Humber estuary the airship transmitted a position report back to Germany. This was picked up by British radio intelligence who informed Fighter Command that the German 'fix' was a few miles off the coast of Yorkshire.

At the Bentley Priory operations table this news caused considerable amusement, as *Graf Zeppelin's* correct position had just been established, in cloud, over Hull itself—well inland. Air Marshal Pretty (then a flight-lieutenant on radar duty at Fighter Command) recalls that 'We were sorely tempted to radio a correction message to the airship but this would have revealed we were actually seeing her position on radar, so we kept silent.'

Off the north-east coast *Graf Zeppelin* turned for home, having picked up nothing but an appalling noise in the receivers. General Martini still did not know whether British radar was operational.

It was assumed that the interference was due to an installation defect and the reflections from the airship's envelope. Modifications were made to the sets and to the aerial and further trial runs were made over Germany.

During one of these the engineer responsible for the aerial, Dr. Sailer, slipped on the ladder between the gondola and the special basket holding the aerial. The altitude was too low for his parachute to open fully, and he fell into a forest, severely injuring his spine. This incident gave rise to later ill-founded rumours of a photographer in the under-basket with a special long-focus lens to record the radar masts on film.

Finally, all was ready for a second run up the east coast. This time Martini was not on board and the senior officer was Oberstleutnant Gosewisch, now Generalmajor retired and regional director of civil defence in Bonn.

At midnight on Wednesday, August 2nd, 1939, the *Graf Zeppelin* again slipped her moorings and steered for the North Sea. Her instructions were to keep close to Britain, but maintaining about fifteen miles distance from the shore. The wave-length strength and position of all high-frequency emissions was to be noted.

The night had been chosen for its poor weather and low cloud which gave adequate protection against sighting from the land. During the morning of August 3rd the airship came abreast of Bawdsey and turned north towards the Wash.

Once again no transmissions were detected and more faults developed in the receivers. Curiously, British radar did not pick up the airship, although the stations were operating.

It was not until three o'clock on the 3rd that the *Graf Zeppelin* was located visually off the coast of Kincardineshire proceeding north towards Scapa Flow. Half an hour later another sighting was obtained by coastguards at Collieston, Aberdeenshire. Two auxiliary air force fighters took off from Dyce, and identified the airship, which was well outside the three-mile limit.

The last sighting was by the lighthouse-keeper at Girdleness who was surprised to see the airship overhead at below 1,000 feet. *Graf Zeppelin* cruised on up to the Scapa Flow base, catching glimpses of British warships through the clouds. In the early evening she turned back to Germany—empty-handed. No high-frequency signals had been detected.

The London *Daily Telegraph* was quick to report the airship's appearance over the islands. At 4 o'clock in the morning Gosewisch had retired to bed after the long flight, but was promptly awakened by General Jeshonnek, air force chief of general staff. The General wanted to know whether *Graf Zeppelin* had in fact crossed the British coast as the newspaper suggested. Gosewisch denied that this had occurred.

On the following day, August 4th, a highly amusing official communiqué was issued concerning the reconnaissance flight. Berlin denied that the *Graf Zeppelin* had intentionally left the Reich or had approached the coast of England. The statement went on: 'The airship cannot leave Germany without special permission. There can be no question of an intention to fly over near British territory. There have, however, been severe storms during the last day or two and it is possible that the airship could have been blown off her course over the North Sea.' A few days later a further flight was carried out, but again with no results.

So ended the Zeppelin's career in radar survey. Within a month war had broken out, and afterwards both *Graf Zeppelin* 1 and *Graf Zeppelin* 2 were destroyed in the sheds at Frankfurt.

Neither side realised that the opening round of the air war against Britain had been fought and lost by Germany.

If the airship's equipment had worked properly in the first place there would doubtless have been many more reconnaissance flights. Radar would then have merited serious study by the Luftwaffe Command staff and intelligence departments.

This in turn would have produced new German tactics for the Battle of Britain, a sustained assault on the coastal radar stations and the employment of airborne jamming devices. Such steps would have deprived the R.A.F. of its long-range-warning cover and the outcome of the Battle of Britain might have been very different.

As it was, the German Air Force made no efforts to investigate the radar chain or the fighter-control system to which it was linked. Bombing of radar stations was abandoned early in the battle. The German High Command chose to ignore the advent of science in warfare.

1   The German Air Force is reborn

The Treaty of Versailles, signed in June 1919, was intended to end German military aviation for ever. The Air Force was disbanded and to the victorious Allies were surrendered over 1,500 aircraft and 27,000 aircraft engines. Peace, like the Charleston, was in the air and in England Geddes of the anti-waste campaign was wielding his axe, reducing the Royal Air Force to a shadow of its former self.

In Germany, however, there was still a Defence Ministry. Here a man of considerable foresight understood the future of air power and determined to see the Air Force reborn. General von Seeckt, Chief of the Army Command, was an infantry soldier by profession, but he could see that one day air power would be of supreme importance in war.

As early as 1921 he began to secrete various promising men in offices of the Reichswehr Ministry in the Bendlerstrasse, Berlin. Their titles were innocuous and to the outside world they were small cogs in the treaty army of 100,000. Three of these officers were destined for high office and their names—Kesselring, Stumpff and Sperrle—were to become unpleasantly familiar in English homes twenty years later as Luftflotten commanders in the Battle of Britain.

Outwardly there was little for the 'secret Air Force' to do but watch technical advances in aviation abroad, produce staff papers and wait. The majority of the former Air Force drifted away to other jobs or stood in the unemployment queue. A much decorated young captain named Hermann Göring went as demonstrator and charter pilot to neutral Sweden.

The Defence Ministry, however, was far from wasting its time. One of its first moves to get round the treaty limitations was to send envoys in December 1921 to Russia to discuss aircraft manufacture and military aviation training for German recruits.

In December 1923 a secret agreement was signed covering military co-operation and the establishment of a flying school at Lipezk, about 200 miles south-east of Moscow. Buildings and land were provided by the Russians, but all equipment, aircraft, practice munitions and supplies were brought in secretly from Germany.

Training of the first entry began in 1924, the specially selected individuals being temporarily 'retired' from the armed forces and 're-enlisted' on their return. Many have tended in post-war years to denigrate the part played by the Lipezk school, but the fact remains that several hundred crews, mechanics and other specialists, were trained in the nine years of its existence. The records show that the majority of officers who later held high rank in the Luftwaffe were Lipezk graduates.

In addition, the embryo air section at the defence headquarters in Berlin was able to carry out much aircraft and equipment development in Russia with the secret co-operation of the German aircraft industry. It is ironic that the Soviet Union should have provided the original facilities for the rebirth of the German Air Force—an Air Force which in 1941 was to all but destroy the Red air fleets.

Parallel to the Lipezk training, a future generation of pilots was being built up through the Deutscher Luftsportverband. Youths flocked to join this promising organisation which ran large-scale courses in glider instruction under Captain Kurt Student, head of the Reichswehr air technical branch. Later he became prominent as a general in command of parachute troops. From small beginnings in 1920 the Luftsportverband grew in nine years to a membership of 50,000.

German aircraft manufacture, contrary to popular belief, never ceased after World War I. On the morning of November 11th, 1918, while the armistice delegates were meeting in the train at Compiègne, Professor Junkers, head of the firm which bore his name, his chief designer Ing. O. Reuter, and a group of engineers, forgathered to survey the future. Junkers informed them that they were to stop all military work and concentrate on the design for a civil transport. Thus, on June 25th, 1919, three days before the signing of the Versailles Treaty, the first post-war German aeroplane took to the air.

A complete breakaway from biplane types, the F-13, as it became known, was an all-metal, six-seater cabin monoplane. During the 1920s it was the most widely used transport aircraft in the world. Orders were at first few in a market glutted with war-surplus machines, but at the end of 1919 Junkers saved the firm closing by obtaining an order from America for six F-13s.

The Inter-Allied Aeronautical Commission then stepped in. All F-13s being built were confiscated, but after much discussion the Commission relented in February 1920 when it was decided that the F-13 was a genuine transport unsuited for military requirements. Its judgment, as usual, was not particularly sound. Within two years the Russians and Japanese were happily operating F-13s equipped with bomb-racks and machine-guns.

Just over a year later the Disarmament Commission thought again and F-13 production, in common with others, was stopped.

The first post World War I German aircraft, the Ju F-13, a six-seater cabin monoplane, which flew in June, 1919. Production was stopped by the Inter-Allied Aeronautical Commission, but later resumed. Widely used commercially, the F.13 was later adapted for military use by Russia and Japan

This did not deter Professor Junkers, who expected just such an edict. A former naval pilot, Gotthard Sachsenberg, Junkers' travelling salesman, with his assistant, Erhard Milch, former air force officer, set about organising other facilities for the F-13. The problem of operating F-13s in the Reich was overcome by selling them to the Danzig Air Transport Company —whose manager also happened to be Erhard Milch.

Other German manufacturers had similar problems with the Disarmament Commission regulations but quickly found methods of circumventing them.

Claude Dornier produced a cabin flying-boat in 1919 and then promptly transferred development and production to Switzerland and Italy. Ernst Heinkel in 1922 began building an aircraft works at Warnemünde on the Baltic coast and also set up a factory in Sweden. In 1924 Heinrich Focke and Georg Wulf jointly founded the Focke-Wulf Company at Bremen. The following year Herr Messerschmitt bought out the Bavarian Aircraft Company and immersed himself in the design and production of high-speed sports aircraft.

Aircraft production went hand in hand with the development of Germany's civil air services. Both were closely surveyed by the small band in the Defence Ministry.

On January 8th, 1919, the Reich Aviation Office licensed a new company, Deutsche Luftreederei, to operate air transport services. These began on February 5th with converted L.V.G. biplanes carrying mails between Berlin and Weimar.

Luftreederei grew at home and abroad where it co-operated with K.L.M., the Danish airline D.D.L. and the British company Daimler Hire. Its success and the subsidies granted by the state led to the mushroom growth of small airlines. By 1923 Luftreederei,

with private capital, began the concentration of resources into two main companies, Deutscher Aero-Lloyd and Junkers Luftverkehr.

Professor Junkers found the operation of various airlines worthwhile for his factory. He sold more aircraft and the regular reports of trained pilots and sevice engineers allowed him to embody operating experience into designs.

Deutscher Aero-Lloyd and Junkers Luftverkehr made considerable progress but they lacked financial backing. The Government, seeing its subsidies being lost, insisted on amalgamation. Accordingly, on January 6th, 1926, Deutsche Lufthansa came into being with $37\frac{1}{2}$ per cent of its shares in Ministry hands.

Behind the formation of Lufthansa was the astute Erhard Milch (later to become Field Marshal) who was appointed chairman of the airline. He wasted no time. Within one year Lufthansa flew four million miles and possessed a fleet of 120 aircraft. Highlights of the year included night passenger services between Berlin and Königsberg, connecting with Deruluft (Deutsche-Russische Luftverkehr) flights to Moscow, the flight of three tri-motor G-24s from Berlin to Peking via Russia, and the dispatch of a Dornier Wal flying-boat to investigate the route to Brazil.

Of even greater significance was the effort put into night and blind flying aids. In this first year these included beacon-lit airways for night operations and the provision of thirteen aviation ground radio stations. Lufthansa, from these small beginnings, was to provide the background and orders for the development of the German aviation electronics industry. Its navigation techniques became standard for the Luftwaffe and its fostering of the Lorenz beam approach system for airports led directly to the 'X' and 'Y' bombing beams of 1940 and 1941 which citizens of Coventry and elsewhere have reason to remember.

To Milch such ideas would have appeared ludicrous in 1926. He was intent on making Lufthansa the leading European airline. In the period from 1926 to 1928 the foreign-route network was expanded and the Baltic and the Alps were covered.

In 1928, however, a financial crisis hit the budding

airline. Government subsidies were reduced from between fifteen and sixteen million Reichsmarks to little over eight and many of the Lufthansa staff were dismissed. Milch lobbied Reichstag deputies to press his case for more funds. One deputy, the thick-set former commander of the famous Richthofen Circus, Hermann Göring, lent a sympathetic ear.

Göring, then one of only twelve Nazi Party deputies in the Reichstag, successfully pursued the cause of Lufthansa. He also told Milch in private that when the Nazis came to power they would create a new German Air Force. Thus was born a friendship which was to have far-reaching effects on Germany's military future in the air.

At the Defence Ministry von Seeckt was not idle during these years. He was anxious to gain as much experience as possible from civil aviation and accordingly in 1924 managed to get his nominee, Captain Brandenberg, appointed to the post of head of the Civil Aviation Department of the Ministry of Transport, thus ensuring co-operation on civil development and ultimately its direction by the Defence Ministry.

The Paris Air Agreement of 1926 provided a setback to von Seeckt's planners, as it heavily restricted the number of army and navy men who were permitted to fly. To overcome this stumbling-block arrangements were made through Captain Brandenberg to train military pilots in special sections of the Lufthansa commercial flying schools.

While the work of the air section of the Defence Ministry went on with varying degrees of success, the Nazi Party was fighting its way—with its own particular methods—to the top. Milch maintained his contacts with Göring until in 1931 he met Hitler. In the following year Göring invited Milch to throw in his lot with the Nazis but he preferred to wait and watch. On January 28th, 1933, Göring called on Milch and told him that the Nazi Party was about to seize power and pressed him to join. Still Milch held back. Two days later, on the morning of January 30th, Hitler was summoned to meet President Hindenberg and within two hours was Chancellor of the Third Reich.

Göring, trusted friend of Hitler, found himself right-hand man in a dictatorship. His devotion in the lean years of the 'twenties was rewarded with no less than four posts—one of which was Special High Commissioner for Aviation.

On his accession to power Hitler personally intervened in an attempt to persuade Milch to accept office. The latter's wish to remain head of Lufthansa was met by his being appointed Göring's deputy as Reichskommissar for Air while retaining the office of chairman of Lufthansa.

In April 1933 the Commissariat for Air was upgraded to the status of Air Ministry with Göring as Minister and Milch as Secretary of State. Milch was also secretly nominated by Hitler's order as Göring's successor in the case of the latter's death.

The die was cast and the wheels had been set irrevocably in motion for the re-formation of the German Air Force. Henceforward military and civil aviation in the Reich moved as one, Lufthansa being the instrument for training air crew, developing aids and proving new aircraft. Göring with his various offices, and fighting the Communists, was far too busy to concern himself with aviation. The task therefore devolved on Milch.

Milch's first step was to create the fabric of an Air Ministry organisation out of the old commissariat with additional departments removed from the Transport Ministry. A central administration department was created with five offices and inspectorates as follows:

1 An office run by an Army Oberst, but later directly under Milch. In this unit the Navy and Army, previously separate, were brought together and gradually became an air operations staff. In the latter part of 1933 Oberst Wever was appointed chief, and in 1935 he became the first Chief of Air Staff.
2 A technical and production office under Oberst Wimmer.
3 Civil aviation and meteorology under Ministerialdirigent Fisch, a department taken over from the Ministry of Transport.
4 Administration, finance, food and clothing including a works department responsible for airfield construction under Kesselring.
5 Personnel was at first headed by a civilian but later by a military commander, Stumpff.

The 'empire' which Milch inherited seemed unimpressive on the surface but the years of secret work had not been wasted. A hard core of army and navy officers with flying experience was immediately available within the Defence Ministry. A large pool of enthusiastic young men learned the elements of aviation in the gliding clubs and the aircraft industry was still healthily in being although on a small scale.

That 20,000 men were included in the new Air Force from its inauguration in 1935 was the result of the Russian training centre and the gliding and sports flying movements. The National Sozialistische Flieger Korps (National Socialist Flying Corps or N.S.F.K.) run by Oberst Bruno Lörzer showed little result, but this organisation took in large numbers of the gliding-school members. The pick of these were sent to the Verkehrsflieger Schule, the German airline pilots' school which before Hitler's accession to power had bases at Brunswick, Warnemünde, Schleissheim and List. The school also continued the work of the Lipezk centre, having special courses for Reichswehr officers temporarily 'discharged' from military service.

Small batches of the civilian trainees at the Verkehrsflieger Schule were sent on short military training courses held at Schleissheim. There they attended lectures on basic military subjects and were given twenty-five hours flying on Albatross and Heinkel biplanes which included combat aerobatics and some air-to-ground firing practice. One of the pupils who graduated from the gliding schools to the airline pilots' school and thence to Schleissheim was a young man named Adolf Galland, later to become known as the Generaleutnant, Inspector of Luftwaffe Fighters.

In May 1933 about seventy Verkehrsflieger Schule pupils were sent to Italy for fighter training but the five months spent on this were almost useless and the experiment was not repeated.

Hitler, during 1933 and 1934, was anxious to con-

The Luftwaffe's proving ground—Spain. Here early production Me 109Es in Condor Legion colours stand on a Spanish airfield in 1938

solidate his position and allay any foreign fears on German rearmament. Thus work had to be continued in the utmost secrecy.

Milch, with a free hand, saw in Lufthansa the instrument on which to base a planned expansion without arousing undue outside suspicion. The so-called Lufthansa training schools, two land and two sea, which were financed with military money, were rapidly extended, new airfields were built, and orders placed with the aircraft industry. Air force training continued with the airline and from 1935 Lufthansa crews were on the military reserve. The second pilot's seats of inland Junkers 52 transports were used to give advanced training to pilots from the elementary flying schools.

Above all Milch wanted a cautious and long-term policy to build up a strategic air force over a period of from eight to ten years. By this time there would be essential continuity of service and a strong cadre of qualified officers to take over senior posts. Some of the Air Ministry staff backed Milch to the full, but they found it impossible to resist Göring, who demanded that a five-year programme be accomplished in twelve months or less, and who roared with laughter at the suggestion that the first two to three years should be devoted solely to training the thousands of air and ground crews.

Göring had tasted the fruits of power. Although with his many appointments he managed to confer with Milch only four times a year he nevertheless sensed that in the new Air Force he would have a weapon of unlimited power which could add further to his laurels.

Any suggestions of steady expansion were ignored. Göring's demands for immediate results were backed up by Hitler himself, who, while largely ignorant about air matters, believed Göring's promises for the future Luftwaffe.

The German aircraft industry in 1933 had a labour force of only about 3,500 workers and its monthly average of production of all types of planes was thirty-one. The foresight of the planners at the Defence Ministry, at Lufthansa, and in the firms themselves, however, assured that the design teams were thoroughly up to date. They were able in a remarkably short time to produce sizable batches of trainers, transports, some biplane fighters and the prototypes of modern bombers such as the Heinkel 111 and Dornier 17. The aircraft that were to fight the Battle of Britain were, in fact, in the advanced design stage in 1933—the year Hitler came to power.

After tooling-up and expansion in 1933, the industry was ready on January 1st, 1934, to receive Milch's first full production programme for 4,021 aircraft covering the years 1934–5. This was intended to provide the basis for building up six bomber, six fighter and six reconnaissance Geschwader (wings) to act as operational instruction units for the increasing numbers of air and ground crews.

No less than twenty-five types of aircraft were included in this first programme. Despite this, production expanded at such a rate that from the monthly average of thirty-one in 1933 the figures increased to 164 a month and 265 a month in 1934 and 1935 respectively. No combat types were produced in 1933, but

Luftwaffe officers tour the Rolls-Royce works at Derby in 1937. Only General Milch realised what the British aviation expansion programme might eventually mean to the Luftwaffe in battle

Göring inspects a batch of future Luftwaffe officers at the secret Schleissheim flying school in the early thirties. This was a Göring in drab civilian clothes lacking his later gaudy uniforms

840 came out of the shops in the following year, and 1,923 in 1935.

For these spectacular results the credit must certainly go to Milch, who not only expanded the factories then in existence with the aid of State loans but encouraged industrial undertakings to form aircraft and component divisions. Foremost among these were Blöhm and Voss the shipbuilders, Henschel the locomotive makers, and Gotha who built rolling stock.

Milch planned to allocate by far the largest number of aircraft, 2,168, to training and a further 1,085 to operational units which would have training duties. A further 115 machines were to go to Lufthansa.

The essence of the interim air force programme was to treat modern bombers as the first line and fighters as the second to have some counter to the growing French Air Force. Milch envisaged fighters assuming priority over bombers about 1937, but by that time his star had waned and those who took over never put the scheme into effect. This had serious consequences in the Battle of Britain.

Things were going so well and output was rising so fast that in January 1935 Milch was able to put into operation a larger and more comprehensive production plan based on the same types of aircraft. This was to raise annual output from 3,183 in 1935 to 5,112 in 1936.

These promising forecasts combined with Hitler's growing security of position and the milk-and-water attitude of most European governments led, in 1935, to the unveiling to the world of the new Air Force.

On February 26th, 1935, Hitler officially created the German Luftwaffe with Göring as commander-in-chief. General Milch was Secretary of State for Air, and became effectively controller of the restyled Air Force. General Wever, the brilliant officer who had risen from an infantry regiment to head the command division of the Air Ministry, was made the first Chief of Air Staff. Some 20,000 officers and men and 1,888 aircraft were incorporated into the new service—a formidable beginning.

An unsuspecting and lethargic world was informed by Berlin on March 1st, 1935, that the Luftwaffe was a force in being. The work of von Seeckt and the 'secret Air Force' had achieved fruition.

The year 1935 was a gala one for the new Air Force. The units secreted in the flying clubs and in various military and para-military organisations were officially incorporated into the Luftwaffe. One of these 'hand-overs' was particularly ostentatious when, on March 28th, 1935, Hitler, accompanied by Göring and Milch, 'accepted' the new Richthofen squadron on the old army parade grounds at Berlin-Döberitz. The unit, equipped with He 51 biplanes, was formerly known as a squadron of the S.A. (Storm Troops).

In the same year an air staff college was opened, and anti-aircraft or Flak arm was subordinated to the

In the mid-thirties Germany developed two promising four-engined long-range bombers, the Dornier 19 and the Junkers 89. The specification called for a radius of action taking in the Urals and the north of Scotland. Both aircraft were capable of long term development and of forming the basis of a strategic bomber force. After the death of Major General Wever in 1936, the big bomber concept was abandoned in favour of larger numbers of much smaller shorter range machines such as the Heinkel 111 and the Dornier 17—a policy which did not pay off. The photograph shows the prototype Do 19 on test

Luftwaffe, the signals service was developed and the basic regional layout of the Air Force was inaugurated. Germany was divided into four main groups (Gruppen-kommandos) with centres controlling flying units at Berlin, Königsberg, Brunswick and Munich. The administration supply and training operations devolved on ten air districts or Luftgaue.

Milch was intent upon training more and yet more air crew. He limited production to trainers and interim combat types such as the He 51 fighter and the Ju 52 transport converted into a bomber, while awaiting assessment of a range of modern prototypes under development in the factories.

The expansion, however, began to get out of hand when Hitler and the General Staff called for the largest striking force in the minimum time. Strategic planning was non-existent. Operations were evolved on the basis

of new equipment available until finally aircraft dictated tactics.

The colossal building of the German Air Ministry which rose in the Leipzigerstrasse, Berlin, was to be one of the causes of German defeat. New staffs and sections which appeared daily were accompanied by new arguments and petty jealousies between department heads. Over all this ruled Göring, the First World War *pour le Mérite* fighter pilot who had no concept whatsoever of strategic air warfare or of up-to-date technical requirements. The ship was under sail but it lacked chart, course and helmsman.

There was one man whose foresight and ability to plan and co-ordinate could have changed the face and fortunes of the Luftwaffe. Major-General Wever was a pilot with an organising brain and an understanding of technology applied to air warfare. As the first Chief of Staff he laid tong-term plans which included the use of heavy four-engined bombers in large numbers. His plans were destined never to mature, for on June 3rd, 1936, he was killed while flying a Heinkel Blitz aircraft which crashed near Dresden.

Wever had been closely associated with an official specification issued in 1935 for a four-engined bomber capable of carrying a sizeable weight of bombs to the north of Scotland and to the Urals from German bases. Prototypes were ordered from Dornier and Junkers. Both these were available for flights trials at the end of 1936. The Dornier 19, with four 650 h.p. Bramo 322 radial engines, had a speed of 199 m.p.h. and a range of 990 miles. Its Junkers counterpart, the Ju 89, had four 960 h.p. Daimler Benz DB600 engines, a top speed of 242 m.p.h. and a range of 990 miles at 200 m.p.h.

The machines required development modification, more tankage and higher-powered engines, but basically one or both could have formed the backbone of the world's first strategic bomber fleet—and in time for the air war over Britain in 1940. Britain did not issue specifications for four-engined heavy bombers until 1936. At that time the Do 19 and the Ju 89 were already well advanced in the erecting shops, giving Germany a clear lead in Europe.

Wever, however, was dead and with him died Germany's heavy bomber fleet. Kesselring succeeded to the post of Chief of Staff and proceeded with Göring and others to examine bombers then under development. It was decided to delete the heavy bomber from the programme and to emphasize the fast medium bombers and Stukas.* Kesselring early in 1937 signed the cancellation order for the Do 19 and the Ju 89.

Colonel Wimmer, head of the technical branch, and other Wever supporters protested that at least a few prototypes should be completed and a full evaluation made. Göring remained adamant and when told by Kesselring that he had the choice between three twin-engined or two four-engined aircraft for the same money and production space remarked: 'The Führer will ask not how big the bombers are, but how many there are.' Even Milch, who had approved the original specification for the big bomber, sided with Göring and produced statistics to show that factory facilities and raw materials were lacking to build it.

With the demise of the heavy bomber, the German Air Ministry became obsessed by what can only be termed 'Stuka madness'.

The Junkers Company, established in Sweden as A. B. Flygindustrie, built the first dive-bomber or Stuka, the K 47, in 1928 and continued test work for some years in co-operation with von Seeckt's staff in the Reichswehr.

After Hitler's rise to power two biplane dive-bomber prototypes were tested and abandoned, although a third, the Henschel 123, was produced and entered service. The Ministry were at first dubious about the whole concept, largely on the grounds of aircraft structural strength, but in 1934 Junkers in Germany designed a successor to the K 47, designated Ju 87. The prototype of this flew late in 1935, but because of lack of a suitable home-built engine a British Rolls-Royce Kestrel motor was purchased and installed. The aircraft crashed due to tail flutter. Further much modified prototypes were built and sent for test at the Rechlin experimental base.

In the meantime Ernst Udet, Germany's most famed stunt flyer and World War I colleague of Göring, in 1933 purchased two American Curtiss Hawk dive-bombers with money put up by the embryo German Air Force. Udet became completely converted to the Stuka concept. His lobbying began to take effect in the Ministry.

Göring, anxious to fill the many vacant chairs in the Leipzigerstrasse, drew in all his 1914 to 1918 confreres. As a result, Udet, in January 1936, received a commission as Colonel and Inspector of Fighter and

* Sturzkampflugzeug = dive-bomber

Stuka Pilots. He pressed his dive-bomber views and gave personal demonstrations, while three firms, Heinkel, Arado and Hamburger Flugzeaugbau (Blöhm and Voss), completed prototypes in addition to Junkers.

After four months as Colonel Inspector, Udet was transferred as head of the Air Ministry technical branch in a general reshuffle which took place after Wever's death. In his new post Udet was in a position to push the dive-bomber programme through and convince Colonel von Richthofen, the chief sceptic, that the system would work.

During competitive dive-bomber trials at Rechlin on the Baltic in June the field was whittled down to the Ju 87 in its new Jumo-engined form and the streamlined Heinkel 118. On June 27th Udet, through pilot error, crashed the 118; the Ju 87 was awarded the production contract and became the Luftwaffe's standard dive-bomber.

The summer and winter of 1936 saw Rechlin carrying out an exhaustive evaluation of a series of prototypes which, in developed form, were to be the backbone of the Luftwaffe's air fleets for the Battle of Britain four years later. The machines were the Me 109 fighter, the He 111 and Do 17 medium bombers, and the Ju 88 high-speed light-medium bomber.

The Heinkel 111 was designed from the outset as a medium bomber, although a civil transport was the first to be announced after the military prototype flew early in 1935. Dornier, who had previously concentrated mainly on flying-boats, produced in 1934 a high-speed six-seat mailplane for Lufthansa. The airline found the type uneconomic. It was only the intervention of an Air Ministry department head that led to a redesign for bombing duties. In 1935 the military version of the Do 17 flew. Its extremely slender fuselage earned it the nickname 'Flying Pencil'. Both the He 111 and the Do 17 were awarded pre-production or 'O' contracts.

The first Ju 88 light bomber was being designed and built in the summer of 1935, the co-designers being Evers, a German, and Alfred Gassner, an *American citizen*. Both men had been employed in the U.S. aircraft industry and applied American techniques to their work. The Ju 88 did not, however, fly until 1936.

Fighters had a much lower priority than bombers as the whole Air Ministry pressure was on offence. In 1934 a design contract for a high-speed single-seat fighter monoplane was placed with Heinkel, Focke-Wulf, Arado, and with Messeschmitt's firm, Bayerische Fleugzeugwerke. Messerschmitt's chances of getting any production orders seemed remote as he had consistently quarrelled with Milch and others in the Air Ministry and, indeed, had been warned that his machine was on a development contract basis only.

Many radical ideas were incorporated into the Messerschmitt design, the Me 109, including automatic wing-slots, a small, light airframe and enclosed cockpit. As in the case of the Ju 87, Junkers could not supply the Jumo engine on time and what was to become one of the world's most famous interceptors took to the air in September 1935 powered by the ever-faithful 695 h.p. British Rolls-Royce Kestrel imported from Derby.

The Rechlin fighter trials soon cut the competition down to a straight fight between the Me 109 and the He 112. As a final decision could not be made, both firms were awarded contracts for ten machines.

Having settled on the development of two bombers, a dive-bomber, two fighters, several army co-operation types and others, the German Air Ministry began planning for industry expansion to a war-production footing and changeover, in late 1937, from production of obsolete types to massive output of the new machines.

Milch, the tough and brilliant organiser, was not destined to supervise the new expansion programme. For some time Göring had been suspicious of Milch's ability and his closeness to Hitler who often asked for the Secretary of State's advice. Milch's enemies in the Leipzigerstrasse lost no opportunity to foster the idea that he was thinking of usurping Göring's throne,* while Göring's many rivals in the Nazi Party hinted openly that the real Air Force commander-in-chief was Milch.

Göring, who had little or no direct hand in the evolution of the Luftwaffe, began to consult and promote others and gradually to divest Milch of his powers, including control of the air staff, the personnel office and the technical department. Göring appointed Udet director of the technical department in charge of production, giving him the rank of Generalmajor.

Göring was not interested in whether Udet was the best man for the job. All he wanted was a trustworthy replacement for Milch. Udet was a first-class pilot, full of humour and the life and soul of any party, but he was no organiser and loathed paperwork. His days were spent flying and visiting factories while lesser lights endeavoured to clear his in-trays as best they could. The German industry, with its deadly rivalries and undercurrents which matched those in the Air Ministry, needed an iron hand to control it. Instead it was presented with a most acceptable velvet glove. By 1939 Udet, far from relinquishing the reins to a more suitable man, had been appointed Luftwaffe Director-General of Equipment in the rank of Generaloberst.

Milch protested bitterly to Göring over his loss of control and demanded the right to return to his own job with Lufthansa. He feared he would continue to be held responsible for any blunders that Göring might make. Göring flatly refused and told him: 'You are not to retire, I will tell you when that is required.' As a parting shot Göring warned his Secretary of State not to feign illness but suggested that he was free to commit suicide if he wished.

Such then were developments when an event occurred which was to have a deep and lasting effect on Luftwaffe tactics, equipment and organisation. In 1936 civil war broke out in Spain and the High Command was presented with a heaven-sent opportunity to operate and train the new air force under modern battle conditions.

Initially, Germany sent eighty-five volunteer air and ground crew to Spain with twenty Ju 52 bomber-transports and six He 51 escort fighters. The Ju 52s'

first task, under the guise of a new airline, Hisma AG, was to transport 10,000 Moorish troops from Tetuan to Seville. The Ju 52s gave valuable service but the He 51s were found to be markedly inferior to American and Russian interceptors employed by the Republicans.

Large-scale assistance to General Franco with up-to-date equipment was the obvious answer. In November 1936 the Legion Condor came into being with General-major Sperrle in command and Lieutenant-Colonel Wolfram von Richthofen as chief of staff. Volunteers were called for, and shortly afterwards a contingent of 370 pilots in civilian clothes sailed for Spain on the liner *Usaramo*, ostensibly on a 'strength through joy' cruise with the code-name 'Union'.

When first set up, the Condor Legion had fifty Ju 52s and about fifty fighters, mainly the obsolescent He 51. Its efforts for the first seven or eight months were poor. It lacked accuracy and co-ordination, the only landmark being the destruction of fortified positions on the northern front by close support He 51s.

This particular staffel (squadron), 3./J 88, was commanded by Lieutenant Adolf Galland. The aircraft each carried four 10 kg. bombs and petrol bombs, these being dropped without the use of bomb-sights from 500 feet. Flying in close V formation all pilots delivered their load when the formation leader nodded his head. Crude as such efforts were, they showed remarkable success and were to lead to the sustained close support operations which smashed the defences of Poland and France in 1939 and 1940. Von Richthofen continued through 1938 to develop close-support techniques in Spain, using ground radio control of formations.

In the summer of 1937 the situation of the Condor Legion changed completely with the arrival of early production Me 109s, He 111s and Do 17s to be followed a few months later by the Ju 87. With these aircraft air superiority was achieved. It was found that the new medium bombers could outpace opposing fighters. They suffered few losses although unescorted. The effect of this was to lull the Luftwaffe into a sense of false security until July and August 1940 provided a rude awakening.

As the Spanish war progressed, the High Command established a routine, posting the best officers to Spain and then replacing them, sending the 'veterans' to training bases as instructors. Modifications to aircraft and equipment were made in the field and heavier armament such as the 20 m.m. cannon was tested on fighters.

While the bomber formations were building up a false reputation for invulnerability, the fighter arm was learning tactics which placed them in advance of any other European air force, including the R.A.F.

The whole question of fighter employment was analysed by Lieutenant Werner Mölders who succeeded Galland as commander of 3./J 88. His first step was to stop the close-formation flying of units of three aircraft and to organise loose formations based on an element of two, the Rotte, and of four, the Schwarm. The formations were also flown with elements at varying heights to give mutual cover and vision. Mölders detailed his experiences in Spain in a lengthy report to

---

* Milch had been appointed General der Flieger early in 1936, which sharpened the jealousies among his colleagues.

Above *Germany's first Sturzkampfflugzeug-dive-bomber—The Henschel Hs 123 which first flew early in 1935. The type saw service in Spain, but was later superseded by the Junkers 87*

Below *The dreaded Stuka, the Ju 87, which wrought havoc in Poland, Belgium, Holland and France, but became an expensive liability over Britain. Illustrated here is the third prototype Ju 87 which flew late in 1935*

the General Staff in 1939. German fighter tactics were henceforward based on this document.

Also from the Spanish campaign the Luftwaffe learned the value of unit mobility and of an efficient signals network for tactical work. By September 1939 every squadron had one or two Ju 52 transports for carrying supplies and personnel. During large scale high intensity operations such as the invasion of France extra Ju 52s acted as radio or D/F stations.

While the Luftwaffe was being built up on the Blitzkrieg theory for a European land-war, the industry in Germany had changed over to the mass production of new types of aircraft. This entailed complete retooling and reorganisation of most factories with consequent dislocation and a marked fall in output in late 1937 and early 1938.

Pre-war German propaganda stressed the massive output of German aircraft factories which went far to frighten air force chiefs in other European countries. In fact aircraft output was not nearly high enough and did not expand even after war began. Britain outstripped Germany in total aircraft output in 1940. Here Junkers 88 fuselages roll down the line

After retooling, the industry should have been driven really hard by the German Air Ministry, but the responsible officer, General Udet, was quite unable to do anything about it. The industry, as was shown later in the war, was quite capable of producing nearly five times as many aircraft as it did in 1939, and this under heavy air attack.

In 1938 to 1939 too many modifications were introduced on combat aircraft, the industry manpower figures did not rise and many able young men were called up for national service. As there was no centralised economic and war potential planning with reserved occupations and direction of labour, the manufacturers did largely what they liked with far-reaching consequences from the Battle of Britain onwards. Even in 1940 the industry succeeded in turning out only 10,826 aircraft whereas Britain doubled its production in that year and outstripped Germany by over 4,000 aircraft.*

The actual strength of the Luftwaffe in the Munich crisis period and after was over-estimated by other European countries and this belief was fostered by the German Propaganda Ministry. In fact, on August 1st, 1938, four months after the occupation of Austria, the total strength of the German Air Force was 2,929 aircraft, of which only 1,669 were serviceable. There were serviceable only 453 fighters, 582 bombers and 159 dive-bombers—hardly sufficient to embark upon a world war.

The breathing space provided by the notorious Munich Agreement was as vital to the Luftwaffe as it was to the R.A.F. Air crew training was extended to bases in Austria, fresh recruits were drawn in from the Austrian population and Austrian aircraft engineers were transferred to a new Messerschmitt factory at Wiener Neustadt. By September 1939 this was turning out Me 109 fighters at the rate of about sixteen per month. In March 1939 Germany invaded Czechoslovakia and took over a fresh batch of airfields and production facilities which were very speedily put to good use. There was, however, little recruiting fodder for the Luftwaffe from the Czech Air Force, and many of the best pilots made their way to France and Britain to become the German Air Force's bitter opponents.

Obsolescent types in 1937 still contributed to a total production of 5,606 aircraft of which 2,651 were combat aircraft. The monthly average for the year was 467 per month. In 1938 the total production fell by nearly 400 to 5,235 with a monthly average down to 436 although combat types represented 3,350 units.

To provide the necessary forces for a European war production of at least 700 aircraft per month was required. This total was achieved only in the autumn of 1939. The average monthly output was 691 for the whole year. Total production rose to 8,295 in 1939 but this was still not good enough. The proportion of fighters was too low.

* British aircraft total production in 1939 was 7,940 and in 1940 reached 15,049

2 Action

On August 22nd, 1939, Hitler addressed his commanders-in-chief at Berchtesgaden with the words:
'. . . I have witnessed the miserable worms Chamberlain and Daladier in Munich; they will be too cowardly to attack and will go no further than blockade. Poland will be depopulated and colonised with Germans . . . and besides, Gentlemen, in Russia will happen what I have practised in Poland. After Stalin's death—he is seriously ill—we will crush the Soviet Union.'

These in a nutshell were Hitler's aims and objects on the verge of World War II. It is recorded that at the end of the meeting 'Göring leapt on a table and gave bloodthirsty thanks and bloody promises; he jumped around like a savage.' The Feldmarschall, it seems, would have been better employed in a Shakespearean play than in his task as head of the Luftwaffe.

The eve of war on September 2nd saw the German Air Force in excellent shape for a short-term close-support conflict over land. It was tailored to destroy and move forward with the ground troops. Air superiority was a necessity to this end. The basic equipment, layout, supply organisation and command were almost exactly those which a year later were to be fighting bitterly for supremacy in the skies over England.

By January 16th, 1939, the Luftwaffe had completed the large-scale reorganisation required by a rapid expansion in both the forces and the area covered. Within the High Command Milch's star was again in the ascendant with his post of Secretary of State supplemented by that of Inspector General. After Kesselring and Stumpff had successively held the office of Chief of Air Staff, the task in February 1939 devolved on General Jeschonnek, an ardent supporter of the high-speed medium bomber and Stuka theories.

New commands had been created to take the place of the Gruppen-kommandos. These emerged as three Luftflotten, or air fleets. They were No. 1 with headquarters at Berlin under General Kesselring, No. 2 at Brunswick under General Felmy and No. 3 at Munich under General Sperrle. There was an additional Air Command in East Prussia subordinate to Luftflotte 1, and in March Luftflotte 4 was inaugurated with headquarters at Vienna. This was commanded by General Loehr, who had come over from the Austrian Air Force after the Anschluss.

Each Luftflotten was a self-contained force with all fighter, bomber and other elements. This was in contrast to the reorganisation of the R.A.F. in 1936 when commands were based on function, i.e. Bomber Command, Fighter Command and so on. It was the integration of all forces in a Luftflotte which led to the great successes in Poland, Belgium and France but which also stultified fighter and bomber operational development along their own specialised lines. It was also the chief reason why adequate fighter defence was not prepared in Germany and not appreciated by the High Command in its dealings with the R.A.F. Luftflotte strength varied according to the task to be undertaken. The basic average was 1,000 aircraft.

Administration and supply for each Luftflotte were carried out by the appropriate Luftgaue (air district) which were extended as more territory was conquered. Within the Luftflotten were the operational complements to the Luftgaue, known as Fliegerkorps, or Fliegerdivisionen. Each air fleet at the outbreak of war contained about two of these 'air divisions' and between two and three Luftgau commands.

The flying personnel of the Luftwaffe were separated from the adminstrative and supply N.C.O.s and officers. In the R.A.F. a promotion from squadron commander to the rank of wing commander would often mean becoming O.C. of a station but in the Luftwaffe the station commander was a non-flying man provided by the Luftgau. If a flying unit was based on his airfield its commander had precedence over him. He possessed real control only when the airfield was empty. From the supply and administration aspect this system was useful but it also tended in wartime to cause ill-feeling where an operational station in the thick of the fight was nominally run by a non-flying officer.

In the Fliegerkorps itself, the basic unit was a Gruppe (group) which approximated to the British wing, and mustered about thirty aircraft. The Gruppen were normally combined into a Geschwader of some 90–120 machines which was roughly equivalent in strength, but not in layout, to an R.A.F. Group. Within the Gruppe the prime unit was a Staffel with nine aircraft, this being smaller than the average British fighter squadron which had sixteen machines.

At the outbreak of the war there was no lack of trained air crew in the German Air Force and the reserve situation was satisfactory. This was largely due to Milch's original policy of concentration on trainer aircraft production and on expanding training bases and facilities. Luftwaffe personnel, excluding those in Flak batteries, totalled nearly 600,000, of which about 15 per cent were aircrew and a further 15 per cent were undergoing training. The schools in 1939 were turning out between 10,000 and 15,000 pilots a year from about 100 schools.

The strength of the Luftwaffe on September 2nd, 1939, as shown in the Quartermaster General's returns, was 4,204 planes including 552 transport aircraft and sundry army co-operation machines.

Reserves varied from 10 to 25 per cent according to the time the type had been in production. There were plenty of He 111 and Do 17 bombers but there were no Ju 88s because the machine was only just coming off the line in its final version.

In addition to air force equipment, the so-called naval Gruppen had a motley collection of 240 flying-boats, seaplanes and land-based aircraft mainly for reconnaissance.

Although the most up-to-date air force in Europe, the Luftwaffe had too few aircraft reserves to fight a long war. The necessity for short campaigns with a low attrition rate was accentuated by three other factors: shortages of oil, bombs and flak ammunition. Although stocks of oil had been accumulated, they were insufficient for heavy fighting on two fronts such as Poland and France, and the possibility of joint action by Britain and France to aid Poland was accepted by the High Command as a calculated risk.

As it turned out, the Allies made no move against Germany in 1939, and the stocks of oil captured in Poland were sufficient to replace the amount used. The long period of the 'phony war' enabled the Luftwaffe to conserve its resources and store current production for the attack in the west.

Unknown to the British and French intelligence authorities, Germany in September 1939 was suffering from an acute lack of bombs. The exact figures are not available but the stocks of all calibres were sufficient only for about three weeks' sustained operations. In the Polish campaign some 60 per cent of these were expended.

Milch had repeatedly tried to get bomb production a higher priority. On July 1st, 1939, while Hitler was inspecting prototype aircraft at the Rechlin experimental station, he had broached the subject with the Führer, much to the annoyance of Göring. Hitler speciously commented that he had no intention of getting involved in a general war, and that bomb production could wait.

Milch pressed his arguments at dinner at Hitler's headquarters in Silesia on September 12th and on several occasions between then and early October but with no result.

It was not until October 12th, over a month after war began, that Hitler finally agreed to a full-scale programme for air force munitions. Milch was placed in charge although he suggested it was Udet's job.

On the same night Milch called a meeting of industrialists, steel, explosives and other experts, in his office at the Air Ministry to plan an emergency programme on munitions. As an interim measure he ordered the production of large quantities of concrete-casing bombs fabricated in moulds. Although several million of these weapons were made between October 1939 and mid-1941, they were not used in any quantity against Britain because nine months conventional bomb programme was sandwiched into six months in good time for the western offensive.

If the Allies had appreciated the position in September and had launched heavy attacks against German military targets the Luftwaffe would have been hard put to it to retaliate.

Apart from these temporary shortcomings, the Luftwaffe went to war with six major defects:

1   An inadequate production programme.
2   No four-engined long-range bombers.
3   Insufficient range for its standard day fighter, the Me 109, and a twin-engined long-range fighter, the Me 110, which was very vulnerable against modern single-engined interceptors.
4   Very little radar equipment; no operational experience in its use, or in radar counter-measures, and a shortage of electronics specialists at all levels.
5   No adequate ground control for fighter aircraft.
6   A shortage of good officers in the middle echelons such as at wing commander and group captain level.

The production programme did not really get under way until Milch took over in 1941 after Udet's suicide. It was then too late. After the French campaign in May 1940 the industry spent much of its time diversifying in the mistaken belief that the war was over. One well-known aircraft company in 1940 built prefabricated aluminium huts for troops who were supposed to occupy most of Africa, while another made aluminium ships, and extending ladders for the Rhineland vineyards. This material should have gone into aeroplanes, but because of the lack of control of raw materials by Udet's directorate considerable wastage occurred.

Germany never succeeded in producing a good heavy bomber after the cancellation of the Ju 89 and Do 19 in 1937—the main effort being poured into the Heinkel 177, a mechanical monstrosity which probably killed more crews in accidents than on operations. Its delivery was years late. If a good four-engined bomber had been available in quantity in 1939 to 1940 the Luftwaffe could have been a considerable nuisance to British ports and shipping. Many of the German fighter escort problems during Dunkirk and the Battle of Britain would have been solved.

The Me 110 was supposed to be the Luftwaffe's best long-range fighter. It was very successful until put up against modern single-seaters like the Spitfire when it became obsolescent except in a night-fighter role. The Me 109 was undoubtedly one of the finest interceptors in the world in September 1939, but its range was far too short. Drop-tanks would have answered the problem but the fighter pilots felt they were dangerous and put them at a disadvantage if 'jumped' by the enemy. Contrary to general belief, jettisonable long-range fuel tanks for the Me 109 were produced during the early stages of the war. They were, however, made of plywood and storage in the open during an advance caused the sun to split the wood and the rain to rot the glue. The result was that they were very unreliable and were scrapped.

While German signals troops had reached a very high pitch of efficiency and had gained field experience in Spain, Austria and Czechoslovakia, there was virtually no radar for offence or defence. Little had been

The crew of a Ju 88 study the map before a raid on Poland in 1939

done to prepare counter-measures against a possible enemy with electronic detection devices.

Radar in Germany began in 1934–5 but at the instigation of the Navy, not the Air Force. The requirement was for two sets, one for gun ranging and target search at sea, the other for air surveillance. The Navy posted an engineer officer to the radio firm of Telefunken to produce a development programme. Instead of continuing with Telefunken, however, the Navy turned to a newly formed company, GEMA, for both development and manufacture. This firm had to start from scratch which considerably lengthened the gestation period.

In 1936 the Flak arm and the Air Force became interested in radar. In that year General Martini saw a demonstration of the GEMA surveillance unit, Freya, which worked on a wavelength of 2.4 metres—considerably shorter than the British Chain Home stations. As a result, the Luftwaffe ordered twelve sets. Meanwhile Lorenz A.G., of Stuttgart, entered the field with an anti-aircraft radar for the Army Weapons Division. In 1937 Telefunken again came on the scene with a contract from the Air Ministry for a combined surveillance and anti-aircraft equipment.

Development was slow, because specifications were constantly changing, numerous departments from the ministries interfered, and there was no co-operation between the firms involved.

It was not until July 1939 that the German Air Ministry wireless section sorted out a simpler surveillance specification which Telefunken could meet. A laboratory set of what was to be named 'Würzburg' was then demonstrated to Hitler and Göring at Rechlin. Some idea of the lack of direction at high level or of any effective radar programme can be gained from the fact that the official responsible for the anti-aircraft warning service was not invited to the demonstration.

Telefunken was ordered to modify its set for one-man operation and 800 Würzburgs were ordered. Simultaneously a contract was placed with GEMA for 200 Freyas.

Production was still delayed because of continual modifications and a complete lack of urgency in the ministries. The work of the scientists was excellent. They proved that radar worked, but in their watertight compartments without any co-ordinating body like the British Tizard Committee, they tended to make very sophisticated sets with built-in problems. A simpler approach with drive behind it would have yielded better results.

British radar was far more crude than that of Germany in 1939, but it worked and was proved operationally. These, in electronics, are the only two things that matter. Very advanced ideas are only useful if they are available off the production line when they are wanted.

An Me 109E being prepared for an exercise just before the war. The unit is 2./JG20

While Britain had a C.H. radar watch twenty-four hours a day round the south and east of the country on September 3rd, 1939, Germany was setting up one or two experimental Freya units on the North Sea coast with a range of seventy-five miles and no indication of altitude.

Throughout the operational installation and development period of German radar, all branches of the service connected with it suffered from an acute shortage of skilled manpower. This was almost entirely due to Göbbels, who had seen fit to ban all amateur radio operators shortly after Hitler's rise to power. The excuse given was that of countering subversive elements during the anti-Communist purge, but the order was never rescinded.

Until the end of the war Germany was short of good quality radio and radar operators and engineers in complete contrast to Britain, where literally thousands of radio 'hams' with first-class working knowledge joined the services and the research establishments.

While communications generally in the Luftwaffe were good, no attempt was made to evolve close ground control of fighters for defence. The basic radar and radio sector system of the R.A.F. did not exist in Germany. Consequently, with the accent on blitzkrieg tactics, fighter operations suffered badly. The discovery of the R.A.F.'s close-knit system in the summer of 1940 came as a distinct shock to the Luftflotten involved, but little was done at High Command level until 1941 when a conference in Russia thrashed out the problem for the first time.

The whole Luftwaffe signals and radar set-up suffered continually from lack of co-operation between departments and open clashes at top level. Milch wanted to absorb signals into the general body of the Luftwaffe and make signals officers into aircrew if necessary for their general training, but this, of course, would never have worked. Martini managed skilfully to keep his autonomy throughout the war though his department was never given the backing and authority it needed. One of the main explanations of this was the complete lack of technical, and particularly electronics, knowledge in the Luftwaffe High Command. Men with sound scientific qualifications were passed over in favour of those with an impressive military career. The hub of the problem could be found in Commander-in-Chief Göring himself, who loathed technicalities of any sort and was totally unable to understand them.

Finally, the abandoning of Milch's ten-year training plans and the early onset of war left the Luftwaffe with a lack of middle echelon men with really good backgrounds. On the one side there were plenty of brave young men to control Staffeln. On the other there was no shortage of ex-army and World War I air force officers to fill the higher ranks and the acres of offices in the Air Ministry.

The younger men needed years to accumulate the experience for organisation rather than fighting while the upper ranks were often hidebound and lacked air force knowledge. In the middle were a limited number of first-class officers equivalent to R.A.F. wing commanders and group captains. For these there were no adequate replacements. Each one killed or captured meant the loss of a future Geschwader or Luftflotte commander, or of a reliable staff officer.

It was in the Battle of Britain that this became painfully evident. The losses at this level affected the structure of the Luftwaffe for the rest of the war.

Despite all these problems, which could only be manifest with time, the German Air Force was launched against Poland on September 1st, 1939, with high hopes of success. In his order of the day, Göring stated:

The wreckage of a Polish hangar after the Luftwaffe had passed

'Born of the spirit of the German airmen in the First World War, inspired by faith in our Führer and Commander-in-Chief—thus stands the German Air Force today, ready to carry out every command of the Führer with lightning speed and undreamed-of might.'

He was not disappointed. In twenty-eight days the campaign in Poland was over. Luftflotten 1 and 4 with a total of 1,538 aircraft destroyed a large part of the Polish Air Force on the ground on the first day of the campaign, gaining complete air supremacy on the second. From September 3rd onwards the Air Force devoted itself to the destruction of the Polish ground forces as the German Army moved forward.

On September 25th came the first large-scale bombing of a major city—Warsaw. On the 27th it capitulated and the myth of the invincible Stuka was born.

This, indeed, was a lightning war. An air force of 400 first-line machines was almost completely destroyed in two days and a country of over thirty-one million occupied in four weeks. Luftwaffe losses were only nineteen aircraft on operations during the whole of the month. So little air opposition was encountered in the later phases of the battle that most fighter units were turned over to ground strafing.

To the Luftwaffe Poland was visible proof of the success of blitzkrieg and the overwhelming superiority of the air arm. To Göring all propaganda claims were vindicated, but in fact the Luftwaffe, although executing a highly efficient attack, learned nothing. The Polish Air Force was inferior in numbers by one to three, largely obsolescent and without any adequate warning system.

Because of the ineptitude and weakness of French and British politicians no air action was taken against Germany from French or British bases. In attacking Poland the Luftwaffe greatly reduced its fighter and bomber forces in the west. The intervention of the R.A.F. and Armée de l'Air could have meant the withdrawal of major fighter units from the east with a consequent easing of the pressure on Polish ground troops and communications.

After September the Luftwaffe deliberately conserved its strength in the west against the forthcoming attack on France and the Low Countries. Only a few

Bombs falling from a Heinkel III over a target in Poland

units were allowed to engage in air combat and there existed a standing order forbidding the frontier to be crossed. Inactivity on the part of the Armée de l'Air and the R.A.F. Advanced Air Striking Force was a godsend to the German Air Force. Fuel, bomb and munitions stocks were built up, new units formed and a complete organisation arranged for the rapid transfer of supplies and fuel to new western bases in preparation for an advance.

Hitler's new objective after Poland was an attack through France and the Low Countries. He was anxious to undertake this as quickly as possible before there was any improvement in the Anglo-French armaments position. It was at first planned that the French invasion should take place in the autumn of 1939 despite vigorous protests from various sections of the Luftwaffe which were still short of supplies.

In a memorandum to his chiefs of staff dated October 9th, 1939, Hitler remarked: 'The attack is to take place in all circumstances (if at all possible) this autumn.' Adverse weather conditions through the autumn and winter, however, meant repeated postponement of the date, much to the relief of the General Staff. When the spring appeared the most opportune time to launch the offensive, planning and preparation were geared to this end.

In the meantime, the High Command had become anxious about its open flank to the north. Norway and Denmark could become a springboard for Allied attacks, thus facing Germany with a war on two fronts. Under conditions of utmost secrecy plans were drawn up for simultaneous surprise attacks on both neutral countries which, if successful, would provide bases for German air and sea warfare against Britain. Already the German High Command envisaged full-scale operations against England. The memorandum of October 9th by Hitler recorded that 'The German Air Force cannot succeed in efficient operations against the industrial centres of England and her southern and south-west ports until it is no longer compelled to operate offensively from our present small North Sea coast by extremely devious routes involving long flights.'

By the end of March 1940 the Danish-Norwegian campaign had been organised in minute detail and an order was issued to the forces concerned by the commander of Fliegerkorps X, General Geisler, under the heading Operation Weser.

Surprise attacks were to be launched at dawn from the sea on seven Norwegian harbours while German troops at the same time occupied the whole of Denmark and made landings at Copenhagen and on the Danish islands. The Luftwaffe support for Denmark was to consist of massive demonstrations of strength in the hope that Göbbel's propaganda efforts would prove sufficient to cow the population into surrender.

Five hundred combat aircraft and 500 Ju 52 transports were allocated for the invasion of Norway. The

Generaloberst Ernst Udet, Director General of Air Force Equipment from 1939 to 1941

Generaloberst Hans Jeschonnek, Chief of the General Staff of the Air Force, 1939–43

Ju 52s were divided into a force of 160 machines from fully trained units for parachute attacks, and 340 were drawn from training establishments which acted as the air supply train for the whole operation.

On April 7th, 1940, reconnaissance aircraft surveyed British naval bases and searched the North Sea in case the Royal Navy had wind of the impending attack. All was quiet, and on the following day Göring delivered an after-dinner speech to his commanders outlining the prospects for the campaign and the methods to be used.

Promptly at 5 a.m. on April 9th, the German Army swept into Denmark by sea and land. The country fell within twelve hours. In Norway, as the seaborne forces fought their way ashore, paratroops and airborne infantry occupied the Stavanger and Oslo airfields following the destruction of the small Norwegian Air Force on the ground.

As in Poland, the Air Force was obliterated before it could get into the air, and the surprise of co-ordinated attack disrupted ground defence. By April 10th four airfields were in German hands and were operating Stukas and fighters. Close watch was kept on the North Sea using the four-engined Focke-Wulf 200 for the

first time. On the opening day of the attacks, Milch, as Inspector General, flew to Aalborg in Denmark in his converted Do 17. On the 12th Göring appointed him temporarily to command the Luftwaffe in Norway with supervisory powers over ground and naval forces.

By April 15th, when the first British landings took place in northern Norway, the Luftwaffe was firmly established and retained full command of the air despite later gallant efforts by No. 263 Squadron's Gladiators and many long-range sorties by Bomber Command.

The Allied landings caused the Luftwaffe hurriedly to strengthen its forces in Norway in the second half of April. By the beginning of May there were 710 combat aircraft on the scene, including 360 long-range bombers and 50 dive-bombers.

The main Allied troops were withdrawn from central Norway on May 2nd and 3rd but in the Narvik area fighting continued with very effective operations by Nos. 46 and 263 Squadrons with Hurricanes and Gladiators respectively. Despite the Narvik problem the Luftwaffe was already perfecting its Norwegian communications and airfields and had set up a full air maintenance unit. On April 24th the staff of a new Luftflotte, No. 5, was flown from Hamburg to Oslo to be followed at the end of the month by their commander, Generaloberst Stumpff. The organisation was already in train for the forthcoming air assault on Britain.

The Norwegian campaign finally closed on June 10th when Narvik was reoccupied by German troops. It had been another brilliant blitzkrieg but with some

Generalleutnant Wever, first Luftwaffe Chief of General Staff. Killed 1936

General der Nachtrichtenfuhrer Martini, head of Luftwaffe Signals

Generaloberst Stumpff, commanded Luftflotte 5 in the Battle of Britain

setbacks from Allied intervention. Luftwaffe losses during the period of the main operations, the month of April, totalled 256, although a few of these were incurred over France and Britain.

Significant factors were the loss of 54 bombers and 35 Ju 52s on operations, and 25 bombers and 33 transports from causes other than enemy action. Although these losses were not severe in numbers they included many of the best crews trained on radio-beam bombing who belonged to Kampfgruppe 100. This unit was thrown into the Norwegian campaign as an ordinary day-bomber unit when it should have been held in reserve for the assault on Britain where long-range beam sorties were to be the order of the day. KGr. 100 had to be completely re-formed for the Battle of Britain and the night blitz using less competent crews. This had a marked effect on the speed of introduction and efficiency of blind bombing.

While operations progressed in Norway the stage had been set for a much greater drama, the assault on France and the Low Countries. Quietly, many units of Luftflotte 5 had been withdrawn early in May and transferred to Luftflotten 2 and 3 under Generals Kesselring and Stumpff respectively.

Luftflotte 2 with Fliegerkorps I and IV and Fliegerdivision IX were to work with Army Group B under von Bock. Luftflotte 3 co-operated with Army Group A under von Rundstedt and Army Group C which faced the Maginot Line. Under Luftflotte 3 came Fliegerkorps II, V and VIII.

For the attacks on Holland and Belgium and for air supply, 475 Ju 52s and forty-five gliders were amassed. These came under the command of a staff known as Zur Besonderen Verwendung (z.b.V.), or Special Operations Group, under General Putzier. The air-landing operations were directed by General Student, who formed the first battalions of the German paratroops in the autumn of 1938.

In all, the Germans had 3,914 serviceable machines* for the campaign in the west out of their total strength of 5,142. About 3,500 of these were used in the assault. This was the largest number of aircraft ever to be used by the Luftwaffe for a single campaign. The bulk of the force was employed on a front of only 200 miles.

The whole strategic concept of the offensive differed from that in Poland. Instead of encirclement, a huge armoured spearhead was to be thrust forward with maximum concentrated air support.

In order to maintain the flying units as they leapfrogged forward, the German Air Force devised a system whereby special Luftgau staffs were organised prior to the offensive so as to act as spearheads for administration and supply. These mobile staffs were to press on close behind the army ground units to reconnoitre and develop airfields and to improvise supplies to these sites so that combat units could fly from them in the shortest possible time. In general, one of these special staffs was allocated to each Fliegerkorps.

Despite the overall plans for attack having fallen into Allied hands in January through the forced landing of a German communications aircraft in Belgium, the High Command, and Hitler in particular, were convinced that surprise could still be achieved and that the Allies were ill-prepared to meet the proposed blitzkrieg movements. The risks were great but the fruits of victory would be incalculable.

The Führer's prophecies held good and on May 10th the avalanche descended on Belgium, Holland and France.

* This figure was made up of 1,120 bombers, 343 Stukas, 42 ground attack aircraft, 248 twin-engined fighters, 1,016 single-engined fighters, 591 reconnaissance aircraft, 401 transports and 154 seaplanes

3 The Trenchard Air Force

The R.A.F., as an independent fighting service, was conceived out of the widespread indignation that swept the country when London was bombed in the early summer of 1917. It was born eleven months later after an inquiry into the defence and co-ordination of the Royal Flying Corps and the Royal Naval Air Service.

General Jan Christian Smuts, the South African soldier and statesman, conducted the investigation at the request of the Prime Minister, Lloyd George.

Smuts concluded his report by recommending the amalgamation of all the air services as a matter of urgency and the creation of an Air Ministry to control and administer all matters connected with air warfare. Strenuous protests were made by the War Office and the Admiralty. On April 1st, 1918, the autonomous and independent Royal Air Force was born.

At the armistice in November 30,122 officers and 263,410 other ranks were serving in the R.A.F. It had 22,000 planes flying with 188 operational squadrons and 199 training units from 675 airfields and stations. With aircraft like the Sopwith Snipe, the D.H.9A and the Handley Page V/1500 its technical superiority was unrivalled.

All three services were shorn of their wartime strength with remarkable alacrity. By the end of 1919 the most powerful air force in the world had been whittled down to 31,500 officers and men, 371 aircraft and twelve squadrons. It would have ceased to exist altogether if the Army, and particularly the Navy, had found a way of bringing their former members back to their respective folds.

To rescue the young service came a man known to posterity as 'The Father of the Royal Air Force'. Marshal of the R.A.F. Viscount Trenchard, then Air Chief Marshal Sir Hugh Trenchard, was tall, broad-shouldered, with shaggy eyebrows and a deep voice that had earned him the nickname of 'Boom'. He had already commanded the Royal Flying Corps and the Independent Bomber Force created to attack strategic targets in Germany when he became the R.A.F.'s first Chief of Staff.

Trenchard saw that a powerful air force could be moulded into a deterrent against future wars. It was he who provided the entire basis on which the Air Force was to develop and on which it was eventually to be tested in the Battle of Britain. His plan covered every aspect of development—the provision of aircraft, air and ground crew training, staff training and the organisation for control.

The mould in which the post-war R.A.F. was cast had its beginnings in a Trenchard memorandum presented to Parliament by Mr. Winston Churchill on December 11th, 1919, as a White Paper. This described in detail the form the new service should take and the duties it should perform. The scheme which covered the whole field of future development was to prove the model for most air forces of the world and to stand the test of time. With few facts and little history for guidance he laid a sound foundation. When in 1936 the R.A.F. opened a chapter of great expansion it was on the sixteen-year-old White Paper that the additions to the structure were built.

The plan aimed to create little more than a skeleton force which would lend itself easily to expansion. Squadrons were reduced to the bare minimum of eighteen, and two seaplane units overseas; a small number of squadrons specially trained in co-operation with the Army and Navy at home and one airship station. The main resources were concentrated on promoting research for which stations were set up to experiment with landplanes, seaplanes, torpedo aircraft and wireless.

The whole system of training for officers and men was intended as a standard one and it had no parallel in Germany. The Cadet College at Cranwell provided the initial training for men who were later to become the commanders of the Air Force, and the Staff College broadened their outlook in mid-career. Technical colleges at Halton, Buckinghamshire; Cranwell, Lincolnshire; and Flowerdown trained the ground crews. Flying training standards were laid down by the instructors of the Central Flying School who carried them through to other training schools.

It was intended to be flexible and to avoid over-specialisation. Schools of wireless, gunnery, and photography were provided for under the scheme, but officers and men were expected to gain experience in any type of squadron, and to move readily from one unit to another. Later on, as new technical discoveries were made and flying became more complicated, a need arose for expert knowledge and concentration by specialist officers upon certain subjects. This was still imposed upon a sound general training, so that no one should become too remote from the main task of flying, nor lack a working knowledge of the service. The system of training was laid down.

The Volunteer Reserve was one of the very few organisations not included in the Trenchard plan. Formed in 1936, it was to become an invaluable source of additional pilots.

Trainers for R.A.F. pilots in the thirties. Below a line-up of Hawker Harts. The trainer version of this famous day bomber first came into service in 1933 and was not superseded by the Harvard and Master until 1939. Above is a formation of Avro Tutors, a basic training type which first came into service in 1933

Other recommendations which were to be of vital importance twenty-one years later foreshadowed the creation of the Auxiliary Air Force, the university air squadrons and the short-service commission. Without these the expansion which was then required would have been impossible.

There was strong opposition to the creation of the Auxiliary Air Force at the outset, on the grounds that military aviation was too complicated and dangerous to be undertaken by amateurs on a part-time basis. But Trenchard's forecast that it would provide an indispensable reinforcement for the regular squadrons of the R.A.F. was amply justified in the Battle of Britain.

The short-service-commission scheme took a man in at eighteen or nineteen, trained him and kept him in the Force for five years. With intensive training he became a proficient pilot in a year and a skilled one in two, so that five years was enough to ensure that the squadrons were adequately manned. The scheme created a first-class reserve of trained officers who were encouraged to return each year to fly and keep abreast of new techniques.

The R.A.F. was small immediately after the war but it was not idle. One of its occupations was to police regions not easily accessible by land forces. Eight squadrons and a small force of armoured cars which were sent out to the Iraq Protectorate allowed British Army strength there to be greatly reduced, for instance.

In the meantime the question of Britain's own defence had cropped up at home. Two factors were responsible, the ascendancy of the bomber as a master-weapon and the fear that the disparity between the R.A.F. and neighbouring air forces might weaken Britain's diplomatic hand.

The French Armée de l'Air had a striking force of 300 bombers and 300 fighters in France. Britain's equivalent was three squadrons or less than forty aircraft.

Hurricane 1's of 79 Squadron lined up at Biggin Hill for the 1939 Empire Air Day display

In the light of these considerations the Government agreed to the Air Ministry's request for a leading role in home defence. In August 1922 a proposal for a metropolitan air force was agreed. This was to consist of fourteen bomber and nine fighter squadrons, the proportion of fighters to bombers reflecting the Air Staff's belief in the principle that the best defence is offence. Even then the force approved for the defence of the country did not come anywhere near to matching the 600 aircraft it was designed to oppose. The total establishment of twenty-three squadrons allowed for a strength of no more than 266 bombers and fighters.

The following year a sub-committee of the Committee of Imperial Defence, under the chairmanship of Lord Salisbury, considered relations between the Navy and the Air Force and the place of air power in national defence. Its report disposed once and for all of attempts by the Army and the Navy to partition the R.A.F. The Committee also advocated the continued control of the naval air units by the Royal Air Force, a recommendation which infuriated the admirals and nearly brought down the Government.

The Government accepted the recommendation of the Committee including that for a Home Defence Air Force. This was to consist in the first instance of fifty-two squadrons 'to be created with as little delay as possible'. They would add thirty-four to the authorised strength of the R.A.F. It was decided that the details of the organisation would be arranged with a view to possible subsequent expansion.

While fully safeguarding the existence of the R.A.F. this reflected the muddle-headedness of the politicians in power.

With his passion for economy Mr. Bonar Law, the Prime Minister, bent on cutting Government expenditure to the bone, appointed Sir Eric Geddes to head what came to be known as the anti-waste campaign. Geddes was loudly applauded each time he wielded his famous 'axe' against the fighting services. When the time came to implement the recommendations of the Salisbury Committee the Air Force had been so mauled by disarmament and crippled by the Geddes axe that

to bring together the broken fragments and to build upon them was a task that involved a long-distance plan of great complexity made all the more difficult by the 'ten-year rule'.

Adopted by Lloyd George's coalition government, the ten-year rule was based on the assumption that, with Germany debarred by the Treaty of Versailles from making war-planes and submarines, it was safe to reduce the R.A.F. to a nucleus for ten years. This became ludicrous because until 1932 successive governments continued the policy effectively extending the ten years indefinitely.

It needed Trenchard's determination to cut through the entanglements that surrounded an expansion programme calling for 394 bombers and 204 fighters by the end of 1928. A complicated task, it involved the recruitment of volunteers, their training and the organisation of all ground services. Many of the airfields which had been sold for a song only a few months earlier had to be bought back at great expense without compulsory powers and in the face of intense local opposition.

For five years the R.A.F. squadrons had to be content with planes left over from the war. Many of them continued in service until well into the 1930s.

A committee created in 1923 under Air Commodore J. M. Steel of the Air Ministry and Colonel W. B. Bartholomew from the War Office produced a plan for defence based on the assumption that any attack on Britain would be delivered across the Channel from the south and the south-east.

It consisted of a defensive belt fifteen miles deep running from Duxford, Cambridgeshire, to Devizes, Wiltshire, in a curve round London parallel to the coast. This belt was called the air fighting zone and it was sandwiched between an inner artillery zone, for the close defence of London, and an outer artillery zone whose purpose was to indicate the presence of the enemy formations and to break them before they reached the air fighting zone. Anti-aircraft artillery was to fire by day only. Night intruders were to be dealt with by fighters assisted by searchlights deployed in the inner artillery and aircraft fighting zones.

To allow the defending fighters time to reach combat heights distant sound locators on the coast and advanced observer posts on the fringes of the belt were to give

Spring 1939 and the R.A.F.'s Spitfire strength grows. Shown here is a complete line-up of the aircraft of 65 Squadron at Hornchurch. 65 were the sixth squadron to be equipped with the type, the first five being Nos. 19 and 66 (Duxford), No. 41 (Catterick), and Nos. 74 and 54 (Hornchurch)

advanced warning of an attack. During the attack the defence control system was to be kept informed of all friendly and hostile aircraft movements. Except for extensions of the belt beyond Devizes to the Bristol Channel and north from Duxford to the Fens this scheme was scarcely altered until the formation of Fighter Command in 1936. The extensions increased the number of sectors in the aircraft fighting zone from eight to ten. Each had a front of about fifteen miles containing the airfields from which the fighters would operate. Two squadrons were allotted to each of the sectors south and south-east of London. The remainder were given one apiece. Three squadrons were to be stationed on coastal aerodromes to attack and harass the enemy on the way to and from targets.

In the light of later developments such as radar it is obvious that this system would have been quite unworkable without much more advanced devices than were then available. There were already indications, however, that science would have to provide new techniques if the Steel-Bartholomew plan was to supply an adequate defence.

All that could be used by way of a warning system were sound locators and visual detection by sky-scanning observers. The locators were mobile. They were reasonably effective when aircraft were within and just beyond earshot but they were quite inadequate for early warning.

Many other measures were considered and tried but none was satisfactory. In short, if the attacking forces could neither be signalled to the authorities in the estimated target areas nor plotted satisfactorily the task of interceptors was impossible.

To minimise these disadvantages another committee, under Major-General C. F. Romer, established a coastal chain of mobile sound locators and laid the foundations of the Observer Corps. But this did little to lift the burden of uncertainty from the shoulders of the R.A.F. The doubtful capacity of the fighters to hold off the enemy even if detected early gave rise to the famous Baldwinism, 'The bomber will always get through'. It also nurtured Trenchard's bias towards the doctrine that the first line of defence lay over an enemy's airfields and aircraft factories. Fighters were vital to Trenchard's architecture but he considered it was the bomber above all that held the key to air power.

A change in the defence structure was introduced in January 1925. Known as the Air Defence of Great Britain (A.D.G.B.), the new command included all air-defence units. It was divided into a fighting area and three bombing areas grouped geographically each with a commander. Air Marshal Sir John Salmond was the first air officer commanding-in-chief.

Fighting Area was further subdivided into advanced fighting squadrons, R.A.F., the ten aircraft sectors, and general officer commanding ground troops. The latter was responsible for the work of the inner and outer artillery zones, the Observer Corps and the technical working of all searchlights.

Harbours and coastal areas were outside A.D.G.B. The air-raid warning organisation which was responsible for collecting and collating raid information involved the three service ministries, the Post Office and the Board of Trade, which had jurisdiction over coastguard stations.

By 1925 relations with France improved and the threatened expansion of the Armée de l'Air appeared to have been shelved. It seemed, furthermore, that the *rapprochement* between France and Germany might pave the way to a decrease in the size of the European arsenals.

In Britain the outcome of these developments was the formation of a committee with Lord Birkenhead as chairman to consider the fifty-two-squadron scheme in the light of changing conditions. In November the committee recommended that although it should not be abandoned, the scheme need not be completed until 1935–6.

Trenchard objected strongly. Postponement would dislocate many of the carefully laid plans, but since there was no German Air Force, the Locarno Treaty was spreading the breath of peace through Europe and Mr. Winston Churchill, then Chancellor of the Exchequer, was relentless in his demands for further economies, the Chief of the Air Staff had no alternative but to accept.

The brake had its compensations, however. The preliminary work on the programme was so extensive that it is doubtful whether the squadrons could have been formed on time without severely hindering the organisation and development of training. It also gave Trenchard the chance to create quality rather than quantity. The reduction of the R.A.F. after the First World War meant starting again from the beginning. Trenchard's main fear was that failure to lay sound foundations might prejudice the high standard at which he aimed. The number of squadrons was never so important to him as the ability to expand them into a much greater air force in the future without sacrificing quality.

What Trenchard did not foresee, however, was that completion of the scheme would be postponed indefinitely, first by Mr. Ramsay MacDonald's second Labour Government which added another two years to the programme and then by the 'armament truce' observed in Britain while the Disarmament Conference sat in Geneva between 1932 and 1934.

From the time the Salisbury programme was allowed to lapse in 1925 until the spring of 1934 world peace was assiduously pursued through the League of Nations. A series of plans, treaties and pacts were drawn up to discourage unprovoked attacks and in February 1932 the Disarmament Conference assembled in Geneva in a last attempt to establish a pledge of world security and peace. In 1933 Adolf Hitler became Chancellor of Germany, which, with Japan, resigned from the League of Nations. In May 1934, after lingering on, achieving nothing, the Conference broke up.

Because the bomber was seen as the ultimate weapon of destruction at that time, German and British military authorities subscribed in varying degree to a theory put forward by an Italian general, Giulio Douhet. This theory was that no effective defence could be devised against the bomber, and that all resources should be invested in it. The British saw that bombers would be able to strike specific military and industrial targets well within enemy territory on such a scale that civilian morale would soon be destroyed. The Germans regarded aircraft mainly as a sophisticated form of long-range artillery which must be subordinated to the land

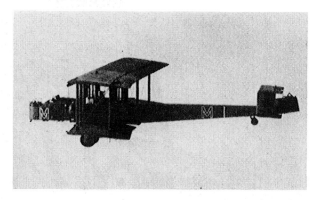

Mainstay of the R.A.F.'s heavy bomber force in the thirties, the Vickers Virginia biplane was in service from 1924 until 1937. It had a maximum speed of 108 m.p.h. and a range of 985 miles. Three Lewis guns and 3,000 lb. of bombs comprised the armament

armies and used tactically to clear a path for the fast-moving armoured spearheads and motorised infantry.

During the nine years of futile disarmament negotiations only the pageants and displays given by the R.A.F. kept it in the public eye. Its value as a first line of defence in any future war was almost disregarded. Likewise the aircraft industry, suffering through a shortage of orders, lost many skilled workers to other industries.

There was, of course, a small band of prophets to warn the nation of the consequences of failing to keep a strong air service. Among them was Mr. Winston Churchill, Member of Parliament for Woodford, Essex, who had just previously been Chancellor of the Exchequer. Even without his persistent warnings no one could ignore the dark signs of trouble gathering over Europe in 1934.

On July 19th the Government announced its intention of increasing the strength of the R.A.F. by forty-one squadrons. The expansion programme would take five years and it would increase the home defences from fifty-two squadrons to seventy-five, and add eight squadrons to the Fleet Air Arm and the R.A.F. overseas. In all it authorised the enlargement of the total first-line strength at home and overseas to 1,304 aircraft by the spring of 1939.

Motions of censure were immediately tabled in both Houses of Parliament, but during the debate on July 30th Churchill drew attention to the danger of Germany's growing strength in the air in no uncertain terms. Germany, he said, had violated the Versailles Treaty, and already possessed a military air force two-thirds as strong as Britain's existing home defence. Furthermore, at the rate at which it was expanding, even if the proposals for increasing the R.A.F. were approved, the German Air Force would nearly equal the home defence force in numbers by the end of 1935, and exceed it substantially by 1936.

Once the Germans established a lead Britain might never be able to overtake them. Their civil aircraft were readily convertible to military duties. They had already overtaken Britain in the numbers of trained pilots and glider pilots.

Britain's main fighter force in 1937 and 1938 relied on fixed undercarriage biplanes. A formation of Gloster Gauntlets of No. 32 Squadron airborne from Biggin Hill in May 1937. The Gauntlet was the last open cockpit fighter biplane to serve with the R.A.F. and it did not go out of service until 1939

It was one thing to be faced with a fleet of aircraft two-thirds of the first-line strength of the home defence squadrons, however, and quite another to be confronted with a trained military force of equivalent calibre. Few German military aircraft were then allotted to units. The secret Luftwaffe was still short of most of the essentials that constitute an air force as opposed to a collection of pilots and aircraft. The situation was worrying but not dangerous.

In the absence of any reliable information on German air strength no one was able to contradict Churchill. The censure motion was defeated and the R.A.F. was assured of its forty-one additional squadrons.

At this period the home defence force stood at forty-two squadrons containing 488 first-line aircraft. There were also at home four flying-boat squadrons for co-operation with the Navy, and five reconnaissance squadrons for co-operation with the Army. Overseas there were six squadrons in Egypt, the Sudan and Palestine, eight in India, five in Iraq, three in the Far East, one in Aden and one in Malta.

In war none of the overseas squadrons could be summoned home to strengthen the Air Defence of Great Britain as they would be hard pressed covering the vast areas to which they were assigned. Accordingly, they did not count in any comparison of strengths with Germany. Nor did the twelve squadrons and six flights of the Fleet Air arm which, though still under R.A.F.

control, were at the disposal of the Navy.

Until 1934 the R.A.F. maintained between 29,000 and 30,000 officers and men by training sixty new pilots and 1,600 men a year. It was backed by an 11,000-strong regular reserve and the Auxiliary Air Force of 1,500. The first-line strength was built up by offering men completing short-service engagements extended terms of service on the active list. This expedient gave the R.A.F. a strength of 55,000 in 1937, and 118,000 in 1939.

A large proportion of short-service men was thus denied to the regular Reserve. This made it necessary to recruit a civilian reserve to train, like the auxiliaries, at week-ends and at two-week annual summer camps. The Royal Air Force Volunteer Reserve was accordingly formed in 1936 to recruit some 800 youths a year for training as air crews.

By 1938 thirty-three volunteer reserve centres were established and by 1939 5,000 volunteers were serving as part-time air crew or in training. At that time all were non-commissioned officers. Many V.R. men were commissioned later. Aircrew, medical equipment and technical courses were established soon after the pilots began training in the spring of 1937. When war broke out the R.A.F. possessed an invaluable reservoir of manpower 63,000 strong. In June 1939 the Women's Auxiliary Air Force, designed to release men for aircrew and front-line ground duties, was formed. In 1949 this became the Women's Royal Air Force.

Until 1934 all pilot training was undertaken by the Royal Air Force but the facilities available were inadequate to meet the requirements imposed by expansion. Elementary flying training was therefore farmed out to civilian flying schools, thirteen of which were in operation by 1936. In addition, five service flying training schools were established. These were run by the R.A.F. to provide advanced training.

When in 1935 training schemes for the Dominions were proposed Australia and New Zealand readily responded by recruiting and training a number of their own people as pilots for the R.A.F. in addition to their own services. Canada did not respond.

When Mr. Mackenzie King, the Canadian Prime Minister, visited Britain for the Coronation of King George VI and the Imperial Conference in 1937, Lord Swinton, Secretary of State for Air, put the plan before him. It was vehemently rejected on the ground that it would commit Canada to war. Backed by Baldwin, Swinton pressed the proposal, offering to pay for the whole commitment including the aircraft. He pointed out that the other Dominion countries were co-operating. This made King more obstinate. He finally threatened to walk out of the Imperial Conference if the matter were even raised or discussed.

That the British Government were not able to put forward their proposals formally, enabled King to say later that the training scheme was never suggested to the Canadian Government before the war.

Beyond training fifty pilots a year, Canada undertook no further commitments for the R.A.F. until December 17th, 1939, when the Empire Air Training Scheme was agreed in Ottawa. Under the agreement Britain supplied all the aircraft and a nucleus of skilled men. The dominions supplied the rest.

Canada, training Canadians, Australians, New Zealanders and a small number of pupils from Britain and Newfoundland, built up thirteen elementary and sixteen service flying training schools, ten air observer, ten bombing and gunnery and two air navigation schools. Australia and New Zealand were too far from Britain to make the training of British citizens there a practicable proposition. Nine elementary, seven service flying training schools, four air observer and four bombing and gunnery schools were formed in Australia, and three elementary and two service flying training schools in New Zealand to train their own men.

Because the earlier stages in flying training were likely to be cramped by enemy action and lack of space, it was clear that some training scheme for British nationals would have to be established abroad. Southern Rhodesia responded immediately by offering to accommodate, administer and partially pay for three service flying training schools staffed and run principally by the R.A.F. At the end of December 1939 South Africa invited the R.A.F. to share in her expanding training organisation.

The first courses started in Canada, Australia and New Zealand on April 29th, 1940. This was too late to help Fighter Command during the Battle of Britain.

In the meantime the expansion programmes of 1934 and 1935 made the administration of the R.A.F. at home too complex to be controlled by one man. By the summer of 1936 the Air Council had swept away A.D.G.B. and the areas, and reorganised on a basis of specialised commands.

Four of these were formed, supported by a maintenance group: Bomber, Fighter, Coastal and Training commands, with headquarters at Uxbridge, Stanmore, Lee-on-Solent, and Tern Hill, Shropshire.

In 1937 the R.A.F. relinquished control of the Fleet Air Arm to the Navy, and in 1938 formed three new commands, Maintenance, Balloon and Reserve. The first dealt with the supply of equipment and armament, the second with balloon squadrons and sites established round the most vulnerable areas, and the third with the administration of the volunteer reserve and the civil elementary flying training schools.

Under this decentralised system the Air Ministry was relieved of detailed administration by delegation to the commands. This simplified the management of the air force and ensured the development of each arm.

At command level the air officers commanding were able to devote themselves to the main task of stragetic planning and direction by delegating as much of the administration as possible to senior air staff officers and air officers in charge of administration. These were the principal subordinates in operational matters.

While the Cabinet therefore decided general strategic policy the Air Council was responsible for its execution through the Chief of the Air Staff. He issued directives for the guidance of commanders and preserved broad control over operational policy. It was then up to the air officer commanding the command to achieve results by using the forces at his disposal.

Each command was divided into a number of subordinate groups. Each group was commanded by an air vice-marshal or an air commodore and consisted of a number of stations or wings under a group captain or a wing commander administering one or more squadrons.

With the exception of some distinctive variations, such as the sector organisation in Fighter Command, the pattern was broadly the same throughout down to group levels. Below this there were marked differences: whereas a Group in Bomber Command might consist of six Blenheim and four Whitley squadrons operating from five airfields, a group in Maintenance Command might contain half a dozen units, each resembling a factory, concerned with overhauling aircraft and engines.

Fighter Command was formed on July 6th, 1936. Seven days later Air Marshal Sir Hugh Dowding, its first air officer commanding-in-chief, paid a visit to Bentley Priory, near Stanmore, Middlesex. This 166-year-old mansion was formerly the headquarters of the Inland Area which moved to Tern Hill as Training Command. It became the Fighter Command headquarters and served as such throughout the Battle of Britain.

The command was divided into two groups. With headquarters at Uxbridge, No. 11 Group assumed operational and administrative control of the southern division. No. 12 Group controlled the northern territories from headquarters at Watnall, Nottinghamshire.

The resources of both groups were too thin, however, to enable them to cover the west and north, but this was resolved after war broke out by the formation of No. 13 Group north of York with headquarters at Newcastle upon Tyne and No. 10 Group west of Oxford based at Box, Wiltshire. Later No. 14 Group north of the Tay and No. 9 Group in the south-west of England completed the picture.

On the verge of war, during the Munich crisis of 1938.
Here No. 79 squadron Hawker Furies formate in their
new—and very hurriedly applied—camouflage. There
had not been time to paint on R.A.F. roundels. In 1931
Fury was the R.A.F.'s first interceptor in Squadron
service to exceed 200 m.p.h. Armament was two
synchronised Vickers machine guns

The groups were subsequently divided into sectors surrounding selected fighter bases known as sector stations.

In the meantime Dowding worked out an 'ideal air defence' scheme at the request of Sir Thomas Inskip, Minister for the Co-ordination of Defence, who in October 1936 had become captured by the piece-meal modifications to the defence programmes.

Dowding showed that broadly at least forty-five fighter squadrons, 1,264 heavy anti-aircraft guns and 4,700 searchlights would be required. Up to 300 twin-barrelled pom-poms seemed likely to be needed for defence against low-flying aircraft, over 400 balloons for the London barrage and an indeterminate number elsewhere. To cover the new defended areas more Observer Corps units would be necessary.

The number of fighter squadrons visualised was small, but it was considered adequate to meet a bomber offensive launched across the North Sea. The possibility that France would fall, bringing Britain within range of enemy fighters, could not have been further from anybody's mind.

Time and energy were required to build Fighter Command into a unified defence mechanism. Time was short but Dowding was endowed with an abundance of energy which he used unsparingly to weld the growing numbers of men and, later, women, airfields, aircraft, radar, balloons, headquarters and communications into a flexible and effective organisation.

The war begins; blackout curtains go up, barrage balloons fly overhead and children are evacuated from London. Here, in September 1939, a group of London children arrive at a station in Surrey complete with labels and the inevitable cardboard gas mask cases

The organisation creaked through its first test, the summer defence exercises of 1937.

The first results were far from spectacular. The infant radar network and fighter control organisation, though promising, were still uncertain of themselves. None of the biplane fighters was able to intercept the new fast twin-engined Bristol Blenheim bombers without being in a position of advantage above them. Even if they chose precisely the right moment to roll over into a vertical diving attack, they were hard pressed to get the speed they needed to use their camera guns within range. The Blenheim formations drew away steadily until the fighters were obliged to give up the chase and return home.

By the summer of 1938 the picture began to change. Hurricanes of Nos. 56, 87 and 111 squadrons gave the controllers a taste of the reality they would be facing two years later.

Several important conclusions were reached after the 1938 exercises. British cities were not considered immune from attack but on the assumption that the Germans would maintain daily raids of 200 machines the defence could count on destroying one-tenth. The

With war came the blackout and air raid precautions. Here an A.R.P. warden sets a black-out clock at an A.R.P. post near London in 1939

exercises also brought out the relative merits of the offensive and the defensive in air warfare and the advantages to the bomber pilot of bad or cloudy weather.

Towards the end of January 1937 Air Chief Marshal Sir Christopher Courtney, then an Air Vice-Marshal as Deputy Chief of the Air Staff and Director of Operations and Intelligence, visited Germany. The Luftwaffe conducted him on a tour of several units and factories, including the Heinkel works at Rostock. On February 2nd he had talks with General Milch.

Milch arrived in England nine months later, on October 18th, with Ernst Udet, the Director of the Technical Department at the Air Ministry, and General Stumpff. The shadow factories impressed him and he was complimentary about the spirit and organisation of the R.A.F. About the aircraft they saw, however, the Germans expressed grave doubts.

A month later the Government bestirred themselves on the question of anti-aircraft defence and Mr. Hore-Belisha, Minister of Defence, announced the formation of an anti-aircraft corps in June 1938.

By the time Anti-Aircraft Command was formed in April 1939 the Munich crisis of September 1938 had ensured that guns were coming off the production lines; they were, however, far too late to fill the gaps even by 1940. With the integration of A.A. Command with Fighter Command, the main components of the

home defence were assembled. Their weapons were good but they needed many more.

The value of the Munich Agreement was that it gave the R.A.F. a year of grace. To oppose the German long-range striking force of 1,200 modern bombers in 1938 Fighter Command could muster, including all reserves, only 759 fighters and of these only ninety-three were Hurricanes. The rest were outdated biplanes. The Hurricanes, being without heating for their guns, could not fight above 15,000 feet, even in summer. No Spitfires were in service.

A year later the Martin-Baker Company produced a design for a utility interceptor, the M.B.2, which could be produced easily and was powered by a Napier Dagger engine. Despite the call for fighters Martin-Baker were not given a production order for reasons dating back to 1932. In that year Sir Frederick Handley Page (then Mr. F. Handley Page) threatened to stop making aircraft on the ground that he was not getting the official support he needed to keep his works going. Fearing that the rest of the aircraft industry might follow Handley Page's example, the Government acted by guaranteeing existing companies all future contracts for first-line aircraft to ensure availability in the event of an emergency. This decision had the effect of creating a closed shop. Any newcomer to aircraft design was virtually precluded from receiving orders for fighting aircraft and had to be content with trainers and gliders.

When Poland was invaded on September 1st, 1939, full mobilisation was publicly proclaimed in the British Isles. But for the R.A.F. the proclamation merely confirmed the call-up notices served on the twenty Auxiliary Air Force squadrons now in Fighter Command, and the Volunteer Reserve on August 24th. By September 1st most of them were in uniform. The units at home and overseas moved to war stations. The air defence system was manned and the look-out began. Coastal Command patrols kept watch for German Naval raiders over the North Sea, and the Air Ministry prepared to requisition civilian aircraft and aerodromes.

During that week ten Fairey Battle light bomber squadrons of the Advanced Air Striking Force and four Hurricane squadrons allotted to the Air Component of the British Expeditionary Force crossed to France. They suffered no interference from the Germans but the engine of one of the Battles failed and the plane came down on the sea. The crew was picked up and shipped to safety. The anticipated appearance of the Luftwaffe did not materialise and as time wore on the feeling of tension gave way to one of boredom.

It no longer seemed possible that Britain, bathing in the peaceful warmth of the sunlit summer, was at war.

The dispatch of eight reconnaissance squadrons of the Air Component by Mid-September brought the strength of the R.A.F. in France up to establishment. It remained thus, except for the addition of another two fighter squadrons by the end of 1939, until after the German invasion.

4 Machines and production

With the exception of a few 'specials' like the Fairey long-range monoplane and the Supermarine Schneider Trophy seaplanes, the only monoplane in service with the R.A.F. in 1934 was the Saro Cloud amphibian trainer, of which there were seventeen. The rest were biplanes. The Air Defence of Great Britain depended on the Bristol Bulldog, the Hawker Fury and Demon fighters, and a variety of bombers ranging from the small Hawker Hart, the Vickers Vildebeest and the Fairey Gordon, to the larger Boulton Paul Overstrand, Vickers Virginia and Handley Page Heyford.

Restrictions during the 1920s severely rationed the resources which the R.A.F. and the aircraft industry devoted to research and development. Progress, which also lacked the stimulus of any change in the basic conceptions of air warfare, was therefore slow. Because there was no financial margin for error, novelties could not be ordered until they had been so thoroughly tested that they were practically obsolescent.

Few advances were made in aerodynamics during the period, and improved performances were derived from increases in engine power. A remarkable exception did appear in 1925, however: the Fairey Fox light bomber whose lines were so clean that it was able to outperform the single-seater fighters of the day. Its secret lay in the American Curtiss D.12 liquid-cooled, in-line engine which lent itself to streamlining impossible to achieve with the popular air-cooled radials employed in contemporary aircraft design.

Although Rolls-Royce had already produced many thousands of liquid-cooled engines during and after the First World War, notably Eagles and Falcons, it was the Fox and its D.12 which accelerated development of the liquid-cooled type in preference to air-cooled engines. In this respect it may be said to have had a relationship with the Rolls-Royce Kestrel which was the parent of the Merlin engine used in the Battle of Britain Hurricanes and Spitfires.

Kestrels powered the Hawker biplanes which were the backbone of the R.A.F. during the 1930s. The first of the breed was the single-engined Hart day-bomber, built to a specification which lifted the speed of this type of machine from the 120 m.p.h. rut and put it up by a good 60 m.p.h.

Hawkers also developed the Fury interceptor. Chosen for delievery in 1931, it was the first R.A.F. fighter to exceed 200 m.p.h.

In the next ten years the Air Ministry adapted the Hart for many different roles and hung it with many attachments. To maintain its performance it had to be boosted with more power, but this was always available from the Kestrel which Rolls-Royce steadily developed from 480 to 765 h.p. Only in the Hawker Hector was the Kestrel replaced by another engine, the air-cooled Napier Dagger.

Within eighteen months of the Kestrel's first bench test a supercharger was boosting its power. Then an automatic boost control was developed which pilots hard pressed in combat were to find a boon. Linked to the throttle, the auto-boost mechanism relieved the pilot of the need to nurse his engine. He could open the throttle to full power with the assurance that the engine would not blow up.

From the Kestrel Rolls-Royce developed the Buzzard and then the 'R' engine, the latter specially for the Schneider Trophy float planes.

The story of the Schneider Trophy's effect on British aircraft design and development of the Spitfire goes back to the sixth contest held in Naples in 1922 when the Supermarine Company deprived the Italians of a third and outright win with a Sea Lion flying-boat of their own design. Without that victory there would never have been the incentive to defend the title and in consequence none of the development work that was to have such repercussions eighteen years later.

The Sea Lion was sturdy and reliable but it was obviously not good enough for the 1923 contest. Something radically new was needed. The late Mr. Reginald Mitchell, Supermarine's chief designer, was convinced a small monoplane built around a 700 h.p. engine was the answer. In the absence of anything better Supermarines entered Sea Lion once more. It performed well but General James Doolittle, then a young lieutenant, won the race and the trophy for America.

Mitchell learned much from the winning Curtiss float-planes, particularly their streamlined engine installations and floats which reduced the frontal area. However, he believed a monoplane could do much better than the Curtiss biplanes.

By August 1925 Mitchell's S.4 was in the air, and on September 13th it set up a new seaplane record of 226 miles an hour. Even land-planes had not yet achieved such a speed, but it crashed as a result of wing-flutter and was unable to join the two Gloster III biplanes representing Britain. America won again.

Despite the fact that all foreign entries were heavily subsidised, the British Government displayed no official interest in the Schneider Trophy. The entire cost of representing Britain fell on Supermarine,

Gloster Aircraft and D. Napier and Son. When national prestige began to be involved, however, it no longer stood aloof. In 1925 the Air Ministry placed an order for seven special high-speed seaplanes, three each from Supermarine and Gloster and one from Short Brothers and Harland. All were powered by 875 h.p. Napier Lion engines except for the Short Crusader, which was fitted with a closely cowled 960 h.p. Bristol Mercury air-cooled radial.

None of the seaplanes was ready for the 1926 contest but the Italians won and gave the trophy a new lease of life by forestalling a third successive win by the Americans and preventing them from taking it back to the United States permanently.

By 1927 Britain had a strong team. Similar in most respects to the S.4, the two Supermarine S.5s then in the contest were low-wing monoplanes with externally braced wooden wings and tailplanes. Duralumin was used elsewhere, including the compact fuselages slimly tailored to fit the cross-section of the Napier Lion engines. Radiators were built into the wing skin, and the fuel was carried in one float so that its weight would counteract the vicious torque delivered by the very coarse pitch propeller and powerful engine.

First and second places were taken by the S.5s flown by Flight Lieutenant Webster and Flight Lieutenant Worsley.

The next Schneider Trophy contest was set for 1929, but the Assistant Director for Engine Development at the Air Ministry, Major G. P. Bulman, did not think enough extra power could be obtained from the Lion to guarantee victory a second time. Napiers had done nothing towards the development of a supercharged version of the engine and Bulman therefore turned to Rolls-Royce.

By August 1929 the Rolls-Royce R engine was developing 1,800 h.p., but during the endurance tests it was found that power dropped off after twenty minutes' running. Fuel troubles were suspected and Air Commodore F. R. Banks, then with the Associated Ethyl Company, was called in for consultations. Instead of pure benzol, Banks suggested the use of several other fuels and finally concocted a suitable blend.

Though similar in overall design as the S.5s the Supermarine S.6s for the 1929 race were all-metal aeroplanes. Mitchell found ingenious answers to problems of streamlining and engine heat dissipation by building the oil cooler into the surface of the tail-fin.

Again the contest was an Anglo-Italian affair and again the Supermarine plane, powered by the 1,900 h.p. Rolls-Royce engine and flown by Flight Lieutenant Waghorn, won at 328.6 m.p.h.

The 1929 competition was one of the most dramatic for Britain, for in addition to international rivalry there was competition between the Supermarine and Gloster aircraft companies and between Rolls-Royce and Napier whose engines powered the planes. Unfortunately for Glosters, who had by this time abandoned the biplane formula, last-minute troubles with the Napier engine forced the withdrawal of their Mk VI Golden Arrow.

Britain now had to win only the 1931 competition

to achieve the three successive victories needed to keep the trophy for good. The Government, however, was suddenly struck with one of the bouts of 'economy fever' that nearly killed the aircraft industry altogether ten years earlier. They withdrew support.

Supermarine could not carry on unsubsidised and consequently little was done until eight months before the race when the late Lady Houston, incensed by the Socialist Government's parsimony, put up £100,000 to cover the cost of development and participation.

There was no time to design anything radically different from the S.6s, but Supermarine built two improved versions designated S.6Bs. The R engine was amenable to further development and Rolls-Royce therefore went to work to build up its power. Banks advised in the matter of fuels.

Banks' pioneer work in this field had important repercussions. From 1929 on the evolution of fuels went hand in hand with engine development and can be conservatively credited with having doubled the power of engines.

After months of feverish activity the Rs developed a maximum 2,300 h.p. for a guaranteed duration of only a few minutes. They also developed so much heat that cooling radiators for the water and oil had to be built into the double skins of wings, floats and fuselage.

The Italians worked desperately under orders from their government to produce an engine to beat the R. Their engines would not stand up to the demands made on them and they were forced to withdraw. The French contender, a Bernard-Hispano, crashed near Marseilles on July 31st, 1931, killing the pilot, M. Bougault. On September 13th, in the absence of any other contenders, it remained only for Air Chief Marshal Sir John Boothman, then a flight lieutenant, to cover the course at 340 m.p.h. to win the Trophy for Britain outright. On the same day Flight Lieutenant Stainforth raised the world speed record to 378 m.p.h. On the 29th, using a different blend of fuel, the R gave 2,530 h.p. and Stainforth achieved 407.8 m.p.h., a speed unexceeded by any other British aircraft until fourteen years later.

Mitchell's seaplane designing days were over but he applied the lessons in aerodynamic efficiency to other types of aircraft. Similarly the Gloster seaplanes were of inestimable value to their designers. The R engines were also of great importance in their effect on the attitude of the Government and the aircraft industry, and Rolls-Royce in particular, towards liquid-cooled engines. They established that only liquid-cooled engines allowed the clean aerodynamic design required for fast planes, especially fighters, and that far greater power could be obtained from them than from any comparable air-cooled types. It was not until 1940 that an air-cooled engine anywhere in the world equalled the 2,783 h.p. maintained during a bench test for an hour by a Rolls-Royce R in 1931.

About the middle of 1932 Rolls-Royce decided on their own initiative that future fighters about the same size as existing types would require a larger engine than the Kestrel. The PV–12 was an almost identical but larger 750 h.p. version of the Kestrel with a 1,649 cubic inches capacity instead of 1,295. It was at first

The tempo of production quickens as war draws near. Here, in 1939, a production Vickers Wellington 1 twin Pegasus-engined bomber takes off from Brooklands, while in the foreground stands the prototype Mk. 2 Wellington with Merlin engines. The Wellington employed a special criss-cross lattice structure developed by Barnes Wallis, later to become famous as the inventor of the spinning bomb which broke the Mohne and Eder dams

to be inverted, but inverted engines were not popular with aircraft designers. After criticism of the mock-up late in 1932, Rolls-Royce reverted to the V arrangement of cylinders.

The 'PV' in the designation indicated that the project was a private venture. Detailed design work on the PV–12 started as Hitler became Chancellor of Germany. A year and a half later it was named the Merlin.

In the meantime the Air Ministry were speculating about the possibilities of applying the experiences of the 1929 Schneider Trophy races to a military aircraft. In 1930 a specification, F7/30, was issued for a plane. This was based on the Rolls-Royce Goshawk engine.

Sir Sydney Camm (then Mr. Sydney Camm), chief engineer for the Hawker Aircraft Company and responsible for the Hart and Fury aircraft, was heavily committed to the development of variants of these types for the R.A.F. and foreign air forces when he received the specification. He responded with a mono-plane design based on the Fury then entering service. As originally planned the Fury monoplane was to have a fixed undercarriage and four guns, two in the fuselage and two in the wings, like Mitchell's independent answer to F7/30 based on the S.6B.

Mitchell found the specification restrictive and insufficiently advanced in concept to produce an aircraft of the highest possible performance. It reflected the uncertain atmosphere of the era in which hindsight ruled any arguments on air warfare and foresight was hemmed in by economics and disarmament. Nevertheless an aircraft was tailored to the specification, but

long before it flew Mitchell's dissatisfaction with it led to a design he believed the R.A.F. should have. It was a neat monoplane with retractable undercarriage, an enclosed cockpit and four machine-guns. Beneath the starboard wing it could carry four small bombs.

Although Camm's preliminary designs never materialised, studies progressed, and when the Merlin came into the picture the geometry began to diverge so sharply from the Fury's that the term 'interceptor monoplane' gained currency. The Merlin also altered Mitchell's plans, which, like the Hawker design, was further modified by a fresh specification following an important conference on armament at the Air Ministry on July 19th, 1934.

The specification was based on the premises that the modern fighter's speed over contemporary bombers was so great that repeated attacks could not be maintained. Decisive results must, therefore, be obtained on the first attack during which a fighter pilot would have the target in the gunsight for only two seconds.

Captain F. W. Hill, senior ballistics officer at the

Aeroplane and Armament Experimental Establishment, Martlesham Heath, Suffolk, was at the conference. He showed that at least eight guns firing one thousand rounds a minute each were needed to destroy a bomber in two seconds. The results of his experiments convinced Air Marshal Sir Ralph Sorley, then a comparatively junior squadron leader at the Air Ministry's Operational Requirements Branch, who set about 'selling' the eight-gun concept to higher authority. This created a furore, particularly among older officers like Air Chief Marshal Sir Robert Brooke-Popham, Commander-in-Chief Air Defence of Great Britain, who thought 'eight guns was going a bit too far'. Brooke-Popham was also against enclosed cockpits.

Sorley pleaded the case vigorously and in 1935 specification F5 34, drawn up round the fast-firing American Browning machine-gun, was issued. It called for a monoplane fighter capable of catching the fastest bomber and destroying it with a two-second burst of gunfire. An enclosed cockpit, eight Brownings with 300 rounds per gun giving a total firing time of roughly fifteen seconds, a reflector sight, retractable undercarriage with wheel-brakes and oxygen for the pilot were specified. No particular engine was called for but the designers were asked to aim for a speed of 275 m.p.h. at 15,000 feet, ninety minutes' endurance, a seven-and-a-half minute climb to 20,000 feet, a ceiling of 33,000 feet, and a landing run of 250 yards. These ideas combined so well with the Camm and Mitchell plans that the Air Ministry, freed of the Government's financial restraint by the 1934 expansion programme, ordered both aircraft.

Mitchell's health, meanwhile, deteriorated following a partially successful lung operation in 1933. He was persuaded to take a holiday on the Continent. There he ran into members of the Deutscher Luftsportverband (German Aviation Sport Association), in whose drive, aggressive spirit and shapely gliders he recognised the menace of the future.

Back in Britain Mitchell was profoundly influenced by another German product—a Heinkel He 70 bought by Rolls-Royce and tested by the R.A.F. at Martlesham Heath. It had eliptical wings, a shape that made those of the Spitfire so distinctive in the air.

Camm and Mitchell worked their way into relatively unexplored territory. Monoplane production, retractable undercarriages, wheel-brakes, wing-flaps, stressed skin construction, blind-flying instruments and radio, all needed detailed attention.

The Hawker prototype, K 5083, was built in eleven months at Kingston, Surrey, and was named the Hurricane. Hawker's chief test pilot, Mr. P. W. S. Bulman, flew it for the first time from Brooklands on November 6th, 1935. He reported remarkable manœuvrability and docility.

Seven months later, on May 5th, 1936, the Spitfire prototype took off on its maiden flight from Eastleigh airfield, Southampton, with Mr. J. 'Mutt' Summers at the controls. Summers was chief test pilot for Vickers-Armstrong, which company had acquired the entire share capital of the Supermarine Company in 1928. He reported enthusiastically on the performance of the small cream-coloured plane.

With the same armament and the same engine the Hurricane and the Spitfire represented two totally different approaches to the same problem. The Spitfire's stressed-skin metal construction was a new and more complex concept based on specialised experience. The Hurricane's fabric-covered tubular steel and duralumin structure was tradition compromising with a modern world. The simplicity of the latter allowed quantity production to start without delay. It also had the advantage of being easily repairable. This allowed battle-scarred aircraft to be back in combat often within hours of being damaged.

Because of the success of the initial trials of the Hurricane, Hawkers felt justified in preparing to tool-up and order material for 1,000 aircraft, although the first Air Ministry contract placed in June 1935 was for no more than 600. A further 400 were ordered in November 1938. Later the Canadian Car and Foundry Company, of Montreal, and the Gloster Aircraft Company were licensed to build the Hurricane. Further contracts were placed with them.

The first production Hurricane made its maiden flight on October 12th, 1937, and in December the type replaced the Gauntlet biplanes of No. 111 Squadron at Northolt. In January 1938 Hurricanes replaced Gloster Gladiators of No. 3 Squadron at Kenley, Surrey. In February Squadron Leader J. E. Gillan, commanding officer of No. 111 Squadron, flew a Hurricane from Edinburgh to Northolt at an average speed of 408 m.p.h.

Sensational though this performance was, a strong tail-wind at 17,000 feet helped to mask the Hurricane's true capabilities. With the 1,030 h.p. Merlin II engine and a wooden, fixed-pitch two-bladed propeller the fighter had a 2,420 feet a minute rate of climb and a maximum speed of 320 m.p.h. at 18,500 feet.

Production Hurricanes differed from the prototype in a number of details in addition to having the Merlin II. In 1939 metal-covered wings began to be fitted on the production line instead of fabric-covered wings.

By the outbreak of war 400 Hurricanes were delivered and eighteen squadrons equipped with them. By August 7th, 1940, 2,309 had been built and the number of Hurricane squadrons had risen to thirty-two.

Supermarine's first production contract for 310 Spitfires placed at the same time as the Hurricane order was due for completion in March 1939. Early manufacturing difficulties, due to the late delivery of wings made by sub-contractors, delayed this, however, until August. A year after the initial contract 200 more were ordered. On April 12th, 1938, the Nuffield Organisation was contracted to build 1,000 at the newly erected Castle Bromwich shadow factory. By October 1939 Spitfire orders increased to 4,000.

Like the early Hurricanes, the first Spitfires to come off the assembly lines had Merlin II engines, two-bladed fixed-pitch wooden propellers and numerous other detailed refinements. No variable-pitch propellers were available for either of the fighters, a position which was characteristic of a period of rapid expansion. The older Spitfires and Hurricanes continued in service until only a few weeks before the invasion of Poland. Even then only the two-pitch propeller was available.

A limited number of variable-pitch propellers were being made before the war but they were reserved for the new bombers which, fully loaded, would never have taken off without them.

A fixed-pitch propeller's main drawback is that the angle at which the blades are set is a compromise. A propeller is literally an airscrew, and like a wood-screw it goes forward a certain amount with each turn. An airscrew designed to travel at 200 miles an hour has coarse pitch blades and moves a long way forward in one revolution. It must therefore be very inefficient at lower speeds.

In 1925 Dr. Hele-Shaw invented a hydraulic variable-pitch propeller which was test flown in Gloster fighter biplanes. It was not only the first variable-pitch propeller, it also had a constant-speed control like the propellers hurriedly fitted to all Merlin-engined fighters in the Battle of Britain. Instead of the pilot selecting his pitch, a governor automatically maintained the engine revolutions at a chosen setting, whatever the speed or attitude of the plane.

Glosters tried to sell the idea, pointing out that pilots would no longer have to watch their engine speed. The authorities were apathetic, however, and development was dropped. This apathy was still in evidence in 1934 when de Havillands asked the Government for support to acquire the rights to make the variable-pitch pro-peller put into production in 1933 by the American Hamilton-Standard Corporation. De Havillands went ahead on their own and began manufacture in 1935.

Spitfires reached the R.A.F. in June 1938 and in August No. 19 Squadron at Duxford, Cambridgeshire, received the first. Another Duxford Gauntlet squadron, No. 66, was re-equipped with Spitfires in October. By the beginning of September 1939 there were nine Spitfire squadrons.

The capabilities of the Spitfire were not appreciated outside the service or the industry until January 1939 when Mr. Geoffrey Quill, the Supermarine test pilot, flew from Le Bourget to Croydon in forty-one minutes —290 m.p.h.—which started the Press speculating. On March 8th an official release gave its maximum speed as 362 m.p.h. at 18,500 feet and its rate of climb to 11,000 feet with full war load as 4.8 minutes. The speed quoted exaggerated the true performances by seven miles an hour.

The type 142M Bristol Blenheim as rolled out in 1936, the first flight taking place on June 25th. The Blenheim, with its two Mercury radials, was fast for its day but not fast enough or suitably protected for the air fighting of World War 2. Nevertheless it bore the brunt of light bombing operations in 1940 and 1941 and served with distinction all over the world

Mitchell did not live to see the first production Spitfire in the air. In March 1937 his tubercular condi-tion was pronounced incurable. On June 11th he died at the age of forty-two.

Mitchell's name will always be linked with the Spitfire, although in the last year of his life he spent most of his creative energy on a bomber. Its lines promised a brilliant future, but the two prototypes were destroyed when the Supermarine factory at Woolston, Hants, was bombed on September 26th, 1940.

The air expansion scheme authorised in Parliament at the end of July 1934 was a step in the right direction, but it failed to satisfy Churchill. Scheme A, as the programme was called, was designed more to impress the Germans than to equip the R.A.F. for early action. Everything ordered was intended for the 'shop-window' behind which there were no reserves.

Throughout the autumn Churchill, reiterating the warnings of early summer, was regarded as 'a bit of a crank about this air business'. Unbeknown to anyone, however, he was being kept thoroughly informed by a private 'intelligence system'.

With the New Year an increase in tempo began with the unveiling of the Luftwaffe on February 15th and Germany's conscription proclamation on March 16th. Eleven days later Hitler in Berlin startled Sir John Simon, the Foriegn Secretary, with a blunt announce-ment that Germany had already reached air parity with Britain and intended to go on building until she had an air force equal to that of France.

Hitler's claim was certainly not justified. It was contradicted by reliable secret information at the Air Ministry's disposal and by German officials, including General Erhard Milch, the Secretary of State for Air. Germany, in fact, had 1,888 aircraft, mainly trainers.

There was little reason to doubt that Hitler would fulfil his aims, however. All available evidence pointed

The Supermarine S.6.B, winner of the Schneider Trophy in 1931. From this seaplane Vickers-Supermarine gained invaluable know-how for the Spitfire and Rolls-Royce for the Merlin engine

to a rapidly accelerating aircraft production programme in Germany. Doubts about the Luftwaffe's capacity to meet the targets Hitler set for it were, nevertheless, entertained by the Air Ministry in London. To reach air parity with France, whose air force numbered 1,500 front-line aircraft, would take the Germans until 1937. It was also considered that although the Luftwaffe might possess a front-line strength of 1,500 first-line aircraft by 1937, two more years at least must elapse before it could be ready for war. The British, therefore, had until 1939 to complete the expansion programme.

Hitler's warning, however, roused the Government, which called for further expansion and for completion of the new programme by March 1937.

This was Scheme C announced by the Air Minister, Lord Londonderry, on May 22nd, 1935. It required the establishment of 49 squadrons of 588 aircraft more than the earlier programme. This represented an air force with a first-line strength of 20 heavy bomber, 18 medium bomber, 30 light bomber, two torpedo bomber and 35 fighter squadrons, with 18 reconnaissance and other units. This was a total of 122 squadrons, containing 1,512 aircraft.

Despite the improvement it achieved little more than to dress the shop-window. There was still no provision for adequate reserves. Only one-third of the squadrons of the home defence force were to be fighter squadrons. The ratio reflected the Air Staff's view that in the long run only offensive power could give the superiority required for safety.

A bomber force would be of scant value if the fighters and the rest of the air defences proved too weak to repulse a succession of surprise attacks by the enemy. Even if the thirty-five fighter squadrons were equipped with the best aircraft available they would not have time to reach combat height before the attacking force crossed the coast or reached the target. The fighter pilots also did not know where to intercept the attackers.

Detection by acoustic means was useless but no one knew whether the experiments in radiolocation beginning at Orfordness on the east coast would be successful. In the light of these circumstances, therefore, it was not surprising that the big bomber enthusiasts held sway.

Unlike the French who, by striving after numbers rather than performance, found themselves near the outbreak of war saddled with a large number of obsolete types, Air Chief Marshal Sir Edward Ellington, Chief of the Air Staff, stressed quality as well as quantity. To minimise the effects of the delay in bringing in new aircraft, squadrons were formed with existing types. Most of these were biplanes like the Gloster Gauntlet, Gloster Gladiator and Hawker Fury fighters, and bombers such as the Hawker Hind and the Handley Page Heyford.

Among the new bombers ordered by the Air Ministry in 1935 was the Bristol Blenheim, whose performance created a stir when it reached the squadrons in 1937.

Like so many of the aircraft that formed the backbone of the R.A.F. in the first two years of the war the Blenheim started as a private venture. In 1933 the Bristol Aeroplane Company had the idea of making an all-metal eight-seater civil transport that would outperform the fastest of the new American airliners. It was backed by Lord Rothermere, the newspaper proprietor.

In 1935 the prototype was named 'Britain First', and service pilots were so enthusiastic about its performance that Lord Rothermere presented the aircraft to the nation. As the Bristol 142 it became the first of the new bombers.

Like the contracts for the production of the Wellesley, Harrow and Whitley bombers and the fighters, the Blenheim order was small—150 aircraft. The Royal Air Force was kept in check by financial considerations dictated by the Government's hope that further rearmament would be rendered unnecessary.

The Abyssinian crisis and the failure of Germany to modify her aims forced the Government to revise their plans. In February 1936 another new air expansion policy was sanctioned. Compared with Scheme C, the new Scheme F strengthened the first line of home defence by substituting medium bombers for light bombers and by placing greater emphasis on fighters. It also had the merit of making better provision for reserves.

Disarmament and the failure of civil aviation to develop rapidly caused the British aircraft industry to dwindle to a shadow of its wartime strength. For fifteen years it survived on repair and overhaul contracts doled out piecemeal by the Air Ministry and an occasional order for new R.A.F. or civil aircraft.

Although designers were filled with inventiveness and ingenuity they were forced to confine designs to the conservative requirements of the Air Ministry.

When Britain began to rearm, therefore, a huge task faced a very small industry employing about 35,000 people. Production techniques did not match the advances made in privately sponsored research. Fabric, wood and tubular metal construction in many cases had to give way to all-metal designs. This presented numerous problems, including those associated with the supply of material. The total British production of aluminium was only 15,000 tons in 1935. Germany and Austria were producing 200,000 tons. Plant, machinery and the output of the industries making vital accessories were also inadequate. The quality of such as was made was good and there were plenty of ideas.

On June 7th, 1935, Sir Philip Cunliffe-Lister became Lord Swinton and replaced Lord Londonderry as Secretary of State for Air. The great significance of the appointment was not subsequently fully appreciated. Swinton brought with him a clear understanding, drive, audacity and imagination which the expansion of the R.A.F. needed. He was chairman of a small Cabinet committee on air armament set up by Mr. Baldwin, the Prime Minister, in 1934. Swinton's initiative did not always meet with the approval of the Prime Minister or the Board of Trade, however, and until the invasion of Austria they were against gearing the industry for war production in peacetime. The result of this and the Treasury's tight-fistedness was that the R.A.F. did not have enough aircraft soon enough.

On taking over the Air Ministry Swinton found that the regular procedure was to build a prototype and test it. When it had been fully tested a number of aircraft were ordered. The result was that even with comparatively simple biplanes five years elapsed between ordering the prototype and the re-equipment of a squadron with the new type. The Air Ministry placed orders only with established firms. They had no reason to do otherwise as the small quantities required were barely sufficient to keep even these aircraft companies fully employed.

It was obvious to Swinton that all this had to be changed if the 1939 deadline for the completion of the 1936 programme was to be met. This called for 124 home-based squadrons, 1,376 first-line aircraft and a 225 per cent reserve. One of his first moves to reduce the time lag before aircraft reached the production stage was to by-pass the long-winded prototype procedure by ordering planes straight off the drawing-board. This meant incorporating essential modifications on the production line, but with time in short supply the practice over-rode all disadvantages.

To ensure that modifications did not disrupt the flow of production only those impinging on safety and essential performance were introduced. Complete aircraft had to be returned immediately for alteration. If the modification was an improvement which was not essential to safety or performance it had to wait until it could be embodied without interrupting the production flow.

The availability of several early models obviated the delay an accident to a prototype might have induced, and enabled several kinds of necessary tests to be made simultaneously. It was impossible to judge accurately how a new type would turn out, however, and it was therefore necessary to insure against failure by ordering more than one type for each specification before choice was made.

Each company preferred to make the aircraft of its own design but in the national interest it was necessary to override any prejudices for one type or another. The final choice rested with the Air Council. Once their minds were made up the manufacturers had to be prepared to build the chosen type whether or not they had designed it. Some mistakes were made in the circumstances. Perhaps the most striking was the choice of the Fairey Battle and the subsequent dismissal of the Hawker Henley as a bomber.

The Fairey Battle day bomber carrying a pilot and a gunner was handicapped by being almost as big as the Blenheim but with no more engine power than the Hurricane. Of extremely simple and clean shape it could carry 1,000 lb. of bombs twice as far as the Harts and Hinds it replaced. The Battle failed in war because the Air Staff did not see the anomaly of ordering multi-gun fighters and a large day bomber with only one fixed gun firing forward and a single Vickers gun firing aft.

The Hawker Henley was intended as a fast monoplane replacement for the Hart biplane bomber series. Its wings were interchangeable with those of the Hurricane, an ingenious way of assisting production, maintenance and repair. The wavering attitude of the Air Ministry in 1936 towards light bombers precluded the Henley from quantity production. Numbers of these fast, heavily armed close-support aircraft might have made all the difference to events in early 1940. The Henley was easily capable of conversion to a two-seat twelve-gun fighter-bomber with a 2,000 lb. bomb load. With a top speed of 290 m.p.h. it was nearly fifty miles an hour faster than the Battle and its range of 950 miles was only 100 miles shorter than that of the Battle.

Two of the Air Staff's re-equipment decisions stand out. The first, taken in 1934, was that the Spitfire and the Hurricane should carry eight guns each instead of two. Without this change the Battle of Britain might well have been lost.

The other, taken in 1938, was the choice of ultra-heavy bombers specified two years earlier as standard aircraft of the home-based striking force. This led to the Short Stirling, Handley Page Halifax and Avro Lancaster bomber offensives against Germany which followed up the battle.

In the Browning gun used in the Hurricane and Spitfire, the R.A.F. had a first-class weapon. It was so reliable that it could be remotely controlled and it had the extremely high rate of fire of 1,260 rounds a minute. The first orders were for American-made guns, but manufacturing rights were soon acquired by the Vickers Company to make them in Britain. It was obvious, however, that heavier armament would replace the rifle calibre Browning. In 1937 Hispano-Suiza were granted facilities to open a factory in Britain for the manufacture of the 20 mm. Oerlikon cannon. These were first tried out during the Battle of Britain on two Hurricanes and thirty Spitfires.

While Swinton was Air Minister, provision was made for engine mountings that were interchangeable. New types of engine could be earmarked provisionally for new aircraft. With the introduction of common mountings alternative engines could be installed if the type of engine originally intended failed to perform as expected and was not available in time. There was in consequence no risk of delaying the output of urgently wanted aircraft.

It became clear that after fifteen lean years the aircraft companies could not be expected to finance unaided the expansion of their productive capacity to meet the later requirements.

To remedy this Lord Swinton devised the 'shadow factory' scheme announced in March 1936. It called for the building of state-owned plants to create a reserve productive capacity. Firms not normally aircraft or component manufacturers, but with experience in a similar field, were given the job of equipping and managing these factories to turn out products designed by an aircraft firm. The motor industry was the most suited to make aircraft engines. Thereby arose the situation in which a shadow factory owned by the state and managed by a motor manufacturer produced aero engines or aircraft designed by other firms.

The industry was required to expand and produce to the limit, and to abandon many of the principles of competitive business. Under the scheme the 'parent' firm in the aircraft industry had to furnish its shadow with drawings, specifications of plant, jigs, tools, processes, test equipment, layout and other technical information, educate key men and give every sort of advice and assistance.

For airframe production the Government built and equipped two large factories at Birmingham and at Speke, Lancashire, both on existing airfields. The first was entrusted to the Austin Motor Company to build Fairey Battle bombers and the second to the Rootes Organisation for the production of Bristol Blenheims.

Swinton invited the Austin, Daimler, Humber (Rootes), Wolseley (Nuffield), Rover and Standard Companies to co-operate in the manufacture of Bristol engines. They received jointly an immediate order for 4,000 engines. For various technical reasons it was decided that each firm would make components for assembly elsewhere rather than complete engines.

Mr. Leonard Lord, a strong supporter of the plan, represented the Nuffield Organisation. It came as a surprise, therefore, when Lord Nuffield refused to let his firm participate unless each company built complete engines. He did not believe that satisfactory results could be obtained with parts manufactured by different firms. That Rolls-Royce relied on seventy or eighty sub-contractors for the production of their engines failed to impress him, although his own lieutenant insisted that the proposal was justified.

The engine shadow scheme went ahead without the aid of the Wolseley Company, but to fill the gap the Bristol Aero Engine Company erected an assembly plant in addition to supervising the whole team. Lord later joined Austins to take charge of airframe production and the engine assembly work.

The February 1936 programme governed expansion until 1939 but by the end of the first year it was clear to the Air Staff that its scope would have to be widened if the strength of the R.A.F. was to keep pace with German rearmament. A fresh plan was drawn up but this was rejected by the Cabinet in February 1937. It was still before the Cabinet when the Germans annexed Austria. Within a few days the original version was approved and the time scales advanced.

It was decided to apply the shadow factory principle within the aircraft industry itself, firms being selected to equip and manage their own shadows. The Rolls-Royce and Bristol engine companies were duplicated. Swinton wished to entrust a very large new factory at Castle Bromwich to Vickers. This was capable of the tremendous output of 1,500 Spitfires by the spring of 1940. Sir Kingsley Wood replaced Lord Swinton as Air Minister in March 1938, and Castle Bromwich was entrusted to the Nuffield Organisation, a decision which was to have far-reaching consequences.

One of the main ways in which increased output was obtained as the threat of war increased and expansion plans grew was the system of farming out component manufacture to smaller firms. Work was spread over more than 15,000 sub-contractors, including small garages and engineering works throughout the country, with the result that rearmament acquired a peculiarly national character.

After the outbreak of war sub-contracting invaded even homes, where it was not uncommon to find women past the age where they could play a more active part holding 'filing parties' to smooth down the rough edges of mysteriously shaped pieces of metal 'for an hour or two after tea'. School workshops were also filled with small boys diligently lipping the sharp edges of stamped-out aircraft seats with fibre-headed hammers that seemed too big for some. It was everyone's war and this work gave a sense of participation.

There were of course mistakes. When the first batch of wings built by the Pobjoy Company under sub-contract was delivered for assembly it was discovered that none would fit the Spitfire fuselages for which they were intended. The error created serious bottlenecks all along the production lines and delayed re-equipment of many squadrons.

Britain relied on the overseas purchase of many raw materials. It was necessary therefore to build up sufficient stocks to meet emergencies. To ensure maximum self-sufficiency manufacturers were encouraged to make goods normally imported. High octane aviation fuel was such a commodity imported before the war but later refined in satisfactory quantities in Britain.

The two vital prototypes from which came the fighters that won the Battle of Britain. Above, the K 5054, the prototype Spitfire which was first flown on March 5th, 1936, and which soon achieved 349 m.p.h. during tests. Below the first Hurricane which flew on November 6th, 1935, and attained 315 m.p.h. while on trial at Martlesham Heath

As it turned out, aviation spirit was to prove no worry for the R.A.F. By July 11th, 1940, the day after the Battle of Britain opened, stocks of 100 octane petrol used in the Merlin engine stood at 343,000 tons. On October 10th, twenty-one days before the battle closed, and after 22,000 tons had been issued, stocks had risen to 424,000 tons. With other grades of aviation spirit total stock available on October 10th, 1940, was 666,000 tons. Oil reserves were 34,000 tons.

The last two pre-war schemes L and M saw production expanded to the limits of peacetime capacity, the chief financial restrictions abandoned and industry much accelerated. The final programme was prepared after the Munich crisis and hurriedly approved following German occupation of Czechoslovakia. It proposed extensions in nearly every direction, but chiefly in the number of fighter aircraft and in bombers of the latest heavy long-range type, such as the Avro Manchester, the Short Stirling and the Handley Page Halifax. By this time the air estimates had risen to a total of £220,626,000.

Meanwhile, in April 1938, a British air mission went to the United States to discuss the purchase of aircraft. The mission visited the entire American aircraft industry and found it in a worse state of depression than Britain's before the expansion programme.

The mission ordered 200 Hudsons and 200 North American advanced trainers, the latter known as the Harvard by the R.A.F.

Three months after the first visit to America another British mission went to Canada to discuss manufacture there of the Hampden bomber, and subsequently the Hawker Hurricane and the Fairey Battle. In May 1939 a joint order for aircraft to be built in Australia was placed by the British and Australian Governments.

Before its new planes could be brought into service the R.A.F. had to build new airfields, training units, camps, bombing and gunnery ranges and other ground installations.

Until 1934 the R.A.F. had found fifty-two airfields adequate for its needs. The bomber squadrons organised in the western area of the Air Defence of Great Britain were, apart from those at Bircham Newton, Norfolk, centred on Wiltshire, Hampshire, Berkshire and Oxfordshire. The fighters of Fighting Area were disposed for the defence of London at airfields in Middlesex, Surrey, Sussex, Kent, Essex and Cambridgeshire.

The position of all these airfields, with the exception of those built during the First World War, was dictated in 1932 by the assumption that any attack on Britain would come from France. With Hitler's rise to power and the possibility of a war, in alliance with France, against Germany the situation was radically changed. By 1939 short-range bombers, intended for continental bases in the event of war, occupied the central airfields. For the long-range bombers a string of new airfields spread across East Anglia, Lincolnshire and Yorkshire.

The dispositions of the fighter bases were determined by a plan recommended in 1935 by the Air Ministry Re-orientation Committee under Air Chief Marshal Sir Robert Brooke-Popham, then commanding

A.D.G.B. They stretched as a continuous system of fighter defence from Southampton east and north as far as Newcastle.

Fighters also guarded the Clyde-Forth area and Bristol. An additional eighty-six new airfields were added, bringing the total in 1939 to 186 excluding civil aerodromes.

Surveying sites, clearing the fields and building hangars, work-shops and living quarters was a complex task. Each had to be strategically placed, fighter airfields where they could best defend probable targets, bomber bases conveniently located for offensives.

Meteorological records had to be studied for those intended for all-weather use. In addition to the fully equipped airfields more than fifty satellite and emergency landing grounds were established. Cleared of obstacles and properly drained they were sown with good grass and leased to farmers.

By early 1940, aircraft production was, nevertheless, causing anxiety. Not enough planes were rolling off the assembly lines. Accordingly, on May 14th, four days after the start of the German offensive in France, the Ministry of Aircraft Production was formed out of the Air Ministry's research and production departments.

A taskmaster was appointed in the person of Lord Beaverbrook to press forward the production of new aircraft. As the head of the new Ministry of Aircraft Production he produced results.

By June 28th, 1940, there were 170 Hurricanes, 97 Spitfires and 20 Defiants in storage units ready for immediate issue to the squadrons. By July 5th the figure rose to 222 Hurricanes, 119 Spitfires and 32 Defiants. These reserves dropped sharply at the height of the Battle of Britain but never to danger point.

Hurricane reserves reached a rock-bottom figure of seventy-eight ready for immediate issue on August 30th. But even then only four days' work was needed to prepare a further seventeen planes for delivery and about a week for another 113. Spitfire reserves were lowest on September 20th when thirty-eight were available for immediate issue.

When the Battle of Britain began on July 10th Fighter Command had 666 aircraft ready for action. They were of high quality, backed by a unique control and reporting system, and flown by pilots trained to the high standards Lord Trenchard decreed essential when he laid the foundations of the R.A.F. in 1919. The one serious defect was a disturbing shortage of trained pilots.

5 Intelligence

GERMAN INTELLIGENCE

In 1940 Germany undoubtedly possessed the most powerful air force in the world but the German intelligence system was disorganised and inefficient. Personal jealousy, poor officers and complete lack of co-operation at all levels were the main reasons for this surprising situation which was to be a major factor contributing to Britain's survival.

Germany possessed two large and wealthy intelligence organisations at top level, the Abwehr under Admiral Canaris and the Sicherheitsdienst (SD) under Heinrich Himmler. Both supplied information to the armed forces and they had separate foreign services and agents. Little or no co-operation existed between the two; on the contrary, there was severe antagonism. Efforts were duplicated and there was no cross check on the accuracy of either. Many of the Abwehr officers were unsuited to their jobs and had little technical ability while the SD was often preoccupied with internal German affairs.

It was against this background that the 5th Abteilung of the Luftwaffe General Staff was established on January 1st, 1938, with a brief to collate information about foreign air forces and to prepare target information for an air war. The Abteilung took over the functions of two small units known as the target data unit and the 'department for foreign air forces' at the Reich Luftministerium (German Air Ministry).

Command of the 5th Abteilung as Chef IC (Intelligence) was given to Major Josef Schmid, who was recommended to Göring by Jeschonnek. He rejoiced in the nickname of 'Beppo' and previously held a ministerial appointment. He was shrewd, ambitious and noted for his 'conviviality', but he spoke no foreign languages and was not a pilot. It is significant of the value placed by the Luftwaffe on intelligence that the appointment was only in the rank of major. In Britain authority at the time was vested in the director of operations, intelligence, with the rank of air commodore.

Schmid found that the two units forming the basis of his department were staffed with civilians and reserve officers who had no clear idea of what they were supposed to be doing. Their files seemed to consist entirely of mountains of newspaper cuttings and foreign magazines.

He began steadily to introduce some sort of order and laid down objectives. Many of the staff were replaced by officers of his own choosing who would not menace his own position.

The first few months of the new organisation were spent in classifying information, sorting out and filing requests for more to the Abwehr. Schmid gradually began to widen the scope of the 5th Abteilung and consolidate his own position through friendship with Göring and as the Marshal's personal general staff officer.

Schmid's ultimate objective was, justifiably, to subordinate all sources which could provide air information. In this he was never completely successful. His only real triumph came in the spring of 1939 when the German air attachés came under his control. Chef IC was allowed no direct contact with foreign technical bodies and even his foreign newspapers were doled out by the SD.

Despite many stumbling-blocks Schmid succeeded in making progress, especially regarding target information on Eastern Europe. After the occupation of Austria, the latter half of 1938 and the first half of 1939 were devoted to studies of Poland and Russia and investigation of Britain. In the case of Poland the date for completion of the study was July 1st, 1939.

While the preliminary work on Britain was proceeding an order was issued by Göring for a high priority examination of the air and industrial armaments capacity of the country. The subject was considered so important that a study committee was formed with Milch, Udet and Jeschonnek as permanent members and with Schmid in the chair. Numerous other officers were called in when their departments were affected.

Milch took a major part in the committee's work because he had toured the R.A.F. and the shadow factories in 1937 with Udet and was personally interested in the subject. Milch's first step was to write to a leading London bookseller on German Air Ministry notepaper requesting several copies of a comprehensive work on British industry. This formed the basis for the committee's report on Britain which appeared in July 1939, with the title of *Studie Blau* (Blue Study). For most of the war *Studie Blau* was the basic reference on which attacks on England were planned.

By the outbreak of war the Luftwaffe possessed considerable information about R.A.F. bases and units from their air attaché, General Wenniger, the Press, and such occasions as Empire Air Days. The airfield and target information was supplemented by a comprehensive photographic reconnaisance of Britain. This was carried out by a unit of special He 111C aircraft under the direction of Oberst Rohwehl. Bearing civil markings, these planes operated from Staaken airfield, Berlin, on 'civil route proving flights'.

With the opening of hostilities the normal channels of information from Britain were cut off and Abteilung 5 had to rely on newspapers, reports from neutral countries, and the German Signals Intelligence Service. This organisation was under the command of General Martini, Director of Luftwaffe Signals, who, as outlined in the Prologue, was responsible for the flights of the *Graf Zeppelin* in 1939.

Signals intelligence, Abteilung 3 of Martini's staff, supplied information to Schmid in the form of daily intelligence summaries and ten-day or monthly surveys. The Service was to provide almost all the useful material available during the Battle of Britain as there were few prisoners of war to interrogate during the period. The Abwehr's juvenile efforts in dropping by parachute low-mentality half-trained spies over England almost without exception ended in disaster. The agents were collected by British security men as they landed, like fond parents meeting homecoming schoolchildren.

Schmid went to war a somewhat surprised man. He had considered with Jeschonnek and others that Britain's grovelling at Munich indicated a strong desire to keep out of the European conflict.

While realising that Britain militarily was a foe to be respected, Schmid had already begun to underestimate the potential and efficiency of the R.A.F., perhaps to please the omnipotent Göring. In the spring of 1939 in a survey of world air forces Schmid stated:

'The English and French air fleets are still much out of date. British air defence is still weak. . . . England will not be able to avoid a conflict with the German Luftwaffe. German aircraft are superior in view of their advantage in armament, armoured fuel tanks and flying instruments. In Germany alone has an overall view been taken of air warfare.'

Separately Schmid issued figures for British air strength computing the total of R.A.F. and Fleet Air Arm aircraft at 5,500 of which 3,600 were first line. He estimated that there were 200 first-line fighters; in fact the R.A.F. mustered 608 at that time. His calculation of 500 first-line bombers was nearer the mark. The correct figure was 536.

As September and October 1939 passed and winter set in both sides realised that the all-out bomber offensive each expected had not materialised. To Britain it was a relief, while to Germany it meant fighters could be concentrated in preparation for 'Operation Yellow', the invasion of France and the Low Countries.

Schmid devoted his time to working out an offensive plan against Britain which would do her most damage regardless of the outcome of Operation Yellow. This document, issued on November 22nd, 1939, as 'Proposal for the Conduct of Air Warfare Against Britain' was far-sighted. It was probably the last in which he was able to make an objective and accurate forecast of the British problem. After reviewing the progress of the war Schmid wrote:

From Germany's point of view Britain is the most dangerous of all possible enemies. The war cannot be ended in a manner favourable to us as long as Britain has not been mastered.

France on the other hand ranks in the second class for unlike Britain she would not be capable of carrying on the war without her allies. Germany's war aim must therefore be to strike at Britain with all available weapons, particularly those of the navy and air force.

In pursuit of this aim it is considered of decisive importance that operations against the British Isles should begin soon, and in as great strength as possible—under any circumstances in the present year. The enemy must not be allowed the time to use past experience to perfect his defences. Furthermore, economic assistance from the British and French colonial empires and from neutrals, particularly the U.S.A., and the encirclement of Germany, must not be permitted to come fully into operation.

The whole theme of Schmid's paper was the strangulation of British supply lines and harbour facilities. He proposed to attack as follows:

(a) The most important ports must be attacked without exception and as far as possible simultaneously. The intermixture of residential areas with dockyards in some British ports is no reason for failing to attack such ports. The most important ports are those of London, Liverpool, Hull, Bristol and Glasgow. In all these ports the primary target will be shipping. As secondary targets, dockyard and warehouse installations, in particular food and oil stores and silos, may be attacked. Raids must be constantly repeated—by day and by night. To achieve the maximum effect, even small formations may be usefully employed.
(b) Warships under repair and under construction on the point of completion are also to be considered as targets worthy of attention.
(c) It is necessary that ports of secondary importance should also be subjected to occasional attack. Nevertheless, in view of their very limited capacity, they should only be considered as secondary or alternative targets.
(d) In view of the superior bad weather flying training of the Luftwaffe it is also possible that we may be able to achieve some purely tactical successes should the enemy air force choose to counter-attack, which is unlikely.

Schmid's hypotheses were correct, but two vital factors were omitted—the radar chain which spelt death for unescorted bombers and the lack of maritime bombers and torpedo aircraft in which Göring was completely disinterested.

The memorandum was read, commented on, and then laid aside. In the offing were bigger fish to fry nearer home and Operation Yellow was fast approaching.

In May 1940 the grey-clad columns poured across the Dutch, Belgian and French borders and the defences of those states crumbled like houses of paper. By mid-June the Wehrmacht was the undisputed master of Europe. The British Expeditionary force, its equipment abandoned, was saved from the holocaust of Dunkirk while the R.A.F. was licking its wounds, trying to fill yawning gaps in the pilots' ranks and feverishly re-forming its squadrons.

The German forces were borne along on a wave of emotion and enthusiasm. The campaign was gloriously successful, every estimate and appraisal having proved correct. It is hardly surprising that this atmosphere should have penetrated even into the intelligence department of the Luftwaffe, where that unit's analysis of French Air Force equipment and morale was confirmed in every detail. Schmid's belief in his own abilities was enhanced. Abeteilung 5 rose in the Luftwaffe's estimation in the general back-slapping that ensued.

As the weeks went by and Britain failed to sue for peace it became clear to the Germans that the R.A.F. would have to be destroyed and if necessary Britain invaded. Schmid concentrated on his *Studie Blau* and on the mass of information that had fallen into German hands on the fall of France. French officers and politicians, smarting and bewildered at their defeat, discussed British war potential openly and agreed with their German victors that the R.A.F. was in a hopeless position. The poor quality of the Spitfire and Hurricane was stressed by a department in General Udet's production ministry under Oberst Ingtschersich, which was responsible for evaluating captured enemy equipment. This department, not attached to IC, had its head in the clouds and wrote only what it hoped Göring and the air staff would like to read.

Having assembled his background information, Schmid compiled in July 1940 an overall survey of the R.A.F. on which the forthcoming offensive would be based. This is an historic document because it reveals all the blind spots and faults of the intelligence system behind the Luftwaffe when it fought the Battle of Britain.

The following is a translation of the entire paper:

Luftwaffe Operations Staff IC *Headquarters.*
 16th July, 1940.

COMPARATIVE SURVEY OF R.A.F. AND LUFTWAFFE STRIKING POWER

I THE MILITARY VALUE OF THE R.A.F.

A *Strength and Equipment*

1 *Fighter Formations*
With 50 fighter squadrons, each having about 18 aircraft, there are 900 first line fighters available of which approximately 675 (75 per cent) may be regarded as serviceable.

About 40 per cent of the fighters are Spitfires and about 60 per cent Hurricanes. Of these two types the Spitfire is regarded as the better.

In view of their combat performance and the fact that they are not yet equipped with cannon guns both types are inferior to the Me 109, and particularly to the Me 109F*, while the individual Me 110 is inferior to *skilfully* handled Spitfires.

In addition to the above formations Blenheim squadrons are available for night fighter tasks as auxiliary heavy fighters and operate in cohesion with particularly intense searchlight defence.

2 *Bomber Formations*
Assuming the average squadron strength to be 20 aircraft, the 55 to 60 bomber squadrons contain about 1,150 first line bombers, of which about 860 (75 per cent) may be regarded as serviceable.

This strength is divided among four types of aircraft of various series, approximately as follows:

Hampden	400
Wellington	350
Whitley	300
Lockheed Hudson	100

Comparison of these types shows that the Hampden has the best qualities as a bomber.

In addition, there is a large number of Blenheim bombers available. Most of these are in training schools but there are also some in operational units. However, in view of its performance, this type can no longer be considered a first line aircraft.

In comparison with German bombers all these types have the following disadvantages:

inadequate armour,
poor bomb-aiming equipment.

However, they usually have strong defensive armament.

3 *Other Formations*
These include coastal formations equipped with Lockheed Hudsons (reconnaissance) and flying-boats and with various obsolescent types of aircraft—close reconnaissance and low-level attack aircraft designed for co-operation with the army.

These need not be taken into consideration in this report.

4 *Anti-aircraft Artillery*
In view of the island's extreme vulnerability to air attack and the comparatively limited amount of modern equipment the number of heavy and light A.A. guns available (1,194 plus 1,114) is by no means adequate to ensure the protection of the island by ground defences.

The large number of efficient searchlights available (3,200) constitutes an advantageous factor in defence at night.

Only limited importance should be attributed to the numerous barrage balloons, as these can be used only at low altitudes (1,000 to 2,000 metres) owing to the medium wind velocities prevailing over the island. The balloons cannot be raised at all at appreciable wind velocities.

B *Personnel and Training*

At present there are no difficulties regarding the number of men available.

From the outset training is concentrated on the production of good pilots and the great majority of the officers in particular are trained solely as such. By comparison tactical training is left far in the background. For this reason the R.A.F. has comparatively well-trained fighter pilots while bomber crews are not up to modern tactical standards. This applies to the bomb-aimers in particular, most of whom are N.C.O.s and men with little service experience. Although there are deficiencies in equipment the comparatively low standard of bombing accuracy may be attributed to this factor.

C *Airfields*

In the ground organisation there is a considerable number of airstrips in the southern part of the island and in some areas in the north. However, only a limited number can be considered as operational airfields with modern maintenance and supply installations.

In general, the well-equipped operational airfields are used as take-off and landing bases, while the numerous smaller airfields located in the vicinity serve as alternative landing grounds and rest bases.

There is little strategic flexibility in operations as ground personnel are usually permanently stationed at home bases.

D *Supply Situation*

1 As regards aircraft, the R.A.F. is at present almost entirely dependent on home production. American deliveries will not make any important contribution before the beginning of 1941.

If deliveries arriving in Britain in the immediate future are supplemented by French orders these aircraft may be ready for operations by the autumn.

* The Me 109F took no part in the Battle of Britain

At present the British aircraft industry produces about 180 to 300 first line fighters and 140 first line bombers a month. In view of the present conditions relating to productions (the appearance of raw material difficulties, the disruption or breakdown of production at factories owing to air attacks, the increased vulnerability to air attack owing to the fundamental reorganisation of the aircraft industry now in progress) it is believed that for the time being output will decrease rather than increase.

In the event of an intensification of air warfare it is expected that the present strength of the R.A.F. will fall and this decline will be aggravated by the continued decrease in production.

2 Unless an appreciable proportion of present stocks is destroyed the fuel situation can be regarded as secure.

3 *Bombs*

Bomb production is limited by the method of manufacture (cast casings).

However, there will be no difficulty in the supply of bombs as long as present stocks are not expended and operations continue on a moderate scale.

It is believed that these stocks would be adequate for intensive operations lasting several weeks.

Most of the bombs available are of medium calibre (112 and 224 kilogrammes), of which a large proportion are of an obsolete pattern with unfavourable ballistic qualities (bombs with fins).

E *Command*

*The command at high level** is inflexible in its organisation and strategy. As formations are rigidly attached to their home bases, *command at medium level* suffers mainly from operations being controlled in most cases by officers no longer accustomed to flying (station commanders). *Command at low level* is generally energetic, but lacks tactical skill.

II THE OPERATIONAL SCOPE OF THE R.A.F.

(a) For its operations the R.A.F. has at its disposal an area of only 200 to 300 km in depth. This corresponds approximately to an area the size of the Netherlands and Belgium.

There is little possibility of Ireland being used in the system of depth owing to the lack of ground organisation and the fact that once R.A.F. units have been transferred there they cannot restore their serviceability.

In contrast the Luftwaffe has at its disposal an area extending from Trondheim, across Heligoland Bay and along the North Sea and Channel coasts to Brest with a practically unlimited zone in depth.

(b) In view of the inferiority of British fighters to German fighters, enemy bomber formations even with fighter escort are not capable of carrying out effective daylight attacks regularly, particularly as escort operations are in any case limited by the lack of long-range single-engined or heavy fighters.

The R.A.F. will therefore be obliged to limit its activity primarily to night operations even in the event of *intensified* air warfare. These operations will doubtless achieve a *nuisance* effect but will be in no way decisive.

In contrast, the Luftwaffe is in a position to go over to decisive daylight operations owing to the inadequate air defences of the island.

III CONCLUSION

The Luftwaffe is clearly superior to the R.A.F. as regards strength, equipment, training, command and location of bases. In the event of an intensification of air warfare the

* High level = Air Staff; Medium level = Group; Low level = Squadron

Luftwaffe, unlike the R.A.F., will be in a position in every respect to achieve a *decisive* effect this year if the time for the start of large-scale operations is set early enough to allow advantage to be taken of the months with relatively favourable weather conditions (July to the beginning of October).

The report contains many inaccurate and misleading statements. In the assessment of strength the R.A.F.'s fighter force was again overestimated. In July only 600 fighters compared with Schmid's 900 could be considered available and reserves were slim.

The suggestion that the Spitfire was inferior to the Me 109 was wishful thinking. The guarded reference to the Me 110 being inferior to 'skilfully' handled Spitfires was naïve and undoubtedly a sop to Göring's pet 'destroyer' units. The bomber statistics were exaggerated, but the selection of the Hampden as having the best qualities as a bomber was yet another feat of Udet's technical evaluation team. The claim that German bombers had better armour than the British was refuted in the battle.

The report underestimated the number of anti-aircraft heavy guns and grossly overestimated the available light weapons, but was correct in assuming a shortage of modern guns. The figures for heavy A.A. guns in A.A. Command after the fall of France were 1,204 and for light guns 581, compared with the German figures of 1,194 and 1,114 respectively.

In item (B) Schmid made one of his cardinal errors of the campaign. Men and not planes were Dowding's nightmare. The R.A.F. flying training schools were slow in expanding. The Civil Air Guard, for instance, was formed before the war to provide pilots for such an expansion but many of its partially trained members who joined the R.A.F. at the outbreak of war were kept waiting on the ground five or six months before their training was continued. Some at least, though inexperienced, could have been available for the squadrons the following summer. When the report was written Fighter Command had already been forced to ask the Fleet Air Arm for the 'loan' of sixty-eight pilots while army co-operation, bomber, and coastal squadrons were being combed for likely talent.

In (C) Schmid did not appreciate the arrangements for the repair and maintenance of fighter aircraft. He failed to realise in the ensuing three months that despite the havoc wrought on British fighter bases repairs went on day and night at sector and satellite airfields and that a network of factories and workshops rebuilt seemingly wrecked machines in a matter of days.

Production of new fighter aircraft was of great importance. German intelligence based its assumptions on pre-war knowledge of industrial expansion. Schmid felt safe in assessing fighter output at between 180 and 300 machines a month and in forecasting 'the continued decrease in production'. He was not aware of the concentration of fighter production taking place in which even small garages, schoolboys and old ladies assembled parts. Above all he had not met Lord Beaverbrook.

Far from decreasing, production soared and stayed up despite attacks on the factories. Instead of the figure of 180–300, which Schmid continued to believe

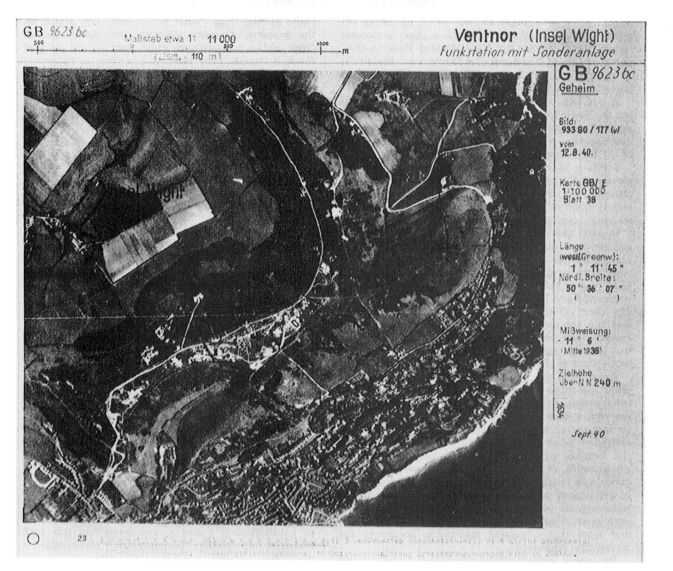

GB 9623 bc

Maßstab etwa 1: 11 000

500   0   500   1000   m

(1 cm = 110 m)

Ventnor (Insel Wight)

funkstation mit Sonderanlage

GB 9623 bc
Geheim

Bild:
933 SG / 177 (w)

vom
12.8.40.

Karte GB/ E
1:100 000
Blatt 38

Länge
(westl. Greenw):
1° 11' 45"
Nördl. Breite:
50° 36' 07"
(   )

Mißweisung:
- 11° 6'
(Mitte 1938)

Zielhöhe
über N N 240 m

Sept. 40

23

A German target photograph of the Ventnor Chain Home radar station on the Isle of Wight taken on August 12th, 1940. This was the day when 15 Ju 88's caused severe damage to the site. The caption to the picture reads as follows :- Radio Station with warning capability 1. 3 transmitter masts 2. 4 small transmitter masts 3. Low level defences 4. Special fuel installation 5. Anti-aircraft position; additional buildings under construction

during the battle, Britain produced 496 fighters in July, 476 in August and 467 in September. Thus the aircraft strength of the R.A.F. presented an enigma which the Germans never solved; Spitfires and Hurricanes which according to the German files had been destroyed or not even built kept appearing from nowhere with monotonous regularity.

On the subject of command (section E), Schmid was completely mistaken. He was not intimately acquainted with the R.A.F. or its members. He based his opinions mainly on air attaché reports and cuttings from publications. His assumption that formations were 'rigidly attached to their home bases' came from published British material which stressed the link between particular squadrons and an airfield. For instance the pre-war home of Nos. 1 and 43 squadrons was at Tangmere. Also the radio interception reports of close ground control tended to confirm this view. The British system was good for morale and competitive reasons but it in no way stopped the transfer of any unit at short notice from one end of the country to the other. Dowding continually switched his squadrons to quieter areas as they became exhausted and replaced them with others which were resting.

The reference to station commanders and officers at group level being 'no longer accustomed to flying' could more readily have been applied to the Luftwaffe than to the R.A.F. Station commanders frequently flew on operations. The generation of station C.O.s somewhat rusty on their 'aviating' had almost entirely disappeared by the end of the first six months of

45

hostilities. Had Schmid known when he wrote his report that in May, two months earlier, a notable 'group level' officer, Air Vice-Marshal Park, A.O.C. of No. 11 Group, had flown over Dunkirk in a Hurricane to view the situation for himself, he might have modified his opinion on this point.

It was, in fact, the Luftwaffe which suffered throughout the battle from top-weight of officers who were not up to flying standards. This included the Luftflotten commanders. Many officers in the 'medium' echelons of the Luftwaffe never learned to fly at all.

Schmid, however, was not employed to look too closely at the shortcomings on his own doorstep. His attitude, like that of Göring, was 'The Luftwaffe is clearly superior to the R.A.F. in strength, equipment, training, command and location of bases.'

Beyond the errors contained in the document an astounding omission becomes apparent. There is not a single mention of the close-knit British defence system with its radar stations, operations rooms, and complex H.F. and V.H.F. radio network. Schmid was not a technician and he lacked such ability among his staff. His chief, Göring, knew even less about radio and was not interested. The German Air Force signals troops under Martini were concerned but their voice was a small one and carried little weight in a strictly non-technical High Command.

Apart from the flights of *Graf Zeppelin* hardly any effort was made to analyse British defence or to obtain information from agents on the spot. The radar research station at Bawdsey was for years wide open to interlopers with no barbed wire and almost unrestricted access from the beach. Holidaymakers on the beaches near Dover amused themselves taking photographs of the unusual lattice masts above the cliffs. Any foreigner in shorts with suitable equipment in a haversack could have picked up and measured the radar signals radiating into space. Almost any radio enthusiast could have deduced the length of the aerials and from this calculated reasonably accurately the wavelength employed.

By 1939 it seemed almost impossible that Germany could lack information on the basic principles of the British scientific defence system. Many people were making the equipment or operating it and so many sites were being requisitioned and built on that a visitor with an adequate electrical engineering background could have pieced much of the jigsaw together. The reliable and security-conscious technical journal *The Aeroplane* remarked in a report on the August 1939 air defence exercises that 'The Observer Corps is an important link in the defence system of communications, and although *there are now other means of learning of the approach of the enemy* the Corps is likely to be used for some time.' The portents went unnoticed in Berlin and the Abwehr continued to produce papers on the decadence and the lack of will to fight of the British people.

The Luftwaffe knew in 1938 that Britain was experimenting with radar, but until July 1940 no efforts were made to assess the system fully or to counteract it. By then it was too late. Even the capture of a British mobile radar station on the beach at Bou-logne in May 1940 failed to stimulate real action on the problem. German scientists considered the set crude and on a wavelength which they felt did not give the best results. They claimed that German radar was superior in performance and thereby lulled still further the senses of the High Command.

With a fighter-defence system hardly worthy of the name and with a force geared entirely to offensive warfare the Luftwaffe turned a blind eye to the unique British layout.

In July radio monitoring stations picked up British high frequency radio telephone chatter and by analysis deduced that fighters operated under close radio control. It was concluded that this made the whole R.A.F. system inflexible, but in fact exactly the opposite was the case.

On August 7th Schmid issued a circular to Luftflotten and Fliegerkorps giving an appreciation of British radio control. This led to the wrong targets being attacked in many cases and it was erroneously assumed that mass attacks would completely swamp the system.

The circular stated:

As the British fighters are controlled from the ground by R/T their forces are tied to their respective ground stations and are thereby restricted in mobility, even taking into consideration the probability that the ground stations are partly mobile. Consequently the assembly of strong fighter forces at determined points and at short notice is not expected. A massed German attack on a target area can therefore count on the same conditions of light fighter opposition as in attacks on widely scattered targets. It can, indeed, be assumed that considerable confusion in the defensive networks will be unavoidable during mass attacks and that the effectiveness of the defences may thereby be reduced.

Having weighed up the estimated potential of the R.A.F. and found it lacking, Abteilung 5 concentrated its energies on providing target and general information to Luftflotten 3, 3 and 5, supplementing this with frequent up-to-date photographic reconnaissance surveys.

The targets were selected on a broad basis to meet dual requirements: the High Command preparations for invasion and Göring's wish to destroy the R.A.F. and bring Britain to her knees by air power alone. These required the British fighter aircraft to be brought to battle, the destruction of fighter airfields and associated installations, attacks on aircraft and munitions factories and the continuous complementary task of wrecking harbours, shipping, dockyards and warships. Certain ports on the south coast were omitted from the list of targets to preserve them for use during the invasion.

Radar stations were included as targets for the first phase of air attacks after an analysis by the signals branch of the Luftwaffe, but the German bombers found that they were extremely difficult to hit. In dive-bombing there was the danger of the aircraft colliding with the aerial masts, while from a height the target appeared small. Even if a near miss was obtained most of the blast went between the lattice girders without causing great damage. The control rooms, power plant

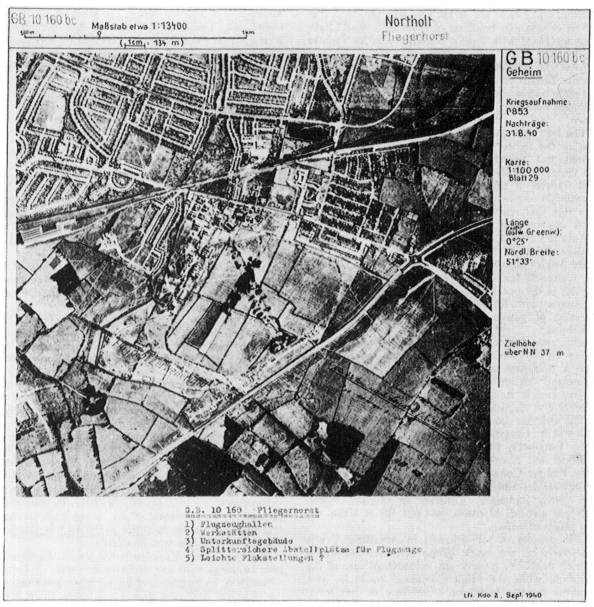

GB 10 160 bc   Maßstab etwa 1:13400

(1cm : 134 m)

G B 10 160 bc
Geheim

Kriegsaufnahme:
0853
Nachträge:
31.8.40

Karte:
1:100 000
Blatt 29

Länge
(östw Greenw):
0°25'
Nördl. Breite:
51°33'

Zielhöhe
über N N 37 m

G.B. 10 160   Fliegerhorst

1) Flugzeughallen
2) Werkstätten
3) Unterkunftsgebäude
4) Splittersichere Abstellplätze für Flugzeuge
5) Leichte Flakstellungen ?

Ln. Kdo 2 , Sept. 1940

*The German reconnaissance photograph of the fighter
airfield at Northolt taken on August 31st, 1940.
The runways have been skilfully painted to merge
with the surrounding countryside*

and other equipment were clustered under the towers
which also made them difficult to distinguish.

After the first assaults attacks were few and not
concerted. The reason for this has up to now been
something of a mystery but the reasoning was logical.
Crews reported having successfully bombed several
radar stations but General Martini's troops later the
same day detected transmissions which they presumed
meant that the stations were still working.

From this intelligence assumed that the radar
operations and equipment rooms were underground

and that further heavy bombing would be wasted as the
aerials could not be put out of action. The layout and
working of the radar sites and the communication
system linking them to fighter defence were unknown
to the Germans. Vital points which might have been
more susceptible to accurate attack therefore remained
undiscovered.

There were no reports from agents on radar and
none could be obtained. Had there been German
intelligence would have been surprised to learn that
the power and receiving rooms were not underground
and that the attacks had damaged some considerably,
particularly at Ventnor, Isle of Wight. Even where the
stations could not detect aircraft, signals were generally
still transmitted in some cases by mobile units. This mis-
led Luftwaffe signals intelligence and the commands.
If, after the bombing, several stations had ceased to

47

transmit and a large gap in the area had appeared, it is almost certain that bombing of radar sites would have been increased with serious consequences for Fighter Command.

After the official opening of the full-scale air war against Britain the only real intelligence came from the radio monitoring service and from reconnaissance, although a number of reconnaissance planes were shot down.

The four days estimated by Göring for the elimination of the fighter forces in southern England soon passed, but Schmid, examining the victory claims, felt certain that the R.A.F. was being bled to death. The transfer of squadrons from northern groups on Dowding's rotation system was incorrectly interpreted as a sign that reinforcements were needed to replace units destroyed in battle. Even the heavy losses of Luftflotte 5 in east coast attacks on August 15th failed to shake Schmid's convictions.

By August 20th German intelligence estimated that the Luftwaffe had destroyed no less than 664 British aircraft in the period August 12th to 19th and that up to August 17th forty-four R.A.F. airfields had been attacked of which eleven had been 'permanently destroyed.'

This extraordinary assessment was lower than the claims put forward by the operations branch (IA). Had it been true it would have meant that Fighter Command was almost finished. In fact, in the period August 12th to 19th only 103 R.A.F. fighters and some bomber and training aircraft on the ground were lost.

The airfields claimed by Schmid as destroyed were Eastchurch, Gosport, Lee-on-Solent, Lympne, Manston, Tangmere, Hawkinge, Portsmouth, Rochester, Driffield and Martlesham Heath. Only five of these were Fighter Command bases. A further twelve airfields were described as 'severely damaged' and twenty-one 'partly damaged'. Contrary to German belief, only one airfield, Manston, was put out of action for any length of time.

The process of self-delusion in Abteilung 5 was accelerated as the battle progressed. Schmid found himself unable to present any cohesive picture of the situation, while the High Command made its own progress reports based on a mixture of 'intuition' and the tales of glorious victory which poured in daily from the operations branch. He was severely hampered by the low status of his department and the fact that none of his officers worked with the groups or squadrons.

The only ray of light in this fog of confusion came once more from the radio monitoring service which, by listening to British radio-telephone chatter, managed to pinpoint the sector stations in No. 11 Group using direction-finding devices. One part of the jigsaw was completed, but as soon as the attacks on these sites were becoming effective the High Command turned the assault on London.

The London raids, which came as a blessed relief to the hardpressed sector stations, were the outcome of the conference of senior air force commanders at The Hague at the beginning of September. The whole position of the air war against Britain was discussed. Luftflotten and Fliegerkorps leaders showed à marked divergence of opinion about the strength of Fighter Command. The complete lack of any accurate information on the subject was revealed by Kesselring's declaration that the R.A.F. fighter force was finished, while Sperrle maintained that it still had 1,000 aircraft.

Schmid considered the figures showed that a large proportion of the fighter strength had been disposed of, but that concentration on R.A.F. targets such as airfields and on aircraft factories should be continued. He also referred frequently to his beloved *Studie Blau*, which was his constant companion throughout the battle.

After heated arguments Kesselring prevailed and Fighter Command was out of action—on paper. The Luftwaffe was then committed to what was hoped would be the final phase, the bombing of London. By this it was expected to wreck in a short time the morale of the capital to such an extent that peace terms would be sought.

In June 1940 Dowding remarked to some of his staff at Bentley Priory: 'The nearness of London to German airfields will lose them the war.' On September 6th this was proved true.

The attraction of London was the German Air Force's undoing. Like an indestructible sponge it absorbed punishment and diverted what might have been the death blow from the sorely tried organism of air defence.

Throughout the campaign the Luftwaffe was groping in the dark. There existed no organisation to sort out the conflicting plans and opinions which emerged on all sides or to impress some sense into Göring.

Intelligence IC was frequently blamed by high air force circles in later years for the defeat in the Battle of Britain, but this was grossly unfair. IC was a product of its own environment and it accurately mirrored the disunity of the High Command. To set up an intelligence organisation for the largest air force in the world, appoint its commanding officer in the rank of major and then deny it the facilities to do the job was sheer folly. The outcome was inevitable.

At no time during the battle was the IC organisation able to assess with any accuracy the state of Fighter Command, its aircraft and pilot reserve position, and its technical resources such as the radar chain. From June onwards Britain was a closed shop with only meagre and mostly inaccurate information from neutral diplomatic and Press sources. The morale of the British people and their ability to repair and improvise under constant attack were misjudged. For this unusually stupid men like Ribbentrop were largely to blame. Luftwaffe intelligence could only accept these views as it knew nothing of the British character and was given little opportunity to learn.

BRITISH INTELLIGENCE

Before 1940 there was little to choose between British and German air intelligence. Extraordinary blunders were made on both sides. Britain relied on agents of the various military intelligence sections, on the Foreign Office, the service intelligence departments and attachés and on ordinary British people from many walks of life who kept their eyes and ears open.

The agents covered a wide field but they were limited by the briefs given them and by the various authorities who lacked knowledge. There was some very brilliant work in the political and economic spheres but where aviation was concerned the results were patchy. Vital scraps of information were often mislaid or misused.

Estimates of Luftwaffe strength in peacetime were greatly exaggerated, as Göbbels intended they should be. This had a boomerang effect because it made the R.A.F. call for faster and greater expansion from 1935 onwards. In many instances the information which Churchill got from his private sources on the Continent was more up-to-date and accurate than that assembled by the Foreign Office and the service departments.

The Foreign Office had some extraordinary 'off' moments. These included a habit of mistranslating German, particularly Hitler's speeches. Prior to the war Hitler in the course of one address declared that he would amaze his potential enemies. This was translated literally by the Foreign Office as a new weapon which would 'blind and deafen'. A scientist who later became one of the principal intelligence experts of the war was sent post-haste to a special retreat in the home counties to look at every intelligence file available in a vain search for the elusive secret weapon. Exhausted, he resorted to a university professor of German who had no trouble in producing a correct translation, to the chagrin of Mr. Neville Chamberlain, then Prime Minister, and Foreign Office officials.

It was, however, in the realm of technical air intelligence that the worst blunders occurred. A well-known aircraft engineer was assisting with investigations into important German projects, including the Me 109, when his meticulous reports disappeared into the depths of Whitehall. They could not be found when they were badly needed in 1940.

Early in 1940 an Me 109 caught fire after it belly-landed. The fuel injector pump was said to have been burned out, although this was difficult to believe because it was made of steel. Not long after, Michael Golovine of Rolls-Royce, who later became an important member of Air Ministry intelligence, found himself sitting in a small café on the outskirts of Belgrade clutching a brown paper parcel containing the Me 109 fuel-pump which had been thrust into his hand by a mysterious stranger who had telephoned and spoken in Russian—Golovine's native language.

Golovine duly presented his precious package to the British Air Attaché, only to be told: 'I don't want the thing. You take it back with you.' Golovine pointed out that he would look extremely stupid carrying a German injector pump through Italy on his way home. Finally he prevailed on the reluctant officer to send it through the usual channels. Through stupidity it never reached England.

Had it done so Spitfires and Hurricanes which were not so equipped in the Battle of Britain might have been able to dive in the same manner as the Me 109 without their engines stopping. Many pilots' lives would have been saved and the R.A.F.'s score against the Luftwaffe increased.

On yet another occasion a complete handbook on the Me 109 became available for twenty-four hours in London. The document was photographed but the copies could not be found in the files when they were required.

Many unusual documents were put away on remote Air Ministry bookshelves and forgotten. When the problems of dealing with unexploded bombs became acute in 1940 there was a lack of information about German fuses. Eventually a copy of the Rheinmetall Company's fuse catalogue was found on the shelves. It had been sent by the company itself and had lain there for months gathering dust.

On radar intelligence before 1940 neither side knew what the other was doing. Germany realised that the R.A.F. had radar but discovered very little about it and came to the wrong conclusions concerning its operation. The R.A.F. gathered that German firms were working on radar detection, but until stations were set up on the German, French and Norwegian coasts late in 1940 the wavelength and other details were not discovered. No efforts were made to use aircraft for interrogation or jamming until the conflict was well advanced.

One of the best efforts of British Air Intelligence was to break the German squadron and radio codes and make a very accurate assessment of Luftwaffe strength.

At the long range wireless intercept 'Y' station in Kent Squadron Leader Maggs could decode as he listened to German radio chatter. When a new unit was formed, say, on the Baltic coast, Maggs would send a message to Wing Commander Bill Coope, the Air Attaché in Berlin, asking him to investigate and see if their aircraft bore a particular fuselage/fin insignia.

The Germans very foolishly had their unit and R/T codes on the aircraft and it was not until 1941, following the escape of a prisoner of war, that the Germans changed their codes to seven letters, although these too were eventually broken.

Wing Commander Coope was a very resourceful officer who spoke fluent German, could more than cope with entertainment and had an aeroplane at his disposal.

He had a remarkable flair for running out of petrol and in the case in question would just make a forced landing and stay for lunch. It took no time at all to find out the codes of aircraft standing around and thus another vital item was added to the Air Ministry Order of Battle for the Luftwaffe.

In the first few months of 1940 a considerable change came over the operational intelligence branch of the R.A.F. Apart from the hard-working regulars a number of newcomers made their appearance. They were civilians hurriedly converted into R.A.F.V.R. officers, each with an extensive knowledge in his particular subject. The organisation was subdivided, the main divisions being, *Technical* run by Wing Commander J. Easton, *Production* under Squadron Leader Allom, *Wireless Intercept* under Wing Commander Maggs, *Order of Battle* with W. Williams, Knights-Whittome and Asher Lee, and *Enemy Equipment Captured* under M. Golovine and H. F. King. Golovine was the son of a General in the Czar's army and a first-class engineer speaking three languages while King was a journalist

Reichmarschall Göring confers with his commanders during the Battle of Britain. On the desk is a map of the battle area. On the extreme right is General Jeschonnek, the chief of Luftwaffe General Staff, while nervously fingering his tunic is Colonel 'Beppo' Schmid, head of Luftwaffe Intelligence

from the editorial staff of the technical paper *Flight*.

Working in close accord with these sections was the P.O.W. Interrogation Unit under Squadron Leader Felkin which produced astounding results using subtlety and common sense in place of threats and coercion. The whole team came under the Director of Operations Intelligence. Originally the intelligence team was headed by Colonel Archie Boyle, an Army officer being given the job because Flak in Germany came under the Luftwaffe! Boyle was later transferred to the R.A.F. as an Air Commodore.

Above this department were several scientists well qualified for intelligence work. One of the most notable was Prof. R. V. Jones, the former pupil of Professor Lindemann, who developed infra-red detection and was in 1940 Deputy Director of Scientific Intelligence, Air Ministry.

Thus from early 1940 onwards British air intelligence grew in stature and reliability while the IC departments in the German Air Ministry steadily declined. The improvement in the R.A.F. was also largely due to the fact that intelligence officers were employed right down the line, at groups, stations and squadrons. In the Luftwaffe there were no representatives of the intelligence organisation stationed at units below the size of Fliegerkorps until 1944.

For the Battle of Britain the major task of R.A.F. intelligence was to obtain a correct Luftwaffe order of battle. The information was combed from secret sources, published documents and radio monitoring.

After months of painstaking assessment and reassessment it was estimated early in August that the Luftwaffe had an operational strength of about 4,500 planes. This was close to the mark, the correct figures being 4,119 on June 29th and 4,295 on August 10th.

Every Gruppe, Staffel and the types of aircraft employed were correctly identified before Eagle Day, August 13th.

What Churchill wanted to know, however, after Dunkirk was how long the air battle would last, when invasion was imminent and when the threat of invasion would recede. In mid-July Air Intelligence completed an assessment for him which, as a piece of prophecy, was almost perfect.

After the Battle of France A.I. had discovered that some seven German units had had to be cannibalised, therefore they deduced, rightly, that there were not 100 per cent. reserves and expansion of the Luftwaffe was at a slower pace than propaganda had suggested. There was a clash of opinion between the Ministry of Economic Warfare and Intelligence over this, the former producing some very exaggerated figures.

Intelligence won the point by providing that replacement machines were being flown direct to units and not, as normally, to aircraft parks—which were the equivalent of R.A.F. Maintenance Units.

In the final report to Churchill, in mid-July, Air Intelligence stated categorically that if the Luftwaffe, in daylight attack, could be held off until mid-September then invasion could not take place in 1940 because of worsening weather, the effects of losses and lack of reserves.

This indeed proved to be the case and the Battle of Britain was the turning point for Air Intelligence within the British High Command.

Both air forces suffered from exaggeration of each other's battle losses during intense air fighting and from differences of opinion between the operational groups and the sleuthing analysts of intelligence. British estimates of German losses were a little less than twice the confirmed figures. The German estimates of the R.A.F.'s losses proved to be five times too great. R.A.F. intelligence after careful study decided that about 50 per cent. of the British claims should be taken as a reasonable figure. This was not far wrong. There was considerable opposition to the assessment from within Fight Command, but it was eventually accepted by the Air Ministry because the claims over land could not otherwise be matched by the wreckage found. Amendments. were not publicly made at the time because it was thought that morale would be adversely affected.

One of the vital elements in deducing the German order of battle was the interception of radio transmissions particularly after the collapse of France and the Low Countries. Before the war Britain, like most countries, possessed a long-range monitoring service. It was one of these receivers which picked up *Graf Zeppelin's* position signals. There was, however, no organisation similar to General Martini's aircraft reporting service with a listening watch on the high-frequency bands. Such an organisation was essential to detect aircraft, ship and even tank H.F. radio-telephone.

It was not until the beginning of 1940 that the Air Ministry turned their attention to this aspect of the intelligence war. Thanks to a healthy peacetime radio industry and large numbers of amateur radio 'hams' in the R.A.F.V.R. there was no shortage of enthusiasts.

Concentration on radio intelligence began in earnest in December 1939, when Flying Officer Scott Farnie (a peacetime member of the volunteer civilian wireless reserve and later Group Captain) was recalled from duties as station signals officer at Oban, Scotland, to report to a deputy director of signals at the Air Ministry. Pulse signals had been coming from Germany. They

were later discovered to emanate from a mountain scientific establishment peacefully engaged in ionospheric research, but they prompted investigation. Scott Farnie was given the job and from this evolved the monitoring system. In February 1940 Scott Farnie, as a flight-lieutenant, was instructed to set up the first listening post at Hawkinge near Dover, Kent.

He found that there were no suitable high-frequency receivers in the R.A.F. and was forced to bargain with Webb's Radio, Ltd., in London, for the whole of their stock of American Hallicrafter 510 civil receivers. This unorthodox step had a sequel two years later when Air Ministry officials were still arguing about who should pay for the equipment.

With Flight Lieutenant Allway, a former B.B.C. engineer, Scott Farnie installed the sets in a hut at Hawkinge and began a listening watch on the forty-megacycle band. The choice of frequencies was fortuitous. There was no certain knowledge of what waveband the Germans used for radio-telephony.

For over two months nothing was heard, but in mid-May, at the height of the Battle of France, German transmissions began to come through loud and clear. Delight in the hut was tempered by the sudden realisation that none of the crew spoke German. This simple point had been overlooked.

One of the staff asked in desperation at the guardroom if anyone spoke German. Surprisingly one army private was a linguist. He was hustled in and the headphones rammed on. He was able to take down and translate the conversations which turned out to be from a formation of Ju 87s making a ground attack.

The private, Mattheson by name, found himself almost overnight transferred to the R.A.F., much to the annoyance of the personnel department of the War Office. He remained with the signals intelligence service until killed later in the war on a reconnaissance flight.

Having established the German radio-telephony frequencies, the Hawkinge unit suffered from an acute shortage of German translators to keep continuous watch. It was decided to recruit women to fill the gaps and to the consternation of the 'queen bees' of the W.A.A.F. suitable candidates were given direct entry in the rank of sergeant. The W.A.A.F.s performed a great service working six-hour shifts and taking down messages in longhand. One operator, Section Officer A. B. Morris, won a well-earned M.B.E. for her work in 1940, but the citation gave no hint of her job.

The success of Hawkinge and the fact that E-boats also worked on the forty-megacycle band led to the establishment of a chain of joint air force and naval monitoring stations along the east coast of England.

With the opening of the Battle of Britain in July it became clear that Hawkinge was too vulnerable, and the unit looked for new premises. Scott Farnie and Flight Officer 'Billy' Conan Doyle of the W.A.A.F. found an old garage at Kingsdowne, near Wrotham, Kent, and the operators were moved in as a temporary expedient. Scott Farnie and Conan Doyle again searched the countryside. They found Hollywood Manor at Kingsdowne and managed to have it commandeered. This became the operations centre for radio-telephony monitoring for the remainder of the war, and from

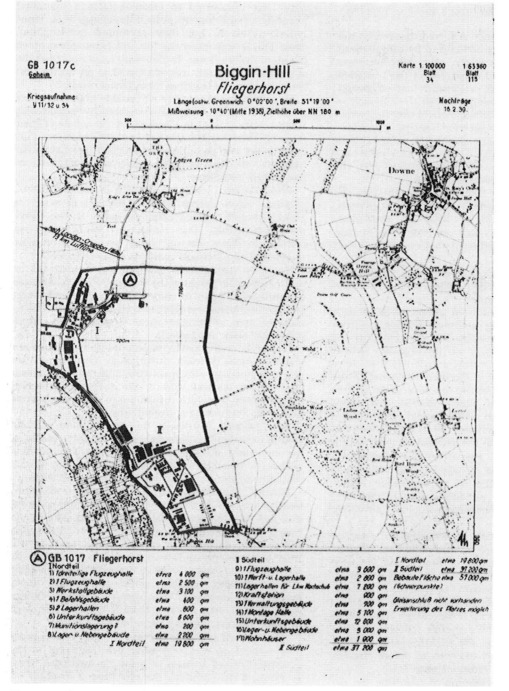

Downe

Ⓐ GB 1017 Fliegerhorst

Two pages from the Luftwaffe airfield-target handbook of Britain. The Biggin Hill map was based on a British Ordnance Survey sheet, while the oblique aerial photographs were taken before the war by a Lufthansa aircraft on its way to Croydon

Kingsdowne information was relayed to all R.A.F. commands and to the other two services.

Radio monitoring apart from its major part in compiling the Luftwaffe order of battle, was to become one of the prime tools of British intelligence. Early in the organisation's life German Air Force codes were successfully deciphered by concentration on the wireless telegraphy signals transmitted by the regular Luftwaffe meteorological flights between Bordeaux, France, and Stavanger, Norway.

The Kingsdowne station also played a part in one of the most successful technical intelligence operations of the war. From 1935 the Luftwaffe worked on radio aids to blind bombing. Three were finally developed, known as Knickebein, 'X' Gerät (instrument) and

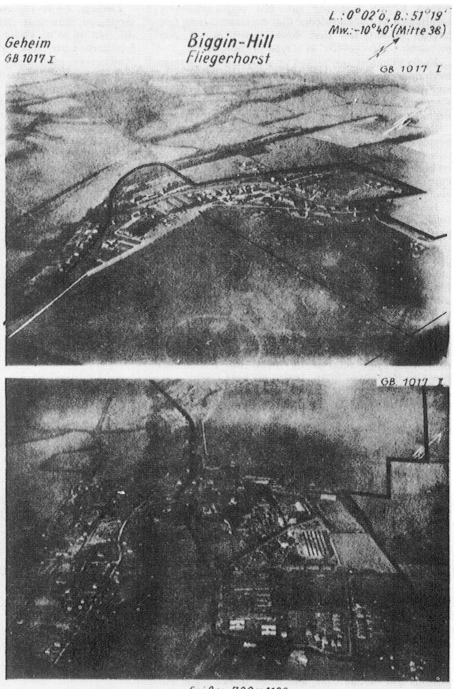

Geheim
GB 1017 I

Biggin-Hill
Fliegerhorst

L.: 0°02'ö, B.: 51°19'
Mw.: -10°40' (Mitte 38)

GB 1017 I

GB 1017 I

Größe: 700 × 1100 m

'Y' Gerät. Of these only Knickebein was available during the Battle of Britain, the 'X' and 'Y' being introduced for the winter blitz.

Basically Knickebein (bent leg) was a system whereby German bombers received long-range signals on their standard thirty-megacycle Lorenz beam approach landing receivers. In the pilot's headphones a continuous note was heard if he was flying along the beam heading for the target. If he deviated to left or right he heard dots or dashes and changed course accordingly. A further note was heard when he was required to drop his bombs. Although Knickebein was accurate only to within about 500 yards of the target it indicated the general position of many sites already receiving the attention of the day bombers, and others such as aircraft and aircraft engine factories, which were beyond the range of day fighter escorts.

Early in June 1940 the Luftwaffe made widespread probing attacks over Britain which led Professor Jones at the Air Ministry to suspect that the aircraft were

53

testing a new bombing aid. His suspicions were heightened by the knowledge that documents from two aircraft of K.G.100 shot down earlier in the year mentioned 'Knickebein' as a type of radio beam.

Radio monitors also picked up a mysterious message beginning 'Willi Knickebein . . .' and giving frequency and position references which indicated Cleve in West Germany and Derby in the midlands, where the Rolls-Royce works were situated.

Professor Jones was certain that directional radio beams were being used but other scientists were equally sure that a beam on the particular frequency could not be bent round the earth's surface to give the range. One enterprising security official started a witch hunt for a clandestine transmitter on the ground at Derby.

Jones refused to let the matter drop. On June 6th a full meeting to discuss the subject was held. Churchill presided. On June 17th Squadron Leader Felkin's interrogation of prisoners of war yielded results which confirmed the existence of Knickebein as a bombing aid. The following day steps were taken to investigate fully the beams using a van receiver and an Anson aircraft of the Blind Approach Aid Development Unit at Wyton.

At Wyton the work came under Flight Lieutenant R. Bluck, who had more experience than anyone in Britain on blind-landing techniques. Using an American thirty-megacycle receiver he found the Knickebein beam on his second flight. It still lay over Derby.

Further discussions between Churchill, intelligence chiefs, scientists and R.A.F. senior officers led in July to the formation of No. 80 Wing under Wing Commander E. B. Addison. This unit was intended to render German bombing aids useless. It was the beginning of Britain's electronic countermeasures organisation which was to play a major part in winning the war.

No. 80 Wing immediately put in hand measures to counteract Knickebein and also to disorganise the German medium frequency beacon system which allowed bombers to navigate by direction-finding methods.

First the wing found the positions of the remaining Knickebein receivers. Staff with radio receivers were sent up the 240-foot high C.H. radar towers to detect the characteristic dots and dashes. By listening in this manner round the south and east coasts by day the bearing of the target for the night could be found and measures taken to nullify the beam's effect. High-powered X-ray apparatus from hospitals which could be made to radiate jamming signals was set up in police stations and mobile vans, and when turned on it was impossible for the German pilot to hear his beam signals.

In some cases the beam was deliberately distorted by nine special transmitters so that it extended over a wide area and became too inaccurate for use. Means were also found to inject a powerful signal short of the target so that bombs were dropped in the open country-side. Fires were lit in the decoy area to assist this ruse.

There is no doubt that the measures taken in August wrecked the Knickebein system and helped to prevent accurate and concentrated German night bombing intended to back up the daylight operations.

German crews reported that the beam was being interfered with and that night fighters were being directed on to it. There was general dissatisfaction in Luftflotte 3 over this. Crews rapidly lost confidence in Knickebein, particularly when reconnaissance showed a target supposedly destroyed to be still standing the following morning.

At first German scientists refused to believe countermeasures had been taken by the R.A.F. because they were certain that Knickebein beams could not be detected by British ground receivers. It was not until several weeks after the Knickebein raids began in August that proof of countermeasures was obtained by sending out experienced Luftwaffe signals officers with the bombers.

6 The advent of Radar

On windswept Romney Marsh in Kent in 1934 an extraordinary concave concrete block 200 feet long and 25 feet high stood facing the Channel. It was one of two sound locators designed by the Army acoustics section.

Much thought and money went into the design and erection. They were then the only means of detecting hostile aircraft beyond the island shores. Unfortunately they were almost useless.

The great sound mirror with microphones along its length could, under ideal conditions and with a great deal of good fortune, give a rough bearing of an aircraft a little over eight miles away but it could not indicate height or range. Temperature variations, the noise of motor-cars, boats and birds allied to make even a bearing doubtful. Aircraft approaching at an acute angle to the reflector could hardly be heard at all.

There was therefore practically no warning of a raid on England, the number of bombers, or their direction and height, until they crossed the coast and could be plotted by the Observer Corps. The warning time was too short for fighters to be scrambled to intercept. The only alternative was to maintain standing patrols over the approaches to London, but this was impossible without many times the fighter force proposed.

The air exercises of 1934 clearly showed the weakness. Not more than two in five of the 'hostile' bombers were intercepted. At this time the standard Vickers Virginia bomber cruised at only 73 m.p.h. and had a full-load ceiling of 7,000 feet. When used in the final night section of the exercises head-winds reduced its speed to just over 60 m.p.h., but despite this 48 per cent of the attacking force reached their targets.

Bomb loads of aircraft were rising and a generation of planes was being developed which would fly higher and would have cruising speeds of 180 m.p.h. or more. These would allow less warning and make the task of the fighter even more difficult.

It was small wonder general opinion held that the bomber was invulnerable. This, with exaggerated claims by all the leading British and European theoreticians for the effects of aerial bombardment, presented a black outlook for R.A.F. fighter defence.

At the Air Ministry there were two men concerned with science, Mr. H. E. Wimperis, Director of Scientific Research since 1924, and Mr. A. P. Rowe, a member of his staff who was the only man in the directorate then employed wholly on armaments.

In June 1934 Rowe informally surveyed the problems of air defence by the simple method of going through the dusty Air Ministry files. Among the thousands he found only fifty-six on the subject. In a memorandum to Wimperis he stated baldly that unless science found some new method of assisting air defence any war within ten years would be lost. The warning did not go unheeded by Wimperis, who instigated a series of developments which were to revolutionise warfare.

Wimperis proposed to the Secretary of State for Air in November that a committee for the scientific survey of air defence be formed within the Air Ministry under a well-known physicist, Mr. H. T. Tizard. The suggestion was approved and the committee appointed, with Tizard as chairman, Rowe as secretary, together with Professor P. M. S. Blackett, Dr. A. V. Hill and Wimperis.

After receiving Rowe's memorandum Wimperis decided to investigate every avenue, even to the extent—not without tongue in cheek—of the possibility of the 'death ray', long the amusement of fiction writers. On this he consulted Mr. (later Sir) Robert Watson-Watt, a forceful Scot who had worked for many years on high-frequency radio and atmospheric research. He was then Superintendent of the National Physical Laboratory's Radio Research Station at Slough, Buckinghamshire.

Watson-Watt was no more enthusiastic than Wimperis about 'death rays' but agreed to have calculations made if only to eliminate the idea. One of the Radio Research Station staff, Mr. A. F. Wilkins, prepared figures which showed that beams of sufficient power to harm human beings and machines could not then be generated but that radio beams might be used for detection.

At the end of a final report Watson-Watt inserted a note suggesting that even if death rays could be produced the target must still be found before they could be put to use. He had ideas on the problem of detecting aircraft from his research into radio wave reflections and asked if the Air Ministry's scientific adviser would be interested. The document was put before the Tizard Committee's first meeting in January 1935 and they immediately requested a paper on the subject.

Watson-Watt showed in Post Office Report No. 233 of June 1932 that aircraft interfered with radio signals and re-radiated them. From this he postulated that an aircraft meeting a short-wave radio pulse would act as a radiator and reflect the signal back to the ground. The time lag measured in microseconds between the emission and reception of the reflected signal could be shown on a cathode ray tube. Thus with a suitable time

The Handley Page Heyford was the R.A.F.'s last biplane heavy bomber and its span of service covered the years 1933 to 1939. One aircraft of this type was used for the first practical demonstration of radar at Weedon near Daventry on February 26th, 1935

base the distance of the aircraft from the radio station could be measured.

The basic knowledge for these assumptions was gained as far back as 1924 from work done by E. V. (later Sir Edward) Appleton at the Radio Research Station in determining the height of the ionised area surrounding the world known as the Heaviside layer. Appleton employed radio pulses to measure the echo's time of travel.

From calculations, again made by Wilkins, Watson-Watt produced an historic document, 'Detection and Location of Aircraft by Radio Methods'. This was submitted to the Air Ministry on February 12th, 1935.

Wimperis was keenly interested in this shaft of light on the bleak defence horizon and requested a demonstration. He and Dowding, then Air Vice-Marshal and Air Member for Research and Development, met Watson-Watt at the Royal Aircraft Establishment, Farnborough, Hants, to discuss the matter.

Watson-Watt pointed out that equipment was nowhere near being designed. What he could justify, however, were the principle and the mathematics.

Accordingly a demonstration was arranged for February 26th. The B.B.C. short-wave overseas radio transmitter, with a power of ten kilowatts, at Daventry, Northamptonshire, was to 'illuminate' the target while the viewers would see the reflected signal on an improvised receiver between ten and twenty miles away. The research station produced a receiver linked to a cathode ray oscillograph, the screen of which was similar to that of a television set. In the centre of the screen was a bright green spot which it was hoped would

be deflected by the radio signal reflected from an aircraft. The plane, if detected, would vary the length of line made by the deflected spot.

In the late afternoon of the 26th a caravan drawn by a Morris car left the Radio Research Station, Slough, on the Bath road and later drew up in a field near Weedon in sight of the Daventry masts. The team consisted of Watson-Watt, Wilkins, and the driver, Mr. Dyer, while the 'examiner' from the Air Ministry was A. P. Rowe.

A lumbering Hayford night bomber from Farnborough was briefed to fly a fixed track of twenty miles up and down the centre-line of the Daventry fifty-metre beam—a boring procedure the reason for which the crew had no idea.

The field watchers heard the aircraft, kept their eyes glued to the screen and waited. Steadily the green spot grew to an inch in length and then receded as the aircraft droned away. The range was about eight miles. To a casual onlooker the inch stub would have meant nothing, but to the five men in the caravan it showed that such a system could be made to work. Thus on a winter's afternoon in the heart of the country a device was born which was in large measure to decide the fate of Britain and the world. In Watson-Watt's words, 'Britain became once more an island'.

Rowe reported his findings to Wimperis, who pressed the Air Ministry to support further development. It says much for the foresight of some senior R.A.F. officers and the gravity of the bomber threat that the sum of £10,000 was allocated to the work.

To ensure security an innocuous name 'radio direction finding' or 'R.D.F.' was applied to the research programme. At the time R.D.F. conveyed a relationship with time-honoured methods of direction finding by means of a ground beacon and a receiver in the aircraft.

An R.D.F. team from the Radio Research Station was formed under Watson-Watt and a home for it was found at Orfordness on the Suffolk coast. The site was near an R.A.F. airfield on a long neck of land joined to the mainland only at its northern tip. To all intents and purposes it was an island and it was not long before the researchers acquired the title of 'the Islanders'.

The team moved in on May 13th, 1935, to what was officially called the new Ionospheric Research Station. Laboratory transmitters and receivers were ready within a fortnight. Practical experiments were possible on June 5th, when a seventy-five-foot radio mast was completed.

The islanders' brief was to obtain approximate continuous plan positions of aircraft at long range, approximate height and strength and a means of distinguishing friend from foe.

On June 15th the Tizard Committee visited Orfordness to inspect progress. An old Vickers Valencia was used for trials but the results were poor due to atmospherics. Some weeks earlier Watson-Watt warned Rowe that several wavelengths would be necessary to combat possible enemy radio interference and much shorter wavelengths for detecting low-flying aircraft. The problem of low-level detection still exercises defence planners of the 1960s. Watson-Watt wanted wavelengths much less than fifty metres and envisaged 200-foot-high masts to obtain maximum efficiency.

While Wilkins and Dr. Bowen, with only four assistants and a part-time help from Slough, were striving to make radar an accomplished fact changes were taking place in the committees of Whitehall which formulated scientific defence policy.

In July Mr. Baldwin, the Prime Minister, told Churchill that Lord Swinton was 'very anxious' for him to join the newly formed sub-Committee of Imperial Defence on Air Defence, despite strong opposition from Neville Chamberlain. Churchill, a dedicated critic of the Government's poor defence policy, agreed to serve if he could reserve his freedom of action. He did not wish to be stifled by a privileged position. Showing unusual public spirit, Baldwin approved, subject to public discussion being avoided of secret matters dealt with by the committee.

Thus Churchill became a member of one of the most exclusive and important defence committees, which was to shape the destiny of Britain. In no other country perhaps could a situation exist where a back-bench member of Parliament and ardent critic of the Government could become privy to the nation's most jealously guarded secrets and participate in their development.

Churchill kept his promise. While his angry voice boomed across the dangerous years warning and demanding, no whisper was heard of radar or of any other device on which the committee worked.

Churchill, however, made it a condition for his joining the Air Defence Committee that his close friend Professor Lindemann (later Lord Cherwell) should become a member of the Tizard Scientific Committee at the Air Ministry. The Prime Minister agreed. Churchill found scientific matters difficult to understand and leaned heavily on Lindemann through the years as his adviser.

Lindemann, however, had his own ideas on air defence and lost no time in putting them forward. He could see the future of radar but differed from Tizard on how it should be developed and applied. He also pressed two of his favourite projects, infra-red detection and parachute bombs for breaking up bomber formations.

One of Lindemann's physicists at Cambridge was a brilliant young man, Professor R. V. Jones. In mid-1935 Jones was engaged in repairing a rudimentary infra-red detector invented by Commander Paul McNeil of the United States Navy. McNeil was demonstrating his gadget in England, but when it broke down resorted to the Cavendish laboratories for assistance.

When Lindemann heard of the apparatus he immediately seized upon it as a possible answer to the aircraft detection problem and introduced the subject to the Tizard Committee. His other notion concerned small bombs on parachutes connected with wire to be dropped in the path of enemy bombers. The wires would foul wings and propellers and the bombs complete their destruction. This was a completely blind alley for research on which valuable time and money were wasted.

Lindemann, after much argument, gained some support for infra-red. Heat detection could not rival radar in range, but Jones managed to get a set working on a Monospar aircraft in 1936 which could detect an aeroplane at a range of half a mile. This was an achievement but the problems were so complex that infra-red was doomed to sink into oblivion until revived by the German Army for night driving and detection in 1944.

In the Tizard Committee Lindemann and Tizard were unable to agree. Both men were brilliant scientists who trained together under Professor Nernst in Berlin. Their very brilliance and contrasting personalities led to violent differences of opinion and clashes on policy and technicalities. In August 1936 Hill and Tizard resigned in protest at the arguments. Lord Swinton, Secretary of State for Air, had the courage to re-appoint the original committee a few weeks later without Lindemann, but with the addition of Professor E. V. Appleton and later of Professor T. R. Merton. The differences of opinion in the Tizard Committee could have had a serious effect on the rapid growth of radar.

The acceptance of scientists for air defence can be largely attributed to Swinton. His was the guiding genius which laid most of the solid foundations of Britain's air rearmament and, above all, he appreciated the need for scientists not as advisers but as an integral part of the fighting machine.

One of Swinton's first acts when he was appointed Air Minister in June 1935 was to bring three scientists into the Air Ministry to sit in on air staff deliberations. This team consisted of Tizard, who became Swinton's personal adviser, Blackett and Hill, while Lord Rutherford took a fatherly interest.

The R.A.F. in 1935 could be likened to an old-established and highly respected company which had been selling the same line too long. It was faced with intense competition from a new and virile rival in another country which threatened to put it out of business. The only alternative to extinction was the rapid development and production of a new sales line.

*Interior of the receiver or 'R' hut at the Dunkirk, Kent
Chain Home radar station in 1940. In the centre are
the 'observer' and the 'converter', with the cathode ray
tube hidden by the W.A.A.F. in the foreground. On
the far wall is the telephone switchboard*

This arrived in the form of radar. The chairman was
Swinton, managing director was Tizard and board
members were Blackett and Hill. The chief engineer-
cum-sales manager was Watson-Watt.

While the top direction sorted itself out in London
there were practical developments in radar and, only
a month after the Tizard Committee's visit of June
1935, Orfordness began to show interesting results. A
record pick-up at thirty-eight miles range was made
and the same plane was followed out to forty-two miles.
For these trials a new and shorter wavelength of twenty-
six metres was used because fifty-six metres was subject
to interference from commercial wireless and atmospherics. On July 24th, while awaiting the return of a
Wallace biplane which was followed out to thirty-four
miles, a new echo was observed at twenty miles. From
its fluctuations the ground operators inferred that the

echo consisted of three aircraft. For the first time radar
had identified a formation. The pilot of the Wallace
confirmed that it consisted of three Hawker Hart
bombers which flew on blissfully unaware that their
passage had been observed by the small group in the
hut at Orfordness.

Two vital problems remained apart from the need
for longer range detection and these were the difficulty
of indicating height and of obtaining accurate bearing.
By September Wilkins had measured the height of
aircraft at 7,000 feet and at fifteen miles range with an
error of 1,200 feet. Direction, or bearing, was far more
difficult. Watson-Watt estimated that two years would
be required to provide direction finding (D.F.).

In September he reported that an aircraft had been
followed out to fifty-eight miles. This shattered the
calculations of the air defence Sub-Committee of the
Committee of Imperial Defence, which estimated that
to detect at fifty miles would take some five years' work.
On the strength of the report the committee recommended that a chain of radar stations should be built
covering the coast from the Tyne to Southampton.
This was just seven months after the first rough
demonstration in a field at Weedon.

By this time it was clear that the facilities at Orfordness were inadequate, also the erection of radar masts was embarrassing the nearby R.A.F. station. In the late summer, Wimperis and Rowe prowled the surrounding countryside looking for an alternative site and their search narrowed to the bizarre manor house at Bawdsey which stood on the mainland seashore south of Orfordness. Local gossip suggested that the owner, Sir Cuthbert Quilter, might be prepared to sell. The Tizard Committee and the Imperial Defence Committee agreed, and by February 1936 an advance party occupied one of the stately towers while the stables and outbuildings were converted into workshops.

Bawdsey itself was designated as one of the stations in the radar chain so that the scientists, instead of working in a secluded laboratory, became an integral part of the defence system. This later had a major beneficial effect on development and the rapid disposal of operational problems.

The first mast was obviously too low for obtaining the best results. The shipbuilding firm of Harland and Wolff of Belfast arranged to erect a 250-foot high lattice mast at Orfordness. It was hoped to complete it by October 1935, but due to delays in the Air Ministry Directorate of Works the mast was not up until February the following year.

A second mast was completed on March 7th, 1936. Six days later Bawdsey achieved the first location of an aircraft beyond sixty-two miles with range and direction, on a Hart flying at 15,000 feet. On the same day the Tizard Committee recommended that Watson-Watt be transferred from the Department of Scientific and Industrial Research (which controlled the Radio Research Station) to the Air Ministry.

Work continued through the summer, although plagued by various snags. During these months a workable radar direction-finding system was evolved by stacking up to six directional aerials arranged on the four points of the compass and working on a six-metre wavelength. A simple goniometer was used at the base, hand rotated, and working in a similar manner to an aircraft-direction-finding loop. With a loop the signal might be coming from one direction or from exactly the opposite direction, but at Bawdsey this ambiguity was overcome by specially sensing the relays in the circuit.

The R.A.F.'s faith in its device was maintained despite slow progress. In the top level reshuffle of 1936 when Lord Dowding became the first commander-in-chief of Fighter Command, Sir Wilfred Freeman took Dowding's place on the Air Council as air member for research and development and radar continued to be accorded the highest priority.

Squadron Leader Raymond Hart (later Air Marshal Sir Raymond Hart) was posted to Bawdsey in July 1936 as the first R.A.F. officer on the staff. His main job was to organise a school for radar training. It was estimated by the Signals Directorate that twelve N.C.O.s, twelve wireless operator-mechanics and twenty-four wireless operators would be required for four stations, Canewdon and Great Bromley, Essex, and Dunkirk and Dover, Kent. The men were posted to Bawdsey and in February 1937 the first radar-training school in the world was officially opened. Hart was to become one of the leading figures in radar operation and a major contributor to the evolution of techniques used in the Battle of Britain.

Watson-Watt suggested that women should be trained as radar operators as three typists at Bawdsey had adapted themselves excellently to the job. The Air Ministry at first objected that women might be emotionally unstable under the strain of operations. They relented, however, and women later proved their fortitude and reliability in the hectic summer of 1940 and throughout the war.

When the original recommendation was made in September 1935 for the erection of a chain of twenty stations covering the area from the Tyne to Southampton the R.A.F. requested a trial stretch over Southwold, Suffolk, to South Foreland by November with three operational stations by June 1936 and seven by August 1936. To ease the load, the requirement was reduced to the four stations mentioned above and Bawdsey.

Much had to be done in a very short time. Inevitably delays occurred while numerous problems were solved and modifications made. The attitude of some officials in Government departments who were quite unused to any sense of urgency, after eighteen years of peacetime plodding, did not help at all. In June Watson-Watt complained to Churchill over a cup of tea at Westminster of the frustration and time wasted by the machinery of officialdom.

Although it was proposed to complete the five 'R.D.F.1' stations of the first programme in time for the annual air-defence exercise, the delays meant that Bawdsey only was operational and had to bear the full brunt of the critical tests.

The results on the first day of the exercise, September 24th, were incomplete, irregular and inaccurate, but after recalibration of the station there was a marked improvement. Ninety reports were given in ninety minutes and on the following day 124 reports came in 115 minutes. With only one station for analysis, and this very much a research prototype, radar was unlikely to alter greatly the familiar pattern of the 1936 exercise: nevertheless Marshal of the R.A.F. Sir Edward Ellington, Chief of the Air Staff, visited Bawdsey in October and pronounced that despite everything radar should go ahead.

The first radar station in the world to form one of a chain was built entirely at the Bawdsey Research Station and handed over to the R.A.F. in May 1937. Dover Chain Home or 'C.H.' followed in July, and Canewdon in August.

It was estimated that a twenty-station chain would take two years to erect, but that with improvements to equipment fifteen stations could do the work of twenty. The remaining five stations could thus incorporate the cumulative results of research.

The whole of air defence was meanwhile being replanned round radar and the evolution of Fighter Command was entirely dependent on its success.

The problems of operating radar were by now multiplying at high rate, and presentation and transmission of information were among the most important. In 1936 Mr. E. J. C. Dixon, who was lent by the G.P.O., formed a separate laboratory at Bawdsey with a working copy of a group operations room. He was assisted by Warrant Officer R. M. Woodley, of the R.A.F.

Squadron Leader Hart, in addition to running the training school, started to develop the all-important 'Filter Centre' where radar information could be checked and analysed before being committed to a plot. An experimental filter room was opened at Bawdsey in July 1937 and passed information collected from the three radar stations to Fighter Command.

To sort out communication Mr. G. A. Roberts of Bawdsey was attached to the G.P.O. research station at Dollis Hill, London, while No. 10 department of the Royal Aircraft Establishment under Squadron Leader Rose co-ordinated ground and building design.

The three stations at Bawdsey, Dover and Canewdon were operating for the August 1937 air exercise. Despite errors which caused apparent failures, the results were promising, with ranges of 100 miles and formations of six or more aircraft observed at 10,000 feet and above.

Immediately after the exercise the Air Ministry drew up specifications for the twenty-station chain, and the scheme was approved by the Treasury on August 12th.

Already in January 1937 it had become apparent that industry's help would have to be invoked to provide essential valves, transmitters and receivers. Metropolitan Vickers Ltd., of Manchester, heard that Watson-Watt was looking for special valves for new radio work. After detailed discussion the company's research department was asked to undertake the development and manufacture not only of the valves but of the complete R.D.F.1 transmitter equipment.

In June 1937 verbal instructions were given to design and produce one set of 'R.D.F. Transmitting Equipment'—a requirement increased in August to twenty-two sets when the Treasury sanctioned expenditure on the chain. A similar contract was awarded to A. C. Cossor Ltd., of Highbury, for receiving sets.

Complete secrecy was required in the two firms and separate buildings were provided for radar work. Only two men, Dr. J. M. Dodds of Metropolitan Vickers, and Mr. L. A. H. Bedford of Cossor, were initiated into the radar secret although others of the team came to know most of it by degrees. To assist security still further one portion of the transmitter, a small box, was designed separately from the rest so that it could be made by a specially hand-picked team. Because of the loyalty of the men in both firms no word leaked out in the ensuing years.

At Cossor's a specially chosen team led by Mr. Puckle set about producing the first receiver in a private house in Highbury Grove, North London. The completed assembly assumed large proportions and holes had to be cut through the house walls for its removal.

Thus with complete co-operation between Bawdsey and the two companies radar passed from the laboratory stage to production.

The massive 350 ft. high transmitter masts of a typical Chain Home (CH) radar station in 1940

7 Radar at work

During the year 1938 radar was transformed from an experimental layout into an operational system capable of being used in war.

In August there was an important change in the management of Bawdsey. Watson-Watt was promoted to the post of Director of Communications, Air Ministry, and his place as Superintendent of Bawdsey was taken by A. P. Rowe.

Although not professing to be an electronics specialist, Rowe was a first-class organiser with an unusual flair for analysing problems and finding the right people to answer them.

He soon realised that many of the trials completed at Bawdsey had been carried out under almost ideal conditions such as would be found in a laboratory. The injection of practical circumstances into exercises showed up marked deficiencies. For instance, attempts to intercept K.L.M. and Lufthansa airliners in the Thames Estuary proved complete failures. If radar was to work it had to be tough and reliable. Dr. E. C. Williams, at that time a young research worker, was given the job of setting-up radar countermeasures designed to make operation of radar as difficult as possible.

Using a modified diathermy set installed in a Sunderland flying-boat, Williams conducted the first electronic countermeasures flight. This showed that 'jamming' could make the cathode ray tube on the ground almost unreadable with dancing lights blotting out signals from aircraft.

An interim solution was found using coloured filters to show up the trace on the screen, but the real answer came later with development by Professor Merton of the long afterglow. With this the echo of the aircraft remained visible for some time and the flickering from jamming could be separated.

July 1938 saw the addition of Great Bromley and Dover radars, thus completing the first five-station chain in time for the highly important air defence exercises on August 5th–7th. The stations were not entirely ready as two were uncalibrated in direction and height-finding. Scientists from Bawdsey were posted to each unit to supervise operation.

The backscreen of sensing relays which cut out the radar stations' view to the rear and avoided confusion between landward and seaward echoes had not been completed. Despite this and poor weather the results were very promising. The only type of aircraft which consistently eluded the watchers at the cathode ray tubes was the low-flier which penetrated below the cover of

radar beams. It became clear that some new type of equipment would be required to deal with this.

A Bawdsey memorandum of August 12th noted that 'it is apparent that filtering is still an art rather than a science'.

Discussing the current situation of radar and the communication requirements revealed by the exercise, a report from Bawdsey ran on August 30th

It is understood that:
1 There will be one map in the filter room covering the whole of the east and south coasts.
2 There will be three Fighter Groups.
3 Information is to be told to groups and thence broadcast simultaneously to sectors.
4 Experience with Biggin Hill has shown that sectors require information accurately and speedily at a rate of one plot per minute per raid.
5 R.D.F. stations will be required by the filter room controller to 'bring in' raids . . .

Information required by the three groups will be obtained by at least 15 R.D.F. stations, the Observers at which, in times of high raid density, will tell plots at a high rate. This information is to be filtered and passed accurately and speedily to groups and sectors simultaneously. This means that on the average when stations are all 'bringing in' raids, the group teller will have to tell the information received from 5 R.D.F. stations and will therefore have to tell information at five times the rate of the R.D.F. observers. . . .

Arguing backwards from the sector, a sector requires information accurately and speedily at the rate of one plot per minute per raid. If each sector can handle even four simultaneous raids, plots must be received at the rate of four per minute.

No. 11 Fighter Group has six sectors, Nos. 12 and 13 have three each. Hence filter room must pass plots at the rate of 12 per minute to Nos. 12 and 13 Groups, and at 24 per minute to No. 11 if all sectors are to be able to work to capacity. These figures include only the plots required by the sectors for interception and take no account of more advance information concerning distant approaching raids, which must be given to fighter group to enable orders for interception to be passed to sectors. . . . It is estimated that, with the proposed method of handling the information, at least two and possibly three lines will be required between filter room, groups and sectors. The actual requirements may vary between groups.

Close on the heels of the exercises came the Munich crisis of September 1938, the five stations being put on continuous watch at 2.30 p.m. on the 26th. They gave warning of attack on London from Suffolk to east Kent at a range of about eighty miles from the coast.

The threat of war caused the building of chain stations to be accelerated and at a meeting at the Air Ministry on October 6th it was decided that 'the R.D.F. chain be hastened so as to be complete by April 1st, 1939'. Compulsory purchase replaced the normal negotiation procedures for sites, and wooden towers were used where steel was not available. The building work went on night and day, and the new stations were under the supervision of No. 2 Installation Unit. This was formed at No. 1 M.U. Kidbrooke under Squadron Leader Rose, transferred from the Royal Aircraft Establishment.

Three kinds of stations were laid down at this stage, 'Advance', 'Intermediate' and 'Final'. Advance sites had wooden huts, seventy-foot or ninety-foot towers, mobile or experimental equipment and no height finding.

Intermediate sites had 240-foot towers, experimental or mobile equipment, improved aerials and height finding.

On the Final stations buildings were protected, the aerials were contained on 350-foot steel towers for transmission and 240-foot wood towers for receiving. Range, direction and height finding were provided together with high-power transmitters and anti-jamming devices. All main equipment was duplicated and four wavebands were to be provided to avoid interference.

In the event only the 10-13.5-metre wavebands were used and the other three abandoned.

The M.B. (mobile base) radar became of increasing importance for Advance and Intermediate sites, for overseas requirements and for replacing chain stations damaged by air attack. The waveband chosen for the mobile stations was under ten metres, and to maintain the range a powerful transmitter, the M.B.2, was used.

Work developing mobiles progressed while Bawdsey was heavily committed on fixed R.D.F. and was solving the many problems of gun-laying, shipborne and airborne interception radars.

Immediately after the Munich crisis it was decided that the filter room must be moved to Fighter Command at Bentley Priory. Accordingly Squadron Leader Hart with several technicians built a rudimentary filter room in what is now the bar at the Priory.

A rough outline of south-eastern England was made in chalk on the floor and five telephone jacks and a wooden table for the map were installed. Within five days, on November 8th, 1938, the Fighter Command filter room was in use. The operators were drawn from those trained by Hart at Bawdsey, and in charge was Group Captain Rudd, then a flight sergeant. While filtering became the responsibility of Fighter Command the operational research behind it went on at Bawdsey. On December 19th, 1938, a provisional scheme was laid down for identification of raids appearing on the operations table.

In the instructions issued from Bawdsey raids first reported by the radar organisation were numbered by the filter room controller and told on to all concerned. On reception raid numbers were treated as provisional until they reached the 'action line' a few miles from the coast, or had been identified as friendly.

Raids undetected by radar and first reported by the Observer Corps were given a number by the controller, Fighter Command, although by 1940 this arrangement had been altered so that Observer Corps groups numbered raids originating in their territory, prefixed by their own code letter. Finally it was decided to use round plotting counters for friendly bombers, square counters for coastal aircraft, and triangular for civil machines.

Radar was fast becoming an integral part of the fighter interception system, but a great deal of work remained to be done before the whole organisation could work smoothly under war conditions. One of the many problems to be dealt with was that of estimating numbers from the radar blips. A good deal of experience had been gained in counting aircraft in numbers up to nine, but not above. To remedy this five small exercises were held by Bawdsey in November and December 1938. Formations of 11, 12, 17, 18, and 24 Blenheims were provided by No. 2 Group Bomber Command, performing a standard flight from the North Hinder Light Vessel to Orfordness or Bawdsey. On an 'unknown' run of 12 aircraft two observers estimated between 9 and 11, one between 10 and 12, and one exactly 12.

With the flight of 24 Blenheims on November 22nd, the response on the cathode ray tube was eight miles wide. The five distinct components in the total echo were each taken as denoting three or more machines. The civilian operators on the exercise little thought that within eighteen months W.A.A.F. and R.A.F. operators would be assessing multiple raids of 100+ with a high degree of accuracy.

A series of controlled interception experiments known as 'lambs' was made in October and November following an earlier one in April when an Anson intercepted a flying-boat—although this could hardly be called representative of fighting conditions. On October 14th a wireless telegraph control test was carried out. One Blenheim was plotted by four radar stations. This was followed by a similar flight on the 24th. Conditions on November 2nd were realistic, with much local flying off Felixstowe, which made selection of the 'Lamb' Blenheim difficult. Hart's report on the run stated 'by sheer luck the correct one was selected and interception was effected at 5,000 feet, twenty miles from the coast'.

An operational research run on November 24th proved less successful. Three Ansons of 220 Squadron were used, but detailed analysis of the run could not be made as unfortunately the photographer at the cathode ray tube turned the film the wrong way round.

Exercises continued throughout 1939 as the chain was extended, but results were patchy and continuous research was necessary to eradicate faults. In the coverage experiments in May affecting Stoke Holy Cross and West Beckham, Norfolk, Stenigot and Staxton Wold, Lincs., and Danby Beacon, Yorks., the report from Bawdsey, dated May 12th, read:

The general comment is that these stations under review are erratic; sometimes they give good results and sometimes bad ones. It is suggested that the cause of complete lack of

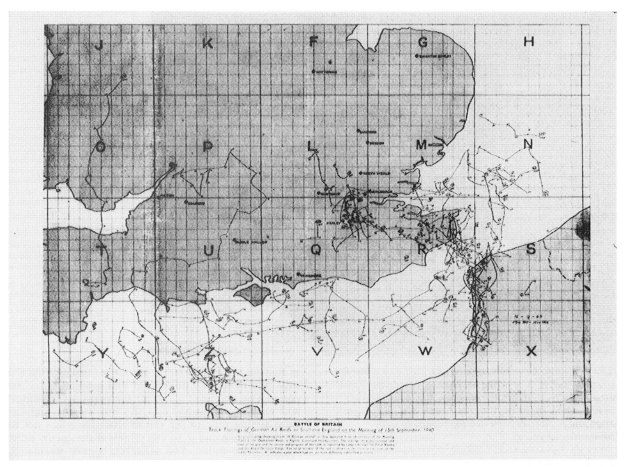

BATTLE OF BRITAIN
Track Tracings of German Air Raids on Southern England on the Morning of 15th September, 1940

Track tracings of Luftwaffe raids on Southern England on the morning of September 15th, 1940, as shown on the operations table at Fighter Command, Stanmore. The tracings show the location and time of the plots and raid progress as reported by the radar stations (via the Stanmore Filter Room) and the Royal Observer Corps. Raid serial numbers are shown in a circle at the beginning of the track. Several tracks are prefixed with the letter 'X' denoting a plot not positively identified as hostile

performance be investigated immediately. While Staxton is so bad there is a huge gap in the coverage of R.D.F. on the Yorkshire coast.

By this time the French armed forces were showing a keen interest in radar as their own detection system, D.E.M., was of little use. A mission arrived from Paris in April 1939, and on May 23rd was shown the underground filter room which had been brought into use three days previously. Two officers from each of the French services attended courses in radar in June, and plans were drawn up for C.H. radar stations to be erected at vital points in France, including Bordeaux. Nothing ever came of this, but the French Air Ministry gave manufacturers details of the equipment, although specifically requested not to by the British Government.

It is only surprising that when the Germans overran France they did not make good use of the information on the British radar system which was freely available there.

The war clouds were gathering, and on Good Friday 1939 the chain of radar stations known as 'Chain Home' or C.H. started a twenty-four-hour watch which was to continue until the end of the war.

The operational research work on control and interception carried out by such Bawdsey scientists as Messrs. G. A. Roberts, E. C. Williams and H. Larnder had not gone unnoticed. Park, then an Air Commodore and Senior Air Staff Officer Fighter Command, arranged with Rowe that the three men should, at the outbreak of war, be transferred to Bentley Priory as an operational research section, Rowe having already teamed them as such. This was to be the beginning of a vital contribution to ultimate victory and a principle adopted later by all the services.

Roberts himself had developed the answer to one of the most pressing problems of reading and passing radar information. In the 1937 and subsequent air exercises the radar station staff used a mechanical converter invented by Mr. L. H. Bainbridge-Bell. With this they had to convert range and bearing of an aircraft seen from the station into a position on the standard grid map used by the R.A.F. The calculations were involved and wasted valuable time.

The first large formation seen on the Bawdsey cathode ray tube during a counting exercise on November 22nd, 1938. The trace shows twenty-four Blenheim aircraft in line astern flying in from the North Sea. By August 1940 radar plotters were dealing regularly with formations of 100 +

Roberts hit on the idea of using rotary switches and relays with metal fingers 'wiping' over contact plates to perform the functions of the calculator automatically when a button was pushed. For the prototype unit he obtained a number of Siemens switches destined for the obsolete army sound locator operations room in London.

The electrical calculator was a simple form of computer which greatly increased the efficiency and speed of radar operation. Inevitably, because of its comparative functions, Roberts's brainchild became known as the 'Fruit Machine'.

A further Bawdsey invention was I.F.F. (Identification Friend or Foe). This involved the use of a small transmitter in R.A.F. aircraft which gave a distinctive character to the blip observed in the radar station. In this way enemy aircraft could be distinguished from friendly machines as they approached the coast. I.F.F. became available during the first year of the war, but in the early stages gave rise to problems. Bomber crews were not told the purpose of the transmitter in their aircraft. They were loath to use it in case the Germans homed on to the signals.

The first taste of operational work came to the radar chain in May 1939 with the flight of *Graf Zeppelin*. This was closely followed by the German air exercises carried out by Luftflotte 2. One lunchtime the watchers at Bawdsey were amazed to see a big formation on the tube fifty to seventy miles away and heading in for the coast. The cry went up 'The Germans are coming!' and everyone crowded into the hut to see. Fighters were at that time under orders from Dowding not to fly over the sea and to intercept only if the enemy came within three miles. The observers gazed, fascinated, as the formation, estimated at about fifty, closed up to seven miles and then turned away, back to Germany.

Work went on unceasingly on the sites to get stations operating and calibrated in time for radar's biggest test so far, the R.A.F. annual exercises held from August 6th to 8th.

For the first time radar plots were married to those of the Observer Corps and warning was given to the Observer operations rooms of aircraft approaching from the sea. 'Lost Property Offices' were set up at Observer groups to show any discrepancies between radar and visual plotting as the Corps was allowed to produce tracks only on aircraft picked up by radar. One such 'Lost Property Office' was run by Mr. G. A. Roberts and Mr. E. Fennessy, another Bawdsey research scientist (now Group Captain Fennessy).

From the radar side the exercise was very successful, and vindicated four years of faith and hard work. I.F.F. was tried out for the first time, and as a result 25,000 sets were ordered for the R.A.F. and the French Air Force, although the latter were not delivered before the collapse in June 1940.

Opposite C.H.L., or Chain Home Low, a rotating aerial radar used in 1940 to search for low flying raiders. The C.H.L. network was built up in a very short period of time and the sets were based on a 1½ metre aerial array developed for coastal defence

A German photograph of the Dover Chain Home radar station taken with a 5-minute exposure on an infra-red camera at a distance of 22 miles. The various buildings silhouetted against the masts are, in fact, a long way in the foreground

The imminence of war meant that even greater scientific effort would be required at short notice. The Royal Society therefore classified the scientific manpower that could be utilised in Britain. Leading scientists from all over the country were shown over the military research establishments, including Bawdsey, and university graduates spent the summer vacations familiarising themselves with the work.

On September 3rd, 1939, the nation began to call on these brains, young and old alike. Many were surprised within six months to find themselves in uniform and commissioned, a number subsequently rising to senior rank.

The declaration of war meant the break-up of the Bawdsey team. The site was considered too vulnerable and it was feared that it might be the subject of an early heavy attack. One section of the team, under Dewhurst, went to Leighton Buzzard, Larnder, Williams and Roberts began operational research at Fighter Command, A. P. Rowe and others set up shop in Dundee, and the War Office section was housed at Christchurch.

The Leighton Buzzard establishment became No. 60 Group R.A.F. in March 1940 and took over all the radar stations which were officially known as 'Air Ministry Experimental Stations' or A.M.E.S.

Before Bawdsey was dismembered trials were in progress with coastal defence and gun-laying radars. The former, known as C.D., measured ships' ranges with an accuracy of about twenty yards. This was achieved by producing new high-power valves; a special aerial array, and using one-and-a-half-metre wavelength. Much of the credit for this went to Mr. C. S. Wright, director of scientific research at the Admiralty.

The success of C.D. radar reached the ears of the Air Ministry. They immediately saw in it the answer to the problem of low-flying aircraft. Relabelled C.H.L. or Chain Home Low, the equipment was ordered on a top-priority basis.

Basically C.H.L. was a searchlight of rays from a rotating aerial, the beam being moved to search for aircraft. Thus it differed from the C.H. conception where fixed masts radiated a floodlight of beams over a wide area.

Professor (later Sir John) Cockcroft from Cambridge took over the C.H.L. programme in the autumn of 1939, cutting all red tape in the process. He requisitioned sites and ordered buildings without the usual preliminary form-filling. This resulted in C.H.L. cover being completed in time for the Battle of Britain, while the Air Ministry accounts department took years to catch up on the bills.

The first C.H.L. was opened on November 1st, 1939, and it gave a range of 100 miles using a Metrovick transmitter giving 100 kw. power to the aerials. C.H.L. was subsequently used for both low-flying aircraft and coastal shipping detection. Coloured counters were used on the filter-room table to denote C.H.L. plots.

As the C.H.L.s were only planned to complete the low cover from C.H. radars, they were linked by telephone with the C.H. stations and their plots passed on from there.

Throughout the first nine months of war the work of rebuilding and modernising C.H. stations, installing 'fruit machines', new aerials and anti-jamming devices progressed. Production of mobile sets was stepped up to meet emergencies.

The main types of radar used in 1940 were as follows:

	Chain Home	*Mobile Radar Units*	*Chain Home Low*
Wavelength	10 to 13.5 m. 5.8 to 10 m.	5.4 to 10 m.	1.5 m.
Frequency	22 to 30 mc/s 30 to 52 mc/s	30 to 56 mc/s	200 mc/s
Power	200 kw.	150 kw with NT77A 250 kw with VT114	40 kw
Pulse length	5.8 or 30 m/secs	6 to 12 m/secs	3 to 5 m/secs
Recurrence rate	12.5 or 25 pulses/sec. Interlocked with other stations	25 P/sec	400 to 1000 P/sec
Transmitting aerial	4 or 6 elements and reflectors	4 elements and reflectors	32 elements and reflector
Receiving aerial	2 crossed dipoles	1 or 2 crossed dipoles	32 elements and reflector
Height	Found height	Found height	No height
Range	120 miles	90 miles	50 miles
CRT	12-inch Afterglow	6-inch Afterglow	12-inch (two)

Considerable difficulty was found in calibrating stations. Friction arose between Fighter Command and the scientists when stations were not operating while undergoing vital modifications and adjustments. Cierva autogyros were brought in as radar calibration aircraft. Trials of all types continued with Poling, near Arundel, used for interception tests, and Ventnor in the Isle of Wight available for long-range exercises.

There were many disappointments, particularly in the length of time taken to get radar plots through the system. One of the main bottlenecks was on the Fighter Command filter table. Early in 1940 three technical assistants with science degrees were given filter training and took up duties at Bentley Priory. The improvement in establishing tracks was immediate and the time lag reduced.

As a result the standards for filter officers were raised, and establishment made for commissioned filterers. Later, liaison officers from the various commands were posted to the filter room to aid in the identification of tracks.

When the Battle of Britain began there were twenty-one operational C.H. stations and thirty C.H.L.s. The only gaps were in the north-west of Scotland, the Bristol Channel and a portion of the Welsh coast, where neither type of radar was installed.

By dint of continuous training exercises and streamlining of techniques a very high state of efficiency was reached. The radar chain provided a long-range 'picture' of the air situation without which defence was almost impossible.

8 Royal Observer Corps

'Early Stone Age' was Churchill's description in 1939 of the aircraft-warning system over land. He was then visiting Bawdsey to see the progress of radar. The great towers on the coast could look far out to sea, but behind them over the countryside and towns they were almost blind.

Special constables who were members of the Observer Corps spent many hours of their spare time watching from hill-tops and plotting in stuffy rooms. They would doubtless have been incensed at Churchill's remark, but, Stone Age or not, their work was vital. Where radar ended at the coast the whole weight of responsibility for accurate records of aircraft movements lay with the Observer Corps and its telephone network.

In common with the rest of the air defence system painstakingly built up between the wars, the Observer Corps was proved in the Battle of Britain. A year later, in April 1941, the prefix 'Royal' was granted in recognition of the Corps' services during the fateful period from July to October 1940.

The idea of visual and aural observation systems was not new. Most countries, including Germany, developed them during and after the First World War. Only in Britain, however, was a layout developed and perfected which could provide accurate continuous tracks and recognition of aircraft types. The German aircraft-reporting service, Flugmeldienst, which was a regular uniformed formation, even in 1944 was plotting only rough bearings and approximate heights. It did not report types or numbers of aircraft. In contrast the volunteer Observer Corps had been able by the Battle of Britain four years earlier to indicate the position of aircraft on a two km. map square, with a good height estimate, the type and strength. Co-operation between two posts provided corrected heights.

The success of the Observer Corps system is accounted for almost entirely by the enthusiasm of volunteers. It was like a large club with an intimate atmosphere and a marked dislike for the more unpleasant feature of military discipline.

The Observer Corps had its roots in World War I when the Admiralty arranged for the police to report aircraft heard or seen within sixty miles of London. In 1915 this scheme was extended to cover the whole of England and Wales. The Admiralty received telegrams and telephone calls from the police and passed relevant information to the War Office. Warnings were issued to railways and Scotland Yard only. Appalling congestion of telephone lines resulted, and

in 1916 the War Office took over. Troops were used instead of police, but they proved inefficient and the responsibility of reporting returned to the police.

In the autumn of 1917 Major General E. B. Ashmore assumed command of the London air defences. Dissatisfied with delays and overlapping, he initiated a new system early in 1918 in which all types of defence units reported through various centres to an operations table at his headquarters. The costly telephone network was not completed until May 19th, 1918, after which date the Gothas and Zeppelins failed to oblige with their presence.

After the armistice the reporting system was swept away and its relics pigeon-holed among the dusty files at the War Office.

On the revival of a semblance of air defence in 1924 it was clear that large areas would lack completely any form of aircraft intelligence. A sub-committee of the Committee of Imperial Defence was therefore set up under Major General C. F. Romer to study the question. One of the members was Ashmore, who was able to give the benefit of his practical experience during the war.

The committee accepted the principle that 'the civil population will be so vitally affected by air attacks that the responsibility for observation and warning cannot be considered exclusively military'.

In August and September 1924 Ashmore organised the first observation experiments. Nine posts were set up in the area between the Romney Marshes and Tonbridge. The village post office at Cranbrook in Kent was used as a control centre. Excellent tracking was obtained by day and night and Ashmore was empowered to organise a system in two zones covering the whole of Kent and Sussex. Each zone consisted of a network of Observer posts connected by direct telephone line to an Observer centre. The centres were linked to the air defence headquarters. All personnel were recruited as unpaid special constables and enrolled by the chief constables of counties and boroughs.

The first two 'groups' had headquarters at Maidstone, Kent, and Horsham, Sussex. Such was the speed at which Ashmore worked that by June 1925 air exercises were being held using the two centres. With three R.A.F. squadrons the coast-watching organisation and part of fighting area headquarters co-operating, the exercises proved very successful.

On the basis of the exercise reports the Home Office and the War Office sanctioned the new Observer Corps. Ashmore set up two further zones, in Hampshire and the eastern counties. By the end of 1925 he and Colonel Day, his signals officer, had created four group headquarters and 100 posts.

The basic organisation of the Observer Corps which later operated in the Battle of Britain was laid down by Ashmore in this period. He obtained direct G.P.O. lines for the posts and centres and introduced the gridded operations room table on which coloured counters were placed for plotting. The counters were exchanged for others of a different colour every five minutes to avoid confusion with stale information. The plotters at the table were each connected to three posts in a 'cluster' and a 'teller' looked down from a precarious box on high to report to Air Defence of Great Britain the tracks as they appeared. This system was to become standard throughout the R.A.F. defence network.

Observers at the posts were provided with an instrument which consisted of a flat circular map table, spindly tripod legs and on top what appeared to be a pantograph stood on end. This plotting apparatus, produced by the War Office at minimum cost, became familiarly known as 'Heath Robinson'.

As the Observer Corps expanded it became evident that the Air Ministry was the authority most competent to control it. Accordingly in January 1929 the R.A.F. took over from the War Office and a Command appointment was created. This was to be filled by a retired R.A.F. officer of air commodore or group captain rank. The first commandant of the Corps, Air Commodore Masterman, was appointed on March 1st, 1929, and retained the position until 1936.

The four existing Observer groups were attached to four of the fighting area stations: No. 1 Group, Maidstone, to Biggin Hill; No. 2 Group, Horsham, to Kenley; No. 3 Group, Winchester, to Tangmere; and No. 18 Group, Colchester, to North Weald.

The Romer Committee envisaged a further fourteen groups but by mid-1931 only the original four groups existed. It was not until May 1931 that permission was given for the formation of a fifth, No. 17, with its centre at Watford. No more were organised until 1933. In the intervening years the original groups soldiered on, participating in various air exercises. There was little to show the existence of an Observer post except for a pair of telegraph wires ending, for no apparent reason, in some out-of-the-way spot, and the last telegraph pole having a small wooden box on it usually filled with earwigs.

When the R.A.F. required the services of its 'eyes and ears' a man would arrive with a bulky box. From this he produced a length of cable and inserted one end into the box on the pole. The tripod was then set up and an extraordinary assortment of men in plus fours, gumboots or perhaps spats proceeded to gaze skywards. One turned the upended pantograph hopefully in the direction of a passing aircraft, another spoke into an antiquated army head and breast telephone set. The Observer Corps was a source of bewilderment to the passing public and high amusement to inquisitive small boys, but it worked.

Gradually the effects of German rearmament began to tell, and a sub-committee under Air Commodore Boyd recommended in January 1935 that eleven new groups should be formed by March 1939, and the Corps should be divided into two areas, north and south.

By the summer of 1935 No. 16 Group, Norfolk and Suffolk, had been added. Groups Nos. 4, 11, 12 and 15 were formed in Oxfordshire, Lincolnshire, Bedfordshire and Cambridgeshire in time for the air exercises of 1936.

Meanwhile in 1935 exercises were planned by the Home Office for the following year with full-scale blackout restrictions and air raid warnings. It was then realised that a raid warning system could only be developed in areas where the Observer Corps operated. Since it was impossible to declare areas immune to attack the only course was to provide complete coverage of the country with the reporting system. This was a recommendation of the Boyd sub-committee.

In 1936 Air Commodore Masterman retired. His place as commandant was taken by Air Commodore Warrington-Morris, who was to guide the Corps in its greatest expansion period and through three years of war. As the pace of rearmament quickened, so did the creation of new Observer groups. In 1937 it was decided to extend the system to the north and west of England and to Scotland. The country was divided into five areas. Each area was administered by a small staff of retired officers but directly controlled from the Corps headquarters, this being removed from Uxbridge to the new Fighter Command headquarters at Stanmore, Middlesex, where it has remained ever since.

The expansion brought many headaches to the small staff of the Corps. Suitable sites for new posts were being surveyed and negotiated throughout the year and these had to be linked with telephone lines to new centres. This placed a massive burden on the G.P.O., while enrolling volunteers, and the provision of even the standard meagre amount of equipment placed a great strain on the Corps officers.

The Munich crisis came during the expansion and on September 26th, 1938, the Observer Corps was called out for the first time as a fully fledged organisation. The system passed the test although faults came to light, particularly in communications, which provided valuable pointers for the future. When by October 1st 'peace in our time' was the slogan the Corps telephone network was restored to normal and the crews were disbanded.

Less than a year later the Corps was out in force for the annual air exercises of August 9th–11th, 1939. For the first time the full warning system was operated. The Corps was given information provided by the Chain Home radar stations, although the rank and file had no inkling of how this was obtained.

Less than a fortnight later the Corps was once more on the alert, this time in earnest. War was inevitable.

On August 24th, 1939, while holiday-makers sunned themselves and one newspaper proclaimed there would be no war, the Observer Corps manned its posts and centres and began a watch on the skies which was to continue unbroken for six long years.

When it was mobilised the Corps consisted of thirty-two centres, over 1,000 posts and about 30,000 observers. There was a nucleus of paid full-time officers

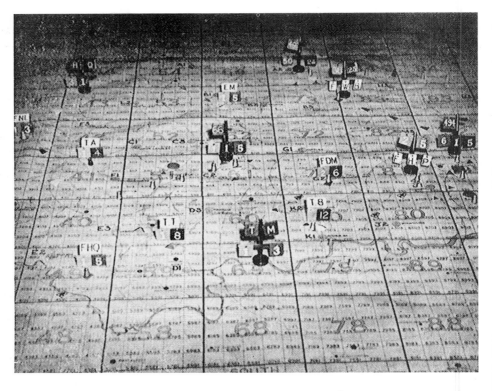

The centre table of No. 17 Group Observer Corps as it appeared during the Battle of Britain. On the right the plaque shows Raid 494 with six hostiles at 15,000 feet, while alongside it are two fighters from Hornchurch climbing through 5,000 feet to intercept. T.8 near the centre is an unidentified sound plot. At the top of the table 50 hostiles are being engaged by 30 fighters from North Weald. On other parts of the table are various friendly aircraft including trainers. Squares 68, 78 etc. have 10 km. sides and are sub-divided into 2 km. squares

and observers but the great majority fitted in part-time duties with their normal work.

From August 24th complete administration including pay and recruiting passed from the Police to the Air Ministry. Observers relinquished their status as special constables. The Corps volunteers objected strongly to being paid and in the commandant's circular for October 5th, 1939, it was noted that 'a member is not bound to claim the hourly rate if he does not wish to do so'.

The Corps layout in September 1939 remained fundamentally the same for the Battle of Britain a year later, but in the intervening months many new posts were initiated and others re-sited for better observation.

Four large gaps existed in the Observer coverage: the whole of north-west Scotland, a large part of south-west Scotland, the whole of west Wales and all Cornwall. These gaps were not completely filled until after 1940.

The Corps structure revolved round the centre at group headquarters where the crews worked on a shift

basis. Here in a small room a plotting table was set up around which sat twelve plotters wearing head and breast telephone sets connected to clusters of two or three posts. A floor supervisor checked the state of the table and the continuity of tracking. Behind him slightly raised on a wooden dais sat the tellers who passed on information to the group and sector operations rooms and to adjacent Observer centres. One centre would provide information for up to six sectors, as in the case of Bromley, Kent, which was linked to Biggin Hill, Hornchurch, North Weald, Kenley, Northolt and Tangmere.

At the end of the line of tellers perched on a wooden box was the recorder who pencilled tracks on grid paper. Two other people of particular importance were the duty controller at the group centre and the Observer Corps liaison officer at Fighter Group headquarters. The latter formed the link between the R.A.F. and the Observer Corps network.

Around the group centre radiated the posts of which there were usually thirty to thirty-four. Each post consisted of some sort of weather protective frame either of wood, sandbags or even railway sleepers. A standard pattern hut was issued, but hard to acquire. The only items common to all posts were the instrument for estimating the position of aircraft, the telephone, binoculars, raincoats, gumboots, a log book and some means of making tea. There is no record of any unit of the Observer Corps being so backward as to be unable to brew tea at frequent intervals. Uniforms were not issued, the only distinguishing marks worn by post observers being armbands and steel helmets, if they were lucky enough to obtain them.

The post might number between fourteen and twenty

observers with a head observer in control. The instrument itself was of improved form compared with the 'Heath Robinson' of the 'twenties. Of all-steel construction, it had a built-in height bar and geared sighting arm, and a device for correcting height estimates when two posts plotted the same aircraft.

The instrument was mounted in the centre of a gridded circular map of ten miles radius on which the five-mile circles of nearby posts were shown. When an aircraft was sighted the observer with the instrument estimated the height and set the bar accordingly. By viewing the aircraft in a ring sight he moved a pointer to a particular 2 km. square of the gridded map. His companion then passed the position indicated, by land-line, to the centre in a standard form; for example, 'B.2 calling, three planes seen 6153 flying north, height 8,000 feet.'

The plotter at the centre placed an arrowed marker on the appropriate square using the colour shown on the clock for the five-minute period, red, yellow, or blue. The marker pointed in the direction of flight. Rectangular counters were added to show eight on blue for the height of 8,000 feet, three on red for the strength, and white on a black letter B to indicate 'bomber'. Other counters denoted variations of this. Enemy raids were shown as numbers allocated by Fighter Command from radar plots or, if initiated by the Observer Corps, with a prefix letter of the group of origin; for example, 'C' for Colchester.

In sound plotting posts gave only a bearing and the direction of flight. The bearing was in the form of a numbered square on a five-mile sound circle on the charts. The centre plotter on receiving this laid a trumpet-shaped counter on the post's circle on the table pointing towards the post itself. When a plot came in from another post, a similar procedure was carried out. At the intersection of the two angles a counter called a 'Halma man' was laid, and a track begun. Special priority was given for low-flying enemy aircraft. The post plots were prefixed by the words 'Low raid urgent'.

This simple basic system for reporting and plotting could be modified to meet different situations. With practice it provided the fastest flow of accurate information obtainable. Reports of plots from the posts to the Observer Corps network often reached over one million in twenty-four hours. A plot obtained by even the most remote post could be transmitted to Fighter Command in less than forty seconds. This was a remarkable achievement.

There was little practice in aircraft recognition in the three services before the war. Its neglect by succeeding R.A.F. directors general of training was to be the cause of many casualties for the first two years. Even Fighter Command's recognition knowledge was scant. The repeated identification of non-existent Heinkel 113s during the summer of 1940 was proof of this.

During the early months of the war 'enemy' tracks appeared frequently on the operations tables throughout the country. Each was the subject of investigation and analysis.

On September 6th, during the 'Battle of Barking Creek', British fighters attacked one another and plots of hostile aircraft were shown at the Bromley centre. The controller, puzzled because no raids developed from the seaward plots shown, sought information from the post reporting hostile aircraft. His comments later read as follows: 'The observer reported a definitely overhead as a bomber. I was doubtful as there were fighter tracks in the vicinity and asked the observer how he knew, and he said: "Because it is black and white underneath and it is being fired at." A nearby post came in and said that they could have told us it was a fighter, but he was not given a chance to report.'

Gradually the Observer Corps grew more proficient at recognition but the R.A.F.'s skill remained comparatively poor in this respect. Among the dozens of tragedies in 1940 through inability to identify aircraft three are worthy of mention.

A Hurricane pilot shot down an unarmed Hudson packed with Australian aircrew. He was convinced the aircraft was a Dornier 17. Two Blenheims mistaken for Ju 88s were chased halfway across the Channel by a Polish Hurricane squadron and shot down in flames. An instructor and pupil flying in a Hawker Hector over a peaceful area passed a strange low-wing monoplane. The stranger shot them down and machine-gunned them after they had taken to their parachutes, killing the pupil and mortally wounding the instructor. Before he died the instructor said he assumed the plane came from a nearby experimental airfield. In fact it was an Me 110.

It was formerly never the Corps' duty to identify aircraft types, machines being classified only as 'friendly fighters', 'bombers', 'hostile' and 'unidentified'. According to the small booklet *Instructions for Observer Posts* which was the only post training manual issued, all bombers were to be regarded as hostile. This scheme worked quite well in peacetime during exercises, but was useless in war.

Many members of the Observer Corps, being enthusiasts, studied cigarette cards, and purchased technical journals such as *Aeroplane* and *Flight*. In 1935 the Corps was issued with an official service silhouette manual which was at that period usually out of date and often very inaccurate.

Shortly after September 1939 officialdom realised that the Corps could identify aircraft as types. Already keen posts were reporting in this fashion. The supply of recognition material began to improve slightly, although in the autumn of 1939 No. 29 Group was moved to invent recognition doggerels, one of which stated:

> There is little to relate
> Of the Junkers 88,
> It's small.
> That's all.

When reprinted in an official Corps document a footnote was added to the effect that this was the 'only information available on the Junkers 88'.

It was left to the members of the Corps to conduct their own schemes of training and proficiency tests.

On December 9th, 1939, a party of forty observers met in the Corona Café, Guildford, to form 'a study

HURRICANE I (MERLIN)
Single-Seat Fighter
Span 40'–0"   Length 31'–5"   Height 11'–3"

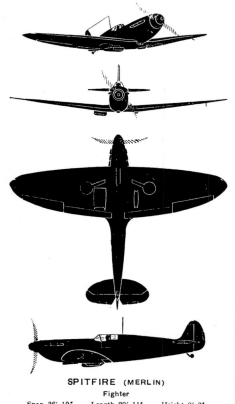

SPITFIRE (MERLIN)
Fighter
Span 36'–10"   Length 29'–11"   Height 9'–3"

Official Air Ministry silhouettes of 1940 showing the Hurricane and Spitfire. By this period recognition material was at last beginning to improve, the pre-war material being hardly identifiable as any type

circle, or club, to provide facilities for members of the Corps to make themselves proficient in the practice of detecting, plotting and identifying aircraft'. The organiser was Mr. H. J. Lowings. Mr. Peter Masefield, then of *The Aeroplane* staff, delivered a lecture on 'The Recognition of Aircraft'.

The study circle became known as the 'Hearkers Club School of Instruction'. It was this kind of enterprise and enthusiasm which enabled the Corps with little official help to separate friend from foe in the Battle of Britain and thus greatly simplify the task of Fighter Command. Ultimately the Hearkers Club became nation-wide and formed the basis for service recognition training.

The main enemy of the Corps in its first eight months of war was not the Luftwaffe but boredom and an appalling winter. A few posts saw German aircraft, particularly over Scotland, but most watched and waited for hour after hour. They stood in the sun, the rain, and then the deep snow and hoar frost at the turn of the year when some posts were snowed up for two days awaiting their relief crews.

The time was not wasted, however. Gaps in coverage were being filled, telephone communications improved, and frequent exercises greatly accelerated and streamlined the plotting at posts and centres. The Corps had its own methods of maintaining relations between units apart from the normal 'Operations Instructions'. One of these was a fortnightly circular issued personally from Bentley Priory by the commandant, Air Commodore Warrington-Morris. This duplicated manuscript was hardly in keeping with the normal turgid and wordy documents pouring out of the headquarters of the services, but well laced with broad humour it typified the volunteer atmosphere of the Corps.

In February 1940 the commandant's circular noted that there was a considerable increase in enemy air activity over the North Sea and that a ship had been attacked in the Channel.

The end of the phoney war was approaching but this was not apparent to the centre crews and post observers who struggled to speed up plotting and reporting and to remove the bugbear of the time lag between sighting an aircraft and its notification on the Fighter Group operations table. A typical report of the period ran:

A daylight exercise carried out by No. 12 Fighter Group on March 1st was disappointing: tracks of the aircraft were not continuous and several were missed altogether. Where large numbers of training aircraft are flying at a low altitude it is difficult for posts' crews to pick up and report aircraft flying at a high altitude but it is a problem to be faced and one that calls for a high degree of co-operation between centre and posts' crews. In addition the handing over of a track from one centre to another is a matter of the greatest importance. The exercise was repeated on March 5th with much better results but 100 per cent efficiency was not attained.

Inside an Observer Corps Operations Room in 1940. This is 17 Group Watford. Around the table are the plotters receiving reports from the posts. A table supervisor leans across to check a plot. At the dais on the right are the liaison officer, the assistant duty controller and the duty controller, while perched on the dais at the left are the tellers

The Corps found by April 1940 that it was reporting many items other than straight plots. Special attention was given to British aircraft lost or in difficulties. Blackout infringements and other suspicious incidents were notified and coastal posts saved lives by reporting promptly aircraft down in the sea. Some posts near sector stations were equipped with paraffin flares to guide night fighters back to their bases, thereby sometimes incurring the wrath of the local populace for breaking the blackout.

Plotting standards on posts varied according to the literacy, eyesight and hearing of the members but surprises could still be sprung on the R.A.F. At one post a new type of aircraft was reported which was still secret and of which no silhouettes or description had been issued. Inquiries elicited the laconic reply 'We are always up to date.' It was later explained that one of the post's crew was working on the aircraft at a nearby factory.

When the Dunkirk evacuation came at the end of

May 1940 the Corps found itself in the front line overnight with the south coast groups facing an enemy rapidly absorbing the whole north coast of France. Urgent instructions went out to posts to protect their weather shelters with earth revetments and to watch for paratroops, troop-carrying aircraft and gliders. Rifles and overalls were issued to posts in the danger areas although the outlook for observers defending their posts in the event of invasion was far from bright, despite promised assistance from the Local Defence Volunteers.

The brief for the Corps was short and to the point. 'Every centre and every post must be continuously manned as long as humanly possible.'

Posts came under fire for the first time in late June when enemy air activity was increasing. A bomb dropping within fifty yards of one was unnoticed by the observers who were busy plotting. At another, where a bomb dropped closer, the Corps commandant noted later that he was asked 'to supply a new pair of trousers'.

German aircraft cruised over England and Scotland throughout July sometimes by day but mainly by night probing, training and dropping bombs and mines. As the month advanced the attacks were concentrated on Channel shipping and the coastal groups of Yeovil, Winchester, Horsham and Maidstone were witnesses to many fierce actions as the convoys fought their way through.

On the 13th August the Luftwaffe officially opened

73

Observer Corps post 17/K.1 in 1940. This post was situated on the top of the Senate House, London University. One Observer is following an aircraft using the post instrument (complete with telescope) while the other Observer reports to centre with a head and breast telephone set. The post is surrounded with sandbags and the numbers hung round the walls indicate 2 km. squares on the British Grid System

its long-awaited offensive against England and for the next three months the Observer Corps' years of practising and exercising were put to their most stringent test.

The volume of information pouring in during those summer days from a comparatively small area was enormous. All of it had to be quickly plotted and analysed. There were scattered raids throughout the length and breadth of the land, but the main daylight concentration was over the areas of the Observer groups within No. 11 Fighter Group R.A.F., namely, No. 1 Maidstone, No. 2 Horsham, No. 3 Winchester, No. 17 Watford, No. 18 Colchester, and No. 19 Bromley.

In these groups, day in day out, the posts queued on the telephone lines to give their plots and the centre staffs worked like machines to convert them into plaques and arrows and pass the information to the Fighter Group headquarters.

With such concentrated activity there were bound

to be problems. Some posts became 'saturated' with aircraft overhead and could only give approximate numbers, others found themselves dealing simultaneously with raiders at tree-top height and 28,000 feet, often while under machine-gun or bomber attack.

Two difficulties were never really overcome. The first concerned persistent unidentified tracks appearing on the Fighter Group operations table and originating in Observer Corps groups. Dowding drew attention to the fact that these must be a lost raid freshly plotted, a raid missed by radar, or a friendly aircraft. The Observer groups without proof by recognition (particularly on cloudy days) were most reluctant to identify a track as friendly because it would then be removed from the operations room table and a hostile machine might get through to its target. If the group labelled it hostile a friendly aircraft might be attacked by the defences.

The second problem concerned height. All Observer visual plots were based on estimation of height before the post instrument could be set to give a map position. Thus wrong estimates not only gave an incorrect altitude for fighters to intercept but misplaced the track on the map. Varying estimates tended to make a track zig-zag on the plotting table and altered its apparent speed.

The estimation of height from the ground is exceptionally difficult even with long practice. At the height of the battle posts had insufficient time to correct

SIGNAL OFFICE DIARY.

DATE 24. 8. 40   STATION Bromley

Watch Times.		REMARKS.	Signature.
		"B" Crew.	
47	15.14	S1 & S3 posts report explosion Q 9381	
48	15.18	To L.O to report explosion in Q9381	
49	15.20	from L.O. Squadron ordered up from Kenley. Inform L.O when they leave.	
50	15.29	S2 & S3 posts report explosion in Q 8777	
51	15.29	To L.O. to report explosion in Q 8777	
52	15.30	To L.O 12 H/c now up from Kenley	
53	16.35	from L.O. "Where are the fighters from Kenley now?" Replied Q 8963	
54	15.40	from L.O "Where are the Kenley fighters now" Replied Q 9965 going N.E.	
55	15.41	Z.2 post report parachutist descending R1385. " " " " plane crashed R0381	
56	15.42	from L.O. Raid X12 is now Raid 12.	
57	15.43	from L.O When are our fighters from Kenley. Replied we fetch pilots. They have probably gone too high.	
58	15.47	To L.O. Raid 8 is Barking Hornchurch.	
59	15.48	Posts report Parachute Descent in R1177	
60	15.52	from L.O. What is B6. Replied we do not know but have passed it to Watford	
61	15.54	To L.O. Our post at M3103 reports many aircraft ours & enemy overhead. we think Kenley	

A page from the Bromley Observer Corps
Centre log book for August 28th, 1940

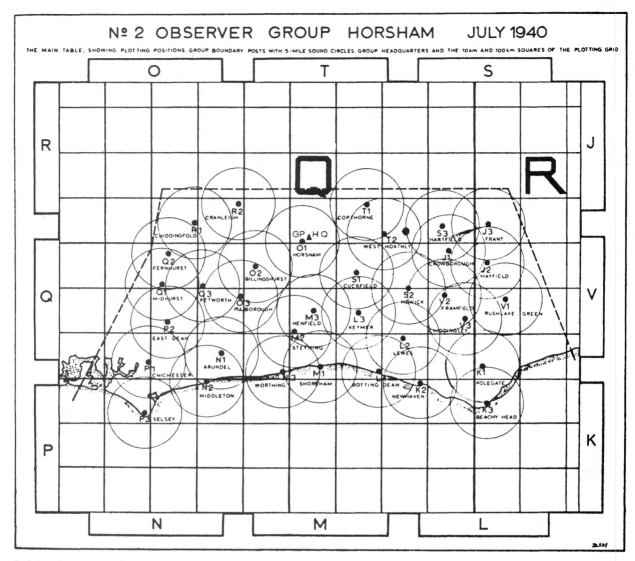

THE MAIN TABLE, SHOWING PLOTTING POSITIONS, GROUP BOUNDARY POSTS WITH 5-MILE SOUND CIRCLES, GROUP HEADQUARTERS AND THE 10km AND 100km SQUARES OF THE PLOTTING GRID

heights by comparison with the instrument readings of neighbouring posts.

Radar in 1940 often gave height incorrectly, sometimes by several thousand feet. This defect in the mechanical and the visual systems was the primary cause of fighters directed to the enemy finding themselves underneath an opposing formation instead of on a level with it or above.

Many pilots complained bitterly of these inaccuracies but it was miraculous that they were not more frequent or that the system, strained to the utmost, could work at all.

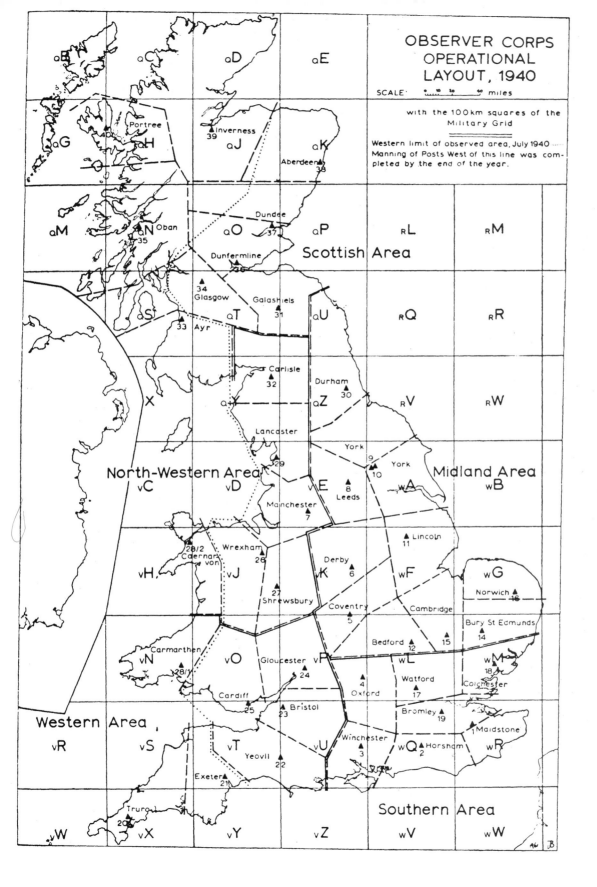

OBSERVER CORPS
OPERATIONAL
LAYOUT, 1940

SCALE: miles

with the 100km squares of the
Military Grid

Western limit of observed area, July 1940 ....
Manning of Posts West of this line was completed by the end of the year.

Scottish Area

Midland Area

North-Western Area

Western Area

Southern Area

9 Radio

Radar and the rapidly expanding Observer Corps network gave the R.A.F., from 1936 onwards, the tools on which to base an air defence system. The service could not, however, operate without certain other vital links, the most important of which was fighter control.

In 1934 Fighting Area headquarters, in its wooden shack at Uxbridge, had no direct telephone lines to its fighter sectors. The communications problem loomed large and it had to be solved.

Information received, whether from electronic or visual sources, was of little use if the fighter controllers were unable to communicate with the aircraft and know their position and other relevant information at any time.

The signals directorate at the Air Ministry was far sighted and industrious. As far back as 1928 experiments were initiated into shortwave direction finders which would accurately fix an aircraft's position.

Squadron Leader Chandler, a signals technical officer, worked on direction finding from its earliest days. With the Marconi Wireless Telegraph Company he evolved the Chandler-Adcock short-wave direction finder. This was designed to operate on the fifty to seventy-metres waveband with a range of up to fifty miles covering the radius of action of fighters of the time.

The set was first used during combined short-wave tests with the Army in August 1932, although it had only just completed experimental trials and no service experience had been obtained. No hut was available for the second stage of this exercise, so the finder was positioned in the middle of a field at Hornchurch, Essex. The Officers and airmen using the equipment had only a few days training and during the tests had to contend with wind, rain and thunderstorms. Nevertheless the results achieved were promising. The report on the exercise recorded that:

'The direction finder can give the direction of the aircraft with an accuracy at least as good as the pilot normally gives his position when he sees the ground.'

Tests continued at Hornchurch through 1933 using Bristol Bulldog and Hawker Hart aircraft and on a long-range sortie with a Vickers Virginia. In addition, foreign short-wave stations in a number of European countries, including Germany, were received to determine the possibility of obtaining bearings.

After painstaking analysis of all the trials, a comprehensive report was prepared by Chandler in August 1933 in which it was recommended that high-frequency direction finders should be set up in each Air Defence

of Great Britain fighter sector. The bearings obtained from three-minute transmissions by the aircraft were to be plotted continuously from a central plotting station which would give the pilot on patrol his position by radio telephone. Chandler ended his report by forecasting that ways might be found of obtaining automatic transmissions from the fighters without action by the pilot. This idea was to become the well-known 'Pip-Squeak' apparatus which surprised the Luftwaffe in 1940.

Thus in 1933 the basic system of fighter direction and control, which was to be used seven years later in the Battle of Britain, was already devised.

The next step was to turn over high-frequency direction finding (H.F./D.F.) to the Air Defence of Great Britain so that the organisation could be developed under operational conditions.

Various improvements were made to the direction finder in the ensuing months and by the late summer of 1935 four stations were operating, at Biggin Hill, Kent, Hornchurch and North Weald, Essex, and Northolt, Middlesex. In January 1935 basic trials with H.F./D.F. for fighters were started and these were followed by night tests in May. 'Homing' to base was tried first and then position 'fixing' using two or more H.F. direction finders. During the 1935 annual air exercises one fighter pilot arranged for unofficial fixes to be relayed to him and succeeded in intercepting a bomber above the clouds at night. On September 30th Hart had been posted to H.Q., Fighting Area, Uxbridge, as deputy chief signals officer with a brief from Air Vice-Marshal Joubert de la Ferté, now Air Chief Marshal Sir Philip Joubert, to assess the efficiency of the warning and control system by a series of co-ordinated tests using H.F./D.F., airborne radio and the Observer Corps.

The Fighting Area control room was contained in a wooden hut at Uxbridge. A gridded map table was installed and Warrant Officer R. M. Woodley worked out a system of reference counters and standardised the sequence of incoming information.

Raids were simulated and fighters scrambled to intercept on information supplied by the Observer centres. Positioning and homing were done by means of H.F./D.F., although because of the shortage of suitable aircraft radio sets and mechanics the precious radios had to be switched from one station to another.

The exercises showed clearly that H.F./D.F. was the answer to control, but far more serious was the report compiled by Hart, which stated that Fighting Area could not hope to intercept any enemy bomber and stop it dropping its load on London unless warning could be given when it was at least thirty-five miles from the Kent coast—and as aircraft speeds increased this minimum distance would rise.

At this time Hart and his colleagues were not fully aware of the existence of radar, but the reports they compiled gave added impetus to the work of Bawdsey and to the setting up of the preliminary chain of five radar stations. Meanwhile on March 17th, 1936, at a meeting at H.Q. Fighting Area, it was decided to fit H.F./D.F. at all sector airfields.

The main task of developing sector operational control devolved on Biggin Hill aerodrome where projects had been undertaken since World War I.

Tizard, whose fertile mind had for many months been occupied with the techniques of using radar information, suggested that full-dress interception experiments should be put in hand. At a conference in August 1936 with the new Fighter Command A.O.C., Dowding, in the chair, it was agreed that experiments should continue to 1937 using Hawker Harts as bombers and No. 32 Squadron Gloster Gauntlet fighters, both based at Biggin Hill. Tizard accordingly set up a team at Biggin Hill in the summer of 1936 for operational research. The members were Squadron Leader Ragg, a navigation expert, Flight Lieutenant W. P. C. Pretty (now Air Marshal), the sector signals officer, and Dr. B. G. Dickens, an Air Ministry scientist. Dickens became what was the world's first operational research civilian and his appointment set a pattern for the future.

Tizard was unable, for security reasons, to tell the team about radar. He therefore requested that they investigate fighter direction and control techniques assuming that bearing, distance and altitude of enemy aircraft could be given to them at guaranteed time intervals from some mysterious source. Even with this information 'elipses of accuracy' had to be drawn which resembled a rugby football 8 in. by 4 in. on the plotting table and within which area the enemy was presumed to be.

The essence of the problem was to take the radar or Observer Corps information in 'filtered' form and convert it into interception courses for the fighters to follow. Three Hawker Harts simulated bomber attacks, while the Gauntlets of No. 32 Squadron undertook the interceptions using radio-telephone information from the ground.

Because no genuine information from radar was available, the bombers' position was fixed by high-frequency radio using the four new H.F. direction-finding stations. Only one channel on one frequency was available, so that the bombers had to be sent out over the North Sea with a given flight plan. As they returned, the wireless operator in the leading aircraft screwed down his morse key to give a continuous wireless transmission. This was picked up by the direction-finding stations, who plotted it and telephoned the information to the Biggin Hill operations room.

There a large horizontal backboard was provided for the actual plots using the range and bearing method. The plotter employed a long wooden ruler with mile notches on it attached at one end to a compass rose which represented Biggin Hill itself. With dividers and protractors suspended on elastic, chalk marks were made on the board to position the bombers and an interception course worked out for the fighters.

The inaccuracies in the direction-finding information and in converting track and ground speed into course and airspeed gave numerous apparent changes of course which confused the plotters and complicated interception. Added to this the fighter pilots had to do their own navigation on dead reckoning.

To bring two fast formations of aircraft together as quickly as possible proved exceptionally difficult. The small group at Biggin Hill laboured for weeks to resolve the 'four vector interception problem' which was the key to the application of radar and visual information. All sorts of weird instruments were devised to do the job including a complex instrument known as the Simmonds-Goudine computer. A large number were produced at £5 each, but were hardly used.

Weeks ran into months but still the solution to successful interceptions was missing. To one man at Biggin Hill trigonometry and computers were distinctly unpleasant subjects. The station commander, Wing Commander E. O. Grenfell, had many tasks to perform but he found time to watch the calculations, exasperation and arguments of the team in the small operations room. As he studied the lines and bearings on the blackboard he became convinced that interceptions could be made by eye based on the D.F. information and the fighter position. To the team worn out with figures and computations this was like a red rag to a bull. To prove the stupidity of the suggestion they suggested that Grenfell try it 'by eye'. Accepting the challenge, he called 'steer seventy degrees' and made further alterations to the fighters' course as he judged necessary.

To the amazement of the onlookers he completed a perfect interception. Away to the east the Gauntlets and Harts met.

Tizard realised that here was the immediate solution. He discarded the computers and the pages of mathematics and evolved a simple rule of thumb known as the 'Principle of Equal Angles', or more colloquially by the staff as the 'Tizzy Angle'. By drawing a line from the bombers to the fighters and making this the base of an isosceles triangle with the fighter angle always equal to the bomber angle, the two formations would meet at the apex of the triangle.

If the bombers altered course the controller could visualise a new triangle on the plotting table and tell the fighters to alter heading accordingly. If the fighters outpaced the bombers and reached the apex first they would be ordered to circle and wait.

This simple system evolved by improvisation proved an extraordinary success. In 100 practical experiments in 1936 using the method Biggin Hill recorded 93 per cent interceptions. Sector control and vectoring procedure later used in the Battle of Britain was evolved on this basis. With it the great importance of the post of sector controller was established. In August 1937 Dowding asked for three H.F./D.F. stations in each fighter sector.

The next step was to link Bawdsey radar station in 1937 with Biggin Hill. The radar picture was trans-

The Sector Operations room at Duxford with the Controller's position, Ops 'A', 'B' and 'B1' and the gun control officer. On the walls are sector maps squadron call signs, a map of R.A.F. airfields in eastern England, recognition silhouettes and the inevitable poster pointing out that 'Careless talk costs lives'

mitted to the airfield operations room from the experimental Bawdsey fighter centre. The H.F. direction-finding network was then free to keep a continuous check on the fighters alone, relaying their positions to the sector controller who could alter his interception triangles accordingly. The fighters were able to disperse with dead reckoning and concentrate on following the controller's instructions.

The blackboard in the operations room proved messy and made plotting difficult. Instead, a vertical ground-glass screen was erected on which the aircrafts' positions were plotted using counters with rubber suction pads. Biggin Hill continued for some years to be the guinea-pig for Fighter Command. Improvements constantly made in equipment and techniques were incorporated at other sector operations rooms. New controllers were trained at Biggin Hill where they were given synthetic as well as 'live' instruction.

While the web of sector operations rooms grew, the H.F. direction-finding system was expanded at a tremendous rate. Co-operation between the experts on radar, fighter control and H.F./D.F. was excellent and there was a continuous exchange of ideas.

Watson-Watt, Rowe and other civilians attended the R.A.F.'s direction-finding conferences. Through Watson-Watt and Bawdsey the service was able to obtain new types of aerials with higher efficiency and the loan of a cathode ray direction finder in 1936 for Northolt. When standardised this speeded up plotting and allowed more fighters to be dealt with by one operator.

By September 1936 plans were in hand for twenty experimental stations to be built for cathode ray installations.

The final arrangement for Fighter Command's direction-finding organisation was already on paper in September 1936, following No. 11 Group's 'Final sector training exercise' on July 27th, 29th and 30th. Eight fighter squadrons operating from Biggin Hill and Hornchurch, the former concentrating upon 'positioning' for interception, and the latter on 'homing' back to base. By September 1937 long-term plans were in hand for a complete H.F./D.F. network for the three R.A.F. commands, to be completed by 1939.

Squadron Leader Chandler's original suggestion in

The heart of radar operations in 1940—the filter room at Bentley Priory. The operations map shows the East and south coasts of England and the network of all-important C.H. and C.H.L. radar stations. On the wall is the 5 minutes colour change clock which was standard throughout all R.A.F. and Observer Corps operations rooms

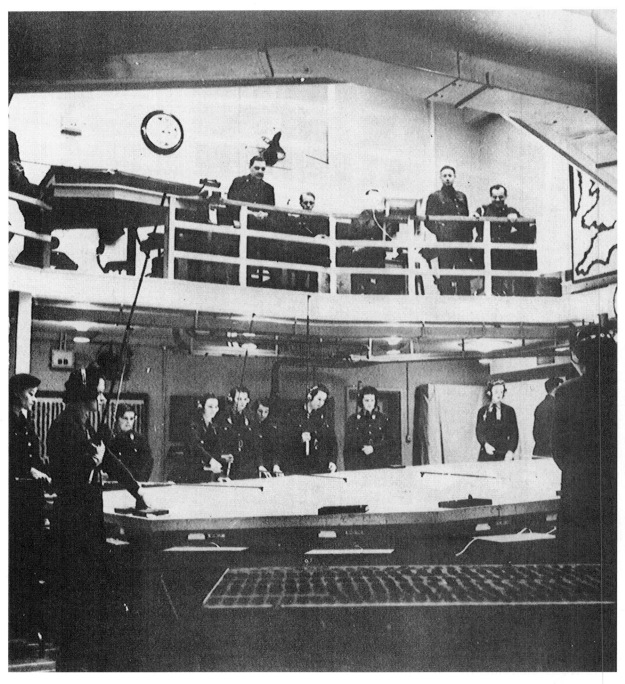

The Operations Room at Fighter Command head-quarters, Bentley Priory, where the final overall picture of the air situation could be seen with filtered radar and the Observer Corps tracks. The officers on the dais look down on the ops table and the W.A.A.F.s with their 'croupier' rakes

1933 that some means might be found for automatic transmission from aircraft of signals for direction finding were echoed in the signals report on No. 11 Group's 1936 exercise:

'It is understood that some thought has been given by the Air Ministry to the idea of incorporating an automatic periodic D.F. transmission in aircraft transmitters. It is thought that such transmissions would enable sector D.F. stations to keep constant check on aircraft positions and so speed up and facilitate the work of interception.'

Chandler, the brain behind the H.F./D.F. network, set to work to evolve a system. This device, 'Pip-Squeak', automatically switched on the H.F. transmitter in the aircraft for fourteen seconds in every minute. During the remainder of the minute the radio set was switched for normal reception and transmission by the pilot. A control was provided so that the pilot could cut out the automatic transmission when necessary.

A clock, similar in principle to the contactor unit in the aircraft, was available in the control room and, where necessary, in the D.F. station. The face was divided into four coloured sectors. A hand rotating once a minute indicated which aircraft should be transmitting at that time.

The 'Pip-Squeak' in the aircraft was arranged so that it could be set to transmit in any quarter-minute period. The pilot was told which period he was to set his control. Four aircraft could transmit in rotation automatically and be identified on the ground by the quarter-minute period in which they transmitted. Each of four aircraft therefore had its position plotted once every minute, the pilots being relieved of the onus of navigation and position fixing. Cockerel was the code word for the device. If a pilot forgot to switch on 'Pip-Squeak' the controller might ask him: 'Is your cockerel crowing?'

The aircraft transmissions enabled a bearing to be taken by each of three D.F. stations in one sector. The bearings were plotted in the sector control room and interception courses passed by radio to the fighters on the 'equal angles' principle as in the early tests at Biggin Hill.

The D.F. network using 'Pip-Squeak' was in existence when war started. Training had been in progress for some time. This system and radar became the keys to all the interceptions made in the Battle of Britain.

One further improvement was considered necessary, however. High-frequency wavebands were becoming overcrowded and were subject to interference and distortion which affected the speed and accuracy with which pilots could talk to sector control.

In January 1937 a requirement was issued for a very high frequency (V.H.F.) radio-telephony set with 100 miles range. The Royal Aircraft Establishment were entrusted with development following its research work over the two previous years. The demand presented problems and by mid-1938 it was reported that it might still take four years to perfect fighter V.H.F. In January 1939 the Director of Communications Development, Air Ministry, decided that a set could be produced more speedily but that it would not be up to the original specification.

The Chief of Air Staff approved revised plans and orders were given for the re-equipping of four sectors each in Nos. 11 and 12 Groups. Hornchurch, North Weald and Debden were to operate both H.F. and V.H.F. simultaneously.

The whole V.H.F. programme became a race against time, which was lost. By August 1939 the first sets, designated TR 1133, were ready for delivery and in October trials began with six Spitfires of No. 66 squadron based at Duxford. The results were excellent. For the second stage of the programme it was anticipated that by May 1940 all Fighter Command aircraft would be equipped with an improved V.H.F. radio, TR 1143.

Serious delays occurred in deliveries of both sets and at the time of Dunkirk V.H.F. was held in reserve.

Aircraft continued with the TR 9 H.F. set. In the main the Battle of Britain was fought using the old and well-tried H.F. network. It was not until the end of September 1940 that sixteen day fighter squadrons had been re-equipped with V.H.F. It was a case of too little too late.

'The war will be won by science thoughtfully applied to operational requirements.' So wrote Dowding to the head of operational research at Fighter Command in November 1940. These few words summed up the essence of the R.A.F.'s survival and victory in the Battle of Britain.

Dowding realised from the inauguration of Fighter Command in 1936 that the country could never be defended against air attack unless the fighter forces could operate as part of an intricate but reliable system. This would have to give continuous warning and control and conserve the forces in combat.

Piece by piece the giant jigsaw puzzle was assembled, each section interlocking exactly with the next. Warning of attack came first from radar. From the coast it was the responsibility of the Observer Corps and the information was passed to Fighter Command and the fighter groups. From there the orders were relayed to the fighting sectors, where with H.F. radio, 'Pip-Squeak' and high-frequency direction finding the controllers could direct the Spitfires and Hurricanes to the attack at the right place and time and guide them safely back to base.

Such ideas are now commonplace but in 1940 they represented an astounding co-ordination of design and organisation which was without parallel in the world. Controlled scientific air defence was unknown in Germany at this time. The accent in the Luftwaffe was always on offence.

Without years of similar experience in building up such a network the Luftwaffe could not anticipate the opposition it would afford nor for a very long time could the full secrets of how it worked be unravelled. The air forces of Poland, Norway, Belgium, Holland and France possessed no worth-while air defence system. Accordingly they were smashed on the ground or shot out of the sky in a matter of days. After these victories the German Air Force might be considered justified in believing the task of demolishing the R.A.F. as well within its capabilities.

It was not until the Luftwaffe radio monitoring service and the German Post Office set up their listening stations on the coast of France in July 1940 that the Luftwaffe realised it was up against something new and of vital importance. First the operators discovered that the ether on the twelve-metre band was alive with signals radiating out across the Channel from the tall and seemingly silent radar masts along the English coast.

The second shock came as the Channel convoy battles developed. British voices could be heard on H.F. accurately directing formations of fighters towards unseen German raiders. The air was full of voices, calmly and systematically placing fighters here and there and guiding others back to base. It dawned on the listeners that this was part of a complex and smooth-running organisation of great size.

In Britain from 1937 onwards no effort had been spared by hard work and trial and error to integrate all the facets of R.A.F. defence. Each succeeding air exercise, so often criticised in the Press, solved one more problem of warning or communications so that by the summer of 1940 the layout was operationally streamlined.

The key to the system of control lay in the fact that from commander-in-chief down to sector controller the display of information was the same and changes were made simultaneously throughout. It was this standardisation and the use of synchronised colour clocks which enabled Fighter Command to bring forces to bear when and where they were necessary and to avoid the waste of standing patrols. An exceptional degree of flexibility was possible. This allowed for the rapid transfer of reinforcements from one group to another and quick appreciation of threats by adjoining groups.

All operations rooms, small and large, were of a similar pattern with the controller and his aides on a raised platform. Below were airmen and W.A.A.F. plotters with their headphones, working day and night moving counters with their long 'rakes' for all the world like croupiers at some weird casino.

Behind all this lay the arteries and veins which fed the heart and limbs, the telephone lines. Until 1938 the R.A.F.'s telephone network was little more than a skeleton with a massive switching of public lines for defence exercises.

Sir Philip Joubert de la Ferté, who took command of the then Fighting Area in 1934, writing of the air exercises of that year, records:

In theory we were supposed to have three lines to each sector: an 'A' line for passing orders, a 'B' line on which to receive the acknowledgement of the orders sent, and an 'I' line for intelligence reports, combat reports and any information regarding the battle. During one hectic half-hour when raids were coming in fast, first the 'A' line, then the 'B' line and finally the 'I' line went dead and I was left without any means of issuing orders to my fighters.

W.A.A.F. plotters at the table in the Duxford sector Operations Room. On the right can be seen the croupier's rakes for moving raid plaques placed on the gridded map. The name Hornchurch and part of the coast are just visible. On the left are racks containing the various discs and plaques used on the ops table

Steady improvements were made after 1934. Permanent lines were installed to the sectors but only a fraction of the communications necessary were available when Munich came. The General Post Office was concerned with planning for the R.A.F. from 1935 with the 'Air Defence Group' but the work was mainly concerned with calculators and other equipment for the radar stations.

In 1938 a complete review was made of existing arrangements for the provision of emergency circuits for all the services. By August 1939 switching was available for some 500 long-distance emergency circuits and a much greater number of similar circuits of under twenty-five miles radius. A large proportion of these were required for the R.A.F. and at the end of August all were turned over to military lines. Within months many switched lines had been converted into permanent private service lines.

To meet a flood of urgent requests for lines, repairs and maintenance on the military communications system the G.P.O. inaugurated the Defence Telecommunications Control (D.T.C.) organisation with regional branches throughout the country.

As well as telephone circuits the services had a heavy requirement for reliable telegraph circuits. The Post Office suggested a new network partially independent of the civil telegraph service, and with voice frequency equipment at the service establishments. On July 14th, 1938, the chiefs of staff of the three services, telephone engineers and six representatives from Standard Telephones and Cables Ltd. met to discuss the vast project.

Treasury authority was given for the scheme, which became known as the Defence Teleprinter Network (D.T.N.). The Post Office and Standards installed for the R.A.F. a teleprinter network serving Fighter, Bomber, Coastal and Maintenance commands with a mass of terminal apparatus. The production and installation of this put a heavy burden on the Post Office engineering department and on the manufacturers.

The first multi-channel telegraph system of D.T.N. was opened on March 31st, 1939, between Uxbridge No. 1 (No. 11 Group) and Faraday Building, London. On April 4th Uxbridge No. 1 was linked with Stanmore No. 1 at Fighter Command Headquarters. From this time on terminals were installed at an increasing rate to link the widely spaced segments of fighter defence.

In the summer of 1940 the D.T.N. was to be flooded with messages, combat reports, intelligence reports, pilot and aircraft replacement requirements, damage assessments and a host of others

A particular headache of the G.P.O. was the maintenance of communications under air attack. The problems of field repairs came under the Post Office War Group headed by Mr. H. R. Harbottle at the engineer-in-chief's office. The War Group became the focal point for the activities of the Defence Telecommunications Control Organisation.

Throughout the Battle of Britain, despite acute manpower problems, the Post Office managed to keep communications going at radar stations, Observer Corps groups, R.A.F. command, group and sector operations rooms and airfields. Bombing caused tremendous damage in the summer of 1940 to radar stations and airfields. Some sector operations rooms were transferred to other buildings but somehow the civilians from the Post Office and R.A.F. signals officers managed to ensure that Fighter Command's system continued to function.

Fighter Command was organised into four fighter groups, Nos. 10, 11, 12 and 13. For tactical control purposes each group was sub-divided geographically into sectors. Each sector contained a main fighter station and sector headquarters with its operations room and direction-finding stations linked to it. In addition one or more satellite airfields with squadrons based on them were controlled by a sector. The number varied to operational and dispersal requirements.

No. 11 Fighter Group covering south-east England bore the brunt of the attacks while the other groups defended their own areas. Where necessary they reinforced No. 11 Group, and supplied fresh squadrons to replace those worn out or depleted by fighting.

At the headquarters of the command and each group and sector was an operations room differing in size and complexity according to its scope. All, however, were provided for the one main purpose of securing the utmost speed in the issue and transmission of orders by landline or radio.

At Bentley Priory, near Stanmore, Middlesex, lay the heart of the system, the Fighter Command operations room. This was the only room where aircraft tracks over the whole of Britain and the sea approaches were displayed. From 1925 to 1936 the Air Defence of Great Britain had its operations room in a wooden hut opposite Hillingdon House, Uxbridge, Middlesex. It was clear that this was of no use for controlling Fighter Command. In 1936 the princely sum of £500 was allocated for an experimental operations room in the ballroom at Bentley Priory. The deputy director of plans at the Air Ministry in desperation asked in June for a permanent arrangement and added: 'We cannot waste any more time, we have had twenty years to decide.'

In the early days of radar the operations room was situated in the ballroom with a rudimentary filter room one floor below in the basement where the bar now stands. To shorten the circuitous route from filter to operations rooms Dowding ordered a hole to be knocked in the walls so that the steps led straight from one room to another.

The Priory was extremely vulnerable. One well-aimed bomb could have wrecked the radar plotting centre and the structure of command. Accordingly the Air Ministry ordained that Fighter Command and Nos. 11 and 12 Groups should have concrete underground operations rooms. The work at Bentley Priory was not to exceed £4,500 in cost! Inexplicably the R.A.F. was loath to give protection to its vitals. It seemed to have a marked aversion to solid safe centres below ground and it was not until March 9th, 1940, that the Fighter Command operations and filter rooms left the Priory and went down to their concrete basement.

The command and the two groups were the only well-protected sites until the end of 1940. The radar stations, the Observer centres and the sector operations rooms remained throughout most of the Battle of Britain naked and above ground and often suffered accordingly.

In one room of the concrete bunker at Bentley Priory was the filter centre where all radar plots of position, strength, height and direction were received from the C.H. and C.H.L. stations. Each radar station was represented by a filter officer at a crescent-shaped filter table. On this was painted the outline of the British Isles, the Channel, North Sea and a large part of northern France. The filter officers checked all information by cross-reference and I.F.F. The filtered plots were then passed direct to the command operations room next door and to the fighter groups by landline.

The identification of hostile aircraft on radar plots by the use of I.F.F. was not always reliable. Unidentified planes reported by radar or observers were treated as hostile until identified. There was no alternative to this method but it meant that the table, particularly in cloudy weather, carried a crop of hostile and unidentified or 'X' plaques which were the nightmare of group and sector controllers.

Each enemy raid picked up by radar was allotted a raid number such as 'hostile 1' or 'hostile 2'. This was supposed to follow it on the plots through its flight over Britain but duplication and confusion often occurred when large numbers of enemy aircraft were involved and tracks were being handed on to the Observer Corps overland.

The command operations room received its Observer Corps information through the fighter groups which disseminated it throughout the system. Dowding and his senior officers thus had a complete picture of the defence position. With it was given full details of squadron availability. During July and August 1940 all information was shown on the main table but by September this was becoming so congested that a slotted blackboard known as the totalisator or tote was erected.

The tote recorded all details of enemy raids and fighters sent to intercept. This left the table map clear except for the raid numbers and symbols for the airborne interceptor squadrons.

In addition to the commander-in-chief and his staff Stanmore operations room housed the commander-in-chief of the anti-aircraft defences, the Observer Corps commandant or their representatives, liaison officers from Bomber and Coastal commands, the Admiralty and an officer from the Ministry of Home Security.

Each had his seat on the dais and telephone lines to his organisation.

The air raid warning system was operated from Stanmore through special trunk exchanges and direct telephone lines. Dowding also exercised general control over the A.A. guns and searchlights through the commander-in-chief of Anti-Aircraft Command and he was responsible for the balloon barrage through the fighter groups.

The operations room at No. 11 Group at Uxbridge was similar to that at the command but with a map showing only the group's area and its adjoining land and water. The information displayed was similar to that at Stanmore except that the area represented was restricted. The tote board showed only the group's squadrons and any units on loan from 10 or 12 Group dealing with German raids in the area.

Park, the group commander, received his filtered radar information from Stanmore and his visual and aural plots direct from the tellers in the Observer groups in his area. He directed sectors to deal with raids as the plaques appeared on the map table.

The final links in the chain were the sectors. These directly controlled the fighter squadrons. Sectors were lettered A to Y from Dorset round the coast and upwards to Edinburgh and Glasgow. Sector operations rooms were usually on or adjacent to the main airfield. They were housed in buildings varying from concrete emplacements to flimsy wooden huts. The emergency stand-bys were even more peculiar, one being housed in a butcher's shop and another sandwiched between a fish frier and a public house.

Sector operations rooms consisted of two separate units. In the direction-finding room the positions of fighter aircraft were obtained from 'Pip-Squeak' bearings and the radio direction-finding stations. The second unit was sector ops which resembled group operations in miniature. The main floor was occupied by the general situation map around which sat about half a dozen plotters. The tracks, raid plaques and other indicators were placed in position according to filtered radar information received from Bentley Priory and from plots 'told on' from adjacent Observer Corps centres. In the centre of a raised dais facing the map table sat the controller flanked by 'Ops A' and 'Ops B'. 'Ops A' was an airman or W.A.A.F. who took down instructions direct from the group indicating the serial number of the operation, squadron or section strength to be employed and the number of the raid to be intercepted. This information was written on a form 'A' and handed to the controller for action. 'Ops B', usually a flight lieutenant, at the controller's right hand manned the communications keyboard while 'Ops B1', a sergeant, controlled the master switchboard with all incoming and outgoing lines including those to the airfield and its satellites. Also on the dais was the local gun-control officer and a man responsible for liaison with the Observer Corps.

Two deputy controllers sat at desks in front of the dais. Each was accompanied by a dead reckoning navigator. They received D/F-'Pip-Squeak' information on the fighter's position, and with tracing paper, rulers, compass rose and pencil worked out the triangula-tions to intercept the raid indicated by the general situation map.

On the wall opposite the controller hung the five-minute colour-change clock, the weather board and the all-important 'state' panels. These last were the sector equivalent to the command and group totes. They consisted of four-foot high boxes, six inches wide and three inches deep, on which were printed the various states of readiness of the squadrons in the sector such as 'Released' and 'Thirty minutes readiness'. One box was allocated to a squadron and under each readiness category were six lamps coloured red, yellow, white, blue, green and black which indicated the flying sections concerned. Thus at a glance the controller could tell the exact state of the units under his jurisdiction.

On receipt of an order number from group the controller would order a selected unit to 'scramble', using its code name for the day. Brief information of the area to be covered and operating height would be given. When hostile aircraft came into the area, perhaps ten minutes later, on receipt of a further order from group, the controller would direct the fighters to the raid using the triangulations worked out at the deputy controller's tables.

The sector controller retained executive authority over the aircraft he despatched until the fighters saw the enemy. Command then automatically passed to the fighter leader in the air, who issued orders over the R/T. Once battle was joined the sector controller listened in. If other enemy formations appeared in the air he would inform the fighter leader.

When combat was broken off the controller resumed command and guided the aircraft back to base. If a machine was damaged, the home airfield put out of action or fuel was running low he would direct them to the nearest airfield.

Sectors were only able to deal with four squadrons using 'Pip-Squeak'. This exhausted the number of automatic transmission periods available. Many times during the Battle of Britain a sector found itself controlling six squadrons in the air. This necessitated quick thinking and much dead reckoning to ensure correct orders for the two squadrons unable to use automatic transmissions for direction finding.

To illustrate the vital and exacting work of sector operations, the following is a dialogue prepared by R.A.F. officers who were controllers during the Battle of Britain.* It faithfully depicts scenes which took place at Biggin Hill during a day in September 1940.

FLOOR SUPERVISOR to Controller: Hostile, sir.
CONTROLLER to Ops B: Ops. B—here they come! Tell the squadrons to be on their toes. I've a feeling it's going to be a repeat of yesterday.
OPS. B to Controller: I've already briefed them, sir. Everything's on the top line and they're quite ready.—Kenley controller for you, sir.
CONTROLLER: Yes, Kenley? I see, thank you. What do you make of these two raids?—Hostiles 132 and 135? (Slight pause.) Yes, I think so too. It looks fairly obvious from the build-up that they're intended for us. I expect Group'll order off something very soon—I'll let you know.

* The script for the Battle of Britain sector operations room reproduction on Horseguards Parade, September 1959

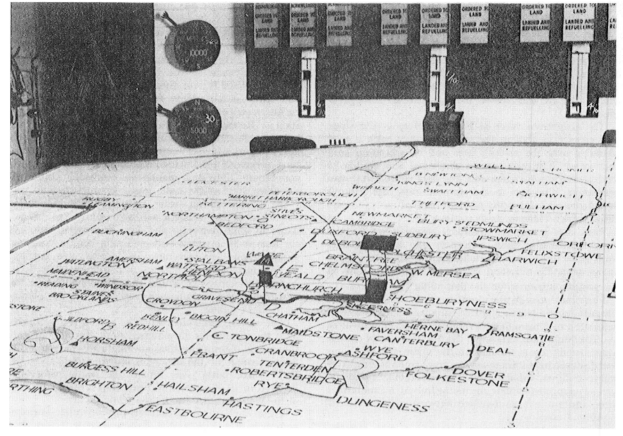

A photograph taken before the war of the operations room table at No. 11 Fighter Group, Uxbridge. The 11 Group sectors are outlined and the 100 km. squares of British Grid System. In the background is the bottom of the 'Tote Board' showing squadrons and their states of readiness

STATION LOOKOUT: Station lookout—testing—testing. Visibility five miles about 3/10th cloud at 20,000 feet. Off.

OPS. A: Biggin Hill—pause—Serial 18—pause—one squadron—intercept hostile 132—Angels 20.† Sir, form A.

CONTROLLER: Right—scramble Tennis squadron, patrol Canterbury Angels 20.

OPS. B: Operations calling—operations calling—Tennis squadron scramble—Tennis squadron scramble—patrol Canterbury Angels 20. One moment, Group—Group controller for you, sir.

CONTROLLER: Smith here, sir.—Getting off now, sir, and the other two squadrons are raring to go. Yes, I think this is it. Right, sir, I'll expect form A.

OPS. A: Biggin Hill—serial 21—one squadron—intercept raid 135—Angels 20. Sir, form A.

Biggin Hill—serial 24—one squadron—patrol base—Angels 15. Form A, sir.

CONTROLLER: Right—scramble Keta squadron vector 140 Angels 20. Scramble Jaunty squadron patrol base Angels 20.

OPS. B: Keta squadron scramble—Keta squadron scramble vector 140 make Angels 20.

Jaunty squadron scramble—Jaunty squadron scramble patrol base Angels 20.

Well sir, that's that—let's hope that Group's hunch is right.

CONTROLLER: Guns! All our aircraft are now committed against hostiles 132 and 135. I expect your turn'll come soon.

GUNS OFFICER: Right sir, I'll tell gun ops.

STATION LOOKOUT: This is the station lookout—12 Spitfires just took off.

R/T TENNIS LEADER: Hello, Short Jack,* Tennis leader calling, Tennis squadron airborne, making Angels 20—over.

DEPUTY CONTROLLER I: Hello, Tennis leader, Short Jack answering, loud and clear. Vector 120—60 plus bandits at 15,000 feet heading west—over.

R/T TENNIS LEADER: Hello, Short Jack, O.K. listening out.

R/T KETA LEADER: Hello, Short Jack, Keta leader calling Short Jack, Keta squadron now airborne. Instructions, 'please—over.

DEPUTY CONTROLLER II: Hello, Keta leader, Short Jack answering, vector 140—25 plus bandits at 12,000 feet heading west—over.

KETA LEADER: O.K. Short Jack. Listening out.

DEPUTY CONTROLLER I: Hello, Jaunty leader—correct, Vector 140 Angels 20.

CONTROLLER: Hello, Group. Yes, sir—they're all off. I understand—we shall do our best. Ops. B—Group Intelligence seem to be right on the ball. They reckon that Hornchurch and ourselves are going to get the lot—I hope they're wrong.

Ops. B—get me the Maidstone Observer Corps centre.

OPS. B: Maidstone, sir.

CONTROLLER: Observer Corps?—This is the Biggin Hill controller—Yes, it is a bit hectic—Group think they're making for us so keep your tracks going, will you?—You're

* Height 20,000 feet

* Biggin Hill call sign

88

Sir Henry Tizard, an eminent scientist largely responsible for the successful working of the air-defence system

Sir Robert Watson-Watt, who began the radar story and laboured unceasingly on its development

doing very well at the moment. Now Ops. B—I want you to ring all dispersals and tell them to get everything into the air that's serviceable; I don't want any aircraft to be caught on the ground.

OPS. B: Right away, sir.

CONTROLLER: Group controller?—Biggin here, sir—I've ordered all other serviceable aircraft into the air as it looks pretty certain now that these raids are heading for us. By the way, sir—I did tell you that our three squadrons are airborne. Right, thank you, sir.

CONTROLLER: Sergeant Brice. How about 72 squadron—have they had any joy yet?

DEPUTY CONTROLLER I: Not yet, sir—they are very close—any moment now I think . . .

TENNIS LEADER: Hello, Short Jack, Tennis leader calling—Tally Ho! Tally Ho! . . . A gaggle of Heinkels with 109s—Dead ahead. Hell, Tennis squadron, B flight take the bombers, A flight take the fighters with me. A flight, line astern—GO.

CONTROLLER: Guns!—Tennis squadron are now engaging hostile 132 so warn the guns of friendly fighters, will you? How about 32 squadron, Sgt. Norris?—Are they into the others yet?

DEPUTY CONTROLLER II: Nearly there, sir—Hello, Keta leader, bandits 12 o'clock 15 miles now heading north—Watch out for top fighter cover—over.

KETA LEADER: This is Keta leader—Understood—no joy yet. Keep your eyes skinned, chaps, and don't straggle. Hello, Short Jack—Keta leader calling—Tally Ho! Tally Ho! A helluva lot of Heinkels and Junkers 88s with fighter escort.

DEPUTY CONTROLLER II: Hello, Keta leader—Short Jack

calling—more friendly fighters are coming to join you. Over.

KETA LEADER: Hello, Short Jack—understood, listening out.

DEPUTY CONTROLLER I: Hello, Jaunty leader—Short Jack calling—60 plus bandits at 20,000 feet still heading west towards base. Are being engaged by your friends. Any joy yet? Over.

R/T VOICE: Hello, Jaunty leader—Ack Ack fire at 12 o'clock—12 o'clock.

JAUNTY LEADER: Hello, Short Jack—Tally Ho! Tally Ho!—just getting into position. Jaunty squadron, line astern—head on attack—going in . . . NOW.

CONTROLLER: Ops. B—Sound the station attack alarm!

OPS. B: This is operations—this is operations. Air raid warning. All station personnel are to take cover immediately.—I repeat—all station personnel are to take cover immediately—enemy attack imminent.

CONTROLLER: Floor supervisor—Get the troops into their battle bowlers right away. Tin hats, everybody.

STATION LOOKOUT: This is the station lookout—enemy aircraft approaching from the south—Five . . . six . . . nine . . . twelve. Blimey, there's dozens of 'em. Explosions.

TENNIS BLUE II: MAYDAY—MAYDAY—MAYDAY. Tennis Blue Two calling. Tennis Blue One has baled out—I am orbiting position and transmitting for fix*—my position is just off Deal.

DEPUTY CONTROLLER I: Hello, Tennis Blue Two—Understood—I have fix on you—stand by.

CONTROLLER: Deal lifeboat?—Biggin here—one of our chaps

* Using 'Pip-Squeak' and D/F

has baled out off-shore. Yes . . . in ROBERT 9070†
Yes, a Spitfire's orbiting the position. Good—thank you.

KETA LEADER: Hello, Short Jack—Keta leader calling—We have all been split up—aircraft are landing at forward base to re-arm and re-fuel, over.

CONTROLLER: Hello, Keta leader—Short Jack controller answering. Understood. Hello, all Keta aircraft—return to this base immediately after re-fuelling and re-arming. Listening out. Well, George—it's been quite a morning! Ring the Watch hut and find out how we fared on the airfield.

The efficiency and foresight of group and sector controllers were of prime importance to the conduct of the battle. They had many factors to bear in mind. Squadrons had to be held in reserve to meet fresh attacks. Feints and diversions had to be assessed for what they were. The right moment had to be chosen for a squadron to be recalled to refuel and rearm and fighter endurance had to be taken into account.

In the early stages of the sytem no great care was taken in recruiting controllers, particularly in the sectors. When Dowding arrived in 1936 there were no operations room staff on establishments. Clerks were mainly used. It was, however, quickly realised that a fighter pilot must have complete confidence in the disembodied voice which he heard by radio from sector operations and that the controller must be an experienced man with full knowledge of flying techniques and problems. This evoked resentment in the Signals Branch, who felt that speaking into microphones and pulling radio switches were their prerogatives.

Fortunately good sense prevailed and controllers without flying knowledge were replaced by former pilots of varying ages. When the Battle of Britain opened relations between 11 Group sector controllers and the fighter pilots were excellent. By a curious coincidence six of the seven sectors in 11 Group had on their strength controllers who were former Reserve or Royal Auxiliary Air Force pilots—a great tribute to the abilities of the spare-time airmen.

John Cherry, formerly of No. 604 Squadron, was at North Weald. At Hornchurch and Northolt respectively were Robert Lee and Heath Compton, both from No. 600 Squadron. The former 601 pilots Anthony Norman and P. R. Foley were at Kenley and Biggin Hill, while David Lloyd, who had flown with the Birmingham Air Squadron, was at Tangmere.

---

* Robert = code for 100 km. sided square on the British Grid system.
9070 = a 2 km. sided square within 'Robert'

11 The great offensive

The fateful month of May 1940 gave the Luftwaffe its greatest success of the war and strained R.A.F. Fighter Command almost to the limit.

When the German assault opened on May 10th, the result was a foregone conclusion although neither the British nor French Governments would admit it. The B.E.F. lacked guns and tanks and the French Army was decayed with the obsolescence of many years.

In the first eight months of war Britain could obtain no satisfaction from the French commander-in-chief, General Gamelin, regarding the yawning gap that lay between the Maginot Line and the Belgian frontier. The French Army had mainly low-grade troops in the area and no real fortifications. The British General Staff wanted to stand firm on the Belgian frontier behind the pill boxes and emplacements which the B.E.F. was building but Gamelin insisted on 'Plan D'. This entailed leaving the prepared lines and marching to the aid of the Belgian Army if that country were attacked.

The whole problem of land and air defence for this sector was never sorted out with the French Government realistically. In *The Second World War*, Volume II, Winston Churchill records: "Looking back, we can see that Mr. Chamberlain's War Cabinet, in which I served, and for whose acts or neglects I take my full share of responsibility, ought not to have been deterred from thrashing the matter out with the French in the autumn and winter of 1939.'

While the situation on the ground was bad enough, in the air it was pitiful. The R.A.F. in France had a maximum strength of 400 aircraft in twenty-five squadrons. Of these no less than eight were equipped with the slow and highly vulnerable Battle light bomber. Six squadrons of Hurricanes made up the fighter protection and the remaining units had Blenheim light bombers and Lysander army-co-operation aircraft. The only advantages that the R.A.F. in France possessed were high courage and good training.

Widely publicised and spoken of as one of the world's major air arms, the French Air Force was a hollow shell which shattered into a thousand pieces at the first blow. It was commanded by men who were completely out of date in their thinking and who succeeded through the years in preventing the promotion of those officers who showed courage and initiative.

The French Air Ministry organisation changed eleven times in ten years and the process of 'friends' influencing contracts reached such a pitch that a furniture maker obtained a contract for an all-metal aircraft and a dope manufacture was awarded one for parachutes.

In a book entitled *Les Erreurs Fatales du Ministre de l'Air* (Fatal Errors of the Air Ministry), published in occupied Paris in 1941, Major Jean Jalbert described how the Ministry officials were so scared of war that they started hiding secret documents at the time of the Munich crisis. One such lorry-load of papers was cached in the wind tunnel at Issy les Moulineaux. Due to an oversight the staff were not informed. The wind tunnel was started and the material was 'scattered over an entire Paris suburb at a speed of 200 m.p.h. . . . and this was the first breath of fresh air that ever blew through the French Air Ministry'.

In September 1939 the Air Force had only 260 first-line bombers and 442 fighters. These were built between 1931 and 1939. From January 1st, 1939, to March 20th, 1940, some 3,300 aircraft were built. Of these it was stated during the Riom Trial in Vichy France, March 1942, that '20 per cent were found to be useless, it is true, but the High Command of the Air Force had been unable to make use of the remaining suitable equipment because the training of air crews lagged behind deliveries'.

In May 1940 the French had thirty-five modern heavy bombers (LeO 45) available. Most of the remaining production LeO 45s were never tested and when required were found to be corroded and lacking vital pieces of equipment. Only after the complete collapse of the French Army and the issuing of an order for withdrawal to North Africa did squadrons begin to get LeO 45s in place of their antiquated Amiot 143s.

France had one good modern fighter, the Dewoitine 520, but this was consistently held back from the flying units by the quantity production office which was comfortably ensconced in the George V Hotel in Paris. After May 14th, when it was too late, 100 520s were suddenly delivered, only to be swallowed up in the holocaust.

The root cause of the complete lack of equipment, apart from the inadequacy of the French Air Force General Staff, was the nationalisation of the aircraft industry by the Communist Air Minister, Pierre Cot, under Léon Blum's government in 1936. All the well-established private firms were swept away and complete chaos ensued up to the time of defeat.

Cot's successor, Guy La Chambre, endeavoured in 1938 to work out a system whereby the French Air Force would have 4,700 new first-line aircraft. This was known as 'Plan 5'. Some of the aircraft never left the

The Luftwaffe moved forward from airfield to airfield keeping pace with the advancing troops in France. The squadrons relied for their supplies largely on transport aircraft. Here bombs are being loaded on board a tri-motor Ju 52

production line and the rest did not reach operational units.

When May 1940 came the Air Force in Europe had the same number of first-line types as at the outbreak of war, about 700, out of a total of 1,450 machines of all types.

Under General Vuillemin the French air command was divided into three air war zones: northern air zone from the Saar to the sea, eastern zone from Saar to Switzerland and air zone of the Alps. The latter was to counteract any Italian intervention.

Thus at the moment of the German attack air support for the critical part of the front in General Augereau's northern air zone consisted of 275 day fighters, 25 'night fighters', 80 reconnaissance aircraft, 15 day bombers and 55 night bombers. This was a total of 450 machines, of which only a moderate proportion were modern. Added to the 400 aircraft of the R.A.F. these gave a maximum of only 850 planes of all types to meet the Luftwaffe's force of 3,824 modern combat aircraft. Of the French force not one fighter group was equipped with the up-to-date Dewoitine 520.

The Dutch Air Force possessed several good types of aircraft but it was numerically too small to cope with the sudden onslaught and the warning system was inadequate. Despite having only 132 aircraft available, a strong fight was put up and German losses, from fighters and flak, were heavy.

The Belgian Air Force was largely composed of obsolescent aircraft and it was tied to an army role of reconnaissance. Dispersal of aircraft was not practised and anti-aircraft protection was limited.

Belgium possessed three 'Regiment d'Aeronautique' with a total operationally available force on May 10th of 82 Fairey Fox, 21 Renard R.31, 15 Gladiator and 23 Fiat CR.42 biplanes. The only monoplane force

consisted of 11 Hurricanes and 14 Battles. On order were 80 Hurricanes, 40 Buffalos and 56 Italian bomber and reconnaissance aircraft.

German attacks on Belgian airfields on May 10/11 destroyed 110 aircraft. Despite this there were many heroic sorties with the remaining machines, some of them being virtually suicide missions.

Air problems were further aggravated by the French system of communications and supply. Apart from the five British mobile radar sets under 80 Wing, which were never fully operational, the aircraft reporting and raid warning layout in France was badly organised and inefficient. Most telephone lines were routed through public exchanges. After three or four days the reporting organisation broke down completely. The Armée de l'Air possessed no radar but spent a good deal of time and money on equipment known as Détection Electromagnétique (D.E.M.). This, however, was useless and played no part in the battle.

The equipment supply and storage units functioned poorly in peacetime and when the storm broke they came almost to a standstill. Many of the replacement aircraft were found to be defective and vital items were often missing, as on the LeO 45. Ammunition, fuel and oil which were supposed to be brought by the army supply columns became completely disorganised as the retreat began.

German objectives in 'Operation Yellow' were to drive westwards through France to the Channel coast at the Somme mouth, while also occupying Belgium and Holland to protect the right flank.

The Luftwaffe was allocated the following tasks based on experience in Poland and Norway:
1 The destruction of the enemy forces and their sources of supply.
2 Indirect and direct support of the army.
3 Attacks on enemy harbours and shipping.

From dawn on May 10th the full weight of Luftflotten 2 and 3 was thrown into hammering the airfields and maintenance depots of the air forces in Belgium, Holland and northern France. The Belgian and Dutch squadrons were largely destroyed on the ground at the outset although a few pilots were able to take off

Hopefully designated a fighter-bomber-reconnaissance aircraft, the Potez 54 twin Hispano-Suiza engined monoplane was typical of the obsolete equipment put into battle in 1940 by the Armée de l'Air. This example was flown to Britain after the French collapse and is shown here at an R.A.F. airfield. In the background is an Avro Anson

Many Dutch air force pilots were trapped when German troops overran Holland in May. Some, however, got away and were absorbed into the Royal Air Force.

One complete unit of Fokker T.8-W seaplanes joined R.A.F. Coastal Command in 1940

The aeroplane which should have been the R.A.F.'s standard light/dive bomber, the Hawker Henley, which had excellent performance and bomb-load and wings interchangeable with the Hurricane fighter. Instead of Henleys the R.A.F. continued with cumbersone Fairey Battle bombers which were shot down like flies in 1940. The Henley, as shown here, was relegated to towing targets for budding fighter pilots

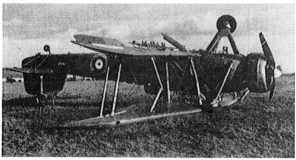

Every type of British operational aircraft was used during the summer months of 1940. The slow but tough and reliable Fairey Swordfish 'Stringbag' naval biplane was used for reconnaissance, bombing, flare dropping and many other roles. Above *A squadron of Swordfish flies over the Hampshire coast on July 26th.* Below *One of the aircraft of this unit upside down in a field in France after a night sortie over Dunkirk*

and fought bravely. While German bomber and fighter bomber units smashed the airfields, paratroops and airborne infantry took and held main roads, bridges and fortresses, such as Fort Eban Emael, Belgium, in preparation for the arrival of armoured forces and mobile infantry.

The R.A.F. Hurricane squadrons (Nos. 1, 73, 85, 87, 607 and 615) were in action all day on the 10th.

They had considerable success, but were vastly outnumbered. On the 11th they were joined by three more Hurricane squadrons from England (3, 79 and 504).

Meanwhile the Battles and Blenheims of the Advanced Air Striking Force chafed at the bit waiting for permission from the French General Staff to attack the advancing grey columns. By midday on the 10th no word had come. Generals Gamelin and Vuillemin, living in a dream world, still hoped to avoid an all-out bomber struggle which had in fact already started. Air Vice-Marshal Playfair in command of A.A.S.F., acting on his own initiative, despatched Battles to bomb a German column in Luxembourg. Thirty-two Battles drawn from Nos. 12, 103, 105, 142, 150, 218 and 226 squadrons with Hurricanes as top cover delivered their attack from 250 feet. No less than thirteen Battles were shot down by flak and most of the remainder were damaged. More Battles were lost later in the afternoon and on the 11th only one aircraft returned from a sortie by eight from Nos. 88 and 218 squadrons.

On May 12th the Belgian Army appealed for help to destroy the bridges over the Albert Canal which were thick with flak batteries. Accordingly five aircraft of No. 12 Squadron performing one of the most gallant flights of the war earned the unit two posthumous V.C.s. None of the Battles returned. By nightfall on the 12th only 206 R.A.F. aircraft in France were serviceable out of 474.

Like the Battles, the Blenheims had been suffering heavy losses on the ground and in the air. In two days' fighting the 135 serviceable A.A.S.F. bombers dwindled to seventy-two and on May 14th the assault forces

Above *Fokker D.XXI of the Royal Netherlands Air Force. This type was standard in Holland at the time of the German invasion*

Right *Mainstay of Armée de l' Air fighter forces in 1940 was the Morane 406 with a maximum speed of 302 m.p.h. and an armament of one 20 mm. cannon and two machine guns. These machines belonged to a Polish Escadrille. Many of the pilots eventually found their way to Britain to fight with the R.A.F.*

of the command were wrecked. The whole of A.A.S.F.'s Battle and Blenheim striking force was sent to support the French operations against German bridgeheads over the River Meuse at Dinant and Sedan. Of the seventy-one aircraft forty were destroyed. This was a death-blow to British air efforts in France.

Such stark tragedy should never have been enacted. The Battle in 1939 showed itself to be a 'flying coffin'. It merited no place in the first-line strength of the R.A.F. If the two-seat Hawker Henley dive-bomber, with a speed of over 280 m.p.h., had been ordered and the Battle relegated to training, the story might have been different. As it was, dozens of first-class pilots were lost who, with their experience of a Merlin-powered retractable undercarriage monoplane, would have swelled the thinning ranks of Fighter Command in the Battle of Britain.

The Armée de l'Air could give no cover to the British bombers because it had been systematically destroyed on the ground and in the air by the Luftwaffe. Extraordinary contrasts were revealed. While some French pilots fought to the death, others retired safely to the estaminet while German bombs rained down on their machines lined up round the airfields.

The rot set in to such an extent that General Augereau, commanding the northern air zone, arrived at the Corap army group on May 16th and announced: 'I have nothing left.' While this was going on, Senator Laurent Eynac, first and last Air Minister of the Third Republic, was holding up the tattered façade of French aerial might in a broadcast to the French people. He stated: 'I have just returned from the front, where I inspected the fighter, bomber and reconnaissance formations. . . . I return with a feeling of absolute confidence in the striking power of our air force.'

The Germans gained air superiority in about two days. The Luftwaffe's effort was then switched almost entirely to the support of the Army, which proceeded

Above *R.A.F. Fairey Battles of No. 88 Squadron, based in France, in formation with escorting French Air Force Curtiss Hawks of GCI/5. The Battles were slaughtered during the German drive into Belgium and France in May*

Below *The only modern monoplane fighters in the Belgian Air Force, a single squadron of Hawker Hurricanes. This unit (2e escadrille, 1e Groupe, 2e. Regiment d'aeronautique) at Schaffen, was largely destroyed on the ground on May 10th, 1940*

to force its way through France with alarming speed. Day-and-night reconnaissance by 300 long-range and 340 short-range aircraft provided a minutely detailed picture of the advance. Fliegerkorps VIII with 380 Stukas was contantly on call in the role of mobile artillery to flatten pockets of resistance.

Flying units were continually on the move, the advance accelerating at a rate which amazed even the German General Staff. The special Luftgauen strove to maintain supplies using masses of Ju 52s, but'the haste meant that some forward units had to be rationed for petrol and ammunition.

Ten R.A.F. Hurricane squadrons were operating in France by May 12th. On the 13th the equivalent of two more squadrons were sent out from England. The French Prime Minister Reynaud requested that ten more squadrons be sent on the 14th, but by this time French air forces in the battle area were almost nonexistent. The loss of these ten squadrons would have crippled Fighter Command. In addition, R.A.F. fighter squadrons were operating from England in support of the fighting in Belgium and were suffering casualties.

By May 24th the German spearheads had passed Arras, captured Boulogne and arrived at the gates of Calais. The B.E.F. was now cut off from the main French army. The R.A.F. in France had been on the retreat for nearly a fortnight and conditions were becoming intolerable.

All that Air Marshal Dowding dreaded had come to pass. There was a pitched battle over France and Belgium and the R.A.F. were outnumbered and without an adequate warning system. Continual reinforcement would have meant the wrecking of Fighter Command and the ultimate destruction of the British economy by the Luftwaffe.

Since the creation of Fighter Command in 1936 Dowding had fought to maintain adequate fighter strength in Britain. He constantly battled with the Air Council for the creation of new interceptor units and the limitation of fighter units in France beyond a certain figure. He estimated that to meet an all-out Luftwaffe *unescorted* assault on England he would need at least forty-six squadrons, but changing circumstances raised this to fifty-two squadrons — a figure which was agreed by the Air Council.

No decision could be taken immediately on M. Reynaud's request for ten squadrons, but the Air Staff ordered that units should be mobile in readiness to go to France.

The Belgian Air Force was largely equipped with obsolete types of aircraft in 1940. When the Luftwaffe attacked on May 10th, tremendous damage was done to units on the ground including the only squadron of Hawker Hurricanes. Pictured here on the left are Fairey Foxes of the 7e escadrille, IIIe Groupe, 1e Regiment, from Gossoncourt. The photograph on the right shows what happened to Foxes of 1 Groupe, 3e Regiment after the Luftwaffe had hit them at Neerhespen on the 10th

Fearing the worst, Dowding hastened to the Air Ministry determined to stop the flow of lifeblood from his command. He was adamant. Any further weakening of the fighter defences at home would be fatal. He requested the opportunity to place his problem before the War Cabinet and on the following day did so with considerable force. He took with him a piece of graph paper showing that if the current rate of losses in France were to continue Fighter Command would cease to exist at the end of July.

The War Cabinet were temporarily won over and the ten squadrons did not leave Britain. On the next day Dowding wrote an historic letter to the Under-Secretary of State at the Air Ministry expressing with exceptional clarity and brevity how grave the situation was:

Headquarters Fighter Command,
Royal Air Force,
Bentley Priory,
Stanmore,
Middlesex.
16th May, 1940.

Sir,

I have the honour to refer to the very serious calls which have recently been made upon the Home Defence Fighter Units in an attempt to stem the German invasion on the Continent.

2. I hope and believe that our Armies may yet be victorious in France and Belgium, but we have to face the possibility that they may be defeated.

3. In this case I presume that there is no one who will deny that England should fight on, even though the remainder of the Continent of Europe is dominated by the Germans.

4. For this purpose it is necessary to retain some minimum fighter strength in this country and I must request that the Air Council will inform me what they consider this minimum strength to be, in order that I may make my dispositions accordingly.

5. I would remind the Air Council that the last estimate which they made as to the force necessary to defend this country was fifty-two squadrons, and my strength has now been reduced to the equivalent of thirty-six squadrons.

6. Once a decision has been reached as to the limit on which the Air Council and the Cabinet are prepared to stake the existence of the country, it should be made clear to the Allied commanders on the Continent that not a single aeroplane from Fighter Command beyond the limit will be sent across the Channel, no matter how desperate the situation may become.

7. It will, of course, be remembered that the estimate of fifty-two squadrons was based on the assumption that the attack would come from the eastwards except in so far as the defences might be outflanked in flight. We have now to face the possibility that attacks may come from Spain or even from the north coast of France. The result is that our line is very much extended at the same time as our resources are reduced.

8. I must point out that within the last few days the equivalent of ten squadrons have been sent to France, that the Hurricane Squadrons remaining in this country are seriously depleted, and that the more squadrons which are sent to France the higher will be the wastage and the more insistent the demands for reinforcements.

9. I must therefore request that as a matter of paramount urgency the Air Ministry will consider and decide what level of strength is to be left to the Fighter Command for the defences of this country, and will assure me that when this level has been reached, not one fighter will be sent across the Channel however urgent and insistent the appeals for help may be.

10. I believe that if an adequate fighter force is kept in this country, if the Fleet remains in being, and if Home Forces are suitably organised to resist invasion, we should be able to carry on the war single-handed for some time, if not indefinitely. But, if the Home Defence Force is drained away in desperate attempts to remedy the situation in France, defeat in France will involve the final, complete and irremediable defeat of this country.

I have the honour to be
Sir,
Your obedient Servant,
(signed) H. C. T. Dowding,
Air Chief Marshal,
Air Officer Commanding-in-Chief
Fighter Command, Royal Air Force.

The Under-Secretary of State,
Air Ministry,
London, W.C.2.

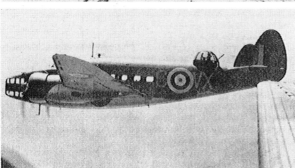

Above *Long lines of British troops stand in the water at Bray near Dunkirk waiting for some form of boat to take them to England. During the evacuation both the Luftwaffe and Fighter Command made all out efforts, the one to destroy and the other to defend. Despite heavy air and naval losses the bulk of the British Expeditionary Force safely crossed the Channel. The Luftwaffe found for the first time that it was up against determined and effective opposition and its casualties rose accordingly*

Above left *Forlorn remnants at Dunkirk when 'Operation Dynamo' had been completed. In the foreground the wrecks of two British motor cars and in the distance a wrecked French destroyer*

Left *While the United States had no modern combat aircraft in production in 1940, certain types for reconnaissance and training proved invaluable. Here a Lockheed Hudson of No. 206 Squadron is on patrol off the Dutch coast. The Hudson was used by the R.A.F. in every theatre of war*

Below *A fighter scramble at an alert during the 'Phoney War'. Pilots of No. 87 Squadron run to their Hurricanes at Lille in the winter of 1939. One Hurricane is an early variant with a two-blade propeller*

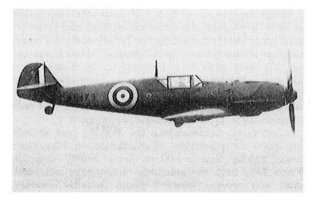

A Fiesler-built Me 109E-3, R.A.F. serialled AE479, which was forced down at Amiens, France, on May 2nd, 1940. It was taken over by No. 1 Squadron of the Advanced Air Striking Force and was subsequently shipped to England for comparative trials at the Aircraft and Armaments Experimental Establishment, Boscombe Down, and later at the Royal Aircraft Establishment, Farnborough. Later still this machine was delivered to the United States for tests. Left hand photograph shows the aircraft at the Royal Aircraft Establishment, Farnborough, with French fin stripes, R.A.F. underwing roundels and the German unit badge (II./JG54) under the cockpit. On the right the machine is seen airborne with full R.A.F. camouflage and markings

The Cabinet decision of May 15th gave Dowding only twenty-four hours' respite from worry. On the following morning, when details of the break-through at Sedan began to filter into Whitehall, Churchill sanctioned the transfer of four fresh squadrons from Britain to France. In the afternoon Churchill sat in a room on the Quai d'Orsay in Paris listening in stunned amazement to the pronouncements of General Gamelin. The Germans had penetrated on a front of about sixty miles, he said, and were deep in France. The French Army was shattered. There was no strategic reserve whatsoever.

The French pleaded for more and yet more British fighters because the Armée de l'Air hardly existed over the main battle front. The bubble was pricked at last, and the fantastic lack of knowledge by the British of their ally's military machine and morale was revealed with all its inevitable consequences. Churchill described himself as 'dumbfounded'. It is ironical that France's enemy should have assessed the position so well while her ally was blind.

Nevertheless, ever faithful to old friends, and with a touch of the quixotic, Churchill left the Quai d'Orsay and its bonfires of official documents to telephone London from the British Embassy. In addition to the four squadrons allocated in the morning, he asked sanction of the War Cabinet for a further six. This would leave Britain with only twenty-five fighter squadrons for home defence.

In *The Second World War*, Volume II, Churchill refers to a conversation with Dowding before the Battle of France in which the latter is claimed to have said that he could defend the islands against the Luftwaffe with twenty-five squadrons. In fact, as documentary evidence shows, Dowding always demanded forty-six to fifty-two squadrons, not twenty-five. Churchill appears to have misunderstood. He describes the orders for the ten extra squadrons as cutting 'to the bone'. Had they been sent it would have been more aptly described as a beheading. The Battle of Britain would have been lost before it began.

Late on the night of the 16th the War Cabinet again met although Churchill was still in Paris. Air Chief Marshal Sir Cyril Newall, Chief of the Air Staff, was now thoroughly alarmed over the fighter situation. Dowding's letter of the 16th convinced him that no more squadrons should be frittered away in the continental debacle. He learned from Air Marshal Barratt of the British Air Forces in France that the British airfields in northern France could take only three more squadrons and that bases could not be found for ten.

Newall suggested as an alternative that three squadrons should fly to France each morning and another three should act as relief in the afternoon. These six squadrons were the only Hurricane units left in the whole of Fighter Command which had not been drawn upon for pilots and aircraft for the French campaign. In this way he hoped that the units might not be lost in the general mêlée, although they would undoubtedly suffer casualties which would reduce their efficiency. The offer was accepted and on the 17th six squadrons of Hurricanes based on southern England were rotating through France. On May 19th Churchill decided finally against the commitment of any more fighters to French bases, although as late as May 18th the A.O.C. of No. 12 Group, Leigh-Mallory, had warned No. 19 Squadron at Duxford that it would be moving to France with its Spitfires.

It became clear that the R.A.F. Component of the B.E.F. could no longer operate from French Airfields. Accordingly, on May 19th, the remaining units retired to continue the fight from southern England, the withdrawal being completed by the 21st. Behind them were left stores, equipment and masses of unserviceable aircraft which could not be flown out. The A.A.S.F. meanwhile retreated westward with the remaining three Hurricane squadrons.

The balance sheet for eleven days of the Battle of France was grim and the total of fighters lost was some 25 per cent of the R.A.F.'s interceptor strength.

While the remains of B.A.A.F. extricated themselves as best they could, the situation on land had taken its final turn. Slowly but surely the B.E.F. and the French 1st Army were pressed back towards Dunkirk and the sea. On May 28th King Leopold of the Belgians, on his own initiative and without prior consultation with the Allies, surrendered his army to the Germans. The whole of the B.E.F.'s left flank was wide open. The only solution lay in rapid withdrawal to the coast.

Lord Gort, commanding the B.E.F., had already discussed the possibility of evacuation on May 19th, when fighter reinforcements were finally stopped. From May 20th the assembly of shipping and small craft was pressed forward under Admiral Ramsay. On May 30th H.Q. in France signalled that all possible British divisions were within the bridgehead area.

Throughout the period from the evacuation of the R.A.F. on the 21st to the 28th strong air cover was provided for the B.E.F. by No. 11 Group in England, and bombers continued to operate mainly by night.

After the withdrawal of all but three squadrons from France, Fighter Command could muster about 600 modern single-engined fighters (Hurricane, Spitfire and Defiant) with 230 aircraft in immediate reserve. Outwardly these figures are impressive but they take no account of the disorganised state of many squadrons returned from the Continent nor the need for rest and replenishment where men and machines were in constant battle for eleven days.

Operation Dynamo, the Dunkirk evacuation, began on the evening of May 26th. The whole weight of air defence over the area fell on Fighter Command. On the 27th sixteen Hurricane and Spitfire squadrons made 287 sorties over north-east France, destroying ten enemy aircraft and losing fourteen. It was impossible, outside the normal operational range of the radar and H.F./D.F. system, to direct the aircraft into battle from the ground. Patrols were the only solution, but these often met superior enemy fighter formations while on their way to intercept the bombers. For the first time Dowding threw in his Spitfires. These had the highest performance of any type he possessed. He had carefully husbanded them while the numerically greater Hurricanes bore the brunt of the continental fighting.

Göring promised to prevent the Dunkirk evacuation by air assault rather than let the B.E.F. be crushed by an all-out tank attack which Hitler feared would be bogged down in marshy ground. Fliegerkorps I, II, IV and VIII were accordingly hurled into the assault using 300 medium and dive-bombers with escorts provided from the 550 Me 109 and Me 110 fighters in the area.

On May 28th the weather deteriorated and much of Dunkirk was obscured by dense black smoke from burning oil tanks. Nevertheless, maximum effort was made by R.A.F. Fighter, Bomber and Coastal commands. Fighters from No. 11 Group flew 321 sorties against large German formations although the attacks petered out as the weather grew worse in the afternoon.

From May 29th, Park, at No. 11 Group, was able to obtain sanction from the Air Ministry to operate up to four squadrons at a time over Dunkirk although with only sixteen squadrons available this entailed periods when fighter cover over the beaches was lacking. Three out of five very large Luftwaffe raids in the afternoon were intercepted but two got through and caused considerable damage. Estimates of the casualties caused by these larger formations of fighter squadrons were exaggerated and it now seems that the principle of using pairs of squadrons, as in the Battle of Britain, would have yielded better results while ensuring continuity of the patrols.

On May 30th bad weather continued and Luftwaffe operations were curtailed. On the 31st, the day when most troops were brought back (68,014), it was fine and clear and in the afternoon the battle was renewed with full fury but only one ship was sunk. The situation worsened on the first day of June when desperate efforts were made by the Luftwaffe to smash shipping. Severe air fighting ensued. More air battles took place on June 2nd, but by evening the British rearguard had been taken off. For the following day the R.A.F. provided cover for the remainder of the French troops to be withdrawn, until at 2.23 a.m. on the 4th the Admiralty reported that Dynamo had been completed.

One R.A.F. pilot, Flight Lieutenant F. J. Howell* of 609 squadron wrote several remarkably frank and humorous letters to his brother in the Army during 1940. The following are extracts from a letter written at Northolt on June 6th which gives a full pilot's picture of the Dunkirk period :-

The next day, [May 31] we went to North Weald, and with another Squadron, flew over to Dunkirk about 2.30 p.m. The place was still burning furiously, a great pall of black smoke stretching 7000 ft. in the sky over Belgium. We again went to 20,000, with two squadrons below us at 10,000 ft. We never saw a single aeroplane within range, and we learnt to our horror that 8 blokes had been killed in a battle below us! So the next patrol we decided to do at about 15,000 ft. It was at 7.45 p.m. that we arrived over there, and I shall never in my life forget the sight. Thousands and thousands of A/A shells were bursting over the town, and we all thought 'here they come'. And here they bloody did come! right over our heads—Wave after wave of 3 bombers escorted by 5 109's. How we all prayed for that extra 5,000 ft. we had decided to do without. My heart gave a terrific thump I can tell you, and we all went full throttle to get above them to 21,000 where there was a thin layer of cloud.

Then below, I saw a Ju 88 twisting and turning—all three of us dived to attack—I put in about 6 seconds fire, and evidently silenced the gunner, for the streams of tracer bullets whistling past me stopped—The next bloke got an engine, and I believe it went down in flames. We all screamed up again as fast as we could go, and saw a terrific dogfight going on a few miles away. I was just about to join in, when tooling along about 3,000 ft. below was one solitary Heinkel, going like a streak of shit for Holland. John was behind me, and when I said I was going to attack, he shouted 'O.K.—I'll guard your tail'. So down I went. Then started the A/A fire and it was so intense that it was just suicide to go into it. After about half a minute, the gunners evidently saw us and it stopped. So down I pissed, and let it have all I had got. Lots of tracer stuff again which again stopped before my ammo ran out. John came down after

* Flight Lt. Howell later commanded 118 squadron at Ibsley and 243 squadron in Malaya. After years in a Japanese prison camp he returned to Britain and in 1948 was killed in an accident while commanding 54 squadron

me, and I think between us, we managed to down it, because before we left, one engine was burning, and it did not look any too happy.

Seeing 'as 'ow we had nearly reached Ostend, we turned tail, and went like a bomb for home.

I landed at Hawkinge, and had a quick pint with Russell, who had got back just before me. From that little do, two of our blokes were missing and had not yet returned.

The next day, we went to Manston, and did a couple of patrols from there—the first was nothing of note, except that Russell mysteriously disappeared after diving at a Heinkel 111. I think a Messerschmitt 110 got him, for another one of our blokes saw one on his tail before he managed to get it. He has since got the D.F.C.

In the afternoon, the weather got very mucky and we only went to 5,000 ft. i.e. two squadrons. I was leading Yellow Section as usual, and we were arse end Charlie. To my everlasting surprise, I looked down to see salvo after salvo of bombs bursting with terrific splashes in the water near some shipping, and there was a Heinkel, only 500 ft. below going in the opposite direction—The other chaps heard 'Crimey, there's a Heinkel', so I did a half roll, and came up its arse, giving it a pretty 2 seconds fire. Y2 came down and put all he had into it, but with no immediate result.

As I pulled out of the dive, there, right above me were three Heinkels 111 in close formation. Another surprise! So I gave one a blip of 2 seconds, which made one engine catch fire. Then the middle one let off a signal of three white puffs, and I thought 'Er, er, where are they?'—looked up, and there were 3 fighters sitting prettily above. I did not wait for them I can tell you, so put the nose down, and disappeared into some cloud like a knife.

Having lost everyone else, and being all on my own—(a most unpleasant position to be in, I thought), I whistled around at 0 feet for a bit about 15 miles off Dunkirk. I thought I saw a boat, just a speck on the water, so went to have a look. There were 8 or 10 Tommies and a sailor rowing for dear life in a ships lifeboat for England about 70 miles away!

The way they were rowing, they would miss England altogether, so I flew three times in the direction. They all stood up and waved and cheered poor devils. I only hope they were picked up all right, as I reported their position as soon as I landed. On the way back I thought I had run into something, as I saw a bomber on the skyline diving at some shipping, but unfortunately, or fortunately for the ship, it was a Hudson. All the way back to England I flew full throttle at about 15 feet above the water and the shipping between England and Dunkirk was a sight worth seeing. Never again shall I see so many ships of different sizes and shapes over such a stretch of water. Paddle boats, destroyers, sloops, tugs towing anything up to four motorless fishing trawlers, river launches—15 ft. motor boats—fire boats, cross-Channel boats, tankers, coal barges, and anything with a motor towing anything without one.

Dover and Ramsgate, Folkestone and all piers round Kent were crowded to overflowing, disembarking the troops and setting off again on the suicide journey. Naturally there were some pretty terrible sights as well, ships on their sides burning furiously, ships sinking and beached, and I even saw a salvo of bombs land smack in the middle of one huge boat—it burst into flames, slowly turned over and sank in about 2 minutes.

Well, the amazing thing about that last patrol was that every one of the other blokes—about 20 in all, never saw a single enemy plane! I just could not understand it.

As you know, it's all over now and I am indeed lucky to have got away scot free. Dizzy was killed and 5 other chaps are missing. We all have hope that they may turn up sometime but as the show is over now, I think there is very little hope left.

One was my Flight Commander so I am now I/C 'A' Flight, and will get another stripe, and it's a rotten way to get it.

We shall be here for a little while I think, and any time off seems hopeless, for we have only twelve pilots now and have to keep twelve machines ready to take off at the longest time of 30 minutes.

So we are on at 4 a.m. until 10.20 p.m.—a long day! If it was not for the truly glorious weather—ceaseless sunshine all day, it would be miserable. . . .

For Fighter Command Dunkirk was the culmination of nearly a month's attrition. British fighter defences on June 4th were at the lowest point in the whole of 1940, the Battle of Britain notwithstanding. Dunkirk had seen the loss of over 100 R.A.F. fighters and eighty pilots. Every squadron of the command except three in Scotland had been in action over the Continent, and on June 3rd twelve squadrons were in the line for the second time.

During the continental battle 320 British pilots were killed, reported missing or died of injuries while 115 more were taken prisoners of war or interned. Altogether 915 air crew members of all categories were lost. When some sorting-out had been accomplished by the 15th, Dowding found he had 1,094 pilots, a deficit of 362 against his alloted establishment.

In the period May 10th to June 20th 944 R.A.F. aircraft operating from Britain and France were lost. Of these 386 were Hurricanes and sixty-seven Spitfires.

On the morning of June 5th Fighter Command could muster only 466 serviceable aircraft of which 331 were Hurricanes and Spitfires. There were thirty-six of these machines in immediate reserve.

It was not until the final evacuation of the A.A.S.F. squadrons on June 18th that the last British fighters in France, from No. 73 Squadron, took off from Nantes and headed for Tangmere in Sussex. Dowding's remaining 'chicks' were home to count. He could begin desperately to rebuild and reorganise with the hope that there might be a momentary respite. As events turned out he had a heaven-sent month in which the whole picture was changed.

12 Britain prepares

Shortly after the Dunkirk evacuation Dowding wrote to the Air Ministry outlining his thoughts on the future of the war. He stated that there were three major threats: invasion for which daylight air superiority was essential to the Luftwaffe; concentrated night bombing which might take months or even a year to achieve decisive results; and the submarine menace.

Of these the most serious immediate threat was invasion combined with the possible destruction of Fighter Command. The German Navy was too weak even to consider opposing the Royal Navy in the Channel or on the east coast without overwhelming air support. For the Royal Navy the prospect of intervening in strength in the narrow waters of the Channel without the support of Fighter Command could only mean the loss of most of the Fleet from air attack. The whole future of Britain therefore rested on Dowding's ability to meet the Luftwaffe, inflict heavy losses on it, and still remain an effective force if invasion should take place.

Fighter Command had to reorganise after Dunkirk. Squadrons needed rest, new crews had to be trained and new units formed. It was necessary to assure maximum production of fighters as well as the immediate repair and salvage of all damaged machines. Mobile radar units had to be ready to take the place of any permanent sites put out of action while the provision of gun defence of all key fighter and radar stations was of paramount importance. The foundations laid by Dowding, Swinton, the Air Ministry and the scientists were now to be tested to the full.

The Government looked anxiously to the United States for support and supplies, especially to its main champion, President Roosevelt. The U.S.A. was divided in its attitude. Some promised maximum aid and others adopted the isolationist point of view. The German Embassy in Washington worked night and day to fan the flames of isolationism and to build up an image of Britain as a tottering country which was hardly worth propping up.

Charles A. Lindbergh openly campaigned on the German side as he was convinced of the Luftwaffe's overwhelming might. He founded 'The Citizens' Committee to keep America out of the War'. Promptly pro-British elements and, in particular, William Allen White, a newspaper editor, set up 'The Committee to Defend Europe by Aiding the Allies'.

In June–July the British Army's position was chaotic with a desperate lack of equipment and most units in process of reorganisation.

The Dunkirk debacle had seen the loss of over 1,000 guns (including A.A.), 850 anti-tank guns and vast quantities of anti-tank rifles.

It was not until the second half of July that the army was able to make any sense of its artillery situation. Out of some 25 infantry divisions only one had its full complement of field guns and of these only a proportion were modern 25-pounders. Another division had 70 guns while the remainder varied between a handful and nil. Medium and heavy regiments were extremely short of guns of all kinds and 2-pounder anti-tank guns were like gold-dust. To add to the problem there was a chronic shortage of towing vehicles and even of guns with pneumatic tyres.

Nationwide searches were made for weapons of all types. The Navy produced (rumour had it from under a coal heap at a Dockyard) over 100 4-inch and 12-pounder guns, while the army unearthed several hundred 6-pounder Hotchkiss guns once mounted on World War I tanks.

All types of guns were mounted for anti-invasion defence including 5.5 in., 6 in., 8 in., 9.2 in., 12 in., 13.5 in., 14 in., 15 in. and even a giant 18 in. howitzer which had its home in a tunnel near Canterbury. Strange guns from long-forgotten wars found their way to operational units.

Apart from 25-pounder, production of which rose steadily, the biggest windfall was the American sale to Britain of 900 75 mm. field guns. Some of these dated from the 1890s, others were British 18-pounders firing 75 mm. ammunition and the remainder U.S. designed weapons.

With the guns (and 1000 rounds of ammunition apiece) came all-important rifles. In batches arrived half a million 1917 P.17 Kennington rifles firing .300 ammunition. The Home Guard took large numbers of these and they also found their way into the three services and organisations such as the Observer Corps.

The British tank situation after Dunkirk was lamentable. Six hundred tanks had been lost and to this figure was later added 617 tanks of 1st Armoured Division wrecked on the Somme. Early in June there were in Britain a total of 963 tanks many of which were obsolete and 618 were thin-armoured light vehicles. Many of these tanks were scattered across the country in training and other second-line establishments.

In Washington Roosevelt was a true friend in need. The release of guns, rifles and ammunition from U.S. reserve stores made a tremendous difference to the British army situation.

In the air, there was nothing the President could do to help Fighter Command. Vast orders had been placed by Britain with American aircraft factories and these served to rebuild the impoverished U.S. industry in time for America's entry into the war in December 1941.

In 1940, however, it was Coastal, and Flying Training commands which began to benefit from transatlantic purchases of aircraft like the Hudson, and Harvard. For Fighter Command there was little to be done. None of the fighter aircraft in service with the United States Army Air Corps or being delivered from the factories were suitable for use against the Luftwaffe. The machines, although widely advertised, were underpowered, undergunned, and lacked armour, speed and high-altitude performance. In addition many of the types had teething troubles which took months to sort out. To have pitted such aircraft as the Brewster Buffalo, the Curtiss Hawk 75 or the Bell Airacobra against the Me 109 would have been suicidal.

New and advanced interceptors were on their way including the famous North American Mustang, which was designed and built to British requirements, but there was nothing ready to take a place in British fighter squadrons in the Battle of Britain.

The United States also suffered from a lack of high-powered engines, especially of the liquid-cooled variety, which hampered the designers from the outset. Britain desperately needed more production facilities for the Merlin engine and the patent rights were released for licensed production in America. In the summer of 1940 Henry Ford I was asked if he would build the Merlin. To his great discredit he refused, stating: 'I want to keep America out of the war'. The British Purchasing Commission turned to the Packard Motor Co. and successfully negotiated for the mass production of the Merlin at Detroit, the plan anticipating 6,000 engines. This and other arrangements could only benefit the R.A.F. many months later. Fighter Command was thus entirely reliant on British production in 1940 and on the ability to put back into the air as many damaged machines as possible.

After the Munich crisis in August 1938 the Air Ministry foresaw the creation of a large-scale repair and salvage organisation staffed entirely with service men and women. When war broke out it became clear that uniformed manpower would not be available and that time was lacking for the creation of a new body of such size and complexity. The Air Ministry therefore requested Lord Nuffield to set up a civilian organisation to run all repair work for the R.A.F. Nuffield was appointed Director-General of Maintenance, Air Ministry, with the managing directors of Morris Motors as Deputy Directors-General.

Morris Motors took control of what became the Civilian Repair Organization, C.R.O. They had to start completely from scratch with motor-car engineers and they created a chain of repair depots from civil airfields, training schools, civil airline bases, garages and a variety of manufacturers whose peacetime production lines now lay idle. Working parties from hundreds of contractors were established to carry out repairs at R.A.F. airfields and three Repairable

Many emergency conversions were made to cope with the dangers of 1940. To provide an aircraft for ground strafing beach landing areas Westland devised a tandem wing version of the ubiquitous Lysander army-co-op aircraft with provision in the rear fuselage for a four-gun Boulton Paul turret. The prototype was flown successfully but development was not proceeded with

Equipment Depots were set up to salvage material of all kinds.

To avoid the possibility of the headquarters of C.R.O. being knocked out by air attack it was rehoused, in May 1940, at Merton College, Oxford. When the Ministry of Aircraft Production was created in the same month C.R.O. was transferred to it from the Air Ministry and Lord Nuffield resigned as Director-General of Maintenance.

C.R.O. under the press of events and of its new energetic head, Lord Beaverbrook, began to show remarkable results. From an output in February 1940 of twenty repaired military aircraft per week, the figure by mid-July rose to 160 per week. Strenuous efforts were made to see that every usable piece of material or equipment was salvaged from wrecks by special teams. Aircraft were broken down in the open or at one of a number of special depots.

Within the C.R.O. were Civilian Repair Units such as No. 1 C.R.U. at the Morris works at Cowley, Oxford. Miracles of repair were worked in 1940. Aircraft apparently beyond repair were returned to the Battle in new condition. The C.R.U.s were more often than not built up with men who had no previous experience of aircraft work and whose only mentors were a handful of aircraft technicians. Tools were made by hand at first and spares were produced straight from unfamiliar aircraft works drawings. The combination of civil contractors and R.A.F. depots worked well.

With the possibility of heavy attacks on airfields and consequent damage to aircraft under repair a new scheme for categorising damaged machines was devised. From May 27th aircraft were divided as follows:

4 Those capable of rapid repair at the station and with station facilities.

5 Those beyond station repair but fit to be flown to an R.A.F. or civil repair depot.

6 Those unfit to be flown.

This superseded the old categories 1, 2 and 3: repairable by unit, repairable by contractor or depot and recommended for reduction and salvage. The scheme was found unworkable in France where airfields became cluttered with unserviceable machines. Repairs under category 4 were limited to those that could be carried out within thirty-six hours. Any repairs taking longer were treated as class 6 and were removed by road. Class 5 consisted of aircraft safe to fly lightly loaded. They became known as 'fly-in' repairs. If an aircraft after delivery at a repair depot was found to be repairable within twenty-four hours the pilot could wait for it and fly it back. In many cases from July onwards pilots brought in machines straight from the Battle and waited while repairs were done in the 'out-patients' department.

Most of the Hurricanes were repaired at R.A.F. Henlow. During the intense periods that station carried out up to twenty fly-in repairs a week, while pilots waited, in addition to major repairs of twelve machines a week. The record for changing both main planes, fitting eight guns and loading with ammunition was 1 hr. 55 min. At Henlow the conversion of Browning guns from Mark II to Mark II Star was undertaken, the Mark II Star giving an increased rate of fire. On an average 300 of these guns were converted each week from May to November 1940.

The salvage organisation was also a vital factor. Eight salvage units were organised before the Battle started. All crashes were reported to headquarters of the group controlling these units and the salvage units' engineer officer decided on the spot the category to which the aircraft were allotted. Salvage units cleared operational airfields of wrecked aircraft, and dealt with crashed German machines after they had been examined by one of the officers from air intelligence.

To assist the Civilian Repair Organisation, No. 50 Maintenance Unit was created responsible to No. 43 Group R.A.F. No. 50 conveyed crashed machines from all over the country to repair depots. Staffed almost entirely by civilians, its home was at Cowley. Control was divided between a civilian superintendent from Morris's and an R.A.F. squadron-leader.

The contribution that C.R.O., the C.R.U.s, R.A.F. repair depots and the salvage teams made to the winning of the Battle cannot be over-emphasised. Between July and December 1940 C.R.O. put back into the line 4,196 damaged planes. Of the total number of aircraft issued to fighter squadrons during the Battle of Britain excluding the fly-in repairs, 35 per cent were repaired and only 65 per cent were new. Of those struck off the strength of the squadrons, excluding the missing aircraft, 61 per cent were repaired and 39 per cent reduced for spares.

Late in the summer British Railways and London Transport were asked to help with repairs and spares. The Great Western Railway turned out 171,000 Hurricane components while London Transport supplied some 400 men for aircraft repairs at an R.A.F. Maintenance Unit.

Without the vast 'spider's web' of C.R.O. there would have been an acute shortage of Spitfires and Hurricanes in 1940. On September 26th, for instance, the Vickers Supermarine works at Woolston, Southampton, was heavily attacked and for a short time production stopped altogether. The flow of Spitfires to squadrons could only be maintained by repair while alternative production facilities round Southampton were organised. As a result of the combined efforts of the aircraft industry, C.R.O. and the R.A.F. mechanics on the airfields, between July and the end of October 1940 fighters were always immediately available to replace losses. No squadrons had to be grounded for lack of aircraft.

Contrary to popular belief, the R.A.F. was never down to its last half-dozen Spitfires and Hurricanes in reserve during the Battle of Britain. The lowest point in the Battle was reached in the week ending September 13th, when there were 127 fighters ready for delivery in storage units. Of these 80 were Hurricanes and 47 Spitfires.

The aircraft industry made tremendous efforts during the summer of 1940 and production rates were kept up despite bombing and extreme fatigue among the workers. The average day shifts were 63.6 hours a week in July 1940, and the night shifts were even higher. Beaverbrook knew that while the threat of invasion and mass air attack existed, precedence should be given to certain R.A.F. aircraft and their equipment and to anti-aircraft defence. Accordingly, on May 31st, the Priority of Production Direction was issued which gave first priority to fighters and bombers, A.A. guns, particularly Bofors, to small arms and ammunition and to bombs. Two weeks later trainers were included on this list. Several types of aircraft under development including four-engined bombers were given low priority gradings which delayed their coming into service. Maximum concentration on the operational types then in full production was however essential. As a result production of fighters rose from 157 in January 1940, to 446 in June, and 496 in July. Output of medium bombers such as the Wellington rose from 96 in January to 239 in June and 242 in July.

One of the greatest disappointments, however, was the Castle Bromwich shadow factory for Spitfire production at Birmingham. Lord Swinton originally intended the works to be run by Vickers-Armstrongs, builders of the Spitfire. In 1938 the new Air Minister, Sir Kingsley Wood, decided instead that it should be controlled by Lord Nuffield and a contract was signed on September 16th of that year.

Continuous delays occurred in the building of the factory under government control and in its operation by Nuffields. Spitfires should have been rolling off the lines in quantity by the beginning of 1940 to meet orders for 1,500 machines. When Beaverbrook came into office in May not one aircraft had been completed.

Soon after Dunkirk German aircraft began to appear over Britain in steadily increasing numbers. On the night of June 19th a Heinkel 111 of 4./KG4 from Merville fought a running battle with Blenheim fighters from No. 23 Squadron. The German gunners succeeded in shooting down one Blenheim and damaging another, but their Heinkel was wrecked and it is seen here in the sea at Blakeney Creek, Clay, Norfolk

The whole of Spitfire production was still centred on the very vulnerable Supermarine factory at Woolston, Southampton. This alone could not possibly meet all R.A.F. requirements. It was for this very reason that Dowding kept the Spitfire out of France and why more squadrons could not be equipped with the type during the Battle of Britain.

Beaverbrook's reaction to the crisis was to telephone Vickers and order them to take over Castle Bromwich immediately. Six days later a belated letter was sent from the Air Ministry at Harrogate regarding the future take-over with an injunction 'to proceed with all speed with the orders which have been allotted to the factory'.

Vickers' reply on the 30th was amusing and indicative of the rising tempo of events with the 'new broom' in the Ministry: 'In accordance with the verbal instructions received from the Minister of Aircraft Production, we took over control of the Castle Bromwich aeroplane factory from Lord Nuffield on the 20th inst., and since that date we have been actively engaged in hastening work on the orders allotted to that factory.'

The new Vickers management cleaned up the line and started to put Spitfires together from the scattered assemblies available. On June 6th the first Spitfire (a Mark II) was flown from the northern factory and by the end of the month nine more had been delivered, with a number of wing sets for fuselages waiting at Woolston.

Plans had been made for building Wellington and

Halifax bombers at Castle Bromwich, but these were cancelled by Beaverbrook in favour of producing Spitfires only.

By dint of tremendous effort Vickers succeeded in turning out 125 Spitfire IIs between the date of take-over and September 30th and this despite air raid damage in August.

The task of meeting the Luftwaffe devolved upon the Spitfire and Hurricane alone because they were the only suitable machines operationally available at the time. Much was expected of the twin-engined Westland Whirlwind but it had continual teething troubles and showed poor performance at height. The Bristol Beaufighter was to make a great name for itself in later years but in 1940 it was only coming off the line in penny numbers, five in July and twenty-three in August. It was also beset with minor snags.

The Boulton Paul Defiant was delivered at the rate of around a dozen a week but with its heavy rear turret and no forward armament it was completely unsuited to daylight operations where the Me 109 was involved.

Finally, there were many expedients on offer in the hour of need. These included advanced trainers with machine-guns installed in the wings and the Miles M.20, a Merlin-powered wooden single-seater. The M.20 was faster than the Hurricane. The time taken to develop the prototype from drawing-board to the first flight was only nine weeks and two days. It was intended for very rapid production using many trainer parts and eliminating hydraulics. Fortunately the R.A.F. had no shortage of Spitfires and Hurricanes and the type was never produced.

Fighter, Bomber and Coastal Commands made detailed preparations for the use of all available forces in the event of invasion and joint service discussions were held as early as May.

Apart from these efforts, Training Command (late

When invasion first threatened at the time of Dunkirk the British Isles were almost defenceless from an army point of view. Parachute and glider landings were feared and every effort was made to obstruct potential air landing areas. Here, at Hatfield, dozens of scrap heap cars were pushed on to the airfield every night and removed in the morning so that flying could start again

in May becoming Flying Training and Technical Commands) on May 15th sent out operational Order No. 1 for the 'Reinforcement of Bomber Command with Training Command aircraft in the event of an invasion of the United Kingdom'.

Originally known as 'ZZ' this scheme was, on May 27th, code-named 'Banquet'. It was intended that as many suitable training aircraft as possible, with experienced pilots should fly to Bomber Command stations and from there undertake bombing and machine gunning sorties.

Aircraft were to move in sections as part of a four-stage transfer and all aircraft in Stage 1 were to be despatched within four hours of receipt of the code-word 'Banquet'. Training Command personnel were told to bring their own bedding, two days' iron rations and 'be prepared to rough it'.

Fourteen bomber stations were to receive a total of 169 aircraft—1 Hampden, 3 Wellingtons, 27 Blenheims, 33 Battles, 48 Ansons, 33 Audax, 12 Harts and 12 Hinds, the last three types being open cockpit biplanes. Armament consisted of fixed and free machine guns and 112 lb. or 20 lb. bombs.

In addition No. 6 (Training) Group was ordered to prepare all its aircraft (Whitleys, Hampdens, Wellingtons, Blenheims, Battles and Ansons) for operations and report its exact state to Bomber Command every 48 hours.

Finally, it was decided to use as many Tiger Moth and Magister basic training aircraft as possible to help repel invasion. In June de Havillands sorted out mid 1930 plans they had made for fitting bombs on Tiger

Moths for a Middle East Government. With modifications these drawings were put out to the shops and in a very short time 1,500 conversion sets for racks with eight 20 lb. bombs had been produced.

On August 9th an order was issued by the Air Ministry for the use of light trainers as part of the Banquet scheme. Approximately 350 Tiger Moths and Magisters in 70 flights of five each were to be deployed under the code name 'Banquet Light'.

The aircraft, manned by flying instructors, were to be under the operational control of Army Co-operation squadron commanders and they were to undertake 'dive and level bombing against enemy troops attempting a landing'.

An extraordinary private venture conversion of June 1940 was the 'paraslasher'. George Reid of Reid and Sigrist conceived the idea of killing parachutists by removing their means of normal descent to earth with a scythe attached to a Tiger Moth. Flight tests proved promising but the idea was not officially adopted.

The fighter production industry in 1940 relied on one engine for its Spitfires and Hurricanes, the Rolls-Royce Merlin. Any breakdown in Merlin deliveries during the Battle of Britain would have been catastrophic. The need for expansion had been foreseen in 1938 when the Rolls-Royce factory at Derby was already stretched to the limit. Rather than have Merlins built by motor manufacturers as was the case with Bristol radial aero engines, Rolls-Royce suggested the building of a shadow factory to be run by themselves. The new works was erected at Crewe. Within eleven months of starting the first Merlin was completed there, on May 20th, 1939.

A second Rolls-Royce shadow factory was put in hand in 1939, at Hillington near Glasgow. Work started in June 1939 but it was not finished until October 1940 when the Battle of Britain was almost over. The British Ford Company's plant for Rolls engines at Trafford Park, Manchester, was also still under construction in the summer of 1940. The whole of the output of Merlins therefore devolved on Derby and Crewe.

To meet the invasion threat plans were made for using every type of aircraft even down to Tiger Moth biplane elementary trainers. In record time de Havillands produced 1,500 conversion sets for Tiger Moths to carry eight 20 lb. bombs. Here bombs are being fitted on the racks under the rear cockpit

There were ninety dispersed workshops and factories around Derby which Rolls-Royce took over to ensure continued production of key items in the event of damage to the main works. Fortunately the Luftwaffe did no damage at Merlin factories during the period July to October. With an all-out effort the R.A.F. had all the power plants it needed. Rolls-Royce built up to the amazing production rate of 400 Merlins per month and held it for the vital period. A full 7-shift week put a great strain on all personnel. One worker in the Merlin assembly shop at Nightingale Road (known as the 'Glasshouse') recalls being finally given a half day off a month and falling asleep within 10 seconds of sitting down in a cinema.

Between September 1939 and September 1940 the Derby and Crewe works produced no less than 2000 Merlins.

While Beaverbrook applied Blitzkrieg techniques to the problems of production bottlenecks, manpower and materials, Dowding was wrestling with a host of operational questions. High and low radar cover was being extended as fast as equipment could be built and operators trained but there were still gaps, mainly in the West Country. The same applied to the Observer Corps network. To aid in picking up aircraft taking off in the area behind Calais two of the new Gun Laying (G.L.) radars were installed on Dover cliffs. These gave five minutes' earlier warning to No. 11 Group than the C.H. station nearby.

Calibration and maintenance of Chain Home and Chain Home Low radars presented a continual problem. While the Observer Corps established a new group centre (No. 21) at Exeter in July 1940 many of the Observer posts there were still in process of formation. Throughout the summer new radar stations, airfields, communications, Observer posts and operations rooms were being built in the north-west, the west and in Wales, while the air fighting was at its height.

No. 10 Fighter Group with headquarters at Box, near Bath, Wiltshire, was brought into operation in July. It controlled three sectors. A fourth, Middle Wallop, was transferred from No. 11 Group in August. The group, however, lacked suitable airfields for modern fighters in its western area. Especially vulnerable was Plymouth with its naval dockyard. The only expedient open to Dowding was to station No. 247 Squadron with Gladiators and six pilots at a small ex-civil airfield called Roborough. These, with the Sea Gladiators of No. 804 Squadron, Fleet Air Arm, were the only British biplane fighters to take part in the Battle of Britain.

An expanding Fighter Command and the network of factories called for greatly increased anti-aircraft defence but only about a quarter of the guns required were available for the defence of the whole island. Every effort was made to give maximum fire power to sector stations and satellites in the south, to radar and other sites. Nevertheless many more guns were needed to give really adequate protection. A number of 20 mm. cannon intended for aircraft, but not yet installed, were released for airfield defence, but were mainly ineffective due to lack of ammunition.

Balloon barrages were set up round certain aircraft factories. In some cases works and fighter airfields were fitted with the Parachute and Cable (P.A.C.) device which consisted of a steel cable and parachutes fired into the air by rockets. The cable then descended slowly attached to the parachutes. With luck the cable could seriously damage an aircraft which crossed its path.

For the fighter pilots and their aircraft there were lessons to be learned speedily, and urgent modifications to be made if losses in combat with the Me 109 were not to be severe.

With the German Army ranged along the Channel coast, defence preparations of every kind were put in hand. Road blocks of every size and shape were erected, including steam rollers and farm carts; poles and wire hoops appeared in the fields to stop gliders; pill-boxes sprouted from roadsides and long anti-tank ditches were dug. Pictured here is a road block outside the Running Horse Inn on the Maidstone–Chatham Road in June 1940

In France and at Dunkirk the R.A.F. learned that the copybook tactics of 'Fighting Area Attacks' were quite useless against the loose formations of the Luftwaffe which had been trained from experience of modern warfare in Spain. Gradually the R.A.F. squadrons which had been in the line learned new tactics by sheer necessity. They also began to keep a continuous watch on their rear mirrors.

When the eight-gun fighter appeared the policy was to disperse the lines of fire so that a comparatively wide area was sprayed with bullets when the guns were fired. But air combat, notably over Dunkirk, showed conclusively that with the short time the target was in line in the gun sight dispersed fire was insufficiently concentrated. Squadrons harmonised their guns on a point 250 yards ahead, which gave them a range of concentration of about 500 yards, the bullets diverging outwards from the point of intersection. Despite the proved lethal effect of 250 yards harmonisation an armament officer from the recesses of Whitehall visited stations in August and demanded to know why the original instructions had not been adhered to. He

received short shrift from the battle-weary pilots.

To combat the two main Luftwaffe fighters, the Me 109 and Me 110, Fighter Command needed comparative trials with the Spitfire and the Hurricane. It was not until May, however, that the Aircraft and Armaments Experimental Establishment was able to procure an intact 109 from France where two such machines had been forced down. The initial flight trials by Messrs. Stanford Tuck and Stainforth showed that the Me 109 was as fast as the Spitfire and climbed at a higher rate, but generally the Spitfire was more manoeuvrable. One great advantage possessed by the 109 was its direct fuel injection pump in place of a carburettor. This item was standard. In the design of the Daimler Benz DB601 engine the supercharger as mounted on the side requiring a pressure carburettor underneath and between the cylinder banks. Rather than waste time on carburettor development the Germans chose to use the Bosch injector pump with which they had much experience.

The Merlin engine on the Spitfire had a normal float carburettor. In a sudden transition from level to diving flight the negative 'G' interrupted the fuel supply. This was a distinct handicap but modifications to overcome it were not forthcoming until some time after the Battle of Britain. In the meantime R.A.F. pilots could not dive sharply away from a pursuer and often lost their own quarry when he dived. The only solution was to turn the Spitfires or Hurricanes on their backs and dive. This was a difficult task under combat conditions. It seems extraordinary that this problem was not tackled earlier or that Rolls-Royce did not fit an injection pump in place of a carburettor.

While the Me 109 was a formidable opponent, the Me 110 was something of an unknown quantity until July 11th, 1940, when a 110 in good condition belly-landed near Wareham, Dorsetshire. The crew endeavoured to set fire to the machine but were shot at by troops from a searchlight battery and captured before doing any harm. A 60 ft. 'Queen Mary' vehicle was despatched from Cowley, Oxford, to collect the aircraft. While the salvage gang removed the wings and loaded the aircraft they received the unwelcome attentions of another Me 110 which circled above. Apparently it had run out of ammunition for no attack was made. With police escort the aircraft was driven to Farnborough, although a concrete tank-trap *en route* and part of a gateway at the destination had to be removed.

As soon as it was generally reassembled the Me 110 was inspected by Sir Archibald Sinclair and Air Ministry experts. Thorough analysis and eventual flight testing revealed that the Me 110 was to be no match for the Hurricane or the Spitfire. It was unwieldy, vulnerable and slower than the latter.

In the trials of the Me 109 one vital aspect of performance testing was omitted, general handling and speed above 20,000 feet. The R.A.F. presumed that air fighting would take place at medium and low altitudes, whereas a great part of it was to be at 25,000 feet and above. In addition, oxygen was not available for the 109 on test which limited the ceiling at which the pilot could operate.

At height the Me 109 with its VDM three-bladed constant speed propeller showed marked superiority even to the Spitfire, which had only a two-pitch propeller, the supplies of constant speed unit having been allocated to the bomber lines.

At the beginning of June all Spitfires, Hurricanes and Defiants were fitted with two-pitch propellers, but on June 9th, 1940, Flight Lieutenant McGrath, an engineer officer at Hornchurch, telephoned the de Havilland propeller division at Hatfield, Herts., to inquire whether a Spitfire could be fitted with a constant speed propeller 'without a lot of paperwork and fuss'. Having answered in the affirmative, de Havillands sent half a dozen picked engineers and a test pilot, Mr. E. Lane-Burslem, to Hornchurch with appropriate equipment to carry out a trial conversion. This was carried out on the night of June 14th, while the Germans were rejoicing over their entry into Paris.

On June 20th Lane-Burslem reported that he had successfully test flown the plane, which was from No. 65 Squadron, and that other pilots, including the commanding officer, Squadron Leader Cooke, had tried it. The results were startling. An extra 7,000 feet was added to the service ceiling and the machine had a better manoeuvrability at height and improved take-off and landing performance. Squadron Leader Cooke was able to give only a brief demonstration in battle of his modified mount. On his second sortie in it he was killed.

Two days after the report, on June 22nd, de Havilland received verbal orders to convert all R.A.F. Merlin-powered fighters in the field with top priority.

The senior technical staff officer at Fighter Command and the company agreed that conversions would start on June 25th and that Spitfires would be done first. Work was to begin simultaneously at twelve stations with a de Havilland supervisory engineer at each. It was estimated that ten days would be required to convert a squadron and that all Spitfire modifications would be completed by July 20th.

Although there was no written contract, de Havillands immediately started to produce 500 conversion sets. These came out at the rate of twenty per day from June 24th onwards. While field conversions went on Supermarines were sent twenty sets a week so that two-thirds of the Spitfires produced rolled off the line with constant-speed propellers.

To start the programme de Havillands used a number of constant-speed units originally ordered by the French Air Force, while the de Havilland engine factory hurriedly set about producing 1,000 sets of engine pipes and quill shafts to drive the hydraulically operated constant-speed units.

As soon as the de Havilland engineer arrived at each station with his precious cargo he was given a picked team of R.A.F. N.C.O.s and fitters who watched him make the first conversion. The R.A.F. ground crew converted the second with his help and the third under supervision. Then, if all was in order, the engineer departed to repeat the sequence at the next station. Lane-Burslem followed, flight testing the first aircraft at each base.

Some Spitfire squadrons in more remote parts of Britain flew their aircraft to the south in ones and twos for conversion. Some even arrived at the Hatfield works.

Averaging fifteen to sixteen hours a day the de Havilland engineers went steadily from station to station. By August 15th 1,051 Spitfires and Hurricanes had been converted, making an average of 20.2 aircraft a day over fifty-two days. This remarkable achievement was of the utmost benefit to Fighter Command when dealing with the Me 109 at high altitude.

Transcending all material problems, however, was the shortage of fighter pilots. This, and not aircraft, could have lost the R.A.F. the Battle of Britain.

Immediately following the Battle of France, Winston Churchill, realising Dowding's predicament, issued an instruction to the air and naval staffs to search for any trained pilots suitable for transfer to fighters.

The Admiralty, which could supply only two squadrons,* due to the obsolescence of its aircraft, rose to the occasion. On June 6th forty-five partially trained and semi-trained naval pilots, including seven ex-R.A.F.V.R. men with the Fleet Air Arm, were transferred to the R.A.F. for completion of training and conversion to eight-gun interceptors. Thirty more were found before the end of June, making a total of sixty-eight, discounting the R.A.F.V.R. crews who were absorbed into the Air Force. Ten of the naval pilots were recalled for service in the Mediterranean in July, leaving a total of fifty-eight first-class naval aircrew who fought through the Battle of Britain with

---

* No. 804 Squadron (Sea Gladiators) and No. 808 Squadron (Fulmars) which for some time were under the operational control of No. 13 Group R.A.F.

On May 14, four days after the German continental invasion started, the mustering of the Local Defence Volunteers was announced. Alternately railed at and derided by the German radio, the L.D.V. (later in the Summer renamed the Home Guard) had vital tasks to perform including observation and reporting of enemy movements and general harassing operations. Their most important job in the summer of 1940, however, was to relieve the hard-pressed British Army of guard duties—on railways, at road blocks, on river bridges, by crashed aircraft and at a multitude of other points.

A large proportion of the L.D.V. were 'old sweats' from World War I who had no small knowledge of the Germans and infantry fighting.

On the right *Reproductions from a typical L.D.V. handbook on sale in 1940 where it is made quite clear what this amateur army was intended to do.*

Below *An identity card issued to a platoon commander in the West Sussex Local Defence Volunteers in August 1940*

This particular platoon was based on a remote hamlet called Madehurst high on the Sussex downs.

Its volunteers included farmers, gamekeepers, woodsmen and gardeners, several of whom were first-class shots.

By September 1940 the unit's armoury consisted of a number of American P.17 Enfield .300 rifles, various shotguns and .22 sporting rifles and one revolver. Grenades were in short supply, while for anti-tank work the platoon was limited to one crate of sticky bombs, home-made from champagne and wine bottles and, adorned with a strip of sandpaper and a couple of matches.

When the L.D.V. was fully established, platoon commanders were commissioned as Lieutenants. On the

HOME GUARD
A HANDBOOK FOR THE
L. D. V.
By JOHN BROPHY

PARACHUTE TROOPS, ANTI-TANK WARFARE, OBSERVATION AND REPORTING, THE RIFLE, THE BREN GUN, THE LEWIS GUN, THE THOMPSON GUN, GRENADES AND 'MOLOTOFFS,' ROAD-BLOCKS, AMBUSHES, STREET FIGHTING, ETC., ETC.

HODDER & STOUGHTON   1/- net

identity card note of this subsequent appointment has been countersigned at the top by Major General E. B. Ashmore, Commander of the London Air Defence Area (L.A.D.A.) in 1918 and founder, in the mid-twenties, of the Observer Corps.

THE LAST WORD

IT is suggested that the substance of this brief postscript be got by heart.

The main duties of the Home Guard are :

1. Guarding important points.
2. Observation and reporting—prompt and precise.
3. Immediate attack against small, lightly armed parties of the enemy.
4. The defence of roads, villages, factories and vital points in towns to block enemy movements.

Every L.D.V. should know :

1. The whole of the ground in his own district.
2. The personnel of his own detachment.
3. The Headquarters of the detachment and where he is to report for duty in the event of an alarm.
4. What the alarm signal is.
5. The form of reports concerning enemy landings or approaches, what the reports should contain, and to whom they should be sent.

6. The personnel of the civil defence services, police, wardens, A.F.S., etc., in his own district.
7. The uniforms and badges of any units of the regular army stationed near at hand, in order to be able to spot enemy agents in disguise.

In the event of an alarm, the L.D.V. might use this check list before he leaves his home or his work. He should take with him :

1. Full uniform, including steel helmet and warm underclothing.
2. His arms and ammunition.
3. His gas-mask.
4. Rations for twenty-four hours.
5. A filled water-bottle.
6. Identity cards.
7. (If a smoker) pipe and tobacco or cigarettes and matches.
8. Two handkerchiefs.
9. A supply of money.
10. Bicycle (or other, means of transport as ordered) in good working order, including front and rear lamps.

All these should habitually be kept handy, ready for an emergency.

Volunteers from the Southern Railway drilling with newly delivered American P.17 rifles in August 1940. The shortage of weapons is evident from the rear rank, patiently waiting their turn

Left *Lord Swinton, far-sighted Secretary of State for Air in the crucial years 1935–8*

Centre *Air Marshal Sir Trafford Leigh-Mallory, commander of No. 12 Group in 1940 and leading offensive tactician*

Right *Air Marshal Sir Keith Park, the brilliant defensive commander of No. 11 Group in 1940*

great distinction and heavy loss. Eighteen of the fifty-eight were killed in the summer and autumn.

Coastal Command transferred some of its best fighter pilots while numbers for training at O.T.U.s were swelled by picked pilots from Bomber Command. Many aircrew under training for Army co-operation were temporarily earmarked for fighters, and a small number from Army co-operation squadrons were brought into Fighter Command in August.

Most welcome additions to the fighting ranks, apart from those from the Dominions, some Belgians and 12 French pilots, came with the fall of France when Czechs and Poles began to arrive. These men did not understand the meaning of the word surrender. They escaped from their respective countries when the Germans marched in. Most joined the French Air Force, but when France too had collapsed, undaunted they cross the Channel to continue the fight.

In the Armée de l'Air they were given poor machines to fly. Their delight on finding themselves in light blue as part of a highly efficient service knew no bounds. To be given Spitfires and Hurricanes was the answer to their dreams. Their enthusiasm had to be tempered somewhat in the early stages as they were often unused to luxuries like variable pitch propellers, retractable undercarriages and H.F. radio. There was a tendency to omit details such as the cockpit check before take-off or following exuberant aerobatics to land with the wheels up. This phase soon passed and the men of the Polish and Czech air forces proved themselves deadly opponents of the Luftwaffe as the summer months went by. By the later stages of the Battle there were five Polish and one complete Czech squadrons in Fighter Command.

In all, Poland and Czechoslovakia contributed more than 200 pilots—defeated nations that never were defeated. Belgium had capitulated, but despite this Belgian pilots in twos and threes began to arrive in Britain by various means. Some came out with the

British troops at Dunkirk while others came via Gibraltar, North Africa and the Congo.

In all 29 Belgian pilots fought in the Battle of Britain and many more were under training with the R.A.F. Nearly all the Belgians spoke English and their flying training had been good with the result that they fitted easily into Fighter Command squadrons.

America was a neutral country, but despite this there were several U.S. citizens who felt the cause strongly enough to leave homes and jobs to fight over England. They were the antithesis of the isolationists.

The U.S. Embassy in London did not look too kindly on its subjects' warlike activities, but undeterred they came in ones and twos to enlist. One such American was Pilot Officer William Fiske of No. 601 Squadron who met his death on August 18th while flying from Tangmere. An amazing trio were Pilot Officers E. G. Tobin, V. C. Keough and A. B. Maimedoff, who, after trying unsuccessfully to join the French Air Force, hitchhiked to the coast in May and caught the last ship to England from St. Jean de Luz. Having sidetracked the American Embassy's efforts to send them back across the Atlantic, the three enlisted in the R.A.F. through the good offices of a member of Parliament. 'Shorty' Keough almost failed his medical board because he was only 4 ft. 10 in. in height. He was, however, prepared for this and with the aid of two cushions showed that he could see over the edge of the cockpit although with only his eyes and helmet showing. All three were qualified pilots and after brief training they were posted to No. 609 Squadron at Warmwell, Dorset, where they participated in the tough summer fighting. In September 1940 the trio travelled to Drem, Scotland, with the honour of being the first three pilots of No. 71 Eagle Squadron. Within a year all were killed.

The cause of Dowding's desperate shortage of pilots lay in the inflexible set-up of Flying Training Command. This has been outlined in chapter three. The assessments of fighter pilot requirements on the outbreak of war

Outwardly this was a typical factory with an Oxford trainer outside. In fact both the factory and the aircraft were made of wood and canvas. This was the 'Q' or dummy site for the de Havilland factory at Hatfield, in open countryside about three miles east of the main works. There were 'Q' sites dotted all over the country for R.A.F. stations, factories, etc. Apart from imitation aircraft and hangars many had dummy runway lights to attract German night raiders

were too low and were largely based on intakes in peacetime. The effect of heavy losses was not fully considered. Because the training of a pilot took about one year, the crucial time for expansion in this respect was September 1939. Once the numbers were decided, the essential system of flying training schools and operational training units could not suddenly expand and produce trained air crew at short notice. In addition the training programme was handicapped by the severe winter of 1939-40.

Dowding fired a barrage of letters on the subject of Fighter Command strength to the Air Ministry in September and October 1939. He deprecated the policy of sending Hurricane squadrons to France and reminded the Ministry that their own estimate for home defence was fifty-two squadrons, of which only thirty-four in all states of efficiency were then available.

If the squadrons for France had been written off as a separate overseas commitment with special reserves built up and Fighter Command had been expanded to fifty-two squadrons solely for the defence of the United Kingdom, it would have had the effect of raising the flow through Training Command for the future. In this case it would have had the crisis period August–October 1940.

On May 27th, 1940, Training Command was split into Flying and Technical Training Commands. Within the former there were the additional problems of having only three Operational Training Units and a poor serviceability rate of not more than 50 per cent.* The handling of some partially trained aircrew also left much to be desired, and some peacetime pilots were

* Memorandum by Winston Churchill to Secretary of State for Air, December 14th, 1940

made to go through the whole of their primary flying syllabus again—although for no very good reason.

In July 1940 Dowding could see where the short-comings lay but there was nothing he could do about it. Apart from scraping the barrel and cutting operational training unit courses from six to three weeks he had to fight with what he possessed and no more.

The tactics of the Battle of Britain were therefore decided before it began. At all costs the force had to be kept in being. The minimum of wastage must be incurred even if it meant some raids getting through and causing damage. As long as Fighter Command was undefeated, invasion could not take place.

In May Dowding showed the Cabinet that if the losses in France were continued Fighter Command would cease to exist by the end of July. The operational research staff at Fighter Command and, in particular, Mr. H. Larnder and Dr. E. C. Williams, from then on maintained special graphs showing current state and future trends. On one side were shown strength in air-crew and aircraft and pilot and aircraft production. This represented the 'Input'. On the other side were the losses in aircraft and pilots which was the 'Output'.

These graphs showed Fighter Command's balance, the most important entries being the numbers of pilots. Throughout the Battle Dowding worked to ensure that the output did not get beyond a minimum. Whenever it was perilously close he and Park changed tactics, as occurred on August 19th when the Luftwaffe was striking at the heart of the fighter defence system and losses were rising.

Apart from the lack of pilots another factor worried Dowding continually. It was clear that pilots would be involved in combat over the sea and that they might be shot down into it. The whole question of air-sea rescue had been sadly neglected.

In August 1936 the first experimental R.A.F. high-speed rescue launch was completed and a further fifteen ordered. Before the war emphasis on the pro-vision of dinghies and other life-saving equipment favoured Bomber and Coastal commands.

On February 28th, 1939, six months before the outbreak of war, the Assistant Chief of Air Staff, Air Vice-Marshal Sholto Douglas (later Marshal of the Royal Air Force Lord Douglas), presided over a con-ference which decided to place air-sea rescue under

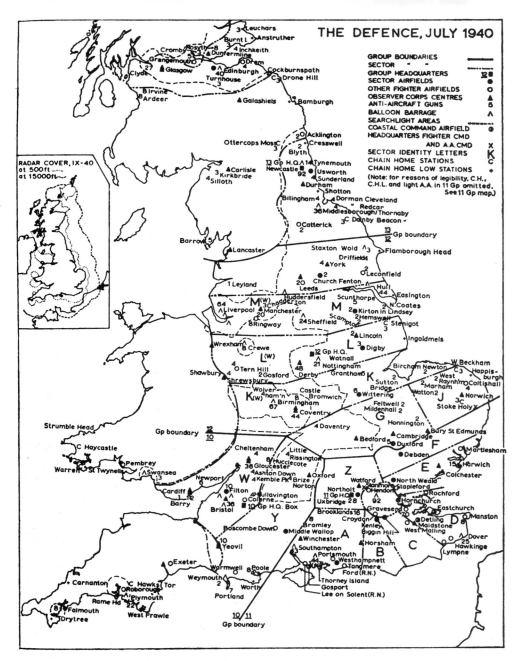

THE DEFENCE, JULY 1940

Coastal Command and acquire a further thirteen launches. The operation of rescue services in wartime was not discussed.

Thus when the Battle of Britain began in July only a skeleton rescue organisation existed with completely inadequate facilities. Fighter pilots did not have dinghies. Many were to lose their lives through drowning in the Channel and the North Sea before an expansion programme was put in hand in December 1940.

At the back of his mind Dowding kept one card in reserve about which he said little. If the losses went over the danger line and stayed there and if invasion was imminent he determined to withdraw his forces north and re-group. Much suffering and damage would undoubtedly have been caused in south England during the course of a few days by the unopposed formations of the Luftwaffe. When, however, the invasion forces struck, Fighter Command would have returned with all its force and air superiority might have been regained although at high cost to both sides. The circumstances did not arise.

As July 1940 opened, Fighter Command and the country as a whole entered on a battle for which there was no precedent in the annals of warfare. The fate of a nation and its Empire depended entirely on the outcome of a strategic conflict in the sky, with the Armies and Navies as onlookers. All the years of planning and preparation were now to be put to the test.

13   One month of grace

On the morning of June 4th, 1940, Generaloberst Milch flew his personal aircraft to Dunkirk, and surveyed the smouldering ruins left after the evacuation. He was surprised to see the enormous quantities of war material which choked the roads and the beaches. It was clear that the British Army had abandoned nearly all its tanks, guns and motor vehicles.

The rapid progress across France made by the German Army in the next ten days convinced Milch that an immediate effort should be made against Britain while the island's defences were still disorganised and the R.A.F. was in the process of re-forming.

Accordingly he went to see Göring on June 18th at command headquarters at Sovet in Belgium, whence the organisation had moved from Polch in the Eifel. France had collapsed and Paris was occupied. Milch proposed that all available paratroops and air landing forces which remained operational after the battles of Belgium and Holland should be despatched immediately to southern England. There they were to take and hold key fighter airfields such as Manston and Hawkinge and be reinforced by normal troops taken over by air in second or third waves.

Stuka formations were to provide the artillery support and both Stukas and Me 109s were to be operated from the airfields as soon as they had been cleared. While Ju 52s maintained supplies of ammunition, fuel and food German ground troops were to be ferried across the Channel in any and every available ship. Milch envisaged that Luftflotten 2 and 3 would transfer the whole of their effort from the French front to the British coast.

The plan involved considerable risk, but it might have succeeded. At that time British ground defence was almost non-existent. At the worst, the troops would be lost, but such would have been the confusion and destruction in Britain that the air war might have been won in 1940. The start of widespread air attack in mid-June would have allowed no rest for Fighter Command and an extra month's good weather for the Luftwaffe.

Göring's reaction was one of blank amazement and he described Milch's suggestions as 'nonsense'. Putting such unpleasant thoughts out of his mind he prepared to enjoy the pleasures of Paris in the early summer. One of the most unusual opportunities in German military history had been thrown away.

To the British public the failure of hordes of German paratroops, fifth columnists and waves of black-crossed bombers to arrive came as a distinct surprise. For nearly 900 years the 'sea-girt isle' had been inviolate. Now a powerful enemy was on the doorstep and from the Army point of view the country was naked on the ground. There were not even enough rifles to equip regular troops let alone the newly formed Local Defence Volunteers. Only the Royal Air Force and the Royal Navy remained to challenge Hitler's might.

The assault was awaited hourly but none came. For over a month, apart from a few night raids, the Luftwaffe stayed away. The sea-borne landing preparations were not completed until September, then to be shelved permanently.

In June 1940 it seemed to Germany and to many in authority in neutral countries that the sun was setting on Britain and her Empire and that the end was only a matter of time. Apart from poor intelligence services the German Government suffered from a complete lack of knowledge of the British way of life and character. This was to cost them dear. Neither Göring nor Hitler had been to the United Kingdom and they did not speak English. While *Mein Kampf* and other inter-war documents showed a marked respect on the Führer's part for the British nation, his regard for its military potential deteriorated rapidly from the time of the Munich crisis. Chamberlain's performance in 1939 and a great deal of pacifist oratory and scribbling led him to believe that the vitality and morale of the British had been undermined.

His view of the island race was further distorted by an extraordinary clique which vigorously campaigned for friendship with Germany before 1939. The British Union of Fascists were loud in voice but few in number. Nevertheless their activities, coupled with those of a small hybrid set of discountenanced and overtaxed aristocracy known as 'the Link', were constantly brought to Hitler's attention by Ribbentrop, the German Foreign Minister. After the outbreak of war the Link was disbanded as an agency of enemy propaganda.

Having no personal knowledge, Hitler came to believe that Britain was still run by aristocracy on a feudal system and that the legally elected House of Commons was in constant danger of being overthrown. He and other members of the party, in particular Rudolf Hess, cultivated the friendship of a certain class of English people, whom they believed held the ultimate reins of Government and would have direct access to the Royal Family. The Nazi party tended to be overawed by titles.

After his visit to England in 1937 General Milch spent two hours with Hitler discussing British war potential and Anglo-German relations. Göring could not be bothered even to look through Milch's reports when they were submitted and did not discuss the R.A.F. with him. Milch was quite certain that the Empire would provide a formidable enemy and that rearmament was well under way. He warned the Führer against underestimating the British and told him that Ribbentrop was the worst possible person to be associated with the British Government. He said: 'If you don't get rid of him now, you will have trouble with England'.

At the time Hitler agreed but nothing was done. Ribbentrop and others continued to foster dissident elements in London, and to believe in them.

In the summer of 1939 a new political party was formed known as the British People's Party. The chairman and a founder member was no less than the Marquess of Tavistock later 12th Duke of Bedford. His associate was Mr. Benjamin Greene, who had for two years been a member of the British Union of Fascists. In a by-election at Hythe the party put up a candidate, Mr. Harry St. John Philby. He lost his deposit but the proceedings did not go unnoticed in Berlin.

After September 3rd, 1936, Tavistock joined the new organisation calling itself 'The British Council for Christian Settlement in Europe'. This had Mr. John Beckett as its secretary and included among its members Captain Gordon Canning, a former member of the Link. A first-class row blew up in Parliament over the new organisation, and many people connected with it were to spend most of the war in Brixton Prison under Section 18 of the Defence Regulations.

While the activities of the various Fascist and pro-Fascist organisations scarcely rippled the surface of the average Englishman's life in the years before 1940, to the German Government they formed part of a definite pattern. This was thrown into sharp relief at the end of 1939 by a one-man peace offensive launched by the Marquess himself. Through an acquaintance who lived in Belfast, he was put in touch with the German Legation in Dublin.

The Legation, on orders from Berlin, propounded a wonderful case which led him to believe that the German Government was prepared to allow Poland and Czechoslovakia full independence provided they remained neutral. Germany would disarm if other major powers would do the same, and she would join a 'reformed' League of Nations. The Germans also expressed themselves ready to hold a plebiscite in Austria and to co-operate to find a national home for the Jews provided former German colonies were returned. The Marquess of Tavistock passed on this information to Lord Halifax, who described his action as 'irregular' but eventually gave him permission to visit Dublin to discover if the terms were authentic.

This the Marquess did in February 1940. The Germans were by now extremely evasive because final preparations were already in hand for the assault on Norway, France and the Low Countries. They ultimately repudiated the so-called 'peace plan'.

The whole affair was released to the Press by an M.P., which caused a further political storm. It is clear that the Marquess was acting misguidedly but true to his opinions. The outcome for Berlin, however, was to stimulate the hallucination of British decadence.

After Dunkirk, when practically all channels of reliable information about Britain dried up, the myth of a widespread movement to oust Churchill and the Government coupled with rumours of general unrest and panic obsessed Hitler and his associates. More fuel was added to this fire by the ever-watchful British secret service, which deliberately allowed certain elements to continue sending messages of the right type through neutral embassies and via Dublin.

On June 19th and 23rd the German Foreign Office noted that according to Swedish sources certain authoritative circles in London were prepared to come to terms. The naval staff war diary on July 21st recorded that there seemed to be a strong group in England who wished to know armistice terms. Winston Churchill's pugnacity damped German hopes but they still looked for a change of heart. This was clearly shown in Hitler's speech to the Reichstag on July 19th in which he launched once again 'an appeal for reason'. He followed it up with a shower of speech reprints from Luftwaffe aircraft at the beginning of August which served only to give as much amusement to English householders as doubtless had the R.A.F. 'bombphlet' raids to the German hausfrau in 1939.

The four German radio stations set up in Europe to simulate an underground radio network in Britain also took up the internal strife theme with great gusto and appealed to non-existent workers' cells and revolutionary organisations. Even Lieutenant-Colonel von Lossberg, an army officer attached to the O.K.W., has recorded that a revolution in Britain was seriously anticipated by Hitler.

Despite everything, the myth still held sway in September when, on the 19th, Ribbentrop informed the Italians in Rome that 'English territorial defence does not exist. One German division will be sufficient to bring about complete collapse.'

It is remarkable that the mutterings and machinations of a few misguided British people and some pro-Fascists, when combined with German misconceptions, should have materially contributed to the invaluable breathing-space which Britain gained in June and July 1940. For one month Dowding was allowed freedom to rest and reorganise his tired squadrons, bring forward more pilots, build up aircraft reserves and extend his control and reporting network. For the country as a whole the respite was even longer. From the beginning of June until mid-August the work of building up vital ground defences, re-equipping Army divisions and increasing war production went on almost unhindered.

Hitler, believing that Britain would sue for an armistice, decided to finish France immediately after Dunkirk. Accordingly, his main forces were switched to the area between the Somme and the Aisne. The decisive battle opened on June 9th, and by the 14th Paris had fallen. On the 17th the Pétain Government asked for terms and the historic railway carriage at Compiègne was used for the signing of the armistice as it had been by the Allied victors in 1918. From June 22nd to 29th Hitler went sightseeing in France

The Luftwaffe during June/July reorganised in France at leisurely pace, occupying and extending French airfields and bringing in munitions and supplies. The wrecks of French Air Force machines were pushed into heaps to make way for German aircraft. This Potez 63 lies wrecked from German fire, while in the background an Me 109 unit has moved in, its personnel being housed in tents

and the O.K.W. free-wheeled for the period. This was an extraordinary procedure if a swift end to the war was to be brought about by military means.

Following a somewhat nebulous directive from the Führer on May 26th which granted 'unlimited freedom of action' to the Luftwaffe to attack England when suitable strength had been built up, preliminary planning for an air assault began.

Five days after the conclusion of the Franco-German Armistice, on June 30th, 1940, Göring issued a general order regarding the air war against the island fortress. In it he stated:

The Luftwaffe war command in the fight against England makes it necessary to co-ordinate as closely as possible, with respect to time and targets, the attacks of Luftflotten 2, 3 and 5. Distribution of duties to the Luftflotten will, therefore, in general be tied to firm targets and firm dates of attack so that not only can the most effective results on important targets be achieved but the well-developed defence forces of the enemy can be split and be faced with the maximum forms of attack.

After the original disposition of the forces has been carried out in its new operational areas, that is after making sure of adequate anti-aircraft and fighter defence, adequate provisioning and an absolutely trouble-free train of command, then a planned offensive against selected targets can be put in motion to fit in with the overall requirements of the commanders-in-chief of the Luftwaffe.

To save us time as well as ensuring that the forces concerned are ready:

(A) The war against England is to be restricted to destructive attacks against industry and air force targets which have weak defensive forces. These attacks under suitable weather conditions, which should allow for surprise, can be carried out individually or in groups by day. The most thorough study of the target and its surrounding area from the map and the parts of the target concerned, that is the vital points of the target, is a pre-requisite for success. It is also stressed that every effort should be made to avoid unnecessary loss of life amongst the civil population.

(B) By means of reconnaissance and the engagement of units of smaller size it should be possible to draw out smaller enemy formations and by this means to ascertain the strength and grouping of the enemy defences. The engagement of the Luftwaffe after the initial attacks have been carried out and after all forces are completely battleworthy has for its objectives:

(a) by attacking the enemy air force, its ground organisations, and its own industry to provide the necessary conditions for a satisfactory overall war against enemy imports, provisions and defence economy, and at the same time provide the necessary protection for those territories occupied by ourselves;

(b) by attacking importing harbours and their installations, importing transports and warships to destroy the English system of replenishment. Both tasks must be carried out separately, but must be carried out in co-ordination one with another.

As long as the enemy air force is not defeated the prime requirement for the air war is to attack the enemy air force on every possible opportunity by day or by night, in the air or on the ground, without consideration of other tasks.

This, therefore, was to be the German plan of campaign: build up the airfields and facilities in France, Belgium and Holland; sound out the defences by using fighters with small bomber formations and then throw the full weight of the Luftwaffe into the destruction of the R.A.F. and its resources including the aircraft industry. Harbours and similar installations were to be attacked simultaneously to cut off vital imports from abroad.

It was a far too ambitious programme for an air force

On the French coast at Wissant, in late July, the German forces installed a Freya radar station shown here on the cliffs. Instead of being used for fighter direction, however, this Freya was restricted to detecting and reporting shipping along the British coast

designed for continental warfare with armies on the move and now faced with a resolute and well-equipped foe. The pattern was to be exactly as in Poland, Belgium, Holland and France—the destruction of the enemy air force at the outset in the air and on the ground.

It is noteworthy that the orders contain none of the sense of urgency which characterised similar documents in earlier campaigns. The Chief of the Army General Staff, Halder, noted on June 22nd: 'The near future will show whether Britain will do the reasonable thing in the light of our victories.'

Göring believed that Britain would sue for peace or be forced to capitulate by air attack. He took little interest in various invasion study papers which were placed before Hitler by the Army chiefs on June 26th.
. He had, however, misjudged the Führer's intentions as became evident on July 2nd when Hitler issued his first brief directive for the invasion of England and called for intensive staff planning and research at High Command level. From this date Göring found that while his prime object, the destruction of the R.A.F., was still at the top of the list, his planning and target selection had to be co-ordinated with the invasion requirements of the Army and Navy.

At this point it is necessary to stress that Germany had every intention of invading if Britain did not sue for peace.

Since the war historians on the Continent have made strenuous efforts to belittle the whole German invasion scheme and suggest that there was no real intention of carrying it out.

If, as has been postulated, the Sealion invasion plan was purely an exercise to frighten and put pressure on Britain, then it must surely have been the most expensive exercise ever.

Whole armies were re-trained and special equipment of all kinds was purchased, while coastal and barge traffic in northern Europe was disorganised for months with very adverse effects on the German economy.

The overall strategic plan was simple. Once Fighter Command had been defeated, the Luftwaffe could overcome the superior strength of the Royal Navy in the Channel. The slow trains of barges etc. would then have faced only the British Army and coastal defences. Once through these, with one or two airfields occupied, then the Luftwaffe could operate from British soil and range far and wide over the country.

Without Fighter Command, R.A.F. bombers would have been assailed over the bridgehead by the full weight of the German fighter forces with inevitable results.

Any half-heartedness evident in German records, particularly those of the naval staff, stemmed only from realisation that invasion could not be launched until Fighter and Bomber commands had been smashed. General Galland, in a post-war article in *Forces Aériennes Francaises*, correctly summarised the situation:

Time was required to complete invasion preparations, especially by the navy. The Luftwaffe was to make good use of this breathing-space by carrying out independent offensive operations aimed at securing air superiority. Though there was no deviation from the original purpose of invading Britain, the nature of operations began gradually to shift the emphasis to the strategic mission of the Luftwaffe.

In an enlightening lecture on the air war against Britain 1940–3, given at Gatow, Berlin, on February 2nd, 1944, Hauptmann Otto Bechtle stated: 'After the western campaign had been successfully concluded, the aim of the German High Command was a speedy decision in the war against Britain. This it hoped to achieve by an invasion of Britain which was to be preceded by German mastery of the air over the British Isles . . . The invasion was scheduled to take place four weeks after the start of planned air attacks against the mainland of Britain.'

The whole position is very well summed up in a German official study of British air defences in 1940–41. It states:

After the victorious conclusion of June 25th, 1940, of the campaign against France, it was the intention of the German General Staff to force a swift defeat on the British by a landing on the mainland of Britain.

Despite the fact that, because of Britain's insular position, the operations that followed met with greater difficulties than on the Continent, the strategic setting of targets was the same as in the previous campaigns. In their attack, the aim of the Luftwaffe was above all to crush the Royal Air Force.

As long as Britain, protected by her Navy, was able to supplement and even to reinforce her power from overseas, the geo-political principle of the protective power of an insular position remained valid; as a sea power, Britain could only be defeated at sea.

But to do this, the German naval forces were inadequate . . .

Thus the only possibility open was to get the British bases into German hands. In these circumstances the German High

A Dornier 17Z bomber of Stab/KG3 being prepared for operations over France in May 1940

Command had to decide to attack the British mainland; for this purpose, they had first to achieve air supriority.

In its conclusions the study notes:

It was unavoidable that the operations of the Army and the Luftwaffe could not be combined. The weaknesses resulting from the operations on the Continent were known to the German High Command. They had to be overcome if Britain was to be defeated. If the wresting of air superiority from the enemy was the first condition for the success of the landing, then the commencement of Army operations could not and dared not coincide with those of the Luftwaffe.

Bearing in mind the effects of Luftwaffe successes in all the campaigns to date and the decisive outcome of the attacks on cities like Warsaw and Rotterdam, Hitler and Göring both felt that air power alone might suffice against Britain. Hitler put the invasion plans in train to provide the finale while Göring was so blinded by success that he was certain a few days of Luftwaffe attacks would see Britain on her knees.

Hitler's determination in July to carry out the invasion is evinced by the opening gambit to his 'Directive No. 16, Preparations for a Landing Operation Against England', issued on July 16th, 1940:

As England, despite her hopeless military situation, still shows no sign of willingness to come to terms, I have decided to prepare, and if necessary to carry out, a landing operation against her.

The aim of this operation is to eliminate the English mother-land as a base from which war against Germany can be continued and, if necessary, to occupy the country completely

While the willingness to mount an invasion was amply in evidence it entirely depended on the substitution of air supremacy for sea supremacy. General Jodl said in Munich in November 1945: 'The landing in England, prepared down to the smallest detail, could not be attempted before the British air arm was completely beaten.'

The growing emphasis on invasion began to show itself in the Luftwaffe's plans early in July. On the 11th the O.K.L. Operations Staff issued its first directive concerning 'Intensive Air War Against England'. This gave orders for preliminary attacks on shipping, particularly in the Channel, and for raids on a limited number of specified places. Detailed planning on large-scale raids and crew briefing on targets was also initiated but no fixed date was given for the commencement of the main assault.

That night Göring gave a party at Karinhall, where Milch and the senior commanders were entertained to an after-dinner speech outlining the preparation for and fulfilment of the operations against England. As he had stated on June 30th, three Luftflotten (2, 3 and 5) were to take part.

From July 11th to July 21st the Luftflotten staffs worked out their plans for a concentrated attack but these had to be modified after the first week when Hitler's 'Directive No. 16' was issued. In this the Luftwaffe, in addition to its role as destroyer of the R.A.F. with its bases and production plants, was required to prevent air intervention in the invasion. It was also to attack British naval forces at their home bases even up to the north of Scotland, overcome coastal defences, break the resistance of ground troops, annihilate advancing reserves and destroy lines of transport.

While the probing in strength of British defences and attacks on Channel shipping began on July 10th in accordance with Göring's orders, planning for the major air attack did not begin until July 21st. This was the day following the creation of eight army and four Luftwaffe field marshals and the announcement of the one and only rank of Reichsmarschall for Göring himself.

On July 21st Milch, Kesselring, Sperrle and Stumpff, together with their Fliegerkorps commanders, assembled at Karinhall to hear Göring's further requirements for the 'Air War Against England'. He outlined once more the basic principles. There were, however, two amendments to his original orders of July 11th, and both were directly connected with the invasion plans. Wherever possible the British Fleet was to be attacked and harbours like Portsmouth were to be rendered unusable as bases from which Royal Navy units might interfere with the invasion fleet.

Certain quay and harbour installations on the south coast originally scheduled for attack were to be deleted from the plan because they would be required by the landing troops. Fliegerdivision IX, which specialised in mine-laying and anti-shipping attack, was ordered not to drop mines on the south coast which might later affect the barges and steamers in Operation Seelöwe (Sealion).

The operations staffs of Luftflotten 2, 3 and 5 were then told to proceed with the first plans for a concentrated assault. The spheres of operation were divided as follows: Luftflotte 2 was to attack targets in the area east of a line from Selsey Bill to Oxford, Birmingham–Manchester and Carlisle, while Luftflotte 3 dealt with all targets west of that line. Luftflotte 5 was to cover a small area bounded roughly by the Humber estuary, the Scottish border and the Lancashire border east of Lancaster.

The planning was not easy. There were too many conflicting requirements and a complete lack of any well-prepared long-term policy for the conduct of aerial warfare against Britain. *Studie Blau* was valuable but as it resembled an encyclopaedia of Britain it gave no idea of how a strategic attack by three Luftflotten should be developed.

The only real study of Britain that had been made was by Luftflotte 2 in 1938 and 1939. Before the annexation of Austria, the threatening attitude of Britain and France led to a directive from the O.K.L. on February 18th, 1938. This was a 'Preliminary Orientation' regarding air war across the Channel. The emphasis was on raids on London and air bases in eastern England because only airfields in west Germany could then be used.

After the Austrian union, the political temperature cooled slightly until the Sudetenland crisis in the summer. On August 23rd the Luftwaffe Chief of Air Staff warned Luftflotte 2 to be prepared to operate three or four bomber Geschwader against England if the Sudetenland situation, known to the Germans as 'Fall Grün' or Green Case, should spark off a war.

General Felmy, then commander-in-chief of Luftflotte 2, submitted a personal paper on the subject on September 22nd, 1938. Felmy concluded that while his command was in no state to achieve decisive results the best targets would be the air armaments industry, the fleet, harbours and merchant ships. These were, in fact, the targets chosen for 1940.

With the Sudetenland crisis passed, the growth of British air rearmament led to the plan by Hitler for a five-fold increase in Luftwaffe strength. This, however, never materialised. Included in this 'Concentrated Aircraft type Programme' were no less than thirteen Geschwader for anti-shipping work. Dearly would the German Air Force have wished to see such a well-trained force available in 1940.

In 'Planstudie 1939', which was issued in February 1939 and outlined Luftwaffe policy for the year, Part 3 dealt with operations against the west. Luftflotte 2 was again responsible for action against Britain. This came under the heading of 'Fall Blau' (Blue Case). The theories were put into training practice in a five-day exercise in May 1939 when simulated raids were made over the North Sea. Some units came within a few miles of the east coast of England, causing considerable excitement at east coast radar stations. In the exercise report produced on May 13th, 1939, it was concluded that Luftflotte 2 was in no position to force a speedy decision on England because of its equipment, training and strength; in particular 'there were not enough aircraft to cope with the large number of targets and the wide area of the theatre of operations'.

General Geisler, the General z.b.V. (special duties general) seconded to Luftflotte 2 in the spring of 1939, examined all the major objectives and problems concerned with war against Britain including the results of the May exercises. His ideas as to objectives (report dated August 7th, 1939) undoubtedly formed the basis for the staff plans in 1940. These were as follows:

1 Gain air superiority.
2 Cripple the British war economy.
3 Cut off shipping.
4 Inflict serious damage on the British fleet.
5 Successfully attack British military transports to the Continent and threaten or carry out an invasion.

While the Luftwaffe took due note of the aims in Geisler's report they ignored his conclusions. These, based on estimates of strength, training and efficiency, were that only partial success could be achieved against Britain in 1940. The Luftwaffe would not become a threat until the second year and then only if 'available forces were strictly concentrated, operations were conducted flexibly and *for a considerable length of time* with gradually increased forces'.

From the outset the Luftflotten produced their own plans of campaign for their areas and submitted them separately. No overall programme was submitted by all three and agreed. Here the merit of the R.A.F. system of division into commands according to function became apparent.

The main Luftflotten (2 and 3) completed their basic studies by July 25th. Their views were received

Adolf Hitler in June 1940 with a group of the airborne troops who captured the Belgian forts at Eben-Emael in a surprise attack on May 10th

by the air force command staff four days later, an indication of the leisurely pace of the whole operation. There were marked divergences of opinion between Kesselring and Sperrle on methods to be adopted and on target selection. These were promptly criticised by the High Command.

While Sperrle was confident about operations against the R.A.F. he wanted maximum effort against ports and supplies, Kesselring at first believed that likely Luftwaffe losses in material and prestige would have far-reaching effects. He preferred to retain the cloak of invincibility covering the German Air Force and instead of mounting a frontal assault, to concentrate on the periphery of the British Isles and to isolate the Mediterranean theatre by smashing Gibraltar. Forced into a corner by the High Command, Kesselring advocated maximum strength over a few given targets instead of dissipating the Luftflotten over a wide area.

After the initial reports the Luftflotten were ordered to revise sections of their studies. On August 1st they were re-submitted to Göring, who made amendments but accepted the documents in principle on the same day.

Luftflotte 2 was not particularly happy about the alterations in its plan of attack. It had originally proposed that London should be the main target to draw the British fighter forces into battle over one vital point as it was thought. Hitler at that time forbade any attacks on London and therefore the main assault was redirected at airfields and military targets in southern England. This would have been Luftflotte 2's second phase in the Battle if their plans had been accepted.

Fliegerkorps II, particularly its Chief of Staff General Paul Deichmann, recognised that the limited range of the Me 109 restricted its escort role to airfield attacks as far north as outer London. He supposed that British fighters would be withdrawn to more northern bases without air superiority having been gained. In fact the argument for attacking London was fallacious as it could only assist in concentrating the forces of Nos. 11 and 12 Groups against large and unwieldy Luftwaffe formations. Throughout the planning and the battle the morale of Londoners and the hopelessness of trying to destroy such an enormous city with the bombs and bombers then available was completely underestimated.

Hitler and his newly promoted commanders after the Battle of France had ended. From left to right: Feldmarschall Milch (Inspector General), Feldmarschall Sperrle (C.-in-C. Luftflotte 3), Adolf Hitler, Reichsmarschall Göring and Feldmarschall Kesselring (C.-in-C. Luftflotte 2)

Having resolved that the battle would be fought in accordance with Göring's original directives, the Führer, on August 1st, 1940, issued his top secret Directive No. 17 for the carrying out of air and naval warfare against England. Ten copies of this document were issued. In it Hitler stated:

To produce the necessary conditions for the reduction of England I consider that the air and sea war against the English motherland must be carried out more firmly than previously. Therefore I order the following: (1) The German Air Forces must with all means in their power and as quickly as possible destroy the English air force. The attacks must in the first instance be directed against flying formations, their ground organisations, and their supply organisations, in the second against the aircraft production industry and the industries engaged in production of anti-aircraft equipment. (2) After achieving air superiority in terms of time and of area the air war should be continued against harbours, especially those which are engaged in the provision of food supplies and also against the installation for food supplies in the heart of the country.

Attacks carried out against harbours on the south coast must bear in mind the future operations that we may wish to carry out and therefore be restricted to the minimum. (3) The war against enemy warships and merchant ships must, however, take second place from the air war point of view so far as it does not concern particularly attractive opportunity targets or so far as it is not an additional bonus to the attacks carried out under paragraph 2 above, or where it is used for training of crews for specialised future tasks. (4) The increased air war is to be carried out so that the air force can support naval operations on satisfactory opportunity targets with sufficient forces as and when necessary. Additionally it must remain battle-worthy for Operation Sealion. (5) Terror raids as revenge I reserve the right to order myself. (6) The strengthening of the air war can start from 5th August. The starting point is to be decided by the air force itself after completion of preparations and bearing in mind weather conditions. The navy will also at the same time carry out an increased scope of operations at sea from the same date.

Receipt of Directive No. 17 by the Luftwaffe High Command gave the green light for orders to the three Luftflotten to be issued on August 2nd. These took the form of a Directive for 'Adlerangriff' or 'The Attack of the Eagles' but no date for 'Adler Tag' or 'Eagle Day' was given. The O.K.W. intention was that battle should begin twelve hours after the Führer's orders, that is twelve hours after the issue of Order No. 17.

Göring, however, appears to have misinterpreted Hitler's intentions in that he thought about eight days should be allowed for final preparations. Adler Tag should have been on August 2nd or 3rd, but arguments were still going on between Kesselring and Sperrle on the strength and composition of raids on various targets, the heights to be flown and the question of escorts. Göring himself seems to have been a little confused over the problems of integrating a strategic air war with the needs for invasion support. It had been made plain to him on August 2nd that Hitler intended to carry through the Seelöwe invasion plans, if necessary four weeks after the beginning of the air war. The Luftwaffe was to provide the full support which was forthcoming in earlier campaigns. To clear the air, and probably his own mind, he called a small conference of senior officers including Milch on August 3rd at Karinhall.

The difficulties were finally sorted out by August 6th and on that day Milch, Sperrle, Stumpff and others were called again to Karinhall for the final analysis on Adlerangriff. No date could be agreed as weather conditions were then unfavourable. Later August 10th was selected as Adler Tag but this was postponed from day to day and from hour to hour until finally fixed for the morning of August 13th.

While the operational staff was endeavouring to produce some cohesive overall plans, the process of building up the Luftwaffe in the newly occupied countries was proceeding leisurely. After France fell large numbers of air and ground crew were granted leave in Germany and much time was spent in organising the great victory parade on the Champs Elysées set for July 18th.

Among the rank and file the rumour was that the war was nearly over and that Britain would sue for peace any day. The knowledge that some soldiers were being demobilised heightened the effect.

Only very gradually were the forces built up along the coast facing England. In many cases elaborate preparations were made at new sites including the construction of railway sidings into airfields. In the months of May and June 1940 the Luftwaffe lost 1,469 aircraft on operations although a large percentage of these were due to flying accidents and other causes. Bomber strength was reduced from 1,002 operational planes on March 30th, 1940, to 841 on June 29th.

The losses were not as high as had been anticipated, but German production was still in low gear and the reserves were drawn on heavily to bring units back to strength. Of aircrew there was no shortage. The flying schools were turning out a steady stream and large numbers of P.O.W.s released during the May/June campaigns returned to their units.

The two air fleets in the west extended their boundaries from Germany across France to the mouth of the Seine. Luftflotte 2 established main H.Q. at Brussels with advanced H.Q. at Cap Gris Nez opposite Dover and Luftflotte 3 had its main H.Q. at Paris with advanced H.Q. at Deauville. The general layout of the Fliegerkorps remained as for the Battle of France except that Fliegerkorps IV was transferred to Luftflotte 3 to carry out its anti-shipping work in the Western approaches and its place in Luftflotte 2 was taken by Fliegerkorps II.

German total first-line strength deployed against Britain on August 10th, 1940, was 3,358 aircraft of which 2,550 were serviceable. The latter figure covered 80 close and 71 long-range reconnaissance aircraft, 998 bombers, 261 Stukas, 31 ground attack machines, 224 twin-engined fighters, 805 single-engined fighters, and 80 coastal reconnaissance aircraft. The total strength of the Luftwaffe in all countries on August 13th was 4,632 of which an average of 3,306 were serviceable.

In addition to these forces there were sundry night fighters and transport aircraft.

The only alteration made to the normal command structure for Adlerangriff was the grouping of fighters in Luftflotten 2 and 3 into tactical fighter commands called Jagdfliegerführer, or Jafu for short. Jafus 2 and 3 in Luftflotten 2 and 3 respectively exercised some independence in their operational planning but were without any radar or radio close control. This resulted in their autonomy being rendered useless as briefings on the ground often bore no relation to the tactical battles that developed.

General Martini's service set up listening stations along the Dutch, Belgian, Danish and French coasts, while engineers of the Luftwaffe signals and the German Post Office began to rig transmitters to jam British radar, although ineffectively because the valves available gave insufficient power for the ranges involved.

A few Freya radars were erected along the coast but they did not fit in with any adequate operational network. They had a range of seventy-five miles and gave bearing and elevation but no altitude information. Particular use was to be made of the Freya transferred in late July from Dieppe to Wissant in the Pas de Calais. This instrument, however, was concentrated on shipping watch and had no function as a fighter director station.

13 GROUP
HEADQUARTERS NEWCASTLE

Wick
3	Hurricane	Wick
504	Hurricane	Castletown

Dyce
603	Spitfire	Dyce (A Flight)
603	Spitfire	Montrose (B Flight)

Turnhouse
141	Defiant	Turnhouse
245	Hurricane	Turnhouse (operational by day only)
602	Spitfire	Drem

Usworth
152	Spitfire	Acklington
72	Spitfire	Acklington

Catterick
41	Spitfire	Catterick
219	Blenheim	Catterick

Church Fenton
249	Hurricane	Church Fenton (operational by day only)
616	Spitfire	Leconfield

12 GROUP
HEADQUARTERS WATNALL

Kirton-in-Lindsey
253	Hurricane	Kirton-in-Lindsey
222	Spitfire	Kirton-in-Lindsey

Digby
29	Blenheim	Digby
611	Spitfire	Digby
46	Hurricane	Digby
266	Spitfire	Digby

Coltishall
66	Spitfire	Coltishall
242	Hurricane	Coltishall

Wittering
23	Blenheim	Wittering
229	Hurricane	Wittering

Duxford
19	Spitfire	Duxford
264	Defiant	Duxford

Debden
85	Hurricane	Debden (B Flight)
85	Hurricane	Martlesham (A Flight)
17	Hurricane	Debden

11 GROUP
HEADQUARTERS UXBRIDGE

North Weald
56	Hurricane	North Weald
25	Blenheim	Martlesham (1 Flight)
25	Blenheim	North Weald (1 Section)
151	Hurricane	North Weald

Hornchurch
65	Spitfire	Hornchurch
74	Spitfire	Hornchurch
54	Spitfire	Rochford

Biggin Hill
600	Blenheim	Biggin Hill
79	Hurricane	Hawkinge
610	Spitfire	Biggin Hill
32	Hurricane	Biggin Hill
604	Blenheim	Gravesend

Kenley
64	Spitfire	Kenley
615	Hurricane	Kenley
111	Hurricane	Croydon

Northolt
1	Hurricane	Northolt
257	Hurricane	Northolt (operational by day only)

Tangmere
43	Hurricane	Tangmere
145	Hurricane	Tangmere
601	Hurricane	Tangmere
F.I.U. Flight Blenheim, Tangmere		

Filton*
87	Hurricane	Exeter
213	Hurricane	Exeter
92	Spitfire	Pembrey
234	Spitfire	St. Eval (1 Section at Hullavington)

Middle Wallop*
501	Hurricane	Middle Wallop
238	Hurricane	Middle Wallop (operational by day only)
609	Spitfire	Warmwell

* These sectors transferred to the operational control of No. 10 Group at Box, Wiltshire, at twelve noon on July 18th. Sector stations in italic

14 First phase—July 10th–August 7th

With France out of the war, Britain in July 1940 no longer had thoughts for anything but her immediate defence against an almost certain assault. Anything that could help to hinder the success of an attack had to be turned into a weapon. Barbed wire and minefields were planted around the south coast, trenches were dug behind them, civilians drew Home Guard uniforms, armed themselves with pikes and pitchforks and set about erecting obstructions on every field a glider could use. On the aircraft industry's airfields old cars salvaged from the unlikeliest rubbish-heaps lined the runways ready to be rolled into the paths of invading aircraft.

At Fighter Command attention had been focused on building up the squadrons. Before Dunkirk the pilot strength of most averaged about seventeen; by the second week in June they had about twenty.

Simultaneously the tasks fighter pilots were called upon to do were amplified; they were not merely to repulse raids levelled at the coasts of Britain, they were to fly special patrols over occupied areas of Belgium and France, and even to reconnoitre the continental coasts by day.

By June 30th Göring had detailed the preparatory work the Luftwaffe would have to undertake to fulfil the Nazis' objectives against England.

Two Fliegerkorps were assigned to establish air superiority over the Channel and close it to British shipping: General Lörzer's II Fliegerkorps based on the Pas de Calais and General Richthofen's VIII Fliegerkorps near Le Havre.

Clearing the Straits of Dover seemed such a simple task that Lörzer did not consider it necessary to commit his whole force. A small battle group under Johannes Fink, Kommodore of the Do 17-equipped Kampf-geschwader 2 based at Arras, was accordingly given the job.

In addition to the Dornier bombers, Fink had at his disposal two Stuka Gruppen and two Me 109 Jagdgesch-wader based on the Pas de Calais. The fighter component was distinguished by the fact that JG26 was led by Major Adolf Galland and JG53 by Major Werner Molders.

The battle group numbered in all about seventy-five bombers, sixty or more Stukas and about 200 fighters. To achieve air superiority over the English Channel Fink was given the impressive title of Kanal-kampführer, or Channel Battle Leader.

Fink established his command post in an old bus near a statue of Louis Blériot erected to commemorate the pioneer's conquest of the Channel in 1909. It stood on top of the cliffs at Cap Blanc Nez and from its windows Fink could follow the progress of his units. In good visibility he could watch the British through powerful binoculars.

Among the first officers to be sent to the Calais area that June was General Major Kurt von Döring. He also set up headquarters on the cliffs near Wissant with a W/T station. One of von Döring's other assignments was to supervise the installation of a maritime radar observation system—Freya—but it was not until the end of July that it came into operation on the cliffs of Wissant to detect Channel shipping.

Richthofen did not dispose of any twin-engined bombers but his Stukas, supported by fighters, were presumed to be capable of establishing air superiority and clearing shipping from the area between Portsmouth and Portland.

On July 2nd the German Air Force Supreme Command issued instructions for the campaign against Britain. By the following day the effect was apparent. Small groups of bombers, covered from above by roving fighter patrols, were out hunting for ships.

On July 3rd a Dornier suddenly dived out of cloud and attacked No 13 EFTS at Maidenhead. One man was killed and half a dozen injured, while six Tiger Moths were destroyed and twenty-five damaged.

On the 4th twenty Ju 88s bombed Portland and two enemy aircraft penetrated as far as Bristol—one of these being shot down by 92 squadron from Pembrey.

One pilot of 601 squadron shot down a Dornier 17 on July 7th and reported that when about 100 yards from the bomber some 20 metal boxes, about 9 inches cube and attached to wires, were thrown out behind. The fighter was hit by the boxes, but remained service-able.

The Luftwaffe's first few incursions over the Channel made it clear that the British radar network was not able to pick up the German aircraft soon enough for the defending fighters to intercept. From July 4th a flight from each R.A.F. sector station was dispatched to operate from its forward landing grounds.

On July 8th Flying Officer Desmond McMullen leading a section of three No. 54 Squadron Spitfires ran into trouble tackling a formation of Me 110s which crossed the coast at Dungeness. The Spitfires were about to intercept when they were attacked from above by Me 109s.

Two of the Spitfires were shot down and the third was damaged. There were no casualties, but one pilot,

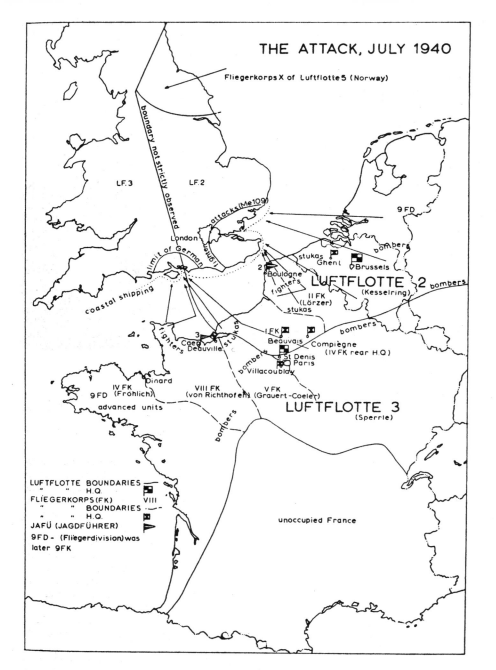

THE ATTACK, JULY 1940

Fliegerkorps X of Luftflotte 5 (Norway)

boundary not strictly observed

LF.3   LF.2

9 FD

limit of German fighter attacks (Me 109)

London

bombers

stukas   Ghent   Brussels

coastal shipping   2   Boulogne   fighters   LUFTFLOTTE 2   bombers
(Kesselring)

II FK
(Lörzer)
stukas

I FK   bombers

3   Caen   Beauvais
fighters   Deauville stukas   Compiègne
(IV FK rear H.Q.)

bombers   St Denis   Paris
Villacoublay

Dinard

9 FD   IV FK   VIII FK   V FK
(Fröhlich)   (von Richthofen) (Grauert-Coeler)   LUFTFLOTTE 3
advanced units   (Sperrle)

bombers

LUFTFLOTTE BOUNDARIES
"   "   H.Q.
FLIEGERKORPS (FK)   VIII
"   "   BOUNDARIES
"   "   H.Q.
JAFÜ (JAGDFÜHRER)
9 FD - (Fliegerdivision) was
later 9 FK

unoccupied France

Flying Officer Coleman, was wounded and put out of action for several weeks.

The Spitfire pilots were caught napping because they were still employing formations and tactics taught before the war and because the lessons learnt at Dunkirk had not been fully digested.

Before the war R.A.F. squadrons flew compact formations based on tight elements of three planes and the tactics employed were standardised in what were known as 'Fighting Area Attacks'. There were five different forms of attack and a flight commander ordered them in combat as he saw fit.

In terms of flying discipline and spectacle they were excellent. They were worthless tactically and when

related to effective shooting. There was never enough time to get the sights on the target since the business of keeping station was the prime requirement.

Following the command 'F.A.A. Attack No. 1—Go', for example, the fighters would swing into line astern behind the leader, follow him in an orderly line up to the bomber, fire a quick shot when their turn came in the queue and then swing gracefully away after the leader again, presenting their bellies to the enemy gunner. They were all based on the belief that modern aircraft, especially fighters, were too fast for the dog-fight tactics of World War I.

Fighting Area attacks were disastrous and it was not long before the British were imitating the Germans.

In the early evening of July 11th Heinkel 111's of KG55 raided Portsmouth. They were intercepted by R.A.F. fighters and this bomber crashed on the beach between Selsey and Pagham, Sussex. Two of the crew were killed and three injured. As the aircraft burns local inhabitants look on—including two firemen with magnificent Victorian-style helmets

By flying their loose formations the Germans found these advantages: they could maintain their positions more easily, they could keep a better look-out and by flying at separated heights they could cover each other and scan a greater area of sky.

The perfect fighter formation was devised by the Germans. It was based on an element of two planes which they called the *rotte*. About 200 yards separated a pair of fighters and the main responsibility of the wingman, or number two, was to cover the leader from quarter or stern attack. The leader looked after navigation and covered his wingman.

The *schwarme* consisted of two pairs, and it was this formation the R.A.F. adopted. The British called it a *finger-four* because each plane flew in a position corresponding to the finger-tips seen in plan view.

In this formation the leader is represented by the longest finger, the number two by the index. Numbers three and four take up the positions of the third and little finger-tips. Number two always flies on the sun side of the leader scanning down-sun. And he positions himself slightly below so that the other pilots can see him well below the glare. That leaves two pairs of eyes stepped-up down-sun of the leader scanning the danger area.

While these lessons were still being learned Fighter Command found itself on July 10th fighting the opening phase of the Battle of Britain.

July 10th

Day Convoy raids off North Foreland and Dover.
Night The east coast, home counties and western Scotland attacked.
Weather Showery in south-east England and Channel. Continuous rain elsewhere.

The first plots to appear on the operations room table indicated that the Luftwaffe were following routine procedure. Skirting the west of England, weather reconnasissance aircraft steered for the Atlantic. Radar tracked them for part of their course but they gave the R.A.F. few opportunities to intercept.

After sunrise a Spitfire from the Coltishall Sector, Suffolk, was directed to a suspect plot. Despite the morning haze it engaged a reconnaissance machine.

Apart from a few other skirmishes the morning was uneventful but activity showed signs of increasing.

A new procedure adopted by No. 11 Group nominated a whole squadron instead of a flight for dawn deployment to forward airfields. The squadron would return home in the evening.

Shortly before 1.30 p.m. radar blips showed a substantial build-up behind Calais. As a west-bound convoy streamed past Dover guarded by six Hurricanes from Biggin Hill about twenty Do 17s escorted by thirty Me 110s and twenty Me 109s arrived.

Within half an hour the Hurricanes were joined by elements of four squadrons from neighbouring sectors, including Hurricanes of No. 56, based at North Weald, but operating from Manston.

Near Newhaven a train was attacked, the driver being killed and the guard injured.

The fight cost the Luftwaffe four fighters. Three Hurricanes were lost, one of them, belonging to No. 111 Squadron, losing a wing after hitting a bomber. Only one small ship was sunk.

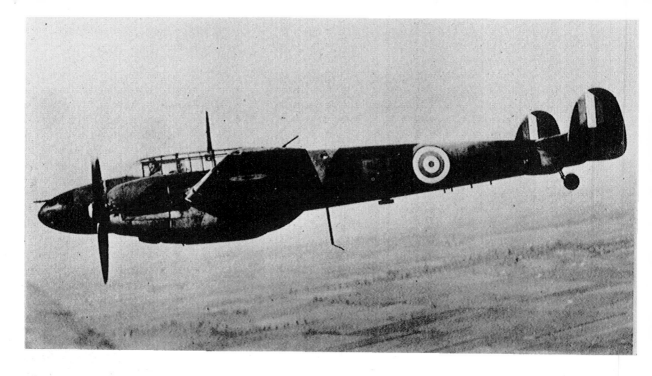

Forced down on July 11th, near Goodwood, Sussex, this Me 110 of 4th Staffel Aufkl. Gr. 14 was repaired and became part of R.A.F.'s circus of German equipment captured. The original German code 5F+CM can just be discerned on the fuselage

Meanwhile seventy German bombers attacked Swansea and Falmouth killing thirty people and damaging shipping, a power station and railways. The Royal Ordnance Factory at Pembrey was hit and seventeen bombs fell on Martlesham.

The most significant event of a day in which Fighter Command flew 609 sorties was the promptness with which Me 110s went into a defensive circle when they were attacked by Hurricanes. It was a clear indication that this long-range fighter needed as much protection as a bomber.

An anti-aircraft battery on the south coast claimed a record by shooting down a 109 in thirty seconds with only eight shells. The battery log-book reads: '1312 hrs.—enemy aircraft seen at 8,000 feet. 1314 hrs.—opened fire on E/A; range 7,000 yards. 1314½ hrs.—cease fire. Enemy had disappeared. 1325 hrs.—enemy reported in the sea.'

Thirteen German aircraft failed to return. Six British fighters were destroyed.

July 11th

Day Convoys attacked off Suffolk. Portland harbour raided.
Night Activity over south-west England, East Anglia, Yorkshire coast and Portsmouth.
Weather Channel overcast. Cloud base 5,000 feet. Visibility fair. Thunderstorms and bright intervals in the midlands and north.

At 7.30 a.m. two Luftflotte 3 formations operating from Cherbourg peninsula were detected by radar heading for a convoy steaming eastwards across Lyme Bay. Six Spitfires and six Hurricanes from Warmwell in the Middle Wallop Sector were scrambled, the Spitfires to patrol the convoy, the Hurricanes to meet the German formation.

The Hurricanes intercepted ten Stukas and about twenty Me 109s shortly before eight o'clock. One Hurricane was shot down almost immediately.

Spitfires arrived as the Stukas were preparing to dive on the convoy. Three Spitfires positioned themselves to attack the dive-bombers while the other three stood by to cover from the rear. Two were shot down when the 109s broke through the rearguard. No ship was sunk.

No. 564 Squadron at Manston flew continuous convoy patrols throughout the day. 'B' Flight, led by Air Commodore A. C. Deere, then a flight lieutenant, ran into trouble on the fourth scramble. It had just crossed the coast at Deal when Deere spotted a silver-coloured seaplane with Red Cross markings flying at wave-top height. Behind it were a dozen Me 109s in loose formation.

There was a fierce fight during which Deere collided head-on with a 109. His engine dead and the propeller blades bent horizontal, he glided back to a crash-landing five miles from Manston, badly bruised, but otherwise unhurt. Two Spitfires were shot down for two Me 109s. The seaplane force-landed.

If the Me 109 pilot came down in the Channel he was probably picked up. The German air-sea rescue organisation was then better than the British.

The Germans used about thirty Heinkel 59 seaplanes to rescue their pilots from the water. Luftwaffe air crews were provided with inflatable rubber dinghies

Pilots of 151 Squadron, North Weald, in July. Fourth from the left is Squadron Leader E. M. Donaldson. On the previous day he had been shot down off Boulogne but was later picked up by a R.A.F. high-speed launch. Fifth from the left is Wing Commander F. V. Beamish, North Weald Station Commander, who flew many sorties during the Battle

and a chemical that stained the sea around them a bright and conspicuous green.

The British system was not fully organised until after the formation of the Directorate of Air-Sea Rescue in the middle of February 1941. Before that R.A.F. crews had to rely on luck, the Navy, the coast-guards or a passing convoy, although Park, by the end of July, had succeeded in borrowing some Lysander aircraft to work with the launches and other craft.

Once located, R.A.F. naval high-speed launches or lifeboats of the Royal National Lifeboat Institution did the rescuing. These vessels were under the operational control of the local naval authorities. They formed a chain round the coast with an important centre at Dover, where a rescue service had been working since May.

Around midday on the 11th fifteen Luftflotte 3 Stukas joined thirty to forty 110s over the Cherbourg peninsula and set course for Portland. Thirty minutes later they surprised six Hurricane pilots of No. 601 Squadron, scrambled from Tangmere to intercept what they thought would be a single aircraft. The controllers of Nos. 10 and 11 Groups sent off more fighters. None intercepted until the Stukas were bombing.

Being up-sun from the Germans, the 601 Squadron Hurricanes exploited the situation by diving on the Stukas and shooting down two before the Me 110s could intervene. A running battle developed.

Luftflotte 3's next raid did not come as such a surprise. Radar warned of a big attack and No. 601 were again sent forward to intercept. As predicted, the Hurricanes found twelve He 111s escorted by twelve Me 110s over the Isle of Wight heading for Portsmouth.

The Hurricanes split into two sections, the first to tackle the bombers and the other to climb and take on the fighters. In confused fighting the Luftwaffe lost eleven aircraft during the day and the R.A.F. four in the course of 432 sorties. At night 30 bombers raided Portsmouth, killing nine and injuring fifty.

July 12th

Day Attacks on convoy off Norfolk-Suffolk coast, shipping off the Isle of Wight and Aberdeen.
Night South Wales and Bristol areas.
Weather Mainly cloudy with early-morning fog in the Channel. Thunderstorms in many districts.

Formation of early-morning fog in the Channel hampered the Germans, and until 8.50 a.m. activity was slight. Several plots were then picked up heading for the convoys 'Agent', off North Foreland, and 'Booty', twelve miles north-east of Orfordness.

The heavier attack was aimed at 'Booty', and sections from Nos. 242, 17, 85 and 264 squadrons were scrambled by No. 12 Group to cover the convoy. No. 151 Squadron from No. 11 Group intercepted.

*During the fighting over Dunkirk at the end of May
and the offensive patrols in June/July the R.A.F.
committed its Spitfire force for the first time. This
Spitfire of 64 Squadron crashed in a beet field in France,
providing a source of particular interest for locally
based Luftwaffe personnel*

*An overshoot during the Battle. A Hurricane of 56
Squadron ends up in a hedge on the Epping road after
attempting a landing at North Weald in July*

Early in July Fighter Command intelligence reports noted that Ju 87 dive bombers had appeared off Portland carrying long-range fuel tanks under the wings to extend their radius of action. The two long-range Stukas shown here were from III/St.G.2 'Immelmann'. Use of long range tanks, however, made no difference to the fate of the Ju 87 in the Battle as, due to heavy losses, the type was withdrawn in August

Later that morning No. 603 Squadron shot down a He 111 belonging to 2./KG26 off Aberdeen, and during the afternoon several more German aircraft were destroyed—among them one off the Isle of Wight. Poor visibility made interceptions difficult and by nightfall these had become impossible. German losses by midnight totalled eight. In the course of 670 sorties the R.A.F. lost six.

The death of two pilots in the seaplane engagement on the 11th had brought No. 54 Squadron's casualties up to six killed and two injured in ten days. The squadron was now down to twelve pilots and eight aircraft, thirteen Spitfires having been lost or damaged in that time.

Before Dunkirk, squadron strengths averaged seventeen pilots. The lull throughout June had enabled most units to train pilots and give newly appointed section leaders an opportunity to obtain experience. Even at this early stage some squadrons were beginning to run short of pilots.

The need for additional fighter pilots was fully realised by Flying Training Command. As early as June the A.O.C.-in-C., Air Marshal L. A. Pattinson, said the command's '. . . . main contribution to the defence of this country is the maximum training output up to the required standards, and that some risks in local defence must be faced in order to meet the main responsibility'.

To the Luftwaffe, who had started serious planning for an all-out assault on Britain only on July 11th, British defences were still an unknown quantity, and it was to probe these defences and train new crews, particularly in navigation, that the Germans increased their activities at night. They were to encounter difficulties.

R.A.F. intelligence had found out before the war that the Germans were using normal broadcasting stations as navigational beacons. All the B.B.C.'s transmitters in Britain were in or near target areas, so a system of synchronising their transmissions was worked out to confuse or deny the Luftwaffe navigators the bearings they needed.

As soon as the operations room at Fighter Command saw that a hostile aircraft had got to within reach of good bearing from a transmitter, the B.B.C. were warned and that station was closed down. Broadcasting services were not interrupted, however. Transmissions were continued by the other stations in the particular group concerned.

In the event of all but one station in a group being closed down, the remaining station was also closed and broadcasting was continued on alternative frequencies used by other groups or stations. Thus, unless hostile aircraft were inside relatively restricted areas broadcasting could continue. Under war conditions the scheme was entirely successful and the Germans were unable to use the B.B.C.'s broadcasting stations as beacons.

July 13th

Day Shipping attacks off Dover and Portland.
Night Minelaying in Thames Estuary.
Weather Early-morning fog in southern England clearing by mid-morning.

British sea power, one of Germany's major problems in launching Operation Sealion without air superiority. Here the Royal Sovereign class 15-inch gun battleship H.M.S. Revenge is seen, on August 5th, 1940, escorting a special fast convoy from America carrying arms and supplies to Britain. The photograph was taken from a Sunderland flying boat of No. 210 Squadron. As the threat of invasion grew during the summer, Revenge was transferred south to Plymouth

Before the battle Park and Brand expressed the view that once the Germans began their offensive it would be as much as they could do to provide enough planes to guard the convoys. The first three days confirmed their fears.

Dowding resisted the temptation to strengthen the south-east sectors at the expense of the others, foreseeing that to do so would invite a flank attack he would be ill prepared to meet. Such changes as he did make were designed chiefly to strengthen the West Country and No. 11 Group's right flank rather than its more obviously threatened centre. Thus he moved No. 152 Squadron with Spitfires from Acklington, Northumberland, to Middle Wallop, Hampshire, on July 12th, and a flight of No. 247 Squadron's Gladiators from Sumburgh in the Shetland Islands to Roborough, Devon, on July 18th.

Roborough, a small grass airfield on the outskirts of Plymouth, was too small for Spitfires and Hurricanes, but it was no problem to the biplane Gladiators whose main task was the local defence of Plymouth.

Park and Brand therefore had to make do with what they had—Park with seven Spitfire, thirteen Hurricane and three Blenheim squadrons, Brand with two Spitfire and two Hurricane squadrons and a flight of Gladiators

directed from No. 10 Group's new headquarters at Rudloe Manor, Box, Wiltshire, inaugurated on this day.

German generals had by now reached Berchtesgaden to confer with Hitler who was still baffled by the British. Wrote General Halder in his diary: 'The Führer is obsessed with the question why England does not want to take the road to peace.'

Hitler, he said, was reluctant to smash Britain because it would lead to the disintegration of the Empire which would benefit America, Japan and other countries at a cost to them only of German blood.

That evening Hitler wrote to Mussolini, declining the Duce's offer to send Italian troops and aircraft for the invasion of Britain.

Pressure on the two groups was much reduced on the 13th owing to a deterioration in the weather. German bombers were, however, out after shipping, and two convoys were attacked off Harwich. There were two air engagements off Dover in which the Germans claimed two Spitfires and six Hurricanes and admitted the loss of five. In fact one British fighter was destroyed while the Germans lost seven aircraft including a FW 200 of I/KG40. At this time pilots reported being fired on by 'old and dirty' Hurricanes which bore no roundels or lettering and had two blade wooden airscrews. No official records exist but it is possible that the Luftwaffe used one or two Belgian Hurricanes repaired after the fighting in May.

July 14th

Day Shipping attacks off Dover and Swanage.
Night Bristol area, Isle of Wight, Kent and Suffolk raided.
Weather Fair all day.

Waiting for the call to scramble, a group of pilots from 610 'County of Chester' Squadron at Biggin Hill in late July

German forces attacked the airfield at Ramsgate and a convoy off Dover. To the west, a destroyer off Swanage was ineffectually bombed, and during the afternoon an attack was directed against the convoy 'Bread'. The Germans inflicted some damage on the convoy, which was guarded by a No. 11 Group patrol. Fighter Command tried to counter every incursion and flew 593 sorties in the attempt. Four Hurricanes were lost in a fight off Deal. German losses totalled two.

Two days had now elapsed since the Heinkel seaplane had been forced down and beached near Deal. The Government decided that they could not recognise the right of He 59s to bear the Red Cross, since it was probable that the planes were being used to report movements of British convoys. On the 14th British pilots were instructed to shoot them down.

July 15th

Day Shipping attacked off Norfolk coast and the Channel. Yeovil bombed.
Night Minelaying.
Weather Low cloud.

Each day German reconnaissance planes would fly at least two patrols, but the use to which the information was put leads to the conclusion that the Germans had too much faith in their intelligence efficiency. Had they fully reconnoitred the airfields, aircraft factories and other vital targets in Britain in July and August they would have been able to concentrate more of their attacks on important objectives instead of wasting time on training stations like Detling.

The British, on the other hand, owed their small but efficient Photographic Reconnaissance Unit to the brilliant work of a few individuals like the adventurous and unorthodox Mr. F. S. Cotton. Based at Heston, Middlesex, the P.R.U. was equipped with special high-altitude Spitfires as well as other aircraft, including Lockheed Hudsons. These planes ranged over the whole of the German-held coastal areas from Spain to Norway. Between July and October the Photographic Reconnaissance Unit flew over 600 sorties for a loss of only seven Spitfires.

Luftwaffe activity on this Monday morning was devoted entirely to reconnaissance. Alerted to some intense shipping movements in the Channel, however, II Fliegerkorps decided to brave the low cloud and heavy rain. They sent fifteen Do 17s of KG2 into action.

The Dorniers reached the convoy 'Pilot' at 2.13 p.m., but their attacks were thwarted by Hurricanes of Nos. 56 and 151 Squadrons. The Hurricanes did not score.

While the Dorniers were busy in the Channel a small force of Luftflotte 3 bombers flew to the Westland Aircraft Works at Yeovil, Somerset, and other targets in the west of England and Wales. A hangar and the runway at Yeovil were slightly damaged. Bombs also fell on the railway at Avonmouth and on the airfield at St. Athan.

The R.A.F. flew 449 sorties and lost a Hurricane from No. 213 Squadron.

Pilot Officer Holland of No. 92 Squadron attacked

A Heinkel 59 seaplane high and dry on the beach at
Deal after being forced down by 54 Squadron on
July 11th. The seaplane had a strong escort of Me 109s
and a running fight ensued with losses to both sides. The
British Government refused to grant immunity to these
seaplanes when operating in the battle area.

Right A German pilot being rescued by an He 59 from
a Seenotflug Kdo. based on Cherbourg. He 59s
operating along the north-east Channel coast bore
red cross markings and civil registrations, while those
farther west were camouflaged and bore Luftwaffe unit
codes and call signs

a Ju 88 and used all his ammunition trying to shoot
it down. All he would claim on returning to Pembrey was
a 'probable'. II/LG1 lost a Ju 88 in that area.

The Germans lost three machines altogether, including a He 111 of 2./KG26 off the Scottish coast.

July 16th

Day Very little activity.
Night Minelaying off the north-east coast.
Weather Fog in northern France, the Straits and south-east
England.

In his 'Directive No. 16' Hitler said of the invasion:
'The landing operation must be a surprise crossing on a
broad front. . . .'

As with all his plans, the Führer chose to ignore the
obvious—that a clandestine crossing of the Channel

*Charred and battered wreckage is all that remains of a
Dornier 17 after being shot down near Portisham,
Dorset, early in July 1940*

was impossible. Or did his statement reflect Göring's
conviction that the R.A.F. would be destroyed before
the invasion fleet set sail?

Later on the 16th the weather cleared sufficiently
to release a few aircraft. Again they went for shipping,
and again the R.A.F. attempted to beat them off.
It was not until 4 p.m. that the first successful interception took place—twenty-five miles east of Fraser-
burgh, Scotland, where an He 111 of III/KG26 was
shot down. Two hours later No. 601 Squadron from
Tangmere destroyed a Ju 88. It went into the Solent
where the one surviving member of the crew took to a
dinghy.

Fighter Command flew 313 sorties and lost two
aircraft. German losses totalled five.

July 17th

Day Search for shipping off Scottish and east coasts.
Night Targets attacked in south-west. Minelaying.
Weather Dull with occasional rain.

Early reconnaissance patrols were impeded by the
weather but it cleared sufficiently later for operations
against shipping to begin.

The scale of these operations was small. Fighter
Command flew 253 sorties, during which one fighter
was lost and Ju 88 and an He 111 were shot down.

By nightfall Fliegerdivision IX minelayers were
flying to the Thames Estuary, Cardiff and Swansea.

In Germany the Army High Command allocated
the forces for Sealöwe and ordered thirteen picked
divisions to embarkation points on the Channel
coast for the first wave of the invasion. The Army
Command completed detailed plans for a broad front
landing on the south coast of England. General von
Brauchitsch told Admiral Raeder the whole operation
would be relatively easy and over in a month.

July 18th

Day Shipping off south and east coasts attacked.
Night Very little activity.
Weather Occasional rain in southern districts. Straits of
Dover cloudy. Cool.

Sporadic raids against the Channel ports and shipping
kept Fighter Command busy. Only one major dog-fight

Pilots of No. 32 Squadron take a breather between patrols at Hawkinge on July 31st, 1940. In the background one of the squadron's Hurricanes

developed—off Deal, where fifteen Spitfires engaged twenty-eight Me 109s. Three British fighters were destroyed in the course of the day, but two Ju 88s, one Do 17 and a Me 109 were lost to the Germans. Between 11 a.m. and 1 p.m. the coastguard station at St. Margaret's Bay was bombed and the Goodwin lightship sunk.

In the north No. 232 Hurricane Squadron stationed at Wick detached a flight to Sumburgh in the Shetlands to replace No. 247 Squadron Gladiators sent to Plymouth.

This was not in the general sense a busy day but for one pilot a lot was involved. In a letter from Middle Wallop, Flight Lieutenant Howell wrote:

Bags of excitement here—almost too much. The other day [July 18], Red Section was sent up to 18,00 over Portland. It was a mucky day, and we had to go up through two layers of cloud. Control gave us a bearing to fly on and said that we ought to meet a jerry, possibly two which were in the vicinity. He had hardly finished speaking when out of the cloud loomed a Ju 88. Whoopee! I told Nos. 2 and 3 to look out for enemy fighters while I made an almost head on attack at it. I don't think he liked that one little bit because he turned over and went split arse for the sea, releasing four large bombs, and doing over 350 m.p.h. I got in another attack, and got his port motor. I was going to do a third when I saw the other chaps screaming down at him. So I let them have a go being a generous chap! Just then I smelt a nasty smell! An 'orrid smell! I looked at the dials and things, and saw that the coolant temperature was right off the clock—about 180°C., and the oil temperature at 95° and going up. The bugger had shot

me in the radiator! White fumes began pouring back into the cockpit, so I thought that that was not really good enough. The poor old motor began to seize up, groaning pitifully. I called up Bandy and said 'Hello Bandy Control, Red 1 calling—I am going to bale out 4 miles off Poole!' The silly C at the other end of course couldn't hear me and asked me to repeat. Bah. Still, I still had 5,000 feet so I told him again and wished him a very good afternoon, and stepped smartly from the aircraft.

I read something somewhere about pulling a ripcord so had a grope—found same—pulled same, and sat up with a jerk but with no damage to the important parts.

Everything was lovely—quiet as a church, a lovely day— a spot of sun—3 ships 2 miles away who would be bound to see me! Found myself still holding the handle, so flung it away— chucked my helmet away but kept the goggles! Undid my shoes, blew up my Mae West, and leaned back and admired the scenery. The water quite suddenly came very close—a swish, and then I began my final swim of the season. I set out with a lusty crawl for Bournemouth, thinking I might shoot a hell of a line staggering up the beach with beauteous barmaids dashing down the beach with bottles of brandy—instead the current was taking me out to sea, and I was unceremoniously hauled on board a 12 ft. motorboat. Still the Navy pushed out a boat and the half tumbler of whisky went down with a rush!

July 19th

Day Dover raided. Defiant squadron largely destroyed.
Night Some activity between Isle of Wight and Plymouth, Thames Estuary and Harwich.
Weather Showery with bright intervals in most cases. Channel winds light—fair.

No. 141 Squadron, newly arrived from Edinburgh with their Defiant two-seater turret-fighters took off

Dover under fire on July 29th, 1940. Ju 87s can be seen banking away after dropping their bombs on the convoy in the harbour. The sky is peppered with bursting anti-aircraft shells

from Hawkinge on their first patrol at 12.32. They were assigned to a height of 5,000 feet on a line south of Folkestone.

The nine Defiants had not long been airborne when they were attacked by twenty Me 109s diving out of the sun. Within minutes five Defiants had gone into the Channel. A sixth crashed at Dover. The remaining three would have shared the same fate but for the timely intervention of No. 111 Squadron with Hurricanes.

The Germans claimed twelve Defiants shot down.

They lost one Me 109 in the engagement. The remains of No. 141 were removed to Prestwick, in Ayrshire, where they could still do good work against unescorted bombers. The other Defiant squadron, No. 264, moved temporarily to Kirton-in-Lindsey and then to Ringway for the defence of Manchester.

Inexplicably, No. 264 was later sent to the Horn-church sector and for a few days was in the thick of the day fighting.

Radar warned of a big gathering of aircraft over Calais at 4 p.m. on the 19th. Dover was their objective, and Nos. 64, 32 and 74 squadrons were scrambled to intercept. Outnumbered nearly two to one, the thirty-five British fighters did not score.

Fighter Command was more heavily committed than ever before; 701 sorties were flown. Total losses for

During the battle Göring confers with, left the Commander of Luftflotte 3, Generalfeldmarschall Hugo Sperrle and centre, the Commander of Luftflotte 2, Generalfeldmarschall Kesselring

the day were eight machines. The Germans lost two—a reconnaissance Do 17 and a He 111 bomber—the ratio of victories contributing to German confidence as Hitler made his 'last appeal to reason' speech at the Reichstag.

July 20th

Day Convoys and shipping at Dover attacked.
Night Widespread minelaying from the Needles, Isle of Wight, to Land's End; Bristol Channel and eastern coastal waters.
Weather Occasional thunderstorms. Straits of Dover cloudy clearing to bright intervals.

There was now so much activity around Dover that it was beginning to get the nickname 'Hellfire Corner'.

In the afternoon a convoy appeared off Dover guarded by two sections of No. 32 Squadron Hurricanes taking turns at escort duty. At 5.40 p.m. it was attacked by Stukas escorted by Me 109s. Two Hurricanes were lost and two damaged.

An hour later forty-eight Messerschmitts clashed with about forty Hurricanes and Spitfires. There was again a lively engagement.

In operations round Britain the R.A.F. lost three and the Germans nine. The Luftwaffe losses included five Me 109s, a Ju 88, a Do 17 and a four-engined FW200, the latter north of Ireland.

The following was the strength of the Luftwaffe on July 20th:

LUFTFLOTTEN 2 AND 3

	Available	Serviceable
Bombers	1131	769
Dive-bombers	316	248
Single-engine fighters	809	656
Twin-engine fighters	246	168
Long-range reconnaissance	67	48

LUFTFLOTTE 5

	Available	Serviceable
Bombers	129	95
Single-engine fighters	84	69
Twin-engine fighters	34	32
Long-range reconnaissance	67	48

KG 40 of Luftflotten 2 and 3 is not included but of its eleven planes only two were serviceable for mine-laying. KGr. 100 with twelve serviceable aircraft out of forty-two is also not included. Though subordinated to Luftflotte 2 it had moved out of the area.

July 21st

Day Raids on Convoys in Channel and Straits of Dover.
Night Targets chiefly at Merseyside.
Weather Fine and fair early, clouding over during the morning. Fair in the evening.

The morning of the 21st followed the usual pattern until after 9 a.m. when three British squadrons intercepted twenty German planes over the convoy 'Peewit'. An Me 109 was shot down.

Later a Hawker Hector biplane was shot down by a Me 109 which, in turn, was destroyed by No. 238 Squadron.

The shattered cockpit of a Dornier 17Z from KG77 which careered across a hop field at Marden, Kent, after a raid on July 3rd, 1940. Altogether the R.A.F. shot down seven Dornier 17s from KG77 on this day

Fighter Command sorties numbered 571, and their losses six. German losses totalled seven.

Control rooms were largely dependent on the W.A.A.F. In the heat of battle they were brave and their services were invaluable.

When the fighting began to get tough and the language of the pilots started to match it, senior officers tried moving the girls beyond earshot of the control room loud-speakers. It was not idle swearing, however, but the voices of men fighting for their lives. The girls refused to leave their jobs and said they did not mind the language as much as the men thought.

July 22nd

Day Shipping off the south coast attacked.
Night Minelaying the whole length of eastern seaboard.
Weather Straits fair; Channel cloudy. Light westerly winds in both. Bright intervals between showers in the east.

Although British fighters flew 611 sorties, hostile aircraft were elusive and in the course of the day only one was shot down. The score was even.

At Wick, Sea Gladiators of No. 804 Squadron Fleet Air Arm flew their first Battle of Britain sortie under the control of No. 13 Group.

July 23rd

Day East coast shipping raided.
Night Minelaying from Dover to the Tyne and Forth Estuary.

Weather Slight haze in Straits of Dover. Cloudy with occasional rain in other districts.

With prospects of a hard fight ahead, a new situation had arisen as a result of the abolition of the western approaches and the transfer of the country's main trade artery to the North Channel. The result of this (Dowding said in a letter to the Chief of the Air Staff) was that convoys would be navigating around the entire coast of Great Britain.

During the winter months, when it would only be necessary to protect convoys on the east coast, the resources of Fighter Command would be strained to the limit in providing standing patrols, even at section strength for these convoys.

At that time, attacks were made by one or two bombers at the most and a section was an ample escort.

It was the policy for the Germans to attack convoys with strong formations of bombers escorted by fighters whenever possible. Defensive measures had to be on a much larger scale if they were not to have sections frequently overwhelmed by sudden attacks in greatly superior numbers.

Bearing in mind the fact that enemy bombers were active almost every night and that units were detailed in every sector for night flying, it appeared that three squadrons per sector were about the minimum requirement to safeguard the passage of convoys off the east coast of England, and that this number would be inadequate north of the Tay and west of the Isle of Wight.

Dowding had about twenty sectors, not counting Northolt, Sumburgh and Coltishall (the latter because he was already counting the sectors behind); and on this basis he should have had about sixty squadrons to cover the coast from the Orkneys to the north shore of the Bristol Channel.

R.A.F. Hornchurch, June 1940. Flight Lt. 'Al' Deere, a New Zealander of 54 Squadron, receives a well-merited Distinguished Flying Cross from King George VI. Next to the King stands Air Chief Marshal Dowding, A.O.C.-in-C. Fighter Command. Al Deere survived an extraordinary number of incidents and crashes and finally retired from the R.A.F. as an Air Commodore

While the R.A.F. was fighting in the skies above, the call to civilians on the ground was for scrap aluminium to build more aircraft. Here is A.R.P. post C 2/3 at Canterbury in July, collecting pots and pans of all shapes and sizes

He had now to expand from St. David's Head to Greenock besides meeting a possible demand for five squadrons in Ireland.

In addition to the above, he could not afford to distribute his squadrons evenly along the front but had to keep some extra strength in the neighbourhood of London to guard against the possibility of invasion in East Anglia or Kent.

It became obvious, then, that the creation of new squadrons should be pressed on with as rapidly as possible to guard against the possibility of invasion.

The Admiralty, said Dowding, had to co-operate with him if any but casual protection was to be afforded to the convoys. They had to start their journeys at definite times and channels had to be swept as close as possible to the coast-lines.

Since it was impossible for some time to be strong everywhere he would have to consider some form of additional mobility within groups so that a sector

The Air Council in session at the Air Ministry, London, in July 1940. Round the top of the table, from left to right: Air Marshal Sir Christopher Courtney (Air Member for Supply and Organisation), Air Marshal E. L. Gossage (Air Member for Personnel), Captain H. H. Balfour (Parliamentary Under Secretary of State for Air), Sir Archibald Sinclair (Secretary of State for Air), Air Chief Marshal Sir Cyril Newall (Chief of Air Staff), Sir Arthur Street (Permanent Under Secretary) and Air Chief Marshal Sir Wilfred Freeman (Air Member for Development and Production)

opposite whose front a convoy was travelling at any time might be temporarily strengthened for the occasion.

German activity during this day was reduced. Concentration being centred on shipping off the east coast. Fighter Command flew 470 sorties and destroyed three enemy machines at no cost to itself.

July 24th

Day Convoys and shipping in the Channel attacked.
Night Nil.
Weather Channel and Straits of Dover cloudy. Coastal and hill fog in western districts spreading east. Rain in most districts.

A sudden break in the weather brought a co-ordinated attack by two bomber formations heavily escorted by fighters—the first against a convoy steaming into the Thames Estuary, and the other against one off Dover.

It was 8.15 a.m. when No. 54 Squadron were scrambled from Rochford. They climbed to 20,000 feet and were just about to intercept the first raid when Deere, leading Red Section, was warned of the second

This formation [he said], the largest I had seen up to that time, consisted of about 18 Dorniers protected by a considerable number of escort fighters weaving and criss-crossing above and behind the bombers. I reported the unpleasant facts to control and requested immediate assistance.

Heavily outnumbered, the squadron split—half taking on one raid, the other half taking on the next. In the

fierce fighting one pilot was killed.

There were several more engagements that day and at the end of it eight German and three British aircraft were destroyed. Fighter Command flew 561 sorties.

Among the targets attacked in Britain that day was Brooklands. A Ju 88 circled it for seven minutes, and then, after lowering its undercarriage, followed several friendly machines going in to land. The moment it was over the airfield buildings it dropped twelve bombs and flew off. Despite the ruse, there was surprisingly little damage.

While only five French pilots took part in the Battle of Britain the Free French Air Force was beginning to appear at St. Athan, Wales. There, a number of French pilots were given clearance to keep in practice with the aircraft in which they had escaped from France, subject to British markings being carried and the planes being painted yellow underneath. The aircraft were two Potez 63, three Dewoitine D 520s, three Caudron Simoun, a Caudron 440 and a Farman F222.

July 25th

Day Convoys and shipping in the Channel raided.
Night Minelaying in Firth of Forth and Thames Estuary. Reconnaissance over Bristol and Channel area.
Weather Fine day with haze in the Straits of Dover. Winds north-westerly and light.

The Luftwaffe concentrated again on shipping and in one attack sank five small vessels and damaged another five in the same convoy. The bombers numbered about sixty and they co-ordinated their efforts with nine E-boats which were engaged by the British destroyers *Boreas* and *Brilliant*.

The two destroyers were dive-bombed and one had to be towed into Dover.

Because the Germans were operating from bases close to their objectives, they were much better placed than the defending squadrons to concentrate their planes above any target, for the British fighters had to rely on continuous patrols in small numbers to find the enemy before calling for reinforcements. These patrols invariably attacked on their own without waiting for help which took some time to arrive.

Fighter Command squadrons flew 641 sorties on the 25th, and destroyed sixteen raiders and lost seven fighters. A curious claim in German records was for a French Breguet 690!

During the night of July 25th–26th mines were laid along the south and east coasts. One raid penetrated to the Forth Bridge and some bombs were dropped in raids on northern Scotland.

July 26th

Day Shipping off south coast attacked.
Night Minelaying in Thames Estuary and off Norfolk coast. Bristol area.
Weather Heavy cloud with rain and poor visibility.

Fliegerkorps VIII took the initiative with attacks on shipping near the Isle of Wight. Two of the convoy raiders were shot down near Portland in the course of 581 sorties by British fighter planes. Two British planes were destroyed. The motor lifeboats *Rosa Woodd* and *Phyllis Lunn* went out after survivors of three steamers sunk in the Channel.

The pattern of German flying during the night pointed to mine-laying in the Thames Estuary, Norfolk and the Bristol Channel.

July 27th

Day Raids on shipping and naval units in Dover harbour and Straits.
Night Attacks on south-west England.
Weather Fair Straits, cloudy in Channel. Slight rain in the midlands and the North Sea.

Richthofen's Fliegerkorps started operations at 9.45 a.m. with an attack on a convoy off Swanage. Simultaneously two convoys off the estuary and Harwich were bombed. The destroyer H.M.S. *Wren* was sunk.

In two attacks on Dover four high-explosive bombs dropped on the harbour and five fell on the barracks. In the second attack the destroyer *Codrington* was hit. A second destroyer was sunk off the east coast and another was damaged, with the result that the Admiralty applied the policy of withdrawing the target. Dover was abandoned as an advanced base for anti-invasion destroyers which relieved Fighter Command of the burden of protecting them. This meant, however, that the defence of the Straits now depended more than ever on the R.A.F. One of the Dover attacks was carried out by six Me 109Es carrying bombs on centre-section racks. This was the first report of 109s being used in this role.

German attacks on Dover were becoming so serious that the Air Ministry issued special instructions to Fighter Command to engage them approaching the port with superior forces whenever possible. To secure this concentration in the south-east meant increasing the number of squadrons to twenty-eight and making more use of Hawkinge and Manston.

Accidents were putting a strain on the repair organisation. To reduce them Dowding ordered the posting of two flying disciplinary flight lieutenants to each station to keep an eye on aircraft handling. At the same time he ordered that pilots were not only to take physical exercise, but to take at least eight hours off a day and twenty-four hours' leave a week.

Early that afternoon Belfast was raided and at about 6 p.m. planes were reported near Wick and Plymouth. The weather deteriorated to such an extent in the south-east of England, however, that those fighters protecting the convoy 'Agent' had to be recalled. Nine Thames barrage balloons were struck by lightning.

During the night several raids were flown over the Bristol Channel and there was some minelaying between Portland and the Lizard, and along the east coast.

By midnight British fighters had flown 496 sorties and destroyed four raiders at a cost of one fighter.

July 28th

Day Shipping attacked off Dover and south coast ports.
Night Minelaying from Thames Estuary to Humber. Scattered raiders over England and Wales.
Weather Fine early. Fair for the rest of the day, clouding over in the evening.

Luftwaffe activity was mainly confined to the Channel and east coasts. At 12 a.m. a large raid set course for Dover, but it turned back when halfway across the Straits and dispersed. At 2 p.m. more than 100 machines approached and were engaged by No. 11 Group in the Straits. There were fifty fighters and fifty bombers in the formation. No bombs were dropped.

Four No. 11 Group squadrons were involved in harassing the Germans—Nos. 74, 41, 257 and 111. They lost four Hurricanes. Fighter Command flew 758 sorties and shot down fifteen. Five British planes were destroyed during the day.

German minelaying aircraft were so active during the night that it was impossible to distinguish all the tracks in the operations room. Other raiders were plotted at Nottingham, Edinburgh, Perth, the Tyne, Newcastle-under-Lyme, Hungerford, Manchester, the Mersey and Plymouth. Some bombs were dropped but with little effect.

July 29th

Day Convoy off Dover raided.
Night Activity on reduced scale over land.
Weather Fair all over Britain. Thames Estuary and Dover hazy.

After weeks of deliberation over an He 59 Red Cross seaplane forced down on July 1st off Hartlepool, the Air Ministry issued this communiqué:

. . . enemy aircraft bearing civil markings and marked with the Red Cross have recently flown over British ships at sea and in the vicinity of the British coast, and that they are being employed for purposes which His Majesty's Government cannot regard as being consistent with the privileges generally accorded to the Red Cross.

His Majesty's Government desire to accord to ambulance aircraft reasonable facilities for the transportation of the sick

A line-up of Spitfires of No. 65 Squadron at Hornchurch in July 1940. The censor of the period has scratched out the serial number of the first aircraft in the line to avoid identification by German intelligence

and wounded, in accordance with the Red Cross Convention, and aircraft engaged in the direct evacuation of the sick and wounded will be respected, provided that they comply with the relevant provisions of the Convention.

His Majesty's Government are unable, however, to grant immunity to such aircraft flying over areas in which operations are in progress on land or at sea, or approaching British or Allied territory, or territory in British occupation, or British or Allied ships.

Ambulance aircraft which do not comply with the above requirements will do so at their own risk and peril.

The first indication of a raid showed on radar at 10.20 a.m. It was intended to surprise Dover. No. 11 Group controllers were quick off the mark, however, the thirty Stukas and fifty Me 109s being intercepted at levels from 5,000 to 15,000 feet before they could line up for an accurate bombing run.

The fighting was fierce and it was made the more dangerous for the British pilots by the heavy anti-aircraft fire of the Dover gunners who, however, hit two Stukas.

At 5 p.m. twenty raiders attacked near Harwich. Seventy-four fighters scrambled to intercept but only No. 151 Squadron engaged. The Germans lost six machines for a loss by the British of three. Sorties flown by the R.A.F. numbered 758.

July 30th

Day Raids on convoys off Orfordness, Clacton and Harwich.
Night South Wales and midlands.
Weather Unsettled, with drizzle and low cloud.

Flying was largely restricted by the weather, but by noon the Germans were hunting in the Channel and the North Sea. At 11 a.m. Ju 88s attacked a convoy without success. Drizzle hampered R.A.F. efforts, but Fighter Command flew 688 sorties and shot down five German machines without loss. One of the raiders, a He 111, was destroyed by No. 603 Squadron north-east of Montrose.

July 31st

Day Widespread attacks on shipping in south, south-east and south-west coastal waters. Dover balloon barrage.
Night South Wales and Thames raided.
Weather Fair all over the country with temperatures slightly above average. Channel and Straits hazy.

Thick haze made flying for both air forces difficult. German aircraft attacked convoys at 11 a.m. At 12.50 p.m. the Luftwaffe was active with reconnaissance planes off the Lizard and between 1 and 4 p.m. flew a number of isolated raids over the North Sea. At 5 p.m. fifteen Me 109s went for Dover, and although five squadrons were sent after them only No. 74 was able to engage.

Fighter Command flew only 365 sorties, shot down five enemy machines and lost three themselves.

A large proportion of the night raiders were mine-layers, and they operated in the Tyne, Humber, Harwich, Thames Estuary and Dover areas. Some scattered raids were flown against random targets in the south-east and East Anglia.

Throughout July the Germans probed and sparred with little achievement. They sank eighteen small steamers and four destroyers, and shot down 145 British fighters for the loss of 270 planes.

For the R.A.F. the planes lost were more than replaced by one week's output from the factories. Only

Hurricanes of No. 56 Squadron take off from North Weald for a patrol in July. Another aircraft from 56 stands at dispersal

the shortage of pilots, who now numbered 1,434, gave cause for concern.

So far as the system was concerned, July gave Fighter Command ample opportunity of putting it to the test. Experience produced confidence, but the defences were not yet fully tried in the face of a heavy onslaught.

August 1st

Day East and south coast shipping attacked.
Night South Wales and midlands targets. Minelaying in Thames Estuary and north-east Scottish coast.
Weather Fair in most districts with Straits and Channel overcast. Low cloud dispersing during the day. Warmer.

Shortly before 1 p.m. Church Fenton sector controllers were alerted to two plots approaching the east coast convoys 'Agent' and 'Arena'. Nos. 616 and 607 Squadrons were scrambled and they intercepted a Do 17 and a Ju 88, but without definite results. Cloud base was down to 1,000 feet and this enabled the raiders to escape.

In the south a No. 145 Squadron section operating from Westhampnett, Sussex, intercepted two raids off Hastings and reported shooting down a Hs 126 and damaging a Ju 88. They lost a Hurricane and its pilot. Simultaneously an attack was developing on Norwich, where a factory, a timber yard and a goods yard were hit. Fire gutted the timber yard.

Minelayers were active again during the night and twelve raids were flown on targets as far apart as Bristol,

144

Southend and Montrose.

In addition to carrying high explosives and incendiaries, planes raiding the West Country scattered Hitler's 'Last Appeal to Reason', a turgid document printed on green-and-yellow paper. The German air crews could scarcely have chosen a less receptive readership, for the majority fell among the grazing cattle of Hampshire and Somerset.

Fighter Command squadrons flew 659 sorties and destroyed five hostile aircraft for the loss of one Hurricane. A sixth, shot down in the vicinity of Mablethorpe by a No. 12 Group plane, was later identified as a Battle belonging to No. 1 Group.

August 2nd

Day Shipping attacked in Channel and east coast.
Night South Wales and the midlands.
Weather Mainly fine in the north but cloudy in the east. Channel cloudy. Drizzle in Dover Straits.

After early-morning reconnaissance and weather sorties by German aircraft an east coast convoy was attacked and a trawler sunk. R.A.F. fighters intercepted several hostile raids in the course of 477 sorties but claimed no victories although four of the planes they damaged failed to reach home. No R.A.F. fighters were lost.

The steamship *Highlander* shot down two He 111s and steamed into Leith harbour with one of the victims on the deck.

Minelayers were active again during the night and eighty were plotted from the Orkneys to Dungeness, together with raids on the R.A.F. Technical College at Halton, the airfields of Catterick, Farnborough and Romford and the Forth Bridge.

August 3rd

Day Mainly shipping reconnaissance in Channel.
Night South Wales, with some raids continuing to Liverpool, Crewe and Bradford areas.
Weather Mainly dull with bright patches. Cloud base 4,000 feet. Visibility two to five miles.

Hostile activity in the morning was largely confined to shipping reconnaissance. Five raids developed in the south-west, but activity was slight except for the occasional pack of about a dozen aircraft over the Channel against which 415 sorties were flown by Fighter Command at no cost to themselves. Four German planes were destroyed in the twenty-four hours.

Minelayers were active again during the night and bombers from Luftflotte 5 attacked the Orkneys and the Firth of Forth. In the south a dozen raids were flown on Harwich, and six each were reported from the Tyne and the Humber. At Gravesend a bomb put an Observer Corps post out of action and incendiaries in Essex set fire to some cornfields.

One enterprising raider dropped a large bundle of leaflets to which was attached an explosive charge; the whole assembly fell in the right place—a sewage farm near Tonbridge.

August 4th

Day Reconnaissance along the south coast and Bristol Channel.
Night Little activity.
Weather Fine to fair early. Cloudy with bright intervals at midday, clearing in the evening.

Sunday, August 4th, gave Fighter Command a respite. A few reconnaissance sorties were flown over the Channel and as far as the west of England, but otherwise the R.A.F. had little to contend with in the course of 261 sorties during which neither side scored.

August 5th

Day Shipping in Straits attacked.
Night Minelaying between the Wash and the Tay.
Weather Temperatures high. Fine with slight haze in the Channel.

In a sharp clash with Spitfires of No. 65 Squadron on patrol over the Straits of Dover a German aircraft was destroyed at 8 a.m.

The squadron was four miles from Calais when the leader caught sight of five Me 109s. Going straight in to the attack, he fired a burst at one Messerschmitt which went straight into the sea. The next 109 hit was last seen heading for the coast with smoke pouring from it, while the third left a trail of debris from the port wing as it headed for France.

At 2 p.m. No. 41 Squadron with Spitfires and No. 151 Squadron with Hurricanes engaged between thirty and forty Germans hunting for shipping in the Channel. Because of the haze the interception was only partially

A typical summer scene at a fighter airfield in 1940. Pilots of 92 Squadron relax on the grass at Bibury, a station in Nl. 10 Group. The pilot on the left is Flight Lt. C. B. F. Kingcombe. In the background is a Spitfire with the trolley accumulator plugged in

successful, but a Me 109 went down in the fighting.

Fighter Command flew 402 sorties. Six German planes were destroyed for one British machine.

August 6th

Day Little activity.
Night Minelaying off east and south-east coasts.
Weather Generally cloudy with fairly strong winds. Cloud ceiling 3,000 to 5,000 feet.

Only seven hostile planes reached the English coast although there was some activity in the Channel against which Fighter Command flew 416 sorties. The score at the end of the day was even at one all, although the only German aircraft lost, an Arado 196 of 1./196, was accidentally wrecked.

August 7th

Day Convoy reconnaissances. Convoy off Cromer attacked.
Night Widespread raids from Thames Estuary to Aberdeen and from Poole, Dorset, to Land's End and Liverpool.
Weather Mainly fair with cloud and thunderstorms in eastern districts. South-eastern districts cloudy. Winds variable.

In the light of subsequent events it is not surprising that German operations were so light, and why they were largely confined during the daylight hours of August 7th to convoy reconnaissance. Preparations were being made for Adlerangriff. Fighter Command squadrons flew 393 sorties, destroying four hostile planes at no cost to themselves.

Broadcasting to the German people on this day, General Sander hinted at the measures to be taken against Britain and indicated that the main weapon would be the bomber. The dawn of Adler Tag was near.

Improvised land defence against invasions.

While the R.A.F. fought its battle in the air, frantic efforts were being made on the ground, in England, to repel the expected invasion.

Ancient armoured vehicles of all types reappeared from sheds and museums. On the Wool–Dorchester Road the vast one and only 'Independent' heavy tank prototype patrolled back and forth; Rolls Royce, Peerless, Crossley and Lanchester armoured cars appeared at many places; at R.A.F. South Cerney, an original 'Little Willie' from World War I provided some measure of airfield defence.

Probably the most unusual 'runner' of the period was a World War I Mk. IV tank presented by the Tank Corps to the Royal Naval Gunnery School, H.M.S. 'Excellent', at Whale Island in 1919. Ever-enterprising, the staff refitted the tank, loaded it with naval 6-pounder ammunition and mounted a Lewis gun on the after hatch. They hoisted the White Ensign over it and the monster went into service as part of 'Excellent's' R.N. Battalion in the defence of Portsmouth. The vehicle can still be seen to this day in full working order.

The photographs show the following :-
A typical scene by a British country road in 1940; an A.13 2-pounder gun cruiser tank of the 2nd Royal Tank Regiment with branches for camouflage.

Originally someone's 'pride and joy'! A 1934 Alvis 'Speed 20' after it had been doctored by the King's Lynn Home Guard. The chicken-wire-lined 'roof' was designed to keep out enemy hand grenades.

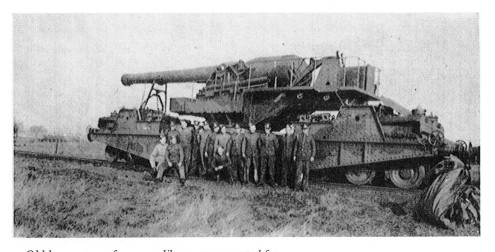

Old heavy guns of many calibres were mounted for anti-invasion defence in 1940. Here is a 9.2 inch on a fully mobile railway mounting at Ashford, Kent. Originally these guns had been used by the Royal Garrison Artillery 1915–1918. The final mobile force of 9.2's in the south east totalled 26 guns.

The remarkably ugly A.11 Matilda 1 heavy tank.
Despite being slow, cumbersome and armed only with
a machine gun, its armour was so thick that no anti-tank
gun of the period could penetrate it. The Matilda Mk. 2
with a 2-pounder gun was also available in small
numbers in 1940.

At first sight a street in Chicago during prohibition,
but in fact a Home Guard-modified Railton Terraplane
motor car at Maidenhead, Berkshire. In the sunshine
roof is a Home Guard with an American Ross rifle
while similar weapons protrude from the side windows.

Between 1939 and 1940 some 40 armoured trains
were produced for coast protection. They were improvised
out of goods wagons and boiler plate. The standard
pattern, as here, mounted light machine guns and a
6-pounder Hotchkiss gun taken from a World War I tank.

13 GROUP,
HEADQUARTERS NEWCASTLE

Wick

3	Hurricane	Wick
504	Hurricane	Castletown
232	Hurricane	Sumburgh (1 Flight only)

Dyce

603	Spitfire	A Flight Dyce
		B Flight Montrose

Turnhouse

605	Hurricane	Drem
232	Hurricane	Turnhouse
253	Hurricane	Turnhouse
141	Defiant	Prestwick

Usworth

79	Spitfire	Acklington (operational by day only)
607	Hurricane	Usworth
72	Spitfire	Acklington

Catterick

219	Blenheim	Catterick

Aldergrove

245	Hurricane	Aldergrove

12 GROUP,
HEADQUARTERS WATNALL

Church Fenton

73	Hurricane	Church Fenton
249	Hurricane	Church Fenton
616	Spitfire	Leconfield

Kirton-in-Lindsey

222	Spitfire	Kirton-in-Lindsey
264	Defiant	Kirton-in-Lindsey (A Flight Ringway)

Digby

46	Hurricane	Digby
611	Spitfire	Digby
29	Blenheim	Digby

Coltishall

242	Hurricane	Coltishall
66	Spitfire	Coltishall

Wittering

229	Hurricane	Wittering
266	Hurricane	Wittering
23	Blenheim	Colly Weston

Duxford

19	Spitfire	Duxford

11 GROUP,
HEADQUARTERS. UXBRIDGE

Debden

17	Hurricane	Debden
85	Hurricane	Martlesham

North Weald

56	Hurricane	Rochford
151	Hurricane	North Weald
25	Blenheim	Martlesham

Hornchurch

54	Spitfire	Hornchurch
65	Spitfire	Hornchurch
74	Spitfire	Hornchurch
41	Spitfire	Hornchurch

Biggin Hill

32	Hurricane	Biggin Hill
610	Spitfire	Biggin Hill
501	Hurricane	Gravesend
600	Blenheim	Manston

Kenley

615	Hurricane	Kenley
64	Spitfire	Kenley
111	Hurricane	Croydon

Northolt

1	Hurricane	Northolt
257	Hurricane	Northolt

Tangmere

43	Hurricane	Tangmere
145	Hurricane	Westhampnett
601	Hurricane	Tangmere

10 GROUP,
HEADQUARTERS BOX, WILTSHIRE

Pembrey

92	Spitfire	Pembrey

Filton

87	Hurricane	Exeter
213	Hurricane	Exeter

St. Eval

234	Spitfire	St. Eval
247	Gladiator	Roborough (1 Flight)

Middle Wallop

238	Hurricane	Middle Wallop
609	Spitfire	Middle Wallop
604	Blenheim	Middle Wallop
152	Spitfire	Warmwell

LUFTFLOTTE 5—NORWAY

X Fliegerkorps
Long-range bombers
    KG26 Stab, I, III   He 111
    KG30 Stab, I, III   Ju 88
Fighters
    ZG76 I   Me 110
    JG77 Stab, I, II   Me 109
Coastal reconnaissance and
    mine-laying
    Kü.Fl.Gr.506   He 115
Long-rang reconnaissance
    Aufkl.Gr.22 with Aufkl. Staffel Obdl.
    1./(F)120
    1./(F)121   He 111 and Ju 88

LUFTFLOTTE 2—HOLLAND, BELGIUM AND NORTHERN FRANCE

I Fliegerkorps
Long-range bombers
    KG1 Stab, I, II, III
          I, II, He 111; III, Ju 88
    KG76 Stab, I, II, III
          Lehrstaffel I, Do. 17;
          II, Ju 88; III, Do. 17
Long-range reconnaissance
    5./(F)122   Ju 88 and He 111
    4./(F)132   Ju 88, He 111, Me 110

II Fliegerkorps
Long-range bombers
    KG2 Stab, I, II, III   Do 17
    KG3 Stab, I, II, III   Do 17
    KG53 Stab, I, II, III   He 111
Dive-bombers
    II/(St.)G.1   Ju 87
    IV/(St.)L.G.1   Ju 87
Fighter-bombers
    Epr.Gr.210   Me 109 and Me 110

IX Fliegerdivision*
Long-range bombers
    KG4 Stab, I, II, III
          I, II, He 111, III, Ju 88
    KGr.100 (up to 16.8.40)†   He 111
Naval co-operation
    KG40 Stab, I   Ju 88
Mine-laying
    KGr.126   He 111
Coastal reconnaissance
    K.Fl.Gr.106   He 115 and Do 18
Long-range reconnaissance
    3./(F)122   Ju 88 and He 111

Jagdfliegerführer 2
Fighters
    JG3 Stab, I, II, III   Me 109
    JG26 Stab, I, II, III   Me 109
    JG51 Stab, I, II, III   Me 109
    JG52 Stab, I, II, III   Me 109
    JG54 Stab, I   Me 109
    ZG26   Me 110

Jagdfliegerführer 1
    In process of formation 22.8.40.

LUFTFLOTTE 3—FRANCE

VIII Fliegerkorps
    (Transferred to Luftflotte 2 29.8.40)
Dive-bombers
    St.G.1 Stab, I, II   Stab, Do 17 and
          Ju 87; I, II, Ju 87
    St.G.2 Stab, I, II   Stab, Do 17 and
          Ju 87; I, II, Ju 87
    St.G.77 Stab, I, II, III   Stab, Do 17
          and Ju 87; I, II, III, Ju 87
Reconnaissance
    II./L.G.2 (at Boblingen,
          Germany)   Do 17
    2./(F)11   Do 17
    2./(F)123   Ju 88
Fighters
    V./(Z)L.G.1   Me 110

V Fliegerkorps
Long-range bombers
    KG51 Stab, I, II, III   Ju 88
    KG54 Stab, I, II   Ju 88
    KG55 Stab, I, II, III   He 111

IV Fliegerkorps
Long-range bombers
    LG1 Stab, I, II, III   Ju 88
    KG27 Stab, I, II, III   He 111
    KGr.806 (under St.G.3)   Ju 88
    KGr.100 (from 16.8.40)   He 111
    St.G.3 Stab   Do 17 and He 111
Naval co-operation
    KG40 I   FW 200
Long-range reconnaissance
    3./(F) (from 8.7.40 to 12.8.40
          under St.G.3)   Me 110 and Do 17

Jagdfliegerführer 3
Fighters
    JG2 Stab, I, II, III   Me 109
    JG27 Stab, I, II, III   Me 109
    JG53 Stab, I, II, III   Me 109
    ZG2 Stab   Me 110

Notes:
* Later IX Fliegerkorps
† KGr.100 Pathfinder and radio beam bombing unit
Stab = Staff flight which was usually operational
Night-fighter gruppen, short-range reconnaissance gruppen (Hs 126)
and transports are not included in these lists

15 Second phase—August 8th–23rd

While the Luftwaffe operations staff anxiously awaited a good weather forecast for the opening of the Adlerangriff, it was not yet committed to an all-out attack on the R.A.F. fighter defence system. For Fighter Command across the Channel a new and serious phase of the battle opened on August 8th when bombing was intensified. Fierce air fighting developed with higher losses to both sides and a month of attrition began in which the British system was strained to the utmost.

To Göring the day held no great significance as he waited impatiently for the belt of high pressure from the Azores which would give him the fine weather required to gain air superiority in 'four days'. He was convinced this aim could be achieved, and outwardly the convoy attacks of July had done nothing to change his views. On the contrary the operations staff and intelligence reports showed heavy British shipping and fighter losses without prohibitive cost to the Germans.

The Reichsmarschall could not know that Dowding on the other side of the Channel was holding his forces in check, and refusing to commit large numbers of fighters to a battle over water where warning time was short, and the enemy usually had the advantage.

By husbanding his resources, Dowding could show a moderate but steady build-up in personnel and surprising increases in aircraft strength and reserves. On August 3rd he had 708 fighters available for operations, and 1,434 pilots, a marked improvement over June 30th, when the respective figures were 587 and 1,200.

On July 10th Fighter Command possessed fifty-two squadrons, but by August 8th three more had been added and six others were under training including No. 1 R.C.A.F. During July the three new squadrons formed were 302 Polish, 303 Polish and 310 Czech.

Most units in the groups rotated through satellite airfields for short periods and the 609 Squadron diarist Flying Officer Dundas recorded:

By the beginning of August 609 were working to a settled operational programme with 238 and 152 Squadrons—609 and 238 Squadrons being based at Middle Wallop, 152 at Warmwell. The routine went as follows—a day on 15 minutes availability at Wallop—a day of release off camp. A day of readiness at Warmwell where we kept a servicing party of thirty airmen under Flight-Sergeant Agar and Sergeant Fitzgerald.

At this time Warmwell possessed, though in rather irregular proportions, the two chief characteristics of a forward station—action and discomfort. Every third day at mid-day the pilots were to set off from Wallop in squadron formation, their cockpits bulging optimistically with sponge-bags, pyjamas,

and other articles of toilet which they got very little opportunity of using.

Sleeping accommodation was provided for visiting squadrons in the sergeants' quarters, but after some experience of this pilots preferred to accommodate themselves as best they could in the dispersal tent, which was furnished with beds, dirty blankets, and an assortment of unreliable telephones.

August 8th

Day Three major attacks on a Channel convoy.
Night Small raids and minelaying.
Weather Showers and bright intervals. Channel cloudy.

The weather in the morning was well suited to German tactics, with visibility six to eight miles and clouds at 2,000 feet giving good cover for enemy aircraft operating from the coast only thirty miles distant.

On the previous night Convoy C.W.9, code-name 'Peewit', had sailed from the Thames Estuary with twenty ships. Its passage did not, however, go unnoticed by operators of the Freya radar set on the cliffs at Cap Blanc Nez, and steps were speedily taken to deal with it. Before dawn on the 8th a pack of E-boats attacked, sinking three ships and damaging others.

At nine o'clock a force of Stukas from Fliegerkorps VIII escorted by Me 109s from JG27 approached from Cherbourg, but was successfully intercepted and broken up by five squadrons from No. 11 Group and one from No. 10 Group.

The bombing was resumed by fifty-seven Ju 87s on a twenty-mile front at 12.45 when the scattered ships were steaming east of the Isle of Wight. Casualties were caused despite the intervention of four and a half British fighter squadrons. Some ships survived, and were duly noted by the departing aircraft. The orders were to sink the convoy completely, if possible, and so a further raid of eighty-two escorted Stukas from Cherbourg moved into the Swanage area at 5 p.m.

Fully alerted, Nos. 10 and 11 groups between them were able to put up seven squadrons, several of which found themselves in excellent positions for attack.

Squadron Leader J. R. A. Peel, commanding No. 145 Hurricane Squadron from Westhampnett, Sussex, reported:

We climbed to 16,000 feet, and, looking down, saw a large formation of Ju 87s approaching from the south with Me 109s stepped up behind to 20,000 feet. We approached unobserved out of the sun and went in to attack the rear Ju 87s before the enemy fighters could interfere. I gave a five-second burst to one bomber and broke off to engage two Me 109s. There was

An Me 110 flying along the Sussex coast near Bexhill during one of the August raids

a dogfight. The enemy fighters, which were painted silver, were half rolling, diving and zooming in climbing turns. I fired two five-second bursts at one and saw it dive into the sea. Then I followed another up in a zoom and got him as he stalled.

A flight-commander of the same squadron brought down two Ju 87s although his own engine had stopped. Despite the engine failure he dived on one Ju 87 which crashed into the sea. His engine re-started and he proceeded to attack another 87 which, instead of bombing a ship, went straight on into the water. After this the engine stopped completely and he glided back to base. No. 145 Squadron was in action three times over the convoy and with No. 43 Squadron caused most of the enemy's losses.

The remains of the battered convoy ploughed its way on, having lost four merchantmen sunk, six badly damaged, with six armed rescue vessels damaged during the day, and three ships sunk by the E-boats. It was the greatest effort made against a single convoy during the whole battle.

While the raids had been going on, German reconnaissance aircraft concentrated on airfields and harbours, the former including Lee-on-Solent, Gosport and Farnborough, and the latter Portsmouth, Portland and Dover. The photographs brought back from these flights and the ensuing four days led to the heavy raids on Lee and Gosport on the 16th and 18th.

The R.A.F. claimed twenty-four German bombers and thirty-six fighters shot down, while the Luftwaffe decided they had shot down forty-nine British fighters. In the upshot the actual losses were nineteen R.A.F. (and one at night) and thirty-one German. These were the highest figures on both sides since the Battle started on July 10th, and Churchill was moved to send a congratulatory message to the Secretary of State for Air.

At night, Fliegerdivision IX laid mines in the Thames Estuary and off the east coast, while small numbers of bombers dropped their loads on Cardiff, Hull, Liverpool, Middlesbrough, Birmingham and the Bristol Aeroplane Company's factory at Filton.

August 9th

Day Quiet. Isolated raids and attacks on the east coast shipping.
Night Minelaying and attacks off east coast.
Weather Cloud and rain showers. Some bright intervals. Channel cloudy.

The Luftwaffe Command staff were preoccupied with the date for Adler Tag. After some discussion, and with Göring's approval, preliminary orders were issued for the commencement of large-scale operations on the 10th. By nightfall, however, these had been cancelled and the action postponed pending the arrival of more favourable weather.

After the dog-fights off the Isle of Wight the previous day, the 9th was quiet. One enemy aircraft reached Sunderland and dropped bombs on the shipyard, causing some damage. Scattered raids were made by Fliegerkorps X on east coast convoys, and two Me 109s attempted to destroy balloons of the Dover barrage without success. Over Plymouth a Ju 88 from 2./LG1 was shot down, also an He 111 from 7./KG26 off the north-east coast.

During the day Fighter Command flew 409 sorties, many of them against 'X' or unidentified raids, which turned out to be mainly reconnaissance patrols. Three R.A.F. fighters were lost (and one at night); five German machines were destroyed. After dark minelaying continued in the same areas as the previous night. Bombers from the Continent hit targets in East Anglia and north of London while Luftflotte 5 attempted to interfere with east coast convoys.

August 10th

Day Shipping and overland reconnaissance.
Night Minelaying.
Weather Squally and thundery, some bright intervals. Channel cloudy.

Senior German officers watching the British coast through binoculars on August 21st, 1940. From left to right: Generaloberst Lörzer, Generalfeldmarschall Milch, Generalfeldmarschall Kesselring and Generalleutnant Wenniger

A very battered Ju 87B of St.G.2 fascinates onlookers of all ages at Bowley Farm, South Mundham, near Chichester, on August 16th. This Stuka was caught by R.A.F. fighters after the strike on Tangmere Aerodrome. Both pilot and observer were hit in the head by bullets, one being dead and the other dying as the aircraft virtually landed itself. The outer wing was ripped off by trees

*A German reconnaissance camera on August 18th
recorded the naval airfield at Ford with hangars smashed
and fuel stores burning. The River Arun can be seen on
the right of the picture. The other photograph shows the
scene on the ground at the same time; outlined against
the pall of smoke are rows of Blackburn Shark biplane
torpedo bombers*

The Sector Station at Middle Wallop, Hampshire, in August. In the first picture a 609 Squadron Spitfire is wrecked and on fire. In the second, three Spitfires of 609 Squadron are seen scrambling to intercept a raid

German activity was limited to shipping reconnaissance off the south and east coasts, eleven bombs from a Dornier 17 falling near West Malling, and a surprise raid being made on Norwich. Fighter Command searched for the elusive raiders in the course of 116 patrols but made no interceptions. There were no losses on either side, although some raiders had tried to find the Boulton Paul factory at Norwich and others flew over Odiham.

Once again at night Fliegerdivision IX laid mines, extending its activities from Harwich and the Thames Estuary to the Bristol Channel. A raid was sent to the Rolls-Royce works at Crewe, but did not find the target.

August 11th

Day Heavy attack on Portland, feints by fighter formations over Dover. Convoy attacks in Thames Estuary and off East Anglia.
Night Harassing attacks on Merseyside. Minelaying.
Weather Fair in morning. Cloudy most of day.

Compared with the lull on the 10th, this Sunday morning started with considerable activity. From 7 to 10.30 a series of probing attacks developed against Dover. First two formations of fifteen + fighters and Me 110 fighter bombers from Gruppe 210 attacked the Dover balloon barrage, followed by a threat to Channel convoys at 8.30 a.m. No sooner had this died down than thirty + of the enemy returned to Dover and were engaged by anti-aircraft fire and by fighters from Nos. 74, 34, 42 and 64 squadrons. The German formation was not really looking for action and only served to draw off British aircraft.

The Luftwaffe plan was to attract as many fighters as possible to the Dover area, while the main strike was delivered much farther west, at Portland. This operation being laid on in place of the mass Adler Tag assault, which had again been postponed.

While three squadrons were hotly engaged over Dover, the radar stations, in particular Ventnor, picked

Hurricanes of No. 501 Squadron taking off past the hangars at Gravesend Aerodrome, Kent, on August 16th

up a large raid heading for the Weymouth area, and Nos. 145, 238, 152, 601, 213, 609 and 287 Squadrons were scrambled to intercept. They found some 150 aircraft, Ju 88s and He 111s escorted by Me 109s and Me 110s. Fierce dog-fights developed as the bombers pressed home their high-level and dive-bomber attacks against docks, oil-tanks, barracks and gasworks at Weymouth and Portland. A resident of one of the houses attacked described the formations as being 'like a swarm of bees in the sky. I counted up to fifty and then stopped.'

When the situation maps showed Portland clear, more fighters appeared off Dover to shoot at balloons from the long-suffering No. 961 Balloon Squadron. A further force attacked the convoy 'Booty' off the Norfolk coast and seriously damaged two ships. A destroyer and two minesweepers off Margate were attacked. They put up a spirited defence but one minesweeper suffered several casualties and the ship was finally beached under the North Foreland.

A typical example of the work of the fighter squadrons involved on the 11th was No. 74 at its forward base at Manston.

The squadron took part in no less than four separate combats from dawn to 2 p.m. and accounted for a number of German aircraft with the loss of only two pilots. The first operational order was received at 7.49 a.m. to intercept a hostile raid approaching Dover. The squadron with twelve aircraft, led by Squadron Leader Malan, climbed to 20,000 feet, and surprised approximately eighteen Me 109s flying towards Dover. Pilot Officer Stevenson's aircraft was hit by enemy fire and he baled out and came down in the sea. He attracted the attention of a motor torpedo-boat by firing his revolver. The second combat took place between 9.50 and 10.45 when twelve aircraft again took off to intercept enemy fighters approaching Dover. Several small groups of Me 109s were sighted in mid-Channel. Owing to R/T difficulties, part of the squadron did not engage.

The third combat started at 11.45 when eleven aircraft took off to patrol the convoy 'Booty' about twelve miles east of Clacton. Forty Me 110s were sighted approaching the

convoy from east in close formation just below cloud base. Enemy aircraft formed a defensive circle on sighting the fighters, but Pilot Officer Freeborne led the squadron in a dive into the middle of the circle. Aircraft landed back at Manston at 12.45. The squadron took off for the fourth time at 1.56 with eight aircraft, to patrol Hawkinge at 15,000 feet and subsequently north-east of Margate where enemy raids were reported. Ten Ju 87s were sighted passing through cloud at 6,000 feet and twenty Me 109s at 10,000 feet. Fighters attacked the 109s, who dived for cloud and a dog-fight ensued.

No. 604 Squadron found a Heinkel 59 rescue seaplane afloat off the French coast with its engines running, and destroyed it, despite interference from the Me 109 escort.

The rest of the afternoon was quiet and that night a few harassing attacks were aimed at Merseyside and more mines were laid in the Bristol Channel.

In the confused fighting, the honours of the day were nearly even—thirty-eight German and thirty-two British losses. This was not the kind of tally sheet which 11 Group liked, or could afford. Fighters had clashed heavily with fighters and thirteen Me 109s had been destroyed (six from JG2) and ten Me 110s. Of the latter two were from the fighter-bomber unit Epr.Gr.210 operating off Harwich.

August 12th

Day Sharp raid on Portsmouth. Convoy in Thames Estuary, radar stations and coastal airfields attacked.
Night Widespread harassing raids.
Weather Fine except for mist patches.

To the harassed staff of the O.K.L., Göring's headquarters, the 12th was an important day. The meteorological forecast showed the first movement of a high-pressure belt in the Azores which would give good clear weather over the United Kingdom on the following day. The operations branch, IA, issued orders to Luftflotten 2 and 3 to be ready for the big attack at at 7 a.m. on the 13th.

In preparation for this the 12th was to be devoted to the first raids on British fighter airfields and radar stations while maintaining pressure against shipping and harbours. The battle area now moved forward over the island itself, and Fighter Command had its

most intensive day since the war began.

The attacks were divided into five phases moving pendulum fashion backwards and forwards along the south coast. Feints began over Dover at 7.30 a.m., and at nine o'clock five radar stations were attacked. Dunkirk radar had two huts destroyed and a 1,000 lb. bomb near the concrete transmitting block moved it inches. No vital damage was done and plotting continued.

At Dover the aerial towers were slightly damaged and huts inside the compound were smashed, while at Rye all huts were destroyed, but miraculously the transmitting and receiving blocks and the watch office were unharmed. A stand-by diesel put the station back on the air by noon. At Pevensey eight 500 kg. bombs were dropped and damage included a cut in the electric main. The airfield at Lympne was also bombed.

After an hour's respite the second phase opened with a formation of Ju 87s attacking convoys 'Arena' and 'Agent' in the Estuary, while Ju 88s from Luftflotte 3, with heavy escort, were flying in towards the Southampton area. Some aircraft diverted to bomb convoys 'Snail' and 'Cable', but the main target was Portsmouth, which received a heavy attack, despite the concentrated fire of every ship and landborne A.A. gun in the harbour. At Margate the lifeboat crew were sitting watching a film of the B.E.F. evacuation from Dunkirk in the town hall when the siren sounded. The crews hurried to their station and the motor lifeboat *J. B. Proudfoot* was launched in time to pick up the survivors of two Admiralty trawlers, *Pyrope* and *Tamarisk*, which had been sunk.

The enemy had approached the target by flying up the Channel in a westerly direction from Spithead and then turned through the gap in the balloon barrage formed by the harbour mouth. Several fires were started in the docks and the city itself, and the harbour station was burnt out. As they saw no fighters over the A.A. area, the citizens of Portsmouth felt that the Germans had been allowed too liberal a use of their air-space.

While Portsmouth was being hit, fifteen Ju 88s dive-bombed the long-range C.H. radar station at Ventnor in the Isle of Wight. Fires were started, and because of lack of water on the site most of the buildings were destroyed and other serious damage done. A German reconnaissance later in the day noted 'craters in the vicinity of the wireless station masts, and the station quarters on fire'.

Shortly after this the coastal airfield at Manston received the first of many raids. A formation of Dorniers came in low at 1.25 p.m. and dropped about 150 high-explosive bombs, pitting the airfield with craters, destroying the workshops and damaging two hangars, all in the space of five minutes. Only one casualty was recorded, but the airfield was unserviceable until the 13th.

No. 54 Squadron had striven to deflect the bombers from Manston, but could not penetrate the heavy escort. On the ground No. 65 Squadron's Spitfires were taxi-ing out for take-off when the first bombs hit. Most of them managed to get into the air and joined in the mêlée of 109s and No. 54 Squadron aircraft above. When the Dornier formation from KG2 turned for home it was without its main escort and came in for a

At lunch time on August 18th two groups of Dornier 17s attacked the sector airfield at Kenley, Surrey. One formation of nine bombers came at tree-top height while the other bombed from high altitude. The first picture taken from a low-level Dornier shows bombs bursting in the dispersal area, just missing a lone 64 Squadron Spitfire standing in its blast pen. The second picture shows the fate of one of these low-level raiders, a Do 17. Hit by a parachute and cable device, A.A. fire and fighters, it crashed in a field at Leaves Green, near Biggin Hill. The pilot, Oberleutnant Lamberty, was injured as were his crew. Out of nine low-level aircraft only one returned intact to base.

The third picture was taken from the high flying Dorniers a few minutes after the first attack. Just below is another Dornier (4) while bomb hits are shown (1, 2 and 3). 2a is marked by the Germans as British wreckage, but is, in fact, believed to be a shot-down Dornier. The Kenley runways have been carefully painted to merge with the surrounding countryside

The hangars at Tangmere sector station, Sussex, smashed and burning after a Stuka attack at mid-day on August 16th. Three aircraft were destroyed and eleven damaged. Alongside the hangars can be seen a Blenheim I fighter and a Blenheim IV bomber

determined attack by the Hurricanes of No. 56 Squadron.

Hawkinge, another advance airfield on the coast, was seriously damaged by Ju 88s which smashed two hangars, destroyed the station workshops and damaged stores. Despite twenty-eight craters on the airfield, Hawkinge was not completely unserviceable and became fully operational again on the morning of the 13th. Four aircraft had been badly damaged, five people killed and seven seriously injured.

Lympne, which had received 141 bombs in the morning, was the subject of a second attack in the fifth phase of the day commencing at 3 p.m. Two hundred and forty-two bombs were dropped in two runs and the airfield rendered unserviceable, although seventy of the bombs fell into surrounding fields. The remainder of the force from Luftflotte 2 bombed Hastings and Dover.

As evening came, the Luftwaffe were jubilant. German radio stations spoke of very heavy damage on the British mainland and claimed seventy-one R.A.F. aircraft, including the whole of No. 65 Squadron at

Manston. The German headquarters report of the 13th claimed that forty-six Spitfires, twenty-three Hurricanes and one Morane 406 had been destroyed on the 12th. In fact the Germans had lost thirty-one machines and the R.A.F., in the course of 732 sorties, had suffered twenty-two casualties.

The attacks had been severe and they provided a foretaste of the main August battle pattern. Of the six radar stations attacked, only one had been knocked out, Ventnor, but this was not apparent to German signals intelligence.

These initial strikes at radar had brought out two important points. First, the aerial towers themselves consistently deflected dive-bombing attacks away from the vital operations rooms underneath. Second, the W.A.A.F. plotters showed courage of the highest order under fire and the ability to keep on reporting a raid until it bombed their own station.

The airfields received many tons of bombs but survived. While it was clear to the R.A.F. that very heavy concentration at frequent intervals would be required completely to wreck a particular field, the Luftflotten staffs in France had already begun the foolhardy process of deleting units and stations on the map after each attack.

That night widespread harassing raids developed overland in addition to the normal crop of minelaying. Small numbers of aircraft dropped bombs on many towns and villages, including Stratford-upon-Avon,

Me 109s of JG53 lined up on a Belgian airfield in September 1940. In the foreground lie the remains of a Belgian Air Force Fairey Fox biplane

Luftwaffe officers confer at the forward headquarters at Cap Blanc Nez. Second from the right is Oberst Theo Osterkamp, a first World War veteran, who commanded JG51 and began fighter escort for the Stukas over the Channel in July

August 13th

Day Opening of 'Eagle Day' misfires. Heavy raid on East-church followed by afternoon raids on Portland, Southampton and airfields in Hampshire and Kent. 1,485 German sorties.
Night Light raids on midlands, Wales and the west.
Weather Mainly fair, early-morning mist and slight drizzle in places. Channel, some cloud.

Luftflotten 2 and 3 were keyed up for the great attack and at dawn all was ready for the opening of the air battle which would crush Britain. Airfield, harbour and shipping targets had been minutely detailed, and the air fleet staffs had worked overtime producing up-to-date photographic maps from films brought back by the reconnaissance groups. Unfortunately, some very poor analyses were made and certain photographic aircraft were shot down with the result that coverage was not complete. Fleet Air Arm, Training Command and Coastal Command airfields were included as fighter stations and many attacks were made on them, the results being overestimated and attributed to Fighter Command.

Typical of the poor reconnaissance interpretations made was contained in the O.K.L. situation report for August 13th. In covering the naval air stations at Ford, Gosport and Lee, twenty-four Hawker Demons

A Dornier 17Z of KG2, based on Cambrai, delivers its load over England

Dornier 17Zs of Stabstaffel/KG3 head out across the Channel for southern England

and ten Spitfires were identified although no such aircraft were based there. Tangmere was credited with no less than fifty-five Hurricanes at the dispersals, a considerable exaggeration.

The incorrect assessment of British control and radio techniques by Schmid at Intelligence IC* had resulted in the assumption that mass attacks would confuse the defences as much as multi-pronged raids over a wide area.

In the morning, formations began to take off to execute the plan, but at the last moment a personal signal from the Reichsmarschall postponed Adlerangriff until the afternoon, when the weather would clear. Three units were, however, already on their way above the cloud-base of 4,000 feet, one headed for the Eastchurch area, another for Odiham, and the third to provide a diversion off Portland.

The main force, seventy-four Dornier 17s from KG2, at Cambrai and St Leger, lost its escort of Me 110s over the coast shortly after 5.30 a.m. Kesselring's headquarters had been frantically radioing instructions to cancel the operation following Göring's message, but only the Me 110s picked it up, and returned to base.

In two separate formations, KG2 made for Eastchurch aerodrome and Sheerness. Because of poor estimating on the part of radar operators and difficulty in plotting by the Observer Corps due to low cloud, the assessments of strength were wrong and insufficient fighters were put up.

No. 74 Squadron, from Hornchurch, found the Dorniers over Whitstable at 7 a.m. as they emerged from cloud. A fierce fight developed with this, the rear formation, but the leaders with General Fink, the commodore of KG2 in command, went on unmolested to Eastchurch. The bombing there was very heavy with a direct hit on the operations room, five Blenheims of No. 35 Squadron destroyed by incendiary bullets, 12 people killed and 40 injured. The Luftwaffe claimed 10 Spitfires destroyed on the ground.

Nos. 111 and 151 squadrons joined in the fight just

Blenheim IF twin-engined fighters were outpaced by German fighters and in certain cases even by Lutwaffe bombers. Despite this, Blenheim-equipped units fought hard; they also bore the brunt of fighting before the advent of the Beaufighter. Shown here is a Blenheim 1 of 604 Squadron based at Middle Wallop

after Eastchurch had been hit and between them the three squadrons shot down four Dorniers and damaged four more as they dodged between the clouds. Eastchurch had been severely damaged and was written off by Luftflotte 2 as a fighter airfield destroyed. In fact it belonged to 22 Group Coastal Command, and housed a composite anti-shipping force of fighters and light bombers. It was operational again ten hours after the raid, despite wrecked buildings, broken communications and fifty bomb craters.

To the west, the Ju 88s of KG54 headed for the airfield at Odiham and the Royal Aircraft Establishment, Farnborough, in Hampshire, in two sections with escort. They were engaged over the coast by No. 43 Squadron and a section from Northolt, these being shortly joined by Nos. 601 and 64 Squadrons. Harried by fighters and disorganised by thick cloud, the two attacks missed their targets.

At 11.40 radar picked up twenty + raiders about eighty miles distant and they were tracked in towards Portsmouth.

The raid on Portland by KG 54 completely misfired as the bombers did not put in an appearance and their escort of Me 110s were picked up by radar over Cherbourg. They were hotly engaged by two R.A.F. squadrons, who dived on them and destroyed six in the space of five minutes, the remainder going flat out for the protection of the French coast.

The real opening thrust of the 'Attack of the Eagles' developed in the afternoon, despite continued poor weather. Mass attacks were made from 3.45 to 5 p.m. on Portland, Southampton, Kent and the Thames Estuary.

After the incursions of the morning, No. 10 Group prepared to put up strong forces to meet formations of

20 +, 50 +, 30 + and 30 + which showed up on the radar screens as coming in from Jersey. No. 152 from Warmwell was over the coast and was joined by Nos. 238 and 213 from Middle Wallop and Exeter respectively, while No. 609 Squadron from Warmwell patrolled over Weymouth. Tangmere sector provided No. 601 Squadron to cover the Isle of Wight.

German bomber formations in three waves were drawn from Lehr Geschwader 1 in the Orleans Bricy area with Ju 88s and Fliegerkorps VIII with Ju 87s. First on the scene was a heavy forward sweep of German fighters which became involved in a fight with Nos. 231 and 152 squadrons, while No. 238's Hurricanes fell in with a force of Me 110s supposedly guarding Ju 87s.

Most of the Ju 88s got through to Southampton where serious damage was done and large fires started in the warehouses and docks.

No. 609 Squadron found a golden opportunity and took it. Thirteen Spitfires found a formation of Ju 87s below them with half the escort well above, and the other half deeply involved with No. 238.

Attacked out of the sun, the Stukas made a perfect target. On the way the Spitfires dived through five Me 109s, breaking them up, Pilot Officer D. M. Crook sending one spinning down into a field on fire. The whole Stuka formation broke up with nine falling in flames or with the crews dead. For once the Spitfires had altitude, position and surprise and they used it to deadly effect. One member of the squadron remarked that he rather missed the 'Glorious Twelfth' this year— 'but the glorious thirteenth was the best day's shooting I ever had'.

The remaining Ju 87s missed their main target, Middle Wallop, and scattered their bombs over three counties. They hit Andover airfield, but this was not a fighter station and little damage was done.

Away to the east the other prong of the divided German attack was coming in in waves from Luftflotte 2 with Detling (near Maidstone) and Rochester as its main targets. The bombers were heavily escorted, and while No. 65 Squadron was engaged with the fighters,

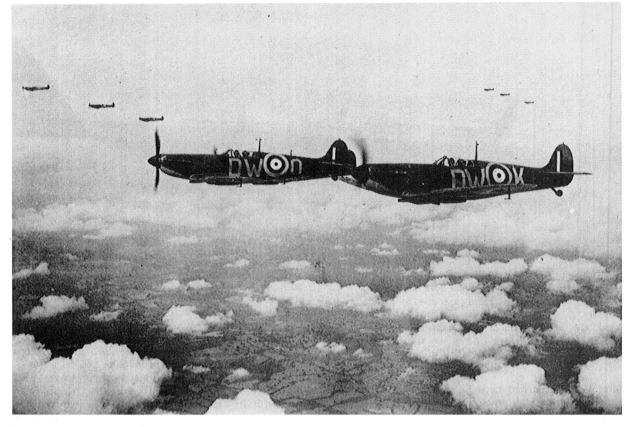

Nine Spitfires of 610 Squadron from Biggin Hill on patrol during August

a bomber force slipped through and got to Detling. Due to cloud, Rochester was not discovered and as the force for this target returned home they were caught by No. 56 Squadron from Rochford and bomb loads were jettisoned over Canterbury. Other bombs fell on Lympne and Ramsgate.

At Detling the commanding officer was killed by dive-bombing and the hangars set on fire. The operations room, the messes and the cookhouse were all destroyed, but essential services, including communications, were working by noon on the 14th.

At the end of a day of severe fighting on both flanks of 11 Group the final score was thirteen R.A.F. fighters lost on 700 sorties and forty-five German aircraft brought down, a definite victory for Fighter Command to which the vulnerable Ju 87 contributed in no small measure.

The Luftwaffe had flown its greatest number of sorties to date—1,485—and it claimed that seventy Spitfires and Hurricanes and eighteen Blenheims had been destroyed, exaggeration by nearly 700 per cent.

At night while thirty-six British bombers flew 1,600 miles to bomb the Fiat and Caproni works at Turin and Milan, German aircraft from Luftflotte 5 raided northern Scotland and machines from the Continent flew to Wales, the West Country, the midlands and

Norwich. The main target was the Spitfire shadow factory at Castle Bromwich where eleven bombs were dropped. One of the British bombers returning from Italy crashed in the Channel in the early morning following. A fishing boat picked up two of the crew and a third was rescued by a Miss Prince who rowed out in a small canoe.

August 14th

Day Targets, south-east England, airfields and communications. Airfields in the west.
Night Little activity.
Weather Mainly cloudy with bright patches. Channel cloudy.

After their efforts of the previous day, the Luftwaffe put in a third the number of sorties with ninety-one bombers and 398 fighters.

O.K.L.IA staff had issued orders to Luftflotten 2 and 3 for attacks on aircraft industry and R.A.F. ground organisation targets. Accordingly at 11.40 formations of bombers and escorts built up over Boulogne and Calais in full view of the coastal radar stations. By noon the attack had developed over Dover and the Kentish airfields in successive waves, mainly consisting of fighters looking for combat. At 1 p.m. a dozen Me 110 fighter bombers from 210 Gruppe slipped through, while Spitfires were occupied with a feint off Dover, and bombed Manston airfield destroying four hangars but losing two machines, one to an Army Bofors gun and one to an R.A.F. aircraft-type Hispano cannon temporarily fitted to a ground mounting.

This Me 110 was brought down in one of the August battles. To stop the machine falling into British hands, a Ju 88 dropped bombs on the field but only succeeded in throwing up great lumps of turf

Three and a half squadrons of 11 Group fighters were in the area, but mainly above cloud dealing with Me 109s and 110s, the Me 109s coming from JG26. Shortly afterwards the main enemy force, which had held back, came in over Folkestone and Dover, shooting down eight barrage balloons and sinking the Goodwin Light Vessel.

In the afternoon it was the turn of Luftflotte 3 and Sperrle's policy was to send in small raids over a wide area in the hope of upsetting the defences. Eight airfields and various railway lines were the main targets.

At Middle Wallop sector station a dive-bombing raid by three machines set on fire the No. 609 Squadron hangar and killed three airmen, while offices were hit and ten airmen at the station headquarters injured. The Luftwaffe, however, reported that it had bombed Netheravon.

Maintenance Command had its first share of the battle at 30 M.U. Sealand, Cheshire, when a Heinkel 111 flew in at 1,000 feet and dropped eight high-explosive bombs and one incendiary in a line, but caused no serious damage. A second Heinkel followed up to more purpose, smashing the sergeants' mess and causing one fatal casualty. Despite water failure and a cut in the main high-tension cable, the station reported a full working day 'with two hours' overtime' on the 15th. Colerne was also attacked but to no good effect. Of the railways, the worst hit was Southampton where the main line was blocked by debris.

Despite hits on various airfields and the problems of bad weather, 10 and 11 Group could show a ratio of over 2:1 in their favour as regards losses, with nineteen German aircraft down against eight R.A.F. fighters.

Although the operational training units were not involved in the struggle, No. 7 O.T.U. at Hawarden, Flintshire, formed a battle flight to deal with emergencies. On the 14th, after hearing explosions and machine-gun fire in the vicinity, Wing Commander Hallings-Pott accompanied by Squadron Leader J. S. McLean and Pilot Officer P. V. Ayerst, took off in Spitfires and intercepted a Heinkel 111, shooting it down near Chester.

Night brought the usual series of small raids over the south of England and Wales. The defences were keyed up for a heavy attack following interception of German radio messages threatening a raid on Liverpool, but nothing developed.

The first week of the second phase had now passed although Fighter Command had no inkling of it and could only see a vista of continued attacks perhaps for six months or more. There were no decisive highs or lows, only more or less fighting.

As the controllers watched the last raids out and awaited first light, they did not know that the morning would bring the combined strength of three Luftflotten against Britain and that all four fighter groups would be in action to score probably the most notable victory of the whole battle.

August 15th

Day Decisive; heavy raids by all three Luftflotten, their greatest effort of the battle. Seventy-five German aircraft lost. Airfields main target.
Night Little activity.
Weather Ridge of high pressure over Britain. Fine, warm weather. Some cloud over Channel.

With clear weather forecast the Luftwaffe exerted its greatest effort of the campaign, throwing in every available fighter, and major portions of the dive-bomber and bomber forces.

Hurricanes of 32 Squadron coming in to land at Biggin Hill after one of the big raids on August 15th. In the right background is a typical blast pen for fighters

The German plan of attack—outlined in a command paper of the previous day—was to produce a series of raids on a wide front—aimed at wrecking airfields and radar and bringing as many British fighters into battle as possible. Luftflotte 5 was to use most of its force to attack targets in the north-east, where it was presumed that fighter defences had been greatly weakened in order to reinforce the south.

The whole perimeter of the German line from Norway to Brittany was a hive of activity at first light, with final briefings, bombing up, and last-minute adjustments to engines and equipment.

In Britain the early hours seemed quiet enough apart from reconnaissance flights but from eleven o'clock onwards five main attacks developed.

First about 100 enemy aircraft, made up of forty Ju 87s with a heavy escort, attacked the forward airfields at Hawkinge and Lympne. At the latter a heavy dive-bombing attack cut all water and power supplies, caused a direct hit on the station sick quarters, and damaged several other buildings. Various sections had to be evacuated to nearby houses and the field was not serviceable for forty-eight hours.

At Hawkinge the damage was far less with one hangar

hit and a small barrack block destroyed. One of the most serious consequences in the area was the shut-down of Rye and Dover C.H. stations and Foreness C.H.L. which suffered a power failure when the electric mains were hit.

Nos. 54 and 501 squadrons met the force, 54 attacking out of the sun on to the dive-bombers, but the devastation at Lympne could not be prevented.

Then followed an attack which was to be the most interesting of the whole day. Banking on tactical surprise and conveniently forgetting the radar chain, Luftflotte 5 launched two simultaneous thrusts in the north and north-east. They expected little opposition and their reception came as a painful surprise.

At eight minutes past twelve radar began to plot a formation of twenty + opposite the Firth of Forth at a range of over ninety miles. As the raid drew closer the estimates went up to thirty in three sections flying south-west towards Tynemouth.

At Watnall the approach of No. 13 Group's first daylight raid was watched on the operations table with particular interest. With an hour's warning the controller was able to put squadrons in an excellent position to attack, with 72 Squadron Spitfires in the path of the enemy off the Farne Islands and 605 Squadron Hurricanes over Tyneside. Nos. 79 and 607 were also put up, but while the latter was right in the path of the raid, No. 79 was too far north.

No. 72 Squadron from Acklington was the first to

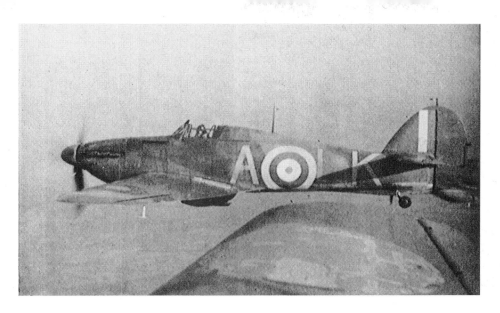

In late August Hurricanes of A Flight, No. 87 Squadron, en route from Exeter to Portland to intercept a raid

make contact and it came as a distinct shock when the thirty materialised as I and III/KG26 with sixty-five Heinkel 111s, and the entire I/ZG76 from Stavanger with thirty-four Me 110s. After a brief pause in which to survey the two massive groups flying in vic formation, Squadron-Leader E. Graham led No. 72 straight in from the flank, one section attacking the fighters and the rest the bombers.

The Me 110s formed defensive circles, while the Heinkels split up. Some of them jettisoned their bombs in the sea and headed back for Norway, leaving several of their number in the sea. The separate parts of the formation finally reached the coast, one south of Sunderland and the other south of Acklington. No. 79 intercepted the northern group over the water while a flight from No. 605 squadron caught it over land. Most of the bombs fell harmlessly in the sea.

The group off Sunderland found Nos. 607 and 41 squadrons waiting for it and they too bombed to little effect apart from wrecking houses. The raiders turned back to Norway, the Me 110s having already departed some minutes before. Of a total force of about 100, eight bombers and seven fighters were destroyed and several more damaged without British loss. The airfield targets such as Usworth, Linton-on-Ouse and Dishforth went unscathed. One Staffel of III/KG26 lost five of its nine aircraft in the course of the fighting.

Farther south, an unescorted formation of fifty Ju 88s from I, II and III/KG30, based on Aalborg, was heading in to No. 12 Group off Flamborough Head. Full radar warning was given and 73 Squadron Hurricanes, 264 Squadron Defiants and 616 Squadron Spitfires were sent to patrol the area, the force being supplemented later by Blenheims from 219 Squadron in 13 Group.

Both No. 616 and a flight of No. 73 engaged, but the enemy split into eight sections. Some turned north to bomb Bridlington where houses were hit and an

ammunition dump blown up. The main force, however, flew to the 4 Group Bomber Station at Driffield, Yorkshire, where four hangars were damaged and ten Whitleys were destroyed on the ground. Heavy anti-aircraft fire was directed against the bombers and one was brought down. Altogether, six of KG30's Ju 88s were shot down, representing about 10 per cent of the force sent over.

In all, the northern attacks lost sixteen bombers out of a serviceable Luftflotte 5 force of 123, and seven fighters of the thirty-four available.

In the south at noon it was the turn of Manston once again. Twelve Me 109s attacked with cannon and machine-gun fire, destroying two Spitfires and causing sixteen casualties.

This was followed at 3 p.m. by a force of Ju 87s, Me 110 fighter bombers and Me 109s attacking the fighter station at Martleshan Heath without being intercepted. The Ju 87s concentrated on an incomplete signals station to the west, while the 110s hit the airfield. The signals station escaped with broken windows and a punctured water tank, but Martlesham itself had workshops and officers' mess wrecked, a burst water main and cut telephone wires. A visiting Fairey Battle blew up, smashing two hangars, the watch office and the night-fighting equipment sheds. The station was engaged on repair work throughout the following day.

Simultaneously about 100 aircraft were approaching Deal to be followed by 150 over Folkestone at 3.30. Only four fighter squadrons were on patrol to deal with this influx, although followed by three more (Nos. 1, 17, 32, 64, 111, 151 and 501) and they were warded off by the escorts through sheer weight of numbers. The German formations broke up to deal with separate targets, one being the Short Brothers and Pobjoy factories at Rochester. The production of four motor Stirling heavy bombers at Rochester suffered a severe set-back due to six complete aircraft and the finished parts store being destroyed. This was a real victory for the Luftwaffe but it had no effect on Fighter Command. Several German machines attacked East-

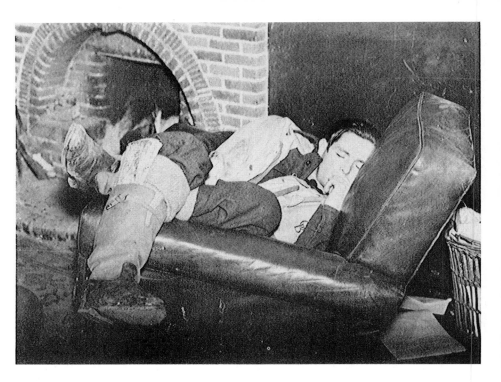

Worn out, Sgt. G. Booth, of No. 85 Squadron, fast asleep after a day's operations in August. He is still wearing his Mae West and his air maps are stuffed into the top of his boot. Sgt. Booth was killed later in the Battle

church and the radar stations at Dover, Rye, Bawdsey and Foreness, although without useful results.

Two further attacks were made in the early evening, the first—a feint—in the south-west and the second against Kent and Surrey. Some 250 aircraft from Luftflotte 3 moved towards the Isle of Wight in two groups at 5 p.m. and spread out over Hampshire and Wiltshire.

Ju 88s with Me 110 escort attacked Middle Wallop but did less damage than the three aircraft of the previous day. No. 609 Squadron got off just before the dive-bombing started, and harried the stragglers out to sea. This raid had been intercepted at intervals by no less than eight R.A.F. squadrons and one section of it which reached Worthy Down caused little damage, while another dropped bombs on Portland. In their combat reports the crews who raided Odiham claimed to have hit Andover instead.

Out of the whole German force twenty-five aircraft were lost against sixteen by Fighter Command. Thirteen Me 110s were brought down of which three fell to the guns of Belgian Lieutenant J. Phillipart of 213 Squadron. Altogether eleven R.A.F. squadrons were put up against these raids, being Nos. 32, 43, 111, 601, 604, 609, 87, 152, 213, 234 and 266.

At 6.15 over seventy aircraft were plotted coming in from Calais, and as most of his forward squadrons were refuelling and rearming, Park switched four squadrons from the eastern sectors following up with

four and a half more as they became available.

Intercepted over the coast by two squadrons, including No. 501, which was almost at the end of its fuel, the Germans split up and missed their primary targets of Biggin Hill and Kenley. Instead they spotted West Malling, Kent, from high altitude and damaged runways and buildings.

Other bombers wandering over Surrey decided to deliver their loads on Croydon, the home of No. 111 Squadron, which unit was officially not yet operational.

Me 110s from Gruppe 210 with Me 109 escort came in at 2,000 feet just after 6.50 p.m. to drop their bombs, which destroyed the Rollason and Redwing factories, together with many trainer aircraft, and a radio component works. Over eighty casualties were caused and it was the first recorded raid on Greater London.

Over the airfield on patrol at 10,000 feet were 111 Squadron's Hurricanes which promptly dived on the raiders and together with 32 Squadron from Biggin Hill shot down four as they went flat out for the coast. This made Gr.210's losses eight Me 110s in five days.

During the day No. 151 Squadron took delivery of the first Hurricane with four 20 mm. cannon which had been rebuilt from a crashed machine. No. 151 already possessed a two-cannon Hurricane, but like 19 Squadron with Cannon Spitfires, the problems of mechanical failure and ammunition feed were not overcome before the end of the Battle.

That night there was no relaxation of German activity with some seventy bombers hitting Birmingham, Boston, Kirton, Beverley, Southampton, Crewe, Yarmouth, Harwich, Bristol and Swansea.

At the time the R.A.F. claimed to have shot down 182 German aircraft in the course of its 974 sorties, but the records show that the actual figure was 75. British losses were less than half, with 34 aircraft lost, 17 pilots

The railways suffered continuously right through the Battle of Britain and the Blitz. Here workers repair the down-line at St. Denys, Southampton, after one of the afternoon trains had been bombed on August 14th

killed and 16 wounded. The Luftwaffe claimed 82 Spitfires and Hurricanes, 5 non-existent Curtiss Hawks and 14 miscellaneous types.

The day's losses for the Luftwaffe covered practically every basic type in operational use—Do 17, He 111, Ju 88, Ju 87, Me 109 and Me 110. In addition an Arado 196, an He 59 and an He 115 (all floatplanes) were destroyed. The He 115 was found wrecked on the coast near Arbroath.

The revised figures in no way detract from the significance of August 15th, which altered the whole course of the Battle. The Luftwaffe had put up 1,786 sorties in the twenty-four-hour period of which 520 were bombers. Practically every available fighter had been used in an attempt to destroy Fighter Command in the air while the ground facilities were being wrecked by bombing. The attacks had covered all four fighter groups and yet despite some airfield damage no success was achieved.

The German Air Force could have committed its whole bomber force to the operation but instead it put in less than half, a tacit admission that all-out bomber operations could not be carried on over Britain until air superiority had been achieved. The full force was in fact never employed on any day throughout the Battle.

The German losses were far heavier than anticipated, and the 15th had three lasting effects on the outcome of the conflict:

1 First and foremost, Luftflotte 5 was to all intents and purposes finished in the daylight battle apart from reconnaissance. Towards the end of August most of its bomber strength and some of the fighters were transferred to France to swell the ranks of Luftflotte 2.

2 The spirited opposition in the north swung the battle back to the south-east of England where heavier loads could be carried over the short ranges and where the Me 109 had sufficient tankage to provide escort.

3 The Stuka and the Me 110 were confirmed as unsuitable for their tasks, and in the latter case it meant that escorts had to be provided for the twin-engined fighters themselves.

From the 15th onwards the Me 109s were allowed less free run over the battle zone, and were brought in closer to the bomber formations. This was the complete antithesis of the purpose for which they were built and instead of bringing the R.A.F. to combat, they had to sit and wait for the attack to come to them.

During the day, while the assault was at its height, Göring was in conference at Karinhall with his senior staff and the Luftflotten commanders.

The Reichmarschall opened his address with a warning against Stuka losses:

The fighter escort defences of our Stuka formations must be readjusted as the enemy is concentrating his fighters against our Stuka operations. It appears necessary to allocate three fighter Gruppen to each Stuka Gruppe, one of these fighter Gruppen remains with the Stukas and dives with them to the attack; the second flies ahead of the target at medium altitude and engages fighter defences; the third protects the whole attack from above. It will also be necessary to escort Stukas returning from the attack over the Channel.

He stressed that 'Operations are to be directed exclusively against the enemy air force including the targets of the enemy aircraft industry. . . . Our night attacks are essentially dislocation raids, made so that the enemy defences and population shall be allowed no respite.'

After directing that the pathfinder unit K.Gr.100

British soldiers remove machine guns, parachute and other equipment from a Dornier 17Z of KG2, brought down at Stodmarsh, Kent, on August 17th. Additional armament was being fitted to all Luftwaffe bombers at this time. The makeshift machine gun position in the rear window has been equipped with a metal safety rail to restrict the field of fire and stop the gunner from shooting holes in his own aircraft

should be thrown into the general attack, Göring proceeded to save the all-important British radar chain from destruction by saying: 'It is doubtful whether there is any point in continuing the attacks on radar sites, in view of the fact that not one of those attacked has so far been put out of action.'

Technicians toiling to repair Ventnor C.H. station on the Isle of Wight would hardly have agreed with these last words, but the R.A.F. could be thankful that its opponent's commander-in-chief understood neither science nor engineering.

Later in the day Göring issued an order prohibiting the presence of more than one officer in any single air crew. This was an attempt to reduce the officer casualties on bombers, which had reached serious proportions.

August 16th

Day Airfields in Kent, Hampshire and West Sussex attacked. Widespread damage. Ventnor radar out of action. Other targets in Oxfordshire, Essex and Suffolk. Göring in conference.
Night Many light attacks.
Weather Mainly fair and warm. Channel haze.

This Friday was a sunny summer day with just the amount of haze that German pilots appreciated. The plotting tables were quiet until 11 a.m. when a series of raids were levelled against Norfolk, Kent and the Greater London area with airfields as the main

targets, including Manston. West Malling, an 11 Group station, was again hit while clearance was still going on after the previous day's attack. Some eighteen bombers dropped high explosives and incendiaries, destroying one aircraft on the ground and putting the station out of action until the 20th. Twelve fighter squadrons were up.

Things were quiet again until midday when the radar screens showed three heavy raids coming in. The first of fifty headed for the Thames Estuary, the second of 150 appeared off Dover, while the third of 100 massed over Cherbourg and proceeded to the Portsmouth–Southampton area. In all, radar was plotting about 350 aircraft simultaneously between Yarmouth and Portland. There was some cloud about, and, despite the despatch of twelve squadrons by Nos. 10, 11 and 12 Groups, many of the bombers succeeded in getting through and causing considerable damage.

London suburbs were bombed, including Wimbledon and Esher, where shops and houses were hit. Bombs on Malden, Surrey, railway station killed staff and passengers and put both lines out of operation. To the north, Gravesend and Tilbury were attacked, and bombs fell on Harwell and Farnborough aerodromes.

The raid off Portland split up and sections arrived over Ventnor, Tangmere, Lee-on-Solent and Gosport. Twelve Ju 88s with Me 110 escort dived out of the sun on Gosport, damaging buildings, killing four people and seriously injuring two. At Ventnor five Ju 87s in a six-minute raid added to the destruction of the 12th. The only habitable buildings left were the diesel house, the receiving block and the protected rooms. Ventnor was thus out of action from August 12th to 23rd, and service was only resumed when a mobile station was rigged nearby at Bembridge. A number of Fleet Air Arm aircraft and hangars were destroyed by fire at Lee-on-Solent.

Tangmere, with its satellite Westhampnett, was an important sector station. The Ju 87s approached from the east and had a clear run up over the airfield dropping

This Junkers 88 of KG54 was hit by anti-aircraft fire and crashed at Portland Bill during the heavy raid on Weymouth and Portland on August 11th

a pattern of bombs which destroyed all the hangars, workshops, stores, sick quarters, pumping station and the officers' mess. The Tannoy broadcasting system, all light, power, water and sanitation were temporarily out of action. Losses in aircraft were heavy, with three Blenheims destroyed and three Blenheims, seven Hurricanes and one Magister damaged. Ten service personnel and three civilians were killed, while twenty others were injured.

The Royal Aircraft Establishment at Farnborough, Hants, was attacked by 8 Ju 88s doing extensive damage to the motor transport yard. The last delayed-action bomb from this raid did not explode until 49 hours afterwards.

In the evening, two Ju 88s carried out the most destructive raid of the day, on Brize Norton, Oxfordshire, a training station and Maintenance Unit in No. 23 Group. Thirty-two bombs burned out forty-six trainer aircraft in the hangars of No. 2 Service Flying Training School, wrecked other buildings and caused ten casualties.

In the twenty-four hours of the 16th, the Luftwaffe put up 1,715 sorties for the loss of forty-five aircraft. The R.A.F. had twenty-two fighters shot down in which eight pilots were killed. The large number of British aircraft destroyed on the ground altered this picture somewhat, but most of them were not fighters. Eight airfields had been hit, but only three of them belonged to Fighter Command, proving that Schmid's intelligence assessments were still wrong.

During the attack on Gosport, Flight Lieutenant J. B. Nicolson of 249 Squadron won Fighter Command's first V.C. of the war. Hit by cannon shells and with the cockpit on fire, he succeeded in shooting down an Me 110 before baling out. Burned and wounded, his immediate reward on reaching the ground was to be shot in the seat by a trigger-happy Home Guard.

The English Channel had by this time become a sort of no-man's land where German seaplanes and British boats competed to pick up survivors. On this day the motor lifeboat Canadian Pacific, off Selsey, Sussex, found a German seaplane and a British naval speed boat on the water—the latter unable to move because of a rope round her propeller. The lifeboat passed two

dead German airmen to the seaplane which took off, while the lifeboat towed the speedboat into harbour.

The two hectic days of effort by Luftflotten 2 and 3 called for a rest for the weary German crews, repairs to damaged aircraft and replacement of lost machines and personnel. Thus the night raids were on a much reduced scale with small attacks on Bristol, Newport, Swansea, Portland, Worcester, Chester, Tavistock, Farnborough and various aerodromes.

In a summary of operations put out by the Luftwaffe Command Staff on the 16th, it was confidently stated that 372 Spitfires, 179 Hurricanes, 9 Curtiss Hawks and 12 Defiants had been destroyed in the period July 1st to August 15th. By a series of extraordinary caulations it was computed that at 10 a.m. on August 16th Fighter Command possessed only 300 serviceable aircraft whereas in fact there were over 700.

August 17th

Day Activity limited to reconnaissance. Fighter Command faces pilot shortage.
Night Light raids midlands, Merseyside, South Wales.
Weather Fine in Channel, haze and some cloud in the east.

The lull continued throughout the day. Reconnaissance flights were plotted and, although Fighter Command flew 288 sorties, Luftwaffe losses amounted to only three machines. The R.A.F. lost none.

At night, raids were scattered and light, the targets being industrial centres in the midlands, Merseyside and South Wales. One raid at 2 o'clock in the morning, first plotted at Hucknall and tracked to Newark, Lincoln and Duxford, was finally shot down off Lincolnshire by a Blenheim night fighter from 23 Squadron.

The serious drain on fighter pilot resources was recognised by the Air Ministry on the 17th. Dowding had been pressing for Fairey Battle pilots to fill the gaps, but the Air Staff felt that wholesale withdrawals from the remaining light bomber squadrons might affect striking power on invasion day.

Finally they agreed to five volunteers each from the four Battle squadrons and three each from Lysander Army co-operation squadrons in No. 22 Group. These were sent for a six-day O.T.U. course at Hawarden and some carried out their first operational patrol within a fortnight of volunteering.

If the unnecessary wastage of the Battle squadrons in France had not occurred there would have been many more first-class pilots available to Dowding without involving a serious strain on Bomber Command's forces.

August 18th

Day Massed formations return. Airfields in south and south-east attacked. Luftflotte 3 against Sussex and Hampshire.
Night Light bombing, Bristol, East Anglia and South Wales. Minelaying.
Weather Fine and fair early. Rest of day cloudy.

The Luftwaffe's all-out efforts to destroy Fighter Command in one week ended with a final flourish on this Sunday. The main objectives were once again airfields with a lesser effort against radar stations.

The first of the massed formations crossed the coast about midday in the Dover area and attacked airfields to the south and south-east of London, including Kenley, Croydon, Biggin Hill and West Malling.

At Kenley two raids of Do 17s with Me 109 escort came in simultaneously at 1.30 p.m., one of about fifty aircraft at altitude and the other low down at 100 feet with nine machines. The Kenley sector controller had detailed all his squadrons—No. 615 to a raid over Hawkinge, No. 64 to intercept the high raid over base and No. 111 to intercept the low raid.

Both raids were met, but 111 Squadron could not effectively deal with the low-flying machines as they

Out of control, a Ju 87 dives to destruction at White House Farm on the outskirts of Chichester, Sussex, on August 18th. The observer baled out but the pilot was killed. All that remained of the aircraft is shown in the second picture where the local Fire Brigade are seen putting out the flames

Sergeant H. J. Mann of 64 Squadron landed this Spitfire at Kenley in mid-August. The nose of a cannon shell had jammed the control column causing a landing on one wingtip and starboard wheel

themselves were too low and too close in over Kenley. As the approach was masked by trees and hangars, the A.A. guns were unable to open fire until the raiders were directly over the camp. Nevertheless the combined efforts of Parachute and Cable and A.A. brought down two aircraft. Both 615 and 64 Squadrons intercepted the high fliers, causing several casualties.

One machine, piloted by Oberleutnant Lamberty, crashed in flames in a field, and the following day it was attributed to rifle-fire by the Home Guard. In fact it is doubtful whether any of the Home Guard hit the aircraft as it was already beyond hope, riddled with Bofors shells and machine-gun bullets.

Intense anti-aircraft fire and the P.A.C. barrage, with the help of the fighters, accounted for two Dorniers straight away and damaged five to such an extent that two fell in the Channel and three force-landed in France. Two aircraft returned safely out of the whole Staffel, one being flown back by the flight engineer with the pilot dead on the floor.

Altogether 100 bombs fell on Kenley aerodrome and buildings, destroying four Hurricanes, one Blenheim, two Magisters and a Proctor and damaging six other aircraft. Ten hangars were total wrecks and many of the camp buildings demolished.

Most of the operations-room communications were cut, nine people were killed and ten injured, including one of the medical officers killed by a hit on a shelter trench near the hospital. Fire broke out and so many local fire brigades answered the SOS that they blocked the roads leading into the airfield. The operations block was moved into a shop and within two and a half days 90 per cent of the lines had been restored by the G.P.O.

While the station was temporarily out of action No.

615 Squadron was ordered to land and refuel at Croydon and No. 64 to go to Redhill. Due to lack of ground staff at Redhill, No. 64 in fact returned to Kenley, landing on a strip marked out between the craters.

Croydon received nineteen bombs, which further damaged hangars and buildings, and some hits were scored at West Malling.

The attack on Biggin Hill was to be carried out in a similar way to that at Kenley with Ju 88s at high level and Do 17s lower down, both formations from KG76. The high-level strike was delayed due to rendezvous difficulties over France, and the Dorniers came in on their own. The airfield defences were fully prepared and on his own initiative the station commander, Group Captain Grice, scrambled Nos. 610 and 32 Squadrons. Group orders did not come through until after the raid, due to the mass of plots on the situation map.

As the firing died down the high-level raid came in and added its quota of bombs, although during both attacks the main damage consisted of airfield craters. KG 76 flew back to France minus four Ju 88s and six Do 17s.

The second major assault also came in the early afternoon, when Luftflotte 3 concentrated on airfields and a radar station in the Hampshire–West Sussex area.

Gosport was still being cleared from the raid on the 16th, when at 2.30 p.m. twenty-one Ju 88s in three groups of seven dive-bombed the airfield, wrecking buildings, engineering shops, aircraft and motor transport, but causing no casualties.

Twenty-five Ju 87s and a flight of Me 109s had Thorney Island, Hampshire, a 16 Group airfield, as their objective. Two hangars were hit, one aircraft destroyed and one damaged.

Ford, a Fleet Air Arm station in Sussex, was heavily bombed, with workshops and a hangar destroyed and thick smoke rising from punctured fuel stores.

An Me 109E of 1./JG52 brought down at Westgate-on-Sea, Kent, on August 24th following a dog-fight over Ramsgate

The only radar station hit was Poling, between Arundel and Littlehampton. Ninety bombs were dropped, including many delayed action. The station was so badly damaged that a mobile unit had to be set up to cover the gap. The Poling radar masts have long since been dismantled, but to this day there is at least one unexploded bomb annually sinking deeper into the soil on the site. In these actions two squadrons, Nos. 43 and 152, between them shot down twelve Stukas, all from St.G.77. A Blenheim accounted for two Ju 87s near Thorney Island.

In the late afternoon the third and last major attack developed when aircraft from Luftflotte 2 approached via the Thames Estuary and again attacked Croydon. Twelve Me 109s sneaked into Manston at ground level, and destroyed two Spitfires on the ground, killing one airman and injuring fifteen others. There was also heavy air fighting over Essex.

At night bombs were dropped on East Anglia, South Wales and Bristol, while mines were laid in the Thames Estuary and the Bristol Channel.

So ended a day which was almost as decisive in its results as August 15th. Fighter Command in 766 sorties, together with A.A., had accounted for seventy-one German aircraft, of which thirty-seven were bombers and eleven were Me 110s. K.Gr.100, the pathfinder unit operating in daylight for the first time, at Göring's behest, also suffered its first loss, a Heinkel 111.

Twenty-seven R.A.F. fighters had been destroyed, with ten pilots killed.

The Luftwaffe had pressed home attacks on airfields using high- and low-level techniques. By far the more dangerous was the hedge-hopping raid which was difficult to plot overland and was often missed by the radar screen. Instead of correctly assessing the value of this type of approach, the German operations staffs felt the losses on the 18th were too great and thereafter formations mainly flew higher and higher

with a close fighter escort.

August 18th was the virtual death-knell of the Ju 87s over Britain. Losses had been mounting at an alarming rate and, apart from a few isolated sorties, they were pulled out of the battle.

In Fighter Command the week had shown up a number of serious problems in defence and in control layout.

In a report after the Kenley raid it was recommended that more Bofors guns and mountings should be provided for the southern approaches to the airfield; the operations room should be removed from the station; new V.H.F. radio buildings and the sick quarters be sited away from the main camp; and that more personnel be made available at unoccupied satellite airfields for refuelling and rearming.

These requirements were put in by one station, but they applied to the whole of Fighter Command. Key sector operations rooms were on the airfields themselves, and while protected from blast and shrapnel at the sides, were wide open to a direct hit on top. The same applied to radio buildings. At Middle Wallop, for instance, the sector control was housed in a hut and the blast of bombs moved the whole building until finally the squadron 'tote board' and its lights collapsed from vibration.

The operations rooms and radio stations should not have been built on the airfields, but as they were, construction should have been underground and in reinforced concrete.

It was only due to German Intelligence's lack of information on the sector layout and on the sites themselves that so many vital buildings and their crews survived the battle.

August 19th

Day Göring again confers. Isolated raids on Britain. Heavy reconnaissance activity.
Night Widespread harassing raids. Minelaying.
Weather Mainly cloudy. Occasional showers in the east.

From August 15th to 18th, inclusive, the Luftwaffe had lost 194 aircraft, and this showed conclusively that, despite the high British casualties claimed, Fighter Command was by no means beaten.

For this Me 109E of 2./JG52 the battle was over. On August 12th it was shot down in a cornfield near the Sussex village of Berwick, midway between Lewes and Eastbourne

When Göring met his fighter commanders at Karinhall on this Monday morning, he stated that: 'Until further notice the main task of Luftflotten 2 and 3 will be to inflict the utmost damage possible on the enemy fighter forces. With this are to be combined attacks on the ground organisation of the enemy bombers conducted, however, in such a manner as to avoid all unnecessary losses.'

The reference to Bomber Command targets was obviously the result of complaints by the other services and by the O.K.W. over the continued attacks by British aircraft. The demand for raids on bomber airfields was nevertheless almost beyond the Luftwaffe's capabilities as most of them were outside the operational radius of action of escorting Me 109s.

Göring concluded by saying: 'There can no longer be any restriction on the choice of targets. To myself I reserve only the right to order attacks on London and Liverpool.' This gave the Luftflotten and Fliegerkorps virtually a free hand and each followed its own particular pattern for target selection.

It was indicated that heavy raids would continue on the R.A.F. ground organisation and that British aircraft production must be disrupted, even to the extent of using single raiders in cloudy weather. Luftflotte 3 was ordered to plan for a night raid on Liverpool and Luftflotte 5 for one on Glasgow.

The Reichsmarschall felt far from happy about the performance of the fighter groups following rising bomber losses. He attributed this to a lack of aggressiveness on the part of pilots when in fact it was nothing of the sort. The Me 110 was a failure but remained in use, while the Me 109s were too few for massive escort and suffered at all times from lack of range.

As occurred throughout the Battle, Göring endeavoured to attribute failures to the operational units instead of to the manifest shortcomings of Luftwaffe Command planning.

In order, as he thought, to boost morale among fighter pilots, he promoted Mölders and Galland, two of his 'star' pilots, each to command of a fighter Gruppe. This was part of a belated policy of promoting younger operational officers to senior rank in place of those who were too old and lacked proper experience. It was a good idea, but it was to have no effect on the outcome of the Battle.

No. 11 Group, meanwhile, had been reassessing the situation in the light of a week's heavy fighting and on the 19th Park issued Instruction No. 4 to his controllers to meet changed requirements.

He began with a note that attacks had been switched from coastal shipping and ports to inland objectives, particularly airfields. His instructions were as follows:

(a) Despatch fighters to engage large enemy formations over land or within gliding distance of the coast. During the next two or three weeks we cannot afford to lose pilots through forced landings in the sea. (Protection of all convoys and shipping in the Thames Estuary are excluded from this paragraph.)

(b) Avoid sending fighters out over the sea to chase reconnaissance aircraft or small formations of enemy fighters.

(c) Despatch a pair of fighters to intercept single reconnaissance aircraft that come inland. If clouds are favourable, put a patrol of one or two fighters over an aerodrome which enemy aircraft are approaching in clouds.

*Dornier 17Z bombers of II/KG3 (Gruppe Finsterwalde)
prepare for take-off from Antwerp/Deurne for a raid
on Britain*

(d) Against mass attacks coming inland despatch a minimum number of squadrons to engage enemy fighters. Our main object is to engage enemy bombers, particularly those approaching under the lowest cloud layer.

(e) If all our squadrons around London are off the ground engaging enemy mass attacks, ask No. 12 Group or Command Controller to provide squadrons to patrol aerodromes Debden, North Weald, Hornchurch.

(f) If heavy attacks have crossed the coast and are proceeding towards aerodromes, put a squadron, or even the sector training flight, to patrol under clouds over each sector aerodrome.

(g) No. 303 (Polish) Squadron can provide two sections for patrol of inland aerodromes, especially while the older squadrons are on the ground refuelling, when enemy formations are flying over land.

(h) No. 1 (Canadian) Squadron can be used in the same manner by day as other fighter squadrons.

For a few days cloudy weather was to lose 11 Group the opportunity of trying out the new tactics on a large scale. On the 19th large numbers of the enemy made threatening moves in the Channel and estuary areas, but only isolated raids came through. The most intense Luftwaffe activity was put up by the long-range reconnaissance Gruppen who carried out photographic sorties.

At 12.30 p.m. sixty+ aircraft were off the coast between Dungeness and North Foreland at 20,000 feet and at 12.50 a further fifty left Calais. Dover was the main target but the formations consisted largely of fighters. A few bombers penetrated to outer London.

Between 2.30 and 3 p.m. a small secondary attack came over Dover while raids approached Portsmouth and the Southampton Docks from Luftflotte 3. One raid succeeded in setting fire to oil-tanks at Pembroke Docks. Three hours later fifty+ approached the east

coast between Dungeness and Harwich and bombs fell on houses and airfields, although without much effect on the latter.

Fighter Command flew 383 sorties, losing three aircraft and destroying six German machines of which two were He 111s from K.Gr.100.

During the night there were continual small raids which operated over a wide area, to the extent that at some times almost three quarters of the country was under a yellow or red air raid warning. Bombs were dropped on Liverpool, Southampton, Hull, Derby, Wolverhampton, Sheffield, Bristol, Leicester and Nottingham. Eight airfields were attacked and at Driffield a hangar was set on fire.

August 20th

Day Scattered raids in morning. Kent and Essex airfields attacked in afternoon.
Night Negligible activity. One or two raids in south-west.
Weather Cloudy generally, rain spreading from north. Channel mainly fine.

The weather was autumnal, with low clouds, strong winds and intermittent rain which restricted German operations. The Luftflotten planning staffs spent the day digesting Göring's requirements outlined on the 19th. These were contained in orders put out by the Luftwaffe Command Staff IA which covered 'the weakening of enemy fighter forces, attacks on the enemy ground organisation, the aircraft industry, and aluminium and steel rolling mills'.

Activity over Britain in the morning was limited to small raids on Cheltenham, Oxford and Southwold, while reconnaissance aircraft surveyed Duxford, Debden, North Weald, Hatfield, Northolt and Hornchurch airfields. At 11.24 bombs were again dropped on the oil-tanks at Pembroke Docks, still burning from the previous day.

During the afternoon several waves of aircraft came in from Calais, starting just after 2 p.m. Objectives were the balloon barrage at Dover and the airfields of

Production of Britain's first four-motor heavy bomber, the Stirling, suffered a serious set-back on August 15th when the Short Brothers factory at Rochester was hit. Here wrecked Stirlings stand on the final assembly line after the raid

Exeter airfield, Devon, in August 1940. A Hurricane of No. 213 Squadron has crashed into the dispersal area of B Flight, No. 87 Squadron, after an air battle over Portland. In the background are Hurricanes of 87 Squadron

Eastchurch, Manston and West Malling. There were also isolated raids on convoy 'Agent' off the east coast and on S.S. *Orford* off Anglesey. Twelve fighter squadrons were despatched to intercept, but due to bad weather only accounted for six enemy aircraft in the course of 453 sorties, although one was a four-engined FW 200 over Ireland. Two R.A.F. aircraft were lost during the day. The Polish Air Force had its first success over Britain, No. 302 Squadron destroying a Junkers 88.

By night German activity was negligible with a few single bombers off the south-west coast.

August 21st

Day Small raids in the east and south. Targets airfields.
Night Slight activity, some in Scotland.
Weather Cloudy, occasional rain.

The bad weather continued throughout the day, and the Luftwaffe resorted to 'tip-and-run' raids round the east and south coasts. Instead of mass attacks, small formations or single aircraft were used in some cases, while others had groups of three divided into two at low level and one stepped up.

Fighter Command had difficulty in meeting this type of attack but 599 sorties yielded thirteen German aircraft destroyed for the loss of one British fighter.

Airfields attacked or threatened were Exeter, St. Eval, Horsham, St. Faith, Bircham Newton, Ford, Coltishall, Stradishall and Watton. Bombs were also dropped on Grimsby, Norwich, Canterbury, Southampton, Newmarket, Bournemouth and Pembroke.

After dark, raiding was again slight with bombers off Harwich, the Humber Estuary and the Firth of Forth.

During the day the operators at Dover radar station would have been intrigued to know that their tall aerial masts were the subject of close scrutiny by a small group of officers on Cap Gris Nez.

SECRET.

COMBAT REPORT.

Sector Serial No. ....(A) ....

Serial No. of Order detailing Flight or Squadron to
Patrol..(B) ....

Date ....(C)   15 - 8 - 40.

Flight, Squadron ....(D) Flight: "A"   Sqdn.: 213

Number of Enemy Aircraft................................(E)   100 or more.

Type of Enemy Aircraft....................................(F) ME110's; ME109's; JU88's; JU87's;

Time Attack was delivered..............................(G)   1745 hours.

Place Attack was delivered..............................(H)   5 miles south Portland Bill.

Height of Enemy...(J)   20,000 ft and various.

Enemy Casualties ....(K)   Conclusive 3 ME110s.
                                                                    Inconclusive 1 ME110.

Our Casualties ....Aircraft..................(L)   2 bullets in cockpit & petrol
                                                                                              tank.

                    Personnel..................(M)   Nil.

~~General Remarks~~   ~~(O)~~

Searchlights. (Did they illuminate enemy; if not, were
        they in front or behind target?)   (N) (i)   Day raid.

A.A. Guns. (Did shell bursts assist pilot intercepting
        the enemy?)   (N) (ii)   No.

Range at which fire was opened in each attack delivered
        on the enemy together with estimated length of burst   (P) From 200 yds to 50 yds.

GENERAL REPORT   (R) Leading yellow section above
~~Portland Bill. I made an attack on the last ME110 of a formation;~~ after a little burst, he
made a flick roll and continued spinning into the sea. I had been attacked from astern
by 4 ME110's. ~~Seeing the tracer bullets coming from astern~~ I made a quick turn and got
on to his tail. After two bursts the starboard engine fired and he went in a slow gliding
turn. I then ~~made a beam attack on the second aeroplane~~ on an echelon starboard
formation of ME110's. The third of that formation turned over on to his back and went
into an inverted dive, pieces falling away. I then ~~engaged a single ME110~~ and had a dog
fight with him. I first stopped his starboard engine; he dived into the clouds; I
remained just above the clouds which were in
patches, and when he reappeared the rear gunner
fired at me when I engaged him. I followed him
beneath the clouds . As the rear gunner was   O.C.
silent I came closer to him but had no more
ammunition. When I left him F/Lt. SING observed
his port engine smoking black and running spasmodically.
I returned to base where they discovered a bullet in my starboard tank and a second
in the cockpit.

Signature (SIGNED) J.A. PHILLIPART P/O.

Section YELLOW
Flight A
Squadron   Squadron No. 213.

R.A.F. Form 1151.
500 PADS 3/60. N/N.

*A typical Form 'F' or Combat Report from the Battle
of Britain. This one was completed by Pilot Officer
J. A. Phillipart, a Belgian pilot with No. 213 Squadron
who, as shown, shot down no less than three Me 110s
on this sortie on August 15th. P/O Phillipart was killed
later in the Battle*

It was the occasion of Göring's first visit to Luftflotte
2's forward headquarters, and with him were Milch,
Kesselring, Sperrle, Lörzer and Wenniger, who had
been the air attaché in London.

A pair of very high-powered naval binoculars had
been set up through which the Dover masts were
clearly visible. The sight does not, however, have
appeared to have influenced the Reichsmarschall to

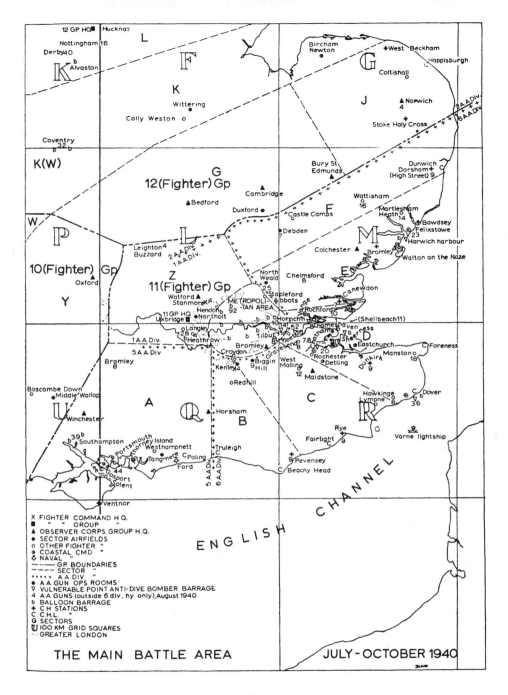

THE MAIN BATTLE AREA   JULY - OCTOBER 1940

X   FIGHTER COMMAND H.Q.
■   "   "   GROUP   "
▲   OBSERVER CORPS GROUP H.Q.
●   SECTOR AIRFIELDS
○   OTHER FIGHTER   "
◉   COASTAL CMD   "
◊   NAVAL   "
── GP BOUNDARIES
─── SECTOR   "
∗∗∗∗ A A DIV.   "
●   A A GUN OPS ROOMS
▽   VULNERABLE POINT ANTI-DIVE BOMBER BARRAGE
4   A A GUNS (outside 6 div. hy only), August 1940
b   BALLOON BARRAGE
✛   C H STATIONS
C   C.H.L.
G   SECTORS
U   100 KM GRID SQUARES
    GREATER LONDON

change his orders of the 15th abandoning heavy attacks on the radar chain.

August 22nd

Day Shipping reconnaissance and attacks on two Channel convoys.
Night Increased activity. Industrial targets in Midlands, north and west. Minelaying.
Weather Cloudy and squally.

At nine o'clock in the morning the convoy 'Totem' was passing through the Straits of Dover and reported being under air attack. Investigation showed that it

was in fact being shelled by the German heavy batteries near Cap Gris Nez. The first bombardment lasted eighty minutes and 100 shells were fired without effect.

Failure of the guns brought the Luftwaffe into action and at 12.40 some forty aircraft attacked the convoy, but were beaten off by Nos. 54 and 65 squadrons.

Apart from a few reconnaissance flights, the day remained quiet until 6.50 p.m. when a series of raids developed against Dover during the course of which Manston was again hit.

Five R.A.F. aircraft were lost for the destruction of two German—a poor repayment for 509 Fighter

After an initial success due to surprise, the Boulton Paul Defiant two-seat turret fighter proved very vulnerable. Units equipped with the type were withdrawn to the north. In the autumn Defiant squadrons returned to southern airfields in a night fighter role. These Defiants of No. 264 Squadron were airborne from Kirton-in-Lindsey on August 9th

Command sorties, which were again hampered by bad weather.

The toll of fighter pilots killed through drowning after being shot down in the sea had been rising steadily during August. The situation became so serious that on the 22nd Air Marshal Harris called a meeting at the Air Ministry to draft some organisation for rescue craft.

It was decided to combine the skeleton rescue service of Coastal Command with the boats of the Naval Auxiliary Patrol and to place R.A.F. launches under the operational control of the local naval authorities.

The R.A.F. retained the responsibility of air search, and twelve Lysanders originally borrowed from Army Co-operation Command were placed under the direction of Fighter Command. The aircraft were stationed at various fighter airfields along the coast and special liaison officers appointed to Nos. 10 and 11 Groups to assist in general handling. It had taken nearly twelve months of war to bring about even this meagre effort.

That night German activity showed a marked increase, with inland bombing, minelaying and shipping attacks. The convoy 'Topaz' was attacked off Wick by aircraft from Luftflotte 5 and the Bristol Aeroplane Company's works at Filton were bombed including the airfield. Other stations visited were Manston, St. Eval, Northcoates and Wick. In the early hours of

the morning one raider flew over and dropped his load on Wealdstone, Greater London. The aircraft was plotted in and the incident duly noted by 17 Group Observer Post D.3 at Harrow.

August 23rd

Day Single raids in the south. Reconnaissance.
Night Main targets South Wales.
Weather Showers and bright intervals. Cloud in Straits, Channel and Estuary.

Low cloud and rain continued throughout this Friday, limiting operations once again to guerrilla warfare by single, or occasionally flights of two or three machines.

Outer London, Tangmere, St. Albans, Portsmouth, Maidstone, Cromer, Harwich, Southampton, Colchester, Biggin Hill and Abingdon reported small attacks, while the east coast convoys were bombed. Of the raiders attempting to penetrate the London defences, several jettisoned their bombs in the suburbs—houses, a bank and two cinemas being hit. Fighter Command's 482 sorties showed five German aircraft destroyed without British loss.

After nightfall twenty-two raids penetrated inland, mainly to South Wales, while the convoy 'Draga' was also bombed. Among the targets hit were Pembroke Dock and the Dunlop Rubber Company's works at Birmingham.

As daylight came, the weather had improved and the Luftwaffe was about to execute its orders of the 20th for the destruction of British fighters and bases. Unknowingly, Dowding's Command was entering upon the third and most critical phase of the Battle of Britain.

16 Third phase—August 24th–September 6th

The cloudy weather from August 19th to 23rd gave some brief respite to both combatants and time to adjust tactics. In Germany senior commanders of the Luftwaffe, and in particular the Jafus and fighter Gruppen commanders, were called to Karinhall on August 19th for discussions on escort problems.

To the Luftwaffe it appeared that Fighter Command had not been fully brought to battle and that, despite the very heavy losses to the R.A.F. shown in the German intelligence reports, a hard core still existed. At all costs this must be engaged and destroyed both in the air and on the ground. The very wide range of targets laid down had meant complete lack of concentration on any particular site, although this was certainly not apparent to Göring. In addition the haphazard use of bombers to raid singly or in threes over the length and breadth of England each night had diluted the bomb capacity in favour of overload fuel.

German bomber losses had been heavy, 127 medium bombers and forty Stukas having been lost between August 10th and 23rd. A major disappointment to the Reichsmarschall was the abject failure of the Ju 87 Stuka. Against modern fighters it was no longer the spearhead of the Blitzkrieg, but a slow, cumbersome and vulnerable machine which had little chance in daylight. To prevent further serious losses in the Stuka formations and to conserve them for the pending invasion, Fliegerkorps VIII (with 220 out of the 280 Ju 87s engaged) was withdrawn from the battle on the 19th, and on August 29th transferred from Cherbourg to Luftflotte 2 in the Pas de Calais. The Stuka had retired from the battle against Britain apart from some isolated sorties by the few remaining units in Luftflotte 3.

As a result of the talks on the 19th, Göring issued a new directive on the following day:

To continue the fight against the enemy air force until further notice, with the aim of weakening the British fighter forces. The enemy is to be forced to use his fighters by means of ceaseless attacks. In addition the aircraft industry and the ground organisation of the air force are to be attacked by means of individual aircraft by night and day, if weather conditions do not permit the use of complete formations.

The Luftwaffe High Command had for some time considered that the main concentration of R.A.F. fighters was in the area around London. Heavy attacks were therefore contemplated as early as August 2nd when an ObdL order was issued to this effect. The timing and implementation were left to the Luftflotten,

and in turn to the individual Fliegerkorps commanders. The order of August 2nd seemed to give the right balance between Göring's dictum of August 20th and the invasion plans for an attack on a narrow front due south of London. Moreover, the detailed planning for attacks on R.A.F. installations round London had now been completed and they could be carried out forthwith.

Fliegerkorps 2, under General Bruno Lörzer, took the initiative and decided to open the attacks as soon as the weather cleared. A new variant was also added to confuse the radar stations, formations of varying size patrolling all day up and down the Straits, and occasionally delivering a feint attack.

To provide overwhelming escorts of Me 109s, it was decided to transfer most of the single-seater fighter strength of Luftflotte 3 to the Luftflotte 2 area. In the following week the units of Jufue 3 were flown across to the Pas de Calais.

In the meantime Fighter Command took stock; in the second phase (August 8th to 18th) no less than ninety-four pilots were killed or missing, and sixty were wounded in varying degrees. Since August 8th the slight improvement in strength at that date had been whittled away and the operational training units were effectively prevented from raising the length of courses from two weeks to four weeks. Squadrons were dog-tired from long hours of fighting each day, and from the constant wear on nerves occasioned by air raids.

Of aircraft there was so far still no shortage despite the loss in the second phase of 54 Spitfires and 121 Hurricanes, 40 Spitfires and 25 Hurricanes damaged beyond unit repair, and a further 30 aircraft destroyed on the ground. Production was beyond schedule, and the repair depots were helping to ensure that any replacements required at the end of each day's fighting were delivered by noon on the following day.

In the field the ground crews performed miracles. Quick servicing had been developed to a fine art—refuelling, rearming, engine checking, including oil and glycol coolant, replacing oxygen cylinders, and testing the R/T set would go on simultaneously. On many occasions all the aircraft of a squadron formation were replenished with fuel and ammunition, and got ready for another battle, in eight to ten minutes after landing. Slit trenches had been dug alongside dispersals so that work could continue until the airfield was under direct attack.

Regular repair and maintenance were carried on day and night with all maintenance personnel pooled on

Liberally sprayed by the fire section, this Spitfire of 92 Squadron came to grief at Biggin Hill during the September battles

Low and fast; a staffel of Me 110s from ZG26 'Horst Wessel' heads inland from the British coast for a raid during late August 1940

each station. The indefatigable station engineer officers detailed parties from the pool to squadrons in accordance with the work required to get them serviceable again.

Most of the maintenance work on the signals equipment of the fighters had to be carried out at night by the light of torches. Trouble was caused by damp, and extreme care was necessary to keep R/T sets dry in rain or dew. Occasionally sets had to be taken to a hot air blower to dry them out.

Wherever possible maintenance was done in the open as hangars were primary targets for German bombs, and many had already been destroyed. Dispersal of aircraft not only to satellite aerodromes, but over wide areas at each of them, combined with lack of transport, increased the labour requirement for a given job. The blackout, damage to power and water mains, and to the station organisation, added to the difficulties.

Initially bomb craters and building repairs were undertaken by the station works and buildings detachments. As the damage grew, these units could no longer cope, and works repair depots were called in. Manned by between 50 and 200 workmen, these depots had lorries, bulldozers, excavators and mobile power generation and water plant.

Appointed Kommodore of JG26 in August 1940, Adolf Galland was one of the best known fighter pilots of the Luftwaffe. He is shown here taxiing in at Audembert after a sortie, and about to leave the cockpit. The Mickey Mouse emblem was much publicised

In many cases the depots performed sterling work, but often during an air raid a gang would retire to the shelters and refuse to budge. They claimed that they were not going to do the job if it was dangerous. There was little thought for the young fighter pilots above being killed or maimed to ensure the labourers' continued freedom of choice in the matter.

Invariably a lot of the crater filling and rubble clearing was carried out by the airmen of the station itself.

To Park at 11 Group, the lull provided by four days of bad weather was a boon, as he was already extremely worried by his rising pilot losses and the damage being caused to his delicate network of communications. The savage attacks on fighter airfields required new tactics if the German intention of bringing as much of Fighter Command's strength as possible into battle and destroying it was not to be realised.

Park's directive of the 19th was therefore of the utmost importance and underlined Dowding's policy of keeping the fighter force in being by any means at his disposal.

On August 24th the weather cleared, and both sides began to try new tactics, the Germans achieving their greatest successes of the Battle of Britain.

August 24th

Day Crucial phase begins. Airfield attacks in south-east. Heavy raid on Portsmouth. Manston evacuated.
Night Heavier attacks, widely spaced targets. Minelaying.
Weather Fine and clear in south. Drizzle in north.

German bomber crews photographed on a sortie over southern England in early September. Above: flying a Heinkel 111 and studying the map; below: gunners on a Dornier 17 searching the sky for the ever-present Hurricanes and Spitfires

Slogans of every type appeared on both sides of the Channel during the Battle of Britain. Some were polite, others were not! Here a Luftwaffe freelance artist is finishing a man size caricature on the side of a van. The caption reads 'When we have shut Churchill's big mouth . . .'

Caught by a British fighter, this Dornier 17Z of KG2 was riddled with bullets from nose to tail, but managed to get back to base

The early part of the Saturday morning was cloudless and fine and the controllers in 11 Group watched anxiously for the inevitable signs of a built-up over France. At 9 a.m. a big raid began to boil up around Cap Gris Nez and some 100 fighters and bombers of Fliegerkorps II advanced on Dover, stepped-up from 12,000 to 24,000 feet. Two formations broke away from the mass in mid-Channel and attacked Dover itself from the north. Eleven fighter squadrons were despatched and the raid broke up at about eleven o'clock.

An hour and a half later a series of feints developed, from which one raid was detached to attack Manston, as No. 264 Squadron's defensive patrol for the airfield landed. The nine Defiants took off before the first bombs were dropped, and were then joined by a Hurricane squadron. The force was driven off with a loss of five bombers and two fighters but not before extensive damage had been done.

At 3.30 another big raid stacked up over Le Havre, and flew to Manston and Ramsgate. The Manston attack was to be the last straw for the station. The living

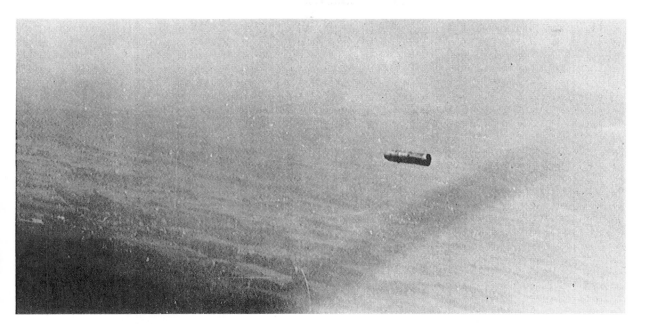

Express delivery! A remarkable series of photographs of a 2½ ton bomb, from loading to delivery over England. The bomb, on the external racks of a special Heinkel 111, was inscribed 'Extra Havana for Churchill'. The thoroughness of German official photographic teams at this period can be gauged from the fact that these pictures are only a selection from a long sequence of the raid right from the bombing-up stage

High level reconnaissance during the Battle of Britain was mainly carried out by specially equipped Dornier 17Ps and He 111s. Here the third staffel of Aufkl.Gr.123 is shown in the hangar at its base in the Paris area

quarters were now badly damaged, hardly any buildings remained intact, all telephone and teleprinter lines were cut and the field was littered with unexploded bombs.

Before the afternoon raid, at 2.15, all communication between Manston and 11 Group ceased. The controller at 11 Group contacted No. 1 Observer Group at Maidstone to see if the Corps could find out what was going on. A mile from Manston was Post A.1, and Observer Foad volunteered to cycle to the airfield and obtain information. Coastal airfields had been reduced to dire straits.

When the cable maintenance inspector at Manston was informed that all lines had gone he took two jointers and went to the particular crater despite the continuing explosion of delayed action bombs. Working like beavers, and with only an occasional glance at a large bomb adjacent to them, the three men got the essential circuits (out of 248 severed) restored in two hours and completed permanent restoration the following day.

As soon as word got through of the state of the station Fighter Command decided to evacuate it, except as an emergency airfield. Administrative personnel were tranferred permanently to Westgate while the remainder of No. 600 Squadron's Blenheims were moved to Hornchurch.

Part of the raiding force split before reaching Manston, and one section attacked the small aerodrome at Ramsgate. The town itself was heavily hit and whole rows of seaside villas were wiped out with a number of casualties.

Concurrently with the south coast attacks, another raid flew to targets north of the Estuary, especially Hornchurch and North Weald, where high-altitude techniques were used. The No. 264 Squadron Defiants, withdrawn from Manston to Hornchurch earlier in the day, found themselves once more in the fray at 3.45, and just airborne as bombs began to rain down.

At North Weald nearly fifty Dorniers and He 111s escorted by Me 110s dropped 150 to 200 bombs. The airmen's and officers' married quarters suffered severely, and the power house was badly damaged. Nine people were killed and ten wounded.

No. 12 Group were called upon to assist over North Weald and Hornchurch, but the Duxford wing was flown in too late to have any major effect.

With the raiders approaching London, the city registered its 11th, 12th and 13th air raid warnings, but the population did not seem unduly perturbed. In Regent's Park, where *A Midsummer Night's Dream* was being performed, few of the audience moved. They seemed to find very appropriate Titania's wish 'To each word a warbling note'.

While the sector stations were under fire a formation of 100 Luftflotte 3 fighters and bombers from North of the Somme headed for Portsmouth and Southampton. They managed to get well towards the coast before their targets were deduced from radar, which was cluttered with other tracks.

A formation of Heinkel 111s from KG53 from Lille moves out across the Channel for one of the September raids

At Portsmouth only one fighter squadron was near enough to intercept, and that was still climbing when fifty bombers were heavily fired on by the anti-aircraft guns. The aircraft jettisoned their loads broadcast over the city, causing much damage and killing 100 civilians.

During the day Fighter Command flew 936 sorties— only slightly less than the Luftwaffe's 1,030—and lost twenty-two fighters to the German total of thirty-eight fighters and bombers.

Luftflotte 3 from this time on began to fade from the daylight picture as the full weight of the assault switched to Luftflotte 2 and the Pas de Calais. After dark on the 24th the attacks were stepped up, and some 170 German aircraft ranged over England from the borderland to Kent. Largely due to bad navigation bombers directed to Rochester and the Thameshaven oil-tanks dropped their loads on the City of London. For the first time since the Gothas of 1918, Central London was damaged in an air raid. Fires burned at London Wall, and boroughs like Islington, Tottenham, Finsbury, Millwall, Stepney, East Ham, Leyton, Coulsdon and Bethnal Green all received their share. It was a foretaste of things to come.

Airfields had been the main focus of the attack in the south, but lack of Knickebein trained crews and general interference with direction-finding aids caused confusion. In the west only Driffield was hit, and this by a single machine. Fighter Command flew forty-five night sorties, but the only interception made was by a Hurricane pilot of No. 615 Squadron who successfully destroyed a Heinkel 111.

August 25th

Day Slight activity in morning. Main raids by Luftflotte 3 in afternoon in south-west.
Night Continued widespread attacks, main concentration the midlands.
Weather Early morning fair. Remainder of day cloudy.

For most of the morning and afternoon of Wednesday the Luftwaffe rested, although the Channel was filled with small formations which kept the radar plotters busy waiting to see which would turn north and become a genuine raid.

At 5 p.m. 50+ appeared near St. Malo and proceeded to Cherbourg where escort and escorted swelled the ranks to 100. Off the Channel Islands another raid of 30+ built up, and behind it further formations of 20, 60 and 20 joined up to form a mass of 100+ aircraft which headed for Weymouth.

Two squadrons, judiciously placed by 10 Group, intercepted, but were unable to get through the fighter screen which numbered nearly 200. A third squadron fared no better and the bombers attacked Warmwell aerodrome, dropping twenty bombs. Two hangars were damaged and the station sick quarters burnt out.

The various stages in the preparations for a Luftwaffe raid. First (A) target maps and photographs are studied, (B) the meteorological staff assess the weather situation, (C) a detailed pictorial lecture on the harbour is given and (D) final briefing to the crews

(A)

(B)

C)

D)

King George VI and Queen Elizabeth walking in the grounds of Bentley Priory with Air Chief Marshal Dowding, the architect of Fighter Command's victory. The date was September 6th, 1940, and a series of German air attacks was in progress

Nine- unexploded bombs were left to be dealt with, and communications were disorganised until noon on the following day. Bombs also fell on Fareham, Pembroke and the Scilly Isles, at the last mentioned a direct hit being scored on the R.A.F. wireless station.

Within an hour a further mass raid of 100 headed from Cap Gris Nez for Dover and the Estuary, but was attacked by several of the eleven fighter squadrons sent up. This final action brought Fighter Command's losses for the day to sixteen with nine pilots dead, four missing and four wounded.

The Luftwaffe left behind twenty aircraft and their crews, but after nightfall they had it all their own way, carrying out widespread attacks without suffering any loss. Some mines were laid on the east, south and west coasts, while most of the sixty-five raids plotted in attacked industrial centres in the midlands, where bombs fell on forty places, including Birmingham, Coventry and towns in southern England, South Wales and Scotland. Montrose, a fighter airfield between Dundee and Aberdeen, was the recipient of an unexpected attack.

While German bombers droned over England, eighty-one twin-engined R.A.F. bombers were heading the other way—for Berlin. Industrial and communications targets were the orders for the night. Cloud prevented accurate identification and bombs were dropped on several sections of the city, some damage

being done to residential property. The R.A.F. raid was a reprisal for the German bombing of London the previous night. This incursion into Germany territory was the first of several and within a fortnight there were to be far-reaching results with changed Luftwaffe daylight tactics, and a reprieve for Fighter Command.

August 26th

Day Airfields in Kent and Essex attacked. Bombs on Dover and Folkestone. Raids in the Solent.
Night Widespread raiding, targets industrial centres and airfields.
Weather Mainly cloudy, but dry. Brighter in south, but Channel cloudy.

This was another day of widespread activity in the course of which the Luftwaffe delivered three main attacks: (a) on Kenley and Biggin Hill, (b) on Hornchurch, North Weald, Debden and east London, and (c) on Portsmouth and the aerodromes at Warmwell in No. 10 Group.

Following several reconnaissance flights, Luftflotte 2 put in an appearance just after 11 a.m. when 150 aircraft were crossing the coast at Deal. Bombs dropped on Folkestone and more balloons were set on fire at Dover, but the main effort was directed at Biggin Hill and Kenley. Six squadrons and three flights from No. 11 Group intercepted well forward, and the raids were broken up.

In the early afternoon a second Luftwaffe concentration was observed by radar to be forming up over Lille. Further units joined it from St. Omer and Calais, until raids of 60+, 20+ and 30+ were being plotted in towards Dover and Harwich.

The main objectives for the bombers from KG2 and KG3 off Harwich were North Weald and Horn-

A Gotha 145 trainer which landed intact on Lewes race-course, Sussex, on August 28th, 1940. The young pilot was delivering German forces mail from the Channel Islands to Strasbourg, but lost his way and was painfully surprised to be greeted by the Home Guard on landing. The second photograph shows the same aircraft being used by the R.A.F.

church, with diversions in the east London area. Their efforts were disorganised by 11 Group which put up ten squadrons and one flight. One section of the raid fared better, however, and despite the attentions of two R.A.F. fighter squadrons it successfully reached the sector station at Debden. Over 100 bombs damaged the landing area, the sergeants' mess, the N.A.A.F.I., a motor transport depot and the equipment section. Both electricity and water mains were hit and five personnel killed.

A squadron from Duxford had been sent up to patrol Debden, but due to late vectoring saw nothing of the enemy. Hurricanes of No. 310 (Czechoslovak) Squadron attempted to catch the raid as it left the Debden area, but most of them were unable to get proper courses to steer as they lacked the right radio-frequencies.

At 4 p.m. 150 aircraft of Luftflotte 3 approached Portsmouth at high altitude while two small diversions were laid on in an attempt to distract the fighters. No. 11 Group despatched five squadrons and No. 10

Almost intact, a Heinkel 111 of KG1 lies in a Surrey field at mid-day on August 30th. The aircraft was one of a large formation that caused heavy damage to Biggin Hill, but was intercepted by 79 and 610 Squadrons. The crew of five were captured but one died from injuries

Group three. Independently three of the squadrons intercepted the formation short of the target, destroying three Heinkel 111s from KG55 and causing many of the bombers to jettison their loads in the sea. By five o'clock the raid had been repulsed. This was Luftflotte 3's last major effort in daylight for some weeks, as its units concentrated on night bombing. To Nos. 10 and 11 Groups it had been one of their most bitter fights with twenty-eight aircraft lost in one engagement, out of thirty-one for the day. Four pilots were killed near Portsmouth, and twelve were wounded. Altogether Fighter Command flew 787 sorties, over 300 more than on the 25th. The losses in pilots were rising alarmingly and replacements were few. German losses for the 26th were 41 aircraft.

On this day another link in the Observer chain was forged through the formation of No. 20 Observer Group H.Q. at Truro with a small nucleus of posts. Gradually the gaps in the warning line were being closed, although the areas in Wales and the north were still without coverage. Communications were uppermost in Fighter Command's mind, as exercises were being held to try out the 'Beetle' emergency signals system which would come into operation on invasion day.

By the 26th Fighter Command was getting a clearer picture of German lines of approach and overall target priorities in this third phase of the battle. Some authorities had suggested that the Luftwaffe was looking for gaps in the defences from the north and west by which to approach London. A full-scale study had been carried out by the operational research staff at Bentley Priory which proved conclusively that the Germans were proceeding to their targets with almost mathematical precision and that the priorities were still airfields and industrial centres.

The operations-room raid tracings and the Observer Corps tracks showed the main entry routed for then current industrial attacks on Birmingham and Coventry at night were either Abbeville-Pevensey-Birmingham, or Cherbourg-Bournemouth-Birmingham, as if drawn with a ruler and pencil.

To prove the point, the raids that night were mainly directed against Bournemouth and Coventry with about fifty bombers aiming at Plymouth. Widespread sorties by other aircraft included an attack against the 15 Group airfield at St. Eval in Cornwall, where the 'Q' site or decoy aerodrome for the station was bombed for several hours. The false flarepath was set on fire, and most of the sixty-two craters made were on open heathland. Some six airfields were on the Luftwaffe's night list to back up the day offensive, but little damage was done due to poor navigation and low clouds.

For some days Park at 11 Group had been worried about the low rate of interceptions compared with sorties flown and the fact that single squadrons had been engaging large formations. This was due to cloud and consequent errors in time and position of Observer Corps plots. To overcome the defect he sent a signal to his controllers requiring that formation leaders should report 'the approximate strength of enemy bombers and fighters, their height, and approximate position immediately on sighting the enemy. A special R/T message would be "Tally Ho! Thirty bombers, forty fighters, Angels 20, proceeding north Guildford." These reports should enable us to engage the enemy on more equal terms and are to take effect from dawn August 27th.'

August 27th

Day Reconnaissance chiefly in Portsmouth-Southampton area.

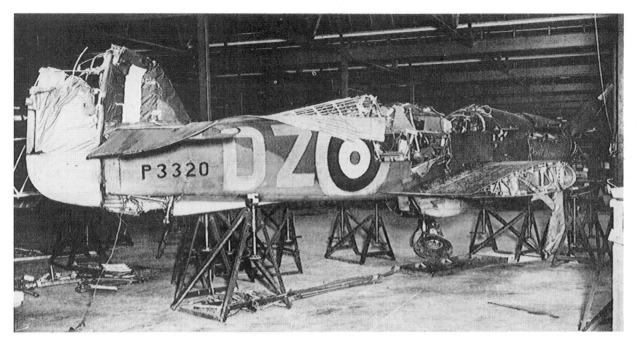

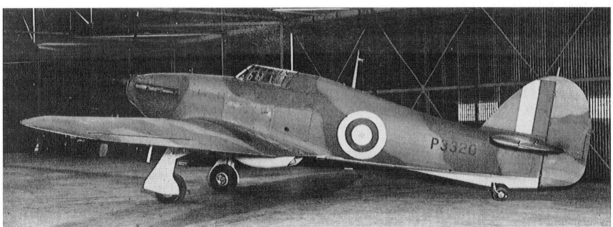

The wreck of a Hurricane of No. 151 Squadron, North Weald. It was crash-landed at Eastchurch by its pilot, Sergeant Davies, after being damaged in a dogfight on August 28th, 1940. The second picture shows the same aircraft completely rebuilt by No. 1 Civilian Repair Unit at Cowley, Oxfordshire

Night Widespread activity industries and airfields from Lincolnshire to Portsmouth.
Weather Central and east England light rain. Some cloud in Channel and haze over Dover Straits.

The Tuesday morning dawned dull and hazy, but no Luftflotte 2 major raids developed. The main effort was devoted to small attacks and photographic reconnaissance at very high altitude to assess the damage done to date.

No. 11 Group had little opportunity to practise its new 'Tally Ho!' procedures but interrupted the flow of aerial pictures back to northern France by destroying three of the long-range aircraft involved, two being Dornier 17s.

Park took the opportunity of the quiet spell to address another instruction to his controllers (No. 7) and this brought into the open the disagreements between himself and Air Vice-Marshal Leigh-Mallory at 12 Group over tactics. Park wanted to be assured of 12 Group squadrons over his north-eastern airfields when raids were being plotted into them, and his own forces were fully engaged elsewhere.

Within 12 Group the pilots were fretting at their lack of activity compared with their southern neighbours. Through Squadron-Leader Bader, the gallant legless C.O. of 242 Squadron, a new system of interceptions at wing strength was shortly to be evolved. Leigh-Mallory had long fostered the idea, based on a maximum strength build-up against large raids instead of squadrons intercepting singly or in pairs. At Air Ministry Air Vice-Marshal Sholto Douglas, the D.C.A.S., lent a sympathetic ear.

One of the main types of night bomber used by the R.A.F. in raids over Germany and the Channel ports in 1940, the Armstrong Whitworth Whitley. This Whitley 5 of 58 Squadron was taking off at dusk from Linton-on-Ouse, Yorkshire

To Park the assembling of large formations of fighters was both time-wasting and unwieldy. In any case with the enemy on his doorstep he could not afford the expensive luxury of testing the scheme with consequent damage to sector stations. His fighters might be massed at one point against raids which could at any time split up and seek separate targets. The warning from radar was far too short to allow for anything but forward interception techniques with reserves on the back patrol lines to meet divided raids, or those not shown early on the group's operations table.

The wing theories were not really born until three days later, but Park's ire had already been aroused by the fact that on two occasions (one of which was the Debden raid of the preceding day) assistance had been requested from 12 Group for patrols over 11 Group airfields. The squadrons requested had not materialised and he suspected that they had gone elsewhere to find a fight.

Accordingly in his instruction of the 27th he did not mince his words. He opened with a note of thanks to 10 Group for their consistent help in covering the Portsmouth area and then went on to deal with the subject of 12 Group co-operation. Up to date, he stated, 12 Group had not shown the same desire to co-operate by despatching their squadrons to the places requested. The result of this attitude had been that on two occa-

sions recently when 12 Group had offered assistance and were requested to patrol over aerodromes their squadrons did not in fact patrol over aerodromes. On both these occasions 11 Group aerodromes had been heavily bombed.

He had decided that rather than argue direct each time over these patrols, he would shift the onus to the shoulders of Command itself, and accordingly he ordered that Controllers were from then onwards immediately to put the requests for 12 Group assistance to the Controller, Fighter Command.

The controversy of wings versus squadron forward attack and 12 Group versus 11 Group was to become a major bone of contention for the rest of the daylight battle and ultimately it was, unjustifiably, to cost Park his command of 11 Group. It was not until 1942 that he had a further chance to prove the correctness of his techniques when he was posted as A.O.C. Malta. There he changed from wing to forward interception and produced remarkable results in two weeks.

While on the evening of the 27th the control-room staff were digesting and discussing Park's forthright instruction, raids began to come in from Cherbourg, and a widespread attack by Luftflotte 3 was made. Bombs were dropped on Gravesend, Calshot, Southampton, the Isle of Wight, Tonbridge, Tiptree and Leighton Buzzard. Some fell within a few miles of Bentley Priory.

August 28th

Day Airfield attacks, Kent, Essex and Suffolk in three phases.
Night First major attack on Liverpool. 150 bombers. Harassing attacks midlands, north-east coast and London.
Weather Fine and fair. Cold. Cloud in Dover Straits.

The men who kept them flying; the groundcrews who laboured day and night rearming, refuelling, maintaining and repairing. This group is from No. 222 Squadron

Once more the Luftwaffe divided its main efforts into three phases. The first began at 8.30 a.m. with a heavy build-up over Cap Gris Nez which became a mass of 100+, the larger proportion being fighters escorting two groups of Dorniers.

One section of the raid, consisting of twenty Dorniers, headed for Eastchurch, while the other with twenty-seven bombers flew to Rochford. Four 11 Group squadrons made desperate attempts to get through the escort screen of the Eastchurch raiders but without success and with the loss of eight aircraft and six pilots, two of which were from the ill-fated No. 264 Squadron with its two-seat Defiants.

The Coastal Command light-bomber station of Eastchurch therefore suffered yet another attack at eight minutes past nine, with two Fairey Battles destroyed on the ground and numerous craters on the airfield. Despite this the station remained serviceable for restricted day flying and there were no casualties.

At 12.30 the second raid developed, with the main objective as Rochford aerodrome near Southend. No. 264 Squadron were again forced to take off, with danger imminent, but fortunately before the bombs began to fall. Several squadrons out of thirteen on patrol intercepted, but the defensive screen was too strong, and most of the bombers reached their target. Despite thirty craters little serious damage was done to Rochford, which continued serviceable. While this was going on, Winston Churchill visited the battered station at Manston to view the damage.

The third attack consisted of large fighter formation sweeps over Kent and the Estuary at 25,000 feet. Seven R.A.F. squadrons attempted to intercept at various

times but lost nine aircraft. On this occasion Park's principle of avoiding combat with German fighters was not adhered to, and the day's losses of twenty Hurricanes and Spitfires was heavy in comparison with German losses of thirty-one for the whole twenty-four hours, although these included twelve bombers. Curiously, the Fighter Command assessment of German casualties was the most accurate of the period at twenty-eight.

The official records show only thirty German aircraft lost on the 28th, but in fact there was one more. A Gotha 145 biplane trainer carrying mail from the German forces in the Channel Islands to Strasbourg was diverted and came down on Lewes racecourse in Sussex, to the surprise of the young German pilot. The contents of mailbags made interesting reading for British intelligence officers.

In Göring's order for the 19th August Liverpool had been singled out for heavy raids (i.e., over 100 tons) and the preparations entrusted to Luftflotte 3. The Germans had long considered Liverpool a major target and it ranked second only to London on their port priority list.

Thus on the 28th Liverpool received the first of four consecutive night raids and about 150 bombers reached the area Liverpool-Birkenhead, causing widespread damage. Simultaneously Luftflotte 2 and a few Luftflotte 3 aircraft attacked Birmingham, Coventry, Manchester, Sheffield, Derby and London, and dropped bombs on a wide selection of other places.

While many of these raids had little or no effect on the British war effort they did disrupt production because of the air raid warning system then in operation. There were three types of warning:

1 *Yellow*, issued by Fighter Command as a preliminary to all areas over which raiders might pass.

2 *Purple*, issued at night to areas in the course of raiders. On receipt of this all exposed lighting in docks,

Mill Street, Maidstone, Kent, after a raid on September 5th, 1940. Miraculously the naval officer driving the car escaped unhurt

factories, sidings, etc., had to be extinguished.
3 *Red*, a public warning upon receipt of which the sirens were sounded.

The information for the various warning signals could only be obtained from Observer Corps plots and at this time the Corps came in for a lot of uninformed criticism by the public and the Press on warnings being in force when no air raid occurred. The responsibility rested with Fighter Command and the liaison officers at Observer Corps centres, and although great discretion was used the problem was not completely solved until after the Battle of Britain, and in the meantime night raids on the midlands or the north-west could mean the greater part of England being under Purple or Red warnings as the bomber stream flew northwards from the coast.

August 29th

Day Quiet morning. Airfield attacks in south and south-east in afternoon.
Night Liverpool again attacked; diversions in the midlands.
Weather Showers and bright intervals. Channel and Straits cloudy.

After the feverish activity of the previous night, the Thursday morning was dull but peaceful. Little activity was reported until after lunch, when at three o'clock radar picked up formations at Cap Gris Nez, Boulogne and the mouth of the Somme. Brightening weather had led Luftflotte 2 to put up massive fighter sweeps in the hope of attracting British fighters to the slaughter. Jafus 1 and 2 operated over Kent with 564 Me 109s and 159 Me 110s respectively.

No. 11 Group sent up forward patrols, expecting a renewal of bomber raids. Thirteen squadrons were despatched and some were involved in combats, but in the main the pilots adhered to Park's order of the 19th and retired when it was clear that no bombers were involved. This incident was particularly noted by the Luftwaffe operations and intelligence staffs who correctly deduced that the R.A.F. was avoiding wastage in fighter versus fighter battles. Thes tactics paid, as Fighter Command losses were only nine machines and German casualties were seventeen for the twenty-four-hour period, of which five were Me 109s from JG3.

After nightfall, Luftflotte 3 delivered its second attack on Liverpool and over 130 bombers reached the target, dropping both high explosives and incendiaries, navigation being assisted by a cloudless night. Diversionary raids on the midlands and outskirts of London were carried on by forty-four aircraft, usually singly.

A group of pilots from No. 310 (Czech) Squadron at Duxford on September 1st, 1940. No. 310 was formed, with Hurricanes, on July 10th

August 30th

Day Feint raids on shipping, then heavy attacks on south-eastern airfields. Raid on Luton.
Night Main target Liverpool. Single raids over wide area.
Weather Fair. Channel and Straits clear.

The day began with a renewal of shipping raids, this time in the Thames Estuary, designed to act as feints for the main assault which was picked up by radar over Cap Gris Nez at 10.30. Three waves totalling 100 aircraft came at half-hour intervals at 14,000 feet.

A cloud-layer at about 7,000 feet meant that the Observer Corps had to rely on sound plotting and it was not until an hour after the build-up over France that the 11 Group controller realised that forces were heading for Kent and Surrey sector stations. Sixteen squadrons were despatched to intercept, of which two, to guard Kenley and Biggin Hill, became involved in a dog-fight over Surrey. One formation of German bombers which had split off from the main group attacked Biggin Hill at noon and was not seen by the 12 Group Squadron flying on airfield protection patrol.

From high altitude delayed-action bombs were dropped which damaged the airfield surface and the village but once again did not render the former unserviceable.

A second mass attack began at 1.30 when raids of 6+, 12+ and 20+ crossed the coast between Dover and Dungeness, and then split up, sections heading for Biggin Hill, Shoreham, Kenley and Tangmere. Eight squadrons of fighters were ordered up and the raids retreated just before four o'clock. During this attack the radar stations at Dover, Pevensey, Rye, Foreness, Fairlight, Whitstable and Beachy Head were out of action due to a mains supply failure.

No sooner was this over than a third attack developed from Dover in waves, the objectives being Kenley, Biggin Hill, North Weald, Slough, Oxford and a convoy code-named 'Bacon'.

Detling airfield was hit by forty to fifty bombs which set fire to oil-tanks, cut the mains cable, cratered the roads and damaged one Blenheim. It was estimated that the station would not be serviceable until 8 a.m. on the 31st.

Far worse than this, one small raid of less than ten confused the defences by flying to the Thames Estuary and then turning south to Biggin Hill where at six o'clock, by low-level bombing with 1,000-pounders, the airfield was reduced to a shambles. Workshops, the transport yard, stores, barracks, the met. office, the

A member of the crew of a Do 17Z-3 of 6./KG3 being escorted ashore. Four men were rescued by local boatmen and the Margate Lifeboat after the aircraft had been shot down in the sea in the course of a raid on Eastchurch and Rochford on August 28th

armoury, W.A.A.F. quarters, and another hangar were wrecked; the power, gas and water mains were severed and all telephone lines north of the camp were cut in three places. Amid the rubble and fires casualties were very heavy, with thirty-nine dead and twenty-six injured—a number of them in a shelter trench which received a direct hit. Somehow the mess was cleared up and the station put back on an operational footing.

During the period another raid had come in over Sheppey, and, although intercepted, part of the force managed to reach Luton, where ten bombs were dropped and one hit the Vauxhall motor works, the total casualties including over fifty dead.

At dusk Fighter Command totted up its losses. Twenty-five fighters had been shot down compared with thirty-six German aircraft destroyed. The only bright spot was the saving of fifteen pilots. Altogether this Friday had been a maximum effort for both sides with the R.A.F. flying 1,054 sorties and the Luftwaffe 1,345.

On the night of the 30th/31st there was no respite for the island, with raiders coming in from 8.30 onwards. A continuous flow of bombers streamed up towards the midlands, South Wales and London, with Liverpool again the main target. Single raiders created diversions by attempting to bomb the airfields Biggin Hill, Debden, North Weald, Hornchurch, Detling, Eastchurch, Thorney Island, Broxbourne, Rochford and Calshot, while others ranged over towns from Derby to Norwich, and Cardiff to Peterborough.

On the 30th another link in the reporting chain had

been forged with the opening of No. 35 Observer Group with its Headquarters at Oban in Scotland.

August 31st

Day Fighter Command's heaviest losses. South-east and eastern airfields again main targets.
Night Heavy raid on Liverpool. Light attacks from north-east coast to Portsmouth.
Weather Mainly fair. Haze in Estuary and Straits.

The odds were weighted even more heavily against Fighter Command on this Saturday and its losses were the heaviest of the whole battle—thirty-nine fighters shot down with fourteen pilots killed. The Germans almost achieved parity, as they lost forty-one aircraft in the whole twenty-four-hour period.

Raiding began at 8 a.m. with waves coming in over Kent and the Estuary, Me 109s amusing themselves shooting down all the Dover balloons both land and water based. Once again airfields such as North Weald, Duxford and Debden were the main targets. Debden received about one hundred high-explosive and incendiary bombs from a formation of Dorniers, the sick quarters and barrack block receiving direct hits and other buildings being damaged. The operations rooms continued, however, to operate right through the attack. The raid steering for Duxford was intercepted by 111 Squadron from Croydon and did not reach its target.

Less than an hour later over 100 machines advanced from Calais and concentrated on Eastchurch where the airfield remained serviceable despite cratering and damage to buildings. Detling received a heavy quota of machine-gun bullets but no bombs.

The third attack, which began soon after noon, was to be the most serious of the day. Over 100 aircraft crossed the coast at Dungeness and flew up two clearly defined corridors.

One section attacked Croydon and Biggin Hill. At the former airfield twelve bombers came in at 2,000 feet demolishing a hangar, damaging other buildings and causing casualties. At Biggin Hill the bombing came from high altitude and to the long-suffering occupants of the airfield it seemed that they must be the A1 priority target for the whole Luftwaffe. Further extensive damage was done to hangars and buildings, the married quarters and officers' mess were bombed and the operations block received a direct hit, extinguishing the lights and filling the rooms with acrid fumes, dust and smoke from the fires which broke out. The temporary telephone lines and power cables put in after the raid on the 30th were destroyed.

At 6.35 Kenley aerodrome advised the Observer centre at Bromley that all lines to Biggin Hill were dead and that the frequency and call-signs of Biggin's 72 and 79 Squadrons were urgently required. Lines from Bromley to Biggin Hill were also found to be out of action, and finally a despatch-rider had to be sent to get the information.

The raiders approaching up the second air corridor over Dungeness headed for Hornchurch, and there they caught 54 Squadron in the act of taking off. Two sections got airborne but the last was blown into the air

German 'Ace' Franz von Werra, adjutant of II/JG3
'Udet', was forced down in this Me 109E in a field
near Marden, Kent, on September 5th. He was
transferred to a prison camp in Canada where he
eventually escaped to Germany. He warned German
intelligence that Britain had broken the Luftwaffe unit
and R/T codes and, as a result, the system was changed.
The fin of von Werra's aircraft shows 13 victories. He
was killed in October 1944

by explosions. One machine was hurled into a field,
another was thrown across the airfield to land on its
belly, while the third, piloted by Flight Lieutenant
Deere, was blown upside down. Miraculously all three
pilots emerged shaken but uninjured and were back
on operations the following morning. The thirty
Dorniers involved dropped about 100 bombs which
left a string of craters and cut the main power cable.
Four Do 17s were shot down.

During the course of these sorties, other German
aircraft made a sharp attack on coastal radar stations,
damaging Pevensey, Dunkirk, Rye, Foreness, Whitstable and Beachy Head C.H.s. The advantage was
not, however, pressed home and the stations were left
to recuperate.

The fourth and last attack of the day was delivered
at 5.30 p.m. by several groups of Ju 88s and bomb-
carrying Me 110s which cratered runways and perimeter
tracks, particularly at Hornchurch, where two more
Spitfires were destroyed on the ground. Both Hornchurch and Biggin Hill were serviceable again the
following morning.

On the night of August 31st/September 1st raids
began coming in at 8.45 p.m. with single aircraft and
groups of up to three. Bombs from twenty-five aircraft
were scattered north and south, keeping many awake
and in the shelters, but achieving little material effect.
Liverpool and the Cammell Laird yards at Birkenhead
received their fourth night raid in succession and
absorbed the main force. Other targets hit by error or
intention included Rotherhithe, Portsmouth, Manchester, Durham, Stockport, Bristol, Gloucester, Here-
ford, Worcester and the York to Leeds arterial road.

One delayed-action bomb fell on the airfield at
Duxford. It was dealt with in the usual way, by being
hitched with 100 yards of rope to an Armadillo vehicle
and then towed to a safe part of the airfield and left to
explode 'at its leisure'.

On the 31st Fighter Command issued orders that the
Defiants were to be used primarily for night fighting.
They could continue to be used by day where suitable,
i.e. where only hostile bombers were involved. The
Defiant Squadrons 141 and 264 henceforth operated
in Nos. 13 and 12 Groups respectively.

The amazing trio of American pilots who fought with No. 609 Squadron. From left to right: Gene Tobin, Vernon Keough and Andrew Mamedoff. All were killed later flying from Britain with the American Eagle Squadron

September 1st

Day Four main attacks on Fighter Command airfields. Heavy damage.
Night Liverpool again. Diversions in midlands and South Wales.
Weather Fair with cloud patches in morning. Fine afternoon.

As September opened, a Fighter Command diarist noted that 'the month of August saw the beginning of a war of attrition'. Dowding's forces were now suffering from accumulated fatigue and the mounting losses in pilots. The Luftwaffe was continuing its time-table concentration on sector airfields, many of which looked on the surface to be complete wrecks: it had become a question of just how long the organisation and the squadrons could continue to operate under continuous bombardment.

During the day, which was warm and sunny, four major attacks developed and these were aimed at Fighter Command airfields. Some 450 aircraft of Luftflotte 2 took part. The first signs of activity came at 10.15 a.m. when radar plotted raids of 20+, 30+, and 12+ forming up over the French coast. Once assembled this force became eleven formations, totalling 120 machines, which flew over Dover and split up to attack Biggin Hill, Eastchurch, Detling and Tilbury Docks. Fourteen and a half Fighter Squadrons were sent up to meet them.

For Biggin Hill it was the sixth raid in three days. No. 610 Squadron had been ordered to Acklington for a rest, but the ground crews were waiting to embus on the north side, and they smartly took cover in the

woods, despite the exhortations of an over-zealous officer brandishing a revolver. One pilot of 610, who had been waiting for a final check on his machine, watched from a shelter as his Spitfire blew up.

The small formation of Dorniers in this action bombed from 12,000 feet and pitted the runways with craters, rendering the airfield unserviceable until the afternoon. No. 79 Squadron's Hurricanes, returning from the fray, were forced to land at Croydon.

At 1 p.m. the usual signs of aircraft taking-off behind Calais were recorded by the gun-laying radar at Dover, and shortly afterwards the C.H. radar reported a concentration of approximately 150+ aircraft over Cap Gris Nez. These followed the same course as the morning raid and headed for the same targets.

The third and fourth attacks in the late afternoon were launched simultaneously, one mixed formation of fifty aircraft bombing Hawkinge and Lympne and another fifty raiding Detling and firing on the Dover balloon barrage. Small formations split off and one of these, consisting of Dorniers, headed for Biggin Hill where it was now realised that 6 p.m. was the regular allotted time for the last daylight Luftwaffe visitation.

The runways were again hit, but, far more serious, the sector operations room was reduced to a shambles, all lines except one out of 13 being severed, and the Defence Teleprinter Network wrecked by a 500 lb. bomb which bounced off a steel safe. Two W.A.A.F. telephone operators, Sergeant Helen Turner and Corporal Elspeth Henderson, worked on until the last moment and then flung themselves flat in time to avoid flying steel, glass and blast. Both received the Military Medal for bravery.

When the crew crawled out of the remains of sector operations they found that four Spitfires had been destroyed, and the armoury was on fire.

First priority was to get the operations room re-established in some form, and here the Post Office engineers came to the rescue. On the night of the 30th

Shot down by Spitfires, this Heinkel 111 of 9./KG27 lies wrecked beside a road in the Mendip Hills near Cheddar on August 25th

the main London-Biggin Hill-Westerham telephone cable had been cut by bombs north of the airfield. The station Post Office maintenance officer, although blown out of a slit trench himself, had made his way through the raid and had got a message to Tunbridge Wells maintenance control. An inspector and six men volunteered to repair the cable, and despite warnings from the Sevenoaks police that an air raid was still in progress they reached the crater after darkness had fallen.

Nothing could be done until dawn due to the presence of both gas and water in the crater. On September 1st the party started work. Despite the morning attack, the effects of coal-gas fumes and lack of food and drink they got the cable restored in seven hours.

Before they had finished, however, the operations room had been smashed, and every G.P.O. engineer was needed to get an emergency set-up working in a village shop. Within an hour some measure of control was once more at the disposal of Biggin Hill Sector, and working through the night, the engineers had by the following day rigged two new switch-boards and restored the telephone services. Meanwhile, the main cable was again severed, but the tireless engineers repaired it and reconnected several Observer posts which had lost their communications.

In daylight on the 1st, Fighter Command sent up 147 patrols involving 700 machines, and suffered fifteen aircraft casualties from which nine pilots were saved. The Luftwaffe reported the loss of fourteen aircraft including night operations which for the first time gave them an advantage on the score card.

Darkness had brought a lull until midnight, but between 9 p.m. and 4 in the morning about 100 aircraft singly attacked industrial targets and laid mines. Bombs fell at Birkenhead, Sealand, Stafford, Sheffield, Burton-on-Trent, Hull, Grimsby, Ashford and Gillingham. The most serious damage was done between Swansea and Neath where six 10,000-ton oil-tanks were set on fire.

September 2nd

Day Once again four main phases of airfield attacks.
Night Scattered raids: Liverpool, midlands and South Wales.
Weather Continuing fine and warm. Early-morning mist and fog patches.

Once again the early morning was warm and hazy, although there were occasional patches of low cloud.

The Luftwaffe stepped up the tempo, determined to eradicate the southern airfields as a source of R.A.F. defence. The day's operations were divided into four main phases intended to stretch No. 11 Group to the maximum. Over 750 aircraft were despatched and the German Air Force mounted 972 daylight sorties—332 more than the previous day.

Instead of the early-morning reconnaissance aircraft which usually preceded attacks later in the morning formations of 30+, 40+, etc., to the tune of 100 aircraft were building up over Calais at 7.15 a.m. These resolved into 40 bombers escorted by about 60 fighters stepped-up from 12,000 to 20,000 feet east of Dover. The formations split and separate raids attacked Eastchurch, North Weald, Rochford and Biggin Hill. 11 Group despatched eleven squadrons, but of these only five made contact.

The problems of dealing with low raids were again brought out during these sorties and special orders were issued from Sectors to the Observer Corps giving priority to low-flying aircraft. The Bromley Observer Centre diary recorded: 'Biggin Hill was caught by a low flight while everybody's attention including our Corps was absorbed by heavy work in dealing with high flights.'

The second attack began to form up over France at noon and at about 12.35 some 250 fighters and bombers converged on Dover and then split up. All the raids were accurately tracked by the Observer Corps over the Isle of Sheppey and the Thames Estuary, but one of them severely damaged Debden aerodrome.

By 3.15 yet another build-up was shown on the radar screens over Calais. Two hundred and fifty German machines transited Dover and then spread fanwise over Kent. One raid penetrated to Biggin Hill, Kenley and Brooklands. At Detling a hangar was hit and damage was caused at both Eastchurch and Hornchurch. At the latter, successful interceptions broke up the raid to such an extent that only six out of a hundred bombs dropped fell within the airfield boundary. Bombs fell at random on other places including Herne Bay, where one crater measured 200 feet across.

Finally at five o'clock in the afternoon a large raid and several small diversions appeared over Dungeness, their targets again being airfields.

Damage to airfields had been considerable with Detling and Eastchurch the worst hit. At Detling thirty aircraft wrecked 'C' Flight hangar and rendered the aerodrome unserviceable for several hours. Eastchurch

received two attacks, the first by eighteen aircraft which exploded a dump of three hundred and fifty 250 lb. bombs, wrecked the N.A.A.F.I. and admin. buildings, smashed water mains and sewers, destroyed five aeroplanes and put most of the communications out of action, including the Defence Teleprinter Network. In the second raid another hangar was hit, and it was decided on the following day to remove G.H.Q. and the accounts section. The camp was transferred to Wymswold Warden and the sick quarters to Eastchurch village. Total casualties for the day at the station were four killed and twelve wounded.

To meet this phased effort against its stations, 11 Group had put up 751 sorties and had lost thirty-one aircraft to the Luftwaffe's thirty-five, eight R.A.F. pilots had been killed and seven wounded. Once again Erprobungs Gruppe 210 had suffered, with eight Me 110s destroyed. On one bomber shot down were found supplies of hand grenades intended to be thrown out at persuing fighters. A coastal raid in the north left two steamers off Aberdeenshire damaged, one of which was burned out.

Night brought a few hours respite until at 1.30 a.m. raiders began to arrive in ones and twos over East Anglia, of which approximately half were engaged in minelaying. Many of the bombers out of the seventy-five despatched were from Luftflotte 3, and their landfall was Swanage in Dorsetshire. Targets were again scattered, including Leighton Buzzard, Digby, Castle Bromwich, Sealand, Birmingham, Liverpool, Monmouth and Cardiff.

September 3rd

Day Heavy attacks on airfields. Losses equal.
Night Main attack Liverpool. Harassing raids on South Wales and the south-east.
Weather Fine and warm. Some cloud and drizzle in north. Haze in Channel and Straits.

At eight o'clock in the morning Luftflotte 2 began the familiar pattern of building up formations over Calais, and one by one the blips appeared on the cathode-ray tubes at the C.H. and gun-laying radar stations at Dover.

The targets were Hornchurch, North Weald and Debden, but through a series of disjointed dog-fights only one intact formation reached its target, North Weald. Here about thirty Dorniers escorted by Me 110s did severe damage. Fire broke out in Nos. 151 and 25 Squadrons hangars, the motor transport yard was badly hit and several other buildings including the main stores were damaged. The new sector operations block received a direct hit but survived, although all communications with the Observer Corps were severed except for one line to Watford Centre. The airfield Tannoy system was destroyed and the vital high-frequency relay system for communication between aircraft and base was cut between the receiver and transmitter. Despite all this and a liberal sowing of delayed-action bombs, the aerodrome remained serviceable for day operations.

One of the pilots from 603 Squadron shot down in

Sgt. C. Babbage of 602 Spitfire Squadron, Westhamp-
nett, Sussex, who baled out into the sea after a Luftflotte 3
attack on Portsmouth on August 26th. He was picked
up by a fishing boat and brought ashore at Bognor
Regis. Note the pier in the background with a large
piece removed to stop its use by a seaborne invading
force

this operation was Pilot Officer Richard Hillary, later
to write the best seller 'The Last Enemy'. His cockpit
in flames Hillary had difficulty in getting the Spitfire's
hood open. When at last he succeeded he fell, badly
burned, into the sea. After over an hour of pain and
misery he, like so many other pilots, was picked up by
an R.N.L.I. lifeboat, the *J. B. Proudfoot,* on temporary
duty at Margate.

In the afternoon a second attack developed in the
same area which was beaten off, and in which action the
Czech pilots of No. 310 Squadron, Duxford, played
a significant part.

Due to continuing bomber losses, the Luftwaffe had
been experimenting with new tactics on this day.
Previously the plan had been to advance in stepped
formations, but this was temporarily replaced by (a)
fighters and bombers flying at the same level and (b)
mixed groups of fighters and bombers. Neither of
these was found to be satisfactory, and a few days
later there was a general resumption of stepped formations. Freiejagd, or freelance patrols of Me 109s and
Me 110s, continued to fly in and then orbit in attempts
to draw R.A.F. fighters away from the main attack.

The losses of the 3rd were nevertheless an ominous
portent for the R.A.F. Sixteen fighters were shot down
with eight pilots saved, while the German casualties
for the whole twenty-four-hour period were also sixteen—the Luftwaffe had achieved parity for the
second time.

The main raid of the night was against Liverpool,
about ninety bombers flying in a steady stream from
Cherbourg. Bombing was, however, not concentrated
and damage was also done at Warrington, Chester
and Sealand.

September 4th

Day Succession of airfield raids in two main phases. Serious
damage at Vickers Works, Brooklands.
Night Further raid on Liverpool. Harassing attacks.
Weather Fine and warm. Occasional rain and strong winds
in north. Haze in Estuary, Channel and Straits.

On September 1st the Luftwaffe Operations Staff IA
had issued an order to the Luftflotten covering the
destruction (if possible) of thirty British factories
making aircraft, aero engines, propellers and ancillary
equipment. This was an attempt to halt a seemingly
endless flow of fighter equipment to the R.A.F.,
despite Intelligence IC statements that the aircraft
were either destroyed or non-existent. The order
covered both fighter and bomber production, and the
necessary target briefings had been completed by
September 3rd.

Accordingly on the 4th the raids by Luftflotte 2
were divided, with both sector airfields and factories
as their targets.

The first big attack of the day concentrated on
airfields, coming in via the Estuary and over Dover.
At Eastchurch bombs from eighteen aircraft demolished
the ration store and produced six craters in the runway,
but there were no casualties. Lympne was shot up, as
were the Dover Balloons.

At lunchtime successive waves of bombers with
fighter escort totalling about 300 crossed the coast
at Dover, Folkestone, Hastings and Beachy Head.
Fourteen squadrons rose to do battle, and nine of them

At mid-day on August 31st, 1940 Squadron Leader
T. P. Gleave of No. 253 Squadron took off from Biggin
Hill leading a formation of seven Hurricanes to intercept
a raid approaching the airfield.

At 12,000 feet was a large formation of Ju 88s. Despite
inferiority in numbers the handful of fighters went into
the attack. Squadron Leader Gleave hit two bombers
of the port line and was laying his sights on a third when
a cannon shell hit his starboard fuel tank.

The aircraft, P3115, burst into flames and the starboard
wing came off. Severely burned, Squadron Leader
Gleave managed to bale out and landed at Mace Farm
just east of Biggin Hill.

One of the Ju 88s he fired at crashed at the village of
Downe to the north.

The 19 Group Bromley Observer Corps log book at
1300 hours recorded: 'Hurricane and hostile bomber
crashed Q8779. Hurricane pilot baled out in
approximately Q9577'.

Squadron Leader Gleave became one of the first plastic
surgery 'guinea pigs' and subsequently returned to
R.A.F. service, rising to the rank of Group Captain.
He presumed that his aircraft had completely broken up,
but in fact the engine and other large sections lay deep
in a thicket on a lonely hillside by the farm. They were
're-discovered' after more than 20 years. In 1967 the
engine was transported to Biggin Hill by the Flairavia
Flying Club and is now a museum piece. Somewhere in
the surrounding fields lie four Browning machine guns
which will doubtless come to light one day.

Aircraft wreckage, bullets, bombs and pieces of uniform
and equipment from 1940 are still being found in the
south of England.

The photographs show left, the Merlin engine of P3115
lying in a thicket at Mace Farm and right, Group
Captain Gleave, in 1967, holding up a piece of the
wreckage

intercepted. In the ensuing confusion at 1.30 p.m.
fourteen Me 110s of 5/LG.1 slipped through at low
level and followed the Southern Railway line over
Guildford, Surrey, to the Vickers Armstrong factory
at Brooklands, where two-thirds of the R.A.F.'s Wellington bombers were produced.

The adjacent sector and Observer Corps operations
tables were 'saturated' with raid plots and the formation
'Bradshawing' up the railway went unnoticed until the
last moment. Due to an unusually quick piece of
recognition by the sergeant in charge of the airfield
guns, the two leading aircraft were shot down almost
immediately and several others jettisoned their bombs
outside the target area when intercepted by No. 253
Squadron's Hurricanes over the village of Clandon. The
bombs dropped, however, scored direct hits on the
machine and erecting shops. Many workers were
buried under rubble and girders while hundreds more
were injured by blast and flying splinters. From the
six bombs in the works area eighty-eight people were
killed and 600 injured, while factory output almost
ceased for four days.

Other small groups of raiders got through to
Rochester, Eastchurch, Shoeburyness, Canterbury,
Faversham and Reigate. At Rochester the target was
again the Short Brothers factory engaged in initial
production of the Sterling four-motor heavy bombers.

In these fierce engagements of the morning and
afternoon, Fighter Command put up a total 678 sorties
and lost seventeen fighters against German losses of
twenty-five—the balance was beginning to improve
slightly.

The night was extremely active with nearly 200
bombers over England, the majority going to Liverpool,
Bristol and South Wales. A number of raiders approached the Thames Estuary but seemed disconcerted
by the London barrage. Parachute flares were dropped
over Hendon and Hatfield, while other bombs fell on

Manchester, Halifax, Newcastle, Nottingham, Tilbury and Gravesend.

September 5th

Day Airfield attacks in two phases. Park orders special cover for fighter factories.
Night Continuous activity over most of England.
Weather Again fine and warm, cloud developing later. Channel and Straits fine.

As on previous days, the Luftwaffe effort was divided up into two major attacks, the sub-formations breaking away and heading for their targets after crossing the coast, in order to confuse the defences.

About 10 a.m. raids developed over Kent heading for Croydon, Biggin Hill and Eastchurch, while others concentrated on North Weald and Lympne. Fourteen R.A.F. squadrons joined the fight and most of the raiders were diverted before reaching their targets as occurred at Biggin Hill where 79 Squadron successfully intercepted.

Just after lunch radar began to track several formations over France, but many came in so high that they were missed by the Observers on the ground and were not plotted on the operations tables. The oil-tanks at Thameshaven were set on fire while Biggin Hill and Detling received further attention.

The bombers dispersed at two o'clock and swarms of Me 109s patrolled the Channel to see them home, as German losses through being shot down into the sea were becoming too frequent to be ignored.

In these engagements fighter Command lost twenty machines to the Germans' twenty-three throughout the twenty-four hour period, although five British pilots were saved.

At night during the 5th/6th there was almost continuous activity, with bombs dropped on Liverpool,

Manchester, London and over forty other towns and cities.

Following the attacks on Weybridge and Rochester, Park, on the 5th, issued instructions passed on from Dowding that maximum fighter cover should be given to the Hawker factories at Kingston, Langley and Brooklands, and to the Vickers-Supermarine works at Southampton. Dowding had correctly diagnosed that part of the enemy's effort had been switched to factories and that more such raids would be forthcoming. The only direct protection he could afford was to ask for two No. 10 Group squadrons to patrol the lines Brooklands–Croydon and Brooklands–Windsor whenever a heavy attack developed south of the Thames.

In his order Park stressed the 'vital' importance to the R.A.F. of the Southampton factories and in particular the Supermarine works at Woolston. Ever helpful, 10 Group had agreed to reinforce the Tangmere sector by up to three or four squadrons whenever a mass raid approached the Southampton–Portsmouth area.

On the 5th, No. 504 Squadron was ordered to move south from Catterick. The procedure was a typical example of unit moves during the Battle. In the early morning a message was received for the squadron to transfer complete to Hendon. Bombay transport aircraft arrived to take part of the personnel, while the remainder entrained after lunch. The pilots flew down at midday and were in action over London on the 7th.

September 6th

Day Three main attacks, largely broken up.
Night Less activity. Harassing raids only.
Weather Fine, but cooler. Haze in Straits and Estuary.

Park's orders on factory defence had been issued none too soon for on Friday the 6th Luftflotte 2 tried to attack the Hawker works at Brooklands where half the total output of Hurricanes was produced. The squadrons on patrol were able to prevent any serious damage being done.

In all there were three main attacks during the day, which cost Fighter Command twenty-three fighters, the pilots of twelve machines being saved. German losses were thirty-five, including sixteen Me 109s and eight He 111s from KG26.

Groups of bombers with fighter escort began to mass at 8.30 in the morning, and they fanned out over Kent trying to get at five of the sector stations around London. Their efforts were frustrated and they therefore made a second attempt at midday and a third in the early evening. No great damage was done due to successful interceptions, as was evidenced at Biggin Hill where most of the bombs overshot the target and fell on the Westerham road where the much repaired main trunk cable was once more severed. An unusual present for the R.A.F. came on this evening in the shape of an Me 109 which landed at Hawkinge when it ran out of fuel.

The night of the 6th/7th was less active than usual with single raiders wandering the counties and dropping bombs sufficient to keep the sirens howling and the shelters occupied. The Fighter Command controllers presumed that the enemy was resting after the long period of sustained activity. They did not know that the Luftwaffe was about to change its policy and that the agonising strain on 11 Group was to be eased at the expense of the citizens of London. The morrow was to provide many surprises.

FIGHTER COMMAND ORDER OF BATTLE Groups and Squadrons September 7th, 1940 (0900 hours)

13 GROUP, HEADQUARTERS NEWCASTLE

Wick

3	Hurricane	Castletown
232	Hurricane	Sumburgh (one flight)

Dyce

145	Hurricane	A Flight Dyce
		B Flight Montrose

Turnhouse

605	Hurricane	Drem
65	Spitfire	Turnhouse
141	Defiant	Turnhouse
615	Hurricane	Prestwick

Usworth

607	Hurricane	Usworth
610	Spitfire	Acklington
32	Hurricane	Acklington

Catterick

54	Spitfire	Catterick
219	Blenheim	Catterick

12 GROUP, HEADQUARTERS WATNALL

Kirton-in-Lindsey

74	Spitfire	Kirton-in-Lindsey
264	Defiant	Kirton-in-Lindsey

Church Fenton

85	Hurricane	Church Fenton
302	Hurricane	Church Fenton (Polish)
64	Spitfire	Church Fenton
		(B Flight Ringway)

Digby

611	Spitfire	Digby
151	Hurricane	Digby
29	Blenheim	Digby

Coltishall

616	Spitfire	Coltishall
242	Hurricane	Coltishall
266	Spitfire	Coltishall (A Flight Wittering)

Wittering

23	Blenheim	Wittering
229	Hurricane	Wittering (B Flight Bircham Newton)

Duxford

19	Spitfire	Duxford
310	Hurricane	Duxford (Czech)

11 GROUP, HEADQUARTERS UXBRIDGE

Debden

17	Hurricane	Debden
73	Hurricane	Castle Camps
25	Blenheim	Martlesham
257	Hurricane	Martlesham (B Flight North Weald)

North Weald

249	Hurricane	North Weald
46	Hurricane	Stapleford

Hornchurch

222	Spitfire	Hornchurch
603	Spitfire	Hornchurch
600	Blenheim	Hornchurch
41	Spitfire	Rochford

Biggin Hill

79	Spitfire	Biggin Hill
501	Hurricane	Gravesend

Kenley

111	Hurricane	Croydon
72	Spitfire	Croydon
66	Spitfire	Kenley
253	Hurricane	Kenley

Northolt

1	Hurricane	Heathrow
1	Hurricane	Northolt (R.C.A.F.)
303	Hurricane	Northolt (Polish)
504	Hurricane	Northolt

Tangmere

601	Hurricane	Tangmere
43	Hurricane	Tangmere
602	Spitfire	Westhampnett

10 GROUP, HEADQUARTERS, BOX, WILTSHIRE

Pembrey

92	Spitfire	Pembrey

Filton

213	Hurricane	Exeter
87	Hurricane	Exeter (B Flight Bibury)

St. Eval

238	Hurricane	St.Eval
247	Gladiator	Roborough (one flight)

Middle Wallop

234	Spitfire	Middle Wallop
609	Spitfire	Middle Wallop
604	Blenheim	Middle Wallop
56	Hurricane	Boscombe Down
152	Spitfire	Warmwell

LUFTFLOTTE 5—NORWAY (at 14.9.40)

X Fliegerkorps
Long-range reconnaissance
Aufkl.Gr.22 Stab, with
1./(F)120	He 111 and Ju 88
2./(F)22	Do 17
3./(F)122	Do 17 and Ju 88
1./(F)121	Do 17 and Ju 88

Coastal reconnaissance
Aufkl.Gr.Ob.d.l.Ku.FlGr.506
(one kette)	He 115
1./506	He 115
2./506	He 115
3./506	He 115

Fighters
II/JG77	Me 109

LUFTFLOTTE 2—HOLLAND, BELGIUM AND NORTHERN FRANCE

(at 3.9.40)

Long-range reconnaissance
Aufkl.Gr.122 Stab
1./(F)22	Do 17 and Me 110
2./(F)122	Ju88
4./(F)122	Ju 88, He 111 and Me 110

I Fliegerkorps
Long-range reconnaissance
5./(F)122	Ju 88 and He 111

Long-range bombers
KG76 Stab, I, II, III	I, III, Do 17; II, Ju 88
KG77 Stab, I, II, III	Ju 88
KG1 Stab, I, II, III	I, II, He 111; III, Ju 88
KG30 Stab, I, II	Ju 88

II Fliegerkorps
Long-range reconnaissance
1./(F)122	Ju 88
7./(F)LG2	Me 110

Long-range bombers
KG2 Stab, I, II, III	Do 17z
KG53 Stab, I, II, III	He 111
KG3 Stab, I, II, III	Do 17z
IV/(St)LG1	Ju 87

Fighter-bombers
LG2 II (Schlacht)	Me 109
Epr. Gr.210	Me 109/110

Dive-bombers
St.G1 Stab, II	Stab, Do 17 and Ju 87; II, Ju 87
St.G26 I, II	Ju 87

VIII Fliegerkorps (In process of transfer from Luftflotte 3 to Luftflotte 2 as from 29.8.40. See Battle order for August)

IX Fliegerdivision
Long-range reconnaissance
3./(F)122	Ju 88 and He 111
KG4 Stab, I, II, III	I, II, He 111; III, Ju 88

Minelaying
KGr.126	He 111
KG40 Stab	Ju 88

Coastal reconnaissance
K.Fl.Gr.106	He 115 and Do 18

Jagdfliegerführer 1
JG76 Stab, II	Me 109
V.(Z)/LG1	Me 110

Jagdfliegerführer 2
JG53 Stab, I, II, III	Me 109
JG51 Stab	Me 109
JG3 (in process of transfer from Luftflotte 3)	Me 109

Luftgaukommando VI
I./JG52 (one Schwarm)	Me 109
III./JG3 (one Schwarm)	Me 109

Luftgaukommando XI
JG1 Stab	Me 109
JG52 II	Me 109
JG51 II	Me 109

Luftgaukommando Holland
JG54 (one Schwarm) each from
I, II, III	Me 109
JG51 II (one Schwarm)	Me 109

Luftgaukommando Belgium
Close reconnaissance aircraft only

LUFTFLOTTE 3 (at 23.9.40)

Long-range reconnaissance
Aufkl.Gr.123 Stab
1./(F)123	Ju 88 and Do 17
2./(F) 123	Ju 88 and Do 17
3./(F)123	Ju 88 and Do 17

Jagdfliegerführer 3

IV Fliegerkorps
Long-range reconnaissance
3./(F)121	Ju 88 and He 111
LG1 Stab, I, II, III and reserve Staffel	Ju 88

Dive-bombers
St.G3 Stab, I, II	Ju 87
St.G2	Ju 87

Long-range bombers
K.Gr.806	Ju 88
KG27 Stab, I, II, III, and reserve Staffel	He 111

Long-range bombers
K.Gr.806   Ju 88
KG27 Stab, I, II, III,
and reserve Staffel   He 111

K.Gr.100   He 111
K.Gr.606   Do 17
Long-range reconnaissance
3./(F)31 (subordinate to 9th Army
H.Q.)   Me 110 and Do 17
Naval-co-operation
I/KG40   FW 200
Fighters
ZG76 Stab, II, III   Me 110
JG53 Stab, I, II, III   Me 109
V./LG1   Me 110

V Fliegerkorps
Long-range reconnaissance
4./(F)121   Ju 88 and Do 17
4./(F)14   Me 110 and Do 17
Long-range bombers
KG51 Stab, I, II, III   Ju 88
and reserve Staffel
KG54 Stab, I, II and   Ju 88
reserve Staffel
KG55 Stab, I, II, III   He 111
and reserve Staffel
Fighters
ZG26 Stab, I, II, III   Me 110
JG2 Stab, I, II, III   Me 109
(operating both Luftflotten
2 and 3)
JG27 Stab, I, II, III   Me 109
(under VIII Fliegerkorps for admin.)

17 Fourth phase—September 7th–30th

The timetable for the German invasion of England was not going to schedule due to the resistance of the R.A.F. during August, and to the High Command it appeared that they were no nearer defeating Fighter Command and achieving the air superiority for the landing. In addition the period August 24th to September 6th had shown 107 German bombers and two Stukas lost.

Intelligence under Schmid had been totally unable to assess the actual state of R.A.F. fighter forces from week to week or that the raids on sector airfields had caused great dislocation and damage with a high rate of pilot casualties. For two months the Luftwaffe had tried every device to bring the main British fighter force into battle when numerical superiority of Me 109s and Me 110s would destroy it.

From the beginning there had been many in the Luftwaffe Command who were of the opinion that only direct and heavy daylight blows against London would achieve the desired results, with the possibility that the raids might cause morale to crack as occurred at Warsaw and Rotterdam. Hitler had consistently forbidden attacks on London as he felt certain Britain would sue for peace without such extreme measures.

The chain which led to a reversal of his policy was actually set off by the Germans themselves. On the night of August 25th a number of bombs had accidentally fallen on central London, due to bad navigation. The R.A.F. had immediately taken up the challenge and flown several night raids over Berlin. Little damage was actually caused, but the effect on both Hitler and Göring was decisive. As the glorious victors of Europe it was embarrassing to say the least to have enemy bombers droning over the Reich night after night practically unscathed.

As early as August 31st the Command Staff of the Luftwaffe issued preliminary orders for Luftflotten 2 and 3 to prepare for a daylight reprisal raid on London. On September 2nd Luftflotten 2 and 3 drew up instructions for the general plan of the attack which covered day and night raids on London and other large centres of population.

Thus, when the Luftwaffe commanders met in The Hague on September 3rd to discuss the progress of the air war against England, an attack on the heart of the British Empire seemed the only logical step. As related in Chapter 5 there were heated arguments between Kesselring and Sperrle over current R.A.F. fighter strength with the former winning the day on a theory that Fighter Command was almost finished. The attacks on sector stations from the south coast up to and around London had cleared the way, so it was thought, for the final assault. British reserves that had apparently been pulled back north out of range of the Me 109 would certainly be thrown into the defence of the city and would incur heavy losses. To Kesselring it seemed the only sensible idea, and one that he had been suggesting ever since the Battle started, i.e. massive attack at full strength against one key objective.

With the Luftwaffe committed to the plan, and the preparations well in hand, it only remained for the Führer to give his sanction. After the first raids on Berlin, Hitler had clearly given Göring permission to put in hand arrangements for such an operation, otherwise the orders of August 31st could not have come from the O.K.L. The Luftwaffe had set the date as September 7th, and five days before that Hitler personally gave orders for 'the start of the reprisal raids against London'.

In England neither Dowding nor Park were aware of any impending change in tactics. All they knew was that the unremitting attacks on airfields and the sector organisation during August had gravely impaired strength and efficiency.

The position was grim in the extreme as from August 24th to September 6th 295 fighters had been totally destroyed and 171 badly damaged, against a total output of 269 new and repaired Spitfires and Hurricanes. Worst of all, during the fortnight 103 pilots were killed or missing and 128 were wounded, which represented a total wastage of 120 pilots per week out of a fighting strength of just under 1,000.

Experienced pilots were like gold-dust, and each one lost had to be replaced by an untried man who for some time would be vulnerable, until he acquired battle know-how. Fresh squadrons, moved in to replace tired units, very often lost more aircraft and pilots than the formations they replaced. For instance, 616 Squadron lost twelve aircraft and five pilots between August 25th and September 2nd and had to be retired to Coltishall in No. 12 Group.

No. 603 Squadron, newly arrived in 11 Group on August 28th, had by September 6th lost sixteen aircraft and twelve pilots, while 253 Squadron at Kenley lost thirteen Hurricanes and nine pilots in the seven days they were in battle, from August 30th.

In contrast the experienced squadrons, while utterly weary and often flying over fifty hours per day, continued to show far better results. No. 54 Squadron, when sent north from Hornchurch on September 3rd,

Above *A Heinkel 111 shot down at Burmarsh, Kent, on September 11th. The Spitfire that shot it down can be seen circling overhead.* Below *Two of the German crew are being led away while the Heinkel burns out in the background*

had lost only nine aircraft and one pilot since August 24th. No. 501 Squadron in the Biggin Hill sector during the complete phase (August 24th–September 6th) had suffered the loss of nine aircraft and four pilots.

During the whole of August no more than 260 fighter pilots were turned out by the O.T.U.s and casualties in the same month were just over 300. A full squadron establishment was twenty-six pilots whereas the average in August was sixteen. The command was literally wasting away under Dowding's eyes and there was nothing he could do about it if southern England was to continue as a defended area.

The ground organisation had also suffered severely and in a report to Headquarters Fighter Command, dated September 12th, Park stated that contrary to general belief and official reports, the enemy's bombing attacks by day had done extensive damage to five forward aerodromes and also to six out of seven sector stations. The damage to forward aerodromes was so severe that

By the second week in September the Luftwaffe air assault on Britain covered a 24-hour cycle. As the last of the daylight raids faded out, the bombers were preparing to deliver their deadly loads by night. Here Do 17s of KG3 are seen on take-off, and heading out towards the Channel. For night operations the white outline of the wing crosses had been blacked over but the white bar denoting first Gruppe on the starboard wing had been retained. In early September KG3 had been transferred from Luftflotte 3 to Luftflotte 2 in the Pas de Calais

Manston and Lympne were for several days quite unfit for fighters. Biggin Hill was so severely damaged that only one squadron could operate from the airfield and the remaining two squadrons had to be placed under the control of adjacent sectors for over a week. Park added that had the enemy continued his heavy attacks to the adjacent sectors, knocked out their operations rooms or telephone communications, the fighter defences of London would have been in a powerless state during the last critical phase, and unopposed heavy attacks would have been directed against the capital.

September 7th

Day Bombing switched to London. Heavy attack on the capital. Pressure on fighter airfields eased.

*A street in west London on September 8th after the
raiders had passed. A double-decker bus has been blown
up into the first-floor windows of a terrace house*

Night London raids continue dusk until dawn. Main objectives east London and docks.
Weather Fair in the south. Some haze.

Göring decided personally to command the assault
against London, and accordingly his immaculate personal train with its cooks, telephones and stocks of wine
rolled north-west to the Pas de Calais. At Cap Gris Nez
the entourage of field marshals, generals and colonels
took their stand while the Reichsmarschall gazed
skyward through his binoculars waiting for the passing
of his aerial armada.

Every available fighter was being used, and bombers
in far greater force than hitherto. The targets lay in
East London, on the banks of the Thames, among the
docks and warehouses.

To the staff on duty in the filter and operations rooms
at Bentley Priory the day began purely as a repetition
of so many others. At 11.15 four raids developed with
Hawkinge airfield as their main target. The fighter
dispositions had been laid down with continued attacks
on sector stations in view, and to this end Park in his
order of September 5th had stressed the need to put
fighter squadrons into battle in pairs, the Spitfires to
deal with the fighter screen and the Hurricanes with

the bombers. 11 Group was ready to deal with sector
and factory raids, with the assistance of 10 Group on
its western flank and 12 Group to the north.

Park was not, however, satisfied that fighters were
being positioned correctly. In the early stages of the
Battle there had been a tendency for radar plots to be
shown with too low a height and many squadrons found
themselves still climbing, with the enemy above. This
had led both pilots and controllers to add a few thousand
feet on to the height given in the hope of arriving above
or on a level with the raid.

By early September the radar plotting and Fighter
Command's filtering had improved still further with
continuous practice, and the heights fed into sector
operations were usually accurate. The habit of 'adding
a bit' nevertheless still went on with the result that
squadrons found themselves going straight into the
high-altitude escort screen while the bombers got
through.

On the 7th a terse instruction was issued by Park to
his controllers. After pointing out that on one occasion
the previous day only seven out of eighteen squadrons
despatched engaged the enemy and on another only
seven out of seventeen got into the right position, he
commented that it was obvious that some controllers
were ordering squadrons intended to engage enemy
bombers to patrol too high. When Group ordered a
squadron to 16,000 feet, sector controller added on one
or two thousand, and the squadron added on another

215

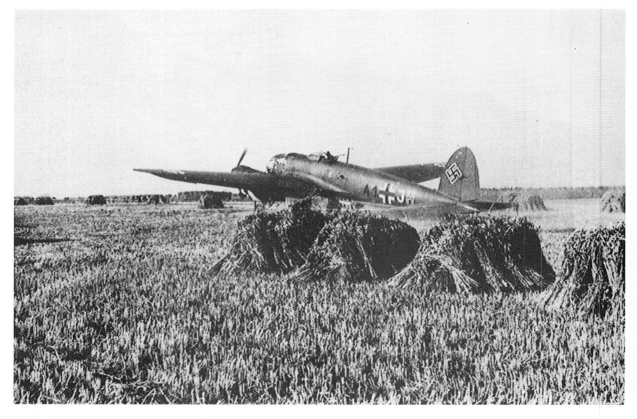

A Heinkel III of KG53 taxies out through a wheatfield in northern France. The dorsal gunner was obviously expecting the worst as he was wearing a steel helmet!

two thousand in the vain hope that they would not have any enemy fighters above them. The net result had been that daily some of the enemy bomber formations slipped in under 15,000 feet, frequently without any fighter escort, and bombed their objectives, doing serious damage, as at Brooklands. In fact the majority of enemy bomber formations had been intercepted only after they had dropped their bombs and were on the way out.

11 Group were also concerned about the prospects of invasion as the barge concentrations across the Channel daily grew larger. In the morning the Air Ministry informed Fighter Command 'Invasion regarded Imminent'. This was followed by standard notifications of states of readiness:

Invasion Alert No. 3—an attack is probable within three days.
Invasion Alert No. 2—an attack is probable within two days.
Invasion Alert No. 1—an attack is imminent.

Fighter Command had plenty on its mind when at 4 p.m. the radar stations picked up several formations of twenty+ over Calais. It was presumed it would adopt the usual tactics of crossing the coast and splitting up straightaway. Gradually it was realised at Bentley Priory that this was no ordinary raid. Over 300 bombers with 600 Me 109s and Me 110s in attendance, stepped up in solid layers, crossed the coast in two waves. The first flew direct to the Estuary and the second, an hour later, passed over central London, then steered back over the Estuary and the East End.

It was too late to alter the carefully prepared dispositions of the fighter squadrons, and as a result many bombers were not attacked until after they had delivered their loads. The sector stations were being well covered, but the road to London was clear. The 11 Group controller got everything he could vector on to the advancing phalanx, but it was in penny numbers compared with the solid masses of the Luftwaffe.

In addition the German fighter screen had adopted new techniques. Both bombers and fighters operated at great height with the former usually at between 16,000 and 20,000 feet.

Escorts were divided into two parts, some operating in close contact with the bombers, and others a few hundred yards away and a little above. Close cover was above, behind—at a lower level—and on both sides of the bombers. If the formation was attacked from starboard the starboard section engaged the attackers, the top section moving to starboard and the port section to the top position. If the attack came from the port side the system was reversed. British fighters coming in to the rear were engaged by the rear section and the two outside sections similarly moved to the rear. If the threat came from above, the top section went into action while the side sections gained height in order to be able to follow the R.A.F. fighters down as they broke away. If attacked themselves, all sections flew in defensive circles. These tactics were skilfully evolved and carried out, and they were extremely difficult to counter.

*Approaching London, a formation of Heinkel 111s
during one of the September raids, with an ever-ready
official cameraman in the nose of this aircraft*

Despite interception by four fighter squadrons and
heavy anti-aircraft fire, the bombers of both waves
made determined efforts to keep formation. High on
the top of the Senate House, London University, the
central London Observer post K.1 had a bird's-eye
view of the attack and passed plots as fast as the operations room could take them.

Bombs rained down upon the London docks, the
oil-tanks at Cliffe and Thameshaven, Beckton gasworks,
and on Poplar, Woolwich, Millwall, Limehouse, Tower
Bridge, Tottenham, West Ham, Barking and Croydon.
Silvertown became a raging inferno and the fires raged
on acting as a beacon for the night bombers, while in
the little streets of the East End the inevitable pattern
of death and destruction was beginning to unfold.

Rows of jerry-built terraced houses of the early
Victorian era suddenly became heaps of tiles and rubble.
Processions of bombed-out families—with a perambu-
lator, a few bundles and the children clinging on for
dear life—threaded their way through the glass and
debris. Wardens, firemen and a host of others dug in
the ruins searching for the injured. London's testing
time had begun, and like the pilots, ground staff and
W.A.A.F.s of the R.A.F., the city was not found
wanting. In curious irony it was a quarter of a century
before, on September 8th, 1915, that Zeppelins had
made their first big raid on London.

Many of the raiders did not fare so well as their
companions who had a clear run over the City. The
12 Group wing at Duxford had been practising their

formation techniques, and had Leigh-Mallory's blessing
to operate *en masse*. No. 242 Squadron which led the
wing had a bitter fight with a large formation of Dorniers
and Messerschmitts and shot down several, although
the remaining two squadrons—19 and 310—could not
gain height in time to join in.

The most successful of the units operating on the
7th was No. 303, the Polish squadron from Northolt.
When the Poles came into the battle they found forty
Dorniers at 20,000 feet with a formation of Me 110s
above and behind, and further back still, at over 25,000
feet, were the Me 109s. The engagement was a first-class
piece of the kind of co-operation Park wanted. A
squadron of Spitfires took on the 109s, while a Hurricane
squadron attacked the rear of the bombers forcing them
to turn back. At this juncture the Poles waded in,
turning their whole unit broadside on to the enemy.

They dived 4,000 feet out of the sun, each pilot
selecting a victim. The squadron commander, Squadron
Leader R. G. Kellett, reported afterwards: 'We gave
them all we'd got, opening fire at 450 yards and only
breaking away when we could see the enemy completely
filling the gunsight. That means we finished the attack
at point-blank range. We went in practically in one
straight line, all of us blazing away.' Nearly a quarter
of the bombers were destroyed or badly damaged.

One of No. 10 Group's squadrons on the factory
protection patrol was also involved in the general
mêlée as the Luftwaffe retired just after 6 p.m. Flight
Lieutenant J. H. G. McArthur, 'Blue Leader' No. 609
Squadron, reported:

Whilst on patrol at 10,000 feet between Brooklands and
Windsor, we saw about 200 enemy aircraft over London
surrounded by A.A. fire. We climbed towards them and I led
the squadron into a quarter attack on a large number of twin-

The two Air Forces meet and vapour trails criss-cross the sky. Older trails fluff out and break up as more aircraft with thin clear contrails take up the battle. These pictures were taken from the R.A.F. station at Manston, Kent

engined and twin-tailed bombers which I think must have been Do 17s. I went for the nearest bomber and opened fire at about 400 yards, meanwhile experiencing very heavy return cross-fire from the bomber formation. After about twelve seconds smoke started to come from the port motor and it left the formation. I broke away as there were many 110s and 109s behind. The bomber with one motor still pouring out thick smoke continued to lose height, so I waited until it got down to about 3,000 feet and then dived vertically on to it and fired off the rest of my ammunition (about 3 to 4 secs.). It kept going on down seemingly still under some sort of control, until it hit the water about ten miles out from the centre of the Thames Estuary.

No. 7 O.T.U. at Hawarden gained their second victory of the Battle, having chalked up an He 111 on August 14th. Sergeant L. S. Pilkington, while instructing a pupil in formation flying, heard on the R/T that a 'bandit' was approaching Hoylake. Having sent the pupil home he intercepted a Ju 88 at 20,000 feet and was able to get in a good burst with his two 20 mm. cannon, which were a rarity at the time. The Ju 88 subsequently crashed in Wales.

While the day had been a frustrating one for Fighter Command with London heavily bombed and nineteen

pilots lost out of twenty-eight fighters shot down, they could show forty-one German aircraft destroyed during the whole day—a not inconsiderable total which led the German radio to report that the attack had entailed 'heavy sacrifices'.

During the afternoon German radio stations had kept up a gleeful commentary on the raids. In the evening Göring, highly delighted, telephoned his wife to report 'London is in flames'. He then broadcast that this was 'a historic hour' and that the Luftwaffe had 'for the first time delivered its stroke right into the enemy's heart'.

Many returning fighter and bomber pilots reported little or no opposition, and for one day at least the Luftwaffe operations and intelligence staff believed that their aim of destroying Fighter Command was nearly achieved.

On the night of the 7th/8th the blitz on London continued with unabated fury, a continuous stream of bombers, totalling 247 in all, stoking the fires in the East End from eight in the evening to nearly five o'clock the next morning. Some 330 tons of high explosives were dropped, and 440 incendiary canisters, the latter contributing to the nine conflagrations (huge spreading areas of flame) which lit up the night sky with a dull glow. Typical of the East End slums which suffered in these early September raids was Tulip Street with its long rows of dingy terraced houses. It had been hit in the August night raids and again on September 7th. Within a few nights it had been reduced to twin rows of shattered roofless walls, and when the debris had finally been cleared away Tulip Street had disappeared for ever.

To add to the confusion the code-word 'Cromwell' was issued at 8 p.m. Many took it that invasion was in progress. Church bells were rung, road blocks put up and Home Guards roamed the countryside with loaded rifles.

Part of Banquet, the Flying Training Command reinforcement programme for invasion, was put into operation. For instance, the Senior Course at No. 3 School of General Reconnaissance at Squire's Gate was on invasion stand-by. Blackpool in 1940 was still a bouncing town in the pre-war mood and Wakes weeks were still celebrated. Stand-by in the Senior Course invariably meant that they spent their week-ends in gay Blackpool.

When the alert came through on the night of Saturday, September 7th, the Senior Course was immediately sent for. No one, however, could be found in his billet. Persistent efforts by the police and the station staff eventually routed all these officers out of bars, night clubs and beds other than their own. Rather the worse for wear, they were hurried into the navigator's seats of Ansons and flown to Thorney Island.

When they reached this southern base they noticed in a somewhat hazy way that the aircraft were being bombed up. Upon enquiry they were informed that they were being readied to attack the German invasion fleet; one man is rumoured to have fainted.

When dawn came there had been no landing but 306 civilians in London were dead and 1,337 seriously injured. Clouds of smoke billowed up over the dock

The Spitfire factory at Woolston, Southampton, after the raid on September 26th. The factory was wrecked, but by dispersal to thirty-five sites and expansion at the Castle Bromwich factory the flow of aircraft to the R.A.F. was maintained. The Luftwaffe would have done better to concentrate on this vital production centre early in the battle

area and the fires burned on, filling the air with acrid fumes and soot. Londoners crawled out of their shelters and picked their way towards their places of work through the hoses and rubble, round the fire engines and the rescue workers still toiling in the wreckage. Some found added difficulty in commuting as three main-line terminal stations were out of action, including London Bridge and Victoria.

Near Waterloo station three lines hung crazily over a large crater, the supporting arches beneath having disappeared. The station was not reopened for passenger traffic until September 19th.

One train from Ramsgate in Kent had bombs go off all round it with an oil bomb eventually falling on the tender. The fire was put out with the engine hose and the guard and fireman, black as soot, delivered the train safely at Charing Cross.

Many eyes looked skywards awaiting the resumption of the day battle, but except for harassing raids and odd attacks which penetrated to the centre, London had had its first and last mass daylight raid; henceforth the Luftwaffe achieved its main results under cover of night.

September 8th

Day Only slight activity. Some small attacks on airfields.
Night Heavy concentration on London, mainly east.
Weather Fair early morning and evening. Rest of day cloudy.

Göring on this day decided that the attacks on London would bear considerable fruit, and accordingly he issued orders for the area covered by bombing to be widened both by day and night. For target purposes the city had been divided into two sections, target area 'A' being east London and the docks and target 'B' west London. Particular emphasis was laid on power stations and railway termini. From the 8th onwards both 'A' and 'B' were bombed. In the morning German radio stations solemnly announced the fact that the Reichsmarschall had assumed command of operations for the first time since the outbreak of war.

Extraordinary contrasts were produced in 1940, even in advertisements in the technical press. On the left is a Vickers-Armstrong's advertisement for the Spitfire which appeared in The Aeroplane *for September 13th, 1940, while on the right is a Junkers advertisement of the period reproduced in* Der Adler

For the R.A.F. the concentration on London was to ease the pressure on hard-hit sector stations, but it could do nothing to increase the flow of new fighter pilots to replace the heavy losses of August and the first week in September. Normally a fighter squadron remained in the line from a month to six weeks, but the intensity of the fighting and resultant losses had required some units to be replaced after a week or ten days. Reluctantly Dowding put into operation a new 'stabilisation' system of classification for fighter squadrons with top priority for groups in the daylight battle zone.

Squadrons were grouped into three categories, viz.:

Category A. Squadrons in No. 11 Group and on its immediate flanks, which bore the brunt of the fighting.

Category B. A small number of squadrons maintained at operational strength to be available as immediate reliefs should this be unavoidable.

Category C. Remaining squadrons, stripped of the majority of their operational pilots for the benefits of the A squadrons and with energies mainly devoted to training new pilots from the O.T.U.s or those transferred from other commands.

The A squadrons were stabilised and were not to be relieved unless circumstances were exceptional, their strength being maintained largely by intakes from the C squadrons. The C squadrons were considered unfit to meet German fighters, but were quite capable of dealing with unescorted bombers.

While the new system tided over a crucial period in the command it was not good for overall morale, as nobody particularly liked belonging to a unit which bore the designation Category C.

By this time the fighter resources were so stretched that Dowding could no longer maintain standing patrols for all the convoys, nor could he divert fighters even to defend such important sites as aircraft storage units.

Believing the danger of invasion to be growing, it was decided to install three retractable machine-gun pill-boxes at each operational airfield to give additional local defence against parachutists and airborne invaders. These elaborate items were raised above ground level to a height of three feet using compressed air.

While Fighter Command examined the records of the London attack the day before, the Luftwaffe somewhat reduced the scale of its efforts on the 8th, partly through fatigue and partly due to bad weather.

Between 11 a.m. and 12.30 Luftflotte 2 put in several raids over Kent with airfields once more the chief objectives. Some fifteen formations of varying size dropped bombs on Sevenoaks, West Malling, Detling, Hornchurch, Dover and Gravesend. Eleven fighter squadrons were sent up and many of the enemy were

Desolation; a London street after Luftflotte 3 had visited it on the night of September 8th. Firemen attempt to damp down the flames

turned back, doing little damage. Compared with its 817 sorties of the 7th, Fighter Command flew 305 on the 8th and lost only two aircraft, the pilot of one returning safely. In contrast Luftwaffe losses for the twenty-four-hour period were fifteen.

At night Luftflotte 3 returned to the assault on London, sending 207 bombers via Rennes, Caen, Le Havre and Dieppe in steady succession from 7.30 p.m. until dawn. In these nine and a half hours high explosives and incendiaries again showered dockland, but many fell on the city proper, leaving twelve conflagrations for the indefatigable fire service to deal with. Three hospitals and two museums were hit, and more than fifty people died when a large bomb wrecked a block of flats in the East End. By Monday morning 412 more Londoners were dead and 747 badly hurt. Whole rows of houses were gutted or knocked down, factories were wrecked, and every railway line southwards out of the city was unserviceable.

September 9th

Day Unsuccessful sorties against London, Thames Estuary and aircraft factories.

Night Main target London, including City and West End. *Weather* Scattered showers. Thundery in the east. Channel fair.

Once more the morning brought respite, and attacks did not develop until the afternoon, when formations began massing in the area Calais–Boulogne. Raids of 30+, 50+, 15+ and 12+ were plotted by the radar stations, and appeared over the coast as groups of escorted and unescorted bombers. A high-flying screen of fighters attempted to draw off British interceptors just before the raids developed.

This time 11 Group were not caught napping. At five o'clock, when the raids began to come in, nine 11 Group squadrons were in position, while units from 10 Group and 12 Group guarded factories and north Thames airfields respectively.

It was the German intention to attack targets in London, the Thames Estuary and the factories at Brooklands, but the fighter interceptions were so successful that most of the formations were broken up long before they reached them. German aircraft sent out a number of distress signals and radio control stations on the French coast ordered formation leaders to break off the attacks 'if the defences are too strong, or if fighter protection is too weak'. These messages were heard with great interest by British radio monitoring receivers in Kent.

Bombs were jettisoned over a wide area, including

A Focke Wulf 200C-1 of KG40. This four-motor bomber, derived from a pre-war Lufthansa transport, was used for bombing, maritime reconnaissance and met. forecasting. Several of these aircraft were forced down during the Battle of Britain, including one which ran out of fuel over the Irish Sea

Canterbury, Kingston, Epsom, Surbiton, Norbiton and Purley, while in central London itself a few fell on Wandsworth, Lambeth and Chelsea.

After the enemy had retired the R.A.F. could show twenty-eight German aircraft destroyed for the loss of nineteen British fighters from which six pilots were recovered. London had been saved from a further onslaught, and the German bomber air crew complained bitterly at their de-briefing of the sudden upsurge of the defences and the apparent shortcomings of their Messerschmitt escorts.

A report of the Luftwaffe Command Staff of September 9th stated:

The maintaining of the attack against London is intended to take place by day through Luftflotte 2 with strong fighter and destroyer units; by night Luftflotte 3 will carry out attacks with the object of destroying harbour areas, the supply and power sources of the city. The city is divided into two target areas, the eastern part of London is target area A with its widely stretched out harbour installations, target area B is the west of London, which contains the power supplies and the provision installations of the city. Along with this major attack on London the destruction raids will be carried on as much as possible against many sectors of the armament industry and harbour areas in England in their previous scope.

On the night of the 9th/10th London was for the third time the main target. Luftflotte 3 had now standardised its techniques. Aircraft came over in small waves at intervals and flew along clearly defined corridors of approach using other routes for the homeward journey. First waves usually flew in over the south coast and out via Essex; the second wave arrived from the east and returned over the Beachy Head area, passing the third incoming wave over that area.

In response to Göring's order of the 8th, that the London coverage be extended, 195 aircraft attacked all districts for eight and a half hours. Familiar landmarks began to suffer, and on this occasion it was the turn of the Royal Courts of Justice and Somerset House. Three hundred and seventy Londoners died and 1,400 were injured, and this was the third night running that total casualties were over 1,700.

September 10th

Day Slight activity. Single raiders over airfields in afternoon.
Night London main objective but also raids on Merseyside and South Wales.
Weather Generally cloudy. Some rain.

The day dawned cloudy, and on the whole it was peaceful over England. In Germany the Luftwaffe Command Staff issued orders that 'if the weather situation does not allow the engagement of strong force of Luftflotten 2 and 3 against England, the Luftflotten must carry out individual attacks against targets of the aircraft production industry'.

Nothing developed until five o'clock in the afternoon when single aircraft of Luftflotte 3, taking advantage of cloud cover, delivered attacks in 10 Group and the western part of 11 Group. One raider machine-gunned Tangmere, and another dropped bombs on West Malling. Poling radar station reported bombs in the vicinity and a few fell in the area of Portsmouth dockyard. In the airfield raids fighters accounted for two Dorniers.

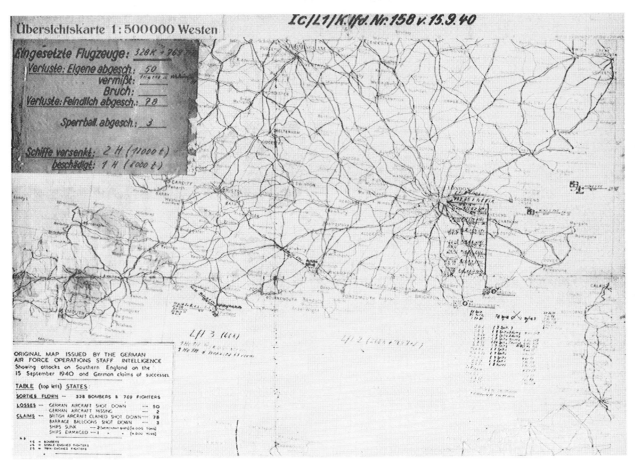

ORIGINAL MAP ISSUED BY THE GERMAN
AIR FORCE OPERATIONS STAFF INTELLIGENCE
Showing attacks on Southern England on the
15 September 1940 and German claims of successes.

TABLE (top left) STATES:

SORTIES FLOWN — 328 BOMBERS & 769 FIGHTERS

LOSSES — GERMAN AIRCRAFT SHOT DOWN — 50
GERMAN AIRCRAFT MISSING — 2
CLAIMS — BRITISH AIRCRAFT CLAIMED SHOT DOWN — 78
BARRAGE BALLOONS SHOT DOWN — 3
SHIPS SUNK — 2 (MERCHANT SHIPS 26,000 TONS)
SHIPS DAMAGED — 1 (8,000 TONS)

Above is a photograph of the original Luftwaffe
operations staff intelligence map for September 15th
showing targets attacked and units operating.

Altogether 328 bomber and 769 fighter sorties were
flown. On the right-hand side is written a detailed
breakdown of units involved, with losses and claims for
British aircraft destroyed.

The figures given for British fighters shot down show
51 Spitfires, 26 Hurricanes and 1 Blenheim—a grand
total of 78, where in fact only 26 R.A.F. fighters were
written off during the day. It is interesting to note that
JG53 and JG51 claimed between them to have destroyed
38 British fighters, twelve more than the complete
Fighter Command total!

German unit losses on this chart amount to 53 whereas
the definitive analysis of total write-offs on operation
in the Quartermaster General's return shows 60. The
R.A.F. claimed no less than 185 German aircraft
destroyed on the 15th. On both sides the claims were
treble the actual losses.

The analysis on the map reads as follows:

Unit	Claims of British aircraft destroyed	Unit losses
JG2	(3 Spitfires)	
JG3	(9 Spitfires and 3 Hurricanes)	4 Me 109
JG26	(3 Spitfires and 2 Hurricanes)	
JG51	(8 Spitfires and 7 Hurricanes)	3 Me 109
JG53	(14 Spitfires and 9 Hurricanes)	6 Me 109
ZG76	(7 Spitfires and 1 Blenheim)	3 Me 110
III/KG2	(1 Spitfire)	6 Do 17
II/KG53	(1 Spitfire)	6 He 111
II/KG3	(4 Spitfires)	6 Do 17
KG26	(1 Spitfire)	1 He 111
JG52	(9 Hurricanes)	3 Me 109
I and III/KG76		6 Do 17
II/KG2		2 Do 17
KG30		1 Ju 88
JG27		2 Me 109
III/KG55		1 He 111 missing
v.d. Wekusta 51		1 He 111 missing

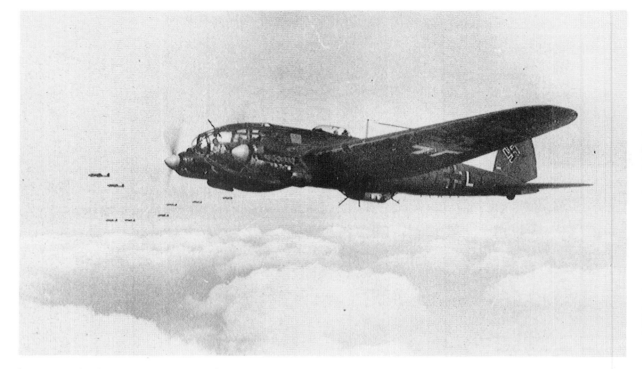

The bomber aimer of this He 111 can be clearly seen getting ready for the run-up to the target. The aircraft is from KG55, V Fliegerkorps, Luftflotte 3

Following these incursions came six small raids from Luftflotte 2, which passed over Dungeness–Beachy Head and flew towards Biggin Hill. One aircraft reached the airfield, but was intercepted some minutes later south of Kenley and shot down. Two small raids appeared near Eastchurch but turned for home without accomplishing anything and these were followed by similar sorties towards south and south-west London.

The rumours of invasion began to assume greater significance at 4.30 p.m. when a Coastal Command aircraft reported twelve merchant vessels plus five destroyers and thirty E-boats off Dieppe.

At night the attack was more varied, and while London received the main weight of bombs from 148 aircraft, others visited South Wales and Merseyside. Many German aircraft avoided detection in the early hours by mixing with a stream of R.A.F. machines returning from Berlin via Orfordness.

September 11th

Day Some bombs on London. Three large raids in south-east. Raids on Portsmouth and Southampton. Seelöwe postponed until the 14th.
Night London attacked and Merseyside.
Weather Mainly fine. Some local showers. Channel and Estuary cloudy.

The spirited defence put up by Fighter Command on the 9th had important repercussions in Germany. Despite all the prognostications of the Luftwaffe C.-in-C., Command Staff and Intelligence, the R.A.F.

had shown itself undefeated and as resolute as ever. This single day's action led Hitler to postpone the warning order for invasion which was scheduled for the 11th. This warning would have led to the laying of a boundary minefield across the Channel for the landing fleet and a final positioning of vital units, in particular, flak.

The Führer decided to issue the warning for the 14th with a view to opening Seelöwe on September 24th —always providing that air superiority had been achieved. He set great store on the effects of the London bombing and hoped that an internal collapse in England would avoid the necessity for a hazardous landing operation. At this time the day and night attacks were regarded as a dual strategic and tactical concept, to destroy British will to fight at all and to bring the R.A.F. fighters into a final pitched battle.

In London itself, the postponement was naturally unknown. All the outward portents showed the preparations across the Channel at an advanced level. Winston Churchill broadcast:

The effort of the Germans to secure daylight mastery of the air over England is of course the crux of the whole war. So far it has failed conspicuously . . . . For him [Hitler] to try and invade this country without having secured mastery in the air would be a very hazardous undertaking. Nevertheless, all his preparations for invasion on a great scale are steadily going forward. Several hundreds of self-propelled barges are moving down the coasts of Europe, from the German and Dutch harbours to the ports of northern France, from Dunkirk to Brest, and beyond Brest to the French harbours in the Bay of Biscay.

While the anti-invasion build-up on land and sea went on day and night, No. 11 Group was tackling the problems of new German tactics initiated on the 7th. After careful study of all available information, Park

The procession; Göring leads a line of officers on an official visit to Luftwaffe units in Luftflotte 3. Second from the left in the picture is Generalfeldmarschall Sperrle

issued a further instruction (No. 16) to his controllers. He outlined that the enemy had changed from two to three separate attacks in one day, to mass raids of 300 to 400 aircraft in two to three waves following in quick succession, the whole engagement covering about forty-five to sixty minutes.

So as to meet the Luftwaffe in maximum strength he ordered paired squadrons to be used wherever possible. The 'Readiness' squadrons were to engage the first wave, Spitfires against fighter screen, Hurricanes against bombers and close escort. The squadrons 'available fifteen minutes' were to be brought to 'Readiness' in pairs and despatched to deal with the second wave, while the 'Available thirty minutes' squadrons were to be sent singly as reinforcements or to protect factories and sector airfields.

Should there be a third wave the last squadrons were to be paired, those from Debden and North Weald together, Hornchurch with Biggin Hill, and Kenley with Northolt.

The squadrons from Tangmere were to be employed within Kenley or the back Tangmere sector to cover factories and to intercept German formations approaching London from the south.

It was left to the group controller to name the base over which paired squadrons would rendezvous. Once sector had linked them up, group detailed the raid, etc., and sector carried the operation through.

There dispositions were timely as the Luftwaffe renewed the attack on London on the same day that they were ordered. In the morning activity was limited to patrolling, with a Henschel 126 tactical reconnaissance aircraft cruising off Dover, and one machine dropping a bomb near Poling radar station.

After the initial heavy raids on radar stations the Germans had concentrated on setting up jamming transmitters on the coast. The work of these became particularly noticeable in September. On this Wednesday morning at eleven o'clock Great Bromley C.H. station reported that it had suffered interference for nearly an hour. Under these conditions the airmen and W.A.A.F.s watching the blips on the cathode-ray tube had to insert coloured slides and strain their eyes to make out the true afterglow trace through the dancing white lights shown up from the jammers. Plotting, however, continued as before and full-scale 'blotting out' of stations was never achieved due to the distance involved and to the German lack of high-power valves.

After reconnaissance flights at lunchtime, Luftflotte 2 put up three big raids and Luftflotte 3 attacked Southampton. At 2.45 p.m. formations began building up over Calais and Ostend and aimed for London. At 3.45 another wave came in over Folkestone, and was shortly followed by a third. Bombs fell on the City, the docks, Islington and Paddington, and others on Biggin Hill, Kenley, Brooklands and Hornchurch.

Simultaneously two raids from Seine Bay and Cherbourg had linked up over Selsey Bill and despite harrying fighters dropped bombs on Southampton and Portsmouth.

A complete Gruppe of KG3 forms up for the journey across the Channel to England. It was the assembly of these formations which gave British radar the warning necessary to put up fighters to intercept

An hour later waves of Me 109s appeared over Kent, some attacking the Dover balloons. Another force attacked a convoy and single aircraft headed for Colerne, Kenley, Detling and Eastchurch. The convoy 'Peewit' was dive-bombed, its escort 'Atherstone' being disabled.

In all this widespread activity, Fighter Command flew 678 sorties. The scoreboard at the end of the day was in reality depressing, R.A.F. losses being 29 aircraft, 17 pilots killed and 6 wounded, compared with German casualties for the 24 hours of 25 aircraft. KG26 was the worst hit, with eight He 111s shot down. At the time it was estimated German losses were far higher, but the red in the British balance sheet on the final reckoning is accounted for by the fact that many squadrons became entangled with the escorting formations who attacked from above.

As the evening drew on jamming of British radar became more general, and four stations reported interference before darkness fell. Throughout the night harassing raids moved up and down the country, while London was receiving a heavy attack from 180 bombers. Merseyside was the secondary target, while single aircraft were over Scotland, the Bristol Channel, Lincolnshire and Norfolk with Fliegerdivision IX minelaying on the south and east coasts in preparation for invasion.

To Londoners there had been one comfort on this Wednesday night; the anti-aircraft defences had been doubled since the 7th and a tremendous barrage was kept going. The Inner Artillery Zone fired no less than 13,500 rounds and although they inflicted little damage on the bombers, they did cause many to drop their loads outside the central area, and others to fly higher than usual.

Once again the bomber stream bound for London mixed with returning aircraft, confusing the plots. On several occasions 11 Group reported that raiders coming in from the south were giving the correct R.A.F. recognition signals and then unloading their bombs.

September 12th

Day Only small raids in south. Reconnaissance.
Night Reduced effort. Main force London. Single aircraft over wide area.
Weather Unsettled, rain in most districts. Channel cloudy.

Thursday proved mainly quiet thanks to cloud and poor weather over the south and east coasts. The morning was marked by continuous German reconnaissance. At lunch three small raids appeared on the operations table, and dropped bombs on the radar station at Fairlight—although without doing any real damage. Fighters chased one raider as far as Cap Gris Nez and there shot it down.

Incursions by single raiders went on during the afternoon and early evening but the 247 R.A.F. sorties flown were hampered by the weather. No Fighter Command machine was lost, and the Luftwaffe for the whole period suffered only four casualties.

A sad task, pulling furniture and belongings from wrecked houses after night raids on north London on September 26th/27th

Neptune Street, Rotherhithe, close by the Commercial Docks in East London. Rescue workers clear the rubble after heavy bombing by Luftflotte 3 on the night of September 8th

Even the Luftwaffe's night efforts were heavily reduced, with fifty-four bombers over London, and singles over the midlands, Merseyside, Essex, Suffolk, Cambridge, Kent and Surrey. One bomber was brought down by 966 Balloon Barrage Squadron at Newport, Monmouthshire.

Of the bombs on London, one, of the delayed-action variety, fell within a few yards of the north wall of St.

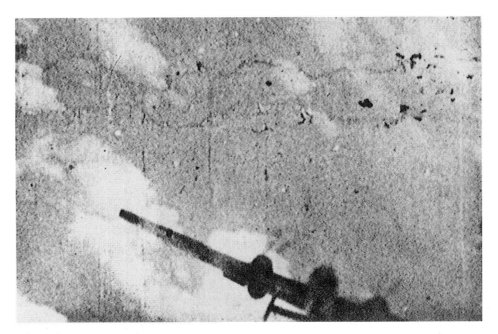

An Me 110 on the point of being shot down over Hastings, Sussex, on the afternoon of September 15th. The camera gun which took the film was mounted on Spitfire R6691 of No. 609 Squadron, piloted by Flt. Lt. F. J. Howell

Paul's Cathedral. It took three days to remove it from a depth of twenty-seven feet. The bomb disposal officer, Lieutenant R. Davies, and his chief assistant, Sapper Wylie, became the first recipients of the George Cross.

September 13th

Day Small raids mainly directed at London. Hitler in conference, discussing air offensive and invasion.
Night Renewed effort against London.
Weather Unsettled. Bright intervals and showers. Rain in Channel. Straits cloudy.

Hitler was far from dissatisfied with the results of the bombing so far, and the reports he received on the operations of the 11th indicated that British opposition was weak and the German casualty rate low. At a luncheon in Berlin attended by a group of naval, army and air force officers (notable among them being Brauchitsch, Göring, Jodl and Milch) Hitler delivered a speech on the current situation. He commented particularly on the need for air superiority and the audience gathered that he was dropping the idea of invasion in view of the success of air bombardment. Nevertheless he indulged in considerable detailed discussion with the army chiefs on their dispositions and strength.

At seven o'clock in the morning the Luftwaffe began its weather reconnaissance for the day's work, aircraft covering the Biggin Hill, North Weald and Hornchurch sectors and another Kenley and Northolt. The weather reports radioed back to France were picked up by the British radio monitoring service although the actual targets could not be deciphered.

Three quarters of an hour later a Focke Wulf 200 of I/KG40, on maritime patrol, bombed the S.S. *Longfort* off Copeland Light near Belfast and fired on a motor vessel in the same area. This was followed from 9.30 to 11.30 a.m. by a stream of single aircraft from Dieppe, passing over Hastings and heading for south London, while simultaneously the Canewdon, Dover and Rye radars suffered jamming.

Near midday, radio monitoring reported that an enemy bomber over Kent was sending messages to the effect that 'cloud is 7/10th at 1,500 metres, and that attack is possible between 1,500 and 2,500 metres'. No. 11 Group were alerted, and sure enough just over an hour and a half later several raids attempted to attack Biggin Hill and the mid-Kent area, while three more, including a few Ju 87s from Luftflotte 3, crossed the coast at Selsey heading for Tangmere. One Heinkel which arrived over Maidstone was promptly shot down by 501 Squadron from Biggin Hill.

At this time a curious report came in from the naval liaison officer to the effect that a long-nosed Blenheim 4, positively identified, had dropped two bombs in Dover harbour. Several Blenheims had been captured on the Continent but there has never been documentary evidence to confirm their use in the Battle of Britain.

In the morning raids single aircraft had penetrated to central London, where bombs hit Downing Street, Whitehall, Trafalgar Square and the Chelsea Hospital. Buckingham Palace had its third bombing, with the Royal Chapel wrecked, and four near-misses.

Due to the intermittent rain and low clouds and the high altitude of the raiders, fighter squadrons had difficulty in finding their prey and only four bombers were destroyed for the loss of one fighter.

During the day the expectation of invasion was sharpened by a report from a coastal post in No. 1 (Maidstone) Observer Group, which had sighted ten large enemy transports each towing two barges from Calais to Cap Gris Nez.

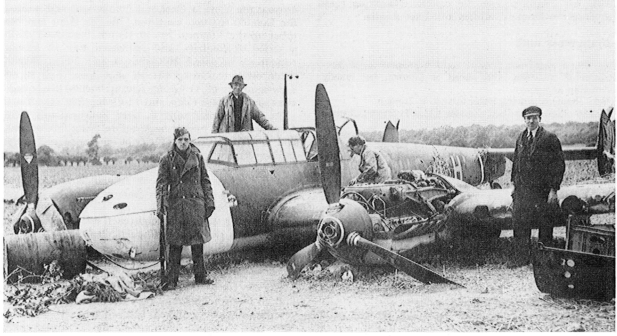

The Me 110s of the Luftwaffe lived a dangerous life
in 1940 with heavy casualties causing eventual unit
amalgamation. Above *a staffel of ZG26 'Horst
Wessel' flies in over southern England;* below *one of
this unit in a field at Lenham, Kent, on September 20th*

Subject of a head-on attack by British fighters, this Ju 88 of KG30 crashed on the beach at Pagham, Sussex, in September

Main targets of the night raiders was again London, with 105 bombers over the capital. Harassing raids covered the Home Counties and East Anglia.

September 14th

Day Hitler postpones Seelöwe until September 17th. Succession of afternoon raids aimed at London, but mainly consisting of fighters.
Night Reduced activity. Main force over London.
Weather Showers and local thunder. Cloud in Straits, Channel and Estuary.

In Berlin Adolf Hitler gathered the Cs.-in-C. of his army, navy, and air force and addressed them on the progress of the war. He pointed out that naval preparations for the invasion were complete and that the 'operations of the Luftwaffe are above all praise'. He felt that four to five days of good weather were required to achieve decisive results, conveniently forgetting that was exactly what Göring had stated before Adler Tag in August.

Hitler blamed the weather for the lack of complete air superiority so far but stressed once again that a 'successful landing means victory, but complete air superiority is required to carry it out'.

Despite contrary opinion expressed by the navy (who had lost eighty barges through R.A.F. action the previous night), Hitler decided to postpone Sealion only until September 17th, and the build-up went on with top priority. It is clear that while Hitler hoped for decisive results from the Luftwaffe, he still put his confidence in a landing if all else failed.

The main German target for the 14th was again London and throughout the morning reconnaissance

aircraft probed the weather and the defences, while between Poling and Great Bromley radar stations there was continual electronic interference. One raider was destroyed over Selsey Bill at lunchtime and bombs were dropped at Eastbourne.

Just after 3 p.m. three raids in quick succession crossed the coast at Deal and Dungeness, and headed for London up two corridors, one via Kent and the other up the Thames. No. 11 Group were involved in a series of combats, and requested two 12 Group squadrons to patrol Hornchurch and North Weald, while other 12 Group aircraft shot down a Ju 88 off Lowestoft. In all, 11 Group sent up twenty-two squadrons against these raids, and 12 Group five squadrons.

At 5.15 a feint came in over Bournemouth from Cherbourg, but turned back before being intercepted, and shortly afterwards a flurry of raids appeared on the Bentley Priory tables with 12+, 20+, 30+, 15+ and 10+ between 17,000 and 20,000 feet. From then until nine o'clock a succession of individual attacks were made covering the south-eastern area, and aimed towards London.

The final score of fourteen to each side was poor from the R.A.F.'s point of view, particularly as 860 sorties were flown. Six R.A.F. pilots were, however, saved. Most of the German aircraft sent over were fighters and these lured the squadrons into combat.

To the Luftwaffe the opposition appeared scrappy and un-co-ordinated, and they felt that during the last few days Fighter Command had begun to collapse. This news was, of course, conveyed to the Reichsmarschall, and via the situation reports to Hitler. Both felt that the hour of destiny was approaching.

That night Luftwaffe activity was at a much lower level, while they prepared for a major blow on the following morning. Fifty-five German bombers attacked London whilst others went to Cardiff, Gloucester, Maidstone, Ipswich and Farnham. One naval patrol vessel was attacked by aircraft from Luftflotte 5 off the Firth of Forth.

The unusually low level of attack was noted by Fighter Command, particularly as the weather was fine, and it could only betoken a great effort on the following day.

September 15th

Day Heavy attacks on London, broken up by Fighter Command. Highest German losses since August 18th. Serious rethinking by German High Command.
Night Main target London. Heavy damage.
Weather Fair but cloud patches. Fine evening.

Now celebrated annually as Battle of Britain Day, Sunday the 15th was remarkable for its ultimate change of German policy and not for its heavy losses, as the 185 German aircraft claimed would lead many to believe.

The weather was misty but promised to be fine and the chance had come for a heavy blow against London which would show once and for all the desperate state of Fighter Command, and perhaps have a decisive effect on British morale. It was to be a repeat of September 7th in German eyes, and a lead-in to invasion.

The usual reconnaissance aircraft patrolled the east and south coasts during the morning, one of which, an He 111, was shot down off Start Point.

At eleven o'clock radar showed mass formations building up over Calais and Boulogne. No. 11 Group put up eleven squadrons, 10 Group one, while No. 12 Group sent five squadrons as a wing to patrol Debden-Hornchurch. No real feints developed and complete attention was devoted to the advancing armadas. The stupidity of large formations sorting themselves out in full view of British radar was not yet realised by the Luftwaffe.

All the way up from the coast, the raids stepped up from 15,000–26,000 feet were constantly under attack, first by two Spitfire squadrons over mid-Kent, next by three more over the Medway towns, then by four Hurricane squadrons over the suburbs of London, and finally by the Duxford wing from 12 Group over London itself. The wing on Leigh-Mallory's instructions was now five squadrons strong. In all, twenty-four fighter squadrons operated and twenty-two engaged the enemy.

Accurate bombing was out of the question, and as formations broke so they scattered their loads on Beckenham, Westminster, Lambeth, Lewisham, Battersea, Camberwell, Crystal Palace, Clapham, Tooting, Wandsworth and Kensington. A heavy bomb damaged the Queen's private apartments in Buckingham Palace, while a second fell on the lawn.

The 609 Squadron diarist recorded that one portion of a Dornier they destroyed during the engagement 'is reported to have reached the ground just outside a Pimlico public house to the great comfort and joy of the patrons'.

No. 504 Squadron had a busy morning. At 11 a.m. Generals Strong and Emmons of the U.S. Army Air Corps and Rear-Admiral Gormley of the U.S. Navy paid a visit to see 'the life of a fighter squadron'. No sooner had introductions been completed than an attack developed with the squadron to patrol North

Weald at 15,000 feet. Using a stop-watch, the Americans recorded that twelve Hurricanes got away in 4 min. 50 sec. from the word 'Go'. No. 504 met a formation of Dorniers between Fulham and Gravesend and shot down several. One pilot, Sergeant R. T. Holmes, attacked and damaged a Dornier, and then found another, which he fired at four times. On the fourth occasion the bomber exploded, sending the Hurricane into an uncontrollable spin.

The Dornier crashed in the station yard at Victoria, with the crew landing by parachute on Kennington Oval cricket ground. Sergeant Holmes baled out and finally came to rest in a dustbin in Chelsea.

Before they could eat lunch the squadron was again engaged with German formations between London and Hornchurch.

After a two-hour break the second attack was seen by radar just after 1 p.m. and began to come in in three waves an hour later. Squadrons were ready to receive them and a running fight took place all the way to the capital. Twenty-three squadrons from 11 Group were airborne, five from No. 12 Group and three from No. 10. Two formations were broken up before reaching London, one turning back in the face of a head-on attack by a lone Hurricane flown by Group Captain Vincent, commander of the Northolt sector.

The remaining bombers were engaged over the city itself by five pairs of squadrons from No. 11 Group and the full five-squadron wing of No. 12 Group. Two squadrons each from 10 and 11 Groups harried the enemy as they retired. Scattering of formations and frequent jettisoning of bombs caused hits over a very wide area in contrast to the concentration achieved on September 7th. West Ham and Erith were the main recipients but other targets were Woolwich, Stepney, Hackney, Stratford, Penge and East Ham—at the last mentioned a telephone exchange and a gasholder being smashed.

While every effort was being made to deal with the attack on London, a force of Heinkel 111s of KG55 from the Villacoublay area set out to bomb Portland. Although seen by radar at three o'clock, the count was only given as six+. The raid detoured and approached Portland from an unusual angle which confused the A.A. gunners. The bombing was inaccurate and only slight damage was done in the dockyard. The one squadron left in the Middle Wallop sector succeeded in intercepting, but after the bombs had dropped.

The final daylight sortie came at about six o'clock when some twenty bomb-carrying Me 110s from Epr. Gr.210 at Denain attempted to hit the Supermarine works at Woolston. They were heavily engaged by the Southampton guns as they dived in and this undoubtedly upset their aim as no bombs fell on the factory. Five R.A.F. squadrons were put up, but most of them were unable to find their quarry, and those that did only encountered the 110s as they were streaking for the safety of the French coast using any available cloud cover.

During the morning Winston Churchill had been on one of his periodic visits to the 11 Group underground operations room at Uxbridge. From the balcony with Park at his side he watched the raids

Bombing up for a raid against the invasion fleet assembled in the Channel ports. This Blenheim IV of No. 110 Squadron is seen here at Wattisham in September 1940. This Squadron carried out the first R.A.F. raid of the war, on September 4th, 1939

pouring in. The operations table became saturated with plots, and two by two the squadrons of 11 Group were committed, followed by the 12 Group wing. Finally the tote board showed all squadrons engaged and that nothing was left in reserve. No new raids developed, however, and slowly the bulbs began to glow again as fighters were re-fuelled and re-armed.

Churchill was greatly impressed with the gravity of such a situation and with the calm methodical way in which 11 Group's nerve centre worked. He recorded the incident at length in Volume II of *The Second World War*, although there had been many similar occasions during the Battle which passed unnoticed.

Families throughout the country listened in to the evening news bulletin and heard '185 shot down'. The figures became the sole topic of conversation and the nation glowed with pride. It was a tremendous and much-needed tonic for civilians and R.A.F. alike.

In the cold light of history the actual German losses of sixty machines make poor reading to the layman. In fact, for a force which had suffered a heavy loss rate

for over two months they were extremely serious, not to mention the numerous aircraft which limped back to France with dead gunners, burned engines and broken undercarriages.

The 12 Group wing under Bader was not so pleased. It felt that it should have earlier warning in order to get at the enemy with the advantages of height and time. Unfortunately most raids kept climbing after the initial radar plots and split up over the coast making interception more difficult. In addition the links between 11 Group and 12 Group were not properly streamlined and 11 Group sectors dealing with raids could not control 12 Group squadrons.

Hitler, Göring and the whole of the Luftwaffe Command had expected great things of the 15th. After the apparently successful efforts of the 12th it seemed that at long last the R.A.F. was ready for the *coup de grace*. Instead the losses were highter than on any day since August 18th. At de-briefing bomber pilots complained of the incessant R.A.F. attacks by squadrons that had long since ceased to exist—if the German radio and intelligence reports were to be believed.

Naturally, but unfairly, they vented their wrath upon the Jafus and the long-suffering fighter pilots. Instead of being allowed full rein, the fighters were ordered to stick even closer to the bomber formations which further nullified their essential space to manoeuvre and attack.

When the tally book was closed at nightfall on the 15th, Fighter Command had lost twenty-six aircraft and saved thirteen pilots; the balance was swinging sharply in favour of the weary defence.

Before the next day's fighting losses in pilots and aircraft had to be made good. One Polish squadron had only four aircraft serviceable by the evening. The remainder had suffered all sorts of damage; control surfaces shot away, radiators smashed, cables cut and wings riddled with bullets. The mechanics worked until dawn patching and repairing so that on the 16th twelve aircraft were ready for operations.

After dark the Luftwaffe returned to the attack, knowing that it was safer than operating in daylight. Some 180 bombers formed long processions from Le Havre and Dieppe–Cherbourg, all heading for London. Once again the barrage opened up, and more scars were added to the city's face. Shell-Mex House and the Embankment were hit, bombs fell on Woolwich Arsenal, and large fires were started in Camberwell, Battersea and Brixton. Other smaller raids dropped their loads on Bristol, Cardiff, Liverpool and Manchester.

September 16th

Day Göring confers on losses of the 15th. Policy changes. Park changes tactics. Only slight air activity.
Night Continuous attacks on London. Smaller raids Merseyside and midlands.
Weather General rain and cloud.

Göring called a conference of his Luftflotten and Fliegerkorps commanders in France and decided to return to a policy of attack against Fighter Command itself. It appeared to the Reichmarschall that the R.A.F. had produced many fresh pilots and aircraft when in reality it was the same force using the new tactics devised by Park.

Bomber formations, Göring outlined, were to be reduced in size, and Gruppen would bomb targets in the London area with maximum fighter escort. 'As many fighters as possible' would be destroyed and he estimated that the R.A.F. fighter force should be finished off in four to five days. Göring was mesmerised by 'four to five days' as this was the time taken in the Polish and French campaigns. He had uttered the self-same words before Adler Tag and nearly five weeks had passed.

His lecture included orders for mass formations only to be used in perfect weather conditions, and for raids to be stepped-up on aircraft production centres. Göring clung to his theory that the Luftwaffe would render Seelöwe unnecessary and went so far as to note that air force operations must not be disturbed by any plans for a landing. For the first time he admitted that air crews were tiring and that for the fighter arm the incessant attacks were 'very exhausting'. Fighter Command pilots were not the only ones weary at this stage.

In England Park took advantage of the lull due to bad weather (rain and cloud-base 300 feet) to issue another instruction, No. 18, to his controllers. Despite the successes of the 15th and the improved loss ratio, he felt that still more interceptions could be made. He listed the faults as he saw them:

Individual squadrons failing to rendezvous.
Single squadrons being detailed to large raids.
Paired squadrons being rendezvoused too far forward, and too low.
High-flying massed formations of German fighters attracting most of the Group while the bombers got through.
Delays in vectoring of paired squadrons on to raids by Group controllers.
Errors in sector reports on pilot and aircraft effective strengths.

To improve the situation he ordered that in clear weather the Hornchurch and Biggin Hill squadrons should attack the high fighter screen in pairs. Rendezvous of pairs was to be made below cloud base in the event of overcast, and at height in clear weather or well in advance of any raids.

Whenever raid information was scanty, fighter squadrons were detailed to short patrol lines, if necessary with two squadrons very high and two squadrons between 15,000 and 20,000 feet.

To deal with high-flying German fighter diversions, Park required several pairs of Spitfire squadrons to be put up while ample Hurricane squadrons were assembled in pairs near sector airfields. The Northolt and Tangmere squadrons were to be despatched as three squadron wings to intercept the second and third waves of attack which experience had shown normally contained bombers.

From this it is quite clear that Park was not averse to using wing formations, where the warning time was sufficient and the type of mass raid required it.

During the 16th the weather precluded any heavy attacks and from the few small raids which penetrated to east London, nine German aircraft were shot down for the loss of one R.A.F. pilot. The dull weather was lightened for both sides by the solemn announcement in the German war communiqué that Göring himself had flown over London in a Ju 88. Apart from lacking the courage for such an enterprise, it was a physical impossibility, as the Reichsmarschall's girth precluded him getting through the door of a Ju 88, and even in the four-motor Condor he had to have a special wide seat with thigh supports.

At night heavy attacks were renewed on London, commencing at 7.40 and going on until 4.30 a.m. Over 200 tons of bombs were dropped by 170 aircraft, while other towns hit by harassing raids included Liverpool and Bristol. Some bombs fell on Stanmore, but did no damage to Fighter Command headquarters. One enemy aircraft was claimed by the balloon barrage, but during the night balloons at ten major centres broke away.

September 17th

Day Slight activity. One large fighter sweep in afternoon. Seelöwe postponed until further notice.
Night Heavy attacks on London. Lighter raids on Merseyside and Glasgow.
Weather Squally showers, local thunder, bright intervals. Channel, Straits and Estuary drizzle.

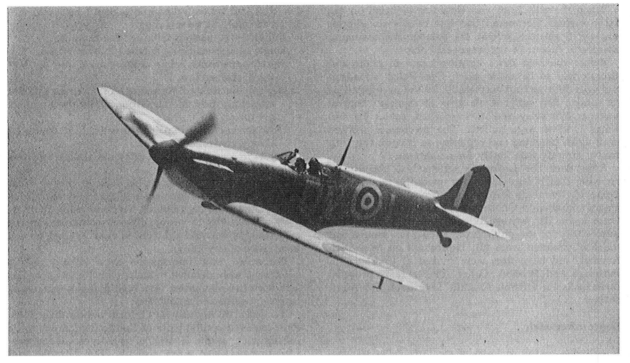

A shapely outline, a Spitfire of 19 Squadron from Duxford photographed during September

The continued strength of both Fighter and Bomber Commands of the R.A.F. and an adverse weather report for the coming week led Hitler on this day to postpone Operation Seelöwe until further notice and he issued a directive to this effect. A high state of preparedness was, however, to be maintained. The naval staff war diary recorded that an order from the Führer to carry out Sealion was still to be expected at any time, and that if the air and weather situations permitted, the invasion might be got under way as late as October.

The weather was unsuitable for mass raids on London, and in accordance with Göring's directive of the 16th, Luftflotte 2 sent waves of fighters across, with a few bombers as bait, in the hope of luring 11 Group into an unprofitable battle.

Seven to eight main raids totalling some 250 aircraft built up over France and crossed the coast at Lympne, Dover and Deal at 15,000 feet. Intercepting R.A.F. fighters found that the majority of the formations were Me 109s and the twenty-eight squadrons put up succeeded in turning them back over Maidstone. A few bombs were dropped, and British losses were only five aircraft (one pilot killed and two wounded) out of the 544 sorties flown. Luftwaffe casualties totalled eight aircraft for the whole twenty-four hours.

By night the German Air Force returned at full strength with 268 bombers over London arriving in a stream via Dungeness and Selsey Bill. Much residential damage was done. It was the turn of the big department stores with John Lewis's in Oxford Street almost completely burnt out, and both Bourne and Hollings-

worth and D. H. Evans hit. By this time 30,000 Londoners had lost their homes.

By way of diversion, a few raiders undertook the long flights to Merseyside and to Glasgow. Fighter Command put up thirty-eight single-engined fighter sorties, but they groped in vain, except for a Defiant of 141 Squadron which shot down a Ju 88 near Barking at 11.30.

While the Germans concentrated on London with the A.A. barrage the only opposition, Bomber Command was out in force attacking the barges, transport and munitions being mustered for invasion. Throughout the Battle and afterwards, in its historical surveys, the Luftwaffe always spoke disparagingly of the R.A.F.'s offensive efforts from July to October 1940. The German naval staff, however, were under no illusions, as they were at the receiving end.

On this night Bomber and Coastal commands, also taking advantage of the full moon, despatched aircraft to Dunkirk, Calais, Boulogne, Cherbourg and den Helder. The following morning the German naval staff described losses as 'very considerable'. At Dunkirk twenty-six barges were sunk or badly damaged and fifty-eight slightly damaged. A tremendous explosion heralded the detonation of 500 tons of stored ammunition, while a ration depot and dock-handling equipment were destroyed. At the other ports buildings were smashed and a steamer and a torpedo-boat sunk.

September 18th

Day Oil targets in Thames Estuary attacked.
Night London and Merseyside raided.
Weather Bright and squally.

At 9 a.m. the first blips appeared on Fighter Command radar screens. They showed a heavy build-up over

Calais. The raiders, mainly fighters, penetrated between North Foreland and Folkestone at 20,000 feet. They were split up over Maidstone and the Estuary and turned for home after running engagements with seventeen R.A.F. squadrons. One was shot down by anti-aircraft fire.

Two hours later radar betrayed four raids totalling 190 planes. They crossed the coast at Deal and attacked Chatham. At least sixty reached the centre of London. The rest roamed over Kent.

At 2 p.m. Luftflotte 2 began to assemble 150 aircraft over Calais. As they climbed to 20,000 feet the Germans sorted themselves into neat formations and set course for Gravesend.

Breaking cloud over Kent the Germans were met in force, and although some of them penetrated the defences, the majority of formations were broken up and repelled.

Flying up the Thames, later, two groups of between twenty and thirty bombers were heading for London when Spitfires and Hurricanes of the Duxford wing attacked them. The wing had taken off at 4.20 p.m. and was patrolling Hornchurch when A.A. fire betrayed the presence of the enemy groups.

Leaving No. 611 Squadron on patrol and No. 19 Squadron to look after the escorts, Bader led his three Hurricane squadrons into an almost vertical diving attack on the first formation. The Germans scattered, leaving only four vics of five aircraft. These were soon broken up and the bombers turned for home.

Sergeant Plzak, a Czech pilot with No. 19 Squadron, fired a couple of bursts at an He 111 and stopped both its engines. The crew baled out and the bomber crashed near Gillingham, Kent.

The Duxford Wing claimed thirty destroyed, six probables and two damaged in the engagement. They lost none. But when the score came to be verified against the German Quartermaster General's records, it was found that only nineteen Luftwaffe machines had actually been shot down during the whole day.

Twelve British fighters went down in the fighting of the 18th, but only three of the pilots were killed, in the course of 1,165 sorties.

No. 7 O.T.U. scored a third victory that day. Squadron Leader McLean, Flying Officer Brotchie and Sergeant Armitage took off from Hawarden, Cheshire, and intercepted a raid flying towards Liverpool. They damaged one Do 17 and shot down another which dived into the sea off the Welsh coast.

Dowding's efforts to remedy the chronic shortage of fighter pilots bore further fruit on the 18th when the Air Ministry agreed to another combing of the Fairey Battle squadrons for Fighter Command's benefit. They also agreed to allot to the Command more than two-thirds of the entire output of the flying training schools in the four-week period ending the middle of October.

On September 7th 984 Hurricane and Spitfire pilots were flying with the squadrons—a deficiency of nearly twenty-two pilots per squadron, and of these 150 were only semi-trained.

On the other side of the Channel German preparations for the invasion were reaching their peak. On the 15th 102 barges were photographed by reconnaissance aircraft in Boulogne. On the 17th there were 150. Calais harbour contained 266. By the 18th the Channel ports held 1,004 invasion craft and a further 600 waited up-river at Antwerp.

From September 7th Blenheims pressed home their attacks by day whenever the weather permitted and Wellingtons, Whitleys, Hampdens and Battles operated at night. Operating under Coastal Command, Fleet Air Arm Swordfishes and Albacores also took part.

During September 60 per cent of the bombing was directed at the invasion ports on which 1,400 tons of bombs were dropped. The remaining effort was concentrated against rail communications, shipyards and oil targets in Germany and occupied Europe.

Night bombing on Britain started on September 18th at 7.30 p.m. and the flow of raids lasted until 5.30 a.m. the following morning. London and Liverpool were the principal targets. Bombs were also scattered over Kent and Surrey and in Middlesex 120 cylindrical parachute mines fell in the vicinity of Stanmore.

September 19th

Day Reduced activity, attacks chiefly over Thames Estuary and east London.
Night London and Merseyside.
Weather Showery.

Piccadilly, Regent Street, Bond Street, North Audley Street, Park Lane and many less famous thoroughfares in the centre of London were blocked after the night's raids. Big cranes surrounded Marble Arch and men of the Civil Defence Corps, Pioneers and Police worked to clear the rubble and rescue the victims trapped in the wreckage.

A lull was expected after the intensity of the previous day's operations. Only seventy hostile planes, flying singly, crossed the coast via Dungeness. A few reached Liverpool and London where a lone roof-top raider machine-gunned Hackney.

Near Bury St. Edmunds, Suffolk, a Ju 88 fell to the guns of No. 302 Squadron. Engine failure compelled another to land intact at Oakington airfield near Cambridge. Losses for the day were eight German and no British.

Rain in the night interfered with German plans, but they managed to despatch 200 aircraft to mine coastal waters. A few went for the Home Counties and London. At Heston aerodrome a parachute mine wrecked or damaged thirteen planes, including five Photographic Reconnaissance Unit Spitfires, a Lockheed 12A and a visiting Wellington bomber. Liverpool sirens sounded for six raids plotted approaching from the Irish Sea.

In Germany, Hitler formally ordered the assembly of the invasion fleet to be stopped, and shipping in the Channel ports to be dispersed 'so that the loss of shipping space caused by enemy air attacks may be reduced to a minimum'.

September 20th

Day One large fighter sweep towards London: otherwise reconnaissance only.

*Dornier 17s of KG 3 flying in over Canning Town on
September 7th, 1940. In the middle of the picture is the
West Ham Stadium while below, partially hidden,
is the Royal Victoria Dock*

Night London.
Weather Fair with bright periods. Showery.

There were few early-morning raids but at 10.30 a.m. the Luftwaffe started massing at Calais. Then twenty planes crossed the coast at Dungeness at 13,000 feet, thirty overflew Dover, at 12,000 feet, and a dozen or more passed over Lympne. The R.A.F. lost seven planes near Kenley, Biggin Hill and the Estuary, and the Germans lost eight.

At night the waning moon was still bright enough to help the Germans but they chose to curtail their activities which were mainly directed against London.

Reporting on his trip to Britain, in New York, Brigadier Strong, Assistant Chief of the U.S. Military Mission sent to London to observe the results of the Luftwaffe's attacks, did much to influence American opinion. The German Air Force, he said, had made no serious inroad on the strength of the R.A.F. and the damage inflicted on military targets was comparatively small. Strong concluded by stating that the British were conservative in claiming German aircraft casualties.

September 21st

Day Slight activity; some fighter sweeps in east Kent.
Night London and Merseyside attacked.
Weather Mainly fine.

London, cloaked in haze, enjoyed a relatively quiet day, as did the rest of the country except for isolated attacks and extensive reconnaissance in coastal areas.

Among the lone raiders was a Ju 88 which bombed the Hawker works at Brooklands in a tree-top-level attack. Fortunately the damage did not affect production.

When an unidentified aircraft was plotted at 4.30 p.m. 25,000 feet over Liverpool, Pilot Officer D. A. Adams of No. 611 Squadron was ordered to investigate. He found a German bomber and sent it crashing into a field near Dolgelly, North Wales.

The bulk of Fighter Command's 563 sorties were flown in the evening when five raids crossed the coast at Dover, Lympne and Dungeness to assail Kenley, Biggin Hill, Hornchurch and central London. Twenty No. 11 Group squadrons, the Duxford Wing and one No. 10 Group squadron scrambled to intercept but only one of them engaged. The German casualties numbered nine while the R.A.F. suffered no loss.

Scattered cloud and moonlight made the night perfect for the raiding, but the Germans chose to exert no more than moderate pressure on London, Liverpool, Warrington, Nottingham, Bolton and Colchester.

September 22nd

Day Slight activity.
Night London bombed.
Weather Dull with fog in morning. Cloudy in afternoon, fair to fine late. Some rain.

Twelve single raiders flying high over London and the noise of No. 234 Squadron's Browning guns shooting down a lone Ju 88 scarcely disturbed this Sunday's congregations. Even the sound of Merlin engines was strangely absent, for the squadrons flew only 158 sorties—the smallest number since the Battle began. German losses were five machines while the R.A.F. lost none.

By midnight the situation had changed; London, in the words of Lord Alanbrooke, was like Dante's Inferno.

Twelve night fighters—Blenheims and Defiants—tried to intercept, but though the Luftwaffe gave them a selection of 123 bombers to shoot at no victories were recorded.

Nazi bombers were still over the capital in the early hours. Others mixed with Bomber Command streams returning from Germany and sneaked through the defences to attack airfields in Lincolnshire, including Digby, where they set fire to a hangar.

September 23rd

Day Fighter sweeps towards London.
Night London and Merseyside.
Weather Fine.

At 9 a.m. a build-up of nearly 200 planes was detected over Calais. Chiefly Me 109s, they came over in four large and two small waves fanned out beyond Dover. Twenty-four squadrons were up to cut them off and ten intercepted. A further force of 109s came in at 7 p.m.

Between 5 and 6 p.m. Uxbridge despatched twelve squadrons in four wings to counter five waves of Messerschmitts intruding through South Foreland, Dover and Hythe. The sweep lasted forty-five minutes but the attackers were elusive.

Eleven British aircraft and three pilots were lost in the day's engagements. Eight of the pilots were wounded. German losses were sixteen.

With London under heavy bombardment the Cabinet were determined to retaliate and they ordered the indiscriminate bombing of Berlin with parachute mines. Nothing could have been less in keeping with Air Staff thinking, which contrasted the effect of four bombs on Fulham power station with several thousand bombs which fell elsewhere.

The dispute ended in compromise. The Air Staff agreed to include Berlin in their forthcoming directives on the understanding that only targets of specific military value were to be bombed. The directive was issued on September 21st and on the night of 23rd 119 Whitleys, Wellingtons and Hampdens took off for the German capital.

In contrast 261 German planes turned London into another inferno and damage was widespread.

September 24th

Day Tilbury and Southampton raided.
Night London and Merseyside attacked.
Weather Early-morning fog in northern France. Channel cloudy, haze in the Straits and Thames Estuary.

British service chiefs, unaware that Seelöwe had been postponed on September 17th, continued to await the invasion. Equinoctial gales which had swept the

Ein Angriff und seine Wirkung

Unsere Aufnahmen haben das große Flugzeugwerk von Filton zum Gegenstand. Das Bild links ist wenige Tage vor dem Angriff aufgenommen, der das Werk vernichtet hat. Deutlich erkennbar sind neben der Bahnlinie die riesigen Werkhallen, deren Tarnbemalung gegen Fliegersicht schützen soll. Das Luftbild beweist aber, daß der Anstrich der Dächer allein nicht genügt. Die Hallen sind vollkommen klar zu erkennen. Das Bild oben ist während des ersten Bombenangriffs aufgenommen. Das Hauptwerk ist in der linken unteren Ecke zu erkennen. Mitten im Werk schlagen Bomben ein. Das etwas kleinere Zweigwerk oberhalb der quer durch das Bild laufenden Bahn ist von Bombensalven vollkommen eingedeckt. Die weißen Stellen in der rechten unteren Ecke des oberen Bildes sind Wolken, die sich zwischen die Erde und die Kampfflugzeuge geschoben haben. Das obere Bild läßt mit aller nur wünschenswerten Deutlichkeit erkennen, daß da unten, im Flugzeugwerk von Filton, die Hölle ist. Einschlag neben Einschlag prasselt in die großen Hallen. Dieses Werk wird nicht mehr viel Flugzeuge herstellen. Die Zahlen bedeuten (1) das Hauptwerk, (2) das Nebenwerk, (3) sieben aufgestellte Flugzeuge, (4) drei Flugzeuge am Boden, (5) Sperrballone am Boden, (6) die Startbahn, die mitten durch den Flugplatz führt

'An Air Raid and it's Results'—the German caption to photographs showing the raid on the Bristol Aeroplane Company, Filton, when production was severely curtailed.

'Our photographs show the large aircraft factories at Filton. The picture on the left was taken a few days before the raid which destroyed the factory.

Easily recognised, close to the railway, are the huge workshops, whose camouflage was intended as protection against aerial observation.

The aerial photograph, however, proves that the paint on the roofs alone is not enough. The workshops are clearly recognisable.

The upper picture was taken during the first bombing attack. The main works can be recognised in the left-hand lower corner. Bombs are seen exploding in the middle of the works. The somewhat smaller branch factory above the railway which crosses the picture is completely covered by salvoes of bombs.

The white patches in the right-hand lower corner of the upper picture are clouds which have drifted between the ground and the bombing planes. The upper picture enables one to recognise with all desirable clarity that hell has been let loose on the Filton works below. Blow after blow rains on the great shops. This factory will not produce many more aircraft.

The numbers indicate :- 1. The main works. 2. Adjoining works. 3. Seven aircraft parked in line. 4. Three aircraft on the ground. 5. Barrage balloons on the ground. 6. The main run-way crossing the middle of the aerodrome'

Channel earlier in the week had now died down and the sea was quieter. By 8.30 a.m. the only sign of enemy activity was in the air where some 200 aircraft, mainly bombers, crossed the coast on a ten-mile front in five formations ranging from three to fifty planes in size.

Flying between 10,000 and 25,000 feet the Germans tried to get through to London, but were repulsed. Three hours later another 200 assembled into five formations over Cap Gris Nez and headed north. Of the eighteen British squadrons sent up to intercept them only two engaged.

Soon after lunch between fifteen and twenty Me 109 fighter-bombers came up the Solent in two waves. Diving singly, they attacked the Supermarine works at Woolston near Southampton. They did little damage to the factory itself but hit a shelter and killed nearly 100 of the staff.

The Messerschmitts then turned over Portsmouth and for twenty minutes trailed their coats. Not a British fighter was to be seen but the A.A. guns blazed away and shot down one German aircraft, making eleven for the day. This brought German losses since September 19th to fifty-nine. In the same period twenty-two British fighters were destroyed of which four were lost on the 24th.

From early evening until 5.30 the following morning there was widespread bombing over the whole country.

September 25th

Day Bristol and Plymouth bombed.
Night London, North Wales and Lancashire attacked.
Weather Fair to fine in most districts. Cool. Channel cloudy with bright intervals; hazy.

Apart from the usual reconnaissance flights and the detection of intense activity over France at 8.20 a.m., the morning was quiet. At 11.20 a large raid crossed the coast.

Fighter-bombers made diversionary attacks on Portland while some sixty Heinkel 111s comprising the three Gruppen of KG55 slipped through the defences with Me 110s of ZG26 and reached Bristol at 11.45. They attacked the Bristol Aeroplane Company's works at Filton with ninety tons of high-explosive and twenty-four oil-bombs.

Production was curtailed for many weeks. The bombing killed or injured more than 250, blocked railways near the factory and cut communications between Filton airfield and No. 10 Group Headquarters. Eight out of fifty completed bombers were badly damaged.

Three No. 10 Group squadrons and a flight of Hurricanes were scrambled in time to meet the attackers. But they were vectored to Yeovil where the Westland aircraft works seemed the more likely target. When the actual objective became known the three squadrons swung into pursuit but only a few of the aircraft caught up with the Germans before they reached Filton. Five of the enemy aircraft were shot down, one of them by anti-aircraft fire.

Although Filton was acting as a temporary sector station, Nos. 87 and 213 Squadrons allocated to it were operating from Exeter and Bibury. To guard against further attack Dowding immediately ordered

No. 504 (County of Nottingham) Squadron to move to Filton from Hendon.

No. 601 Squadron engaged twelve bombers and twelve Me 110s at Start Point near Plymouth at 4.30 p.m. At the same time No. 74 Squadron, operating from Duxford, joined Nos. 611 and 19 squadrons to intercept a raid coming in over London at 20,000 feet.

By dusk Fighter Command had flown 668 sorties. The score was four British to thirteen German planes destroyed.

On the night of the 25th the highest number of people sheltering in tube stations was recorded. A Home Security operations room weekly report on this day records:

> The German attack upon London has had no fundamental ill effect either upon the capital or on the nation. Its first impact caused bewilderment and there was some ill-temper . . .

> This loss of temper . . . has almost completely vanished and a general equanimity prevails . . . Nothing has affected the unconquerable optimism of the Cockney nor has anything restricted his ready if graveyard humour . . . Without over emphasis people take the obvious precautions to ensure sufficient sleep. Having done so they regard the event philosophically. During the day they continue their ordinary business . . . It is still necessary to canvas some classes of the people to leave London.

September 26th

Day Supermarine works at Southampton attacked and wrecked.
Night London and Merseyside.
Weather Mainly fair to cloudy in the south.

It was obvious to the Germans as they studied reconnaissance photographs of Southampton that Supermarine's Woolston factory remained intact.

In the afternoon seventy-six planes—He 111s, Ju 88s and Me 109s—assembled over Brittany and set course for the Solent. By 5.45 they had delivered a 'pattern bombing' attack on the home of the Spitfire. It was all over in a few minutes with seventy tons of bombs dropped to such good purpose that for a short time production was completely stopped. In addition more than thirty people were killed and a nearby warehouse filled with grain was destroyed.

Engaged on the way in by anti-aircraft fire only, the attackers were intercepted after the bombing by four No. 10 and No. 11 Group squadrons. One of these was No. 303 (Polish) Squadron which had left Northolt in the middle of an inspection by the King. Three German aircraft were shot down. The R.A.F. lost six. The day's engagements cost both air forces nine planes each, the R.A.F. flying 417 sorties.

Only three Spitfires on the Woolston production line were destroyed. Many others were damaged by the blast and debris but they were soon repaired and delivered to the squadrons.

In August 149 Spitfires had been produced, mostly at Woolston, as the shadow factory at Castle Bromwich was only just coming into production. In October 139 Spitfires were built. The Southampton facilities were dispersed to thirty-five sites and by the end of the year production was back to normal.

September 27th

Day Heavy attacks on London and one on Bristol.
Night London, Merseyside and the midlands.
Weather Fair in extreme south and south-west. Cloudy in the Channel with haze. Slight rain in southern England.

The first sign of German activity appeared on the operations table at No. 11 Group as the 8 a.m. watch took over.

The planes were bomb-carrying Me 110s escorted by Me 109s. Harried by fighters from Dungeness to the outskirts of London they scattered their bombs indiscriminately.

Some Me 109s stuck tenaciously to the London area. They had orders to protect two succeeding formations of Do 17s and Ju 88s, but the bombers did not make the rendezvous. 11 Group was ready for them and they were intercepted over the coast by a powerful assembly of Spitfires and Hurricanes which broke up the tidy German formations and compelled them to jettison their bombs.

Badly mauled, the Messerschmitt pilots over London were obliged to split up and dive for the safety of a ground-level retreat.

Having failed to clear the skies by sending fighters ahead of the bombers in the first assault, the Germans reverted at 11.30 to a split raid, sending eighty aircraft to Bristol and 300 to London.

No. 10 Group squadrons fought the Bristol raiders across the West Country and only ten Me 110s and some 109s managed to get through. These were intercepted on the outskirts of Bristol by the Nottingham squadron, which compelled them to release their bombs unprofitably on the suburbs. The survivors were harried all the way back to the coast and out to sea.

The majority of the London raiders got no further than the middle of Kent where they were so severely mauled that they retreated in confusion. Some reached the outskirts of the city and twenty slipped through to the centre.

With fifty-five German aircraft missing (including twenty-one bombers) the Channel was alive with air-sea rescue planes and boats in the evening. Most of the twenty-eight British planes lost came down on land.

September 28th

Day London and the Solent area attacked.
Night The target London.
Weather Fair to fine generally. Channel, Straits of Dover and Thames Estuary cloudy. Winds moderate.

Delighted by the results of the 27th, Churchill was moved to send the Secretary of State this message: 'Pray congratulate the Fighter Command on the results of yesterday. The scale and intensity of the fighting and the heavy losses of the enemy . . . make 27th September rank with 15th September and 15th August, as the third great and victorious day of the Fighter Command during the course of the Battle of Britain.'

By that evening, however, sixteen fighters and nine pilots had been lost resisting two major raids on London and one on Portsmouth.

This, coupled with the fact that only three German planes were shot down, was an indication that the British pilots were exhausted by the intensity of the demands made on them.

The Luftwaffe's losses for the day in fact totalled ten machines. Seven of them were destroyed accidentally.

Another important factor to be found in these results lay in the composition of the German formations. As a result of their losses—accentuated on the 27th—the Germans were forced to admit that their large bomber formations were not paying big enough dividends to justify the heavy losses they had incurred. New tactics were accordingly ordered, involving smaller bomber formations consisting of thirty of the faster Ju 88s, escorted by 200 to 300 fighters.

Evidence of this change in tactics did not become apparent until midday when several large formations of Me 109s appeared between Deal and Dungeness escorting some thirty bombers. The raiders were driven off before they reached central London, but not without difficulty for the British, who were placed at a disadvantage by the heights at which the German escorts were flying.

All No. 11 Group squadrons were involved, as well as five squadrons from No. 12 Group.

At 2.45 p.m. fifty Me 110s were intercepted en route for Portsmouth and driven back by squadrons of No. 10 Group assisted by five No. 11 Group units diverted to help.

From 5 p.m. until nightfall the Germans concentrated on reconnaissance. At 9 p.m. they began night operations which were centred on London.

September 29th

Day Reduced activity in south-east and East Anglia.
Night London and Merseyside attacked.
Weather Fine and fair early. Fair late. Cloudy for the rest of the day.

The Germans, after a morning harassing convoys, struck out with several high-flying formations. Nine of their aircraft failed to return home and that night Weybridge A.A. gunners added a bomber to the score. Five British fighters were destroyed.

September 30th

Day Fighter sweeps towards London but few bombs dropped.
Night London attacked.
Weather Generally fair but cloudy. Winds light.

An hour separated the first two major raids which began at 9 a.m. In the first there were thirty bombers and 100 fighters; in the second sixty planes.

Crossing the coast at Dungeness the two raids were met in force. Split and harried, neither reached London.

At 10.50 a.m. radar warned of another attack—this time approaching Dorset from Cherbourg. The planes were Me 110 fighter-bombers escorted by 109s. They were so severely handled by the R.A.F. that they turned back before reaching the coast.

Midday came and with it a fierce battle over Kent. Then at 3.10 p.m. a series of minor sorties was followed by a major raid of more than 100 planes. Thirty reached,

London. Within fifty minutes 180 more bombers and fighters were plotted approaching Weybridge and Slough on a front of eight miles.

One hundred miles west, forty escorted Heinkel bombers crossed the coast heading for the Westland works at Yeovil. Cloud obscured the target and the Germans were obliged to bomb blind. Sherborne, some miles from Yeovil, took the full impact of the attack.

The Germans had to fight their way in against four British squadrons and they were beset by another four on the way out. Four Hurricanes fell to their gunners and an Me 110 shot down another.

Two of the British pilots baled out and the third, Wing Commander Constable-Maxwell, shot down by a single bullet puncturing the oil system of his aircraft, force-landed his Hurricane on a beach.

By dusk the last great daylight battle was over and the score was forty-seven German aircraft destroyed for a loss of twenty R.A.F. fighters and eight pilots killed or wounded.

Just as the Stuka had been withdrawn from the battle so now were the twin-engined bombers to be relegated to the night offensive—except for those rare occasions when they could use the clouds to cover their sorties over Britain.

And as if to mark the occasion the King appointed Dowding Knight Grand Commander of the Bath.

At night there were heavy raids on London, East Anglia, Liverpool and Bristol. The attack was mounted mainly by Luftflotte 2 whose 250 aircraft penetrated between Beachy Head and the Isle of Wight.

Attempting to reach London 175 of the raiders met with heavy anti-aircraft fire and stalking night fighters. A few broke through to bomb Acton and Westminster, but most of them were content to release their loads on the suburbs.

13 GROUP, HEADQUARTERS NEWCASTLE

Wick
232	Hurricane	Castletown
		(one flight only)

Dyce
145	Hurricane	A Flight Dyce
		B Flight Montrose

Turnhouse
65	Spitfire	Turnhouse
3	Hurricane	Turnhouse
141	Defiant	Turnhouse
		(A Flight only)
111	Hurricane	Drem
263	Hurricane	Drem (one flight only)
615	Hurricane	Prestwick

Usworth
43	Hurricane	Usworth
32	Hurricane	Acklington
610	Spitfire	Acklington

Catterick
54	Spitfire	Catterick
219	Blenheim	Catterick
		(B Flight Acklington)

12 GROUP, HEADQUARTERS WATNALL

Kirton-in-Lindsey
616	Spitfire	Kirton-in-Lindsey
264	Defiant	Kirton-in-Lindsey
		(B Flight only)

Church Fenton
86	Hurricane	Church Fenton
302	Hurricane	Leconfield (Polish)
64	Spitfire	Leconfield (A Flight;
		B Flight, Ringway,
		Cheshire)

Digby
151	Hurricane	Digby
29	Blenheim	Digby
611	Spitfire	Digby (A Flight,
		B Flight, Turnhill,
		Salop)

Coltishall
74	Spitfire	Coltishall
242	Hurricane	Coltishall

Wittering
266	Spitfire	Wittering
1	Hurricane	Wittering

Duxford
19	Spitfire	Duxford
310	Hurricane	Duxford (Czech)

11 GROUP, HEADQUARTERS UXBRIDGE

Debden
17	Hurricane	Debden
73	Hurricane	Castle Camps

257	Hurricane	Castle Camps

North Weald
249	Hurricane	North Weald
46	Hurricane	Stapleford
25	Blenheim	North Weald (one flight
		Martlesham re-equipping
		with Beaufighters)

Hornchurch
41	Spitfire	Hornchurch
603	Spitfire	Hornchurch
222	Spitfire	Rochford

Biggin Hill
72	Spitfire	Biggin Hill
92	Spitfire	Biggin Hill
66	Spitfire	Gravesend

Kenley
253	Hurricane	Kenley
501	Hurricane	Kenley
605	Hurricane	Croydon

Northolt
1	Hurricane	Northolt (R.C.A.F.)
303	Hurricane	Northolt (Polish)
229	Hurricane	Heathrow
264	Defiant	Luton (A Flight)
241	Defiant	Gatwick (B Flight)

Tangmere
607	Hurricane	Tangmere
213	Hurricane	Tangmere
602	Spitfire	Westhampnett
23	Blenheim	Ford (one flight
		Middle Wallop)

10 GROUP, HEADQUARTERS BOX, WILTSHIRE

Pembrey
79	Hurricane	Pembrey

Filton
504	Hurricane	Filton
601	Hurricane	Exeter
87	Hurricane	Exeter
		(B Flight Bibury)

St. Eval
234	Spitfire	St. Eval
247	Gladiator	Roborough (one flight)

Middle Wallop
238	Hurricane	Middle Wallop
609	Spitfire	Middle Wallop
604	Blenheim	Middle Wallop
152	Spitfire	Warmwell
56	Hurricane	Boscombe Down

LUFTFLOTTE 5—NORWAY

X Fliegerkorps
Bombers
11./KG26	He 111

Long-range reconnaissance
Aufkl.Gr.22 Stab
1./(F)120	He 111 and Ju 88
2./(F)22	Do 17
3./(F)22	Do 17
1./(F)121	He 111 and Ju 88

Fighters
11./JG77	Me 109
9./ZG76	Me 110

LUFTFLOTTE 2—HOLLAND, BELGIUM AND NORTHERN FRANCE

Long-range reconnaissance
Aufkl.Gr.122
2./(F)122	Ju 88 and He 111
4./(F)122	Ju 88, He 111 and Me 110
1./(F)22	Do 17 and Me 110
7./(F)LG2	Me 110

II Fliegerkorps
Long-range bombers
KG2 Stab, I, II, III	Do 17
KG3 Stab, I, II, III	Do 17
KG53 Stab, I, II, III	He 111
IV./LG1	

Long-range reconnaissance
1./(F)122	Ju 88

VIII Fliegerkorps
Dive-bombers
St.G2 Stab, I, III	Stab, Ju 87 and Do 17; I, III, Ju 87
St.G77 Stab, I, II, III	Ju 87

Long-range reconnaissance
2./(F)11	Do 17

IX Fliegerkorps (name changed from IX Fliegerdivision 16.10.40)
KG4 Stab, I, II, III	I, II, He 111; III, Ju 88
KG40 Stab	Ju 88
KG30 Stab, II, III	Ju 88

Minelaying
KGr.126	He 111

Coastal reconnaissance
KGr.106	He 115

Jagdfliegerführer 2
Fighters
JG3 Stab, I, II, III	Me 109
JG26 Stab, I, II, III	Me 109
JG27 Stab, II, III	Me 109
JG51 Stab, I, II, III	Me 109
JG52 Stab, I, II	Me 109
I./LG2	Me 109
JG54 Stab, II	Me 109
JG53 Stab, I, II, III	Me 109
JG77 I	Me 109

Ground attack
II./LG2	Me 109
Epr.Gr.210	Me 110

Luftgaukommando XI
Fighters
JG1 Stab	Me 109
JG54 I	Me 109
ZG76 II	Me 110

Luftgaukommando VI
Fighters
JG3 I (one Schwarm)	Me 109

Luftkommando Holland
Fighters
JG54 III	Me 109

C.A.I. Verb. Stab (Corpo Aero Italiano)
Bombers
KG43 (43 Stormo)	Fiat BR 20
KG13 (13 Stormo)	Fiat BR 20

Fighters
JG56 Stab	
18/JG56 (18 Gruppo)	Fiat G.50
20/JG56 (20 Gruppo)	Fiat CR.42

Reconnaissance
Aufkl.St. 172 (172 Squadriglia)	Cant Z.1007 bis

LUFTFLOTTE 3—FRANCE

Long-range reconnaissance
Aufkl.Gr.123 Stab
1./(F)123	Ju 88 and Do 17
2./(F)123	Ju 88 and Do 17
3./(F)123	Ju 88 and Do 17

Long-range bombers
KG1 III (10 and 12 Staffeln on special duties)	Ju 88

Jagdfliegerführer 3
I Fliegerkorps
Long-range reconnaissance
5./(F)122	Ju 88 and He 111

Long-range bombers
KG1 Stab, I, II, III and reserve Staffel	Stab, I, II, He 111; III, Ju 88
KG26 Stab, II, III and reserve Staffel	He 111
KG76 Stab, I, II, III and reserve Staffel	Do 17
KG77 Stab, I, II, III and reserve Staffel	Ju 88

IV Fliegerkorps

Long-range reconnaissance

3./(F)121	Ju 88 and He 111
3./(F)31	Me 110 and Do 17

Long-range bombers

LG1 Stab, I, II, III and reserve Staffel	Ju 88

KG27 Stab, I, II, III
    IV and reserve
    Staffel
	He 111

KGr.100	He 111

Naval co-operation

KG40 I	FW 200
K.Fl.Gr.606	Do 17

Fighters

JG27 I, II	Me 109

Long-range reconnaissance

Aufkl.Gr.31 Stab	Me 110 and Do 17

(subordinate to H.Q. 9th Abteilung)

V Fliegerkorps

Long-range reconnaissance
(subordinate to 9th Army)

4./(F)121	Ju 88 and Do 17
4./(F)14	Me 110 and Do 17

Long-range bombers

KG51 Stab, I, II, III and reserve Staffel	Ju 88
KG54 Stab, I, II	Ju 88
KG55 Stab, I, II, III and reserve Staffel	He 111
K.Gr.806	Ju 88

Dive-bombers

St.G.3 Stab, I, II	Stab, Do 17 and He 111; I, II, Ju 87

Fighters

ZG26 Stab, I, II, III and reserve Staffel	Me 110
JG2 Stab, I, II, III and reserve Staffel	Me 109
5./JG53 (subordinate to Luftflotte 2)	Me 109

Coastal reconnaissance

K.Fl.St.2./106	Do 18

18   Fifth phase—October 1st–31st

Three months less ten days had now elapsed since the start of the Battle of Britain, but for all the German effort there was little to set against the loss of 1,653 aircraft. Germany had not established the superiority she needed in the air. To avoid further bomber losses, Göring resorted to the use of fighter-bombers operating at high altitude.

These tactics were difficult to counter because of the height at which the German fighters flew. Above 25,000 feet the Me 109 with a two-stage supercharger had a better performance than even the Mk. II Hurricanes and Spitfires then coming into service. Moreover, raids approaching at 20,000 feet or more had a good chance of minimising the effect of radar observation and were difficult for the Observer Corps to track, especially when there were clouds about. Secondly, the speed at which the formations, unencumbered by long-range bombers, flew was so great that at best the radar chain could not give much more than twenty minutes warning before they released their bombs. Thirdly, Park and his controllers had no way of telling which of the several approaching formations contained bomb-carrying aircraft and should therefore be given preference.

A step towards the solution of the second and third problems was taken at the end of September when No. 421 Flight (later No. 91 Squadron) was formed to spot approaching formations and report their height and strength to Uxbridge by R/T. Although told to fly high and avoid combat, pilots so employed were sometimes at a disadvantage. After four had been shot down in the first ten days of October they began to work in pairs, a practice generally adopted later. But in any case their efforts were not sufficient answer to the problem of intercepting raiders which flew too high for detection by the radar chain.

Compared with its efficiency as an instrument of defence in daylight Fighter Command was woefully weak at night. The R.D.F. chain still only covered the coastal areas and inland there were only a handful of gun-laying radars, sound locators and the Observer Corps. In the darkness of this cloudy autumn the Observer Corps' binoculars were, so to speak, *hors de combat*.

Six Blenheim and two Defiant squadrons strengthened by a flight of Hurricanes were available for night fighting in October 1940, but none of the aircraft was designed or equipped for the purpose. The planes were gradually being fitted with Air Interception radar which at that time was no more than promising.

Between September and November, therefore, the number of interceptions was disappointingly few. Improved equipment, including the Bristol Beaufighter specially suited to night operations, was coming into service, but local ground-control radar was needed to put the planes within operating limits of A.I. It was to be some time before these local ground-control radar stations were installed.

It was not until 1941 that the night-fighter squadrons began to have telling effects on the Luftwaffe.

In the meantime some of the more experienced Hurricane and Spitfite pilots attempted to convert themselves to night fighting without being trained for the job or even having the basic essentials for approach and landing at their airfields. It is doubtful whether the risks they took in bad weather justified their courageous efforts, for they had little success, even on bright moonlit nights.

The Germans therefore had little opposition to contend with. What there was of it came from the anti-aircraft defences. But even this was ineffective owing to the inadequacy of the sound locators and the lack of gun-laying radar sets.

There is evidence to show, however, that the anti-aircraft guns did force the Germans to fly higher and some of the half-hearted crews to turn back. For the Londoners at least the guns were comforting.

Searchlights were even more limited than guns. They could not penetrate cloud or hold a bomber in their beams long enough to help the artillery or the night fighters, and by flying above 12,000 feet the bombers escaped their pointing fingers altogether.

October 1st

Day London raids. Southampton and Portsmouth also targets.
Night London, Liverpool, Manchester main targets.
Weather Mainly fair but generally cloudy.

German patrols began to appear between Beachy Head and Southwold from about seven in the morning. They gave no trouble but at 10.45 a force of 100 aircraft operating from Caen attempted to bomb Southampton and Portsmouth. They met stiff opposition.

There was a marked difference in the composition of this raid. The machines were mostly Me 109s and Me 110s, some of them carrying bombs. The Germans were beginning to reserve their bombers for night operations and place the whole burden for the daylight offensive on the fighter arm which had converted one

Hit by British anti-aircraft fire, this Heinkel 111 of KG 55 force-landed in Holland in October

staffel of each gruppe or one gruppe of each geschwader to fighter-bomber duties.

A third of the German fighters—250 aircraft—were so converted, Me 109s to carry a 250 kg. bomb and Me 110s a total bomb-load of 700 kg.

Flying at great height and taking every advantage of the cloudy weather, these aircraft set Fighter Command new and difficult problems and imposed many fruitless hours of climb and chase upon the British pilots. But they did little else and Fighter Command continued the recovery which had started on September 7th.

From 1 to 3 p.m. a steady stream of aircraft crossed the coast between Deal and Selsey Bill. The first three waves, consisting of fifty Me 109s, reached Maidstone before 2 p.m.

Forty minutes later about seventy-five planes flew in from Calais and split some thirty miles inland. The raiders were intercepted and retired towards Maidstone but bombs landed at Brixton, Wandsworth, Camberwell and Lambeth.

The third attack was a half-hearted effort to penetrate over Dungeness and the Germans turned back before the R.A.F. could reach them.

In the north three raids were plotted over Aberdeenshire and three in the Moray Firth. One of these, a single aircraft, was seen returning to Brittany across Wales and Devon.

At 5 p.m. more than fifty aircraft assembled over Cap Gris Nez at 20,000 feet. No sooner had they crossed the coast than Luftflotte 2 massed for a follow-through with another thirty to fifty Me 109s and Me 110s. For each attack the R.A.F. were up in force.

Night raiders started coming in just after 7.30 p.m. mainly over the Isle of Wight, Beachy Head and Dungeness, 175 of them weaving and turning in the general direction of London. Liverpool and Manchester were visited by a further twenty-five, while Glasgow and Swansea had two raiders each. Bombs dropped on the Mersey side of Manchester and Grantham. In the course of 723 sorties during the day the R.A.F. lost four aircraft. Luftwaffe casualties were six machines.

A variety of weapons was tried out at this period against enemy bombers. One device was an airborne adaptation of the rocket-fired parachute and cable which was supposed to form a barrier to German bombers. Known as 'Mutton', this weapon consisted of a parachute with a bomb dangling at the end of 2,000 feet of piano wire.

The idea was to launch these in the path of an approaching enemy formation. The bomb would be brought up to explode near the aircraft—at least in theory.

No. 420 Flight was formed to use the equipment and on October 1st Flight Lieutenant Burke, the commanding officer, collected the first Harrow bomber equipped to use it from the Royal Aircraft Establishment, Farnborough.

Although several 'Mutton' sorties were flown it was difficult in practice to make effective use of the weapon.

October 2nd

Day High-flying and fighter sweeps on south-east London and Biggin Hill.

A crippled Me 109E, one undercarriage leg hanging down, descending into the sea off Folkestone Harbour in October. The Spitfire that shot it down circles above. An army officer jumped off the jetty and rescued the German pilot

Night London main target. Manchester, Usworth and Aberdeen also attacked.
Weather Brilliant blue skies during the day, turning to cloudy later.

The first warning came through at 8.30 a.m. when aircraft of Luftflotte 2 began to mass over Cap Gris Nez. Climbing to between 20,000 and 30,000 feet the German machines attacked Biggin Hill and south-east London from 9 a.m. until lunch-time. Seventeen formations, ranging from one aircraft to more than fifty, penetrated inland in a continuous stream. They were back in smaller numbers during the afternoon, a few of them penetrating as far as the centre of London. Eight of the day's raiders fell in combat to some of the 154 patrols sent up by Fighter Command. Altogether seventeen German aircraft were lost against only one British fighter.

Between 7.15 p.m. and 6.15 the next morning 180 bombers came over. More than 100 attacked London, dropping bombs on Willesden, Woolwich, Fenchurch Street, Rotherhithe, Stanmore and the districts near airfields like Northolt, Kenley, Walton, Hendon, Brooklands, Redhill, Eastchurch, Hornchurch and

Pilots of No. 303 (Polish) Squadron at Northolt in October 1940. Second from the left is Flight Lieutenant (later Group Captain) J. A. Kent commanding A flight. In the background is his Hurricane which bears the 'Kosciuszko' crest just below the aerial on the fuselage. A flight carried on the traditions of the Polish 111 Kosciuszko squadron while B flight did the same for 112 Salamander squadron.

The crest includes a Polish hat and thirteen stars and stripes for the original States of the U.S.A. Kosciuszko had been Washington's adjutant in the War of Independence and subsequently became Dictator of Poland. Thus it was that the Stars and Stripes flew to war in the skies over Britain long before December 7th, 1941

Duxford. Manchester, Usworth and Aberdeen were also hit. Thirty-three night fighters were scrambled during the night but they were unable to intercept.

October 3rd

Day Scattered raids on East Anglian and southern England targets.
Night London and suburbs attacked.
Weather Rain and drizzle in the Channel. Visibility in England reduced to 500 yards.

Routine patrols and reconnaissance flights off the east coast opened the action for the day. Later raiders coming singly or in pairs, mostly from Belgian and Dutch bases, attacked targets over a widespread area. These included Thameshaven, Cosford, Cambridge, Cardington, Bedford, Leamington, Worcester, Reading, Harrow and Tangmere. The weather was too bad to intercept successfully, or to protect a convoy in the Channel at 5.20 p.m.

One raider, however, reached the de Havilland works at Hatfield. At 50 feet altitude a Ju 88 of KG77 machine-gunned workers as they ran for the trenches and bounced four bombs into a sheet metal shop and the Technical School—killing 21 people and wounding 70. The 88 was hit by 40 mm. Bofors shells, 303 machine-gun bullets from an R.A.F. detachment and even rounds from a Hotchkiss manned by the Home Guard. The burning aircraft crashed at Hertingfordbury.

Low cloud during the night hampered the Luftwaffe but not enough to prevent sixty bombers getting through, for the most part singly, at 10,000 feet and penetrating the inner artillery zone. Bombs were dropped mainly in the suburbs, and at Feltham, Middlesex, the General Aircraft Company was hit. No R.A.F. aircraft were lost during 173 sorties but the Luftwaffe suffered nine casualties.

October 4th

Day Single raiders in stream on London and south-east.
Night London again main target, with Liverpool as subsidiary target.
Weather Mist, rain and poor visibility throughout the day. Fog at night.

Seelöwe was still very much in Hitler's mind, but he was reluctant to come to a decision despite Army and Navy recommendations to call it off altogether. Holding troops on the Channel coast 'under constant British air attack', they pointed out, 'led to continual casualties'.

Remarked the Italian Foreign Minister, Count Galeazzi Ciano, in his diary, after the Hitler-Mussolini meeting at the Brenner Pass on October 4th, 'there is

Pilots of No. 616 Squadron relax in the ready hut at Kirton-in-Lindsey on October 15th, 1940

no longer any talk about a landing in the British Isles'.

After two attacks on convoys at 9 a.m. German fighters and fighter-bombers flying singly for the most part headed for London in an almost continuous stream. Altogether sixty to seventy crossed the coast, and at 1 p.m. twelve penetrated the inner artillery zone to drop bombs on London. Canterbury, Folkestone, Hythe and Reigate were also hit. Later in the afternoon R.A.F. fighters made interceptions and brought down two Ju 88s, making a total of twelve for the day against three British machines lost.

To counteract the Luftwaffe's latest tactics Park issued new instructions:

HEIGHT OF FIGHTER PATROLS

1. With the prevailing cloudy skies and inaccurate heights given by the R.D.F. the group controllers' most difficult problem is to know the height of incoming enemy raids. Occasionally reconnaissance Spitfires from Hornchurch or Biggin Hill are able to sight and report the height and other particulars of enemy formations. Moreover the special fighter reconnaissance flight is now being formed at Gravesend (attached 66 Squadron) for the purpose of getting information about approaching enemy raids.

2. Because of the above-mentioned lack of height reports and the delay in the receipt of R.D.F. and Observer Corps reports at group plus longer time recently taken by squadrons to take off, pairs and wings of squadrons are meeting enemy formations above, before they get to height ordered by group.

3. Tip-and-run raids across Kent by Me 110s carrying bombs or small formations of long-range bombers escorted by fighters give such short notice that the group controller is sometimes compelled to detail even single fighter squadrons that happen to be in the air to intercept the enemy bombers before they attack aircraft factories, sector aerodromes, or other vital points such as the docks, Woolwich, etc. Normally, however, group controller has sufficient time to detail from one to three pairs (two to six squadrons) to intercept raids heading for bombing targets in the vicinity of London.

4. Whenever time permits I wish group controllers to get the readiness squadrons in company over sector aerodromes, Spitfires 25,000 feet, Hurricanes 20,000 feet, and wait until they report they are in good position before sending them to patrol lines or to intercept raids having a good track in fairly clear weather.

5. This does not mean that the controller is to allow raids reported as bombers to approach our sector aerodromes or other bombing targets unengaged because pairs or wings of squadrons have not reported they have reached the height ordered in the vicinity of sector aerodromes or other rendezvous.

6. I am sending a copy of this instruction to all sector commanders and controllers also squadron commanders in order that they may understand why their squadrons have sometimes to be sent off to intercept approaching bombers before they have reached the height originally ordered or perhaps have joined up with the other squadron or pair of squadrons of a wing. Our constant aim is to detail one or more pairs of squadrons against incoming bomb raids, but the warning received at group is sometimes not sufficient and our first and primary task is to intercept and break up bombers before they can deliver a bombing attack against aircraft factories, sector aerodromes, docks, etc.

7. Circumstances beyond the control of group or sector controllers sometimes demand that the squadrons engage

249

*Leader of the 'Big wig' protagonists, Squadron Leader
Bader is shown here with some of his pilots from
242 Squadron on October 4th, 1940. The other
photograph shows the whole of 242 Squadron airborne
from Coltishall*

A 19 Squadron Spitfire is refuelled from a petrol bowser at Duxford on October 9th, 1940

enemy bombers before they have gained height advantage and got comfortably set with the other squadrons detailed by group.

8. I wish the squadron commanders and sector controllers to know everything humanly possible is being done by group to increase the warning received of incoming enemy raids. Meanwhile squadrons can help by shortening the time of take-off, assembly and rendezvous with other squadrons to which they are detailed as pairs or wings.

It was Luftflotte 2's turn to mount the night raids on the 4th and between 8 and 9 p.m. over 100 raiders passed over Dieppe and Le Havre steering for London. The weather made night interception impossible and so the anti-aircraft guns were given permission to fire at unseen targets.

Despite fog and intermittent rain a further 200 machines crossed the coast heading for London later that night. One-third of the formation split from the main assembly and steered for Liverpool. Parachute mines were dropped on Woolwich and Enfield.

October 5th

Day Targets in Kent and Southampton attacked.
Night London and East Anglian aerodromes raided.
Weather Local showers in most districts. Bright periods. Winds light and variable.

Thirty raiders flying singly at 10,000–15,000 feet were plotted off the coast before 9 a.m. Half an hour later another raid began to boil up at Calais and by 10 a.m. two raids of twenty and fifteen bombers and fighters were tracked inland by the Observer Corps to West Malling and Detling airfields.

At 11 a.m. a forceful attack developed on Kent. Raids of 40, 30, 50, and 12 machines crossed the coast near Lympne and fanned out over southern England to attack Detling and Folkestone. The third attack came at 1 p.m. with a fighter sweep of twenty-five Me 109s which were followed by a wave of a further 100 machines, thirty of which carried bombs. Fifty aircraft reached the centre of London. Simultaneously two formations of fifty and thirty aircraft set course from Cherbourg to attack Southampton.

With no further need to go for bombers at all costs the Spitfires and Hurricanes were now free to fight directly with the Messerschmitts. The fighter-bombers, almost helpless with their awkward loads, usually let their bombs go the moment they were engaged. The fighters on the other hand took on the British machines in spirited fashion. There were bitter dog-fights, and in clear weather the people of London and the Home Counties watched the great swirls and streaks of vapour trailing across the pale blue of the autumn sky.

In the fourth attack at 3.30 p.m. on Kent and East Sussex a mixed force of fifty bombers and fighters from Luftflotte 3 flew in over Ashford and Tonbridge. They were met by Spitfires and Hurricanes which split them up and drove them off. Hostile operations ended with an attack in the Selsey/Southampton area at 5 p.m. by two formations of thirty aircraft each, mainly Me 110s. By sunset Fighter Command had flown 1,175 sorties and lost nine aircraft. Nine German planes were also destroyed.

Flying under cover of darkness, cloud and rain, over 200 bombers went for south London and East Anglian aerodromes during the night. Fires flared up in the London docks and the East End districts.

*The view from one of Winston Churchill's windows
at No. 10 Downing Street, on the morning of October
18th after single night raiders had penetrated to the
heart of London. The wrecked building was part of
the Treasury offices.*

*A full squadron turn-out by Hurricanes of No. 85
Squadron on October 23rd, 1940*

Day Single raiders or small formations attacked London and East Anglia.
Night Very quiet.
Weather Dull with continuous rain all day.

Early in the morning a large raid formed up across the Straits, but whatever the Luftwaffe's original intention the weather did not lend itself to serious business. Only single raiders and small formations dashed to the London airfields in the morning.

An entry in Biggin Hill's operations book recorded 'a low-flying attack by single enemy bomber. Three barrack blocks destroyed. No. 1 parachute and cable post came into action, and hit an enemy aircraft, but failed to bring it down. One aircraft was damaged, slight damage to the aerodrome surface'.

By midday there were again signs of a big concentration at Cap Gris Nez. This resolved into smaller units, some of which attacked Middle Wallop with high-explosive and oil-bombs. Northolt and Uxbridge were also targets for small formations.

An intercepted German wireless message made it clear, however, that Luftwaffe operations were more or less cancelled for the day owing to the continuous rain and low cloud. In spite of German tactics and the weather the R.A.F. lost one plane only. German losses were six aircraft.

Considering the weather German bombing was remarkably accurate that night. A powder factory was hit at Waltham Abbey, Hertfordshire, and de Havilland's aircraft works had a narrow escape. Disturbed by no more than seven bombers, however, Londoners slept well.

253

A typical anti-aircraft gun site during the Battle. These mobile 3.7 inch guns are shown on October 23rd 1940. In the background flies a barrage balloon. As air attack over Britain intensified in the summer months, the accuracy of AA increased and the Luftwaffe developed considerable respect for British guns

October 7th

Day Mixed force of bombers and fighters attacked Yeovil.
Night Main targets London and Merseyside, otherwise raids scattered from Harwich to Newcastle and the Firth of Forth.
Weather Occasional showers. Visibility fair. Variable cloud.

In the morning 127 German planes were engaged by eighteen No. 11 Group squadrons over Kent and Sussex.

The attack resumed at 12.30 when Luftflotte 2 again sent over a series of small waves from Calais to Dover. More than 150 Me 109s flew in and No. 11 Group had to call upon No. 12 Group to stand by. For the third attack at 3.30 p.m. the Luftwaffe again used Me 109s and sent in fifty via Dymchurch.

These machines made for Biggin Hill and London. At the same time a mixed force of Ju 88s, Me 109s and Me 110s from Cherbourg in formations stepped up to 26,000 feet delivered an attack with eighty high-explosive and six oil-bombs on the Westland air-craft works at Yeovil.

Between 5 and 9 p.m. seven raids were plotted from Cherbourg to Swansea, eleven from Le Havre to Selsey Bill, twenty-seven from Dieppe to Beachy Head, two from Cap Gris Nez to Dungeness, twenty-six from Holland to Harwich, Newcastle and Spurn Head, and seven from Denmark to the Firth of Forth. Hostile efforts were mainly concentrated on London and Merseyside although bombs on Hatfield damaged three Lysanders belonging to No. 239 Squadron, an aircraft was destroyed at Ford and other bombs fell on West-hampnett, Tangmere, Eastleigh and Lee-on-Solent. Bomber Command countered the flow of traffic with a raid of 147 bombers on the German capital and the invasion ports.

In Berlin, meanwhile, Göring put a new five-point plan for the war against Britain. In it he frankly admitted that the demoralisation of London and the provinces was one aim and he described the air operations against the islands as 'merely an initial phase'.

The plan he outlined demanded:

A Heinkel 111 H brought down over Britain and put back into flying condition by the R.A.F. The aircraft was from KG 26 'Löwen–Geschwader'

1 Absolute control of the Channel and the English coastal areas.
2 Progressive and complete annihilation of London, with all its military objectives and industrial production.
3 A steady paralysing of Britain's technical, commercial, industrial and civil life.
4 Demoralisation of the civil population of London and its provinces.
5 Progressive weakening of Britain's forces.

Far from being progressively weakened, the R.A.F. was fighting back with increased strength. On the 7th Fighter Command flew 825 sorties and lost 17 planes to the Luftwaffe's 21 one of which was an He 115 seaplane.

Examination of eight Me 109s shot down on the 7th revealed that they were from LG2 and each carried a 250 kg. bomb. They were operating in small formations of 6–18 aircraft and flying 2–3 sorties per day.

October 8th

Day London.
Night Widespread raids on London and the suburbs.
Weather Cloudy in the south-east but fair. Winds high.

After the usual morning patrols and reconnaissance flights, two formations of fifty and 100 aircraft penetrated inland from Dymchurch and approached London via Kenley and Biggin Hill at 8.30 a.m. Bombs fell on Charing Cross Underground Station, Horse Guards Parade, the War Office and the Air Ministry's Adastral House. Tower Bridge was also hit and so was the B.B.C.'s Bush House. Two hours later a second attack with thirty aircraft developed on London. An hour later another twenty attacked and at 12.30 two formations of twelve took up where the others left off. Fighter Command scrambled 639 sorties and lost four machines. Fourteen German aircraft were destroyed.

From Uxbridge came another order from Park:

When a Spitfire squadron is ordered to readiness patrol on the Maidstone line its function is to cover the area Biggin Hill–Maidstone–Gravesend, while the other squadrons are gaining their height, and protect them from the enemy fighter screen. The form of attack which should be adopted on the high enemy fighters is to dive repeatedly on them and climb up again each time to regain height.

The squadron is not to be ordered to intercept a raid during the early stages of the engagement, but the sector controller must keep the squadron commander informed as to the height and direction of approaching raids.

The object of ordering the squadron to patrol at 15,000 feet while waiting on the patrol line for raids to come inland is to conserve oxygen and to keep the pilots at a comfortable height. Pilots must watch this point most carefully so that they have ample in hand when they are subsequently ordered to 30,000

Ju 88 A-4 dive bombers of KG 51. The aircraft in the foreground and in the distance have had swastika, cross and code markings painted out in black for night operations. It is curious that wing crosses have been retained.

feet which is to be done immediately enemy raids appear to be about to cross our coast.

When other squadrons have gained their height and the course of the engagement is clear, the group controller will take a suitable opportunity to put this Spitfire squadron on to enemy raids where its height can be used to advantage.

It was a rough and windy night but aircraft from Cherbourg, Le Havre, Calais and Holland converged on Britain. Over 100 raids were entered in the Fighter Command controller's log which shows that the stream did not cease until four o'clock the next morning. The main objectives were again London and the suburbs, and as on previous nights anti-aircraft batteries were given permission to fire at unseen targets. A formidable barrage was put up.

October 9th

Day London and airfields attacked.
Night Heavy raid on London.
Weather Cloudy in Channel with rain in northern France and the Straits. Winds high. Squalls.

Targets in Kent and London were again on the Luft-waffe's agenda and from 11 a.m. until 1.15 p.m. 120 Me 109s flew in. By 2.20 p.m. they had returned in

greater numbers.

Between 160 and 180 aircraft were involved and the damage they did to some of the airfields was as serious as that inflicted during August and September.

Over 400 Hurricane and Spitfire sorties were flown. Nine German planes were destroyed for the loss of one British fighter.

In Berlin, meanwhile, Göring had consulted the calendar. As his Luftflotten were preparing for their night raids on Britain he issued directives for heavy attacks on London during the next full moon. The moon was then in its first quarter, which meant London could expect some exceptionally noisy nights from about October 15th.

October 10th

Day Hostile operations over east Kent, London suburbs and Weymouth.
Night London, Liverpool, Manchester and fifteen airfields also attacked.
Weather Showery with bright intervals. Haze in the Thames Estuary and East Anglia.

Having failed to get through *en masse* the Luftwaffe was now infiltrating in continuous streams. These tactics were difficult to combat and the decrease in the rate of German loss was worrying Fighter Command.

In the course of 754 sorties the R.A.F. lost five machines, against the Luftwaffe's four.

Manchester, London and Liverpool were again assailed, and following up on Göring's directive, fifteen R.A.F. airfields were bombed.

Because of bomber losses the Luftwaffe turned to fighter bombers for the assault. Initially standard Me 109s were converted to carry bombs as 109E-4/B, but later aircraft were delivered from the factory fully equipped as fighter bombers. On this 109E-4/B the bomb is just being attached to the belly rack

October 11th

Day Targets in Kent, Sussex and Weymouth attacked.
Night Main objectives London, Liverpool, Manchester and Tyne and Tees.
Weather Mainly fair apart from showers chiefly in coastal areas. Mist in Straits and Estuary early, clearing later. Fog developed in the night.

Four fighter sweeps over Kent and Sussex and two over Weymouth by Me 109s flying at heights of up to 33,000 feet occupied the southern sector fighters throughout the day.

At 10 a.m. 100 Me 109s assembled at Cap Gris Nez and crossed the coast at Hastings. They attacked Folkestone, Deal, Canterbury and Ashford. An hour later another stream went for Biggin Hill and Kenley. At 2.15 p.m. about 100 aircraft reached Southend and by 4 p.m. a similar number penetrated as far as Maidstone and Tonbridge.

No. 611 West Lancashire Squadron, based at Ternhill, Shropshire, had a lively evening. Their terse combat report tells the story.

'A' Flight took off from Ternhill at 17.30 hrs. to patrol Anglesey. At about 18.20 hrs. at 17,000 feet, three enemy aircraft, Do 17s, were sighted about twelve miles away approaching from the south-west. Yellow section attacked out of sun, meeting fire from enemy leader. E/A broke formation and were attacked by both sections. Yellow leader opened fire at 15 degrees deflection and hit E/A's starboard engine and return fire ceased. Yellow 3 followed with No. 3 and then No. 1 attack, and Yellow 1 from above attacked causing E/A to lose height but return fire had recommenced.

Yellow 1 saw E/A jettison five bombs into the sea and then crash into the water. Yellow 3 received an explosive bullet or shell in the bottom of his cockpit, making his airspeed indicator unserviceable.

Red section carried out two No. 1 attacks on another E/A whose starboard engine stopped, and he finally crashed in the hills south of Caernarvon. They then attacked E/A leader and on the third attack saw two crew bale out and both engines on fire. Aircraft glided down and crashed in flames near Capel Curig.

Altogether seven German aircraft were destroyed. Fighter Command squadrons, which flew 949 sorties, lost nine machines, but only three pilots. Six pilots were wounded.

October 12th

Day London and suburbs again main target.
Night Fairly quiet but National Gallery damaged.
Weather Widespread mist and fog during the day, clearing with light winds off the North Sea.

The point had now been reached where Hitler had to decide on his next course of action. It was evident towards the end of September that Seelöwe could not be accomplished before the end of the year. Bomber

Command had sunk 214 barges and twenty-one transports of the invasion fleet which in any case had been forced to disperse. He was thus compelled in October to choose between stopping this dispersal or postponing the whole project indefinitely.

As the bombs fell on Biggin Hill, Chatham and Piccadilly, Keitel circulated Hitler's decision:

The Führer [he wrote] has decided that from now until the spring, preparations for Sealion shall be continued solely for the purpose of maintaining political and military pressure on England.

Should the Invasion be reconsidered in the spring or early summer of 1941, orders for a renewal of operational readiness will be issued later. In the meantime military conditions for a later invasion are to be improved.

The significance of this memorandum was not to be realised at the War Office, damaged at nine o'clock that evening by a direct hit, nor at Bentley Priory, until very much later. Hitler had admitted defeat nineteen days before the Battle of Britain officially came to a close.

Despite mist and fog, October 12th was a day of almost uninterrupted German activity the R.A.F. did not find easy to counter. Raids on London and the south-east started at 8.45 a.m. and went on until late afternoon.

Met in force by the British, who flew 797 sorties, the Germans had difficulty reaching their objectives. They lost eleven planes. British aircraft destroyed numbered ten.

October 13th

Day Targets in London and Kent attacked.
Night London, Bristol, Wales, Liverpool, Birmingham and Birkenhead raided.
Weather Almost cloudless but foggy early. Fine in the morning. Fair at midday, clouding over later.

Although Hitler had unofficially conceded victory to Fighter Command, Park, still striving to work out effective counter-measures to the Germans' high-flying tactics, could certainly not have agreed that the Luftwaffe was defeated. The Germans had simply been prevented from achieving their objectives but they were still taking every opportunity to harass the R.A.F.

The first threats on this day were small and they developed off the east coast where a convoy was attacked. London was then selected for the next three raids which began at 12.30 a.m. when a force of fifty Me 109s reached Woolwich. An hour later a slightly larger force fanned out over Kent and made its way to the capital. The third formation of twenty-five Me 109s got to the centre of London at 4 p.m. in spite of spirited opposition.

The all-clear had not long sounded when 100 night raiders flew in. Assisted by a waxing moon they were better placed to find their targets, including Stanmore, where a bomb undoubtedly intended for the heart of Britain's air defence organisation landed plumb in the middle of the railway station.

About thirty bombers were tracked by the Observer Corps to Bristol, Wales, Liverpool, Birmingham and Birkenhead; also to Dundee.

The moon did not prove to be much of an asset to the

twenty-two night fighters scrambled to intercept the raiders. They were singularly unsuccessful, but they brought the number of sorties for the day to 591. German planes destroyed totalled five. The British lost two.

October 14th

Day Widespread small attacks.
Night Widespread and serious damage in London. Coventry also damaged.
Weather Occasional rain or drizzle spreading to the south-east. Rain in the Channel, misty in the Straits and the Estuary. Cloudy in the North Sea.

It was 10.15 a.m. before the Germans showed signs of serious business. Fifty small raids were then picked up heading for the south-east and the south midlands. Some passed over north London aerodromes, including North Weald, which was by now showing the effects of nearly 400 accurately aimed bombs. Hardly a building had escaped so that dispersal and improvisation were necessary to keep the four squadrons going.

More than 100 patrols involving 272 fighters were flown. They neither scored nor lost. Three German aircraft were destroyed, nevertheless, in accidents.

Although the East End of London bore the main burden of the early German attacks, it was not long before the West End was sharing its bombing experiences with the poorer sections of the capital.

From the clear moonlight skies of October 14th there rained a load of high explosives and incendiaries which caused widespread and serious damage to many parts of the city. More than 220 members of the Conservative Carlton Club were in the building when it was destroyed by a direct hit. By some miracle they all crawled out from beneath the rubble unhurt. A Labour M.P. remarked rather cynically: 'The devil looks after his own'.

Other Londoners were not so lucky. Five hundred were killed and 2,000 seriously injured. This was a foretaste of even worse things to come and marked the beginning of the blitz which is outside the scope of this book.

October 15th

Day Hostile elements penetrate to London targets and targets in Kent and the Estuary.
Night Unusually heavy attack on London and Birmingham.
Weather Fair but cloudy in the Straits. Winds southerly and variable. Moonlit night.

Sector controllers on the early shift had hardly had time to read Park's latest instructions when the first signs of trouble showed on the radar screens as a build-up over Cap Gris Nez. It soon faded and for an hour they were able to assimilate and discuss the orders their group commander had penned the previous day.

Said Park:

Owing to the very short warning given nowadays by the R.D.F. stations, enemy fighter formations (some carrying bombs) can be over London within twenty minutes of the first R.D.F. plot, and have on occasion dropped bombs on south-east London seventeen minutes after the first R.D.F. plots.

By day and night the attack went on with Luftflotte 3 being concentrated on British cities during the hours of darkness. Here a Heinkel 111 on a French airfield prepares for take-off for a British target.

Under these circumstances, the only squadrons that can intercept the enemy fighters before they reach London or sector aerodromes are the squadrons in the air on readiness patrol, or remaining in the air after an attack, plus one or two squadrons at stand-by at sectors on the east and south-east of London.

In these circumstances it is vitally important for the group controllers, also sector controllers, to keep clearly in mind the time taken for squadrons and other formations to climb from ground level to operating height. The following times are those for a good average squadron of the types stated:

(a) Spitfire (Mark 1)	13 minutes to 20,000 feet.	
	18 minutes to 25,000 feet.	
	27 minutes to 30,000 feet.	
(b) Hurricane (Mark 1)	16 minutes to 20,000 feet.	
	21 minutes to 25,000 feet.	

Pairs: The rate of climb for a pair of squadrons in company will be 10 per cent to 12 per cent greater than the time given above.

Wings: The rate of climb of wings of three squadrons is between 15 per cent and 18 per cent greater than the times given above.

Rendezvous:
In view of the above, controllers will see the importance of ordering pairs or wings to rendezvous over a point at operating height in order that they climb quickly, singly, and not hold one another back by trying to climb in an unwieldy mass. Bitter experience has proved time and again that it is better

to intercept the enemy with one squadron above him than by a whole wing crawling up below, probably after the enemy has dropped his bombs.

At 9 p.m. thirty Messerschmitts were heading for Hornchurch and central London. They hit Waterloo Station and blocked all but two of the lines. At 9.45 another fifty went for the city and at 11.20 more came in to attack points in Kent and the Estuary. By 12.20 a.m. 110 were plotted in the Straits but these did not mature into a full-scale attack.

At 6.30 p.m. Göring's plans to use the full moon were developing. The attack on London was heavy and the destruction of two bombers by night fighters did little to compensate for the serious and widespread damage inflicted on the city. Train services were stopped at the five main stations. Traffic from others was cut by more than two-thirds. The city's Underground railway system was severed at five places. Roads were blocked throughout the city and a reservoir, three gasworks, two power stations and three important docks were hit. There were 900 fires in London that night. Over 400 people were killed and more than 800 badly wounded.

In the day and night operations of Fighter Command 643 sorties were flown against the Luftwaffe, whose units lost fourteen machines—one less than the number lost by the R.A.F.

October 16th

Day Quiet
Night Limited attack on London by single raiders.
Weather Fog widespread in Germany and France. Warm front lying the length of French coast. Wet and misty night.

Fog kept all but the more confident and competent Luftwaffe pilots on the ground. Those who flew struck out for Kent and the west of England. Seven caught by the R.A.F., who flew 275 sorties, failed to return. Six were destroyed in accidents. British losses numbered one plane.

It was not much better during the evening but at least 200 bomber crews chanced the mist and drizzle to raid the British Isles. R.A.F. bombers returning from Italy met with difficulties. Eight Whitleys crashed and a Czech-crewed Wellington came down on the Fight Command headquarters' tennis court.

October 17th

Day Fighter-bomber attacks on Kent and London.
Night Targets in No. 11 Group area, Liverpool and Birmingham.
Weather Bright intervals. Local showers.

Limited visibility did much to mask the Luftwaffe whose raids started soon after breakfast. Ninety Me 109s and Me 110s raided Margate, Broadstairs and Stanmore.

They were back after lunch and throughout the afternoon appeared in large and small concentrations or in streams, feinting, weaving, splitting up and then rejoining, using cloud to maximum effect, employing every ruse to elude and confuse the defences.

At one of London's key arteries, Waterloo Station, a bomb smashed all automatic signalling and signal telephones. Fourteen inexperienced station staff and a handful of soldiers somehow kept trains moving using flags.

British fighters enjoyed a moderate success. They destroyed five enemy aircraft and lost three of their own in combat. Luftwaffe losses for the day totalled fifteen.

The speed and height at which the Messerschmitts flew continued to trouble Park, and in yet another attempt to counter their activities he issued these instructions:

ENGAGEMENT OF HIGH FIGHTER RAIDS

The general plan is to get one or two Spitfire squadrons to engage enemy fighters from above about mid-Kent, in order to cover other Spitfire and Hurricane squadrons whilst climbing to operating height at back patrol lines east and south of London.

Preparation

Whenever the cloud conditions are favourable for high raids by fighters the following preparations will be made:

(1) *Reconnaissance Aircraft:* One or two reconnaissance aircraft to be kept on patrol near the Kentish coast, height depending on cloud layers.

(2) *Readiness Patrol:* A patrol by one or two squadrons to be maintained on Maidstone line at 15,000 feet, between 0800 hours and 1800 hours.

(3) *Stand-by Squadron:* One squadron at sector providing patrol at (2) to be standing-by during the peak periods—breakfast, noon and early tea-time.

(4) *London and Debden Squadrons:* State of readiness of Hurricane squadrons to be *advanced state* whenever cloud conditions are suitable for very high fighter raids.

Attack

Immediately enemy formations are plotted over the French coast or Dover Straits, the following action will be initiated:

(1) *Reconnaissance Aircraft:* Despatched to the area enemy raids are plotted, to locate, shadow and report.

(2) *Readiness Patrol:* Ordered to climb to 30,000 on the Maidstone patrol line to cover other squadrons whilst climbing over base patrol lines.

(3) *Stand-by Squadrons:* Despatched to operating height over base, and then to join the readiness squadrons at 30,000 feet.

(4) *Readiness Squadrons:* Despatched to rendezvous over base at 20,000 to 27,000 feet, and when assembled, detailed to raids or forward patrol lines.

(5) *Squadrons at Available, Spitfires:* To be brought to readiness, and if necessary despatched to assemble in pairs on back patrol lines at 25,000 to 30,000 feet, and then detailed to raids.

(6) *Squadrons at Available, Hurricanes:* Brought to readiness, and if there is a second or third wave, assembled in pairs over back patrol lines so as to protect sector aerodromes and London area whilst climbing.

(7) *Hurricane Squadrons from Tangmere and Debden:* Despatch in wings or pairs at 20,000 to 27,000 feet according to time and weather conditions, of one of the following purposes:

    (a) To reinforce London sectors if there is a second or third wave of enemy raids;

    (b) To protect sector aerodromes and London area whilst the earlier squadrons are refuelling.

(8) *Close Defence of Important Bombing Objectives:* If enemy raids are approaching aircraft factories, London area, sector aerodromes, etc., single Hurricane squadrons that have not been included in pairs or wings should be detailed to protective patrols between 15,000 and 18,000 feet depending on clouds.

With recollections of the Luftwaffe's August tactics, Park felt the Germans might renew their massed bomber raids. Accordingly he ordered the engagement of the enemy's

high fighter screen with Spitfire squadrons from Hornchurch and Biggin Hill half-way between London and the coast, and so enable Hurrican squadrons from North Weald, Kenley and Northolt to attack bomber formations plus close escort before they reach the line of fighter aerodromes east and south of London.

The squadrons from Debden and Tangmere (if disengaged) to be despatched and employed in wings or pairs so as to form a screen east and south-east of London to intercept third or fourth wave coming inland, also the retreating earlier waves.

Spitfire Squadrons:

Assembled at height in pairs on the back patrol lines, then detailed to engage high fighter screen at 30,000 feet.

Role: To protect pairs or wings of Hurricane squadrons whilst climbing up, also while attacking bombers plus escort. If the high fighter screen withdraws to the coast a proportion of the Spitfires may be detailed to attack the escorts to incoming bomb raids.

Hurricane Squadrons:

Squadrons at readiness to be despatched in pairs to back patrol lines covering line of aerodromes. Immediately pairs have reached operating height, detail to bomb raids or to forward patrol lines under Spitfires. Squadrons at available to be brought to readiness and assembled in pairs at operating height on back patrol lines covering sector aerodromes, and detailed to second wave of bomb raids.

Whilst gaining height the latter squadrons may have to be

Luftwaffe personnel show members of the Regia Aeronautica over a German airfield in Belgium. The subject of interest is a collection of bullet holes made by the R.A.F. in a Heinkel III. The Italian Air Force's participation in the Battle of Britain was extremely brief and unfortunately not very effective

detailed to split raids by bombers that attempt to attack vital points on the flank of the mass of bombers plus escort.

Hurricane Squadrons from Flank Sectors (Debden, Tangmere, and possibly Northolt):

Despatch in pairs or wings, according to clouds, to patrol mid-Kent patrol lines at 20,000 to 25,000 feet to engage:

    (i) Third or fourth wave attacks of bombers plus escort;
    (ii) Retreating bomb raids of first and second waves;
    (iii) To protect fighter aerodromes whilst the earlier Hurricane and Spitfire squadrons are refuelling.

Reinforcements from other Groups:

Immediately the enemy numbers appear to be more than 150, request two to three squadrons to cover the northern approaches to London, or the south-western group of vital points near London, as directed in Controllers' Instructions No. 7, dated August 27th, 1940.

In these orders can be seen the flexibility of mind displayed by Park. He was sometimes surprised by German tactics, but they never caught him off balance. He was equal to every challenge.

October 18th

Day Relatively quiet.
Night Raids on a reduced scale.

Weather Fog in Straits of Dover and Estuary; also in North Sea. Visibility poor.

After a fairly busy night the morning was unusually quiet. Between lunch and tea thirty-five raids were counted flying high over East Anglia. Forty-five R.A.F. fighter patrols were flown. Some intercepted and shot down four Luftwaffe machines. Total German losses were fifteen. The British lost four.

Night raids were on a reduced scale also, and by 1.45 a.m. the 160 bombers counted had returned home.

It is clear from an address to his aircrews that Göring did not realise what little impression his night bombers were making on British morale.

In the past few days and nights [he said] you have caused the British world enemy disastrous losses by your uninterrupted destructive blows. Your indefatigable, courageous attacks on the heart of the British Empire, the City of London, with its eight and a half million inhabitants, have reduced British plutocracy to fear and terror. The losses which you have inflicted on the much-vaunted Royal Air Force in determined fighter engagements are irreplaceable.

October 19th

Day Isolated patrols and reconnaissance.
Night London, Liverpool, midlands and Bristol main targets.
Weather Cloudy in Channel, mist in northern France clearing later.

Swirling mists gave the Germans an easy morning but where possible they mounted some patrols. One bomber sent out was brought down over Kent.

At lunchtime it began to clear and by 2 p.m. fourteen

October was the month when the attack in daylight changed over largely to fighter-bomber attacks. One of the aircraft employed was the Me 110 with a belly bomb rack. Here an Me 110 of III/ZG 26 'Horst Wessel' is being loaded with a bomb prior to a raid on southern England

Me 109s had assembled over the Pas de Calais for a sweep on England. They steered for London unopposed but dropped no bombs. Later, a dog-fight over Beachy Head developed and two British fighters were shot down, bringing Fighter Command's losses to five for the day. Two Germans failed to return home.

October 20th

Day Fighter-bomber raids on south-east and London.
Night Heavy attacks on London and industrial centres in the midlands.
Weather Mainly cloudy in most districts. Channel and Straits cloudy, Hazy.

All was quiet until 9.35 a.m. when the first of five Messerschmitt waves were plotted on R.D.F. In the afternoon high-flying raiders again penetrated inland.

Squadrons of Fighter Command flew 475 sorties and lost four of their machines. German losses were fourteen aircraft.

Nearly 300 bombers gave London a bad night. Traffic was dislocated by severe damage to the railways.

In Coventry the Armstrong-Siddeley and Singer Motor Works were hit.

Eleven night-fighter sorties were flown, but they were not successful. Dowding reported that the Beaufighter squadrons were having trouble with their airborne interception radar equipment and their aircraft.

Quoting the case of No. 219 Squadron, Dowding said that at 4 p.m. on October 19th the unit had four Beaufighters ready for night operations. By dusk they were all unserviceable.

Although there was not a single item for which a cure would not be found, it was the aggregation of defects which hindered rapid progress.

What depressed Dowding was that the Germans could fly and bomb with considerable accuracy in weather which prevented British fighters leaving the ground.

Fighter Command's task, he said, would not be finished until 'we can locate, pursue and shoot down the enemy in cloud by day and by night'. The A.I. had to become a gunsight. They had a long way to go before approaching this ideal, but nothing less would suffice for the defence of the country.

Every night Dowding spent watching attempts at interception strengthened his conviction that haphazard methods would never succeed in producing more than an occasional fortunate encounter and that night interception depended on the laborious development of a system, the defects of which would have to be eliminated by means of practical trials and thoughtful analysis of the results.

While the Battle of Britain dragged on, the weapons of reprisal were being forged. The first squadron of four-engined Stirling bombers was in formation by September and trials were advanced with the Manchester and Halifax long-range bombers. One of the most potent weapons of the air war, the Mosquito, was nearing the flight test stage in an imitation barn at Salisbury Hall, five miles west of Hatfield. The picture shows the prototype de Havilland Mosquito under construction in October 1940. This prototype first flew on November 25th, 1940

October 21st

Day Sporadic raids on capital, Liverpool and West Country.
Night London, Wolverhampton, Coventry, Birmingham and Liverpool main targets.
Weather Mainly cloudy with fog and intermittent rain. Visibility poor.

Taking advantage of the overcast, single aircraft and small formations of bombers despatched by Luftflotten 2 and 3 reached widely separated targets in England.

Between 11 a.m. and 1 p.m. the number of raids increased. About sixty machines flying singly flew in from the Continent and dropped bombs on London and the suburbs. About fifteen were detected going to the West Country.

The weather clearly put the British at a disadvantage and in the course of the day Fighter Command squadrons flew only 275 sorties. They lost no aircraft whereas six German planes were destroyed. One of these, a Ju 88 which had been posing as a Blenheim and machine-gunning the airfield at Old Sarum, Hampshire, from a height of about fifty feet, was shot down by Flight Lieutenant F. J. Howell and Pilot Officer S. J. Hill.

Howell dived to decide what it was [says the No. 609 Squadron record book] and even after making sure that it was a Ju 88 with a big cross, was surprised to see the rear gunner signalling with smoke cartridges. Both pilots attacked in turn and after an unusual chase above and below the tree-tops the enemy aircraft hit the ground and blew up near Lymington.

Fog and intermittent rain did not hinder the Luftwaffe during the night. London, the midlands and Liverpool were raided. Bombs on the south-east coast temporarily affected several radar stations.

October 22nd

Day Quiet morning and afternoon.
Night London, Coventry and Liverpool main targets.
Weather Widespread fog in the south, clearing to rain later. Visibility poor.

With No. 12 Group now receiving the same indications of hostile activity as No. 11 Group, it must have been galling for the Duxford Wing to be grounded by a thick fog which closed all but Tangmere, Kenley and Biggin Hill and the airfields of No. 10 Group.

The morning was therefore quiet with the Luftwaffe content to despatch a few small fighter-bomber raids. At 2 p.m., however, a big formation began to form up over north-east France and three raids totalling thirty-six aircraft were plotted. The expected raid on London

October 5th, 1940; children settle down to sleep on the platform of a London Underground station. Every night thousands of people sought shelter in this way and in the mornings climbed blinking into the daylight to resume their normal lives; many found their homes destroyed

did not materialise, but a convoy off Dover and two in the Estuary were unsuccessfully attacked.

At 4 p.m. four small raids of about thirty-three machines were plotted flying high. Convoy 'Fruit' off Dover called for help and Uxbridge diverted two squadrons to cover it. Six other squadrons intercepted the main German formation and a dog-fight developed over Dungeness.

The Luftwaffe lost eleven aircraft—four in combat, the rest in operational accidents. Fighter Command lost six planes.

Poor weather limited night operations, but Coventry, Liverpool and London were raided.

October 23rd

Day Mainly reconnaissance.
Night London and Glasgow raided. Minelaying off Yorkshire coast.
Weather Low cloud and drizzle. Visibility poor.

For Fighter Command this was the quietest day of the Battle of Britain. Hampered by the weather, the squadrons flew ninety sorties. They lost six planes, however. The Germans, who made some minor raids on London, the midlands and the Thames estuary, lost four machines.

London Bridge, St. Pancras Station, Victoria Docks, East Ham and Watford were hit by night raiders. In the north Glasgow was bombed by Stavanger-based aircraft. One fouled a balloon cable and crashed into the sea.

October 24th

Day Very quiet.
Night London and Birmingham main targets.
Weather Overcast and hazy in Channel, clearing to starlit sky at night.

Apart from a few reconnaissance patrols, the morning was quiet. A single raider crossed the coast at Southwold, Suffolk, and penetrated as far as the midlands. It was shot down at St. Neots, Huntingdonshire, on its return flight.

During the afternoon nuisance raids over the southeast and East Anglia kept British pilots on the alert. They flew 476 sorties without loss and shot down two hostile aircraft. The Germans, nevertheless, lost eight operational machines.

Nearly a month had now elapsed since Park and Leigh-Mallory had clashed over their respective tactics. But Dowding had been so preoccupied that he had been able to do little about the controversy. The lull on the 24th gave him an opportunity to pen a memorandum.

In it he asked Park to give Leigh-Mallory as much notice as possible of a 'probable intention to call for assistance', and warned Leigh-Mallory that Park would seldom be able to tell whether he needed help until preliminary symptoms indicated the manner in which an attack would develop. 'It may often happen,' said

The railway bridge at Blackfriars with wrecked trams and other vehicles. The picture was taken on the morning of October 25th and the cameraman himself narrowly missed injury as the bomb burst

Dowding to his group commanders, 'that the first raid had been met in strength by No. 11 Group and that the assistance of No. 12 Group is required when it is seen that further raids are building up over the Straits of Dover.'

Park, he continued, had to remember Leigh-Mallory's requirements with regard to warning; even if there were doubts about the need for help, Dowding asked that warning should be given to enable No. 12 Group to bring units to readiness at stand-by.

Leigh-Mallory, he continued, should not send less reinforcements than asked for if he is in a position to meet the requirements, but he may send more at his discretion.

'It may be imperatively necessary,' Dowding went on, 'that No. 12 Group shall keep No. 11 Group informed of the position of his formations which should not normally penetrate beyond the range of R/T control.'

To save time communications between groups were to be direct. Only in cases of inability to comply with a request for reinforcements, or a difference of opinion, was the channel of communication to be through Fighter Command's operations room, concluded the commander-in-chief.

London was attacked again during the night. About fifty machines were over the capital. Seventy other bombers were detected heading for widely separated targets, including Birmingham.

Only one successful interception was made—by an A.I. equipped Beaufighter of No. 219 Squadron off Beachy Head. The pilot reported damaging the enemy plane.

October 25th

Day Fighter-bomber raids on Kent and London.
Night Italian Air Force raids Harwich.
Weather Fair but overcast.

How far the Luftwaffe succeeded in reducing business and industrial output cannot be calculated. Suffice it to say that the Germans certainly succeeded in disrupting the normal industrial life of the country more often than most Britons would care to reckon.

One thing they did not succeed in doing, however, was to undermine morale. After each raid, whatever the district hit and whatever the suffering, the inhabitants cheered the Civil Defence forces, went on planting flowers round their Anderson air raid shelters and shouting defiance at Hitler and the German Air Force in the fruitiest of Cockney terms. And so they continued as on this day a sprinkling of Do 17s surrounded by fighters renewed the Luftwaffe's assault on the capital.

Signs of activity showed on the radar screens as the

first business commuters were disgorging from London's deepest shelters—the Underground railway stations. High over Kent they flew, only to be dispersed by Hurricanes and Spitfires, several of them newer and more powerful than those which had borne the brunt of the earlier battles.

Kent took the full force of the bombs released indiscriminately as the R.A.F. dived on the German bombers and fighters, although London came in for a share.

Raids continued throughout the day, during which 809 Fighter Command sorties were flown. Twenty German machines were destroyed. Ten R.A.F. machines were lost.

In Belgium, meanwhile, an excited band of Italians of the Reggia Aeronautica's Corpo Aereo Italiano prepared for their first direct action against Britain. They were there more as a political gesture than as a serious military effort, and had been despatched by Mussolini as a reply to the embarrassing raids Bomber Command were flying against industrial targets in northern Italy.

The two Fiat BR.20 bomber units, Nos. 13 and 43 Stormos, were allocated the bases of Moelsbroek and Chievres. No. 18 Gruppo with Fiat CR.42 biplane fighters went to Moldegchen and No. 20 Gruppo with Fiat G.50 fighters was sent to Usel. A fifth unit, No. 172 Squadrillia, equipped with CZ.1007 Bis aircraft was allocated Chievres.

On this October Friday 16 BR.20s were despatched to bomb Harwich. One of them crashed on take-off and two were abandoned over the sea after running out of fuel.

According to Milch, Mussolini's contingent was more of a liability than an asset. The men themselves were not to blame. They were excellent pilots, but they had not been trained to fight.

That their presence was unheralded is understandable. They were indistinguishable from the streams of German night bombers that crossed into Britain from bases in France, the Low Countries and Scandinavia.

October 26th

Day Fighter-bomber raids on London and Kent.
Night Targets in London, the midlands, Manchester and Liverpool.
Weather Cloudy with local showers chiefly in the north and east. Bright intervals in the west. Channel hazy. Cool.

The whole of London was now under the lash of Göring's night blitz and as the German News Agency put it inadvertently at the time: 'Bombs fell all over the place.' The *New York Herald Tribune* summed up the situation more accurately, 'What appears to be happening,' it said, 'is that the Germans have found the defences too strong for their daylight attack, permitting accurate fire, and so are putting their effort into night attack . . . But against a people with courage it is unlikely to prove fruitful . . . and there is no doubt of British courage.'

The Luftwaffe was keeping up the pressure in daylight, but now it has to reckon with a greater measure of co-ordination between Park and Leigh-Mallory.

Part outlined the arrangements made for the Duxford wing operating in the No. 11 Group area.

The No. 12 Group Controller [he instructed] will advise the A.O.C. or the Duty Controller of the hours between which the Duxford wing will be at readiness. This information will if possible be given by 0900 hours daily in order to fit the Duxford wing into the programme for the day.

As soon as the Group Controller gets a clear indication of raids building up over the French coast he is to request No. 12 Group Controller to despatch the Duxford wing to patrol east of London on approximate line north and south through Hornchurch. The arrival of the wing patrol will be communicated to No. 11 Group Controller who will indicate to the No. 12 Group Controller the best position in the Estuary or northern Kent to which the wing should be directed to effect an interception.

The No. 12 Group Controller will inform No. 11 Group immediately the Duxford wing has left the ground.

No. 11 Group Controller is then to inform Senior Controller of Hornchurch who is to fix the position of the Duxford wing. This will be possible as two aircraft of the VHF squadron in the Duxford wing are fitted with Hornchurch fixer crystals (one working, one in reserve).

On arrival on the patrol line Hornchurch will give zero to the Duxford wing on its operational frequency. Hornchurch will hold a crystal of the leading squadron's frequency in the Duxford wing and set up a channel on air frequency with R/T facilities as indicated. Hornchurch Controller will be able to fix the Duxford wing and inform the Observer Corps liaison officer, flank sector and group operations of the position of the Duxford wing at frequent intervals.

On the 26th the Luftwaffe kept the whole of south-east England on the alert. Raids started early in the morning and began to intensify after 10 a.m. when high-flying fighter sweeps started to penetrate from the Channel. Maidstone, London and convoys in the Thames estuary were bombed, and off the north-west coast of Ireland a FW 200 bombed and set fire to the 42,000 ton liner *Empress of Britain*.

Fighter Command mounted 732 sorties. Ten German and two British planes were destroyed.

Although airborne in reasonable numbers British night-fighter pilots again had the galling experience of failing to intercept the raids which disturbed the Saturday-night pleasures of thousands all over Britain.

October 27th

Day Mainly fighter and fighter-bomber sweeps.
Night Widespread raids with London the principal target.
Weather Cloudy all day except for fair period in late morning.

The two Luftflotten made an early start and by 7.45 a.m. were raiding London and convoys in the estuary with a series of formations of as many as fifty aircraft.

By 9 a.m. the London suburbs had been hit and the docks damaged. Further sweeps were flown later in the morning and early in the afternoon. At 4.30 p.m. the Germans raided Southampton, London and Martlesham Heath simultaneously.

To repulse the attackers Fighter Command pilots flew 1,007 sorties. Ten British aircraft were shot down, but only five of the pilots were killed. The Germans lost fifteen machines.

Unknown to Fighter Command, however, they

A postman searches in vain for the residents of a smashed house in London in October. Even postmen had been issued with steel helmets and of course carried the inevitable gas mask. On the railing outside the ruin hangs a Union Jack

had driven off the penultimate major assault in the Battle of Britain.

The night was marked by the usual attacks on London, the south-eastern counties, Liverpool and Bristol, but they differed in detail. In addition to bombing, the Germans made a point of machine-gunning aerodromes in eastern England, including Leconfield, Driffield, Coltishall, Hawkinge, Kirton-in-Lindsey, Feltwell and Honington.

October 28tn

Day Convoy off Dover and shipping in the Estuary attacked. London the main afternoon target.
Night Widespread attacks throughout the country.
Weather Misty in northern France. Fog over Estuary and Straits, clearing later. Cloudy.

Mist in northern France restricted the Germans to nuisance raids by single aircraft which also attacked some ships in the Channel.

They were more active in the afternoon when two raids of twenty and one of forty aircraft flew in over Kent. At 4.30 p.m. fifty more planes crossed the coast at Folkestone and headed for London. They were followed by more than 100 German machines which flew in in four waves.

British fighters, which flew 639 sorties, fought off the Messerschmitts and lost two planes in the fighting. Eleven German aircraft were destroyed.

That night Nos. 85 and 247 squadrons intercepted and fired on two bombers caught by searchlights. The daylight battle was dying out but Fighter Command was only just beginning to get the measure of the task it had to undertake at night.

October 29th

Day London and Southampton main targets.
Night Heavy raids on the capital and midlands.
Weather Channel overcast. Haze in northern France and Dover Straits. Winds southerly.

In what seems in retrospect like a last convulsive spasm, the Luftwaffe pilots gave of their best. By 11 a.m. thirty of them were fighting it out with British fighters over Kent, although some managed to escape the net to attack Charing Cross bridge.

On the morning of October 3rd a Junkers 88 of
Stab/KG 77 took off from Laon to attack Reading.
Bad visibility led the aircraft astray and, by accident,
Hatfield appeared. At about 60 feet the Ju 88 made
two runs hitting the sheet metal shop and the technical
school building, killing 21 and wounding 70. Hit by
A.A. guns and small arms fire the aircraft crashed,
on fire, at Hertingfordbury. The above photograph shows
the damage at Hatfield while the picture below
is of the burned-out Ju 88.

In the second phase of the day's assault ninety minutes later, No. 602 City of Glasgow Squadron distinguished themselves by shooting down eight Messerschmitts in ten minutes. With three other squadrons No. 602 were given a tactical advantage by their positioning and height. Moreover, they were able to achieve greater success by working in pairs.

The encounter developed thus: No. 222 Squadron climbed to deliver an attack on the enemy from the rear. No. 602 attacked simultaneously from above, just as Nos. 615 and 229 Squadrons were climbing for height. Outmanoeuvred, the invaders turned for home, whereupon No. 602 gave chase and shot a further four down into the Channel.

While Luftflotte 3 were raiding Portsmouth with two groups of fifty and twelve machines, fifteen Italian BR.20 bombers and seventy-three Fiat fighters attacked Ramsgate.

It was not until November that the first Italians were shot down on British soil. They included three Fiat CR.42 biplane fighters and three Fiat BR20 bombers, all of which came down in East Anglia. One of the bombers carried the surprisingly large crew of six. They wore tin hats and were armed with bayonets.

By the end of the day Fighter Command had recovered its old ratio of victories and destroyed nineteen of the enemy for a loss of seven of its own machines.

October 30th

Day Nuisance raids on reduced scale.
Night Activity reduced.
Weather Low cloud and continuous drizzle in all areas.

It was not until 11.30 a.m. that the first plots began to appear on the operations rooms tables. They were comparatively small. At midday eighty raiders flew into the Estuary and at 12.15 two waves of fifty and sixty machines penetrated via Dymchurch. Ten R.A.F. squadrons were on patrol at the time, and of these six sighted the raiders. No. 81 Squadron shot down two of them.

Luftflotte 3 fighters were responsible for the next flurry of activity when they despatched a succession of raids totalling 130 machines. These started to cross the coast at 4.15 p.m. and some reached London.

Eight German planes were destroyed. The British lost five.

The first night raiders appeared soon after dark, but the weather was closing in and by midnight none was left over Britain.

October 31st

Day Fighter bomber and fighter sweeps.
Night Activity greatly reduced.
Weather Drizzle in the Channel. Haze in the Estuary and Dover Straits.

The rains came, as it were, to douse the last remaining embers of a bonfire. A few of them spat, however, into sixty half-hearted incursions across the Channel. By nightfall the Battle of Britain was over.

For all the effort put into this phase the Germans achieved singularly little of strategic value. They were no nearer invasion and the sky was no less fraught

with danger for the long-range daylight bombers than it had been in earlier phases.

It would be inaccurate to suggest the Germans relaxed the pressure on Fighter Command or indeed that October was an anticlimax. On the contrary, in many ways October gave British fighter pilots one of the most severe tests of the whole Battle of Britain.

The physical strain of fighting at great heights was exacting. The continuous German fighter sweeps and rapid fighter-bomber attacks called for far greater vigilance and operational activity.

When the weather was clear and the Luftwaffe was able to multiply its attacks, British fighter squadrons of twelve aircraft averaged forty-five hours flying a day and occasionally as much as sixty hours. The volume of operational flying was also increased by the need to maintain standing patrols over Kent.

These counter-measures were an effective reply to the high-flying tactics of the Luftwaffe, but they shattered one of the basic principles of Fighter Command organisation, namely economy of effort by keeping planes grounded until they were needed.

The casualties and damage inflicted on the fighter squadrons by the night raiders were insignificant, but the bombing kept many awake and this had an effect on efficiency. Fatigue began to tell not only on the pilots but on staff in the operations rooms.

German losses in October were comparatively large— 325 planes. Fighter Command's losses in terms of pilots were 100 killed and eighty-five wounded—more than half of them in No. 11 Group.

During the war the Air Ministry claimed that between July 10th and October 31st a total of 2,698 German aircraft had been destroyed. Actually the Germans lost 1,733. Luftwaffe's claims were even more exaggerated. The German High Command's figures for the period were 3,058 British planes destroyed. In fact the R.A.F. lost 915.

Both air forces were bereaved of irreplaceable men, most of them in the flower of their youth. Counting pilots alone, Britain lost 415.

In contrast it is interesting to note that 451 pilots went through the whole of the Battle and that 217 had been operational since the outbreak of war. The record for service goes to Flight Lieutenant J. C. Freeborn. He was posted to No. 74 Squadron on October 29th, 1938, and was still with the squadron at the end of November 1940.

It was estimated in the summer of the Battle that every pilot kept in action for more than six months would be shot down because he was exhausted or stale, or even because he had lost the will to fight. In terms of flying hours the fighter pilot's life expectancy could be measured at eighty-seven.

During that crucial summer the average pilot rarely got more than twenty-four hours off in seven days, or seven days a quarter—if he could be spared from constant availability, readiness and actual fighting.

Among public figures Churchill was the first to grasp the significance of the job they had done. He summed it up in what was perhaps his most famous speech of all. 'Never in the field of human conflict was so much owed by so many to so few.'

14 GROUP, HEADQUARTERS INVERNESS

Wick

3	Hurricane†	Castletown

Dyce

145	Hurricane†	A Flight Dyce
		B Flight Montrose

13 GROUP, HEADQUARTERS NEWCASTLE

Turnhouse

607	Hurricane†	Turnhouse
65	Spitfire†	Turnhouse
232	Hurricane†	Drem (one flight)
263	Hurricane†	Drem (one flight)
1	Hurricane†	Prestwick (R.C.A.F.)

Usworth

43	Hurricane†	Usworth
32	Hurricane†	Acklington
610	Spitfire†	Acklington

Catterick

54	Spitfire†	Catterick
600	Blenheim*	Catterick
		(one flight Acklington)

12 GROUP, HEADQUARTERS WATNALL

Kirton-in-Lindsey

616	Spitfire†	Kirton-in-Lindsey
85	Hurricane*	Kirton-in-Lindsey

Church Fenton

303	Hurricane†	Leconfield (Polish)

Digby

151	Hurricane*	Digby

Coltishall

72	Spitfire†	Coltishall
64	Spitfire†	Coltishall

Wittering

1	Hurricane†	Wittering
266	Spitfire†	Wittering
29	Blenheim*	Wittering (one flight)

Duxford

242	Hurricane	Duxford
310	Hurricane	Duxford (Czech)
19	Spitfire	Duxford

11 GROUP, HEADQUARTERS UXBRIDGE

Debden

25	Blenheim and Beaufighter*	Debden
73	Hurricane*	Castle Camp

North Weald

257	Hurricane	North Weald
249	Hurricane	North Weald
46	Hurricane	Stapleford
17	Hurricane	Martlesham

Hornchurch

264	Defiant*	Hornchurch
41	Spitfire	Hornchurch
603	Spitfire	Hornchurch
222	Spitfire	Rochford

Biggin Hill

74	Spitfire	Biggin Hill
92	Spitfire	Biggin Hill
141	Defiant*	Gravesend
66	Spitfire	West Malling
421	Hurricane‡	West Malling (flight)

Kenley

253	Hurricane	Kenley
501	Hurricane	Kenley
605	Hurricane	Croydon
219	Blenheim and Beaufighter*	Redhill

Northolt

229	Hurricane	Northolt
615	Hurricane	Northolt
302	Hurricane	Northolt (Polish)

Tangmere

145	Hurricane	Tangmere
213	Hurricane	Tangmere
602	Spitfire	Westhampnett
23	Blenheim*	Ford
422	Hurricane*‡	Tangmere (one flight)

10 GROUP, HEADQUARTERS BOX, WILTSHIRE

Pembrey

79	Hurricane†	Pembrey

Filton

504	Hurricane†	Filton
601	Hurricane†	Exeter
87	Hurricane	Exeter
		(one flight Bibury)

St. Eval

234	Spitfire†	St. Eval
247	Gladiator†	Roborough (one flight)

Middle Wallop

609	Spitfire	Middle Wallop
604	Blenheim*	Middle Wallop
56	Hurricane	Boscombe Down
238	Hurricane	Middle Wallop
152	Spitfire	Warmwell

9 GROUP, HEADQUARTERS PRESTON

Speke

312	Hurricane†	Speke (Czech)

Ternhill

611	Spitfire†	Ternhill
29	Blenheim*	Ternhill (one flight)

* Denotes Night Fighter Squadron.
† Denotes C Class Squadron.
‡ Flights during the Battle of Britain and not squadrons—which they became later with different numbers.
All other squadrons were A except for 65 and 87, which were B.

19 Conclusions

By November the Battle of Britain was over. It petered out as the Luftwaffe withdrew from the daylight assault and winter set in.

Losses during the Battle were heavy and German and British crews suffered severely from physical and nervous strain. The Luftwaffe, which was a tactical air force, for four months fought a strategic battle but had little to show for its all-out effort. Britain was not invaded and Fighter Command, though weary and battered, was undefeated.

Early in November Göring issued new orders for the attack on Britain, by night. They showed a clear-cut change of policy with the whole weight of the offensive concentrated on bombing major cities, industries and ports.

The Luftwaffe and the R.A.F. began to rebuild and reorganise. In Britain there was continued expansion for the rest of the war while the German Air Force was brought back to the operational strength it enjoyed before France was invaded.

The High Command made no changes in the structure of the air force or its equipment. If Germany had learned the lessons of the Battle radical changes would have been made. The fighter force would have been doubled and four-engined planes would have replaced the medium bombers such as the Do 17 and He 111. As winter set in Hitler focused his attention on the invasion of Russia. The problems presented by Britain and the R.A.F. were pigeon-holed.

In the final analysis the outcome was dependent on political systems and personalities. In Germany the Nazi party was all-powerful. Hitler considered himself a military genius but his knowledge of air warfare was extremely limited. He disliked aircraft and air weapons. The direction of air warfare he left to Göring who as a commander and strategist had few qualifications. His flying knowledge was out of date and his understanding of technical subjects non-existent. The correct application of the air force which Milch built up was more than he could grasp.

The Luftwaffe lacked any long-term directive on economic warfare or any real guidance from above. After Colonel Wever's death in 1936 battle planning became a hand-to-mouth affair. The whole organisation was bedevilled with petty jealousies and intrigues arising from the haphazard way in which officials acquired senior jobs. Instead of providing central direction and efficiency the totalitarian state produced only rigidity of thought and disorganisation on a grand scale.

Göring's commanders, Kesselring and Sperrle, who bore the brunt of the air war against Britain, also lacked a positive strategic plan of action. They committed the errors of underestimating the enemy and being inflexible in their thinking.

The prime example of German inflexibility occurred over radar. Nothing was done to provide an operational system to work with the warning stations. German equipment was brilliantly conceived but laboratory instruments took years to develop. In a country noted for scientific achievement the application of radar was strangely disregarded.

The R.A.F.'s radar may have lacked polish and refinement but it worked and was appreciated. By improvisation, co-operation and experiment British radar remained one step ahead of Germany's throughout the war. Through what was little short of German naïvety and conceit the integration of radar into the British defence system remained undetected.

Britain was an easy-going democracy where central direction and concise planning might have appeared illogical. Sufficient work on rearmament and expansion was done, however, by such men as Lord Swinton to ensure a fair chance of survival. From 1935 to 1940 money and effort were directed towards combating the menace of the bomber.

With the arrival in power of Winston Churchill overall direction of the war effort was obtained without the loss of democratic freedom. The British system was sufficiently flexible to allow for improvisation and rapid changes of plan where necessary.

Churchill trusted Dowding and left the task of air defence almost entirely to him in the summer of 1940. Churchill interfered only where he thought assistance could be given to Fighter Command's efforts. Such an instance occurred in July when he directed a memorandum to the three services calling for fighter-pilot reinforcements.

He drew the reins of High Command together and above all raised public morale and instilled a sense of purpose into a country bored and depressed by Chamberlain and the 'phoney war'.

Dowding was comewhat of an enigma. To the outside world he carried the air of a University don. This was misleading. He was dedicated to the task of defending Britain against air attack and he would go to any lengths to ensure that the forces were matched to the task. From 1936 he nursed the 'system' into a working entity'

Dowding was not a familiar figure to the pilots he

commanded. He was seldom seen in the squadrons and he did not mix easily with his subordinates. There was, in fact, an extraordinary contrast between the A.O.C.-in-C. and the pilots of Fighter Command.

The pilots cultivated a rakish and light-hearted approach to life. They affected to despise the external manifestations of service discipline and disregarded the more pompous conventions of King's Regulations whenever possible.

Dowding did not fit their ideal at all. He was withdrawn and aloof. He had distinguished himself more as a staff officer than as a pilot and wild parties were certainly not in his line.

Nevertheless there existed between these two extremes a close bond of mutual respect and admiration. Nothing was too good for Dowding's pilots. He would fight any opposition and risk the displeasure of the highest authorities to get them what they needed. Churchill once called them his chicks.

In turn the pilots called him 'Stuffy', not in contempt but rather affection for a trusted 'father figure'.

Dowding and Park received scant recognition for their efforts. After the Battle Dowding was retired and asked to do various mediocre jobs including the investigating of service waste and touring the United States.

For Park there were only brickbats. Archibald Sinclair and Leigh-Mallory, supported by Sholto Douglas, decided that much greater losses could have been inflicted on the Luftwaffe if the 'big wing' theories had been adopted in No. 11 Group.

At one meeting Park was subjected to criticism for his handling of the Battle and Squadron Leader D. Bader was called in to give his views. The presence of a squadron leader among such senior officers was unprecedented.

The meeting had already made up its mind about the outcome and from this time forward the big wings held sway. Park was posted to Flying Training Command, Leigh-Mallory took over No. 11 Group and Sholto Douglas became Air Officer Commanding Fighter Command in place of Dowding.

In retrospect it is clear that Park was correct in his handling of No. 11 Group and that the full-scale introduction of wing tactics into the southern battle would have been disastrous. In most cases the wings would have become unmanageable as the squadrons were on different radio frequencies and could not communicate with one another.

To allow the Germans to destroy vital targets at will was the complete negation of air defence regardless of the number of aircraft shot down afterwards. If such tactics had been pursued in 1940, the whole sector airfield and control system would have been reduced to a shambles by the Luftwaffe.

With control gone and airfields scarce, the big wings would have been hard put to it to get airborne or find the enemy. The obvious choice for the German Air Force if such tactics were used would have been to disperse the bombers immediately after the attack and fly in further waves of fighters to meet the wings.

Throughout the Battle of Britain the Germans were mainly concerned by their failure to attract enough British fighters into action at one time to make a real impression on Fighter Command. Park's forward interception caused fighter and bomber formations to be broken up before they reached the target and in many cases the fighter escort became involved at such an early stage that bombers flew on alone and vulnerable.

Big wings would have suited the Luftwaffe far better. Its plans were laid in the hope that Park would put up large formations to deal with one mass attack over one area while another equally large force attacked another.

If Park had succumbed to the big wing theories he would have had one pitched battle with serious casualties on both sides while in a different area one or two major raids would have got through inscathed. As it was, a very high proportion of all raids were intercepted on the way in despite feints and attacks on a broad front. The classic example of this occurred on August 15th.

The essence of the controversy between Nos. 11 and 12 Groups lay in personalities. Park was a brilliant defensive tactician while Leigh-Mallory had leanings towards offence. The two were incompatible.

The objects of a fighter force in 1940 were twofold (a) Defence and (b) Offence.

The first task of a fighter force commander in defence was to prevent an enemy bombing force hitting its assigned targets. To do this he had often to forgo tactics which would involve heavier enemy losses in order to concentrate on preventing hostile bombers achieving their objectives.

A fighter commander had to consider the number of serviceable fighters he possessed and could maintain from day to day as compared with enemy bomber forces, the time available based on geography and the performance of his fighter aircraft, between warning of approach of enemy bombers and the point of interception, and the width of front to be covered.

The number of serviceable fighters determined the deployment in width of front while the time required for interception determined the deployment of squadrons in depth. Formation size was a function of time available for forming up. This was usually very little.

In the initial stages and for most of the Battle the ratio of serviceable R.A.F. fighters to the known size of the German bomber force prevented Park from using other than small formations, often single squadrons. The time required for interception made the rapid deployment of the first-line squadrons south of the Thames imperative and the extensive width of front ruled out the employment of large formations.

Towards the end of the Battle Park was able to employ wings of two, three or more squadrons more often, but this was only made possible by the changed tactics of the Luftwaffe.

In offence the primary task of Fighter Command was to destroy as many enemy aircraft as possible. In these circumstances large fighter formations were more economical than small ones.

In the 'trailing the coat' campaign over France 1941 to 1944 Fighter Command was not faced with the problem of interception. It was therefore able to use the distance from British fighter bases to the south coast to form up. Moreover, the 'width of front' problem vanished together with the paramount requirement for preventing enemy bombers flying in unimpeded.

The Battle of Britain and the 'trailing the coat' campaign were two entirely different 'wars'.

At all costs Park, in 1940, had to preserve the physical well being of his pilots. To assist this he laid down State of Preparedness whereby at each station there was one squadron at Readiness and two other squadrons at 15 and 30 minutes Available respectively.

It was found under this scheme that the two Readiness squadrons (from Biggin Hill and Hornchurch) had to make a very rushed air rendezvous.

The states were therefore modified so that, in the morning, there were two Readiness squadrons at Hornchurch and one at 15 minutes, while Biggin Hill had one squadron at Readiness and two at 15 minutes Available. The positions were reversed in the afternoon. The three Hurricane squadrons at Kenley and North Weald maintained similar states.

The essence of all this was to get a high flying pair of Spitfire squadrons up above the danger spot at an early stage in the proceedings.

Leigh Mallory at 12 Group was well clear of the main bombing area and was obsessed with wing formations.

His task was to come to the assistance of 11 Group when enemy raids had built up to about 150 aircraft. A 12 Group wing was thereupon supposed to assist in attacking later enemy formations and guard 11 Group airfields while refuelling and rearming was going on.

In the event the 12 Group wings never seemed to appear when the need was desperate. Park became suspicious and called for close plotting by the Observer Corps. The Observer tracks thus produced often showed the 12 Group wing looking for the enemy in the Thames Estuary or beyond when they should have been back around Tilbury.

Park was furious and expressed his feelings in a very strong letter to Fighter Command. A copy of this letter is understood to have reached Leigh Mallory, which only served to increase the enmity between the two Group commanders.

The vindication of Park's basic theories came in 1941. Leigh Mallory, by then at 11 Group, decided to run a paper battle exercise using the actual attacks which took place on one day in September 1940.

He controlled the 'battle' using big wing tactics. To his chagrin the Luftwaffe hit his three main airfields while the fighters were still on the ground. Leigh Mallory found himself trying to order wings of three squadrons off each station when one was at Readiness, the second at 15 minutes and the third at 30 minutes Available. Needless to say such paper exercises were not repeated.

British fighter pilots had no fear whatsoever of the German bombers which were easy prey for the Hurricanes and Spitfires. The He 111s, Do 17s and 215s and the Ju 88s were not fast enough, particularly when operating in formation. Moreover, they were indifferently armed. They could rarely bring more than one gun to bear on an attacking fighter.

The attitude towards the Me 109 was different.

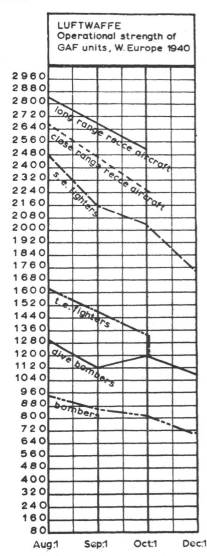

LUFTWAFFE
Operational strength of GAF units, W. Europe 1940

This type was very effective and accounted for most of the losses suffered by Fighter Command during the battle. It was as fast as the Spitfire, considerably faster than the Hurricane and it would out-dive and out-climb either. Its armament was formidable. Half a dozen explosive shells from its cannon could do far more damage than the equivalent length of burst of Browning rounds. On the other hand, the firing rate of the Brownings was much higher, which gave the British pilots a better chance of scoring with a short burst.

In one vital respect the Me 109 was at a disadvantage. It could be out-turned by the Spitfire and the Hurricane. This was a serious handicap to the Luftwaffe pilots assigned to escorting bombers. Their freedom of action was curtailed. They were therefore unable to pursue the tactics best suited to their aircraft. They never found a way round this problem and their difficulties were aggravated when Göring, infuriated by the losses inflicted on his bombers, ordered the fighters to stay closer still to their charges.

At the beginning of the battle the German fighters used their speed to advantage which, coupled with

273

their more recently evolved tactics, played havoc with the antiquated practices of Fighter Command.

British tactics were completely wrong when the Battle began, but steadily improved. Fighter Command squadrons at the outset flew in tidy tight formation, so close that only the leader could see where he was going and what was going on. The other members of the formation concentrated on keeping station.

This was a hand-over from peacetime. It looked good at an air display but in combat formation of aircraft is easier to see. The result was that many unsuspecting pilots were 'bounced'.

Since the Battle the importance of the Hurricane to victory has been slowly undermined. The Spitfire tends to hold pride of place to the extent that a fallacy runs the risk of becoming accepted as historical fact.

There were more Hurricanes in the Battle of Birtain than Spitfires. The Hurricane Mk. I, with a constant-speed propeller, was a fine fighting aircraft, an excellent gun platform and it was magnificently manœuvrable up to 20,000 feet. It was extremely strong and could take an extraordinary amount of punishment.

As Wing Commander Roland Beamont remarks in his book 'Phoenix into Ashes':

The Hurricane had an altogether exceptional combination of manœuvrability, rugged strength, stability, ease of control and gun aiming, and viceless landing characteristics which went far towards offsetting the fact that its climb, level and altitude performance were slightly lower than the Spitfire and Me 109.

This was the view of a first class most experienced combat pilot. It cannot be stressed too highly that the real key lay in the pilots themselves. Those with sharp reflexes and long experience in a Hurricane were more than a match for their average opposite numbers on Me 109s. Exactly the same situation existed in reverse.

In the winter of 1940 Luftwaffe daylight activity was limited to sneak raids and to fighter sweeps at high altitude, the latter proving very difficult to combat. Squadron Leader (now Group Captain retired) H. J. Wilson O.C. Aerodynamics Flight, Experimental Section, Royal Aircraft Establishment, was put on temporary attachment with No. 74 squadron, Biggin Hill, to study fighter requirements.

In his report Squadron Leader Wilson called for improved cannon armament and more powerful engines etc., particularly for the Spitfire. He concluded with remarks which summarise the whole position as it existed in the Battle of Britain:

It can hardly be said that the R.A.F. Spitfire squadrons have superior fighting material to the enemy, and it is my considered opinion that the only reason why we are just managing to maintain the balance of fighter power is due entirely to the outstanding flying and leadership of the pilots.

The popular picture which has grown up in Britain around the Battle is not a true one. The picture is of a small band of invincible aces, brilliant, debonair and gay, flying into battle again and again, with vapour trails across the blue skies, shooting down German after German, and occasionally falling themselves when outnumbered.

Some squadrons of course were pre-eminent, usually because they were exceptionally well led. Because of their success they were kept longest in the forefront of the battle, and scored the greatest number of successes. In such squadrons as these there existed an élite who survived longest and carried individually the heaviest burden of the Battle.

Most of the squadrons were not like that, however. Many went into action confident and gay and withdrew as a battered remnant ten days or a fortnight later.

There were the very young and over-confident and inexperienced with little idea what it was all about. There were the many thoroughly competent pilots, courageous and determined, but who lacked the speed and instinct needed to live long in action. But at the end of it they could nearly all claim that they had given a little better than they received.

Scores of humble and unknown young pilots made up the squadrons. If they succeeded in scoring a victory or two before going down themselves, it was this that set the seal of victory on the preparations made before the war.

There is no doubt that Göring and his commanders overrated the effectiveness of their own fighters in relation to the British. This may be deduced from the number of Messerschmitts assembled for the Battle. A total of nearly 1,000 against a defending force of little more than 600 gave a degree of superiority, particularly because less than two-thirds of Dowding's aircraft were at any time within range of the battle area. But it was not a degree of superiority which a cautious commander would have accepted as sufficient for the job in hand unless he thought the defending fighters were much inferior. In this uneven proportion of fighters and bombers may be found the fundamental reason for Göring's failure to achieve his objectives. He thought the Hurricanes and Spitfires could be quickly brushed aside. He misjudged the quality of the planes, the spirit of the pilots who flew them and the men on the ground who backed them up.

It has been suggested that Germany should have returned to the assault on Britain in the spring of 1941 and that this would have settled matters once and for all. In May of that year the Luftwaffe was operating the same aircraft as it had in 1940, with the exception of an improved fighter, the Me 109F.

Its tasks would have been exactly the same as those laid down in August 1940, the destruction of the R.A.F. and the substitution of air power for sea power.

Britain, on the other hand, had greatly increased her strength. Compared with the 708 fighters and 1,434 pilots available on August 3rd, 1940, by March 31st, 1941, there were 1,240 fighters on establishment and 1,702 pilots, with a steady flow of trained air crew from the schools in Canada, South Africa, Southern Rhodesia, Australia and New Zealand.

The radar coverage over Britain was greatly extended. Ground Control Interception radar was installed and operations rooms moved underground.

For a land battle the Army could muster in the same month nearly two million men. The German opportunity after Dunkirk was lost irretrievably. Never again was Britain's margin of safety so narrow.

Appendices

*Notes on performance of aircraft used operationally by Fighter Command and the Luftwaffe,
July/October 1940*

German aircraft detailed are those actually employed on
sorties or met in combat over the Channel. Night fighters
and close reconnaissance aircraft are not included. The lists
of sub-types actually used in the Battle of Britain are taken
from Luftwaffe Quartermaster General's returns for the
period.

VICKERS-SUPERMARINE SPITFIRE MK. I

After winning three successive Schneider Trophy contests
with their high-speed record-breaking seaplanes, Supermarines built to Air Ministry Specification F7/30, a cranked-
wing fixed-undercarriage fighter, K2890, with a 600 h.p.
Rolls-Royce Goshawk steam-cooled engine. This aircraft
fulfilled its specification requirements, but its designer,
R. J. Mitchell, did not consider that it was the thing for
future combat. Accordingly, he set about designing the
interceptor he thought the R.A.F. ought to want. This was
to have an enclosed cockpit, retractable undercarriage and
four machine-guns. This met Air Ministry Specification
F5/34. The advent of the Rolls-Royce PV-12 Merlin dictated
changes in the design, and around Mitchell's later plans a new
specification, F37/34, was written. The result was the Spitfire,
and the prototype, K5054, flew for the first time on March
5th, 1936. It bore the Vickers-Supermarine type number, 300.

On K5054 the engine was a Merlin C giving 1,030 h.p.
at 16,250 feet, and the propeller was a de Havilland fixed-pitch
two-blade wooden type. A tail-skid was fitted, the cockpit
canopy was flat-topped and the exhausts were flush.

In 1937 production of the Spitfire Mk. I with the Merlin II
engine and a wooden propeller began. Deliveries started from
the Eastleigh factory in 1938, and Nos. 19 and 66 squadrons
at Duxford were the first to receive them. These aircraft
bore the same type number (300) as the prototype Spitfire,
and it was allocated to the 1,531 aircraft built.

Tests carried out to improve take-off and climb were made
by fitting the prototype with a de Havilland three-blade two
position propeller. These were fitted from the seventy-
seventh aircraft to come off the assembly line. A bubble cockpit
hood also became standard on later models, this type having
replaced the flat canopy.

The Spitfire Mk. Is in service had four .303 machine-guns,
but this was changed to eight .303 Browning guns in the
Mk. IA. In February 1939 one aircraft was fitted experi-
mentally with two 20 m.m. guns, and this version, also carrying
four .303s, became the Mk. IB, thirty of which were delivered
in August 1940 for operational trials in the Battle of Britain.
The experimental 20 m.m. cannon Spitfire shot down a
Dornier Do 17 in March 1940.

Two main differences distinguished the Spitfire Mk. II
from the Mk. I. It was fitted with a Merlin XII engine and was
built exclusively at Castle Bromwich.

The Mk. II incorporated some detailed refinements, and
whereas the Mk. I had armour plating added in service, the
Mk. II had it fitted on the production line.

Altogether 920 Mk. IIs were built; 750 as Mk. IIAs with
eight machine-guns, and 170 as Mk. IIBs which carried four
Brownings and two Hispano 20 m.m. cannon.

Deliveries of the Mk. II to the R.A.F. began on June 3rd,
1940.

In July 1940 Fighter Command possessed nineteen Spitfire
squadrons. These were 19, 41, 54, 64, 65, 66, 72, 74, 92, 152,
222, 234, 266, 602, 603, 609, 610, 611, 616.

Data: SPITFIRE MK. I

Manufacturers: Supermarine Division of Vickers-Armstrong
Ltd., in factories at Southampton, Winchester, Swindon,
and Castle Bromwich. Widely sub-contracted.
Power Plant: Rolls-Royce Merlin II and III with single speed
supercharger and Glycol cooling. Combat rating on 80
octane fuel. 1,030 h.p. at 16,250 ft. Merlin III was identical
with Merlin II except for the propeller shaft and the
accessory drive. First seventy-seven aircraft fitted with
two-blade fixed-pitch wooden propeller.
Dimensions: Span, 36 ft. 10 in. length, 29 ft. 11 in. height, 11 ft.
5 in. wing area 242 sq. ft.
Weight: Empty: 5,067 lb.; Loaded: 6,409 lb.
Performance: Maximum speed 355 m.p.h. at 19,000 ft.;
time to 20,000 ft. 9.4 mins.; maximum range 575 miles,
range, including take-off and 15 mins. combat, 395 miles;
service ceiling 34,000 ft.

Mk. II
As for Mk.I except:
Power Plant: 1,175 h.p. Rolls-Royce Merlin XII, fitted with
Coffman starter, driving a three-bladed Rotol propeller.
Weights: As for Mk. I. + 75 lb.
Performance: Maximum speed (IIA) 370 m.p.h. Initial rate
of climb 2,600 ft./min.

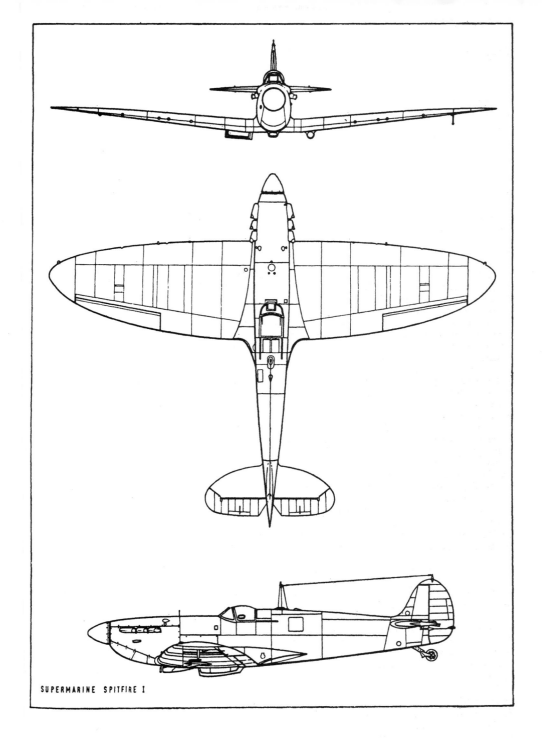

SUPERMARINE SPITFIRE I

BRISTOL BLENHEIM FIGHTER

The Bristol Blenheim had its origins in the generosity and foresight of a private individual, Lord Rothermere. In 1934 he ordered from the Bristol Aeroplane Company the prototype of a high-speed 6/8 seat civil transport of advanced design, and powered by two 560 h.p. Mercury 4 radials. This machine flew in April 1935, and was an immediate success, having the then phenomenal speed of 307 m.p.h. at 14,000 ft. All metal, the transport bore the number 142, and was a low-wing monoplane with refinements like a retractable undercarriage.

Performance of the 142 proved so good that Lord Rothermere presented the aircraft to the nation, as a gift. It was refitted with 640 h.p. Mercury 6.S.2 motors and had its civil registration G-ABCZ replaced by the serial K7557. Known as the 'Britain First' the aircraft served as a test-bed for its direct development, the Blenheim, for which Specification B.28/35 was evolved.

Only major external differences between the 'Britain First' and the prototype Blenheim I light bomber, lay in the raising of the wing to mid-position, and the modification of the engine nacelles for twin Mercury 8s, which developed 840 h.p. each. The Blenheim had the type number 142A and the prototype, K7022, flew for the first time in June 1936.

Production version of the Blenheim was the type 142M and the first—K7037—left the factory in November 1936. Seating three, the Mk. I had an all-up-weight of 12,500 lb., top speed of 277 m.p.h. at 20,000 feet, and a maximum range of 1,165 miles at 200 m.p.h.

The sturdiness and good all-round qualities of the type prompted the Air Ministry to order a number of Blenheims as fighters, to be known as the Mk. 1F. These had an armoured nose and four .303 Browning guns in a ventral gun pack, in addition to the bomber's single Browning in the port wing and single-gun dorsal turret.

Blenheim fighters pioneered airborne radar, and achieved their first success on the night of July 22nd, 1940. They went into squadron service in 1938 and equipped the following squadrons: Nos. 23, 25, 29, 64, 68, 145, 219, 222, 600, 601, and 604.

Data: BRISTOL BLENHEIM FIGHTER

Manufacturers: Bristol Aeroplane Company Ltd., Filton, Bristol. Sub-contracted by Avro and Rootes.
Power Plant: Two 840 h.p. Mercury VIII.
Dimensions: Span, 56 ft. 4 in. length, 39 ft. 9 in. height, 9 ft. 10 in. wing areas 469 sq.ft.
Weights: Empty, 8,100 lb. Loaded, 12,500 lb.
Performance: Maximum speed, 260 m.p.h. Cruising 200 m.p.h. Initial climb, 1,540 ft./min. Range 1,125 miles. Endurance, 5.65 hrs. Service ceiling, 27,280 ft.

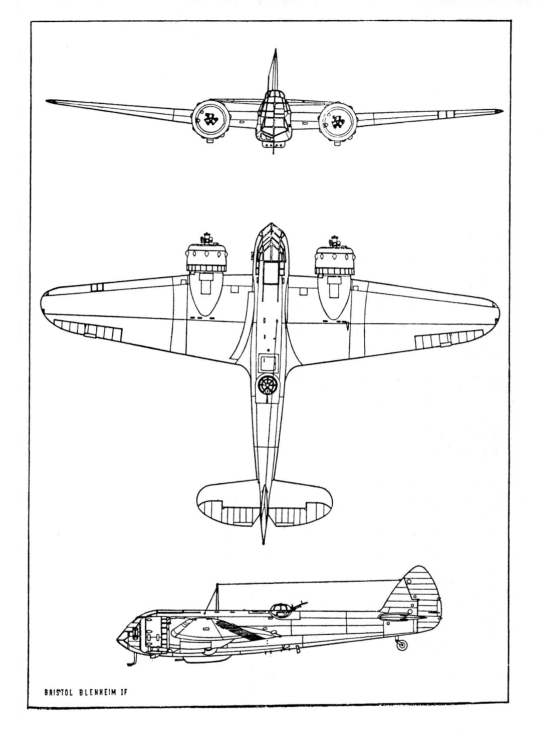

BRISTOL BLENHEIM IF

THE GLOSTER GLADIATOR

Designed as a private venture, the Gloster Gladiator was found to conform to specification F.7/30, to which the original Goshawk engine Blackburn and Westland biplanes, and the original inverted gull-wing Spitfire had been designed.

An aerodynamically cleaned up development of the Gloster Gauntlet which made such a spectacular début at the S.B.A.C. Display in 1933, it had a cantilever single-strut undercarriage with Dowty internally-sprung wheels, a single-bay wing cellule, and double the armament standard on R.A.F. aircraft over the previous two decades—two Vickers guns in the fuselage and two Lewis guns under the wings.

Powered by a 645 h.p. Bristol Mercury VI S enclosed by a short chord cowling, the prototype (K5200) first flew in September 1934 designated the D.S.37. In July 1935 the Gladiator was ordered for the R.A.F. to Spec. 14/35, the initial contract being for twenty-three machines. A further 186 were ordered in September 1935 and production continued until April 1940, by which time 311 Gladiators had been delivered to the R.A.F.

The production model was fitted with the 840 h.p. Mercury IX engine and a medium chord cowling. It also differed from the prototype in having an enclosed cockpit and four Browning .303 machine-guns.

The basic structure of the Gladiator was orthodox—steel tube and strip construction with fabric-covered wings and rear fuselage assembly, and metal skinning for the front fuselage. A feature not usually found in biplanes was the trailing edge flaps on both upper and lower wings.

In 1938, the Fleet Air Arm took an interest in the Gladiator as a shipboard fighter, and thirty-two production Gladiator IIs were fitted with temporary arrester hooks for use as interim deck-landing fighters. These were followed by sixty Sea Gladiator IIs which carried a dinghy in a fairing beneath the fuselage, and featured other modifications dictated by their naval role. They were delivered to the Navy during 1939–40.

Largely replaced in Fighter Command by the outbreak of war, Gladiators went to France with Nos. 607 and 615 Squadrons of the Advanced Air Striking Force. During the Battle of Britain they equipped No. 247 Squadron at Roborough, charged with defending the Royal Naval dockyards at Plymouth.

Sea Gladiators in the Battle of Britain belonged to 804 Squadron, Fleet Air Arm.

Data: GLADIATOR MK. I AND MK. II

Manufacturers: Gloster Aircraft Co. Ltd., Hucclecote, Gloucester. Makers' designation S.S.37.
Power Plant: One 840 h.p. Bristol Mercury IX.
Dimensions: span, 32 ft. 3 in. length, 27 ft. 5 in. height, 10 ft. 4 in. wing area, 323 sq. ft.
Weights: Empty, 3,450 lb. Loaded, 4,750 lb.

Performance: Maximum speed, 253 m.p.h. at 14,500 ft.; Cruising, 210 m.p.h.; Initial climb, 2,300 ft./min.; 9.5 mins. to 20,000; Endurance, 2 hrs.; Service ceiling, 33,000 ft.

Sea Gladiator
As for the Gladiator Mk. II except:
Weights: Empty, 3,745 lb. Loaded, 5,420 lb.
Performance: Maximum speed, 245 m.p.h. at 15,000 ft. Cruising speed, 212 m.p.h. at 15,500 ft. Range, 425 miles. Service ceiling, 32.000 ft.
Mk. I. Gladiator fitted with fixed-pitch wooden propeller.
Mk. II. Gladiator fitted with three-bladed Fairey-Reed metal fixed-pitch airscrew.

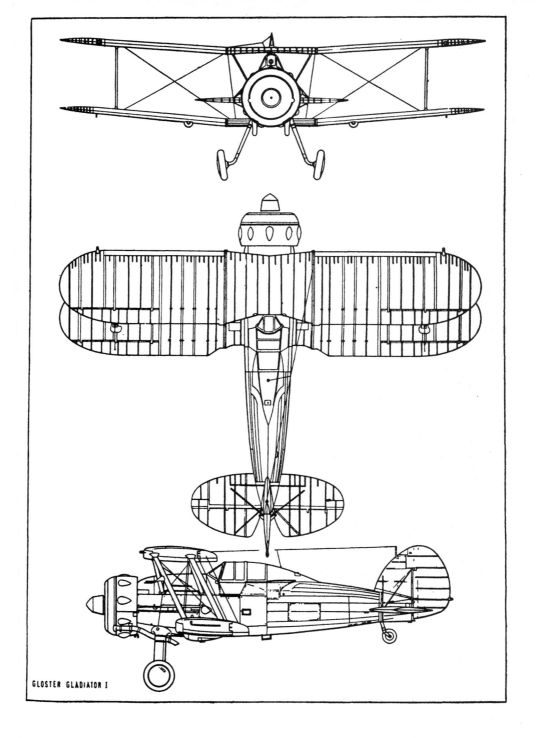

GLOSTER GLADIATOR I

THE HAWKER HURRICANE

Many of Britain's most famous military aircraft owe their existence to 'private ventures' initiated by far-sighted men and firms in industry. This was the case with the development and production of the Hawker Hurricane, which played such an important part in the Battle of Britain.

The Hurricane was originally designed as a Rolls-Royce Goshawk-engined monoplane version of the Fury biplane, to carry four machine-guns. The advent of the Rolls-Royce PV-12 Merlin offered substantial improvements, however, and the fighter was redesigned around it.

Official views on single-seater fighter performance requirements were revised in 1934, and out of these changes came Air Ministry specification F5/34. The specification was investigated by Hawkers who prepared a new design, but the earlier plan showed greater promise. It was recognised by the Air Ministry when specification F36/34 was written around it, and they ordered a prototype—K5083, to be equipped with eight .303 machine-guns in the wings. K5083 flew on November 6th, 1935, powered by a Merlin C of 1,045 h.p.

Encouraged by its performance and the rearmament programmes Hawkers prepared to lay down a production line for 1,000 aircraft in anticipation of an order which was later justified.

Progressive development of the basic Hurricane type had started in 1935 when stressed-skin wings were first investigated. Metal wings began to replace fabric-covered wings on the production line in 1939.

First production Hurricane — L1457 — with Merlin II engine flew on October 12th, 1937. It differed from the prototype in having stub exhausts, strengthened canopy, modified rudder mass balance and altered undercarriage doors. Later a ventral fin was added to improve spin recovery. Armour-plating and bullet-proof windscreens were fitted in 1938, and as part of an attempt to increase fire power, one Hurricane was fitted with one 20 m.m. cannon slung beneath each wing.

The first Hurricane entered service with No. 111 Squadron at Northolt. The re-equipment of other squadrons was rapid and by September 3rd, 1939, 497 Hurricanes had been delivered and eighteen squadrons equipped. All these aircraft were of the Mk. I type with eight .303 Browning machine-guns and alternative propeller installations: a Merlin II driving a Watts wooden two-bladed fixed-pitch airscrew, or a Merlin II of similar power with a standardised shaft for de Havilland or Rotol three-bladed metal airscrews.

The Hurricane Mk. II differed from the Mk. I in having a Merlin XX engine, a strengthened fuselage and a choice of wings—one pair designed for twelve Browning machine-guns and the other for four 20 m.m. cannon, both types capable of supporting 500 lb. weight in bombs.

The Hurricane Mk. IIA was an interim production version with strengthened fuselage to permit conversion to a later Mark, but fitted initially with eight-gun armament. Aircraft fitted with twelve Brownings were designated Mk. IIBs and those with four Hispanos Mk. IICs.

Delivery of Mk. IIAs to R.A.F. units began in August 1940, but the more heavily armed IIB and IIC did not reach the squadrons until 1941, although the IIC was first delivered to the R.A.F. in October 1940.

When war broke out the Hurricane was quickly in action with Nos. 1 and 73 Squadrons. In the Battle of Britain they equipped the following squadrons: Nos. 1, 3, 17, 32, 43, 46, 56, 73, 79, 85, 87, 111, 145, 151, 229, 232, 242, 245, 253, 257, 263, 302, 310, 312, 501, 504, 601, 605, 607, 615 and No. 1 Squadron, Royal Canadian Air Force.

Data: HURRICANE MK. I

Manufacturers: Hawker Aircraft Limited, Kingston, Surrey. Sub-contracted to Gloster Aircraft.

Power Plant: Rolls-Royce Merlin II or III with single speed supercharge and Glycol cooling.
Weight, 1,375 lb.
Combat rating on 80 octane fuel. 1,030 h.p. at 16,250 ft.
Merlin III was identical with Merlin II except for the propeller shaft and the accessory drive.
First production models fitted with Watts two-bladed fixed-pitch wooden airscrew. Three-blade de Havilland and Rotol two position propellers came later, and variable pitch airscrews. On June 24th, 1940, conversion to constant-speed propellers started. Conversion completed in August. Fuel capacity, 69 gallons plus. 56 gallons reserve.

Dimensions: Span, 40 ft. length, 31 ft. 5 in. height, 13 ft. 1½ in. wing area, 257½ sq. ft.

Weights: Empty, 4,670 lb.; Loaded, 6,600 lb.

Armament: Eight .303 Browning machine-guns.

Performance: Maximum speed—

D.H. Hamilton three-blade metal propeller (variable pitch)	320 m.p.h.
Rotol three-blade wooden propeller (variable pitch)	325 m.p.h.

Cruising speed, 230 m.p.h.
Initial rate of climb, 2,420 ft./min.
Service ceiling, 34,000 ft.
Range, 600 miles.

Mk. IIA

As for Mk. I except:

Power Plant: Rolls-Royce Merlin XX delivering 1,185 h.p.

Performance: Maximum speed, 342 m.p.h.; cruising speed, 232 m.p.h.; initial rate of climb, 2,380 ft./min.; service ceiling, 35,000 ft.

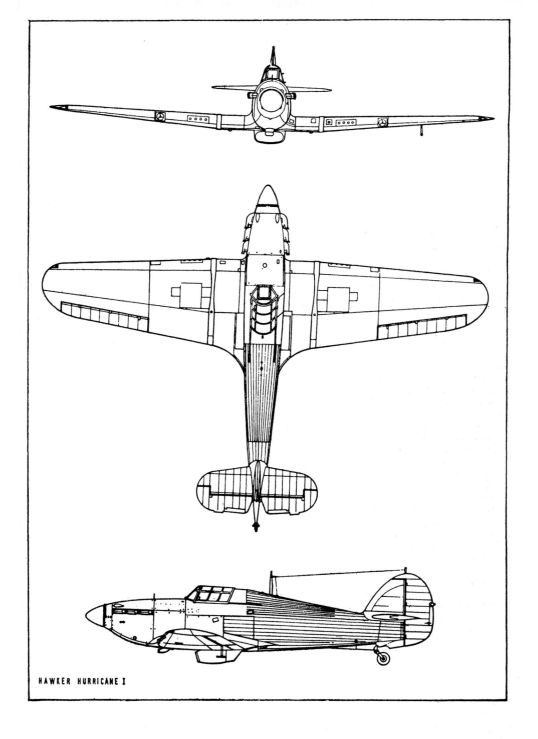

HAWKER HURRICANE I

283

THE FAIREY FULMAR

The Fairey Fulmar was designed at Heaton Chapel, Stockport, to meet specification o8/38 for a general purpose fleet fighter-bomber. Developed from a light bomber specification P4/34 the prototype made its maiden flight on January 4th, 1940, from Ringway near Manchester. The second prototype flew on April 6th and was delivered at Boscombe Down on May 3rd.

Production of the Fulmar as a two-seat fighter fitted with eight .303 Brownings in the wings, went ahead and in May the first production aircraft was delivered to the Service Trials Unit at Lee-on-Solent near Southampton.

The first three Fulmars for operational service were delivered to Worthy Down early in June 1940 for No. 806 Squadron. Fulmars also replaced Blackburn Skuas which 808 Squadron had used at Dunkirk. In the Battle of Britain Fulmars operated from Wick with No. 808 Squadron, Fleet Air Arm, under the control of No. 13 Group.

Data: FAIREY FULMAR MK. I

Manufacturers: The Fairey Aviation Company Limited, Hayes, Middlesex and Stockport, Cheshire.
Power Plant: Rolls-Royce Merlin VIII. 1,010 h.p.
All-up Weight: 9,804 lb.
Dimensions: Span, 46 ft.; length, 40 ft. 3 in.; height, 14 ft.; wing area, 342 sq. ft.
Performance: Maximum speed at sea level: 213 m.p.h.
    Maximum speed at 10,000 ft.: 245 m.p.h.
    Maximum speed at 20,000 ft.: 220 m.p.h.
    Initial rate of climb to 5,000 ft.: 4 mins. 24 secs.
    Initial rate of climb to 20,000 ft.: 26 mins. 26 secs.
    Service ceiling: 22,400 ft.
Range: 830 Statute miles.
Endurance: 4 hrs. 45 mins., on normal fuel load of 155 gallons.

THE BOULTON PAUL DEFIANT MK. I

Encouraged by the success of the four-gun power-operated turrets being made for bombers, the R.A.F. decided to try them out in small, fast single-engined aircraft. As two-seater fighters they were intended to replace the Hawker Demon bi-planes.

The Hawker Hotspur and the Boulton Paul Defiant met the specification, F9/35, and after their initial flights the Defiant was selected.

The prototype flew for the first time on August 11th, 1937. The first production model first flew on July 30th, 1939.

The Defiant, whose turret was also designed and made by Boulton Paul, was superficially rather like the Hawker Hurricane and was about the same size. The crew of two were over the wing and a retractable fairing was fitted behind the turret which, when lowered, widened the four Browning guns field of fire.

The Defiant introduced a new tactical concept in two-seat fighters whereby no forward armament was carried. All offensive power was concentrated in the rear cockpit.

No. 264 Squadron took the first Defiants into action from Manston on May 12th, 1940, and found the idea paid handsome dividends during early engagements. On May 29th they put up the amazing record of destroying thirty-seven German aircraft. The Germans mistook the squadron for twelve exceptionally careless Hurricanes and dived on their supposedly defenceless tails only to be destroyed in a withering concentration of fire. By May 31st Defiants had shot down sixty-five aircraft, mainly bombers, over Dunkirk.

The Defiant's success was short lived, however. The Luftwaffe found its weakness and on July 19th scored heavily against No. 141 Squadron by attacking from the front. Its other weakness was the the brain flying it was not the brain firing the guns. It was withdrawn from daylight operations in August 1940 but as an A.I. radar-equipped night fighter it did extremely well, shooting down more raiders per interception than any other night fighter in the winter of 1940–1.

Data: BOULTON PAUL DEFIANT MK. I

Manufacturers: Boulton Paul Aircraft Ltd., Wolverhampton.
Power Plant: Rolls-Royce Merlin III.
Dimensions: Span, 39 ft, 4 in.; length, 35 ft. 4 in.; height, 12 ft. 2 in.; wing area, 250 sq. ft.
    Weights: Empty, 6,282 lb.; loaded, 7,110 lb.
    Performance: Maximum speed, 304 m.p.h. at 16,500 ft.; Cruising speed, 240 m.p.h.; Initial rate of climb, 2,120 ft./min.; Time to 18,000 ft., 10.2 mins.; Maximum range, 600 miles; Service ceiling, 30,200 ft.

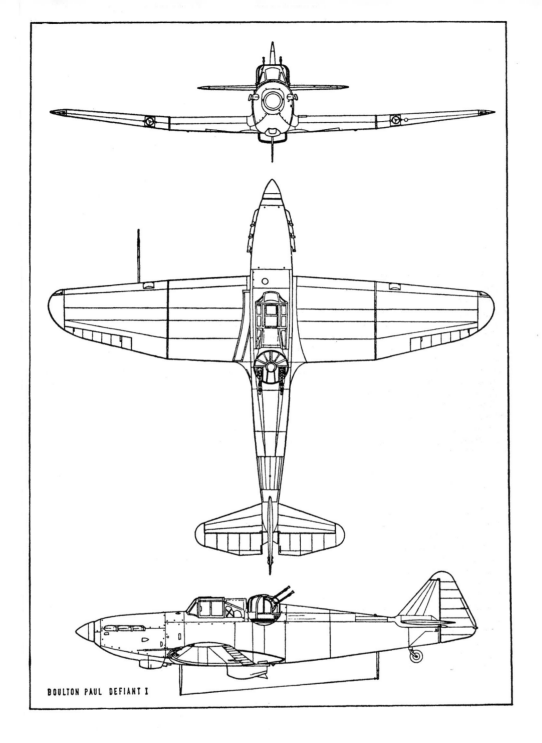

BOULTON PAUL DEFIANT I

THE GRUMMAN MARTLET MK. I

No. 804 Squadron, Fleet Air Arm, which operated with Sea Gladiators from Wick under the control of No. 13 Group, started re-equipping with Grumman Martlets in October 1940.

The Martlet thus became the only American fighter to go into action against the Luftwaffe during the Battle of Britain for one week.

Developed from the Grumman G-36 (XF F-3) the G-36A Martlet was ordered by the British Government for the Fleet Air Arm in 1939. The first two reached Britain at the end of August 1940. By October 15th, fifteen had been delivered and by the 19th a further sixteen had reached the Navy.

Modified to British specifications, the Martlet differed from the U.S. Navy version in having bullet-proof windscreen, armour-plate, light bomb racks and British-type deck-arrester gear. The armament was increased to four guns by the removal of the .50 calibre guns in the fuselage and the addition of four .303 Brownings in the wings.

Operationally the Martlet was highly efficient and had a considerable margin of speed over the Fulmar.

Data: GRUMMAN MARTLET MK. I

Manufacturers: Grumman Aircraft Engineering Corporation, Bethpage, Long Island, New York.
Power Plant: One Wright Cyclone G-205A. R-1820 air-cooled radial motor developing 1,000 h.p. at 4,500 ft. with a Hamilton Hydromatic, three-bladed propeller.
Dimensions: Span, 38 ft.; length, 28 ft. 10 in.; height, 9 ft. 2½ in.
Weight: Empty, 4,649 lb.; loaded, 5,876 lb.
Performance: Maximum speed, 325 m.p.h. at 13,500 ft.; cruising speed, 285 m.p.h.; initial rate of climb, 3,300 ft./min.; service ceiling, 28,000 ft.; range at cruising speed, 1,150 miles.

DORNIER 17

In July 1937 a new German medium bomber, the Do 17, caused a sensation at the Zürich international flying meeting. The slim machine outpaced most of the first-line interceptors in the show, although the onlookers did not know that it was operating at low weight and with special engines.

Nicknamed the 'Flying Pencil', the Do 17 was originally conceived as a high-speed commercial aircraft for Lufthansa and it flew for the first time, in civil guise, in the autumn of 1934. Its potentialities as a bomber were realised only after the prototypes had been stored away as unacceptable for civil use.

The first bomber version was flown in 1935 and the Luftwaffe received the Do 17E-1 at the end of 1936. This was slow (top speed 220 m.p.h.) and carried only two machine-guns. Its reconnaissance counterpart was the Do 17F.

Despite its speed the Do 17 performed well in the Spanish Civil War, and managed to avoid interception by fighters. In service the 17E was followed by the Do 17M-1 which had Bramo 323A radials of 900 h.p. in place of the earlier 750 h.p. BMW VI-7.3 engines.

Re-engined with BMW 132N radials the Do 1/P emerged and was built in quantity.

Following this came a re-design of the front fuselage which was more bulbous, with a ventral underhang, and accommodation for a crew of four. In this form the aircraft first appeared as the Do 17S of which only three were built, with DB 600 engines.

Fifteen pathfinder versions of the 17S were built as the 17U and these had an extra radio operator.

As in the case of the Heinkel 111, endeavours were made to restrict the use of DB 600 series engines to fighters and the next Do 17 to appear reverted to Bramo 323P radials. Known as the Do 17Z this variant was widely employed over Britain.

Armament was increased to six 7.9 m.m. machine-guns, two firing forward, one dorsal, one ventral and two through side windows. During the Battle of Britain two additional free-mounted machine-guns were added and some aircraft had the lower front machine-gun replaced by a 20 m.m. cannon. Among the measures adopted by Do 17 crews to try and shake off R.A.F. fighters was the carrying of stick hand grenades which were thrown out in the wake of the aircraft.

Like the He 111 the Do 17 had its crew grouped forward, was inadequately armed, and suffered accordingly.

Three Kampfgeschwader, one bomber Gruppe (K.Gr.606) and a number of long-range reconnaissance Staffeln were equipped with Do 17s for operations over Britain.

The following variants of Do 17 were operated in the Battle of Britain.

Do 17E-2 Slim nose. 1,760 lb. bomb-load. Two 750 h.p. BMW VI-7.3.

E-3 Similar to above.

M Bramo 323A.

P-1 Reconnaissance. Cameras in bomb-bay. BMW

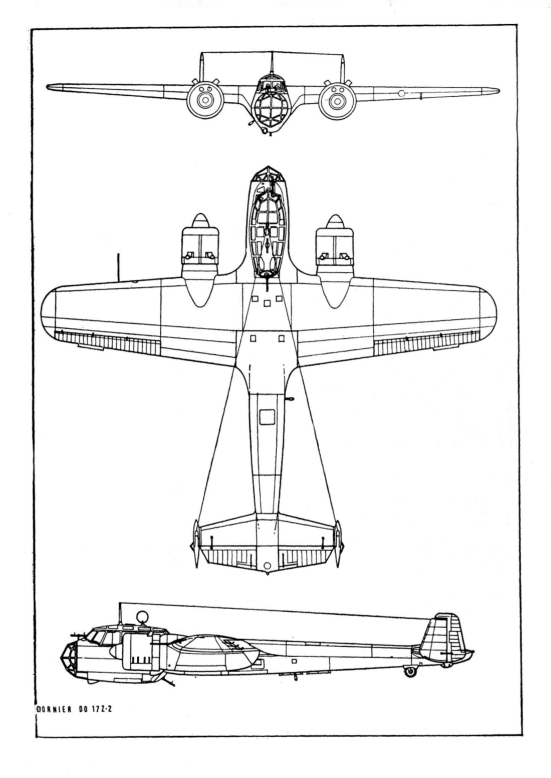

DORNIER DO 17Z-2

287

132N engines.

U   New bulged forward fuselage. Five crew. Path-finder aircraft. DB 600A.

z-1   Bramo 323A radials.

z-2   Bramo 323P radials. Four crew. Six machine-guns. One variant for special missions.

z-3   Reconnaissance version. Cameras in bomb-bay.

Data: DORNIER 17z-2

Manufacturers: Dornier-Werke G.m.b.H., Neuaubing and Friedrichshafen.

Power Plant: Two Bramo 1,000 h.p. 323P radials. Fuel capacity: total fuel 1,550 litres, with extra fuel tank, 2,445 litres for long-range reconnaissance.

Dimensions: Span, 59 ft.; length, 53 ft. 5½ in.; height, 15 ft. 9 in.; wing area, 592 sq. ft.

Weights: Empty, 11,484 lb.; normal loaded, 18,913 lb.; overloaded, 19,481 lb.

Bomb Load: (Internal) maximum, 2,200 lb.; with maximum fuel, bomb load reduced to 1,100 lb.

Performance: (At normal loaded weight) maximum speed, 265 m.p.h. at 16,400 ft.; maximum cruising speed, 236 m.p.h. at 14,200 ft.; service ceiling, 26,740 ft.; range, normal 745 miles, with overload tank 1,860 miles.

DORNIER 215

The Do 215 was in all main respects similar to the Do 17z except for its power plant of two DB 601A inline engines. The 215 was originally an export model taken over by the Luftwaffe, and was seen only in small numbers during the Battle of Britain, in most cases in a reconnaissance role.

The variants used were:

Do 215B-1   Reconnaissance bomber with cameras.

215B-4   Different camera equipment.

Data: DORNIER 215B 1

Manufacturers: Dornier-Werke G.m.b.H., Friedrichschafen and Neuaubing.

Power Plant: Two 1,150 h.p. Daimler Benz DB 601 inline engines.

Dimensions: Span, 59 ft.; length, 53 ft. 5½ in.; height, 15 ft. 9 in.; wing area, 592 sq. ft.

Weights: Empty, 11,685 lb.; normal loaded, 18,960 lb.

Bomb Load: 2,200 lb.

Performance: Maximum speed, 275 m.p.h. at 15,000 ft.; service ceiling, 28,000 ft.; range, 1,450 miles with 1,100 lb. of bombs, or 900 miles with 2,200 lb. of bombs.

DORNIER 18

One staffel (2/106) of Do 18s operated alongside the HE 115 from Brittany in the summer of 1940 on minelaying and coastal reconnaissance work. Originally flown as a transatlantic mail carrier, the Do. 18 had a crew of four. Two machine-guns were carried and bombs or mines hung under the sponsons.

Data: DORNIER 18

Manufacturers: Dornier-Werke G.m.b.H., Friedrichschafen.

Power Plant: Two 865 h.p. BMW 132N radials in tandem driving tractor and pusher propellers.

Dimensions: Span, 77 ft. 9 in.; length, 63 ft. 1 in.; height, 17 ft. 9 in.; wing area, 1,054 sq. ft.

Weights: Empty, 12,600 lb.; loaded, 30,000 lb.

Performance: Maximum speed, 186 m.p.h. at 7,200 ft.; cruising, 161 m.p.h.; service ceiling, 17,400 ft.; range, 2,700 miles.

FOCKE-WULF 200

A civil transport (the Condor) converted to military use, the FW 200 was the only four-motor aircraft used for bombing in the Battle of Britain. The FW 200C-1 first appeared late in 1939 and only a few were available to take part in the Norwegian campaign.

After the fall of France 1./KG40 was established at Bordeaux with seven FW 200Cs for maritime reconnaissance and shipping strike. Several of the unit's aircraft were shot down over Britain during the Battle. In order to put in a maximum effort against Merseyside on the nights August 28th–31st, 1940, aircraft of 1./KG40 were used as ordinary bombers.

The aircraft carried a crew of five and mounted three machine-guns and one 20 m.m. cannon.

Data FW 200C-1

Manufacturers: Focke-Wulf Flugzeugbau G.m.b.H., Cottbus.

Power Plant: Four 870 h.p. BMW 132H-1 radials.

Dimensions: Span, 108 ft. 3 in.; length, 78 ft. 3 in.; height, 23 ft. 4 in.; wing area, 1,290 sq. ft.

Weight: Loaded, 48,500 lb.

Bomb Load: Maximum, 2,750 lb.

Performance: Maximum speed, 250 m.p.h.; cruising, 180 m.p.h.; service ceiling, 21,500 ft.; maximum range, 2430 miles.

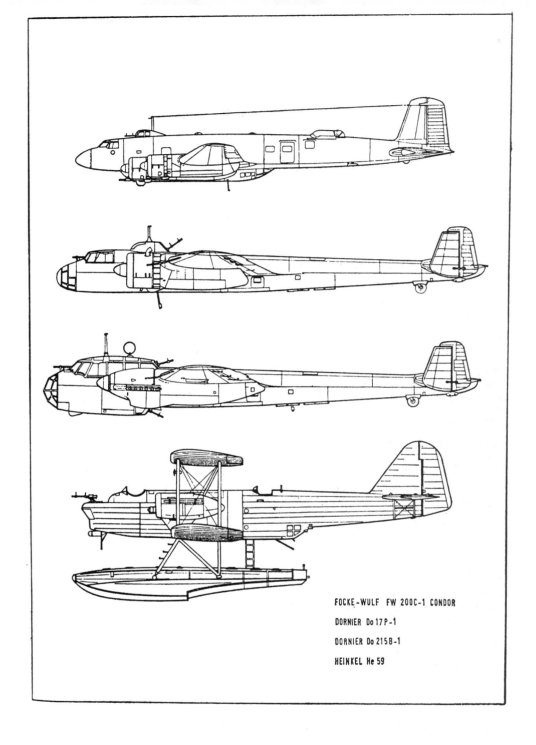

FOCKE-WULF FW 200C-1 CONDOR

DORNIER Do 17 P-1

DORNIER Do 215 B-1

HEINKEL He 59

HEINKEL 59

The obsolete Heinkel 59 float biplane was used by the Luftwaffe for air-sea rescue in the Channel. Several were brought down by R.A.F. fighters following a British Government protest at the use of the red cross for the recovery of valuable aircrews and 'reconnaissance'. The 59 had originally been produced as a torpedo and general purpose bomber in the Luftwaffe's early days.

Data: HEINKEL 59

Manufacturers Ernst Heinkel Flugzeugwerke G.m.b.H., Marienehe.
Power Plant: Two 660 h.p. BMW VI engines.
Dimensions: Span, 77 ft. 6 in.; length, 56 ft. 6 in.; wing area, 1,615 sq. ft.
Weight: Loaded, 19,620 lb.
Performance: Maximum speed, 137 m.p.h.; range, 1,090 miles at 106 m.p.h.

HEINKEL 111

Heinkel 111s from five Geschwader operated over Britain during the summer of 1940, together with many more of the type from reconnaissance staffeln.

First flown early in 1935, the He 111 was in operational service with the Luftwaffe in 1937. In its early versions, it had a stepped cockpit, elliptical wings and 'dustbin' gun-turret.

Early in 1939 the He 111P came into service with revised straight-tapered wing, unstepped cockpit and ventral gun cupola. To avoid a shortage of Daimler Benz DB 601 liquid-cooled engines, which were required for the Me 109 and Me 110 fighters, a further variant, the 111H, was introduced with Jumo 211 motors. The 111H began to equip squadrons in the autumn and winter of 1939, and it was in full-scale production throughout 1940 and ensuing years.

The He 111H was a low wing all-metal monoplane carrying a crew of five or six made up of pilot, bomb-aimer, radio operator and two or three gunners. Armament consisted of five 7.9 mm. machine-guns, one in the nose, one each ventral and dorsal positions, and two firing from the side windows.

During the Battle of Britain efforts were made to increase the armament while at the same time armour protection was given to the crew. On some aircraft a 20 mm. cannon was fitted in place of the nose machine-gun and on others a remotely controlled machine-gun was mounted in the tail.

In the Polish, Belgian and French campaigns the He 111 had not suffered too badly, but when flown against the R.A.F. it was shown to be very vulnerable, as its speed was not high enough for it to escape British fighters. Its armament was inadequate and without powered turrets the hand-operated

guns were difficult to use. Some Heinkel crews resorted to throwing out tin boxes attached to reels of wire, in the hope that they would catch in a fighter's propeller.

As a night bomber the He 111 was more successful in 1940–1 and the pathfinder gruppe K.Gr.100 used Heinkels carrying the 'X' and 'Y' beam navigation/bombing systems. For mine-laying and anti-shipping strike, the He 111 was used by KG4 and KG26 respectively.

Some Heinkels used over Britain were of the early 'D' variant produced in 1937. The sub-types operated in the Battle of Britain were as follows)

He 111D	Stepped cockpit. Elliptical wing. 'Dustbin' turret. Two 1,050 h.p. DB 600Ga engines.
P-1	First version with unstepped cockpit and straight-tapered wings. Two 1,150 h.p. DB 601A. Basic armament three machine-guns but this increased retrospectively after delivery.
P-2	As for P-1, but modified wireless.
P-5	Detail modifications.
H-1	Similar to P series. Two Jumo 211A-1s of 1,000 h.p. each.
H-2	Additional guns through side windows, although this modification retrospectively fitted to most earlier sub-types. Two Jumo 211A-3. Modified wireless equipment.
H-3	Some fitted with 20 mm. cannon in nose. Jumo 211D-1 engines of 1,200 h.p. each. Certain H-3 had an additional machine-gun firing forward from the ventral cupola.
H-4	Uprated engines: 1,340 h.p. Jumo 211F-2. Equipped to carry two 2,000 lb. or one 4,000 lb. bomb externally.
H-5	Reverted to Jumo 211D-1. External bomb load 5,510 lb.

Data: HEINKEL 111H-3

Manufacturers: Ernst Heinkel Flugzeugwerke G.m.b.H. Marienehe and Oranienburg.
Power Plant: Two 1,200 h.p. Junkers Jumo 221D-1. Fuel capacity, 762 gallons.
Dimensions: Span, 74 ft. 3 in.; length, 54 ft. 6 in.; height, 13 ft. 9 in.; wing area, 942 sq. ft.
Weights: Empty, 14,355 lb.; normal loaded, 25,520 lb.; maximum overload, 27,400 lb.
Bomb Load: (Internal, fitted vertically in the centre section) 4,400 lb.; with full tanks load decreased to 2,134 lb.
Performance: (at normal loaded weight) Maximum speed, 255 m.p.h. at 16,000 ft.; cruising speed, 225 m.p.h. at 16,000 ft.; service ceiling, 25,500 ft.; range, normal, 1,540 miles; with overload tanks, 2,640 miles; with 4,400 lb. of bombs range was reduced to 760 miles.

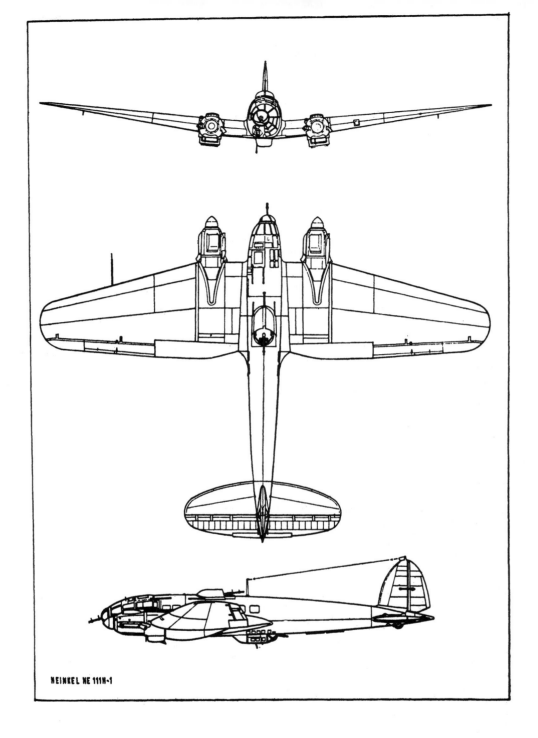

HEINKEL HE 111H-1

HEINKEL 113

In many combat reports for the period August-October 1940 reference was made to combats with and sightings of Heinkel 113s. The myth of the 113 has been perpetuated in several books since the war. Designated He 100D, the so-called He 113 was an attractive and very fast interceptor, first flown in January 1938. Seven prototypes, three pre-production and twelve production He 100s were built, but not one was accepted by the Luftwaffe for operational use. Six prototypes were sold to Russia, and the three pre-production machines to Japan.

The batch of twelve remaining, known as the He 100D, formed into a unit for the defence of the Heinkel Marienehe works and were flown by Heinkel test pilots. To give the impression that the 100 was in service with the Luftwaffe, a flood of propaganda pictures was issued showing the line up of He 100s with full camouflage and false unit markings. The type was given the spurious designation He 113. The He 113s reported in the Battle of Britain resulted from faulty aircraft recognition and were, in fact, Me 109s.

HEINKEL 115

Employed for coastal reconnaissance and minelaying, the He 115 seaplane was used by five Küstenfliegerstaffeln employed by Luftflotten 2, 3 and 5.

Developed from a civil main seaplane, the 115 carried a crew of three and mounted two machine-guns, one forward and one dorsal. Two variants were operated, the 115B-1 and C.

Data: HEINKEL 115

Manufacturer: Ernst Heinkel Flugzeugwerke G.m.b.H., Marienehe.
Power Plant: Two 880 h.p. BMW 132 radials.
Dimensions: Span, 75 ft. 10 in.; length, 57 ft.; height, 23 ft. 4 in.; wing area, 946 sq. ft.
Weights: Empty, 11,670 lb.; loaded, 20,020 lb.
Performance: Maximum speed, 217 m.p.h. at 11,150 ft.; cruising, 186 m.p.h.; service ceiling, 21,320 ft.; normal range, 1,300 miles.

JUNKERS 87

The Junkers 87 Stuka was a prime weapon in the Luftwaffe armoury until the summer of 1940, when its poor performance and vulnerability led to heavy casualties. Employed in the convoy battles of July and the strikes against southern England in August, the Ju 87 began to fade out of the picture on August 19th, and the main units with the type (under Fliegerkorps

VIII) were withdrawn to the Pas de Calais on August 29th. Some raids with the remaining Ju 87 units were made on the 30th.

The Stuka never reappeared over Britain and confined its activities to fronts where opposition was less intense.

Descended from the K.47 built in Sweden in 1928, the Ju 87 had many staunch adherents in the Luftwaffe, as where air supremacy was assured it offered a cheap and easy method of precision bombing. First flown with a Rolls-Royce Kestrel engine in 1935, the Ju 87 went into service in 1937 as the Ju 87A powered by a 635 h.p. Jumo 210 inline engine. Both the 87A and the 87B participated in the Spanish Civil War, the latter having more power, spatted in place of trousered undercarriage, altered hood and many detail modifications.

The Ju 87B swept a path for the armoured divisions through Poland, Holland, Belgium and France, and six Stukakampfgeschwader were finally ranged against Britain. With its cranked wing and prominent undercarriage, the Ju 87 bore an unmistakable outline. It carried a crew of two and was armed with two fixed and one movable machine-guns.

The variants flown over Britain were:
Ju 87 B-1   First used in Spain in 1938.
B-2   Broader propeller blades, ejector exhausts and minor modifications to the undercarriage.
R   As for B-2, but underwing fuel-tanks and single bomb under the fuselage. R= Reichweite or range.

Data: JUNKERS 87B

Manufacturers Junkers Flugzeug und Motorenwerke, A. G., Dessau.
Power Plant: One 1,150 h.p. Jumo 211Da inline engine.
Dimensions: Span, 45 ft. 4 in.; length, 36 ft. 5 in.; height, 12 ft. 9 in.; wing area, 344 sq. ft.
Weights: Empty, 6,085 lb.; loaded, 9,370 lb.
Bomb Load: Either one 1,100 lb. bomb under the fuselage, or one 550 lb. bomb under the fuselage and four 110 lb. bombs under the wings. Maximum bomb load for short ranges, 2,205 lb.
Performance: Maximum speed, 232 m.p.h. at 13,500 ft.; cruising, 175 m.p.h. at 15,000 ft.; service ceiling, 24,500 ft.; range with 1,100 lb. of bombs, 370 miles; with external tanks (Ju 87R), 875 miles.

JUNKERS 88

The Junkers 88 was designed as a medium/dive bomber with the speed of a fighter. While the 88 was under development, however, the new generation of British fighters caught up with and surpassed it with the result that serious losses were suffered over Britain in 1940.

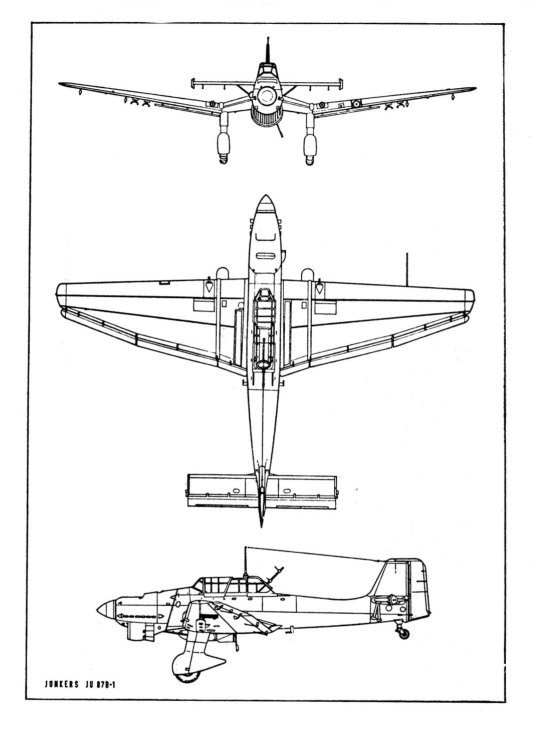

JUNKERS JU 87B-1

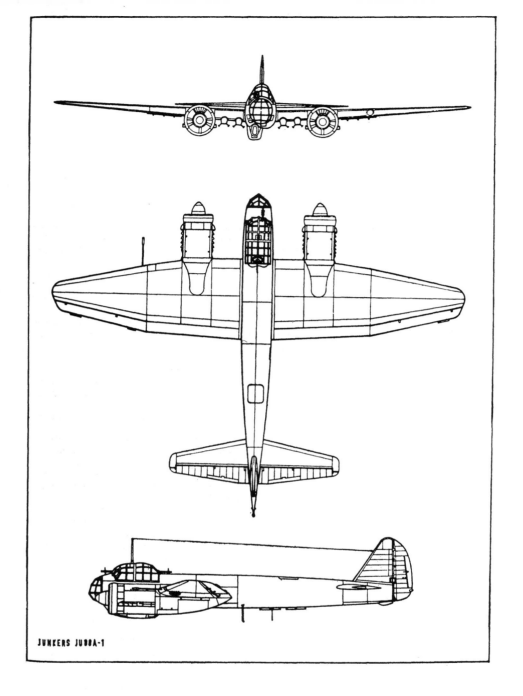

JUNKERS JU88A-1

First flown in December 1936, the Ju 88 was only at the pre-production batch stage on the outbreak of war. The first ten Ju 88A-1s were hurriedly put into service and attacked the *Ark Royal* in September 1939.

The A-1 variant was that mainly used in the Battle of Britain. It had twin Jumo engines, slatted wing dive brakes, and a crew of four grouped, as usual, in the nose. Armament comprised three machine-guns, nose, ventral and dorsal, although an additional gun was later fitted in the dorsal position. Armour protection was increased during August and September 1940.

Against the Spitfire and Hurricane the Ju 88 was vulnerable, but it could outpace the obsolescent Blenheim 1F which tried to intercept it.

Variants used:

Ju 88 1-1   In large-scale use. First production model.
    A-5   Wing span increased to 65 ft. 10½ in. Armament four/five machine-guns. Outer wing bomb carriers. Improved armour. Strengthened undercarriage.

Data: JUNKERS 88A-1

Manufacturer: Junkers Flugzeug and Motorenwerke, A. G. Dessau, etc.

Power Plant: Two 1,200 h.p. Jumo 211B-1 inlines (in radial cowlings).

Dimensions: Span, 59 ft. 10¾ in.; length, 47 ft. 1 in.; height, 15 ft. 5 in.; wing area, 540 sq. ft.

Weight: Maximum loaded, 27,500 lb.

Bomb Load: Normal, 3,968 lb. (main load on four external carriers inboard of the nacelles, plus small load in the fuselage); maximum bomb load, 5,510 lb.

Performance: Maximum speed, 286 m.p.h. at 16,000 ft.; service ceiling, 26,500 ft.; range, 1,553 miles.

MESSERSCHMITT 109

In the period 1939–40, the Me 109 was undoubtedly one of the finest single-seat fighters in the world, and it was a most worthy opponent of the Hurricane and Spitfire. Due to lack of production organisation and any sense of urgency, however, the Me 109 was not available in sufficient numbers to decide the outcome of the Battle of Britain.

Flown initially in 1935, the Me 109 proved its worth in 109B and C forms in the Spanish Civil War. The type was steadily developed up to 1939 when the E series came into service and these formed the bulk of the fighter formations used in the summer of 1940.

Among the 109s advantages were speed, rate of climb, and the ability to go straight into a dive due to a direct injection fuel pump. Its faults lay in delicate handling qualities which required much experience to master. Unlike the Hurricane and Spitfire, the Me 109 had the petrol tank behind the pilot, and it was vulnerable.

In the later stages of the Battle, improved engine ratings gave the 109 a better rate of climb than the Spitfire above 20,000 ft. Originally, protection for the pilot was lacking, but in July armour was fitted behind the fuselage petrol tank, and armour plates were added round the pilot's head and neck— although these interfered with the view from the cockpit. Throughout, the Me 109 suffered from lack of range and the non-availability of suitable drop tanks.

No less than ten Jagdgeschwader were used against Britain, and many 109s operated as fighter-bombers in October 1940.

Variants used:

Me 109B   First issued to 2./JG88 in Spain, April 1937. 650 h.p. Jumo 210DA.
    E-1   DB 601A of 1,050 h.p. Armament: two machine-guns in the cowlings and two 20 mm. cannon in the wings.
    E-1/B   Carried 4 × 110 lb. or one 550 lb. bomb. Machine-guns only.
    E-3   Main variant in the Battle of Britain. DB 6/1Aa. Additional cannon through airscrew hub, but this was generally removed by July 1940.
    E-4   Engine cannon deleted. Wing cannon fitted.
    E-4/B   Fighter-bomber, war load as for E-1/B including wing cannon.
    E-4/N   DB 601N, higher compression ratio.
    E-5   Reconnaissance. Armament only two machine-guns. One large camera.
    E-7   Similar to E-4 but DB 601N and drop tank, 551 lb. bomb fitting.

Data: MESSERSCHMITT 109E-3

Manufacturers: Messerschmitt A. G., Augsburg, Regensburg, etc.

Power Plant One 1,150 h.p. Daimler Benz DB 601 Aa inline.

Dimensions: Span, 32 ft. 4 in.; length, 26 ft. 8 in.; height, 7 ft. 5½ in.

Weights: Empty, 4,421 lb.; loaded, 5,520 lb.

Performance: Maximum speed, 354 m.p.h. at 12,300 ft.; cruising, 298 m.p.h.; initial rate of climb, 3,100 ft./min.; time to 16,500 ft., 6.2 mins.; service ceiling, 36,000 ft.; cruising range, 412 miles (no combat allowances).

MESSERSCHMITT 110

Like the Junkers 87, the Messerschmitt 110 started the war with a false aura of invincibility. In the Zerstörer, or Destroyer, class, the 110 was intended as a long-range escort fighter to clear the path for the bomber formations. When they first came into service in 1939 the Me 110s had hand-picked crews who

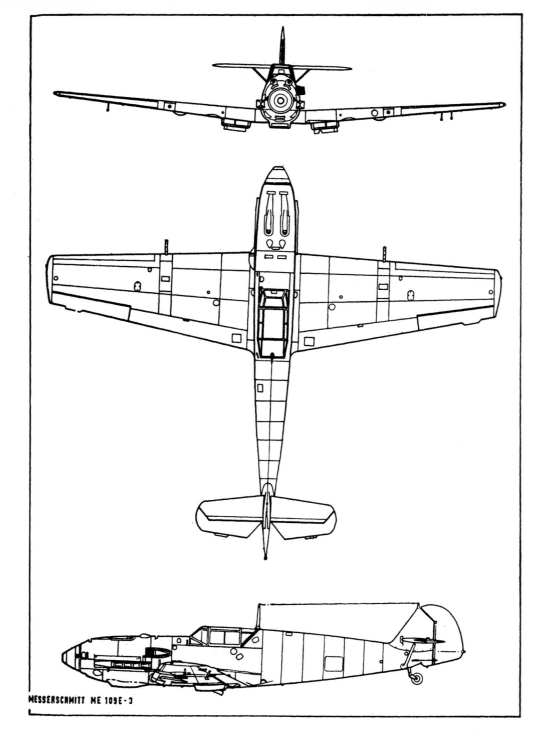

MESSERSCHMITT ME 109E-3

were supposed to represent an élite corps.

The Zerstörer's reputation was maintained until the attacks opened on Channel convoys in July, when it was rudely shattered. Throughout the period July–October Zerstörergruppen suffered severe losses out of all proportion to the effect they achieved and in the end they themselves had to be escorted by Me 109s.

The Me 110 should have been withdrawn from service in the west in August, but overall shortage of fighters necessitated their retention. In addition the High Command was impressed by the success claims which Z.Gruppen put in—these being grossly exaggerated.

The Me 110 was first flown in May 1936, but due to engine changes, etc., it was not in large-scale production until 1939. In the Battle of Britain three Zerstörer Geschwader were operated together with several Me 110 reconnaissance staffeln and the ground attack unit Erprobungsgruppe 210 which had Me 110 and Me 109. In October many Me 110s were converted into fighter-bombers.

Lack of manoeuvrability and speed and structural weakness, particularly in the tail, were the main faults of the 110. Two crew were carried and the armament was four machine-guns and two 20 mm. cannon in the nose, plus a free mounted machine-gun in the dorsal position.

Main variants used:

Me 110 C-1 First version in service.

C-2 Revised electrics. FuG 10 radio.

C-4 Main variant operated. Similar to C-1 but with improved MG FF cannon.

C-4B Fighter bomber. DB 601N engines. 1,100 lb. of bombs.

C-5 Fighter reconnaissance. Camera replacing nose cannon.

D-0 A pre-production variant. Only a few used. No cannon. 230 gallon fixed ventral fuel-tank and provision for underwing tanks.

D-1 No ventral tank but provision for underwing tanks.

Data: MESSERSCHMITT ME 110C-4

Manufacturer: Messerschmitt A. G., Augsburg, Regensburg, etc.

Power Plant: Two 1,100 h.p. Daimler Benz D.B. 601A inlines.

Dimensions: Span, 53 ft. 5 in.; length, 40 ft. 4 in.; height, 11 ft. 6 in.; wing area, 413 sq. ft.

Weight: Loaded, 15,290 lb.

Performance: Maximum speed, 340 m.p.h. at 22,000 ft. and 294 m.p.h. at sea level; cruising speed, 285 m.p.h. at 16,500 ft.; service ceiling, 32,000 ft.; time to 18,000 ft., 8.5 mins.; economic cruising range, 680 miles; highspeed cruise range, 565 miles at 301 m.p.h. at 23,000 ft.

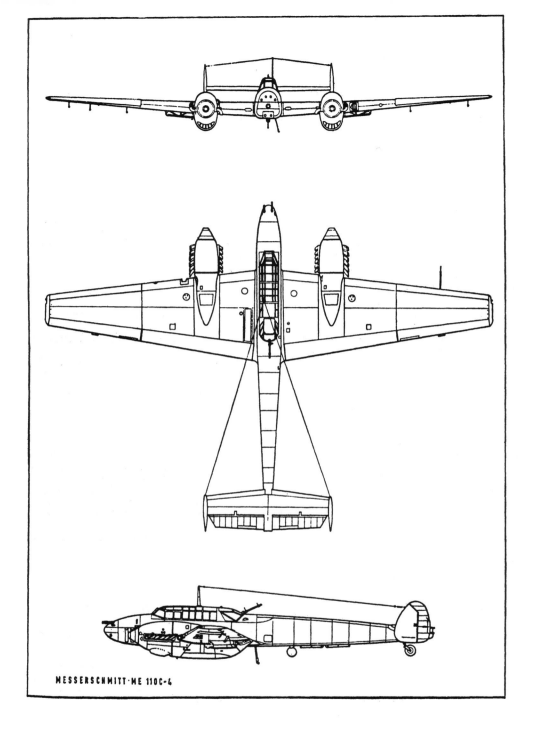

MESSERSCHMITT·ME 110C-4

FIAT BR.20 CICOGNA (STORK)

Early in October 1940 Mussolini despatched a force of seventy-five BR.20 bombers to participate in the air war against Britain. The move was more political than military and the Luftwaffe was somewhat embarrassed by the arrival of its new comrades in arms. The BR.20s were supplemented by Squadriglia 172 with five CZ-1007 Bis reconnaissance bombers, but these did not operate against Britain.

Stationed in the Brussels area, the BR.20s belonged to 13 Stormo and 43 Stormo re-designated KG13 and KG43 respectively. They operated first by night on October 25th, against Harwich, and then by day on October 29th, when fifteen bombers approached Ramsgate with a heavy escort of Italian and German fighters. On the latter occasion none were shot down, but many were damaged by A.A. fire.

The BR.20s made one more daylight raid after the Battle of Britain was over (on November 11th) and lost three aircraft out of ten despatched. After this they raided only by night, putting up seven small sorties between November and January when they were withdrawn to Italy.

One of the most modern Italian aircraft at the time, the BR.20 was not, however, suitable for use against the R.A.F. It lacked defensive armament and armour. Of all-metal construction, it carried a crew of five and mounted three machine-guns, one nose, one dorsal and one ventral.

Data FIAT BR20 CICOGNA (STORK)

Manufacturer: Aeronautica d'Italia S.A. (Fiat), Turin.
Power Plant: Two 1,030 h.p. Fiat A.80 R.C.41 radials.
Dimensions: Span, 70 ft. 6 in.; length, 52 ft. 10 in.; height, 14 ft. 1 in.; wing area, 796 sq. ft.
Weights: Empty, 14,300 lb.; loaded, 22,220 lb.
Bomb Load: Maximum, 2,550 lb.
Performance: Maximum speed, 255 m.p.h. at 13,500 ft.; cruising speed, 220 m.p.h. at 13,450 ft.; service ceiling, 15,000 ft.; range cruising, 1,350 miles with 2,200 lb. of bombs.

FIAT CR.42 FRECCIA (ARROW)

As part of the escort for the seventy-five BR.20 bombers in their raids on Britain, the Regia Aeronautica provided fifty Fiat CR.42 biplane fighters which were based in Belgium at the beginning of October 1940. They formed the 18th Gruppo alternatively designated 18./JG56.

A delightful machine to fly, and one of the most manoeuvrable, the CR.42 was completely out-classed by modern monoplanes. When attacked it could only do flick rolls and tight turns to keep out of the way. Even when presented with a target, the two machine-guns in the engine cowling were insufficient to do much damage.

The CR.42 made only one sortie during the Battle of Britain, on October 29th, escorting bombers to Ramsgate. On their second and last daylight raid on November 11th, three were shot down by British fighters.

Data: FIAT CR.42 FRECCIA (ARROW)

Manufacturer: Aeronautica d'Italia SA. (Fiat), Turin.
Power Plant: One 840 h.p. Fiat A.74 RC.38 radial
Dimensions: Span, 31 ft. 10 in.; length, 27 ft. 3 in.; height, 10 ft.
Weight: Normal loaded, 5,100 lb.
Performance: Maximum speed, 270 m.p.h. at 13,100 ft.; cruising, 232 m.p.h.; climb to 13,000 ft., 5.5 minutes; service ceiling, 32,000 ft.; cruising range, 460 miles.

FIAT G.50 FALCO (FALCON)

The most up-to-date portion of the escort for Italy's BR.20 bombers in Belgium was the 20th Gruppo (20./KG56) with forty-eight Fiat G.50 Falco single-seat fighters.

Although a low monoplane with retractable undercarriage, the G.50 had a top speed only 20 m.p.h. faster than that of the CR.42 biplane. The main advantage of the G.50, as with other Italian types, was its manoeuvrability.

The G.50 carried four machine-guns, two in the fuselage and two in the wings.

Data: FIAT G.50 FALCO (FALCON)

Manufacturer: Aeronautica d'Italia S.A. (Fiat), Turin.
Power Plant: One 850 h.p. Fiat A.74 R.C.38 radial.
Dimensions: Span, 35 ft. 2 in.; length, 25 ft. 7 in.; height, 9 ft. 9 in.
Weights: Empty, 3,528 lb.; loaded, 5,291 lb.
Performance: Maximum speed, 290 m.p.h. at 14,760 ft.; maximum cruising, 205 m.p.h.; initial rate of climb, 1,080 ft./min.; time to 16,400 ft., 5.2 mins.; maximum range (with overload fuel), 420 miles.

APPENDIX 2

Detailed layout of R.A.F. Fighter Command and its subsidiary formations at 0900 hours, September 15th, 1940

Air Officer Commanding-in-Chief : Air Chief Marshal Sir Hugh Caswall Tremenheere Dowding, G.C.V.O., K.C.B., C.M.G., Principal Air Aide-de-Camp to the King.
Headquarters : Bentley Priory, Stanmore, Middlesex.

FORMATIONS UNDER COMMAND (Block letters denote Sector Headquarters)

NO. 9 GROUP

Air Officer Commanding : Not yet appointed.
Headquarters : Barton Hall, Preston, Lancashire.
Stations and Squadrons : None.

NO. 10 GROUP

Air Officer Commanding : Air Vice-Marshal Sir Christopher Joseph Quintin Brand, K.B.E., D.S.O., M.C., D.F.C.
Headquarters : Rudloe Manor, Box, Wiltshire.

Stations	Officers Commanding Stations	Squadrons	Officers Commanding Squadrons
PEMBREY	W/Cdr. J. H. Hutchinson	No. 79	S/Ldr. J. H. Heyworth
FILTON	G/Capt. R. H. Hanmer, M.C.		
Exeter	S/Ldr. R. S. Mills, D.F.C. (temporarily in command)	No. 601 (County of London)	S/Ldr. Sir A. P. Hope, Bart.
		No. 87 ('B' Flight)	(see 'A' Flight)
Bibury		No. 87 ('A' Flight)	S/Ldr. R. S. Mills, D.F.C.
Colerne[1]	W/Cdr. C. E. St. J. Beamish,[2] D.F.C.		
St. Eval[3]	G/Capt. L. G. Le. B. Croke (O.C. Fighter Section H.Q.)	No. 234	F/Lt. C. L. Page
Roborough[4]		No. 247	F/Lt. H. A. Chater
MIDDLE	W/Cdr. D. N. Roberts, A.F.C.	No. 238	S/Ldr. H. A. Fenton
WALLOP		No. 609 (West Riding)	S/Ldr. H. S. Darley
		No. 604 (County of Middlesex)	S/Ldr. M. F. Anderson
		No. 23 ('A' Flight)	S/Ldr. G. Heycock
Warmwell	G/Capt. G. V. Howard, D.F.C.	No. 152	S/Ldr. P. K. Devitt
Boscombe Down[5]	G/Capt. R. S. Sorley, O.B.E., D.S.C., D.F.C. (Commanding Aeroplane and Armament Experimental Establishment)	No. 56	S/Ldr. H. M. Pinfold

		Operational Training Units	Officers Commanding Operational Training Units
Aston Down	G/Capt. G. W. Murlis-Green, D.S.O., M.C.	No. 5	W/Cdr. P. J. H. Halahan, D.F.C.
Sutton Bridge	G/Capt. B. B. Caswell	No. 6	W/Cdr. J. H. Edwardes-Jones, D.F.C.
Hawarden	G/Capt. W. J. Seward	No. 7	W/Cdr. J. R. Hallings-Pott, D.S.O.

NO. 11 GROUP

Air Officer Commanding : Air Vice-Marshal Keith Rodney Park, M.C., D.F.C.
Headquarters : Hillingdon House, Uxbridge, Middlesex.

Stations	Officers Commanding Stations	Squadrons	Officers Commanding Squadrons
DEBDEN	W/Cdr. J. L. F. Fuller-Good	No. 17	S/Ldr. Miller
Castle Camps	(Satellite of Debden)	No. 73	S/Ldr. M. S. W. Robinson
Martlesham	W/Cdr. A. D. Farquhar, D.F.C.	No. 257	F/Lt. R. R. S. Tuck, D.F.C.
Heath		No. 25 ('A' Flight)	S/Ldr. W. W. Loxton

[1] Forming as Sector Station for eventual replacement of Filton
[2] On temporary duty at Filton   [3] Station in Coastal Command
[4] Fleet Air Arm Station
[5] Station in Flying Training Command

Stations	Officers Commanding Stations	Squadrons	Officers Commanding Squadrons
NORTH WEALD	W/Cdr. F. V. Beamish, D.S.O., A.F.C.	No. 25 ('B' Flight) No. 249	(see 'A' Flight) S/Ldr. J. Grandy
Stapleford Abbotts	(Satellite of North Weald)	No. 46	S/Ldr. J. R. MacLachlan
HORNCHURCH	G/Capt. C. A. Bouchier, O.B.E., D.F.C.	No. 603 (City of Edinburgh)	S/Ldr. G. L. Denholm
Rochford (Southend)	(Satellite of Hornchurch)	No. 41 No. 222	S/Ldr. D. O. Finlay S/Ldr. J. H. Hill
Manston	S/Ldr. G. A. L. Manton		
KENLEY	W/Cdr. T. B. Prickman	No. 253 No. 501 (County of Gloucester)	S/Ldr. G. R. Edge, D.F.C. S/Ldr. H. A. V. Hogan
Croydon	W/Cdr. T. B. Prickman	No. 605 (County of Warwick)	S/Ldr. W. Churchill, D.S.O., D.F.C.
West Malling	F/Lt. V. Mercer-Smith[1]		
BIGGIN HILL	G/Capt. R. Grice, D.F.C.	No. 72 No. 92 No. 141 ('B' Flight)	S/Ldr. E. Graham S/Ldr. P. J. Sanders (see 'A' Flight)
Gravesend (Satellite)		No. 66	S/Ldr. R. H. A. Leigh
Redhill[2]		No. 600 (City of London)	
Hawkinge	S/Ldr. E. E. Arnold, D.F.C.		
Lympne	S/Ldr. D. H. Montgomery		
TANGMERE	W/Cdr. J. A. Boret, M.C., A.F.C.	No. 607 (County of Durham) No. 213	S/Ldr. J. A. Vick
		Special Unit The Fighter Interception Unit[3]	*Officer Commanding Unit* W/Cdr. G. P. Chamberlain
		Squadrons	*Officers Commanding Squadrons*
Westhampnett	(Satellite of Tangmere)	No. 602 (City of Glasgow)	S/Ldr. A. V. R. Johnstone, D.F.C.
Ford[4]	Capt. A. G. E. Burton, R.N.	No. 23 ('B' Flight)	(see 'A' Flight)
NORTHOLT	G/Capt. S. F. Vincent, A.F.C.	No. 229 No. 1 (Canadian) No. 303 (Polish)	S/Ldr. H. J. Maguire S/Ldr. E. O. McNab S/Ldr. Z. Krasnodebski and S/Ldr. R. G. Kellett, D.F.C.
	G/Capt. S. F. Vincent, A.F.C.	*Special Unit* The Air Fighting Development Unit[5]	*Officer Commanding Unit* W/Cdr. G. H. Vasse
		Squadrons No. 264 ('B' Flight)[6]	*Officers Commanding Squadrons* (see 'A' Flight)
Hendon	G/Capt. Ryder Young	No. 504 (County of Nottingham)	S/Ldr. J. Sample, D.F.C.

NO. 12 GROUP

Air Officer Commanding : Air Vice Marshal Trafford Leigh-Mallory, C.B., D.S.O.
Headquarters : Watnall, Nottingham, Notts.

Stations	Officers Commanding Stations	Squadrons	Officers Commanding Squadrons
DUXFORD	W/Cdr. A. B. Woodhall	No. 19[7] No. 310 (Czech) No. 312 (Czech)[5]	S/Ldr. B. J. E. Lane, D.F.C. S/Ldr. G. D. M. Blackwood S/Ldr. J. Ambrus and S/Ldr. F. H. Tyson
COLTISHALL	W/Cdr. W. K. Beisiegel	No. 74 No. 242	S/Ldr. A. G. Malan, D.F.C. S/Ldr. D. R. S. Bader
WITTERING	W/Cdr. H. Broadhurst, D.F.C., A.F.C.	No. 1 No. 266[8]	S/Ldr. D. A. Pemberton, D.F.C. S/Ldr. H. W. Mermagen, A.F.C. (temporarily in command)

[1] For discipline and administration. Station in other respects a satellite of Kenley employed as forward aerodrome for Kenley and Biggin Hill
[2] Employed as forward aerodrome for Kenley
[3] Nominally non-operational
[4] Fleet Air Arm Station
[5] Non-operational
[6] Nominally non-operational until 17.9.40, but operated on night 15/16 September.   [7] Operating from satellite at Fowlmere.
[8] Half-squadron available for operations in Duxford Sector, remainder non-operational.

Stations	Officers Commanding Stations	Squadrons	Officers Commanding Squadrons
DIGBY	W/Cdr. I. R. Parker	No. 151	S/Ldr. West
		No. 611 (West Lancashire)	S/Ldr. J. E. McComb
		No. 29	S/Ldr. S. C. Widdows
KIRTON-IN-LINDSEY	W/Cdr. S. H. Hardy	No. 616 (South Yorkshire)	S/Ldr. Burton
		No. 264 ('A' Flight)	S/Ldr. G. D. Garvin
		No. 307 (Polish)[1]	S/Ldr. G. C. Tomlinson, D.F.C.
Speke	F/Lt. E. Travers-Smith	No. 308 (Polish)[1]	F/Lt. S. Laskiewicz
Ringway[2]	W/Cdr. J. Blackford	No. 64 ('B' Flight)	(see 'A' Flight)
CHURCH FENTON	G/Capt. C. F. Horsley, M.C.	No. 85	S/Ldr. P. W. Townsend, D.F.C.
		No. 306 (Polish)[3]	S/Ldr. Scott
Leconfield[3]	W/Cdr. L. G. Nixon	No. 302 (Polish)	S/Ldr. W. A. J. Satchell
	F/Lt. A. J. Sayer	No. 64 ('A' Flight)	S/Ldr. A. R. D. MacDonnell, D.F.C.
Yeadon			

NO. 13 GROUP

Air Officer Commanding : Air Vice-Marshal Richard Ernest Saul, D.F.C.
Headquarters : Blakelaw Estate, Ponteland, Newcastle-on-Tyne.

Stations	Officers Commanding Stations	Squadrons	Officers Commanding Squadrons
CATTERICK	W/Cdr. G. L. Carter, A.F.C.	No. 54	S/Ldr. F. P. R. Dunworth
		No. 219 ('A' Flight)	S/Ldr. J. H. Little
USWORTH	W/Cdr. B. S. Thynne, A.F.C.	No. 43	S/Ldr. T. F. D. Morgan, D.F.C.
Acklington	W/Cdr. H. J. Pringle, A.F.C.	No. 32	S/Ldr. M. N. Crossley, D.S.O., D.F.C.
		No. 610 (County of Chester)	S/Ldr. J. Ellis, D.F.C.
		No. 219 ('B' Flight)	(see 'A' Flight)
TURNHOUSE	W/Cdr. The Duke of Hamilton and Brandon, A.F.C.	No. 65	S/Ldr. A. L. Holland
		No. 3	S/Ldr. S. F. Godden
		No. 141 ('A' Flight)	S/Ldr. W. A. Richardson
Drem	W/Cdr. R. L. R. Atcherley, A.F.C.	No. 111	S/Ldr. J. M. Thompson, D.F.C.
		No. 263[3]	S/Ldr. H. Eeles
WEST FREUGH[4]	G/Capt. E. R. Openshaw, A.F.C. (O.C. Fighter Sector H.Q.)		
Prestwick[4]		No. 615 (Auxiliary)	S/Ldr. J. R. Kayll, D.S.O., D.F.C.
DYCE[5]	G/Capt. F. Crerar (O.C. Fighter Sector H.Q.)	No. 145 ('B' Flight)	(see 'A' Flight)
Montrose[4]	G/Capt. F. H. Coleman, D.S.O.	No. 145 ('A' Flight)	S/Ldr. J. R. A. Peel, D.F.C.
WICK[5]	G/Capt. E. Digby Johnson, A.F.C. (O.C. Fighter Sector H.Q., W/Cdr. Ambler, A.F.C.)	No. 804[6]	Fleet Air Arm
Castletown		No. 808[6]	Fleet Air Arm
Sumburgh[5]	W/Cdr. S. H. V. Harris	No. 232[7]	F/Lt. M. M. Stephens, D.F.C.
ALDERGROVE[8]	G/Capt. C. S. Richardson, M.B.E. (O.C. Fighter Sector H.Q.)	No. 245	

NO. 14 GROUP[9]

Air Officer Commanding : Air Vice-Marshal Malcolm Henderson, C.I.E., D.S.O.
Headquarters : Drunmossie Hotel, Inverness.

Stations	Officers Commanding Stations
Castletown	W/Cdr. D. F. W. Atcherley
Skaebrae	W/Cdr. C. F. H. Grace

Squadrons : None

Other operational fighter units in Fighter Command: No. 421 Flight, No. 422 Flight.

[1] Non-operational.
[2] Station in No. 22 Group (Independent Group).
[3] 'A' Flight non-operational, 'B' Flight operational.
[4] Station in Flying Training Command.
[5] Station in Coastal Command.
[6] Under 13 Group for operations.

[7] Established on half-squadron basis.
[8] Station in R.A.F. in Northern Ireland, administered from Air Ministry.
[9] Responsible for administration of various units under operational control of No. 13 Group besides those stations shown.

APPENDIX 3

Bomber Command Order of Battle—September 15th, 1940

Unit	Parent Station	Temporary Location	Est.	Aircraft	Remarks
NO. 1 GROUP	HUCKNALL			Battles	
12 Squadron	Binbrook	Binbrook	16	,,	Operational
142 ,,	Binbrook	Binbrook	16	,,	,,
103 ,,	Newton	Newton	16	,,	,,
150 ,,	Newton	Newton	16	,,	,,
300 (Polish)	Swinderby	Swinderby	16	,,	,,
301 ,,	Swinderby	Swinderby	16	..	,,

(Nos. 12 and 142 earmarked as reinforcement for North Ireland.
Nos. 103 and 150 re-arming with Wellingtons in late September.)

Unit	Parent Station	Temporary Location	Est.	Aircraft	Remarks
NO. 2 GROUP	HUNTINGDON			Blenheims IV	
107 Squadron	Wattisham	Wattisham	16	,,	Operational
110 ,,	Wattisham	Wattisham	16	,,	,,
21 ,,	Watton	Lossiemouth	16	,,	,,
82 ,,	Watton	Watton	16	,,	,,
40 ,,	Wyton	Wyton	16	,,	,,
15 ,,	Wyton	Alconbury	16	,,	,,
57 ,,	Wyton	Lossiemouth	16	,,	,,
114 ,,	Horsham St. Faith	Oulton	16	,,	,,
139 ,,	Horsham St. Faith	Horsham	16	,,	,,
18 ,,	West Raynham	Gt. Massingham	16	,,	,,
101 ,,	West Raynham	West Raynham	27	,,	,,
105 ,,	Watton	Watton	16	,,	,,
218 ,,	Oakington	Oakington	16	,,	,,

Unit	Parent Station	Temporary Location	Est.	Aircraft	Remarks
NO. 3 GROUP	EXNING			Wellingtons I.A. and I.C.	
99 Squadron	Mildenhall	Newmarket	16	,,	Operational
149 ,,	Mildenhall	Mildenhall	16	,,	,,
38 ,,	Marham	Marham	16	,,	,,
115 ,,	Marham	Marham	16	,,	,,
9 ,,	Honington	Honington	16	,,	,,
37 ,,	Feltwell	Feltwell	16	,,	,,
75 N.Z.	Feltwell	Feltwell	16	,,	,,
214 Squadron	Stradishall	Stradishall	24	,,	,,
311 (Czech.)	Honington	Honington			Non-Operational

Unit	Parent Station	Temporary Location	Est.	Aircraft	Remarks
NO. 4 GROUP	YORK			Whitleys V	
51 Squadron	Dishforth	Dishforth	16	,,	Operational
58 ,,	Linton	Linton	16	,,	,,
10 ,,	Leeming	Leeming	16	,,	,,
77 ,,	Linton	Tholthorpe	16	,,	,,
102* ,,	Leeming	Prestwick	16	,,	,,
78 ,,	Dishforth	Dishforth	16	,,	,,
7 ,,	Leeming	Leeming	16	Stirlings	Non-Operational

Unit	Parent Station	Temporary Location	Est.	Aircraft	Remarks
NO. 5 GROUP	GRANTHAM			Hampdens	
61 Squadron	Hemswell	Hemswell	16	,,	Operational
144 ,,	Hemswell	Hemswell	16	,,	,,
49 ,,	Scampton	Scampton	16	,,	,,
83 ,,	Scampton	Scampton	16	,,	,,
44 ,,	Waddington	Waddington	16	,,	,,
50 ,,	Lindholme	Lindholme	16	,,	,,

* No. 102 Squadron under control of Coastal Command.

Appendix 3 continued.

Unit		Parent Station	Temporary Location	Est.	Aircraft	Remarks
106	,,	Finningley	Finningley	24	,,	Operational in emergency
271	,,	Doncaster	Doncaster			Transport

Unit		Parent Station	Temporary Location	Aircraft
NO. 6 GROUP	ABINGDON			
10 O.T.U.		Abingdon	Abingdon	Ansons—Whitleys
11	,,	Bassingbourn	Bassingbourn	,, —Wellingtons
12	,,	Benson	Benson	,, —Battles
15	,,	Harwell	Harwell	,, —Wellingtons
18	,,	Hucknall	Hucknall	,, —Battles (Polish)
19	,,	Kinloss	Kinloss	,, —Whitleys
20	,,	Lossiemouth	Lossiemouth	,, —Wellingtons
304	,,	Bramcote	Bramcote	Battles (Polish) Non-Operational
305	,,	Bramcote	Bramcote	,, (Polish) Non-Operational
NO. 7 GROUP	BRAMPTON			
13 O.T.U.		Bicester	Bicester	Ansons—Whitleys
14	,,	Cottesmore	Cottesmore	,, —Hampdens—Herefords
16	,,	Upper Heyford	Upper Heyford	,, —Hampdens—Herefords
17	,,	Upwood	Upwood	,, —Blenheims

TOTALS — 40 Operational Squadrons
11 O.T.Us.
4 Non-Operational Squadrons
—
55
—

Totals of Operational Squadrons by Types   *Establishment*

No. 1 Group	Battles	6 Squadrons	96 Aircraft
No. 2 ,,	Blenheims	13 ,,	219 (+ 36 I.R.)
No. 3 ,,	Wellingtons	8 ,,	136 Aircraft
No. 4 ,,	Whitleys	6 ,,	96 ,,
No. 5 ,,	Hampdens	7 ,,	120 ,,
		40	667 (+ 36 I.R.)
		—	—— (Blenheims)

APPENDIX 4

Squadron, flights and units which took part in the Battle of Britain

1, 1 (R.C.A.F.) (later 401), 3, 17, 19, 23, 25, 29, 32, 41, 43, 46, 54, 56, 64, 65, 66, 72, 73, 74, 79, 85, 87, 92, 111, 141, 145, 151, 152, 213, 219, 222, 229, 232, 234, 235, 236, 238, 242, 245, 247, 248, 249, 253, 257, 263, 264, 266, 302 (Polish), 303 (Polish), 310 (Czech), 312 (Czech), 501, 504, 600, 601. 602, 603, 604, 605, 607, 609, 610, 611, 615, 616, 421 Flight (became 91 Squadron), 422 Flight (became 96 Squadron), Fighter Interception Unit (F.I.U.), 804 Squadron Fleet Air Arm (under the operational control of No. 13 Group), 808 Squadron Fleet Air Arm (under operational control of No. 13 Group).

APPENDIX 5

Fighter production, June/November 1940

Week ending	Total	Types					Imports				
		D	H	S	B	W	B	M	H	ML	T
June 1	282	8	87	22							
8	285	2	79	22	2	1			1		
15	258	7	67	25							
22	261	8	75	21		1			3		
29	292	13	68	26							
July 6	281	12	65	32							
13	230	12	57	30		1					
20	270	11	67	41	1	1	10	3	3		
27	269	14	65	37	4	1	2	2			
Aug. 3	262	13	58	41	3						
10	230	10	54	37	5			5	4		
17	222	11	43	31	5			18	2		
24	265	8	64	44	5			14	9		
31	243	3	54	37	5	1		12	9	2	
Sept. 7	203	11	54	36	5	1				3	
14	221	10	56	38	6	1			1		1
21	211	6	57	40	4	1	1	1			
28	214	10	58	34				8			
Oct. 5	210	12	60	32				12		6	
12	201	11	55	31	4	1	5	14		4	
29	202	8	55	25	6		4	9		16	
26	241	16	69	42	9		2	9	1	9	
Nov. 2	208	10	56	41	3	4		13		1	

Types

D—Boulton Paul DEFIANT
H—Hawker HURRICANE
S — Vickers-Supermarine SPITFIRE
B — Bristol BEAUFIGHTER
W—Westland WHIRLWIND

Import Types

B — Brewster BUFFALO
M—Curtis MOHAWK
H—Hawker HURRICANE (Canada)
ML—Grumman MARTLET
T — Curtiss TOMAHAWK

APPENDIX 6

Monthly output of fighter aircraft, June/October

Operational

	P	A	C
June	1,164	1,163	−1
July	1,061	1,110	+49
August	1,143	1,087	−56
September	1,195	908	−287
October	1,218	917	−301

P—Planned;   A—Actual;   C—Actual compared with planned.

Types

	Beaufighter			Defiant			Hurricane			Spitfire			Whirlwind		
	P	A	C	P	A	C	P	A	C	P	A	C	P	A	C
June	8	2	−6	30	30	—	300	309	+9	135	103	−32	8	2	−6
July	14	5	−9	50	56	+6	220	272	+52	140	160	+20	4	3	−1
Aug.	21	23	+2	65	38	−27	270	251	−19	155	163	+8	6	1	−5
Sept.	24	15	−9	65	41	−24	280	252	−28	175	156	−19	8	3	−5
Oct.	40	21	−19	50	48	−2	300	250	−50	231	149	−82	10	1	−9

APPENDIX 7

Number of aircraft available for operations in fighter squadrons

DAILY AVERAGES

Week ending		*In total initially equipped operationally fit squadrons*	*Total Aircraft available for operations*
June	22	814	565
	29	814	587
July	6	871	644
	13	901	666
	20	1,052	658
	27	1,052	651
August	3	1,061	708
	10	1,106	749
	17	1,113	704
	24	1,169	758
	31	1,181	764
September	7	1,161	746
	14	1,046	725
	21	1,048	715
	28	1,048	732
October	5	1,048	734
	12	1,054	735
	19	1,056	734
	26	1,064	747
November	2	1,064	721

APPENDIX 8

Operational aircraft in storage units

Week ending		Defiant				Hurricane				Spitfire			
		1	2	3	4	1	2	3	4	1	2	3	4
June	28	20	4	2	3	170	25	59	39	97	10	7	3
July	5	32	2	—	2	222	21	74	45	119	21	13	3
	12	45	—	2	1	186	18	79	39	122	4	10	7
	19	52	1	12	—	174	20	84	37	107	17	30	12
	26	56	—	17	—	176	26	89	38	80	15	27	15
August	2	72	—	4	—	164	26	128	36	100	8	49	16
	9	80	—	11	—	160	23	150	33	132	11	51	13
	16	73	1	24	—	98	17	119	36	118	34	21	6
	23	79	1	18	4	86	17	113	33	84	11	28	8
	30	40	—	18	35	78	22	127	31	73	19	24	15
September	6	67	1	13	17	86	21	56	24	41	21	24	19
	13	81	1	14	10	80	17	68	8	47	10	15	9
	20	54	3	30	11	100	21	81	5	38	17	23	6
	27	66	—	40	6	116	17	109	5	43	9	34	4
October	4	74	—	31	7	111	22	82	8	51	13	20	5
	11	77	1	39	7	119	19	102	3	52	7	39	9
	18	82	1	40	6	156	24	80	3	71	3	26	8
	25	92	—	44	4	152	15	85	18	61	16	31	7
November	1	103	—	41	4	158	21	90	19	50	16	30	12

Class 1—Ready to current acceptable standard.
Class 2—Estimated ready within 4 days to above standard (Equipment
      in sight).
Class 3—Under preparation for issue.
Class 4—Awaiting repair or modification.

APPENDIX 9

Anti-Aircraft Command. Gun dispositions, 11 July–9 October, 1940

A.A. Division	H.A.A. Gun Zones	11 July	21 Aug.	11 Sept.	9 Oct.
4th	BARROW	—	—	8	8
	LIVERPOOL	52	56	58	76
	MANCHESTER	20	20	20	20
	CREWE	8	16	8	8
	DONNINGTON	—	—	—	4
	BIRMINGHAM	64	71	64	64
	COVENTRY	44	32	24	24
R.A.F. Stations	Ringway	4	4	4	4
	L.A.A. Guns[1]	52	80	84	92
	A.A.L.M.G.s[2]	376	389	397	411
5th	MILFORD HAVEN	—	—	4	4
	SWANSEA	—	16	24	24
	CARDIFF	12	26	26	30
	NEWPORT	4	16	20	22
	BROCKWORTH	36	24	24	24
	BRISTOL	36	32	32	32
	FALMOUTH	8	12	8	8
	PLYMOUTH	18	46	26	24

[1] Bofors, Vickers 2-pdr. (Mk. VIII, and 3 inch (Case 1) guns: deployed
for the defence of industrial and communication V.P.s, R.A.F. stations
and R.D.F. radar stations.
[2] Lewis and Hispano guns: deployed chiefly at searchlight sites and
R.A.F. stations.

A.A. Division	H.A.A. Gun Zones	11 July	21 Aug.	11 Sept.	9 Oct.
	YEOVIL	—	4	4	4
	PORTLAND	6	14	14	16
	HOLTON HEATH	8	8	8	8
	SOUTHAMPTON	43	39	31	32
	PORTSMOUTH	44	44	40	40
	BRAMLEY	8	8	8	8
R.A.F. Stations	Tangmere	4	4	4	4
	Farnborough	—	—	4	4
	Brooklands	16	16	16	16
	L.A.A. Guns	136	181	190	184
	A.A.L.M.G.s	560	547	553	521
6th	DOVER	18	18	14	14
	THAMES & MEDWAY (S)	70	72	72	72
	THAMES & MEDWAY (N)	46	48	48	48
	HARWICH	17	15	8	8
R.A.F. Stations	Biggin Hill	4	4	8	8
	Hawkinge	7	7	7	7
	Manston	8	8	8	8
	West Malling	2	2	2	2
	Rochford	4	4	4	4
	North Weald	4	4	8	8
	Martlesham	4	4	4	4
	Ipswich	4	2	2	2
	L.A.A. Guns	101	133	141	145
	A.A.L.M.G.s	437	415	397	443
1st	LANGLEY	28	28	28	28
	HOUNSLOW	4	4	4	4
	STANMORE	4	4	4	4
	I.A.Z.*	92	92	199	199
	L.A.A. Guns	34	38	44	60
	A.A.L.M.G.s	183	167	161	161
2nd	LEIGHTON BUZZARD	4	4	4	4
	NORWICH	—	—	4	4
	NOTTINGHAM	16	16	16	16
	DERBY	40	40	32	32
	SHEFFIELD	23	27	27	28
	SCUNTHORPE	—	24	—	—
	HUMBER	38	38	26	26
	Mobile Battery	8	8	—	—
R.A.F. Stations	Duxford	2	2	2	2
	Watton	2	2	2	2
	Marham	2	2	2	2
	Feltwell	2	2	2	2
	Daventry	4	4	4	4
	Wattisham	4	4	4	4
	Grantham	4	4	4	4
	Horsham St. Faith	—	2	2	2
	L.A.A. Guns	82	78	82	82
	A.A.L.M.G.s	788	765	835	839
7th	LEEDS	20	20	20	22
	TEES	30	30	30	30
	TYNE	54	50	50	46
	Mobile Guns	—	4	—	—
R.A.F. Stations	Linton	4	4	4	4
	Driffield	4	4	—	—
	Topcliffe	—	—	2	2
	Dishforth	—	—	2	2
	Thornaby	4	4	4	—
	Acklington	2	2	2	2
	L.A.A. Guns	50	62	55	55
	A.A.L.M.G.s	321	270	277	263

* Inner Artillery Zone, London.

Appendix 9 continued.

A.A. Division	H.A.A. Gun Zones	11 July	21 Aug.	11 Sept.	9 Oct.
3rd	BELFAST	7	7	7	12
	LONDONDERRY	—	—	4	4
	CLYDE	28	27	34	40
	ARDEER	4	8	8	8
	KYLE OF LOCHALSH	4	4	4	4
	ABERDEEN	4	4	4	4
	SCAPA	88	88	88	88
	SHETLANDS	12	12	12	12
R.A.F. Stations	Kinloss	2	2	2	2
	Lossiemouth	2	2	2	2
	Wick	4	2	2	2
	Castletown	—	2	2	2
	L.A.A. Guns	119	122	132	132
	A.A.L.M.G.s	368	378	367	375

APPENDIX 10

Fighter Command casualties

A. AIRCRAFT DESTROYED OR BADLY DAMAGED ON GROUND BY ENEMY ACTION*—
15 August–25 September, 1940

Week ending	Hurricane Cat. 2	Cat. 3	Spitfire Cat. 2	Cat. 3	Blenheim Cat. 2	Cat. 3	Total
21 August	8	12	9	3	5	5	42
28 August	2	2	Nil	1	Nil	2	7
4 September	1	2	1	2	Nil		6
11 September	Nil		Nil		Nil		Nil
18 September	Nil		Nil		Nil		Nil
25 September	Nil		Nil	1	Nil		1
TOTAL	11	16	10	7	5	7	56

B. FIGHTER PILOT CASUALTIES—GROSS- MONTHLY CASUALTIES *July—October, 1940*
(Number of pilots made casualties in the air and on the ground by enemy action and flying accidents in all squadrons of Fighter Command.)

	Killed, P.O.W., Missing	Wounded and injured
July	74	49
August	148	156
September	159	152
October	100	65
TOTAL	481	422

C. FIGHTER PILOT CASUALTY RATES, *August—October, 1940*

	August	September	October
Casualties per 100 miles flown	6.5	6.6	3.9
Casualties as percentage of pilot strength	22.4	24.4	10.5
Actual casualties as percentage of postulated	172.2	163.3	84.7

* Operational Types only.

APPENDIX 11

Fighter Command establishment, strength and deficiency of fighter pilots, June/November 1940

Date		Establishment	Strength	Deficiency or surplus
June	15	1,456	1,094	−362
	30	1,482	1,200	−282
July	6	1,456	1,259	−197
	13	1,456	1,341	−115
	20	1,456	1,365	− 91
	27	1,456	1,377	− 79
August	3	1,588	1,434	−154
	10	1,588	1,396	−192
	17	1,588	1,379	−209
	24	1,588	1,377	−211
	31	1,588	1,422	−166
September	7	1,588	1,381	−207
	14	1,662	1,492	−170
	21	1,662	1,509	−153
	28	1,662	1,581	− 81
October	5	1,714	1,703	− 11
	12	1,714	1,752	+ 38
	19	1,700	1,737	+ 37
	26	1,727	1,735	+ 8
November	2	1,727	1,796	+ 69

APPENDIX 12

Casualties* to R.A.F. Aircraft operating from United Kingdom and France
10th May–20th June, 1940

	A.A.S.F.			R.A.F. Component			Bomber Command			P.R.		Fighter Command				Coastal Command			
May 10	21	0	3	0	4	2	4	0	0	0	0	0	1	0	6	0	1	0	0
11	7	18	1	0	1	8	2	0	1	0	0	1	5	0	0	0	0	0	0
12	12	8	4	0	2	6	11	0	0	1	0	1	0	0	0	0	1	2	0
13	2	0	1	1	1	2	0	0	0	0	0	1	1	5	0	0	0	0	0
14	35	5	5	2	3	11	9	0	0	0	0	1	0	0	0	0	0	0	0
15	0	1	6	2	2	12	3	0	0	2	1	0	0	0	0	0	0	0	0
16	0	0	0	3	3	8	0	0	0	0	0	0	1	0	0	0	0	0	0
17	0	0	2	1	0	50†	11	0	0	0	0	0	1	0	0	0	0	0	0
18	0	0	1	1	2	50†	3	0	1	0	0	0	7	0	0	2	1	0	0
19	7	1	3	8	1	50†	0	0	3	0	1	0	12	0	0	1	0	0	0
20	0	0	0	0	0	2	0	0	1	0	0	0	1	0	0	0	0	2	0
21	0	0	0	1	2		1	3	1	0	0	0	3	0	0	0	0	0	0
22	5	1	0	2	5		4	2	2	1	0	1	5	0	0	1	0	0	0
23	0	1	0	0	1		3	1	1	2	0	5	9	0	0	0	0	0	0
24	7	0	2	0	3		1	1	0	1	0	7	2	0	1	0	1	0	0
25	0	0	2	0	1		3	0	0	0	0	3	2	0	0	1	0	1	0
26	4	0	2	2	3		0	1	0	2	0	4	3	0	0	0	0	0	1
27	0	0	1	4	2		2	0	0	0	0	5	11	0	0	0	1	0	0
28	2	0	0	1	0		1	0	0	0	0	3	9	0	0	0	0	0	0
29	1	0	0	1	1		1	0	1	0	0	7	9	3	0	0	3	2	0
30	1	0	0	0	0		1	3	0	0	0	1	0	0	0	1	0	2	0
31	1	0	0	4	0		0	1	0	0	0	7	9	5	0	0	0	1	0
June 1	1	0	3	3	0		0	2	0	0	0	11	8	0	0	0	2	0	0
2	0	0	0	0	1		2	0	0	0	0	7	2	0	0	0	0	0	0
3	0	0	4	0	0		0	0	0	0	0	0	1	0	0	0	0	0	0
4	0	0	0	0	0		0	0	1	2	0	1	0	0	0	0	0	0	0
5	2	0	5	1	0		0	0	1	0	0	0	0	0	0	0	1	0	0
6	0	0	0	0	1		5	1	0	1	0	0	5	0	0	2	0	0	1
7	6	0	0				1	0	0	0	0	0	12	0	0	0	0	1	0
8	4	0	4				7	0	1	1	0	0	4	0	0	0	0	0	0
9	1	0	1				3	0	0	0	0	0	0	0	0	0	0	0	0
10	2	0	4				0	0	1	1	0	0	0	0	0	0	0	0	0
11	3	0	0				6	1	1	0	0	0	1	0	0	3	0	0	0
12	1	0	0				3	0	2	1	0	0	0	0	0	0	1	0	0
13	8	0	0				5	0	0	1	0	0	0	0	0	0	0	1	1
14	3	0	1				4	2	0	0	0	0	1	0	0	1	0	0	0
15	1	0	0				0	1	1	0	0	0	0	0	0	3	1	0	0
16	0	2	0				0	0	0	0	0	0	0	0	0	0	0	1	1
17	0	0	0				0	0	0	0	0	0	1	0	0	0	0	0	0
18							0	0	2	0	0	0	2	0	0	0	0	0	0
19							1	2	2	0	0	1	0	0	3	0	0	0	0
20							0	1	2	0	1	0	0	0	0	1	0	0	0
TOTAL	137	37	55	35	39	201	97	22	25	16	3	67	128	13	10	18	13	11	4

GRAND TOTAL 931

* These casualties include aircraft which failed to return from operations, aircraft destroyed on the ground and aircraft irreparably damaged. In France this latter category is taken to include aircraft reported as repairable away from unit since it was not in fact possible to get these aircraft repaired.

† These figures are 'balancing figures', spread over three days to adjust the reported Hurricane losses to the total of Hurricanes which failed to return from France.

APPENDIX 13

Fighter Command battle casualties : weekly

TOTAL AND BY TYPES

Date	Fighters total Cat.2	Cat.3	Blenheim 2	3	Defiant 2	3	Hurricane 2	3	Spitfire 2	3
June 6	10	73	—	2	1	5	5	42	4	24
13	1	20	—	1	—	—	1	19	—	—
20	3	14	2	5	—	—	—	7	1	2
27	2	16	1	9	—	—	1	5	—	2
July 4	3	9	—	3	—	—	2	4	1	2
11	22	48	3	6	—	—	11	22	8	13
18	22	23	2	9	—	—	11	9	9	5
25	13	35	—	4	—	6	4	12	9	13
Aug. 1	11	27	5	6	—	—	4	7	8	14
8	13	35	—	7	—	—	5	13	8	15
15	68	122	1	18	—	—	37	71	30	33
22	61	90	4	17	—	—	25	49	32	24
29	42	120	4	9	3	14	20	56	15	40
Sept. 5	109	167	3	4	—	1	61	96	45	66
12	64	109	2	7	—	—	34	70	28	32
19	45	69	2	4	—	—	23	42	20	22
26	36	44	1	4	—	—	14	20	21	20
Oct. 3	60	82	2	4	1	—	38	52	19	26
10	34	49	3	4	—	2	16	21	15	22
17	39	50	1	2	1	—	25	27	12	20
24	25	20	1	4	—	—	17	7	5	9
31	40	50	1	1	2	—	19	29	18	20
Nov. 2	22	33	1	2	1	—	9	24	11	7

Category 2—Repairable by depot or contractor
Category 3—Reduced to produce

APPENDIX 14

Battle casualties. Metropolitan Air Force, July 1–October 31, 1940

Cat. 2 = repairable by depot or contractor.
Cat. 3 = missing or wrecked beyond repair (i.e. total loss)

Cumulative totals at dates shown

Date	Bombers Cat. 2	Cat. 3	Fighters Cat. 2	Cat. 3	Other Op. Types Cat. 2	Cat. 3	Total Cat. 2	Cat. 3
July 1	82	358	56	517	16	104	154	979
11	87	386	78	565	20	108	185	1059
18	92	396	100	588	23	112	215	1096
25	95	413	113	623	26	116	234	1152
Aug. 1	102	435	130	650	29	120	261	1205
8	106	448	143	685	31	128	280	1261
15	124	487	211	807	35	137	370	1431
22	133	510	272	897	37	145	442	1552
29	144	534	314	1017	38	147	496	1698
Sept. 5	153	563	423	1184	39	153	615	1900
12	161	595	487	1293	41	161	689	2049
19	167	611	532	1362	43	164	742	2137
26	176	624	568	1406	49	169	793	2199
Oct. 3	179	648	628	1488	51	178	858	2314
10	183	661	662	1537	56	184	901	2382
17	·185	689	701	1587	58	189	944	2465
24	192	701	726	1607	63	190	981	2498
31	198	725	766	1657	66	200	1030	2582
Grand totals for period	116	367	710	1140	50	96	876	1603

APPENDIX 15

(A) Fighter aircraft casualties, August 1940

	Hurricanes Cat. 2	Spitfires Cat. 2	Defiants Cat. 2	Blenheims Cat. 2
COMBAT	49	55	4	4
ACCIDENT	38	35	3	9
*E/A ON GROUND	10	10	0	5
Total Cat. 2:	97	100	7	18
	Cat. 3	Cat. 3	Cat. 3	Cat. 3
COMBAT	220	118	9	8
ACCIDENT	18	14	1	11
*E/A ON GROUND	15	5	0	7
Total Cat. 3:	253	137	10	26

	Total Cat. 2	Total Cat. 3
(a) In combat	112	355
(b) Flying Accident	85	44
(b) *E/A on Ground	25	27
	222	426

Personnel	killed or missing	wounded
In combat	157	137
In training	24	8
	181	145

(B) Fighter aircraft casualties, September 1940

	Hurricanes	Spitfires	Defiants	Blenheims	Beaufighters
	Cat. 2	Cat. 2	Cat. 2	Cat. 2	Cat. 2
COMBAT	95	80	0	0	0
ACCIDENT	60	56	6	9	3
*E/A ON GROUND	1	0	0	0	0
Total Cat. 2:	156	136	6	9	3
	Cat. 3	Cat. 3	Cat. 3	Cat. 3	Cat. 3
COMBAT	228	130	0	2	0
ACCIDENT	21	13	1	7	1
*E/A ON GROUND	1	2	0	0	0
Total Cat. 3:	250	145	1	9	1

Plus 1 Battle and 14 training aircraft—Total   319 Cat. 2
                                                    412 Cat. 3

	Total Cat. 2	Total Cat. 2
(a) In combat	175	360
(b) Flying Accident	143	48
(c) *E/A on Ground	1	4
	319	412

Personnel	killed or missing	wounded
In combat	156	150
In training	24	10
	180	160

* Destroyed by enemy action on the ground.

APPENDIX 16

German losses during the Battle of Britain

CLAIMED AND DEFINITE

Date	R.A.F. claimed Destroyed	Actual* Destroyed		Damaged
10 July—7 August	188	192	(63)	77
8 August—23 August	755	403	(213)	127
24 August—6 September	643	378	(243)	115
7 September—30 September	846	435	(243)	161
1 October—31 October	260	325	(134)	163
Total	2692	1733	(896)	643

Figures in brackets denote losses publicly admitted by the German High Command at the time of the battle, i.e. just over half the actual total.
* The figures are taken from the German Quartermaster General's returns.

APPENDIX 17

British and German sorties—weekly totals

Date		BRITISH			GERMAN		
	Bomber	Fighter	Coastal	Bomber	Fighter	GR
Sept. 8	642	5513	921	2855	2355	310
15	882	3152	871	2115	875	315
22	953	4513	789	2930	1190	400
29	911	4877	865	3137	820	420
Oct. 6	497	4631	823	1845	1540	270
13	757	4734	745	1735	1560	265
20	514	2760	601	2060	1060	300
27	662	3260	600	1570	920	230
Nov. 3	470	4500	639	1380	1660	335
10	471	3777	618	1430	695	235

APPENDIX 18

German aircraft casualties, July/October 1940

1940	Destroyed				Damaged			
	Due to enemy action	On operations but not due to enemy action	Total on operations	Not on operations	Due to enemy action	On operations but not due to enemy action	Total on operations	Not on operations
July								
C.R.	—	—	—	2	—	—	—	1
L.R.	18	8	26	4	2	4	5	1
S.E.F.	34	12	46	7	6	8	14	16
T.E.F	19	1	20	2	4	2	6	2
N.F.	—	—	—	—	—	—	—	—
B.	76	17	93	20	12	14	26	28
D.B.	12	4	16	5	8	2	10	5
G.A.	—	1	1	—	—	—	—	—
T.	1	—	1	3	1	—	1	3
C.	11	3	14	2	—	—	—	1
M.	1	—	1	—	—	—	—	3
Aug.								
C.R.	1	1	2	1	—	2	2	1
L.R.	13	3	16	2	1	1	1	1
S.E.F.	177	34	211	20	24	33	57	23
T.E.F.	114	6	120	5	32	9	41	2
N.F.	1	1	2	1	—	1	1	—
B.	183	45	228	31	48	34	82	36
D.B.	47	4	51	7	14	3	17	8
G.A.	—	—	—	—	—	—	—	—
T.	2	1	3	2	—	1	1	4
C.	19	11	30	8	2	3	5	6
M.	1	—	1	3	1	—	1	4
Sept.								
C.R.	—	1	1	2	—	1	1	7
L.R.	16	3	19	3	3	3	6	3
S.E.F.	187	33	220	14	17	42	59	16
T.E.F.	81	2	83	5	17	—	13	1
N.F.	1	1	2	1	—	—	—	1
B.	165	65	230	19	58	70	128	34
D.B.	—	2	2	7	—	1	1	8
G.A.	—	—	—	—	—	—	—	—
T.	—	—	—	6	—	—	—	2
C.	8	15	23	4	2	3	5	5
M.	1	1	2	5	—	—	—	12
Oct.								
C.R.	1	3	4	3	1	3	4	7
L.R.	8	5	13	5	1	6	7	4
S.E.F.	104	19	123	22	24	28	52	22
T.E.F.	10	2	12	5	1	3	4	4
N.F.	1	13	14	2	—	2	2	2
B.	64	78	142	29	24	66	90	18
D.B.	—	—	—	6	—	3	3	2
G.A.	—	—	—	—	—	—	—	—
T.	1	—	1	5	—	—	—	3
C.	7	9	16	8	—	1	1	1
M.	—	—	—	4	—	—	—	4

From statistics compiled from original records kept by the Quarter-master General's Department of the German Air Ministry.

Key:

C.R. Close reconnaissance (army co-op)
L.R. Long-range reconnaissance
S.E.F. Single-engine fighters
T.E.F. Twin-engine fighters

N.F. Night fighters
B. Bombers
D.B. Dive Bombers
G.A. Ground attack

T. Transport
C. Coastal
M. Miscellaneous

APPENDIX 19

Glossary of German operational commands

ObdL : Oberbefehlshaber der Luftwaffe; C. in C. German Air Force.
Luftflotte : Operational and administrative command, an air fleet, e.g. Luftflotte 2.
Fliegerkorps : Subsidiary operational command. Mobile and containing any required units, e.g. VIII Fliegerkorps.
Fliegerdivision : Operational command smaller in size than a Fliegerkorps. The Fliegerkorps were formed by enlarging existing Fliegerdivisionen, e.g. IX Fliegerdivision.
Geschwader : Operational unit comprising two to four Gruppen usually of one type of aircraft, e.g. KG2 (Kampfgeschwader 2) = bomber geschwader No. 2
Gruppe : Subsidiary operational unit to Geschwader, or may be independent. Comprises three to four Staffeln, e.g. II/KG2 = the second Gruppe of KG2 or Independent Unit KGr.2 = Bomber Group 2.
Staffel : Smallest operational unit. Nine aircraft. Staffeln are denoted with Arabic numerals while Gruppe have Roman, e.g. II/JG53 = second Gruppe of Jagdgeschwader 53, while 2./JG53 = second Staffel of the Jagdgeschwader.
Schwarm : Formation of five aircraft.
Kette : Formation of three aircraft.
Rotte : Tactical formation of two aircraft.

APPENDIX 20

(A) Luftwaffe operational strength, September 19th, 1938·

Flying Units	Strength	Serviceability
Long-range reconnaissance	222	177
Close reconnaissance	289	238
Ground attack	195	164
Fighter	810	717
Bomber	1,235	1,019
Dive-bomber	247	227
	2,998	2,542
Transport	317	293
	3,315	2,835

(B) Luftwaffe operational strength, September 2nd, 1939

Flying Units	Establishment	Strength	Serviceability
Close reconnaissance (Luftwaffe)	183	190	146
Close reconnaissance (Army)	297	285	164
Long-range reconnaissance (Luftwaffe)	192	297	235
Long-range reconnaissance (Army)	120	115	109
	792	887	654
Ground attack	39	40	36
Heavy fighter	438	408	377
Fighter	811	771	676
Bomber	1,239	1,180	1,008
Dive-bomber	381	366	318
	3,700	3,652	3,069
Transport	554	552	540
	4,254	4,204	3,609

(C) Luftwaffe operational strength, May 11th, 1940

Flying Units	Strength	Serviceability
Close reconnaissance	304	253
Long-range reconnaissance (Army)	153	124
Long-range reconnaissance (Luftwaffe)	180	105
	637	482
Ground attack	50	45
Heavy fighter	355	263
Fighter	1,346	1,076
Bomber	1,615	1,031
Dive-bomber	414	345
	4,417	3,242
Transport	408	285
	4,825	3,527

(D) Luftwaffe forces against Britain, August 10th, 1940

Flying Units	Establishments	Strength	Serviceability
Close reconnaissance	120	95	80
Long-range reconnaissance	126	100	71
Fighter	1,011	934	805
Heavy fighter	301	289	224
Bomber	1,569	1,481	998
Dive-bomber	348	327	261
Ground attack	40	39	31
Coastal	94	93	80
	3,609	3,358	2,550

All figures taken from Luftwaffe Quartermaster General 6th
Abteilung returns.

APPENDIX 21

Location of German units, Order of Battle in the West, 1940

Unit	Mid-August	Mid-September
KG26	Stavanger	
KG30	Aalborg	Brussels and Gilze-Rijen
ZG76	Stavanger	Le Mans, Abbeville and Laval
JG77	Stavanger	(I) Northern France
K.Fl.Gr.506	Stavanger	Stavanger, Trondheim
I./(F)120	Stavanger	
I./(F)121	Stavanger and Aalborg	Stavanger
KG1	Montdidier and Rosieres-en-Sainterre	
KG76	Beauvais, Creil and Cormeilles-en-Vexin	Beauvais, Creil and Cormeilles-en-Vexin
5./(F)122	Haute Fontaine	Haute Fontaine
4./(F)122	Holland	Brussels
KG2	Arras, Epinoy and Cambrai	St. Leger and Cambrai
KG3	Le Culot, Antwerp and Saint-Trond	Le Culot, Antwerp and Saint-Trond
KG53	Lille	Lille
IV/(St.)LG1	Tramecourt	Tramecourt
Epr.Gr.210	Monchy-Bréton	Valenciennes
KG4	Soesterberg, Eindhoven and Schipol	Soesterberg, Eindhoven and Schipol
K.Gr.100	Vannes	Vannes
KG40	——	(I) Bordeaux
K.Gr.126	——	
K.Fl.Gr.106	Brest and Borkum	Brest
3./(F)122	Eindhoven and Zeelst	Eindhoven and Zeelst
JG3	Samer and Desvres	Pas de Calais
JG26	Audembert, Marquise and Caffiers	Northern France
JG51	Wissant, Desvres and St. Omer	St. Omer, St. Inglevert and S. Holland
JG52	Coquelles and Peuplingne	Pas de Calais and Laon
JG54	Guines and Hermalinghen	South Holland
ZG26	Lille, St. Omer and Barley Arques	Abbeville, St. Omer and Crécy-en-Ponthieu
StG1	Angers	St. Pol and Pas de Calais
StG2	St. Malo and Lannion	Tramecourt, St. Omer and St. Trond
StG77	Caen	——
II/LG2	Boblingen	St. Omer
2./(F)11	Boblingen	
V./(Z)LG1	Caen	Ligescourt and Alençon
KG51	Orly, Melun Villaroche and Etampes	Orly, Melun, Villaroche and Etampes
KG54	Evreux and St. Andre de l'Eure	Evreux and St. Andre de l'Eure
KG55	Villacoublay, Dreux and Chartres	Villacoublay, Dreux and Chartres
LG1	Orleans-Bricy and Chateaudun	Orleans-Bricy and Chateaudun
KG27	Tours and Dinard	Tours, Dinard, Bourges and Rennes
K.Gr.806	Nantes and Caen	Nantes and Caen
StG3	Dinard (Stab only)	Dinard
I/KG40	Bordeaux	Bordeaux
3./(F)31	St. Brieuc	St. Brieuc
JG2	Beaumont-le-Roger and Le Havre	Beaumont-le-Roger and Le Havre
JG27	Guines and Crepon	Etaples, Montreuil and Sempy
JG53	Cherbourg, Rennes, Dinan and Brest	Dinan
ZG2	Tousée-le-Noble, Amiens and Guyancourt	Amiens, Caen and Guyancourt
1./(F)22		Lille
1./(F)122		Holland
2./(F)122		Brussels
7./(F)LG2		——
StG26		——
KG77		Laon and Asch

APPENDIX 22

German figures of bombs dropped on British targets, August–October, 1940*

Target	Type of Bomb	August		September		October	
London	H.E. Bombs						
	(Metric tons)	12	(12)	6,501	(691)	7,242	(1,118)
	Incendiary[1]	12	(12)	9,540	(685)	4,869	(305)
Liverpool	H.E. Bombs	454	(94)	326	(326)	210	(210)
	Incendiary	1,029	(301)	787	(787)	300	(300)
Birmingham	H.E. Bombs	94	(94)	14	(14)	339	(339)
	Incendiary	204	(204)	7	(7)	864	(864)
Coventry	H.E. Bombs	89	(89)	19	(19)	163	(163)
	Incendiary	277	(277)	18	(18)	536	(536)
Manchester	H.E. Bombs	6	(6)	12	(12)	—	—
	Incendiary	—	—	10	(10)	—	—
Southampton	H.E. Bombs	—	—	117	(117)	6	(6)
	Incendiary	—	—	77	(77)	—	—
Plymouth	H.E. Bombs	—	—	49	(49)	14	(14)
	Incendiary	—	—	12	(12)	62	(62)
Bristol	H.E. Bombs	—	—	110	(110)	25	(25)
	Incendiary	—	—	68	(68)	58	(58)
Zerstörungziele[2]	H.E. Bombs	406	(406)	292	(292)	77	(77)
	Incendiary	261	(261)	83	(83)	88	(88)
Ausweichziele[3]	H.E. Bombs	397	(397)	1,112	(1,112)	769	(769)
	Incendiary	2,492	(2,492)	1,202	(1,202)	188	(188)
Ships	H.E. Bombs	86	(86)	24	(24)	30	(30)
	Incendiary	—	—	—	—	—	—
Airfields	H.E. Bombs	1,004	(1,004)	333	(333)	182	(182)
	Incendiary	321	(321)	122	(122)	56	(56)
Total	H.E. Bombs	2,548	(2,188)	8,909	(3,099)	9,057	(2,933)
	Incendiary	4,596	(3,868)	11,926	(3,071)	7,021	(2,457)

* These figures do not necessarily mean that the weight of bombs shown actually fell on the different targets, due to navigation errors, casualties, etc.
[1] The number of incendiaries is given in terms of incendiary containers, each of which held 36 1 Kilogramme incendiary bombs.
[2] *Zerstörungziele*: targets in harassing raids (*Störangriffen*). In this type of operation specific industrial targets, especially aircraft and aero engine works, were attacked by single aircraft.
[3] *Ausweichziele*: Alternative and secondary targets. Railway communications were the chief objectives here.
Figures in brackets denote amount dropped in attacks of under 100 tons of H.E. bombs. Attacks over 100 tons were referred to as Grossangriffen.

APPENDIX 23

Aircrew who flew operationally under Fighter Command control in the Battle of Britain, July 10th to October 31st, 1940

Roll Up

Nationalities of Pilots and aircrew	*Number of each nationality who took part in the Battle*	*Number of each nationality killed in the Battle*
United Kingdom, including Commonwealth pilots and aircrew serving in the Royal Air Force who cannot be identified separately	2,365	397
United Kingdom, serving in the Fleet Air Arm but also including F.A.A. personnel seconded to R.A.F. squadrons	56	9
Australian	21	14
New Zealander	103	14
Canadian	90	20
South African	21	9
Southern Rhodesian	2	—
Jamaican	1	—
Irish	9	—
American	7	1
Polish	141	29
Czech	86	8
Belgian	29	6
Free French	13	—
Palestinian	1	—
	2,945	507

Approximate number of wounded—all nationalities	500
Approximate total casualties killed and wounded—all nationalities	1,007

Aircrew who fought under Fighter Command operational control in the Battle of Britain,
July 10th–October 31st, 1940. List of names

ADAIR, Sgt. H. H. British. 213–151. Killed
ADAMS, P/O D. A. British. 611–41
ADAMS, P/O H. C. British. 501. Killed*
ADAMS, F/Lt. J. S. British. 29
ADAMS, Sgt. R. T. British. 264. Killed
ADAMS, Sgt. E. H. British. 236
ADDISON, Sgt. W. N. British. 23
AEBERHARDT, P/O R. A. C. British. 19. Killed*
AGAZARIAN, P/O N. le C. British. 609. Killed
AINDOW, Sgt. C. R. British. 23
AINGE, Sgt. E. D. British. 23
AINSWORTH, Sgt. S. British. 23
AITKEN, Sgt. A. British. 219
AITKEN, Sgt. H. A. British. 54
AITKEN, Wg/Com. M. British. 601
AKROYD, P/O H. J. British. 152. Killed*
ALBERTINI, Sgt. A. V. 600
ALDOUS, P/O E. S. British. 610–41. Killed
ALDRIDGE, P/O F. J. British. 610–41
ALDRIDGE, P/O K. R. British. 32–501
ALDWINCLE, P/O A. J. M. British. 601
ALEXANDER, P/O J. N. E. British. 151
ALEXANDER, Sgt. E. A. British. 236. Killed
ALLAN, F/O J. H. L. N/Zealander. 151. Killed*
ALLARD, P/O G. British. 85. Killed
ALLCOCK, P/O P. O. D. British. 229. Died
ALLEN, F/O J. L. British. 54. Killed*
ALLEN, P/O H. R. British. 66
ALLEN, Sgt. J. W. British. 266
ALLEN, Sgt. L. H. British. 141
ALLEN, Sgt. K. M. British. 43–257–253
ALLGOOD, Sgt. H. H. British. 85–253. Killed*
ALLISON, Sgt. J. W. British. 611–41. Killed
ALLSOP, S/Ldr. H. G. L. British. 66
ALLTON, Sgt. L. C. British. 92. Killed*
AMBROSE, P/O C. F. British. 46
AMBROSE, P/O R. British. 25. Killed
AMBRUS, P/O J. K. Czech. 312
ANDERSON, P/O D. J. British. 29
ANDERSON, Sgt. J. D. British. 604
ANDERSON, S/Ldr. M. F. British. 604
ANDERSON, Sgt. J. A. British. 253
ANDREAE, P/O C. J. D. British. 64. Killed*
ANDREW, Sgt. S. British. 46. Killed*
ANDREWS, Sgt. M. R. N/Ze-lander. 264
ANDREWS, P/O S. E. British. 32–207. Killed
ANDREWS, P/O S. E. British. 257. Killed
ANDRUSZKOW, Sgt. T. Polish. 303. Killed*
ANGUS, Sgt. R. A. British. 611–41. Killed*
ANGUS, Sgt. J. G. C. British. 23
APPLEBY, P/O M. J. British. 609
APPLEFORD, P/O A. N. R. L. British. 66
ARBER, Sgt. I. K. British. 602. Died
ARBON, P/O P. W. British. 85
ARBUTHNOT, Sgt. J. British. 1–229. Killed

ARCHER, Sgt. H. T. British. 23. Killed
ARCHER, Sgt. S. British. 236
ARIES, P/O E. W. British. 602
ARMITAGE, F/Lt. D. L. British. 266
ARMITAGE, Sgt. J. F. British. 242. Killed
ARMSTRONG, P/O W. British. 54. Died
ARNFIELD, Sgt. S. J. N/Zealander. 610. Died
ARTHUR, P/O I. R. British. 141
ARTHUR, P/O C. J. British. 248. Killed*
ASH, F/Lt. R. C. V. British. 264. Killed*
ASHCROFT, Sgt. A. E. British. 141. Killed
ASHFIELD, F/O G. British. F.I.U. Killed
ASHTON, F/O D. G. British. 266. Killed*
ASHTON, Sgt. D. K. British. 32. Killed
ASHWORTH, Sgt. J. British. 29
ASLETT, Sgt. A. T. R. British. 235
ASLIN, Sgt. D. J. British. 257–32
ASSHETON, P/O W. R. British. 222
ATKINS, Sgt. F. P. J. British. 141. Killed*
ATKINSON, P/O R. British. 242. Killed*
ATKINSON, F/Lt. M. R. British. 43. Killed
ATKINSON, Sgt. G. British. 151. Killed
ATKINSON, P/O H. D. British. 213. Killed*
ATKINSON, P/O G. B. British. 248
ATKINSON, P/O R. British. 111–213. Killed*
ATKINSON, P/O A. A. British. 23. Killed*
AUSTIN, P/O. British. 151
AUSTIN, Sgt. A. T. British. 29
AUSTIN, Sgt. A. L. British. 604. Killed*
AUSTIN, F/O F. British. 46. Killed
AUSTIN, Sgt. S. British. 219. Killed
AYERS, Sgt. D. H. British. 600–74. Killed*
AYLING, Sgt. C. A. H. British. 43–66–421 Flt. Killed*

BABBAGE, Sgt. C. F. British. 602
BACHMANN, P/O J. H. British. 145. Killed
BACON, P/O C. H. British. 610. Killed*
BADDELEY, Sgt. D. H. British. 25. Killed
BADER, S/Ldr. D. R. S. British. 242
BADGER, F/Sgt. I. J. British. 87
BADGER, S/Ldr. J. V. C. British. 43. Killed*
BAILEY, P/O C. G. British. 152
BAILEY, Sgt. G. J. British. 234–603
BAILEY, P/O J. C. L. D. British. 46. Killed*
BAILEY, P/O J. R. A. British. 264–85
BAILEY, P/O G. G. British. 56. Killed
BAILEY, P/O H. N. D. British. 54
BAILEY, Sgt. C. British. 23
BAILLON, P/O P. A. British. 609. Killed
BAIN, P/O G. S. P. British. 111
BAINES, S/Ldr. C. E. J. British. 238
BAIRD, P/O G. H. British. 248
BAKER, P/O. British. 600
BAKER, P/O H. C. British. 421 Flt.

* Personnel killed during the Battle of Britain.

BAKER, Sgt. A. C. British. 610
BAKER, P/O H. C. British. 41
BAKER, Sgt. R. D. British. 56. Killed*
BAKER, P/O S. British. 54–66. Killed
BAKER, Sgt. B. British. 264. Killed*
BAKER, Sgt. E. D. British. 145. Killed*
BAKER, P/O C. C. M. British. 23
BAKER, Sgt. L. V. British. 236
BALL, F/Lt. G. E. British. 242 Killed
BAMBERGER, Sgt. C. S. British. 610–41
BANDINEL, P/O J. J. F. H. British. 3. Killed
BANHAM, F/Lt. A. J. British. 264–229
BANISTER, Sgt. T. H. British. 219
BANKS, Sgt. W. H. British. 245–32–504
BANN, Sgt. E. S. British. 238. Killed*
BARALDI, P/O F. H. R. British. 609
BARANSKI, F/Lt. W. Polish. 607
BARBER, P/O R. H. British. 46
BARCLAY, P/O R. G. A. British. 249. Killed
BARKER, Sgt. J. K. British. 152. Killed*
BARKER, P/O G. L. British. 600. Killed
BARKER, Sgt. F. J. British. 264
BARNARD, Sgt. E. C. British. 600
BARNES, P/O W. British. 405
BARNES, Sgt. L. D. British. 257–615–607
BARNES, F/O J. G. C. British. 600
BARNETT, S/Ldr. R. E. British. 234
BARON, P/O R. V. British. 219. Killed*
BARRACLOUGH, Sgt. S. M. British. 92
BARRACLOUGH, Sgt. R. G. V. British. 266
BARRAN, F/Lt. P. H. British. 609. Killed*
BARRETT, Sgt. W. E. British. 25
BARRON, Sgt. N. P. G. British. 236
BARROW, Sgt. H. I. R. British. 607–43–213. Killed
BARRY, F/O N. J. M. S/African. 3–501. Killed*
BARTHROPP, F/O P. P. C. British. 602
BARTLETT, Sgt. L. H. British. 17
BARTLEY, P/O A. C. British. 92
BARTON, P/O A. R. H. British. 32–253. Killed
BARTON, F/Lt. R. A. British. 249
BARTOS, P/O J. Czech. 312. Killed
BARWELL, P/O E. G. British. 264–242
BARY, P/O R. E. British. 229. Killed
BASHFORD, Sgt. H. British. 248
BASSETT, F/O F. B. British. 222. Killed
BATCHELOE, P/O G. H. British. 54. Killed
BATT, Sgt. L. G. British. 238
BAXTER, Sgt. S. British. 222. Killed*
BAYLES, F/O I. N. British. 152
BAYLEY, Sgt. E. A. British. 32–249. Killed*
BAYLISS, P/O D. British. 604
BAYLISS, Sgt. E. J. British. 248. Killed
BAYLY, Sgt. J. N/Zealander. 111
BAYNE, F/Lt. A. W. A. British. 17
BAYNE, S/Ldr. D. W. British. 257
BAYNHAM, P/O G. T. British. 234–152
BAZIN, F/Lt. J. M. British. 607
BAZLEY, F/Lt. S. H. British. 266. Killed
BEAKE, P/O P. H. Canadian. 64
BEAMISH, Wg/Com. F. V. Irish. 151–249–56. Killed
BEAMISH, Sgt. R. British. 601
BEAMONT, F/O R. P. British. 87
BEARD, Sgt. J. M. B. British. 249
BEARDMORE, P/O E. W. B. Canadian. 1 (Can.) (401)
BEARDSLEY, P/O R. A. British. 610–41
BEATTY, Sgt. M. A. British. 266
BEAUMONT, P/O W. British. 152. Killed*
BEAUMONT, F/Lt. S. G. British. 609
BEAZLEY, P/O H. J. S. British. 249
BEDA, Sgt. A. Polish. 302

BEE, Sgt. E. H. British. 29
BEECHEY, Sgt. A. F. British. 141
BEER, Sgt. C. S. F. British. 235. Killed*
BEGG (F.A.A.), Sub/Lt. H. W. British. 151. Killed
BELC, Sgt. M. Polish. 303. Killed
BELCHEM, S/Ldr. L. G. British. 264. Killed
BELEY, P/O W. G. Canadian. 151. Killed*
BELL, F/O C. A. British. 29
BELL, Sgt. C. H. British. 234. Killed
BELL, F/O J. S. British. 616. Killed*
BELL, Sgt. D. British. 23. Killed
BELL, Sgt. R. British. 219
BELL-SLATER, F/O D. B. British. 253
BELL-WALKER, Sgt. H. J. British. 72
BENN, Sgt. G. W. British. 219
BENNETT, P/O C. C. Australian. 248. Killed*
BENNETT, Sgt. H. E. British. 43. Killed
BENNETTE, F/O G. R. British. 17. Killed
BENNIONS, P/O G. H. British. 41
BENNISON, Sgt. A. A. N/Zealander. 25
BENSON, P/O N. J. V. British. 603. Killed*
BENSON, P/O J. G. British. 141
BENT, Sgt. B. British. 25
BENZIE, P/O J. Canadian. 242. Killed*
BERESFORD, F/Lt. H. R. A. British. 257. Killed*
BERGMAN, P/O V. Czech. 310
BERKLEY, Sgt. T. C. E. British. 85. Killed
BERNARD, Sgt. F. A. Czech. 238–601
BERNAS, P/O B. Polish. 302
BERRIDGE, Sgt. H. W. British. 219. Died
BERRY, F/Sgt. F. G. British. 1. Killed*
BERRY, P/O R. British. 603
BERRY, Sgt. A. British. 264. Killed*
BERWICK, Sgt. R. C. British. 25. Killed
BEVERIDGE, Sgt. C. British. 219
BEYTAGH, S/Ldr. M. L. British. 73. Died
BICKERDYKE, P/O J. L. N/Zealander. 85. Killed*
BICKNELL, Sgt. British. 23
BICKNELL, S/Ldr. L. C. British. 23
BIDGOOD, P/O E. G. British. 253. Killed
BIDGOOD, Sgt. I. K. British. 213. Killed
BIGGAR, S/Ldr. A. J. British. 111
BIGNALL, Sgt. J. British. 25. Killed
BINHAM, Sgt. A. E. British. 64
BIRCH (F.A.A.), Lt. R. A. British. 804. Killed
BIRD-WILSON, P/O H. A. C. British. 17
BIRKETT, P/O T. British. 219. Killed
BIRRELL (F.A.A.), Mid/Ship. M. A. British. 804–79
BISDEE, P/O J. D. British. 609
BISGOOD, P/O D. L. British. 3. Killed
BITMEAD, S/Ldr. E. R. British. 266–310–253. Died
BLACK, Sgt. A. British. 54. Killed
BLACK, Sgt. H. E. British. 46–257–32. Killed*
BLACKADDER, F/Lt. W. F. British. 607
BLACKWOOD, S/Ldr. G. D. M. British. 310–213
BLAIR, P/O C. E. British. 600. Killed
BLAIR, P/O K. H. British. 151. Died
BLAIZE, W/O P. Free French. 111
BLAKE (F.A.A.), Sub/Lt. A. G. British. 19. Killed*
BLAKE, S/Ldr. M. V. N/Zealander. 238–234
BLAND, P/O J. W. British. 601–501. Killed*
BLANE, Sgt. W. H. British. 604
BLATCHFORD, F/O H. P. Canadian. 17–257. Killed
BLAYNEY, P/O A. J. British. 609
BLENKHARN, Sgt. F. British. 25
BLOOMELEY, P/O D. H. British. 151
BLOOR, Sgt. E. British. 46. Killed
BLOW, Sgt. K. L. O. British. 235. Killed
BODDINGTON, Sgt. M. C. B. British. 234
BODIE, P/O C. A. W. British. 66. Killed

BOITEL-GILL, F/Lt. B. P. A. British. 152. Killed
BOLTON, Sgt. H. A. British. 79. Killed*
BOMFORD, Sgt. British. 601
BON-SEIGNEUR, P/O C. A. Canadian. 257. Killed*
BOOT, P/O P. V. British. 1
BOOTH, Sgt. J. J. British. 23–600
BOOTH, Sgt. G. B. British. 85. Killed*
BORET, P/O R. J. British. 41. Killed
BOROWSKI, F/O J. Polish. 302. Killed*
BOSWELL, Sgt. R. A. British. 19
BOULDING, F/O R. J. E. British. 74
BOULTER, F/O J. C. British. 603. Killed
BOULTON, F/O J. F. British. 603–310. Killed*
BOUQUILLARD, Adj. H. Free French. 615–249. Killed
BOWEN, P/O F. D. British. 264. Killed
BOWEN, P/O N. G. British. 266. Killed*
BOWEN, F/Lt. C. E. British. 607. Killed'
BOWEN-MORRIS, Sgt. H. British. 92
BOWERMAN, Sgt. O. R. British. 222
BOWMAN, Sgt. L. D. British. 141
BOWRING, F/O B. H. British. 111–600
BOYD, F/Lt. R. F. British. 602
BOYD, F/Lt. A. H. McN. British. 145-600
BOWYER, F/O W. S. British. 257. Killed
BOYLE, Sgt. C. British. 236
BOYLE, F/O J. G. Canadian. 41. Killed*
BRACTON, Sgt. British. 602
BRAHAM, S/Ldr. J. R. D. British. 29
BRAMAH (F.A.A.), Sub/Lt. H. G. K. British. 213
BRANCH, F/O G. R. British. 145. Killed*
BRASH, Sgt. G. B. British. 248. Killed*
BREEZE, Sgt. R. A. British. 222. Killed
BREJCHA, Sgt. V. Czech. 43. Killed
BRENNAN, Sgt. J. S. N/Zealander. 23
BRETT, F/O P. N. British. 17
BREWSTER, P/O J. British. 615–616. Killed
BRIERE, P/O Y. J. Free French. 257. Killed
BRIESE, F/O. Canadian. 1 (Can.) (401)
BRIGGS, P/O M. F. British. 234. Killed
BRIGGS, Sgt. D. R. British. 236. Killed
BRIGHT, F/O V. M. British. 229. Killed
BRIMBLE, Sgt. G. W. British. 242. Killed
BRIMBLE, Sgt. J. J. British. 73. Killed*
BRINSDEN, F/Lt. F. N. N/Zealander. 19
BRITTON, P/O H. W. A. British. 17. Killed
BRITTON, F/O A. W. N. British. 263. Killed*
BROADHURST, S/Ldr. H. British. 1
BROADHURST, P/O J. W. British. 222. Killed*
BROOKER, F/O R. E. P. British. 56. Killed
BROOKMAN, Sgt. R. W. A. N/Zealander. 253
BROOM, Sgt. P. W. British. 25
BROTHERS, F/Lt. P. M. British. 32–257
BROWN, Sgt. C. B. British. 245
BROWN, F/Lt. G. A. British. 253
BROWN, F/Sgt. F. S. British. 79. Died
BROWN, F/O D. P. Canadian. 1 (Can.) (401)
BROWN, P/O M. K. Canadian. 242. Killed
BROWN, F/Lt. M. H. Canadian. 1. Killed
BROWN, P/O B. W. British. 610–72
BROWN, P/O M. P. British. 611–41
BROWN, P/O R. C. British. 229
BROWN, P/O R. J. W. British. 111
BROWN, P/O A. W. British. 25
BROWN, Sgt. J. W. British. 600. Killed
BROWN, Sgt. C. W. D. British. 236. Killed
BROWN, Sgt. R. S. British. 604
BROWN, Sgt. P. G. F. British. 234. Killed
BROWN, F/O D. M. British. 1
BROWNE, Sgt. C. British. 219
BROWNE, P/O D. O. M. British. 1. Killed*

BRUCE, F/Lt. D. C. British. 111. Killed*
BRUMBY, Sgt. N. British. 615–607. Killed*
BRUNNER, P/O G. C. British. 43
BRYANT-FENN, P/O L. T. British. 79
BRYNE, Sgt. E. L. British. F.I.U.
BRYSON, P/O J. Canadian. 92. Killed*
BRZEZINA, F/Lt. S. Polish. 74. Killed
BRZOZOWSKI, Sgt. M. Polish. 303. Killed*
BUCHANAN, P/O J. British. 29. Killed
BUCHANAN, P/O J. R. British. 609. Killed*
BUCHIN, P/O M. S. H. C. Belgian. 213. Killed*
BUCK, Sgt. J. A. British. 43. Killed*
BUCKNOLE, Sgt. J. S. British. 54. Killed
BUDD, F/Lt. G. O. British. 604
BUDZINSKI, Sgt. J. Polish. 605–145
BULL, P/O J. C. British. 600
BULL, F/Lt. C. H. British. 25. Killed
BULMER (F.A.A.), Sub/Lt. G. G. R. British. 32. Killed*
BUMSTEAD, Sgt. R. F. British. 111
BUNCH, Sgt. D. C. British. 219
BUNCH (F.A.A.), Sub/Lt. S. H. British. 804. Killed
BUNGEY, F/O R. W. Australian. 145
BURĐA, P/O F. Czech. 310
BURDEKIN, Sgt. A. G. British. 600
BURGESS, Sgt. J. H. H. British. 222
BURGOYNE, P/O E. British. 19. Killed*
BURLEY, Sgt. P. S. British. 600
BURNARD, F/Sgt. F. P. British. 74–616
BURNELL-PHILLIPS, Sgt. P. A. British. 607. Killed
BURNETT, F/O N. W. British. 266–46. Killed
BURNS, Sgt. W. R. N/Zealander. 236
BURNS, Sgt. O. V. British. 235
BURT, Sgt. A. D. British. 611–603
BURTENSHAW, Sgt. A. A. British. 54. Killed
BURTON, F/Sgt. C. G. British. 23
BURTON, S/Ldr. H. F. British. 66
BURTON, F/Lt. H. British. 242
BURTON, F/O P. R. F. S/African. 249. Killed*
BURTON, P/O L. G. N/Zealander. 236. Killed
BURTON, Sgt. L. British. 248
BUSH, P/O C. R. N/Zealander. 242
BUSH, Sgt. B. M. British. 504
BUSHELL, Sgt. G. D. British. 213. Killed
BUTTERFIELD, Sgt. S. L. British. 213. Killed*
BUTTERICK, Sgt. A. F. British. 3–232. Killed
BUTTERWORTH, Sgt. K. British. 23
BYNG-HALL, P/O P. British. 29. Died

CAIN, Sgt. A. R. British. 235. Killed
CAISTER, P/O J. R. British. 603
CALDERHEAD, P/O G. D. British. 54. Killed
CALDERWOOD, Sgt. T. M. British. 85
CALE, P/O F. W. Australian. 266. Killed*
CALTHORPE, Sgt. British. 25
CAMBELL, Sgt. D. C. O. British. 66
CAMBRIDGE, F/Lt. W. P. British. 253. Killed*
CAMERON, Sgt. N. British. 1–17
CAMERON, F/Sgt. M. British. 66
CAMERON, Sgt. J. D. British. 604. Killed
CAMPBELL, P/O A. R. McL. Canadian. 54
CAMPBELL, St. A. N/Zealander. 264
CAMPBELL, F/Lt. A. M. British. 29
CAMPBELL, Sgt. D. B. N/Zealander. 23
CAMPBELL, P/O/ G. L. British. 236. Killed
CAMPBELL, P/O N. N. Canadian. 242. Killed*
CAMPBELL-COLQUHOUN, F/Lt. E. W. British. 264–66
CANDY, P/O R. J. British. 25
CANHAM, Sgt. A. W. British. 600
CANNON, Sgt. B. British. 604

CAPEL, Sgt. B. British. 23
CAPON, P/O C. F. A. British. 257. Killed
CAPSTICK, P/O H. Jamaican. 236. Died
CARBURY, F/O B. J. G. N/Zealander. 603
CARDELL, P/O P. M. British. 603. Killed*
CARDNELL, P/O C. F. British. 23. Killed*
CAREY, F/Lt. F. R. British. 43
CARLIN, P/O S. British. 264 Killed
CARNABY, F/O W. F. British. 264–85. Killed
CARNALL, Sgt. R. British. 111
CARPENTER (F.A.A.), Sub/Lt. J. C. British. 229–46. Killed*
CARPENTER, P/O J. M. V. British. 222
CARR, F/O W. J. British. 235. Killed
CARR-LEWTY, Sgt. R. A. British. 41
CARRIERE, P/O J. C. Canadian. 219
CARSWELL, F/O M. K. N/Zealander. 43
CARTER, P/O V. A. British. 607
CARTER, Sgt. L. R. British. 610–41. Killed
CARTER, P/O C. A. W. British. 611
CARTER, P/O P. E. G. British. 73–302. Killed*
CARTHEW, P/O G. C. T. Canadian. 253–145
CARVER (F.A.A.), Lt. R. H. P. British. 804
CARVER, P/O K. M. British. 229
CARVER, F/O J. C. British. 87. Killed
CASE, P/O H. R. British. 64–72. Killed*
CASSIDY, F/O E. British. 25
CASSON, P/O L. H. British. 616–615
CASTLE, Sgt. C. E. P. British. 219. Killed
CAWSE, P/O F. N. British. 238. Killed*
CAVE, P/O J. G. British. 600
CEBRZYNSKI, F/O A. Polish. 303. Killed*
CHABEPA, Sgt. F. Czech. 312
CHADWICK, Sgt. D. F. British. 64
CHAFFE, P/O R. I. British. 245–43. Killed
CHALDER, P/O H. H. British. 266–41. Killed*
CHALUPA, P/O S. J. Polish. 302
CHAMBERLAIN, P/O J. T. R. British. 235
CHAMBERLAIN, Wg/Com. G. P. British. F.I.U.
CHANDLER, Sgt. H. H. British. 610
CHAPMAN, Sgt. V. R. British. 246
CHAPPELL, P/O A. K. British. 236
CHAPPELL, P/O C. G. British. 65
CHAPPLE, Sgt. D. W. E. British. 236. Killed
CHARD, Sgt. W. T. British. 141
CHARLES, F/O E. F. J. Canadian. 54
CHARNOCK, Sgt. G. British. 25
CHARNOCK, Sgt. H. W. British. 64–19
CHATER, F/Lt. G. F. S/African. 3
CHEETHAM, Sgt. J. C. British. 23. Killed
CHELMECKI, P/O M. Polish. 257–17–6
CHESTERS, P/O P. British. 74. Killed
CHETHAM, P/O C. A. G. British. 1. Killed
CHEVRIER, P/O J. A. Canadian. 1
CHEW, Sgt. C. A. British. 17. Killed
CHIGNELL, S/Ldr. R. A. British. 145. Killed
CHILTON (F.A.A.), Sub/Lt. P. S. C. British. 804
CHIPPING, Sgt. D. J. British. 222
CHISHOLM, P/O R. E. British. 604
CHLOPIK, F/Lt. T. P. Polish. 302. Killed*
CHOMLEY, P/O J. A. G. British. 257. Killed*
CHORAN, F/Sgt. French. 64
CHRISTIE, Sgt. J. McBean. British. 152. Killed*
CHRISTIE, F/Lt. G. P. British. 66–242. Killed
CHRISTMAS, P/O B. E. British. 1 (Can.) (401)
CHRYSTALL, Sgt. C. British. 235
CHURCHES, P/O E. W. G. British. 74. Killed
CHURCHILL, S/Ldr. W. M. British. 605. Killed
CIZEK, P/O E. Czech. 1. Killed
CLACKSON, F/Lt. D. L. British 600
CLANDILLON, F/O J. A. British. 219. Killed

CLARK P/O H. D. British. 213
CLARK, Sgt. W. T. M. British. 219
CLARK,P/O C. A. G. S/African. F.I.U. Killed
CLARK, Sgt. G. P. British. 604
CLARKE, S/Ldr. D. de B. British. 600
CLARKE, Sgt. H. R. British. 610
CLARKE, S/Ldr. R. N. British. 235. Killed
CLARKE, P/O A. W. British. 504. Killed*
CLARKE, Sgt. G. S. British. 248. Killed*
CLARKE, P/O R. W. British. 79. Killed
CLARKE, Sgt. G. T. British. 151. Killed
CLEAVER, F/O G. N. S. British. 601
CLENSHAW, Sgt. I. C. C. British. 253. Killed*
CLERKE, F/Lt. R. F. H. British. 79
CLIFT, F/O D. G. British. 79
CLIFTON, P/O J. K. G. British. 253. Killed*
CLOUSTON, S/Ldr. A. E. N/Zealander. 219
CLOUSTON, F/Lt. W. G. N/Zealander. 19
CLOWES, P/O A. V. British. 1. Died
CLYDE, F/O W. C. British. 601
COATES (F.A.A.), Lt. J. P. British. 804. Killed
COBDEN, P/O D. G. N/Zealander. 74. Killed*
COCHRANE, P/O A. C. Canadian. 257. Killed
COCK, P/O J. R. Australian. 87
COCKBURN (F.A.A.), Lt/Com. J. C. British. 804
COCKBURN (F.A.A.), Sub/Lt. R. C. British. 808
COGGINS, P/O J. British. 235. Killed
COGHLAN, F/O J. H. British. 56. Killed
COKE, F/O The Hon. D. A. British. 257. Killed
COLE, Sgt. C. F. J. British. 236
COLEMAN, P/O E. J. British. 54. Killed
COLEBROOK, P/O British. 54
COLLARD, F/O P. British. 615. Killed*
COLLETT, Sgt. G. R. British. 54. Killed*
COLLINGRIDGE, P/O L. W. British. 66
COLLINS, S/Ldr. A. R. British. 72
COLLYNS, P/O B. G. N/Zealander. 238. Killed
COMELY, P/O P. W. British. 87. Killed*
COMERFORD, F/Lt. H. A. G. British. 312
COMPTON, Sgt. J. W. British. 25
CONNELL, P/O W. C. British. 32
CONNOR, F/O F. H. P. British. 234
CONNORS, F/Lt. S. D. P. British. 111. Killed*
CONSIDINE, P/O B. B. Irish. 238
CONSTANTINE, P/O A. N. Australian. 141. Killed
COOK, Sgt. A. W. British. 604
COOK, Sgt. H. British. 66–266
COOK, Sgt. R. V. British. 219
COOKE, P/O C. A. British. 66
COOKE, Sgt. H. R. British. 23
COOMBES, Sgt. E. British. 219. Killed
COOMBS, Sgt. R. J. British. 600
COONEY, F/Sgt. C. J. British. 56. Killed*
COOPE, S/Ldr. W. E. British. 17. Killed
COOPER, Sgt. C. F. British. 600. Killed*
COOPER, Sgt. T. A. British. 266
COOPER, Sgt. S. F. British. 253
COOPER, Sgt. D. C. British. 235
COOPER, Sgt. J. E. British. 610 Killed
COOPER, Sgt. R. N. British. 610. Killed
COOPER-KEY, P/O A. M. British. 46. Killed*
COOPER-SLIPPER, P/O T. P. M. British. 605
COOTE, Sgt. L. E. M. British. 600. Killed
COPCUTT, Sgt. R. British. 248. Killed*
COPELAND, Sgt. P. British. 616–66. Killed
COPELAND, Sgt. N. D. British. 235
COPEMAN, P/O J. H. H. British. 111. Killed*
CORBETT, F/Lt. V. B. Canadian. 1 (Can) (401)
CORBETT, P/O G. H. Canadian. 66. Killed*
CORBIN, Sgt. W. J. British. 610–66

CORCORAN, Sgt. H. British. 236. Killed*
CORDELL, Sgt. H. A. British. 64
CORFE, Sgt. D. F. British. 73–66–610. Killed
CORK (F.A.A.), Sub/Lt. R. J. British. 242. Killed
CORKETT, P/O A. H. British. 253
CORNER, P/O M. C. British. 264. Died
CORY, P/O G. W. British. 41
CORY, P/O. British. 25
COSBY, Sgt. E. T. British. 3–615
COSBY, F/Lt. I. H. British. 610–72
COTES-PREEDY, P/O D. V. C. British. 236
COTTAM, Sgt. G. British. 25
COTTAM, P/O H. W. British. 213. Killed
COURTIS, Sgt. J. B. N/Zealander. 111
COURTNEY, F/O R. N. H. British. 151
COUSSENS, Sgt. H. W. British. 601
COUZENS, P/O G. W. British. 54
COVERLEY, F/O W. H. British. 602. Killed*
COVINGTON, P/O A. R. British. 238
COWARD, F/Lt. J. B. British. 19
COWEN, Sgt. W. British. 25
COWLEY, Sgt. J. British. 87
COWSILL, Sgt. J. R. British. 56. Killed*
COX, Sgt. D. G. S. R. British. 19
COX, P/O G. J. British. 152
COX, P/O K. H. British. 610. Killed*
COX, F/O P. A. N. British. 501. Killed*
COX, Sgt. R. C. R. British. 248. Killed*
COX, Sgt. British. 421 Flt.
COX, Sgt. G. P. British. 236
COX, Sgt. W. E. British. 264. Killed
COXON, Sgt. J. H. British. 141. Killed
CRABTREE, Sgt. D. B. British. 501. Killed
CRAIG, Sgt. J. T. British. 111. Killed
CRAIG, F/O G. D. British. 607
CRANWELL, Sgt. E. W. British. 610
CRAWFORD, P/O H. H. N/Zealander. 235. Killed
CRESTY, Sgt. K. G. British. 219. Killed
CRESWELL, Sgt. D. G. British. 141. Killed
CREW, P/O E. D. British. 604
CRISP, Sgt. J. L. British. 43. Killed
CROCKETT, P/O R. F. British. 236. Killed
CROFTS, F/O P. G. British. 615–605. Killed*
CROKER, Sgt. E. E. N/Zealander. 111
CROMBIE, Sgt. R. British. 141. Killed*
CROOK, P/O D. M. British. 609. Killed
CROOK, Sgt. V. W. J. N/Zealander. 264
CROOK, Sgt. H. K. British. 219
CROSKELL, Sgt. M. E. British. 213
CROSSEY, P/O J. T. British. 249
CROSSLEY, F/Lt. M. N. British. 32
CROSSMAN, Sgt. R. G. British. 25. Killed
CROSSMAN, P/O J. D. Australian. 46. Killed*
CROWLEY, P/O H. R. British. 219–600
CROWLEY-MILLING, P/O D. W. British. 242
CRUICKSHANKS, P/O I. J. A. British. 66. Killed*
CRUTTENDEN, P/O J. British. 43. Killed*
CRYDERMAN, P/O L. E. Canadian. 242
CRYSTALL, Sgt. C. British. 235
CUDDIE, P/O W. A. British. 141. Killed
CUKR, Sgt. V. Czech. 253
CULLEN, Sgt. R. W. British. 23
CULMER, Sgt. J. D. British. 25
CULVERWELL, Sgt. J. H. British. 87. Killed*
CUMBERS, Sgt. A. B. British. 141
CUNNINGHAM, F/Lt. J. L. G. British. 603. Killed*
CUNNINGHAM, F/Lt. W. British. 19
CUNNINGHAM, F/Lt. J. British. 604
CUNNINGHAM, Sgt. J. British. 29
CUNNINGTON, Sgt. W. G. British. 607. Killed
CUPITT, Sgt. T. British. 29
326

CURCHIN, P/O J. British. 609. Killed
CURLEY, Sgt. A. G. British. 141. Killed*
CURRANT, P/O C. F. British. 605
CURTIS, Sgt. F. W. British. 25
CUTTS, F/O J. W. British. 222. Killed*
CZAJKOWSKI, P/O F. Polish. 151. Killed
CZERNIAK, P/O J. M. Polish. 302. Killed
CZERNIN, F/O Count M. B. British. 17. Died
CZERNY, F/Lt. H. Polish. 302
CZERWINSKI, F/O T. Polish. 302. Killed
CZTERNASTEK, P/O. Polish. 32

DAFFORN, F/O R. C. British. 501. Killed
DALTON, Sgt. R. W. British. 604
DALTON-MORGAN, F/Lt. T. F. British. 43
DALY, Sgt. J. J. British. 141
DANN, Sgt. J. E. British. 23
DANNATT, Sgt. A. G. British. 29
D'ARCH-IRVINE, F/O B. W. J. British. 257. Killed*
DARGIE, Sgt. A. M. S. British. 23. Killed
DARLEY, S/Ldr. H. S. British. 609
DARLING, Sgt. A. S. British. 611–603. Killed
DARLING, Sgt. E. V. British. 41. Killed
DARWIN, P/O C. W. W. British. 87. Killed
DASZEWSKI, P/O J. Polish. 303
DAVEY, P/O B. British. 257–32. Killed
DAVEY, P/O J. A. J. British. 1. Killed*
DAVID, P/O W. D. British. 87–213
DAVIDSON, Sgt. H. J. British. 249. Killed
DAVIES, P/O R. B. British. 29
DAVIES, P/O A. E. British. 222. Killed*
DAVIES, P/O C. G. A. British. 222
DAVIES, Sgt. M. P. British. 1–213. Killed
DAVIES, F/Lt. J. A. British. 604. Killed
DAVIES, F/O P. F. M. British. 56
DAVIES, Sgt. L. British. 151
DAVIES-COOK, P/O P. J. British. 72–610. Killed*
DAVIS, Sgt. P/O. British. 222. Killed
DAVIS, F/Lt. C. R. S/African. 601. Killed*
DAVIS, F/O C. T. British. 238. Killed
DAVIS, Sgt. W. L. British. 249
DAVIS, Sgt. J. N. British. 600
DAVIS, Sgt. J. British. 54
DAVIS, Sgt. P. E. British. 236
DAVIS, Sgt. A. S. British. 235
DAVISON, P/O. British. 235
DAVY, P/O T. D. H. British. 72–266. Killed
DAW, P/O V. G. British. 32. Killed
DAWBARN, P/O P. L. British. 17
DAWICK, Sgt. K. N/Zealander. 111
DAWSON, Sgt. T. British. 235
DAWSON-PAUL (F.A.A.), Sub/Lt. F. British. 64. Killed*
DAY, P/O R. L. F. British. 141. Killed
DAY, Sgt. F. S. British. 248. Killed
DEACON, Sgt. A. H. British. 85–111
DEACON-ELLIOTT, P/O R. British. 72
DEANSLEY, F/Lt. E. C. British. 152
DEBENHAM, P/O K. B. L. British. 151. Killed
DEBREE, P/O. British. 264
DEE, Sgt. O. J. British. 235. Killed
DEERE, F/Lt. A. L. N/Zealander. 54
DE GRUNNE, P/O R. C. C. Belgian. 32. Killed
DE JACE, P/O L. J. Belgian. 236. Killed
DE LA BOUCHER, W/O F. H. Free French. 85. Killed
DE LA PERRELE, P/O V. B. N/Zealander. 245
DELLER, Sgt. A. L. M. British. 43
DE MANCHA, P/O R. A. British. 43. Killed*
DEMETRIADI, P/O R. S. British. 601. Killed*
DEMOULIN, Sgt. R. J. G. Belgian. 235. Killed

DE MOZAY, 2nd Lt. J. E. French. 1
DENBY, P/O G. A. British. 600. Killed
DENCHFIELD, Sgt. H. D. British. 610
DENHOLM, S/Ldr. G. L. British. 603
DENISON, F/Lt. R. W. British. 236. Killed
DENTON, Sgt. D. A. British. 236. Killed
DERBYSHIRE, P/O J. M. British. 236
DERMOTT, P/O. British. 600
DE SCITIVAUX, Capt. C. J. M. P. French. 245
DESLOGES, F/O. Canadian. 1 (Can) (401)
DE SPIRLET, P/O F. X. E. Belgian. 87. Killed
DEUNTZER, Sgt. D. C. British. 247
DEVITT, S/Ldr. P. K. British. 152
DEWAR, W/C J. S. British. 87–213. Killed*
DEWAR, P/O J. M. F. British. 229. Killed
DEWEY, P/O R. B. British. 611–603. Killed*
DEWHURST, F/O K. S. British. 234
DEXTER, P/O P. G. British. 603–54. Killed
DIBNAH, P/O R. H. 1–242
DICKIE, P/O W. G. British. 601. Killed*
DICKINSON, Sgt. J. H. British. 253. Killed*
DIEU, P/O G. E. F. Belgian. 236
DIFFORD, F/O I. B. S/Afrian. 607. Killed*
DIGBY-WORSLEY, Sgt. M. P. British. 248. Killed*
DITZEL, Sgt. J. W. British. 25
DIXON, Sgt. F. J. P. British. 501. Killed*
DIXON, P/O J. A. British. 1
DIXON, Sgt. C. A. W. British. 601
DIXON, Sgt. G. British. F.I.U.
DIXON, Sgt. L. British. 600
DODD, P/O J. D. British. 248. Killed
DODGE, Sgt. C. W. British. 219
DOE, P/O R. F. T. British. 234–238
DOLEZAL, P/O F. Czech. 19
DOMAGALA, Sgt. M. Polish. 238
DON, P/O R. S. British. 501. Killed
DONAHUE, P/O A. G. American. 64. Killed
DONALD, F/Lt. I. D. G. British. 141. Killed*
DONALDSON, S/Ldr. E. M. British. 151
DOSSETT, Sgt. W. S. British. 29
DOUGHTY, P/O N. A. R. British. 247
DOUGLAS, P/O W. A. British. 610
DOULTON, P/O M. D. British. 601. Killed*
DOUTHWAITE, P/O B. British. 72
DOUTREPONT, P/O G. L. J. Belgian. 229. Killed*
DOWDING, P/O The Hon. D. H. T. British. 74
DOWN, P/O P. D. M. British. 56
DRABY, Sgt. British. 25
DRAKE, P/O G. J. S/African. 607. Killed*
DRAKE, F/O B. British. 213–1
DRAPER, P/O B. V. British. 74. Killed
DRAPER, F/O G. G. F. British. 41–610
DRAPER, Sgt. R. A. British. 232
DREDGE, Sgt. A. S. British. 253. Killed
DREVER, F/O N. G. British. 610
DREW, S/Ldr. P. E. British. 236. Killed*
DROBINSKI, P/O B. H. Polish. 65
DRUMMOND, F/O J. F. British. 46–92. Killed*
DUART, P/O J. H. British. 219
DUBBER (F.A.A.), P/O R. E. British. 808. Died
DUCKENFIELD, P/O B. L. British. 501
DUDA, P/O J. Czech. 312
DUFF, P/O S. S. British. 23
DUKE-WOOLLEY, F/Lt. R. M. B. D. British. 253–23
DULWICH, Sgt. W. H. British. 235. Killed
DUNCAN, Sgt. British. 29
DUNDAS, P/O J. C. British. 609. Killed
DUNDAS, F/O H. S. L. British. 616
DUNLOP-URIE, F/Lt. J. British. 602
DUNMORE, Sgt. J. T. British. 22. Killed

DUNN, Sgt. I. L. British. 235
DUNNING-WHITE, F/O P. W. British. 145
DUNSCOMBE, Sgt. R. D. British. 213–312. Killed
DUNWORTH, S/Ldr. T. P. R. British. 66–54
DUPEE, Sgt. O. A. British. 219
DURRANT, Sgt. C. R. N/Zealander. 23. Killed
DURYASZ, F/Lt. M. Polish. 213
DUSZYNSKI, Sgt. S. Polish. 238. Killed*
DUTTON, S/Ldr. R. G. British. 145
DUTTON, Sgt. G. W. British. 604
DU VIVIER, P/O R. A. L. Belgian. 229. Killed
DVORAK, Sgt. A. Czech. 310. Killed
DYE, Sgt. B. E. British. 219. Killed
DYER, Sgt. N/Zealander. 600
DYGRYN, Sgt. J. Czech. 1
DYKE, Sgt. L. A. British. 64. Killed*
DYMOND, Sgt. W. L. British. 111. Killed*

EADE, Sgt. A. W. British. 266–602
EARP, Sgt. R. L. British. 46
EASTON, Sgt. D. A. British. 248
ECKFORD, F/Lt. A. F. British. 32–253–242
EDGE, F/Lt. G. R. British. 253–605
EDGE, F/O A. R. British. 609
EDGLEY, Sgt. A. British. 601–253
EDGWORTHY, Sgt. G. H. British. 46. Killed*
EDMISTON, P/O G. A. F. British. 151
EDMOND, P/O N. D. Canadian. 615. Killed*
EDMUNDS, P/O E. R. N/Zealander. 245–615
EDRIDGE, P/O H. P. M. British. 222. Killed*
EDSALL, P/O E. F. British. 54–222. Died
EDWARDS, F/O R. L. Canadian. 1 (Can) (401). Killed*
EDWARDS, P/O H. D. Canadian. 92. Killed*
EDWARDS, Sgt. F. British. 29
EDWARDS, Sgt. British. 604
EDWARDS, P/O K. C. British. 600
EDWARDS, Sgt. H. H. British. 248
EDWARDS, P/O I. N. British. 234
EDWARDS, F/Lt. R. S. J. Irish. 56
EDWARDS, Sgt. British. 247
EDY, P/O A. L. British. 602. Killed
EGAN, Sgt. E. J. British. 600–501. Killed*
EIBY, P/O W. T. N/Zealander. 245
EKINS, Sgt. V. H. British. 111–501
ELCOMBE, Sgt. D. W. British. 602. Killed*
ELEY, Sgt. F. W. British. 74. Killed*
ELGER, P/O F. R. C. Canadian. 248
ELIOT, P/O H. W. British. 73. Killed
ELKINGTON, P/O J. F. D. British. 1
ELLACOMBE, P/O J. L. W. British. 151
ELLERY, P/O C. C. British. 264
ELLIOTT, F/O G. J. Canadian. 607
ELLIS, Sgt. R. V. British. 73
ELLIS, F/Lt. J. British. 610
ELLIS, Sgt. J. H. M. British. 85. Killed*
ELLIS, Sgt. W. T. British. 92
ELLIS, F/O G. E. British. 64
ELSDON, F/O T. A. F. British. 72
ELSDON, Sgt. H. D. B. British. 236. Killed*
ELSE, Sgt. P. British. 610
EMENY, Sgt. C. N/Zealander. 264
EMMETT, F/O W. A. C. British. 25. Killed
EMMETT, Sgt. G. British. 236
ENGLISH, P/O C. E. British. 85–605. Killed*
ENSOR, F/O P. S. B. British. 23. Killed
ETHERINGTON, Sgt. W. J. British. 17
EVANS, P/O H. A. C. British. 236
EVANS, Sgt. W. R. British. 85–249
EVANS, P/O D. British. 607–615. Killed

EVANS, Sgt. C. R. British. 235. Killed
EVANS, Sgt. G. J. British. 604
EVERITT, Sgt. G. C. British. 29. Killed
EVERITT, Sgt. A. D. British. 235
EYLES, Sgt. P. R. British. 92. Killed*
EYRE, F/O A. British. 615. Killed

FAJTL, F/Lt. F. Czech. 17–1
FALKOWSKI, F/O J. P. Polish. 32
FARLEY, F/Lt. British. 151–46
FARMER, F/Lt. J. N. W. British. 302
FARNES, Sgt. P. C. P. British. 501
FARNES, P/O E. British. 141
FARQUHAR, Wg/Com. A. D. British. 257
FARROW, Sgt. J. R. British. 1–229. Killed*
FARTHING, Sgt. J. British. 235
FAWCETT, Sgt. D. R. British. 29. Killed
FAYOLLE, W/O F. E. Free French. 85. Killed
FEARY, Sgt. A. N. British. 609. Killed*
FEATHER, Sgt. J. L. British. 235. Killed*
FECHTNER, P/O E. Czech. 310. Killed*
FEJFAR, F/O S. Czech. 310. Killed
FENMORE, Sgt. S. A. British. 245–501. Killed*
FENN, Sgt. C. F. British. 248
FENTON, S/Ldr. H. A. British. 238
FENTON, Sgt. British. 604
FENTON, P/O J. O. British. 235. Killed
FENWICK, P/O C. R. British. 610
FENWICK, F/O British. 601
FERDINAND, P/O R. F. British. 263. Killed
FERGUSON, Sgt. E. H. British. 141. Killed
FERGUSON, F/O P. J. British. 602
FERIC, P/O M. Polish. 303
FERRIS, F/Lt. H. M. British. 111. Killed*
FILDES, Sgt. F. British. 25
FINCH, F/O T. R. H. British. 151
FINLAY, S/Ldr. D. O. British. 41–54
FINNIE, P/O A. British. 54. Killed*
FINNIS, F/Lt. J. F. F. British. 1–229
FINUCANE, P/O B. E. Irish. 65. Killed
FISHER, P/O A. G. A. British. 111
FISHER, P/O G. British. 602
FISHER, F/O B. M. British. 111. Killed*
FISKE, P/O W. M. L. American. 601. Killed*
FITZGERALD, F/Lt. T. B. N/Zealander. 141
FIZELL, Sgt. J. F. British. 29
FLEMING, P/O J. British. 605
FLEMING, P/O R. D. S. British. 249. Killed*
FLETCHER, Sgt. J. G. B. British. 604. Killed*
FLETCHER, F/Lt. A. W. Canadian. 235
FLETCHER, Sgt. British. 3
FLETCHER, Sgt. W. T. N/Zealander. 23
FLINDERS, P/O J. L. British. 32
FLOOD, F/Lt. F. W. Australian. 235. Killed*
FLOWER, Sgt. H. L. British. 248
FOGLAR, Sgt. V. Czech. 245
FOIT, P/O E. A. Czech. 310
FOKES, Sgt. R. H. British. 92. Killed
FOLLIARD, Sgt. J. H. British. 604
FOPP, Sgt. D. British. 17
FORBES, S/Ldr. A. S. British. 303–66
FORD, Sgt. R. C. British. 41
FORD, Sgt. E. G. British. 3–232. Killed
FORDE, F/O D. N. British. 145–605
FORREST, Sgt. D. H. British. 66
FORRESTER, P/O G. M. British. 605. Killed*
FORSHAW, F/O T. H. T. British. 609
FORSTER, F/O A. D. British. 151–607
FORSYTH, Sgt. C. L. M. N/Zealander. 23. Killed

FORWARD, Sgt. R. V. British. 257
FOSTER, P/O R. W. British. 605
FOTHERINGHAM, Sgt. British. 3
FOWLER, Sgt. R. J. British. 247
FOWLER, F/O A. L. British. 248. Killed
FOX, Sgt. P. H. British. 56
FOX, Sgt. L. British. 29
FOXLEY-NORRIS, F/O C. N. British. 3
FOX-MALE, P/O D. H. British. 152
FRANCIS, P/O C. D. British. 253. Killed*
FRANCIS, Sgt. D. N. British. 257
FRANCIS, Sgt. C. W. British. 74
FRANCIS, Sgt. J. British. 23
FRANCIS, Sgt. British. 3
FRANCIS, P/O N. I. C. British. 247. Killed
FRANKLIN, F/O W. D. K. British. 74
FRANKLIN, P/O W. H. British. 65. Killed
FRANTISEK, Sgt. J. Czech. 303. Killed*
FRASER, Sgt. R. H. B. British. 257. Killed*
FREEBORN, F/Lt. J. C. British. 74
FREEMAN, Sgt. R. R. British. 29
FREER, Sgt. P. F. British. 29. Killed
FREESE, Sgt. L. E. British. 611–74. Killed
FRENCH, Sgt. T. L. British. 29. Killed
FREY, F/Lt. J. A. Polish. 607
FRIEND, Sgt. J. R. British. 25. Killed
FRIENDSHIP, P/O A. H. B. British. 3
FRIPP, Sgt. J. H. British. 248
FRISBY, P/O E. M. British. 504. Killed
FRITH, Sgt. E. T. G. British. 611–92. Killed*
FRIZELL, P/O C. G. Canadian. 257
FROST, P/O J. L. British. 600
FULFORD, Sgt. D. British. 64. Killed
FULFORD, Sgt. British. 19
FUMERTON, P/O R. C. Canadian. 32
FURNEAUX, Sgt. R. H. British. 3–73
FURST, Sgt. B. Czech. 310–605

GABSZEWICZ, F/O A. Polish 607
GADD, Sgt. Pilot J. British. 611
GAGE, P/O D. H. British. 602. Killed
GALLUS, Sgt. British. 3
GAMBLEN, F/O D. R. British. 41. Killed*
GANE, P/O S. R. British. 248. Killed*
GANT, Sgt. E. British. 236
GARDINER, F/O F. T. British. 610. Killed
GARDINER, Sgt. G. C. British. 219. Killed*
GARDINER, Sgt. W. M. British. 3
GARDNER, Sgt. B. G. D. British. 610. Killed
GARDNER, P/O P. M. British. 32
GARDNER (F.A.A.), Sub/Lt. R. E. British. 242
GARDNER, P/O J. R. British. 141
GARFIELD, Sgt. W. J. British. 248. Killed*
GARRARD, P/O A. H. H. British. 248. Killed
GARSIDE, Sgt. G. British. 236
GARTON, Sgt. G. W. British. 73
GARVEY, Sgt. L. A. British. 41. Killed*
GARVIN, S/Ldr. G. D. British. 264
GASH, Sgt. F. British. 264
GASKELL, P/O R. S. British. 264
GAUNCE, F/Lt. L. M. Canadian. 615. Killed
GAUNT, P/O G. N. British. 609. Killed*
GAUNT, Sgt. W. D. British. 23
GAVAN, Sgt. A. British. 54
GAWITH, P/O A. A. N/Zealander. 23
GAYNER, F/O J. R. H. British. 615
GEAR, Sgt. A. W. British. 32
GEDDES, P/O K. I. British. 604
GEE, Sgt. V. D. British. 219. Killed

GENNEY, P/O T. British. 604. Killed
GENT, Sgt. R. J. K. British. 501–32. Killed
GIBBINS, Sgt. D. G. British. 54–222
GIBBONS, Sgt. C. M. British. 236
GIBSON, F/Lt. J. A. A. British. 501
GIDDINGS, F/Lt. H. S. British. 615–111. Killed
GIL, P/O J. Polish. 229–43
GILBERT, P/O E. G. British. 64
GILBERT (F.A.A.), Mid/Ship. P. R. J. British. 111
GILBERT, P/O H. T. British. 601. Killed
GILDERS, Sgt. J. S. British. 72. Killed
GILL, Sgt. J. V. British. 23. Killed
GILLAM, F/Lt. D. E. British. 312–616
GILLAM, Sgt. E. British. 248. Killed
GILLAN, P/O J. British. 601. Killed*
GILLEN, F/O T. W. British. 247
GILLESPIE, P/O J. L. British. 23. Killed
GILLIES, Sgt. British. 421 Flt.
GILLIES, F/Sgt. J. British. 602. Killed
GILLIES, F/Lt. K. M. British. 66. Killed*
GILLMAN, P/O K. R. British. 32. Killed*
GILROY, P/O G. K. British. 603
GILYEAT, Sgt. H. R. British. 29
GIRDWOOD, Sgt. A. G. British. 257. Killed*
GLASER, P/O E. D. British. 65
GLEAVE, S/Ldr. T. P. British. 253
GLEDHILL, Sgt. G. British. 238. Killed*
GLEED, F/Lt. I. R. British. 87. Killed
GLEGG, P/O A. J. British. 600
GLENDENNING, Sgt. J. N. British. 54–74. Killed
GLEW, Sgt. N. British. 72. Killed
GLOWACKI, Sgt. W. J. Polish. 605–145. Killed*
GLOWACKI, Sgt. A. Polish. 501
GLYDE, F/O R. L. Australian. 87. Killed*
GMUR, Sgt. F. Polish. 151. Killed*
GNYS, P/O W. Polish. 302
GODDARD, F/Lt. H. G. British. 219
GODDARD, P/O W. B. British. 235. Killed
GODDEN, S/Ldr. S. F. British. 3
GOLDSMITH, F/O C. W. S/African. 54–603. Killed*
GOLDSMITH, Sgt. J. E. British. 236. Killed
GONAY, P/O H. A. C. Belgian. 235. Killed
GOODALL, P/O H. I. British. 264. Killed*
GOODERHAM, Sgt. A. T. British. 46
GOODERHAM, Sgt. A. J. British. 25. Killed
GOODMAN, Sgt. G. British. 85
GOODMAN, P/O G. E. Palestinian. 1. Killed
GOODMAN, Sgt. M. V. British. 604
GOODWIN, P/O H. Mc.D. British. 609. Killed*
GOODWIN, Sgt. C. British. 219. Killed*
GOODWIN, Sgt. S. A. British. 266
GOODWIN, Sgt. R. D. British. 64
GORDON, S/Ldr. J. A. G. Canadian. 151. Killed
GORDON, P/O W. H. G. British. 234. Killed*
GORDON, Sgt. S. British. 235. Killed
GORE, F/Lt. W. E. British. 607. Killed*
GORRIE, P/O D. G. British. 43. Killed
GORZULA, P/O M. Polish. 607
GOSLING, P/O R. C. British. 266
GOTH, P/O V. Czech. 501–310. Killed*
GOTHORPE, Sgt. British. 25
GOULD, P/O D. L. British. 601–607
GOULD, F/O C. L. British. 607–32. Killed
GOULD, Sgt. G. L. British. 235
GOULDSTONE, Sgt. R. J. British. 29. Killed*
GOUT, P/O G. K. British. 234. Killed*
GOWERS, P/O A. V. British. 85. Killed
GRACIE, F/Lt. E. J. British. 56. Killed
GRAHAM, F/Lt. E. British. 72
GRAHAM, P/O L. W. S/African. 56

GRAHAM, Sgt. J. British. 236. Killed
GRAHAM, P/O K. A. G. British. 600. Killed
GRANDY, S/Ldr. J. British. 249
GRANT, Sgt. E. J. F. British. 600. Killed
GRANT, P/O S. B. British. 65
GRANT, Sgt. N/Zealander. 151
GRANT (F.A.A.), Sub/Lt. M. D. British. 804
GRASSICK, P/O R. D. Canadian. 242
GRAVES, Sgt. British. 235
GRAVES, P/O R. C. British. 253
GRAY, F/O A. P. British. 615
GRAY, P/O C. F. British. 54
GRAY, P/O C. K. British. 43
GRAY, P/O D. Mc.T. British. 610. Killed
GRAY, Sgt. M. British. 72. Killed*
GRAY, Sgt. K. W. British. 85. Killed
GRAY, P/O T. British. 64
GRAYSON, F/Sgt. C. British. 213. Killed
GREEN, F/Lt. C. P. British. 421 Flt.
GREEN, Sgt. W. J. British. 501
GREEN, P/O M. D. British. 248. Killed*
GREEN, P/O W. V. British. 235. Killed*
GREEN, Sgt. H. E. British. 141
GREEN, Sgt. G. G. British. 236
GREEN, Sgt. F. W. W. British. 600
GREENWOOD, P/O J. D. B. British. 253
GREENSHIELDS (F.A.A.), Sub/Lt. H. la Fore. British. 266.
                                Killed*
GREGORY, P/O F. S. British. 65. Killed*
GREGORY, Sgt. A. E. British. 219
GREGORY, Sgt. A. H. British. 111. Killed
GREGORY, Sgt. W. J. British. 29
GRELLIS, P/O H. E. British. 23 Died
GRETTON, Sgt. R. H. British. 266–222
GRIBBLE, P/O D. G. British. 54. Killed*
GRICE, P/O D. H. British. 32
GRICE, P/O D. H. British. 600. Killed*
GRIDLEY, Sgt. R. V. British. 235. Killed
GRIER, P/O T. British. 601. Killed
GRIFFEN, Sgt. J. J. British. 73. Killed
GRIFFITHS, Sgt. G. British. 17–601
GRIFFITHS, Sgt. British. 32
GROGAN, P/O G. J. Irish. 23
GROSZEWSKI, F/O. Polish. 43
GROVE, Sgt. H. C. British. 501–213. Killed
GRUBB, Sgt. E. G. British. 219
GRUBB, Sgt. H. F. British. 219
GRUSZKA, F/O F. Polish. 65. Killed*
GRZESZEZAK, F/O B. Polish. 303
GUERIN, Adj. C. Free French. 232. Killed
GUEST, P/O T. F. British. 56
GUNDRY, P/O K. C. British. 257. Killed
GUNN, P/O H. R. British. 74. Killed*
GUNNING, P/O P. S. British. 46. Killed*
GUNTER, P/O E. M. British. 43–501. Killed*
GURTEEN, P/O J. V. British. 504. Killed*
GUTHRIE (F.A.A.), Sub/Lt. G. C. M. British. 808
GUTHRIE, Sgt. N. H. British. 604
GUY (F.A.A.), Mid/Ship. P. British. 808. Killed
GUY, Sgt. L. N. British. 601. Killed
GUYMER, Sgt. E. N. L. British. 238

HACKWOOD, P/O G. H. British. 264. Killed
HAIG, P/O J. G. E. British. 603
HAIGH, Sgt. C. British. 604. Killed*
HAINE, P/O R. C. British. 600
HAINES, F/O L. A. British. 19. Killed
HAIRE, Sgt. J. K. British. 145. Killed
HAIRS, P/O P. R. British. 501

HALL, P/O R. M. D. British. 152
HALL, F/Lt. N. M. British. 257. Killed*
HALL, P/O R. C. British. 219
HALL, Sgt. British. 235
HALL, Sgt. British. 29
HALL, P/O W. C. British. 248. Killed
HALLAM, F/O I. L. Mc.G. British. 222. Killed
HALLIWELL, P/O A. B. British. 141
HALLOWES, Sgt. H. J. L. British. 43
HALTON, Sgt. D. W. British. 615. Killed*
HAMALE, Sgt. R. E. de J'a Belgian. 46. Killed
HAMAR, P/O J. R. British. 151. Killed*
HAMBLIN, Wg/Com. British. 17
HAMER, Sgt. British. 141
HAMILL, P/O J. W. N/Zealander. 299. Killed
HAMILTON, F/Lt. H. R. Canadian. 85. Killed*
HAMILTON, Sgt. J. S. British. 248. Killed
HAMILTON, Sgt. C. B. British. 219. Killed
HAMILTON, P/O A. L. Australian. 248
HAMILTON, P/O A. C. British. 141. Killed*
HAMILTON, P/O C. E. British. 234. Killed
HAMLYN, Sgt. R. F. British. 610
HAMMERTON, Sgt. J. British. 615. Killed
HAMMERTON, Sgt. J. British. 3. Killed
HAMMOND, P/O D. J. British. 253–245
HAMPSHIRE, Sgt. C. W. British. 85–111–249
HANBURY, P/O B. A. British. 1
HANBURY, P/O O. V. British. 602. Killed
HANCOCK, P/O N. P. W. British. 1
HANCOCK, P/O N. E. British. 152–65
HANCOCK, P/O E. L. British. 609
HANNON, P/O G. H. British. 236
HANSON, F/O D. H. W. British. 17. Killed*
HANUS, P/O J. Czech. 310
HANZLICEK, Sgt. O. Czech. 312. Killed*
HARDACRE, F/O J. R. British. 504. Killed*
HARDCASTLE, Sgt. J. British. 219. Killed
HARDIE, Sgt. British. 232
HARDING, Sgt. N. D. British. 29
HARDING, F/O N. M. British. 23. Killed
HARDMAN, P/O H. G. British. 111
HARDWICK, Sgt. W. R. H. British. 600
HARDY, P/O R. British. 234
HARDY, Sgt. O. A. British. 264
HARE, Sgt. M. British. 245
HARGREAVES, P/O F. N. British. 92. Killed*
HARKER, Sgt. A. S. British. 234
HARKNESS, S/Ldr. H. Irish. 257
HARNETT, F/O T. P. Canadian. 219
HARPER, F/Lt. W. J. British. 17
HARRIS, P/O P. A. British. 3. Killed
HARRISON, Sgt. A. R. J. British. 219
HARRISON, P/O J. H. British. 145. Killed*
HARRISON, P/O D. S. British. 238. Killed*
HARROLD, P/O F. C. British. 151–501. Killed*
HART, F/O J. S. Canadian. 602–54
HART, P/O K. G. British. 65. Killed
HART, P/O N. Canadian. 242. Killed
HARTAS, P/O P. Mc.D. British. 603–421 Flt. Killed
HARVEY, Sgt. L. W. British. 54
HASTINGS, P/O D. British. 74. Killed*
HATTON, Sgt. British. 604
HAVERCROFT, Sgt. R. E. British. 92
HAVILAND, P/O J. K. American. 151
HAVILAND, P/O R. H. S/African. 248. Killed
HAW, Sgt. C. British. 504
HAWKE, Sgt. P. S. British. 64
HAWKE, Sgt. S. N. British. 604. Killed
HAWKINGS, Sgt. R. P. British. 601. Killed*
HAWLEY, Sgt. F. B. British. 266. Killed*

HAWORTH, F/O J. F. J. British. 43. Killed*
HAY, F/O I. B. D. E. S/African. 611
HAY (F.A.A.), Lt. R. C. British. 808
HAYDEN, Sgt. L. H. British. 264
HAYES, S/Ldr. British. 242
HAYES, F/O T. N. British. 600
HAYLOCK, Sgt. R. A. British. 236
HAYSON, F/Lt. G. D. L. British. 79
HAYTER, F/O J. C. F. N/Zealander. 605–615
HAYWOOD, Sgt. D. British. 504
HAYWOOD, Sgt. D. British. 151
HEAD, Sgt. F. A. P. British. 236. Killed*
HEAD, Sgt. G. M. British. 219. Killed
HEAL, P/O P. W. D. British. 604
HEALY, Sgt. T. W. R. British. 41–611. Killed
HEATH, F/O B. British. 611
HEBRON, P/O G. S. British. 235
HEDGES, P/O A. L. British. 245–257
HEIMES, Sgt. L. British. 235
HELCKE, Sgt. D. A. British. 504. Killed*
HELLYER, F/Lt. R. O. British. 616
HEMINGWAY, P/O J. A. Irish. 85
HEMPTINNE, P/O B. M. de. Belgian. 145. Killed
HENDERSON, P/O J. A. Mc.D. British. 257
HENDRY, Sgt. D. O. British. 219
HENN, Sgt. W. B. British. 501
HENNEBERG, F/O Z. Polish. 303
HENSON, Sgt. B. British. 32–257. Killed
HENSTOCK, F/Lt. L. F. British. 64
HERON, P/O H. M. T. British. 266–66
HERRICK, P/O M. J. British. 25. Killed*
HERRICK, P/O B. H. N/Zealander. 236. Killed
HESLOP, Sgt. V. W. British. 56
HESS, P/O A. Czech. 310
HETHERINGTON, Sgt. E. L. British. 601. Killed
HEWETT, Sgt. G. A. British. 607
HEWITT, P/O D. A. Canadian. 501. Killed*
HEWLETT, Sgt. C. R. British. 65. Killed
HEYCOCK, S/Ldr. G. F. W. British. 23
HEYWOOD, P/O N. B. British. 32–607–257. Killed*
HEYWORTH, S/Ldr. J. H. British. 79
HICK, Sgt. D. T. British. 32
HIGGINS, Sgt. W. B. British. 253–32. Killed*
HIGGINSON, F/Sgt. F. W. British. 56
HIGGS, F/O T. P. K. British. 111. Killed*
HIGHT, P/O C. H. N/Zealander. 234. Killed*
HILES, P/O A. H. British. 236. Killed
HILKEN, Sgt. C. G. British. 74
HILL, P/O H. P. British. 92. Killed*
HILL, S/Ldr. J. H. British. 222
HILL, P/O S. J. British. 609. Killed
HILL, P/O M. R. S/African. 266. Killed
HILL, Sgt. C. R. N/Zealander. 141
HILL, P/O A. E. British. 248. Killed
HILL, Sgt. A. M. British. 25
HILL, Sgt. G. British. 65
HILL, P/O G. E. British. 245. Killed
HILLARY, P/O R. H. British. 603. Killed
HILLCOAT, F/Lt. H. B. L. British. 1. Killed*
HILLOCK, F/O F. W. 1 (Can) (401)
HILLMAN, Sgt. R. W. British. 235. Killed
HILLWOOD, Sgt. P. British. 56
HIMR, P/O J. J. Czech. 56. Killed
HINDRUP, Sgt. F. G. N/Zealander. 600
HINE, Sgt. British. 65
HIRD, Sgt. L. British. 604. Killed
HITHERSAY, Sgt. A. J. B. British. 141
HLAVAC, Sgt. J. Czech. 56. Killed*
HLOBIL, P/O A. Czech. 312
HOARE-SCOTT, P/O J. H. British. 601. Killed

HOBBIS, P/O D. O. British. 219. Killed
HOBBS, Sgt. S. J. British. 235. Killed
HOBBS, P/O J. B. British. 3. Killed
HOBBS, Sgt. W. H. British. 25
HOBSON, P/O C. A. British. 600. Killed*
HOBSON, S/Ldr. W. F. C. British. 601
HOBSON, F/Lt. D. B. British. 64
HODDS, Sgt. W. H. British. 25
HODGE, Sgt. J. S. A. British. 141. Killed
HODGKINSON, P/O A. J. British. 219. Killed
HODGSON, P/O W. T. N/Zealander. 85. Killed
HODSON, Sgt. C. G. British. 229–1
HOGAN, S/Ldr. H. A. V. British. 501
HOGG, F/O E. S. British. 152
HOGG, Sgt. R. D. British. 17–257–56. Killed
HOGG, P/O R. M. British. 152. Killed*
HOGG, P/O D. W. British. 25. Killed*
HOGG, Sgt. J. H. British. 141. Killed
HOGG, Sgt. R. V. British. 616. Killed
HOLDEN, F/Lt. E. British. 501
HOLDEN, P/O K. British. 616
HOLDER, Sgt. R. N/Zealander. 151. Killed
HOLDER, P/O G. A. British. 236
HOLDERNESS, F/Lt. J. B. S/Rhodesian. 1–229
HOLLAND, S/Ldr. A. L. British. 501–65
HOLLAND, P/O D. F. British. 72. Killed*
HOLLAND, Sgt. K. C. Australian. 152. Killed*
HOLLAND, P/O R. H. British. 92. Killed
HOLLAND, Sgt. R. M. British. 600
HOLLIS, Sgt. E. J. British. 25
HOLLOWAY, Sgt. S. V. British. 25
HOLLOWELL, Sgt. K. B. British. 25
HOLMES, P/O F. H. British. 152. Killed
HOLMES, Sgt. R. T. British. 504
HOLMES, P/O G. H. British. 600. Killed
HOLMES, Sgt. G. British. 25
HOLMES, Sgt. E. L. British. 248. Killed
HOLROYD, Sgt. W. B. British. 501–151
HOLTON, Sgt. A. G. V. British. 141
HOMER, F/O M. G. British. 242–1. Killed*
HONE, P/O D. H. British. 615
HONOR, F/O D. S. G. British. 145
HOOD, S/Ldr. H. R. L. British. 41. Killed*
HOOK, Sgt. A. British. 248. Killed
HOOKWAY, P/O D. N. British. 234
HOOPER, F/O B. G. British. 25
HOPE, F/O R. British. 605. Killed*
HOPE, F/Lt. Sir A. P. British. 601
HOPEWELL, Sgt. J. British. 616–66. Killed
HOPGOOD, Sgt. British. 64
HOPKIN, P/O W. P. British. 54–602
HOPTON, Sgt. B. W. British. 73. Killed
HORNBY, Sgt. W. H. British. 234
HORNER, Sgt. F. G. British. 610
HORROX, F/O J. M. British. 151. Killed
HORSKY, Sgt. V. Czech. 238. Killed*
HORTON, F/O P. W. N/Zealander. 234. Killed
HOUGH, P/O H. B. L. British. 600. Killed
HOUGHTON, P/O C. G. British. 141
HOUGHTON, Sgt. O. V. British. 501. Killed*
HOWARD, P/O J. British. 74–54. Killed
HOWARD, Sgt. British. 235
HOWARD-WILLIAMS, P/O P. I. British. 19
HOWARTH, Sgt. E. F. British. 501. Killed
HOWE, P/O B. British. 25. Killed
HOWE, P/O D. C. British. 235
HOWELL, F/Lt. F. J. British. 609. Killed
HOWELL, Sgt. F. British. 87
HOWES, P/O P. British. 54–603. Killed*
HOWES, Sgt. H. N. British. 85–605. Killed

HOWITT, P/O G. L. British. 615–245
HOWITT, P/O I. E. British. 41
HOWLEY, P/O R. A. Canadian. 141. Killed*
HOYLE, Sgt. H. N. British. 257
HOYLE, Sgt. G. V. British. 232. Killed
HRADIL, P/O F. Czech. 19–310. Killed
HRUBY, P/O O. Czech. 111
HUBACEK, Sgt. J. Czech. 310
HUBBARD, F/O T. E. British. 601
HUBBARD, Sgt. B. F. R. British. 235. Killed
HUCKIN, Sgt. P. E. British. 600
HUGHES, F/Lt. J. McM. British. 25. Killed
HUGHES, F/Lt. D. P. British. 238. Killed*
HUGHES, P/O F. D. British. 264
HUGHES, F/Lt. P. C. Australian. 234. Killed*
HUGHES, Sgt. D. E. N/Zealander. 600. Killed*
HUGHES, F/Sgt. W. R. British. 23
HUGHES, P/O D. L. British. 141
HUGHES, Sgt. A. J. British. 245
HUGHES-REES, Sgt. J. British. 609. Killed
HUGO, P/O P. H. S/African. 615
HULBERT, Sgt. F. H. R. British. 601
HULBERT, Sgt. D. J. British. 257–501
HULL, S/Ldr. C. B. S/African. 263–43. Killed*
HUMPHERSON, F/O J. B. W. British. 32–607. Killed
HUMPHREY, P/O A. H. British. 266
HUMPHREYS, P/O J. S. N/Zealander. 605
HUMPHREYS, P/O P. C. British. 32
HUMPHREYS, P/O J. D. British. 29. Killed
HUMPHREYS, F/O P. H. British. 152. Killed
HUNT, Sgt. D. A. C. British. 66
HUNT, P/O D. W. British. 257
HUNT, P/O H. N. British. 504. Killed
HUNTER, F/Lt. British. 600
HUNTER, S/Ldr. P. A. British. 264. Killed*
HUNTER, Sgt. British. 604. Killed
HUNTER, Sgt. D. J. British. 29
HUNTER, P/O A. S. British. 604. Killed
HUNTER-TOD, F/Lt. British. 23
HURRY, Sgt. C. A. L. British. 43–46
HURST, P/O P. R. S. British. 600. Killed
HUTCHINSON, Sgt. I. British. 222
HUTCHINSON (F.A.A.), Sub/Lt. D. A. British. 804. Killed
HUTLEY, P/O R. R. British. 32–213. Killed*
HUTTON, Sgt. R. S. British. 85. Killed
HYBLER, P/O J. Czech. 310
HYDE, Sgt. R. J. British. 66
HYDE, P/O J. W. British. 229
HYDE, F/O. Canadian. 1 (Can) (401)

IEVERS, F/Lt. N. L. Irish. 312
IGGLESDEN, F/O C. P. British. 234
IMRAY, Sgt. H. S. British. 600
INGLE, F/O A. British. 605
INGLE-FINCH, P/O M. R. British. 607–151–56
INNES, Sgt. R. A. British. 253
INNESS, P/O R. F. British. 152
INNISS, F/O A. R. de. H. British. 236
IRVING, F/Lt. M. M. British. 607. Killed*
ISHERWOOD, Sgt. D. W. British. 29
ISAAC, Sgt. L. R. British. 64. Killed*
IVESON, Sgt. T. C. British. 616
IVEY, Sgt. R. British. 248

JACK, F/O D. M. British. 602
JACKSON, Sgt. P. F. British. 604. Killed
JACKSON, Sgt. A. British. 29. Killed*
JACKSON, P/O P. A. C. British. 236

JACOBS, P/O H. British. 219–600
JACOBSON, Sgt. N. British. 29. Killed*
JAMES, Sgt. R. H. British. 29
JAMES, Sgt. R. S. S. British. 248. Killed
JAMESON, S/Ldr. P. G. British. 266
JANICKI, P/O Z. Polish. 32
JANKIEWICZ, F/O J. S. Polish. 601. Killed
JANOUGH, P/O S. Czech, 310
JANUSZEWICZ, P/O W. Polish. 303. Killed*
JARRETT, Sgt. G. W. J. British. 501–245. Killed
JASKE, P/O J. A. Czech. 312
JASTRZEVSKI, F/Lt. F. Polish. 302. Killed*
JAVAUX, P/O L. L. G. Belgian. 235. Killed
JAY, P/O D. T. British. 87. Killed*
JEBB, F/O M. British. 504. Killed*
JEFF, F/Lt. R. V. British. 87. Killed*
JEFFCOAT, P/O H. J. British. 236. Killed
JEFFERIES, P/O C. G. St. D. British. 3–232
JEFFERIES, F/Lt. J. (ex. J. LATMER). British. 310
JEFFERSON, Sgt. G. British. 43
JEFFERSON, P/O S. F. British. 248
JEFFREY, F/O A. J. O. British. 64. Killed*
JEFFERY-CRIDGE, Sgt. H. R. British. 236
JEFFERYS, Sgt. G. W. British. 46–43. Killed*
JEKA, Sgt. J. Polish. 238
JENKINS, P/O D. N. O. British. 253. Killed*
JENNINGS, Sgt. B. J. British. 19
JERAM (F.A.A.), Sub/Lt. D. N. British. 213
JERECZEK, P/O E. W. Polish. 229–43
JESSOP, Sgt. E. R. British. 253–111–43–257. Killed
JICHA, P/O V. Czech. 1. Killed
JIROUDEK, F/Sgt. M. Czech. 310
JOHNS, Sgt. G. B. British. 229
JOHNSON, P/O A. E. British. 46. Killed
JOHNSON, P/O J. E. British. 616
JOHNSON, Sgt. J. I British. 222. Killed*
JOHNSON, P/O C. E. British. 264. Killed*
JOHNSON, Sgt. W. J. British. 145
JOHNSON, Sgt. R. B. British. 222
JOHNSON, Sgt. G. B. N/Zealander. 23
JOHNSON, P/O S. F. British. 600. Killed
JOHNSON, Sgt. R. A. British. 43
JOHNSON, Sgt. C. A. British. 25
JOHNSON, Sgt. A. E. British. 23. Killed
JOHNSON, Sgt. R. K. H. British. 235. Killed
JOHNSTON, P/O J. T. Canadian. 151. Killed*
JOHNSTONE, S/Ldr. A. V. R. British. 602
JOLL, P/O I. K. S. British. 604
JONES, P/O W. R. British. 266
JONES, F/O D. A. E. British. 3–501
JONES, Sgt. H. D. B. British. 504. Killed
JONES, P/O C. A. T. British. 611
JONES, P/O J. S. B. British. 152. Killed*
JONES, P/O R. E. British. 605
JONES, P/O R. L. British. 64–19
JONES, Sgt. E. British. 29. Killed
JONES, P/O J. T. British. 264. Killed*
JONES, F/O. British. 616
JOTTARD, P/O A. R. I. Belgian. 145. Killed*
JOUBERT, P/O C. C. O. British. 56
JOWITT, Sgt. L. British. 85. Killed*
JULEFF, P/O J. R. British. 600

KAHN, P/O A. H. E. British. 248. Killed
KANE, P/O T. M. British. 234
KANIA, F/Sgt. J. Polish. 303
KARASEK, Sgt. L. R. British. 23. Killed*
KARUBIN, Sgt. S. Polish. 303. Killed
KARWOSKI, P/O W. E. Polish. 302

KAUCKY, Sgt. J. Czech. 310
KAWALECKI, P/O T. W. Polish. 151
KAY, P/O D. H. S. British. 264. Killed
KAY, P/O J. K. British. 111–257
KAY, Sgt. A. British. 248. Killed*
KAYLL, S/Ldr. J. R. British. 615
KEARD, P/O J. A. British. 235. Killed
KEARSEY, P/O P. J. British. 607–213. Killed
KEARSEY, Sgt. A. W. British. 152
KEAST, Sgt. F. J. British. 600. Killed*
KEATINGS, Sgt. J. British. 219
KEE, Sgt. E. H. C. British. 253. Killed
KEEL, Sgt. G. E. British. 235. Killed*
KEELER, Sgt. R. R. G. British. 236
KEIGHLEY, P/O G. British. 610
KELLETT, S/Ldr. R. G. British. 303–249
KELLETT, F/O M. British. 111
KELLIT, Sgt. W. H. British. 236
KELLOW, F/O R. W. British. 213
KELLS, P/O L. G. H. British. 29. Died
KELLY, F/Lt. D. P. D. G. British. 74
KELSEY, Sgt. E. N. British. 611. Killed
KEMP, P/O J. R. N/Zealander. 141. Killed*
KEMP, P/O N. L. D. British. 242
KEMP, P/O J. L. British. 54
KENDAL, P/O J. B. British. 66. Killed
KENNARD, P/O H. C. British. 66
KENNARD-DAVIS, P/O P. F. British. 64. Killed*
KENNEDY, Sgt. R. W. British. 604. Killed
KENNEDY, F/Lt. J. C. Australian. 238. Killed*
KENNER, P/O P. L. British. 264. Killed*
KENNETT, P/O P. British. 3. Killed
KENSALL, Sgt. G. British. 25. Killed
KENT, F/Lt. J. A. Canadian. 303
KENT, P/O R. D. British. 235
KEOUGH, P/O V. C. American. 609. Killed
KEPRT, Sgt. J. Czech. 312
KER-RAMSAY, F/Lt. R. G. British. 25. F.I.U.
KERSHAW, P/O A. British. 1. Killed
KERWIN, F/O B. V. Canadian. 1 (Can) (401) Died
KESTIN (F.A.A.), Sub/Lt. I. H. British. 145. Killed*
KESTLER, Sgt. O. Czech. 111. Killed
KEYMER, Sgt. M. British. 65. Killed*
KEYNES, Sgt. J. D. British. 236. Killed
KIDSUN, P/O R. N/Zealander. 141. Killed*
KILLICK, Sgt. P. British. 245
KILLINGBACK, Sgt. F. W. G. British. 249
KILMARTIN, F/Lt. J. I. Irish. 43
KILNER, Sgt. J. R. British. 65
KINDER, P/O M. C. British. 607
KINDER, P/O D. S. British. 73
KINDERSLEY (F.A.A.), Lt. A. T. J. British. 808. Killed
KING, S/Ldr. E. B. British. 249–151. Killed*
KING, F/O P. J. C. British. 66. Killed*
KING, P/O F. H. British. 264. Killed*
KING, P/O R. British. 238
KING, F/O L. F. D. British. 64. Killed
KING, P/O M. A. British. 249. Killed*
KING, P/O W. L. British. 236. Killed
KINGABY, Sgt. D. E. British. 266–92
KINGCOMBE, F/Lt. C. B. F. British. 92
KINGS, P/O R. A. British. 238
KIRK, Sgt. T. B. British. 74. Killed*
KIRKPATRICK, P/O J. C. Belgian. 235. Killed*
KIRKWOOD, P/O M. T. British. 610. Killed
KIRTON, Sgt. D. I. British. 65. Killed*
KITAL, Sgt. S. Polish. 253
KITSON, P/O T. R. British. 245. Killed
KLELZKOWSKI, P/O S. Polish. 302
KLEIN, Sgt. Z. Polish. 234–152. Killed

KLOZINSKI, Sgt. W. Polish. 54
KNIGHT, F/Lt. R. A. L. British. 23. Killed
KNOCKER, P/O W. R. A. British. 264
KOMAROFF, Sgt. L. A. British. 141. Died
KOMINEK, F/Sgt. J. Czech. 310
KONRAD, Sgt. Polish. 501
KOPECKY, Sgt. V. A. Czech. 111–253
KOPRIVA, Sgt. J. Czech. 310
KORBER, Sgt. Czech. 32
KORDULA, P/O F. Czech. 17–1
KOSARZ, Sgt. Polish. 302. Killed
KOSINSKI, F/Lt. Polish. 32
KOUKAL, Sgt. F. Czech. 310. Killed
KOWALSKI, F/O J. Polish. 302
KOWALSKI, Sgt. J. Polish. 303
KOZLOWSKI, P/O F. Polish. 501
KRAMER, P/O M. British. 600. Killed
KRASNODEBSKI, S/Ldr. Z. Polish. 303
KRATKORUKY, Sgt. B. Czech. 1. Killed
KREDBA, F/Lt. M. Czech. 310. Killed
KREPSKI, P/O W. Polish. 54. Killed*
KROL, P/O W. Polish. 302
KUCERA, Sgt. J. V. 111–238
KUCERA, Sgt. J. Czech. 245. Killed
KUMIEGA, P/O L. British. 17
KUSTRZYNSKI, F/O Z. Polish. 607
KUTTLEWASCHER, Sgt. K. M. Czech. 1. Died
KWIECINSKI, Sgt. J. Polish. 145. Killed*

LACEY, Sgt. J. H. British. 501
LACEY, Sgt. E. R. British. 219
LACKIE, Sgt. W. L. British. 141
LAFONT, Adj. Henrie G. Free French. 615
LAGUNA, F/Lt. Polish. 302
LAING, F/O A. J. A. British. 64
LAING, Sgt. A. British. 151
LAKE, F/O D. M. British. 219. Killed
LAMB, P/O R. L. British. 600
LAMB, Sgt. A. British. 25
LAMB (F.A.A.), Sub/Lt. R. R. British. 804. Killed
LAMB, F/O P. G. British. 610
LAMB, P/O O. E. N/Zealander. 151. Killed
LAMBERT, F/Lt. H. M. S. British. 25. Killed*
LAMBIE, P/O W. G. M. British. 219. Killed
LAMMER, P/O A. British 141
LANDELS, P/O L. N. British. 32–615. Killed
LANDSELL, Sgt. J. British. 607. Killed*
LANE, F/Lt. B. J. E. British. 19. Killed
LANE, P/O R. British. 43. Killed
LANGDON, P/O. British. 43
LANGHAM-HOBART, P/O N. G. British. 73
LANGLEY, Sgt. L. British. 23. Died
LANGLEY, P/O G. A. British. 41. Killed*
LANNING, P/O F. C. A. British. 141
LAPKA, P/O S. Polish. 302
LAPKOWSKI, P/O W. Polish. 203
LARBALESTIER, P/O B. D. British. 600
LARICHELIERE, P/O J. E. P. Canadian. 213. Killed*
LATTA, P/O J. B. Canadian. 142. Killed
LAUCHLIN, F/O J. H. British. 235
LAUDER, Sgt. A. J. British. 264
LAURENCE, P/O. British. 234
LAURENCE, Sgt. G. British. 141. Killed
LAW, P/O K. S. British. 605
LAWFORD, Sgt. D. N. British. 247
LAWLER, Sgt. E. S. British. 604
LAWRENCE, Sgt. N. A. British. 54. Died
LAWRENCE, Sgt. British. 235

LAWRENCE, Sgt. British. 235
LAWS, Sgt. G. G. S. British. 501–151. Killed
LAWS, P/O A. F. British. 64. Killed
LAWSON, P/O W. J. British. 19. Killed
LAWSON, P/O R. C. British. 601. Killed
LAWSON-BROWN, P/O. British. 64. Died
LAWTON, F/O P. C. F. British. 604
LAYCOCK, P/O H. K. British. 79. Killed
LAYCOCK, F/O. British. 87
LAZORYK, F/Lt. W. Polish. 607
LEARY, P/O D. C. British. 17. Killed
LEATHART, S/Ldr. J. A. British. 54
LEATHAM, P/O E. G. C. British. 248
LEATHER, F/Lt. W. J. British. 611
LE CHEMINANT, Sgt. J. British. 616
LECKRONE, P/O P. H. American. 616. Killed
LECKY, P/O J. G. British. 610–41. Killed*
LE CONTE, Sgt. E. F. British. F.I.U.
LEDGER, Sgt. L. British. 236
LE DONG, Sgt. T. British. 219. Killed
LEE, P/O K. N. T. British. 501
LEE, Sgt. M. A. W. British. 72. Killed
LEE, Sgt. M. A. British. 421 Flt.
LEE, F/Lt. R. H. A. British. 85. Killed*
LEES, S/Ldr. R. B. British. 72
LEES, P/O A. F. Y. British. 236
LE FEVRE, P/O P. W. British. 46. Killed
LEGG, P/O R. J. British. 601
LEGGETT, P/O P. G. 245
LEIGH, S/Ldr. R. H. A. British. 66
LEIGH, Sgt. A. C. British. 64–72
LE JEUNE, Sgt. O. G. Belgian. 235. Killed
LENAHAN, P/O J. D. British. 607. Killed
LENG, Sgt. M. E. British. 73
LENNARD (F.A.A.), Mid/Ship. P. L. British. 501. Killed
LENTON, P/O E. C. British. 56
LE ROUGETEL, F/O S. P. 600
LE ROY DU VIVIER, P/O D. A. R. G. Belgian. 43
LERWAY, Sgt. F. T. British. 236
LESLIE, Sgt. G. M. British. 219. Killed
LEVENSON, Sgt. S. A. British. 611. Killed
LEWIS, P/O A. G. S/African. 85–249
LEWIS, Sgt. W. G. British. 25. Killed
LEWIS, Sgt. C. S. British. 600
LEWIS, P/O R. G. Canadian. 1 (Can) (401). Killed
LEYLAND, Sgt. R. H. British. F.I.U.
LILLE, Sgt. British. 264
LILLEY, Sgt. R. British. 29. Killed
LIMPENNY, Sgt. E. R. British. 64
LINDSAY, P/O A. I. British. 72. Killed
LINDSEY, P/O P. C. British. 601. Killed*
LINES, F/O A. P. British. 17
LINGARD, P/O J. G. British. 25
LINNEY, P/O A. S. British. 229
LIPSCOMBE, Sgt. A. J. British. 600 Killed
LISTER, S/Ldr. R. C. F. British. 92–41
LITCHFIELD, P/O P. British. 610. Killed*
LITSON, Sgt. F. W. R. British. 141
LITTLE, F/O B. W. British. 609
LITTLE, P/O A. G. British. 235
LITTLE, Sgt. R. British. 238. Killed*,
LITTLE, F/O T. B. Canadian. 1 (Can) (401). Killed
LITTLE, S/Ldr. J. H. British. 219. Killed
LITTLE, S/Ldr. British 600
LLEWELLYN, Sgt. R. T. British. 213
LLEWELLYN, F/O. British. 29
LLOYD, Sgt. D. E. British. 19–64
LLOYD, Sgt. P. D. British. 41. Killed*
LLOYD, P/O J. P. British. 72–64

LLOYD, Sgt. British. 29
LOCKHART, P/O J. British. 85–213. Killed
LOCHMAN, F/O P. W. Canadian. 1 (Can) (401). Killed
LOCK, P/O E. S. British. 41. Killed
LOCKTON, Sgt. E. E. British. 236. Killed*
LOCKWOOD, Sgt. J. C. British. 54. Killed
LOFTS, P/O K. T. British. 615–249. Killed
LOGAN, P/O C. British. 266. Killed
LOGIE, P/O O. A. British. 29
LOKUCIEWSKI, P/O W. Polish. 303
LONG, Sgt. British. 236
LONSDALE, Sgt. R. V. H. British. 242–501
LONSDALE, P/O J. British. 3. Killed
LOOKER, P/O D. J. British. 615
LOUDON, F/Lt. M. J. British. 141
LOVELL, P/O A. D. J. British. 41. Killed
LOVELL-GREGG, S/Ldr. T. G. N/Zealander. 87. Killed*
LOVERSEED, Sgt. J. E. British. 501
LOVETT, F/Lt. R. E. British. 73. Killed*
LOWE, Sgt. J. British. 236
LOWETH, P/O P. A. British. 249
LOWTHER, Sgt. W. British. 219
LOXTON, S/Ldr. W. W. British. 25
LUCAS, P/O R. M. M. D. British. 141
LUCAS, Sgt. S. E. British. 32–257
LUKASZEWICZ, F/O K. Polish. 501. Killed*
LUMSDEN, P/O D. T. M. British. 236
LUMSDEN, Sgt. J. C. British. 248
LUND, P/O J. W. British. 611–92. Killed
LUSK, P/O H. S. N/Zealander. 25
LUSTY, P/O K. R. British. 25
LYALL, F/Lt. A. Mc. L. British. 25
LYALL, P/O A. British. 602. Killed
LYNCH, Sgt. J. British. 25. Killed
LYONS, P/O E. B. British. 65
LYSEK, Sgt. A. Polish. 302

MacARTHUR, F/O M. R. British. 236
MacCAW, F/O D. C. British. 238. Killed*
MACCONOCHIE, Sgt. A. R. D. British. 235
MacDONALD, Sgt. A. S. British. 601
MacDONALD, P/O D. K. British. 603. Killed*
MacDONALD, F/Lt. H. K. British. 603. Killed*
MacDONELL, S/Ldr. A. R. D. British. 64
MacDOUGAL, Sgt. C. W. British. 111. Killed
MacDOUGALL, P/O L. N. British. 141
MacDOUGALL, S/Ldr. R. I. G. British. 17
MACEJOWSKI, Sgt. M. K. Polish. 111–249
MacFIE, P/O C. H. British. 616–611
MacGREGOR, Sgt. A. N. British. 19
MACHACEK, P/O J. Czech. 145. Died
MACHIN, Sgt. W. H. British. 264. Killed*
MACINSKI, P/O J. Polish. 111. Killed*
MacKAY, P/O. British. 234
MacKENZIE, P/O. British. 43
MacKENZIE, P/O D. C. N/Zealander. 56. Killed
MacKENZIE, P/O K. W. British. 501
MacKENZIE, P/O J. N. N/Zealander. 41
MacKINNON (F.A.A.), Lt. A. Mc. L. British. 804
MacKINNON, Sgt. D. D. British. 236. Killed*
MacLACHLAN, S/Ldr. A. M. British. 92
MacLACHLAN, F/O J. A. F. British. 73–145. Killed
MacLAREN, P/O A. C. British. 604
MacLACHLAN, S/Ldr. J. R. British. 46
MacLEAN, P/O C. H. British. 602
MacNAMARA, F/O B. R. British. 603
MacPHAIL, P/O F. J. British. 603. Died
MacRAE, Sgt. I. N. British. F.I.U.
MacRORY, Sgt. H. I. British. 23. Killed

MADLE, P/O S. J. British. 615–605
MAFFETT, P/O G. H. British. 257. Killed*
MAGGS, P/O M. H. British. 264
MAGUIRE, S/Ldr. H. J. British. 229
MAHONEY (F.A.A.), Petty/Off. T. J. British. 804
MAIN, Sgt. A. D. W. British. 249. Killed*
MAIN, Sgt. H. R. British. 25. Killed
MAITLAND-WALKER, P/O W. H. British. 65
MAKINS, Sgt. British. 247
MALAN, F/Lt. A. G. S/African. 74
MALENGREAU, P/O R. F. F. G. Belgian. 87
MALES, P/O E. E. British. 72. Killed*
MALINOWSKI, Sgt. B. Polish. 43
MALINSKI, P/O J. L. Polish. 302
MALLETT, Sgt. R. S. British. 29. Killed
MALY, P/O J. M. Czech. 310. Died
MAMEDOFF, P/O A. American. 609. Died
MANGER, F/O K. British. 17. Killed*
MANN, P/O H. J. British. 1
MANN, Sgt. J. British. 92–64
MANSEL-LEWIS, P/O J. British. 92
MANSFIELD, Sgt. M. J. Czech. 111
MANSFIELD, Sgt. B. M. British. 236. Killed
MANSFIELD, Sgt. D. E. British. 236
MANTON, S/Ldr. G. A. L. British. 56
MANTON, Sgt. E. British. 610, Killed*
MARCHAND, P/O R. A. British. 73. Killed*
MAREK, Sgt. F. Czech. 310–19. Killed*
MARKIEWICZ, Sgt. A. L. Polish. 302
MARLAND, Sgt. R. G. British. 222. Killed
MARPLES, P/O R. British. 616. Killed
MARRS, P/O E. S. British. 152. Killed
MARSH, Sgt. British. 152
MARSH, Sgt. W. C. British. 236
MARSH (F.A.A.), Lt. A. E. British. 804
MARSH, Sgt. H. J. British. 238. Killed*
MARSHALL, Sgt. A. E. British. 73. Died
MARSHALL, P/O J. E. British. 85. Killed
MARSHALL, Sgt. T. R. British. 219. Killed
MARSHALL, Sgt. T. B. British. 235
MARSHALL, P/O J. V. British. 232
MARSLAND, P/O G. British. 245–253
MARSTON, F/O K. J. British. 56. Killed
MARTEL, P/O B. Polish. 603–54
MARTIN, F/O J. C. N/Zealander. 257. Killed
MARTIN, P/O A. W. British. 235
MARTIN, Sgt. British. 264
MARTIN (F.A.A.), Sub/Lt. R. M. S. British. 808. Killed
MASLEN, Sgt. T. A. British. 235. Killed
MASON, Sgt. W. British. 235. Killed
MASSEY, Sgt. K. British. 248
MATHER, P/O J. R. British. 66. Killed*
MATHERS, Sgt. J. W. British. 29–23
MATHESON, F/Lt. G. C. British. 222. Killed
MATTHEWS, Sgt. H. G. British. 236
MATHEWS, P/O K. L. British. 23
MATTHEWS, P/O H. K. F. British. 54–603. Killed*
MATTHEWS, F/O P. G. H. British. 1
MATTHEWS, Sgt. I. W. British. 64. Died
MAXWELL, P/O M. C. British. 56
MAXWELL, Sgt. W. British. 264. Killed*
MAXWELL, P/O D. A. British. 611–603. Killed
MAXWELL, S/Ldr. H. L. British. 600
MAYERS, P/O H. C. British. 601. Killed
MAYHEW, P/O P. F. British. 79. Killed
MAYNE, W/O E. British. 74
McADAM, Sgt. W. D. British. 23. Killed
McADAM, Sgt. J. British. 41. Killed
McALLISTER, Sgt. P. J. British. 29–23
McARTHUR, F/Lt. J. H. G. British. 609–238

McCALL, P/O S. V. British. 607
McCANN, Sgt. T. A. British. 601. Died
McCARTHY, Sgt. T. F. British. 235. Killed
McCARTHY, Sgt. J. P. British. 235
McCAUL, Sgt. J. P. British. 219. Killed*
McCHESNEY, Sgt. R. I. N/Zealander. 236. Killed
McCLINTOCK, P/O J. A. P. British. 615. Killed
McCOMB, S/Ldr. J. E. British. 611
McCONNELL, Sgt. J. British. 145
McCONNELL, P/O W. W. Irish. 607–245–249
McCORMACK, Sgt. J. B. British. 25. Killed
McDERMOTT, Sgt. J. N/Zealander. 23
McDONOUGH, P/O B. M. Australian. 236. Killed*
McDOUGALL, P/O R. British. 3–232
McDOWALL, Sgt. A. British. 602
McFADDEN, P/O A. British. 73
McGAW, P/O C. A. British. 73–66. Killed
McGIBBON, P/O J. British. 615. Killed
McGLASHAN, P/O K. B. British. 245
McGOWAN, F/O R. A. British. 46
McGOWAN, P/O H. W. British. 92
McGRATH, P/O J. K. British. 601
McGREGOR, F/Lt. G. R. Canadian. 1 (Can) (401)
McGREGOR, P/O P. R. British. 46
McGREGOR, S/Ldr. H. D. British. 213
McGREGOR, P/O A. J. British. 504
McGUGAN, Sgt. R. British. 141
McHARDY, P/O E. H. N/Zealander. 248
McHARDY, P/O D. B. H. British. 229
McINNES, P/O A. British. 601–238
McINTOSH, Sgt. P. R. C. British. 151–605. Killed
McINTYRE, P/O A. G. British. 111
McKAY, Sgt. D. A. S. British. 501–421 Flt.
McKELLAR, F/Lt. A. A. British. 605. Killed
McKENZIE, P/O J. W. British. 111. Killed*
McKIE, Sgt. E. J. British. 248
McKNIGHT, P/O W. L. Canadian. 242. Killed
McLAUGHLIN, Sgt. J. W. British. 238
MacLEOD, Sgt. G. S. M. British. 235. Killed
McLURE, P/O A. C. R. British. 87. Killed
McMAHON, Sgt. British. 235
McMULLEN, F/O D. A. P. British. 222–54
McNAB, S/Ldr. E. A. Canadian. 1 (Can) (401)–111
McNAIR, Sgt. R. J. British. 249–3
McNAY, Sgt. A. British. 73. Killed*
McPHEE, Sgt. J. British. 249–151
McPHERSON, F/Sgt. R. R. British. 65. Killed
MEAKER, P/O J. R. B. British. 249. Killed*
MEARES, S/Ldr. British. 54
MEASURES, F/Lt. W. E. G. British. 74–238
MEDWORTH, Sgt. J. British. 25
MEESON, Sgt. C. V. British. 56. Killed
MELVILLE, P/O J. C. British. 264
MELVILLE-JACKSON, P/O G. H. British. 236
MERCER, Sgt. British. 609
MERCHANT, Sgt. H. J. British. 1
MEREDITH, Sgt. A. D. British. 242–141
MERMAGEN, S/Ldr. H. W. British. 266–222
MERRETT, Sgt. J. C. British. 235
MERRICK, P/O C. British. 610
MERRYWEATHER, Sgt. S. W. British. 229. Killed
MESNER, Sgt. B. W. British. 248. Killed*
METCALFE, Sgt. A. C. British. 604
METHAM, Sgt. J. British. 253. Killed
MEYER, Sgt. R. H. R. British. 236. Killed
MICHAIL, Sgt. British. 501
MICHIELS, Sgt. A. C. A. Belgian. 235. Died
MIDDLEMISS, Sgt. W. British. 235
MIDDLETON, P/O. British. 266
MIERZWA, P/O B. Polish. 303

MILBURN, Sgt. R. A. British. 601
MILDREN, P/O P. R. British. 54–66. Killed
MILEHAM, P/O D. E. British. 41. Killed
MILES, Sgt. E. E. British. 236
MILES, Sgt. S. F. British. 23
MILEY, P/O M. J. British. 25. Killed*
MILLAR, F/O W. B. N. Canadian. 1 (Can) (401)
MILLARD, P/O J. G. P. British. 1
MILLER, F/Lt. A. G. British. 17–F.I.U.
MILLER, P/O R. F. G. Australian. 609. Killed*
MILLER, Sgt. A. J. British. 23
MILLER, Sgt. A. C. British. 604
MILLER, Sgt. T. H. British. 25. Killed
MILLER, F/Lt. R. R. British. 3. Killed
MILLINGTON, P/O W. H. Australian. 79–249. Killed*
MILLIST, P/O K. M. British. 73–615. Killed
MILLS, S/Ldr. R. S. British. 87
MILLS, Sgt. J. P. British. 43–249
MILLS, Sgt. J. B. British. 23
MILNE, P/O J. A. Canadian. 605
MILNE, F/O R. M. British. 151
MILNES, Sgt. A. H. British. 32
MITCHELL, P/O/ H. T. Canadian. 87
MITCHELL, F/O R. G. British. 257. Killed*
MITCHELL, F/O P. H. G. British. 266
MITCHELL, S/Ldr. H. M. British. 25
MITCHELL, Sgt. G. British. 23
MITCHELL, P/O G. T. M. British. 609. Killed
MITCHELL, Sgt. R. R. British. 229
MITCHELL, Sgt. H. R. N/Zealander. 3
MITCHELL, Sgt. British. 65
MOBERLEY, F/O G. E. British. 616. Killed*
MOLSON, F/O H. de M. Canadian. 1 (Can) (401)
MONK, P/O E. W. J. British. 25. Killed
MONK, Sgt. D. A. British. 236
MONTAGU, S/Ldr. G. W. British. 236. Killed
MONTAGUE-SMITH, F/Lt. A. M. British. 264
MONTBON, Sgt. Xavier de. Free French. 64
MONTGOMERY, Sgt. H. F. British. 43. Killed*
MONTGOMERY, P/O C. R. British. 614. Killed*
MOODY, P/O H. W. British. 602. Killed*
MOODY, Sgt. D. G. British. 604
MOORE, Sgt. A. R. British. 245–615–3
MOORE, P/O W. R. British. 264
MOORE, Sgt. P. J. British. 253. Killed
MOORE, F/O W. S. British. 236. Killed
MORE, S/Ldr. J. W. C. British. 73. Killed
MOREWOOD, F/Lt. R. E. G. British. 248
MORFILL, F/Sgt. P. F. British. 501
MORGAN, P/O P. J. British. 238
MORGAN-GRAY, P/O H. 46. Killed
MORRIS, P/O E. J. S/African. 79
MORRIS, P/O G. E. British. F.I.U.
MORRIS, P/O J. British. 248
MORRISON, Sgt. N. British. 54–74–72. Killed
MORRISON, Sgt. J. P. British. 46–43. Killed*
MORROUGH-RYAN, P/O O. B. British. 41. Killed
MORTIMER, P/O P. A. British. 257. Died
MORTON, P/O J. S. British. 603
MOSS (F.A.A.), Sub/Lt. W. J. M. British. 213. Killed*
MOSS, Sgt. R. C. British. 29
MOTT, Sgt. W. H. British. 141
MOTTRAM, P/O R. British. 92. Killed
MOUCHOTTE, Adj. R. Free French. 615. Killed
MOULD, Sgt. E. A. British. 74. Killed
MOULTON, Sgt. E. W. British. 600
MOUNSDON, P/O M. H. British. 56
MOUNT, F/O C. J. British. 602
MOWAT, F/Lt. N. J. N/Zealander. 245
MOWAT, Sgt. R. I. British. 248

MOYNHAM, Sgt. H. F. J. British. 248. Killed
MRAZEK, P/O K. Czech. 46
MUDIE, P/O M. R. British. 615. Killed*
MUDRY, Sgt. M. Polish. 79
MUIRHEAD, F/Lt. I. J. British. 605. Killed*
MUMLER, W/Com. M. Polish. 302
MUNGO-PARK, F/O J. C. British. 79–74. Killed
MUNN, F/Sgt. W. S. British. 29
MURCH, F/O L. C. British. 253. Died
MURLAND, Sgt. W. J. British. 264
MURRAY, Sgt. J. British. 610
MURRAY, P/O T. B. British. 616
MURRAY, S/Ldr. A. D. British. 73–501
MURRAY, Sgt. P. H. British. 23. Killed

NAISH, Sgt. K. E. British. 235
NARUCKI, P/O A. R. Polish. 607
NAUGHTIN, Sgt. H. T. British. 235. Killed
NEER, Sgt. British. 29
NEIL, P/O T. F. British. 249
NELSON, F/O W. H. Canadian. 74
NELSON, F/Sgt. D. British. 235
NELSON-EDWARDS, P/O G. H. British. 79
NENAGE, Sgt. T. N. British. 29. Killed
NESBITT, F/O A. D. Canadian. 1 (Can) (401)
NEVILLE, Sgt. W. J. British. 610. Killed*
NEWBURY, P/O J. C. British. 609
NEWBURY, P/O M. A. British. 145. Killed
NEWHAM, Sgt. E. A. British. 235
NEWLING, P/O M. A. British. 145. Died
NEWPORT, Sgt. D. V. British. 235
NEWTON, Sgt. H. S. British. 111
NEWTON, Sgt. E. F. British. 29
NICHOLAS, F/O J. B. H. British. 65
NICHOLLS, Sgt. T. G. F. British. 23. Killed
NICHOLLS, Sgt. D. B. F. British. 151
NICHOLS, Sgt. D. H. British. 56
NICOLSON, F/Lt. J. B. British. 249. Killed
NICOLSON, Sgt. P. B. British. 232. Killed
NIEMIEC, F/O P. Polish. 17
NIGHTINGALE, P/O F. G. 219. Killed
NIVEN, P/O H. G. British. 601–602
NIXON, Sgt. W. British. 23. Killed
NOBLE, Sgt. W. J. British. 54
NOBLE, P/O B. R. British. 79
NOBLE, Sgt. D. British. 43. Killed*
NOKES-COOPER, F/O B. British. 236. Killed*
NORFOLK, P/O N. R. British. 72
NORRIS, F/O R. W. Canadian. 1 (Can) (401)
NORRIS, F/Lt. S. C. British. 610
NORRIS, Sgt. P. P. British. 213. Killed*
NORTH, P/O G. British. 257. Killed
NORTH, P/O H. R. British. 43
NORTH-BOMFORD, Sgt. D. J. British. 17
NORWELL, Sgt. J. K. British. 54–41
NORWOOD, P/O R. K. C. British. 65
NOSOWICZ, P/O Z. Polish. 56
NOWAK, P/O T. Polish. 253
NOWAKIEWICZ, Sgt. E. J. A. Polish. 302
NOWELL (F.A.A.), Sub/Lt. W. R. British. 804
NOWIERSKI, P/O T. Polish. 609
NUNN, P/O S. G. British. 236
NUTE, Sgt. R. R. J. British. 23. Killed
NUTTER, Sgt. R. C. British. 257

OAKS, Sgt. T. W. N/Zealander. 235
O'BRIAN, F/O P. G. St. G. Canadian. 247–152
O'BRIEN, S/Ldr. J. S. British. 92–234. Killed*

O'BRIEN, F/Lt. 247
O'BRYNE, Sgt. P. British. 73–501
O'CONNELL, F/O A. British. 264
OBELOFSE, P/O J. R. S. S/African. 43. Killed*
ODBERT, S/Ldr. N. C. British. 64
OFFENBERG, P/O J. H. M. Belgian. 145. Killed
OGILVIE, P/O D. B. British. 601
OGILVIE, F/O A. K. Canadian. 609
OLDFIELD, Sgt. T. G. British. 64–92. Killed*
O'LEARY, Sgt. A. A. British. 604
OLENSEN, P/O W. P. British. 607. Killed
OLENSKI, F/O Z. Polish. 234–609
OLEWINSKI, Sgt. B. Polish. 111. Killed
OLIVE, F/Lt. C. G. C. Australian. 65
OLIVER, P/O P. British. 611
OLIVER, Sgt. G. D. British. 23. Killed
OLVER, P/O. British. 603
O'MALLEY, F/O D. H. C. British. 264. Killed*
O'MANNEY, Sgt. R. J. British. 229. Killed
O'MEARA, P/O J. J. British. 421 Flt.–64–72
O'NEILL, F/O D. H. British. 611–41. Killed*
O'NEILL, F/Lt. J. A. British. 601–238
ORCHARD, Sgt. H. C. British. 65. Killed
ORGIAS, P/O E. N/Zealander. 23. Killed*
ORTMANS, P/O V. M. M. Belgian. 229. Killed
ORZECHOWSKI, P/O J. Polish. 607
OSMAND, P/O A. I. British. 3–213
OSTOWICZ, F/O A. Polish. 145. Killed*
OTTEWILL, Sgt. P. G. British. 43
OVERTON, P/O C. N. British. 609
OWEN, Sgt. A. E. British. 600
OWEN, Sgt. H. British. 219
OWEN, Sgt. W. G. British. 235
OXSPRING, F/Lt. R. W. British. 66

PAGE, P/O A. G. British. 56
PAGE, Sgt. W. T. British. 1. Killed
PAGE, Sgt. V. D. British. 610–601
PAGE, Sgt. A. J. British. 257. Killed
PAGE, F/Lt. C. L. British. 234
PAGE, Sgt. A. D. British. 111. Killed
PAIN, P/O J. F. British. 32. Killed
PAISEY, Sgt. F. G. British. 235
PALAK, Sgt. J. Polish. 303–302
PALLISER, Sgt. G. C. C. British. 249–43
PALMER, Sgt. N. N. British. 248. Killed
PALUSINSKI, P/O J. H. Polish. 303
PANKRATZ, F/Lt. W. Polish. 145. Killed*
PANNELL, Sgt. G. C. N/Zealander. 3
PARKE (F.A.A.), Sub/Lt. T. R. V. British. 804. Killed
PARKER, Sgt. K. B. British. 64–92. Killed*
PARKER, P/O T. C. British. 79
PARKER, Sgt. D. K. British. 66
PARKER, P/O V. British. 234. Killed
PARKER, Wg/Com. L. R. British. 611
PARKES, Sgt. British. 501
PARKIN, P/O E. G. British. 501
PARKINSON, Sgt. C. British. 238. Killed*
PARNALL, P/O S. B. British. 607. Killed*
PARNALL, F/Lt. D. G. British. 249. Killed*
PARR, Sgt. L. A. British. 79
PARR, Sgt. D. J. British. 29. Killed
PARROTT, F/O D. T. British. 19. Killed
PARROTT, P/O P. L. British. 145–605
PARROTT, Sgt. R. J. British. 32. Killed
PARRY, Sgt. M. E. British. 604
PARRY, Sgt. E. British. 23. Killed
PARSONS, Sgt. E. E. N/Zealander. 23

PARSONS, Sgt. C. A. British. 66–610. Killed
PARSONS, F/O P. T. British. 504. Killed
PARSONS, Sgt. J. G. British. 235
PASSY, F/O C. W. British. 605
PASZIEWICZ, F/O L. W. Polish. 303. Killed*
PATEREK, Sgt. E. Polish. 302–303. Killed
PATERSON (F.A.A.), Lt. B. British. 804
PATERSON, F/Lt. J. A. N/Zealander. 92. Killed*
PATRICK, Sgt. L. F. British. 222
PATSON, Sgt. A. G. British. 604
PATTEN, F/O H. P. F. British. 64
PATTERSON (F.A.A.), Mid/Ship. P. J. British. 242. Killed
PATTERSON, P/O R. L. British. 235. Killed*
PATTERSON (F.A.A.), Sub/Lt. N. H. British. 804. Killed
PATTERSON, Sgt. L. J. British. 501. Killed
PATTISON, F/O A. J. S. British. 616–23–92. Killed*
PATTISON, Sgt. K. C. British. 611. Killed*
PATTISON, F/O. Canadian. 1 (Can) (401)
PATTISON, F/O J. G. British. 266
PATTULLO, P/O W. B. 151–249–46. Killed*
PAVITT, Sgt. British. 235
PAVLU, Sgt. O. Czech. 1. Killed
PAYNE, Sgt. A. D. British. 610
PAYNE, Sgt. R. I. British. 23. Killed*
PAYNE, P/O R. A. British. 602. Killed
PEACHMENT, P/O C. B. G. British. 236
PEACOCK, Sgt. W. A. British. 46. Killed*
PEACOCK, F/O R. J. British. 235. Killed
PEACOCK, Sgt. D. C. 605
PEACOCK-EWARDS, P/O S. R. British. 253–615
PEARCE, Sgt. L. H. B. British. 32–249. Killed
PEARCE, Sgt. P. G. British. 600. Killed
PEARCE, Sgt. W. J. British. 236–23. Killed
PEARCE, Sgt. R. British. 29
PEARCY, Sgt. D. J. British. 219. Killed
PEARMAN, P/O S. J. British. 141
PEARSE, Sgt. L. L. British. 236
PEARSON, Sgt. D. E. British. 236
PEARSON, Sgt. G. W. British. 501. Killed*
PEARSON, Sgt. P. British. 238. Killed
PEASE, P/O A. P. British. 74–603. Killed*
PECHA, Sgt. J. Czech. 310
PEEBLES, Sgt. W. British. 235. Killed
PEEL, S/Ldr. J. R. A. British. 145
PEEL, F/O C. D. British. 603. Killed*
PEGGE, P/O/ C. O. J. British. 610. Killed
PEMBERTON, S/Ldr. D. A. British. 1. Killed
PENFOLD, P/O P. E. British. 29
PENFOLD, Sgt. W. D. British. 236
PENFOLD, F/Sgt. V. W. R. British. 23
PENNINGTON, P/O D. A. British. 253–245
PENNINGTON-LEIGH, F/Lt. A. W. British. 232–248. Killed
PENNYCUICK, Sgt. B. British. 236
PERCY, P/O H. H. British. 264. Killed
PERKIN, Sgt. F. S. British. 73–421 Flt.
PERRIN, Adj. G. Free French. 615–249
PERRY, Sgt. H. T. British. 23. Killed*
PETERS, F/O G. C. B. British. 79. Killed*
PETERSON, F/O O. J. Canadian. 1 (Can) (401). Killed*
PETTET, P/O A. H. British. 248. Killed
PETTIT, Sgt. H. W. British. 605–1. Killed
PEXTON, F/O R. D. British. 615
PFEIFFER, P/O J. Polish. 257–32
PHILLIPART, P/O J. A. L. Belgian. 213. Killed*
PHILLIPS, Sgt. A. British. 604
PHILLIPS, F/Sgt. N. T. British. 65. Killed*
PHILLIPS, Sgt. R. F. P. British. 602
PHILLIPS, P/O E. R. British. 235. Killed
PHILLIPS, Sgt. J. British. 25. Killed
PHILLIPSON, Sgt. J. R. British. 604. Killed

PHILO, P/O R. F. British. 151
PIATKOWSKI, P/O S. Polish. 79.
PICKERING, Sgt. T. G. British. 501–32
PICKERING, Sgt. J. British. 64
PICKERING, P/O J. H. British. 66. Killed
PICKFORD, Sgt. J. T. British. 604
PIDD, Sgt. L. British. 238. Killed*
PIGG, F/O O. St. John. British. 72. Killed*
PILKINGTON, Sgt. A. British.23
PILKINGTON-MIKSA, P/O W. J. Polish. 303
PILCH, P/O E. Polish. 302. Killed
PINCKNEY, F/O D. J. C. British. 603. Killed
PINFOLD, F/Lt. M. H. British. 56
PINKHAM, S/Ldr. P. C. British. 19. Killed*
PIPA, Sgt. J. British. 43
PIPER, Sgt. A. H. British. 236
PIPPARD, P/O H. A. British. 29
PIPPETT, F/O J. G. British. 64. Killed
PISAREK, F/O M. Polish. 303
PITCHER, F/O P. B. Canadian. 1 (Can) (401)
PITTMAN, P/O G. E. British. 17
PLANT, Sgt. R. E. British. 611–72. Killed
PLEDGER, P/O G. F. C. British. 141. Killed
PLINDERLEITH, Sgt. R. British. 73
PLUMMER, F/O R. P. British. 46. Killed*
PLZAK, Sgt. S. Czech. 310–19. Killed
POCOCK, Sgt. M. H. British. 72
POLLARD, P/O P. S. C. British. 611. Killed
POLLARD, Sgt. J. K. British. 232. Killed
POND, F/Sgt. A. H. D. British. 601
PONTING, P/O W. A. British. 264. Killed*
POOL, P/O P. D. British. 266–72
POOLE, Sgt. E. R. L. British. 604
POPLAWSKI, P/O J. Polish. 111–229
PORTER, Sgt. J. A. British. 615–19–242
PORTER, Sgt. E. F. British. 141. Killed
PORTER, Sgt. O. W. British. 111. Killed
POSENER, P/O F. H. S/African. 152. Killed*
POULTON, P/O H. R. C. British. 64
POUND, Sgt. R. R. C. British. 25
POWELL, F/Lt. R. P. R. British. 111
POWELL, Sgt. S. W. M. British. 141
POWELL, P/O R. J. British. 248. Killed
POWELL, Sgt. E. British. 25. Killed
POWELL, Sgt. S. W. M. British.141
POWELL-SHEDDEN, F/Lt. G. British. 242
POWER, F/Lt. R. M. Australian. 236
PRCHAL, Sgt. E. M. Czech. 310
PREATER, Sgt. S. G. British. 235
PREVOT, P/O L. O. J. Belgian. 235
PRIAK, P/O K. 32–257. Killed
PRICE, P/O A. O. British. 236
PRICE, Sgt. N. A. J. British. 236
PRICE, Sgt. R. B. British. 245–222–73. Killed
PRICE, Sgt. J. British. 29
PRIESTLEY, F/O British. 235
PRITCHARD, F/Lt. C. A. British. 600
PROCTOR, Sgt. J. British. 602. Killed
PROCTOR, P/O J. E. N/Zealander. 32
PROSSER, Sgt. P. R. British. 235. Killed
PROUDMAN, Sgt. D. H. British. 248. Died
PROWSE, P/O H. A. R. British. 266–603
PTACEK, Sgt. R. Czech. 43. Killed
PUDA, Sgt. R. Czech. 310–605
PUDNEY (F.A.A.), Sub–Lt. G. B. British. 64. Killed
PUGH, Sgt. J. S. British. 25
PUGH, F/Lt. T. P. British. 263. Killed
PUSHMAN, P/O G. R. Canadian. 23
PUTT, F/Lt. A. R. British. 501
PUXLEY, Sgt. W. G. V. British. 236

PYE, Sgt. J. W. British. 25
PYMAN, P/O L. L. British. 65. Killed*
PYNE, Sgt. C. C. N/Zealander. 219

QUELCH, Sgt. B. H. British. 235
QUILL, F/O J. K. British. 65
QUINN, Sgt. J. British. 236

RABAGLIATI, F/Lt. A. C. British. 46. Killed
RABONE, P/O P. W. British. 145. Killed
RABONE, F/O J. H. M. British. 604
RADOMSKI, P/O J. Polish. 303
RADWANSKI, P/O G. Polish. 151–56–607
RAFTER, P/O R. F. British. 603
RAINE, Sgt. W. British. 610. Killed
RAINS, Sgt. D. N. British. 248. Killed
RALLS, Sgt. L. F. British. 605
RAMSAY, Sgt. N. H. D. British. 610–222
RAMSAY, P/O J. B. British. 151. Killed*
RAMSAY, Sgt. J. S. British. 235. Killed
RAMSHAW, Sgt. J. W. British. 222. Killed*
RASMUSSEN, Sgt. L. A. W. N/Zealander. 264. Killed*
RAVENHILL, P/O M. British. 229. Killed*
RAWLENCE, P/O A. J. British. 600
RAWNSLEY, Sgt. C. F. British. 604
RAY, Sgt. British. 56
RAYMOND, F/O P. British. 609
RAYNER, P/O R. M. S. British. 87
READ, F/O W. A. A. British. 603
REAM, Sgt. C. A. British. 235
REARDON-PARKER (F.A.A.), Sub/Lt. J. British. 804
REDDINGTON, Sgt. L. A. E. British. 152. Killed*
REDFERN, Sgt. E. A. British. 232. Killed
REDMAN, P/O J. British. 257–245–43. Killed
REECE, Sgt. L. H. M. British. 235. Killed*
REED, Sgt. H. British. 600
REES, P/O B. V. British. 610
REID, P/O R. British. 46. Killed
REILLEY, P/O H. W. Canadian. 64–66. Killed*
REILLY, Sgt. C. C. N/Zealander. 23. Killed
RENVOIZE, Sgt. J. V. British. 247
REYNELL, F/Lt. R. C. Australian. 43. Killed*
REYNO, F/Lt. E. M. Canadian. 1 (Can) (401)
RHODES, P/O R. A. British. 29. Killed
RHODES-MOOREHOUSE, F/O W. H. British. 601. Killed*
RICALTON, P/O A. L. British. 74. Killed*
RICH, Sgt. P. G. British. 25
RICHARDS (F.A.A.), Sub/Lt. D. H. British. 111. Died
RICHARDS, Sgt. W. C. British. 235. Killed
RICHARDSON, Sgt. E. British. 242
RICHARDSON, S/Ldr. W. A. British. 141
RICHARDSON, Sgt. R. W. British. 610
RICHARDSON, Sgt. British. 141
RICKETTS, Sgt. H. W. British. 235. Killed
RICKETTS, P/O V. A. British. 248. Killed
RICKS, Sgt. L. P. V. J. Canadian. 235
RIDDELL-HANNAM, Sgt. J. D. British. 236
RIDDLE, F/O C. J. British. 601
RIDDLE, F/O H. J. British. 601
RIDLEY, Sgt. M. British. 616. Killed*
RIGBY, P/O R. H. British. 236. Killed*
RILEY, F/Lt. W. British. 302. Killed
RILEY, P/O F. British. 236. Killed
RIMMER, F/Lt. R. F. British. 229. Killed*
RINGWOOD, Sgt. E. A. British. 248. Killed*
RIPLEY, Sgt. W. G. British. 604. Died
RIPPON, P/O A. J. British. 601. Killed
RISELEY, Sgt. A. H. British. 600

RITCHER, P/O G. L. British. 234
RITCHIE, Sgt. R. D. British. 605. Killed
RITCHIE, P/O I. S. British. 603
RITCHIE, P/O J. R. British. 111
RITCHIE, P/O T. G. F. British. 602. Killed
RITCHIE, P/O J. H. British. 141
RITCHIE, P/O J. R. British. 600
ROACH, P/O R. J. B. British. 266
ROBB, P/O R. A. L. British. 236
ROBBINS, P/O R. H. British. 54–66
ROBERTS, Wg/Com. D. N. British. 609–238
ROBERTS, Sgt. A. J. A. British. 29
ROBERTS, P/O R. British. 615–64
ROBERTS, Sgt. D. F. British. 25. Killed
ROBERTS, Sgt. E. C. British. 23
ROBERTS (F.A.A.), Mid/Ship. G. W. British. 808. Killed
ROBERTSON, Sgt. F. N. British. 66. Killed
ROBERTSON, Sgt. British. 56
ROBERTSON, Sgt. B. L. British. 54. Killed
ROBINSON, F/Lt. A. I. British. 222. Died
ROBINSON, Sgt. D. N. British. 152
ROBINSON, Sgt. J. British. 111. Died
ROBINSON, P/O J. C. E. British. 1. Killed
ROBINSON, F/Lt. M. L. British. 610–619–238–66. Killed
ROBINSON, P/O G. British. 264
ROBINSON, S/Ldr. M. W. S. British. 73
ROBINSON, F/Lt. P. B. British. 601
ROBINSON, Sgt. P. E. M. British. 56. Killed
ROBINSON, Sgt. P. T. British. 257
ROBINSON, S/Ldr. M. British. 616
ROBSHAW, P/O F. A. British. 229
ROBSON, P/O N. C. H. British. 72. Killed
RODEN, Sgt. H. A. C. British. 19. Died
ROFE, P/O B. J. British. 25. Killed
ROGERS, P/O B. A. British. 242. Killed
ROGERS, Sgt. G. W. British. 234. Killed
ROGERS, P/O E. B. British. 501–615
ROGOWSKI, Sgt. J. Polish. 303–74
ROHACEK, P/O R. B. Czech. 238–601. Killed
ROLLS, Sgt. W. T. E. British. 72
ROMAN, P/O C. L. Belgian. 236
ROMANIS, Sgt. A. L. British. 25. Killed
ROOK, F/Lt. A. H. British. 504
ROOK, P/O M. British. 504. Killed
ROSCOE, F/O G. L. British. 87. Killed
ROSE, F/O J. British. 32–3
ROSE, P/O S. N. British. 602
ROSE, Sgt. J. S. British. 23. Killed
ROSE, P/O E. B. M. British. 234. Killed
ROSE-PRICE, P/O A. T. British. 501. Killed*
ROSIER, S/Ldr. F. E. British. 229
ROSS, P/O J. K. British. 17. Killed
ROSS, P/O A. R. British. 25–610. Killed
ROTHWELL, P/O J. H. British. 601–605–32. Killed
ROUND, Sgt. J. H. British. 248. Killed*
ROURKE, Sgt. J. British. 248
ROUSE, Sgt. G. W. British. 236
ROWDEN, P/O J. H. British. 64–616. Killed
ROWELL, Sgt. P. A. British. 249
ROWLEY, P/O R. M. B. British. 145. Killed
ROYCE, F/O M. E. A. British. 504
ROYCE, F/O W. B. British. 504
ROZWADOWSKI, P/O M. Polish. 151. Killed*
ROZYCKI, P/O W. Polish. 238
RUDDOCK, Sgt. W. S. British. 23
RUDLAND, Sgt. C. P. British. 263
RUSHMER, F/Lt. F. W. British. 603. Killed
RUSSELL, F/Lt. H. a'b. British. 32
RUSSELL, F/O B. D. Canadian. 1 (Can) (401)
RUSSELL, Sgt. N/Zealander. 264

RUSSELL, P/O G. H. British. 236
RUSSELL, Sgt. A. G. British. 43
RUSSELL, P/O. British. 141
RUSSELL (F.A.A.), Lt. G. F. British. 804. Killed
RUST, Sgt. C. A. British. 85–249
RUSTON, F/Lt. P. British. 604. Died
RUTTER, P/O R. D. British. 73
RYALLS, P/O D. L. British. 29–F.I.U. Killed
RYDER, F/Lt. E. N. British. 41
RYPL, P/O. F. Czech. 310

SADLER, P/O N. A. British. 235. Killed
SADLER, F/Sgt. H. S. British. 611. Killed
ST. AUBIN, F/O E. F. British. 616. Killed
ST. JOHN, P/O P. C. B. British. 74. Killed*
SALMON, F/O H. N. E. British. 1–229
SALWAY, Sgt. E. British. 141. Killed
SAMOLINSKI, P/O W. M. C. Polish. 253. Killed*
SAMPLE, S/Ldr. J. British. 504. Killed
SAMPSON, Sgt. A. British. 23
SANDERS, S/Ldr. F. J. British. 92
SANDERS, F/Lt. J. G. British. 615
SANDIFER, Sgt. A. K. British. 604
SARGENT, Sgt. R. E. B. British. 219
SARRE, Sgt. A. R. British. 603
SASAK, Sgt. W. Polish. 32. Killed
SATCHELL, S/Ldr. W. A. J. British. 302
SAUNDERS, P/O C. H. British. 92
SAUNDERS, F/Lt. G. A. W. British. 65
SAVAGE, Sgt. T. W. British. 64. Killed
SAVILL, Sgt. J. E. British. 242–151
SAVILLE, Sgt. British. 501. Killed
SAWARD, Sgt. C. J. British. 615–501
SAWICZ, F/O T. Polish. 303
SAWYER, S/Ldr. H. C. British. 65. Killed*
SAYERS, F/Sgt. J. E. British. 41
SCHOLLAR, P/O E. C. British. 248
SCHUMER, P/O F. H. British. 600. Killed
SCHWIND, F/Lt. L. H. British. 257–213. Killed*
SCLANDERS, P/O K. M. Canadian. 242. Killed*
SCOTT, Sgt. A. E. British. 73. Killed
SCOTT, Sgt. G. W. British. 64–19
SCOTT, Sgt. N/Zealander. 246
SCOTT, Sgt. E. British. 222 Killed*
SCOTT, Sgt. J. A. British. 611–74. Killed*
SCOTT, F/Lt. D. R. British. 605
SCOTT, P/O A. M. W. British. 3–607. Killed
SCOTT, P/O D. S. British. 73
SCOTT, F/O W. J. M. British. 41. Killed*
SCOTT, F/O R. H. British. 604
SCOTT, Sgt. British. 422 Flt.
SCOTT-MALDEN, P/O F. D. S. British. 611–603
SCRASE, F/O G. E. T. British. 600. Killed
SEABOURNE, Sgt. E. W. British. 238
SEARS, P/O L. A. British. 145. Killed*
SECRETAN, P/O D. British. 72–54
SEDA, Sgt. K. Czech. 310
SEDDON, P/O J. W. British. 601. Killed
SEGHERS, P/O E. G. A. Belgian. 46–32. Killed
SELLERS, Sgt. R. F. British. 46–111
SELWAY, F/O J. B. British. 604
SENIOR, Sgt. J. N. British. 23. Killed
SENIOR, Sgt. B. British. 600
SEREDYN, Sgt. A. Polish. 32
SERVICE, Sgt. A. British. 29. Killed
SEWELL, Sgt. D. A. British. 17. Killed
SHANAHAN, Sgt. M. M. British. 1. Killed*
SHAND, P/O British. 54
SHARMAN, P/O H. R. British. 248

SHARP, P/O L. M. British. 111. Killed
SHARP, Sgt. B. R. British. 235. Killed*
SHARP, Sgt. R. J. British. 236
SHARPLEY, Sgt. H. British. 234. Killed
SHARRATT, Sgt. W. G. British. 248. Killed
SHAW, P/O R. H. British. 1. Killed*
SHAW, F/O I. G. British. 264. Killed*
SHAW (F.A.A.), Petty/Off. F. J. British. 804. Killed
SHEAD, Sgt. H. F. W. British. 257–32
SHEARD, Sgt. H. British. 236. Killed
SHEEN, F/O D. F. B. Australian. 72
SHEPHERD, Sgt. F. W. British. 264. Killed
SHEPLEY, P/O D. C. British. 152 Killed*
SHEPPARD, Sgt. British. 236
SHEPHERD, Sgt. J. B. British. 234. Killed
SHEPPERD, Sgt. G. E. British. 219. Killed*
SHEPPHERD, Sgt. E. E. British. 152. Killed*
SHEPHERD, Sgt. F. E. R. British. 611 Killed*
SHERIDAN, Sgt. S. British. 236
SHERRINGTON, P/O T. B. A. British. 92
SHEWEL, Sgt. British. 236
SHIPMAN, P/O E. A. British. 41
SHIRLEY, Sgt. S. H. J. British. 604. Killed
SHORROCKS, P/O N. B. British. 235. Killed*
SHUTTLEWORTH, P/O Lord R. U. P. KAY-. British. 145. Killed*
SIBLEY, Sgt. F. A. British. 238. Killed*
SIKA, Sgt. J. Czech. 43
SILK, Sgt. F. H. British. 111
SILVER, Sgt. W. G. British. 152. Killed*
SILVESTOR, Sgt. G. F. British. 229
SIM, Sgt. R. B. British. 111. Killed*
SIMMONDS, P/O V. C. British. 238
SIMPSON, F/O G. M. N/Zealander. 229. Killed*
SIMPSON, F/Lt. J. W. C. British. 43. Died
SIMPSON, P/O P. J. British. 111–64
SIMPSON, P/O L. W. British. 141–264
SIMS, Sgt. I. R. British. 248. Killed
SIMS, P/O J. A. British. 3–232
SINCLAIR, F/O G. L. British. 310
SINCLAIR, P/O J. British. 219
SING, F/Lt. J. E. J. British. 213
SIZER, P/O W. M. British. 213
SKALSKI, P/O S. Polish. 501–615
SKILLEN, Sgt. V. H. British. 29. Killed
SKINNER, Sgt. W. M. British. 74
SKINNER, F/O C. D. E. British. 604
SKINNER, F/Lt. S. H. British. 604. Killed
SKOWRON, Sgt. H. Polish. 303. Killed
SLADE, Sgt. J. W. British. 64. Killed
SLATTER, P/O D. M. British. 141. Killed*
SLEIGH (F.A.A.), Lt. J. W. British. 804
SLOUF, Sgt. V. Czech. 312
SLY, Sgt. O. K. British. 29. Killed*
SMALLMAN, Sgt. J. British. 23
SMART, P/O T. British. 65. Killed
SMITH, Sgt. A. D. British. 66. Killed*
SMITH, P/O D. N. E. British. 74. Killed
SMITH, P/O E. British. 229
SMITH, F/O D. S. British. 616. Killed*
SMITH, S/Ldr. A. T. British. 610. Killed*
SMITH, P/O E. B. B. British. 610
SMITH, F/Lt. F. M. British. 72
SMITH, P/O I. S. N/Zealander. 151
SMITH, P/O J. D. Canadian. 73. Killed
SMITH, F/Lt. R. L. British. 151
SMITH, Sgt. K. B. British. 257. Killed*
SMITH, P/O R. R. Canadian. 229
SMITH, F/Lt. W. A. British. 229
SMITH, P/O P. R. British. 25. Killed
SMITH, F/Lt. C. D. S. British. 25. Killed

SMITH, P/O A. W. British. 141. Killed
SMITH (F.A.A.), Sub/Lt. F. A. British. 145. Killed*
SMITH, P/O A. J. British. 74
SMITH, Sgt. R. C. British. 236. Killed
SMITH, P/O E. L. British. 604
SMITH, Sgt. W. B. British. 602
SMITH, F/O E. S. British. 600
SMITH, Sgt. L. E. British. 234–602
SMITH, Sgt. St. James. British. 600. Killed
SMITH, Sgt. F. British. 604. Killed
SMITH, Sgt. G. E. British. 264
SMITH, A. British. 600. Killed
SMITH, Sgt. L. British. 219
SMITH, Sgt. P. R. British. 236. Killed
SMITH, Sgt. N. H. J. British. 235
SMITH, Sgt. E. C. British. 600
SMITH, F/Lt. W. O. L. British. 263. Killed
SMITHERS, P/O J. L. British. 601. Killed*
SMITHERS, F/O R. Canadian. 1 (Can) (401). Killed*
SMITHSON, Sgt. R. British. 249. Killed
SMYTH, Sgt. R. H. British. 111
SMYTHE, Sgt. G. British. 56
SMYTHE, P/O R. F. British. 32
SMYTHE, F/O D. M. A. British. 264
SNAPE, Sgt. W. G. British. 25. Killed
SNELL, P/O V. R. British. 501–151
SNOWDEN, Sgt. E. G. British. 213. Killed
SOARS, Sgt. H. J. British. 74
SOBBEY, Sgt. E. A. British. 235. Killed
SODEN, P/O J. F. British. 266–603. Killed
SOLAK, P/O J. J. Polish. 151–249
SOLOMAN, P/O N. D. British. 17. Killed*
SONES, Sgt. L. C. British. 605
SOUTHALL, Sgt. G. British. 23. Killed
SOUTHORN, Sgt. G. A. British. 235
SOUTHWELL, P/O J. S. British. 245. Killed
SPEARS, P/O British. 421 Flt.
SPEARS, Sgt. A. W. P. British. 222
SPEKE, P/O H. British. 604. Killed
SPENCE, P/O D. J. N/Zealander. 245. Killed
SPENCER, S/Ldr. D. G. H. British. 266
SPENCER, Sgt. G. H. British. 504
SPIERS, Sgt. A. H. British. 236
SPIRES, Sgt. J. H. British. 235
SPRAGUE, Sgt. M. H. British. 602. Killed*
SPRAGUE, P/O H. A. Canadian. 3
SPRENGER, F/O Canadian. 1 (Can) (401)
SPURDLE, P/O R. L. N/Zealander. 74
SPYER, Sgt. R. A. British. 607. Killed
SQUIER, Sgt. J. W. C. British. 64
STANGER, Sgt. N. M. N/Zealander. 235
STANLEY, P/O D. A. British. 64. Killed
STANLEY, Sgt. D. O. N/Zealander. 151. Killed
STANSFELD, F/O W. K. British. 242–229
STAPLES, Sgt. R. C. J. British. 72
STAPLES, Sgt. L. British. 151
STAPLES, P/O M. E. British. 609. Killed
STAPLETON, P/O B. G. British. 603
STARLL, Sgt. British. 601
STARR, S/Ldr. H. M. British. 245–253. Killed*
STAVERT, P/O C. M. British. 1–504
STEADMAN, Sgt. D. J. British. 245
STEBOROWSKI, F/O M. J. Polish. 238. Killed*
STEELE, Sgt. R. M. British. 235
STEERE, F/Sgt. H. British. 19. Killed
STEERE, F/Sgt. J. British. 72
STEFAN, Sgt. J. Czech. 1
STEGMAN, P/O S. Polish. 111–229
STEHLIK, Sgt. J. Czech. 312
STEIN, P/O D. British. 263. Killed

STENHOUSE, F/O J. British. 43
STEPHEN, P/O H. M. British. 74
STEPHENS, P/O M. M. British. 232–3
STEPHENS, Sgt. C. British. 23. Killed*
STEPHENSON, F/Lt. P. J. T. British. 607
STEPHENSON, F/O I. R. British. 264. Killed
STEPHENSON, P/O S. P. British. 85
STERBACEK, P/O J. Czech. 310. Killed
STEVENS, Sgt. G. British. 213
STEVENS, P/O L. W. British. 17. Killed
STEVENS, P/O R. P. British. 151. Killed
STEVENS, P/O E. J. British. 141
STEVENS, Sgt. W. R. British. 23
STEVENS, Sgt. R. E. British. 29. Killed*
STEVENSON, P/O P. C. F. British. 74. Killed
STEWARD, Sgt. G. A. British. 17. Killed
STEWART, Sgt. C. N. D. British. 604. Killed
STEWART, P/O C. N/Zealander. 222–54. Killed
STEWART, P/O D. G. A. British. 615. Killed
STEWART, Sgt. H. G. British. 236
STEWART-CLARKE, P/O D. British. 603. Killed
STICKNEY, F/Lt. P. A. M. British. 235
STILLWELL, Sgt. R. L. British. 65
STOCK, Sgt. E. British. 604
STOCKS, Sgt. N. J. British. 248. Killed*
STOCKWELL (F.A.A.), Petty/Off. W. E. J. British. 804
STODDART, F/Lt. K. M. British. 611
STOKES, P/O R. W. British. 264. Killed
STOKOE, Sgt. J. British. 603
STOKOE, Sgt. S. British. 29. Killed
STONE, F/Lt. C. A. C. British. 249–254
STONE, Sgt. T. F. E. British. 72
STONES, P/O D. W. A. British. 79
STONEY, F/Lt. G. E. B. British. 501. Killed*
STOODLEY, Sgt. D. R. British. 43. Killed*
STORIE, P/O J. M. British. 607–615
STORRAR, Sgt. British. 421 Flt.
STORRAR, P/O J. E. British. 145–73
STORRAT, S/Ldr. British. 501
STORRIE, P/O A. J. British. 264. Killed
STRAIGHT, P/O W. W. British. 601
STRANGE, P/O J. T. N/Zealander. 253
STREATFIEND, S/Ldr. V. C. F. British. 248
STRETCH, Sgt. R. R. British. 235
STRICKLAND, P/O C. D. British. 615. Killed
STRICKLAND, P/O J. M. British. 213. Died
STRIHAUKA, F/Sgt. J. Czech. 310
STROUD, Sgt. G. A. British. 249
STUART, Sgt. M. British. 23
STUCKEY, Sgt. S. G. British. 213. Killed*
STUDD, P/O J. A. P. British. 66. Killed*
SUIDAK, Sgt. A. Polish. 302–303. Killed*
SULMAN, J. E. British. 607. Killed
SUMMERS, Sgt. R. B. G. British. 219
SUMNER, Sgt. F. British. 23. Killed
SUMPTER, Sgt. C. H. S. British. 604
SURMA, P/O F. Polish. 151–607–257. Killed
SUTCLIFFE, Sgt. W. A. British. 610. Killed
SUTHERLAND, P/O I. W. British. 19. Killed*
SUTTON, P/O F. C. British. 264
SUTTOH, P/O F. B. British. 56
SUTTON, P/O J. R. G. British. 611. Killed
SUTTON, P/O N. British. 72. Killed*
SUTTON, Sgt. H. R. British. 235
SUTTON, F/O K. R. N/Zealander. 264
SUTTON, P/O N. British. 611
SWANWICK, Sgt. G. W. British. 54
SWANWICK, Sgt. British. 141
SWITON, Sgt. L. Polish. 54
SWORD-DANIELS, P/O A. T. British. 25

SYDNEY, F/Sgt. C. British. 266–92. Killed*
SYKES (F.A.A.), Sub/Lt. J. H. C. British. 64
SYKES, Sgt. D. B. British. 145
SYLVESTER, P/O E. J. H. British. 501. Killed*
SYLVESTER, Sgt. British. 245
SYMONDS, Sgt. J. E. British. 236
SZAFRANCIEC, Sgt. W. Polish. 151–56–607. Killed
SZAPOSZNIKOW, F/O E. Polish. 303
SZCZESNY, P/O H. Polish. 74
SZLAGOWSKI, Sgt. J. Polish. 234–152
SZULKOWSKI, P/O W. Polish. 65. Killed

TABOR, Sgt. British. 152
TABOR, Sgt. G. British. 65
TAIT, F/O K. W. British. 87
TALMAN, P/O J. M. British. 213–145. Killed
TALMAN, P/O. British. 151
TAMBLYN, P/O H. N. Canadian. 242–141. Killed
TANNER, F/Sgt. J. H. British. 610. Killed*
TATE, Sgt. British. 604
TATNELL, Sgt. R. F. British. 235. Killed
TAYLOR (F.A.A.), Petty/Off. D. E. British. 808
TAYLOR, F/O D. M. British. 64
TAYLOR, P/O R. British. 235. Died
TAYLOR, Sgt. K. British. 29
TAYLOR, Sgt. R. N. British. 601. Killed
TAYLOR, Sgt. R. H. W. British. 604. Killed
TAYLOR, Sgt. G. N. British. 236
TAYLOR, Sgt. G. S. N/Zealander. 3
TAYLOR, Sgt. E. F. British. 29–600. Killed
TAYLOUR (F.A.A.), Lt. E. W. T. British. 808. Killed
TEARLE, Sgt. F. J. British. 600
TEMLETT, P/O C. B. British. 3. Killed
TERRY, Sgt. P. A. R. R. A. British. 72–603
TEW, F/Sgt. P. H. British. 54
THATCHER, P/O. British. 32
THEASBY, Sgt. A. J. British. 25. Killed
THEILMANN, F/Sgt. J. G. British. 234
THOMAS, Sgt. British. 247. Killed
THOMAS, Sgt. British. 236
THOMAS, Sgt. G. S. British. 604
THOMAS, F/O E. H. British. 222–266
THOMAS, F/Lt. F. M. British. 152
THOMAS, P/O S. R. British. 264
THOMAS, F/O C. R. D. British. 236. Killed*
THOMAS, P/O R. C. British. 235. Killed*
THOMPSON, F/O A. R. F. British. 249
THOMPSON, F/Lt. J. A. British. 302
THOMPSON, F/O R. A. British. 72
THOMPSON, S/Ldr. J. M. British. 111
THOMPSON, P/O P. D. British. 605–32
THOMPSON, F/O T. R. British. 213
THOMPSON, P/O F. N. British. 248
THOMPSON, Sgt. W. W. British. 234
THOMPSON, Sgt. J. B. British. 25. Killed
THOMPSON, Sgt. J. R. British. 236. Killed
THORN, Sgt. E. R. British. 264. Killed
THOROGOOD, Sgt. L. A. British. 87
THORPE, Sgt. British. 145
TIDMAN, P/O A. R. British. 64. Killed
TILL, Sgt. J. British. 248. Killed
TILLARD (F.A.A.), Lt. R. C. British. 808. Killed
TILLETT, P/O J. British. 238. Killed
TITLEY, P/O E. G. British. 609. Killed
TOBIN, P/O E. Q. American. 609. Killed
TOMLINSON, P/O P. A. British. 29
TONGUE, P/O R. E. British. 3–504
TOOGOOD, Sgt. British. 43. Killed
TOOMBS, Sgt. J. R. British. 236–264

TOPHAM, P/O J. G. British. 219
TOPOLNICKI, F/O J. Polish. 601. Killed
TOUCH, Sgt. D. F. British. 235. Killed
TOWER-PERKINS, P/O W. British. 238
TOWNSEND, S/Ldr. P. W. British. 85
TOWNSEND, Sgt. T. W. British. 600
TRACEY, P/O O. V. British. 79. Killed
TREVANA, F/O. Canadian. 1 (Can) (401)
TROUSDALE, P/O R. M. N/Zealander. 266. Killed
TRUEMAN, F/O A. A. G. Canadian. 253. Killed*
TRUHLAR, Sgt. F. Czech. 312
TRUMBLE, F/Lt. A. J. British. 264
TRURAN, P/O A. J. J. British. 615
TUCK, F/Lt. R. R. S. British. 92–257
TUCKER, F/O A. B. British. 151
TUCKER, P/O B. E. British. 266–66
TUCKER, Sgt. R. Y. British. 235. Killed*
TUCKER, Sgt. F. D. British. 236
TURLEY-GEORGE, P/O D. R. British. 54
TURNBULL, Sgt. R. N. British. 25
TURNER, F/O R. S. Canadian. 242
TURNER, F/Sgt. G. British. 32
TURNER, F/Lt. D. E. British. 238. Killed*
TURNER, Sgt. R. C. British. 264. Killed*
TWEED, Sgt. L. J. British. 111
TWITCHETT, Sgt. F. J. British. 229–43
TYRER, Sgt. E. British. 46
TYSON, S/Ldr. F. H. British. 213–3

UNETT, Sgt. J. W. British. 235. Killed
UNWIN, F/Sgt. G. C. British. 19
UPTON, P/O H. C. British. 43–607
URBANOWICZ, F/O W. Polish. 145–303–601
URWIN-MANN, P/O J. R. British. 238
USMAR, Sgt. F. British. 41

VAN-DEN HOVE, P/O. Belgian. 501–43. Killed*
VAN-LIERDE, P/O W. E. Belgian. 87
VAN-MENTZ, P/O B. Belgian. 222. Killed
VAN-WAYEN BERGHE, P/O A. A. L. Belgian. 236. Killed
VARLEY, P/O G. W. British. 247–79
VASATKO, P/O A. Czech. 312. Killed
VELEBRNOVSKI, P/O A. Czech. 1. Killed
VENESOEN, Sgt. F. A. Belgian. 235. Killed
VENN, P/O J. A. British. 236
VERITY, P/O V. B. S. N/Zealander. 229
VESELY, P/O V. Czech. 312
VICK, S/Ldr. J. A. British. 607
VIGORS, P/O T. A. British. 222
VILES, Sgt. L. W. British. 236
VILLA, F/Lt. British. 72–92
VINCENT, G/Capt. S. F. British. 229
VINDIS, Sgt. F. Czech. 310
VINYARD, Sgt. F. F. British. 64. Killed*
VLAD, P/O. Czech. 501
VOKES, P/O A. F. British. 19. Killed
VOPALECKY, W/O. Czech. 310
VRANA, F/O. Czech. 312
VYBIRAL, P/O T. Czech. 312
VYKOURAL, P/O K. J. Czech. 111–73. Killed

WADDINGHAM, P/O J. British. 141. Died
WADE, P/O T. S. British. 92. Killed
WADHAM, Sgt. J. V. British. 145. Killed*
WAGHORN, Sgt. British. 249–111
WAGNER, Sgt. A. D. British. 151. Killed
WAINWRIGHT, P/O A. G. British. 151. Killed

WAINWRIGHT, P/O M. T. British. 64
WAKE, Sgt. British. 264
WAKEFIELD, P/O H. K. British. 235
WAKEHAM, P/O E. C. J. British. 145. Killed*
WAKELING, Sgt. S. R. E. British. 87. Killed*
WALCH, F/Lt. S. C. Australian. 238. Killed*
WALKER, Sgt. S. British. 236. Killed
WALKER, Sgt. A. N/Zealander. 600
WALKER, F/O J. H. G. British. 25. Killed
WALKER, Sgt. N. Mc. D. British. 615. Killed
WALKER, P/O W. L. B. British. 616
WALKER, P/O J. A. Canadian. 111
WALKER, P/O J. R. Canadian. 611–41. Killed
WALKER, P/O. British. 616
WALKER, Sgt. G. A. British. 232
WALKER, P/O R. J. British. 72
WALKER-SMITH, Sgt. F. R. British. 85. Killed
WALLACE, P/O C. A. B. Canadian. 3. Killed
WALLACE, Sgt. T. Y. British. 111. Killed
WALLEN, F/Lt. D. S. British. 604

WALLENS, P/O R. W. British. 41
WALLER, Sgt. G. A. British. 29
WALLEY, Sgt. P. K. British. 615. Killed*
WALLIS, Sgt. D. S. British. 235. Killed
WALSH, Sgt. E. British. 141
WALSH, P/O J. J. Canadian. 615. Died
WALSH (F.A.A.), Sub/Lt. R. W. M. British. 111
WALTON, Sgt. British. 152
WALTON, Sgt. H. British. 87
WANT, Sgt. W. H. British. 248. Killed*
WAPNIAREK, P/O S. Polish. 302. Killed*
WARD, Sgt. R. A. British. 66. Killed*
WARD, Sgt. W. B. British. 604
WARD, F/O D. H. N/Zealander. 87. Killed
WARD, P/O J. L. British. 32. Killed
WARD, S/Ldr. E. F. British. 601
WARDEN, Sgt. N. P. British. 610. Killed
WARD-SMITH, Sgt. P. British. 610
WARE, Sgt. R. T. British. 3
WAREHAM, P/O M. P. British. 1. Killed
WAREING, Sgt. P. T. British. 616
WARING, Sgt. W. British. 23
WARMSLEY, Sgt. H. W. British. 248. Killed
WARNER, F/Lt. W. H. C. British. 610. Killed*
WARREN, Sgt. S. British. 1
WARREN, Sgt. T. A. British. 236
WARREN, Sgt. J. B. W. British. 600. Killed
WARREN, P/O C. British. 152
WARREN, P/O D. A. P. British. 248. Killed
WATERSTON, F/O R. McGregor. British. 603. Killed*
WATKINS, F/O D. H. British. 611
WATKINSON, P/O A. B. S/African. 66
WATLING, P/O W. C. British. 92. Killed
WATSON, Sgt. J. G. British. 604
WATSON, P/O A. R. British. 152. Killed
WATSON, P/O E. J. British. 605. Killed
WATSON, P/O L. G. British. 29
WATSON, P/O R. F. British. 87
WATSON, P/O. British. 64
WATSON, P/O F. S. Canadian. 3. Killed
WATTERS, P/O J. N/Zealander. 236
WATTS, P/O R. F. British. 253
WATTS, Sgt. E. L. British. 248. Killed
WATTS, Sgt. R. D. H. British. 235. Killed*
WAY, P/O L. B. R. British. 229
WAY, F/Lt. B. H. British. 54. Killed*
WCZELIK, F/O. Polish. 302. Killed
WEAVER, F/Lt. P. S. British. 56. Killed*
WEBB, F/O P. C. British. 602
WEBBER, P/O W. F. P. British. 141

WEBBER, Sgt. J. British. 1
WEBER, P/O F. Czech. 145
WEBSTER, F/Lt. J. T. British. 41. Killed*
WEBSTER, P/O F. K. British. 610. Killed*
WEBSTER, Sgt. H. G. British. 73. Killed
WEBSTER, Sgt. E. R. British. 85
WEDGEWOOD, F/Lt. J. H. British. 253. Killed
WEDLOCK, Sgt. G. V. British. 235
WEDZIK, Sgt. M. Polish. 302
WEIR, P/O A. N. C. British. 145. Killed
WELCH, Sgt. E. British. 604. Killed
WELFORD, P/O G. H. E. British. 607
WELLAM, P/O G. H. A. British. 92
WELLS, P/O E. P. N/Zealander. 41–266
WELLS, F/O P. H. V. British. 249
WELLS, P/O M. L. British. 248
WELSH, P/O T. D. British. 264
WENDEL, P/O K. V. N/Zealander. 504. Killed*
WEST, S/Ldr. H. British. 151–41
WEST, P/O D. R. British. 141
WESTCOTT, Sgt. W. H. J. British. 235
WESTLAKE, P/O G. H. British. 43–213
WESTLAKE, P/O R. D. British. 235
WESTMACOTT, F/O I. B. British. 56
WESTMORELAND, Sgt. T. E. British. 616. Killed*
WHALL, Sgt. B. E. P. British. 602. Killed*
WHEATCROFT, P/O N. R. British. 604. Killed
WHEELER, P/O N. J. British. 615
WHELAN, Sgt. J. British. 64–19
WHINNEY, P/O M. T. British. 3
WHIPPS, Sgt. G. A. British. 602. Killed
WHITBREAD, P/O H. L. British. 222. Killed*
WHITBY, Sgt. A. W. British. 79
WHITE, P/O B. E. British. 504. Killed
WHITE, Sgt. J. W. British. 32–3–F.I.U.
WHITE, S/Ldr. F. L. British. 74
WHITE, Sgt. J. British. 72. Killed
WHITE, Sgt. British. 604
WHITE, Sgt. R. British. 235
WHITE, Sgt. J. British. 248. Died
WHITEHEAD, Sgt. C. British. 56. Killed
WHITEHEAD, Sgt. R. O. British. 253–151
WHITEHOUSE, P/O British. 32
WHITEHOUSE, Sgt. S. A. H. British. 501
WHITFOELD, Sgt. J. J. British. 56. Killed*
WHITLEY, S/Ldr. E. W. N/Zealander. 245
WHITLEY, P/O D. British. 264. Killed*
WHITNEY, P/O D. M. N/Zealander. 245
WHITSUN, Sgt. A. D. British. 236. Killed
WHITTICK, Sgt. H. G. British. 604
WHITTINGHAM, F/O C. D. British. 151
WHITTY, F/O W. H. R. British. 607
WHITWELL, Sgt. P. N/Zealander. 600. Killed
WICKINGS-SMITH, P/O P. C. British. 235. Killed*
WICKINS, Sgt. A. S. British. 141
WICKS, P/O B. J. British. 56. Killed
WIDDOWS, S/Ldr. S. C. British. 29
WIGG, P/O R. G. N/Zealander. 65
WIGGLESWORTH, P/O J. S. British. 238. Killed
WIGHT, F/Lt. R. D. G. British. 213. Killed*
WIGHTMAN (F.A.A.), Mid/Ship. O. M. British. 151. Killed
WILCOCK, Sgt. C. British. 248. Died
WILCOX, P/O E. J. British. 72. Killed*
WILDBLOOD, P/O T. S. British. 152. Killed*
WILDE, P/O D. C. British. 236
WILKES, Sgt. G. N. British. 213. Killed*
WILKINSON, S/Ldr. R. L. British. 266. Killed*
WILKINSON, Sgt. W. A. British. 501
WILKINSON, Sgt. K. A. British. 616
WILKINSON, F/Lt. R. C. British. 3

WILLANS, P/O A. J. British. 23. Killed
WILLCOCKS, Sgt. P. H. British. 610–66. Killed
WILLCOCKS, Sgt. C. P. L. British. 610
WILLIAMS, S/Ldr. C. W. British. 17. Killed*
WILLIAMS, P/O D. G. British. 92. Killed*
WILLIAMS, F/Sgt. E. E. British. 46. Killed*
WILLIAMS, F/O T. D. British. 611
WILLIAMS, P/O W. D. British. 152
WILLIAMS, P/O W. S. N/Zealander. 266. Killed
WILLIAMS, Sgt. G. T. British. 219
WILLIAMS, P/O D. C. British. 141. Killed
WILLIAMS, P/O A. British. 604
WILLIS, Sgt. N/Zealander. 600
WILLIS, Sgt. R. F. British. 219. Killed
WILLIS, Sgt. W. C. British. 73–3. Killed
WILSCH, P/O British. 141
WILSDON, Sgt. A. A. British. 29. Killed
WILSON, F/O D. S. British. 610
WILSON, P/O R. R. Canadian. 111. Killed*
WILSON, P/O D. F. British. 141
WILSON, Sgt. W. C. British. 29
WILSON, Sgt. W. British. 235
WILSON-MACDONALD, S/Ldr. D. S. British. 213
WINGFIELD, Sgt. V. British. 29. Killed
WINN, P/O C. V. British. 29
WINSKILL, P/O A. L. British. 603–54–72
WINSTANLEY, Sgt. J. British. 151

WINTER, P/O D. C. British. 72. Killed*
WINTER, P/O R. A. British. 247
WISE, Sgt. J. F. British. 141. Killed*
WISEMAN, P/O W. D. British. 600
WISSLER, P/O D. H. British. 17. Killed
WITHALL, F/Lt. L. C. Australian. 152. Killed*
WITORZENC, F/O S. Polish. 501
WLASNOWOLSKI, P/O B. Polish. 607–32–213. Killed
WOJCICKI, Sgt. A. Polish. 213. Killed*
WOJCIECHOWSKI, Sgt. M. Polish. 303. Killed
WOJTOWICZ, Sgt. S. Polish. 303. Killed*
WOLFE, S/Ldr. E. C. British. 141–219
WOLTON, Sgt. R. British. 152
WOOD, Sgt. S. V. British. 248
WOOD, Sgt. K. R. British. 23. Killed
WOODGATE, Sgt. J. E. British. 141. Killed
WOODGER, P/O D. N. British. 235. Killed*
WOODLAND, Sgt. N. N. British. 236
WOODS-SCAWEN, P/O C. A. British. 43. Killed*
WOODS-SCAWEN, F/O P. P. British. 85. Killed*
WOODWARD, F/O H. J. British. 64–23. Killed*
WOODWARD, P/O R. S. British. 600. Killed
WOOLLEY, Sgt. A. W. British. 601. Killed
WOOTTEN, P/O E. W. British. 234
WORDSWORTH, P/O D. K. A. British. 235. Killed
WORRALL, S/Ldr. J. British. 32
WORRALL (F.A.A.), Sub/Lt. T. V. British. 111. Killed
WORRALL, P/O P. A. British. 85–249. Killed
WORSDELL, P/O K. W. British. 219. Killed*
WORTHINGTON, F/O A. S. British. 219
WOTTON, Sgt. H. J. British. 234. Killed
WRIGHT (F.A.A.), Lt. A. J. British. 804
WRIGHT, Sgt. B. British. 92
WRIGHT, F/Lt. A. R. British. 92
WRIGHT, Sgt. E. W. British. 605
WRIGHT, Sgt. J. British. 79. Killed*
WRIGHT, Sgt. D. L. British. 235. Killed
WRIGHT, P/O W. British. 604. Killed
WRIGHT, Sgt. R. R. British. 248
WROBLEWSKI, P/O Z. T. A. Polish. 302
WUNSCHE, F/Sgt. K. Polish. 303
WYATE, Sgt. J. P. British. 25. Killed*
WYATT-SMITH, P/O P. British. 263. Killed

WYDROWSKI, P/O. Polish. 607
WYNN, P/O R. E. N. E. British. 249. Killed

YAPP, D. S. British. 253–245
YATES, Sgt. T. M. British. 64
YATES, Sgt. G. British. 248
YATES, Sgt. W. British. 604
YORK, Sgt. R. L. British. 610. Killed
YOUNG, P/O C. R. British. 615–607–46. Killed
YOUNG, P/O M. H. British. 264
YOUNG, Sgt. R. B. M. N/Zealander. 264. Killed*
YOUNG, Sgt. R. C. British. 23
YOUNG, F/O J. R. C. British. 249
YOUNG, P/O J. H. R. British. 74. Killed*
YOUNG, P/O J. S. British. 234
YUILE, F/O A. Canadian. 1 (Can) (401)
YULE, P/O R. D. British. 145. Killed

ZAK, P/O W. Polish. 303
ZALUSKI, Sgt. J. Polish. 302. Killed*
ZAORAL, P/O V. Czech. 310. Killed
ZAVORAL, Sgt. A. Czech. 1. Killed
ZENKER, P/O P. Polish. 501. Killed*
ZIMA, Sgt. R. Czech. 310
ZIMPRICH, P/O S. Czech. 310. Killed
ZUKOWSKI, P/O A. Polish. 302. Killed*
ZUMBACH, P/O J. Polish. 303
ZURAKOWSKI, P/O J. Polish. 234–609

This list has been compiled for the Battle of Britain Fighter Association by Flight Lt. J. H. Holloway, M.B.E.

Bibliography

BOOKS

Empire of the Air (Viscount Templewood) Collins 1957
Assignment to Catastrophe (Major-General Sir Edward Spears) William Heinemann 1954
Wing Leader (Group-Captain J. E. Johnson) Chatto and Windus 1956
Nine Lives (Group-Captain A. C. Deere) Hodder and Stoughton 1959
Sailor Malan (Oliver Walker) Cassell 1953
Fighter Pilot (Paul Richey) Hutchinson 1955
Air Challenge and the Locusts (H. W. Bayly) Bodley Head 1939
The Rise and Fall of the German Air Force Air Ministry 1946
The Sky Suspended (Drew Middleton) Secker and Warburg 1960
Luftmacht Deutschland (Heinz Bongartz) Essener Verlagsanstalt
Famous Bombers of the Second World War (W. Green) Macdonald First and Second Series 1958 1960
Operation Sea Lion (Ronald Wheatley) Oxford 1958
Trumpf oder Bluff (Lt.-Gen. H. J. Rieckhoff) Interavia S.A.
Spitfire Pilot (Flight-Lieutenant D. M. Crook) Faber 1942
Blitz on Britain (Asher Lee) Four Square 1960
Duell im Dunkel (Cajus Bekker) Gerhard Stalling
Evidence in Camera (C. Babington Smith) Chatto and Windus 1958
Development of Aircraft Engines and Fuels (Schlaifer and Heron) Harvard 1950
The Struggle for Europe (Chester Wilmot) Collins 1952
Reach for the Sky (Paul Brickhill) Collins 1957
The Dangerous Skies (Air Commodore A. E. Clouston) Cassell 1954
Air Power, Key to Survival (A. P. de Seversky) Herbert Jenkins 1952
Fighter Command (P. Wykeham) Putnam 1960
The Third Service (P. Joubert de la Ferté) Thames and Hudson 1955
The Second World War, Vols. I and II (W. Churchill) Cassell 1948 1949
Royal Air Force 1939–45 (D. Richards) H.M.S.O. (3 vols.) 1953 1954
Invasion 1940 (P. Fleming) Rupert Hart Davis 1957
Forewarned is Forearmed (T. Winslow) Hodge 1948
Aircraft of the Royal Air Force (O. Thetford) Putnam 1957
The Fated Sky (P. Joubert de la Ferté) Hutchinson 1956
Survivor's Story (Air Marshal Sir P. Gibbs) Hutchinson
R.A.F. Biggin Hill (G. Wallace) Putnam 1957
Three Steps to Victory (R. Watson-Watt) Odhams 1958
The Fatal Decisions (F. Freiden and W. Richardson editors) Michael Joseph 1956
I Remember (Lord Swinton) Hutchinson 1948
British War Production (M. M. Postan) H.M.S.O. 1952
The Defence of the U.K. (Basil Collier) H.M.S.O. 1957
Broken Swastika (W. Baumbach) Robert Hale 1960
Udet-eines Mannes Leben (Herlin) Henri Nannen Verlag
The First and the Last (Lieutenant General A. Galland) Methuen 1955
Observers' Tale (produced privately by 17 Group R.O.C. Watford)
Contribution to Victory (Metropolitan Vickers)
Strike from the Sky (A. McKee) Souvenir Press 1960
Design for Flight (H. Conradis) Macdonald 1960
One Story of Radar (A. P. Rowe) Cambridge 1948
The Hitler I Knew (Otto Dietrich) Methuen 1957
The Rise and Fall of the Third Reich (W. Shirer) Secker and Warburg 1960
Berlin Diary (W. Shirer) Hamish Hamilton 1941
Warplanes of the Second World War
Fighters (W. Green) Macdonald 1960 1961
Science at War (D.S.I.R.) H.M.S.O. 1948
Marshal Without Glory (E. Butler and G. Young) Hodder and Stoughton 1956
Spitfire—The Story of a Famous Fighter (B. Robertson) Harleyford 1960

Spitfire (J. W. R. Taylor and M. E. Allward) Harborough 1946
These and Other Things were Done (Reekie) Standard Telephones
Calling All Arms (E. Fairfax) Hutchinson 1945
The Magic of a Name (H. Nockolds) G. T. Foulis 1950
The Battle of Britain (E. Bishop) Allen and Unwin 1960
The Battle of Britain (Air Ministry pamphlet 156) August 1943
The Battle of Britain (Air Ministry) H.M.S.O. 1941
The Battle of Britain (Dowding (Despatch)) Supplement to *London Gazette* 1946
Handbooks for Observer Posts and Centres (1937, 1938, 1939)
Jane's all the World's Aircraft (1933–41 and 1945) Sampson Low
L'Aviation d'Assault Française dans le campagne de 1940 (Editions Berger Lavrault)
Les Forces Aériennes Françaises de 1939–45 (Editions Berger Lavrault)
L'Aviation de Bombardment Française en 1939–40 (Editions Berger Lavrault)
L'Aviation de Chasse Française en 1939–40 (Editions Berger Lavrault)
Mölders und Seine Männer (Major Fritz von Forell) Steinische Verlagsanstalt
The Fighter Pilots (Edward H. Sims) Cassell 1967
Ack-Ack (General Sir Frederick Pile) Harrap 1949
The Breaking Wave (Telford Taylor) Wiedenfeld & Nicolson 1967
Hitler Confronts England (Walter Ansel) Duke University Press 1960
The Tiger Moth Story (Alan Bramson/Neville Birch) Cassell 1964
Eagle Day (Richard Collier) Hodder & Stoughton 1966
Phoenix into Ashes (Roland Beamont) William Kimber 1968
Margings and Camouflage Systems of Luftwaffe Verlag Dieter Hoffmann
Aircraft in World War II Vols. 1, 2 and 3 (Karl Reis Jr.) 1965, 1966, 1967
Dora Kurfurst und Rote 13 (Karl Reis Jr.) Verlag·Dieter Hoffmann 1964
Shorts Aircraft since 1900 (C. H. Barnes) Putnam 1967
Vickers Aircraft since 1908 (C. F. Andrews) Putnam 1969
Squadron Histories R.F.C., R.N.A.S. and R.A.F. since 1912 (Peter Lewis) Putnam 1968
Aircraft Camouflage and Markings 1907–54 (Bruce Robertson) Harleyford Publications 1956
Icare—The Battle of Britain The French Airline Pilots Association 1965

PERIODICALS, ETC.

The Aeroplane (various issues 1937–40)
Flight (various issues 1937–40)
Interavia Air Letter (various issues 1934–42)
Interavia Review (various issues 1946–7–50)
Interavia ABC (1939)
Air Pictorial (various issues 1950–60)
R.A.F. Flying Review (various issues 1953–60)
Wehr Wissenschaftliche Rundschau (various issues)
Luftwaffen Revue (various issues 1959–60)
Aircraft Recognition—The Inter Services Journal (various issues 1942–3)
The Journal of the Royal Observer Corps (various issues 1941–2)
Commander's Circular, Observer Corps (various issues 1939–40)

BIBLIOGRAPHY

Acknowledgements for photographs

Lufthansa, 4
Group Captain J. Kent, 22, 25, 56, 218
Kent Messenger, 23, 108, 111, 139, 140, 168, 170, 198, 201, 129
Vickers-Armstrongs, 24, 33, 36, 39, 219
Air Commodore P. M. Brothers, 26
The Press Association, 28, 30
Central Press Photos, 29, 98, 135, 166, 221, 227, 252, 264, 267
Hawker Siddeley, 39, 106, 107, 113, 263, 268
British Lion Films, 50
Imperial War Museum, 58, 74, 80, 85, 89, 94, 96, 98, 112, 129, 132, 133, 140, 141, 143, 144, 146, 157, 159, 164, 180, 192, 196, 197, 199, 202, 232, 234, 236, 249, 250, 251, 253, 255
Crown Copyright, 60, 63, 72, 81, 82, 88, 223, 248
AEI, 65
Dr. Gaertner, 66
London News Agency Photos, 73
Fox Photos, 89, 136, 165, 193, 194, 213, 268
Wing Commander Havercraft, 93, 163
Bundesarchivs, 94, 117, 118, 119, 130, 131, 134, 161, 162, 176, 182, 183, 184, 185, 186, 187, 188, 189, 190, 191, 214, 216, 217, 224, 225, 226, 229, 246, 256, 257, 269, 261, 262
Lt. Col. Aviateur BEM M. Terlinden, 96, 97

Group Captain Wilson, 99, 193
Westland Aircraft, 103
Royal National Lifeboat Institution, 105, 200
Hodder and Stoughton, 110, 111
Dennis Knight, 127, 156, 160, 247
Air Commodore Donaldson, 130
Syndication International, 134
Associated Press, 137, 171, 175
Field Marshal Milch, 138, 154
T. Angelle Weisse, 145, 182
A. W. Capel, 149
R.A.C. Tank Museum, 147, 148
Topix, 154, 172
Lalouette, 155, 205, 230
Wing Commander R. P. Beamont, 167, 177
The Museum of British Transport, 169, 265
Captain J. H. Mann, 173
Associated Newspapers, 174
Short Brothers and Harland, 177
Force Aerienne Belge, 178
British Leyland Motor Corporation, 195
T. H. McLellan, 206
A. Wilson, 207
Radio Times Hulton Picture Library, 215
Barratt's Photo Press, 254

Index